D0376282

# CARIBBEAN CRUISE PORTS OF CALL

Portions of this book appear in *Fodor's Caribbean*.

# Fodor's CARIBBEAN CRUISE PORTS OF CALL

**Design:** Tina Malaney, *Associate Art Director*; Erica Cuoco, *Production Designer*

**Photography:** Jennifer Arnow, *Senior Photo Editor*

**Maps:** Rebecca Baer, *Senior Map Editor*; Mark Stroud (Moon Street Cartography), David Lindroth, *Cartographers*

**Production:** Angela L. McLean, *Senior Production Manager*; Jennifer DePrima, *Editorial Production Manager*

**Sales:** Jacqueline Lebow, *Sales Director*

**Business & Operations:** Chuck Hoover, *Chief Marketing Officer*; Joy Lai, *Vice President and General Manager*; Stephen Horowitz, *Head of Business Development and Partnerships*

**Writers:** Laura Adzich-Brander, Carol M. Bareuther, Carol Buchanan, Susan Campbell, Linda Coffman, Greg Devilliers, Lynda Lohr, Elise Meyer, Amy Peniston, Ann L. Phelan, Rika Purdy, Jessica Robertson, Laura Rodini, Paul Rubio, Paulina Salach, Julie Schwietert Collazo, Jordan Simon, Richard Sitler, Eileen Robinson Smith, Roberta Sotonoff, Robin Sussman, Jeffrey Van Fleet, Jane E. Zarem

**Editor:** Douglas Stallings

**Production Editor:** Carrie Parker

Copyright © 2017 by Fodor's Travel, a division of Internet Brands, Inc.

17th Edition

ISBN 978-0-14-754658-6

ISSN 2331-9275

PRINTED IN THE UNITED STATES OF AMERICA

10 9 8 7 6 5 4 3 2 1

# CONTENTS

## MAPS

# ABOUT THIS GUIDE

## Fodor's Recommendations

Everything in this guide is worth doing—we don't cover what isn't—but exceptional sights, hotels, and restaurants are recognized with additional accolades. **Fodor'sChoice★** indicates our top recommendations. Care to nominate a new place? Visit Fodors.com/contact-us.

## Trip Costs

We list prices wherever possible to help you budget well. Hotel and restaurant price categories from **$** to **$$$$** are noted alongside each recommendation. For hotels, we include the lowest cost of a standard double room in high season. For restaurants, we cite the average price of a main course at dinner or, if dinner isn't served, at lunch. For attractions, we always list adult admission fees; discounts are usually available for children, students, and senior citizens.

## Hotels

Our local writers vet every hotel to recommend the best overnights in each price category, from budget to expensive. Unless otherwise specified, you can expect private bath, phone, and TV in your room. For expanded hotel reviews, facilities, and deals visit Fodors.com.

| Top Picks | | Hotels & |
|---|---|---|
| ★ **Fodor's**Choice | | **Restaurants** |
| | | 🖼 Hotel |
| **Listings** | | 🛏 Number of |
| ✉ Address | | rooms |
| 📬 Branch address | | ¶◎¶ Meal plans |
| ☎ Telephone | | ✗ Restaurant |
| 🖷 Fax | | ⌕ Reservations |
| ⊕ Website | | 🏛 Dress code |
| ✍ E-mail | | ⊟ No credit cards |
| 🎟 Admission fee | | ⑤ Price |
| ⊙ Open/closed | | |
| times | | **Other** |
| Ⓜ Subway | | ⇨ See also |
| ⊹ Directions or | | ☞ Take note |
| Map coordinates | | 🏌 Golf facilities |

## Restaurants

Unless we state otherwise, restaurants are open for lunch and dinner daily. We mention dress code only when there's a specific requirement and reservations only when they're essential or not accepted.

## Credit Cards

The hotels and restaurants in this guide typically accept credit cards. If not, we'll say so.

## EUGENE FODOR

Hungarian-born Eugene Fodor (1905–91) began his travel career as an interpreter on a French cruise ship. The experience inspired him to write *On the Continent* (1936), the first guidebook to receive annual updates and discuss a country's way of life as well as its sights. Fodor later joined the U.S. Army and worked for the OSS in World War II. After the war, he kept up his intelligence work while expanding his guidebook series. During the Cold War, many guides were written by fellow agents who understood the value of insider information. Today's guides continue Fodor's legacy by providing travelers with timely coverage, insider tips, and cultural context.

# PLANNING YOUR CARIBBEAN CRUISE

By Linda
Coffman

If you're considering a cruise but can't decide whether it's really for you, it's tempting to ask, "What's so special about a cruise vacation?" It's a good question. Until the age of the airplane, ocean travel was simply a means to get to your far-flung destination—often the only way. But even in the early decades of the 20th century, venerable ocean liners such as the Normandie offered the occasional round-trip cruise to an exotic locale.

Passengers on those earliest cruises didn't have a fun-in-the-sun mind-set as they sailed to faraway ports. They sailed to broaden their horizons and learn about ports of call that couldn't be reached by overland travel. Perhaps they booked a cruise to Panama to observe the construction of the canal or, like the *Normandie's* passengers, were bound for Brazil and the daring excitement of Carnaval.

Regardless of why they were cruising, early cruisers steamed toward the unfamiliar with many fewer comforts than contemporary passengers enjoy. On the *Normandie*, air-conditioned comfort was available only in the ship's first-class dining room, though at least passengers could find relief from Rio's heat by taking a dip in one of the era's few outdoor swimming pools at sea. In those days, if an ocean liner had a permanent swimming pool, it was often indoors and deep in the hull.

Carnival Cruise Lines executives like to reminisce about the tiny "gyms" on their early ships, which were converted ocean liners, and then point to how far ship designs have evolved. I remember the old ships well. It was even difficult to find the casino on Carnival's first "Fun Ship," *Mardi Gras*, let alone locate the indoor swimming pool. That's hardly the case today. Designed for contemporary travelers and tastes, modern cruise ships carry passengers amid conveniences unheard of in the heyday of the North Atlantic ocean liner or even in the earliest vessels permanently dedicated to cruises. As more than 16 million passengers discovered when they went to sea in 2011, there's a lot to like on ships these days.

The allure of a modern sea cruise is its ability to appeal to a wide range of vacationers as a safe and convenient way to travel. Today's cruise ships are lively and luxurious floating resorts that offer something to satisfy the expectations of almost everyone. The first thing you'll find is that although cruise ships differ dramatically in the details and how they craft and deliver the cruise experience, most ships have the same basic features. And although the decisions and considerations in booking one cruise over another can be complex, the more you know about cruise travel in general, the better prepared you will be when it comes to making your choices.

# CHOOSING YOUR CRUISE

Just as Caribbean islands have distinct histories and cultures, cruise ships also have individual personalities. Determined by their size, the year they were built, and their style, on one hand, they can be bold, brassy, and exciting—totally unlike home, but a great place to visit. Big ships offer stability and a huge variety of activities and facilities. On the other hand, small ships feel intimate, like private clubs or, more appropriately, personal yachts. For every big-ship fan there is someone who would never set foot aboard a "floating resort." Examine your lifestyle—there's sure to be a cruise ship to match your expectations.

After giving some thought to your itinerary and where in the Caribbean you might wish to go, the ship you select is the most vital factor in your Caribbean cruise vacation, since it will not only determine which islands you will visit, but also how you will see them. Big ships visit major ports of call, such as St. Thomas, St. Maarten/St. Martin, Nassau, and San Juan; when they call at smaller islands with shallower ports, passengers must disembark aboard shore tenders (small boats that ferry dozens of passengers to shore at a time). Or they may skip these smaller ports entirely. Small and midsize ships can visit smaller islands, such as St. Barths, St. Kitts, or St. John, more easily; passengers are sometimes able to disembark directly onto the pier without having to wait for tenders to bring them ashore.

## ITINERARIES

You'll want to give some consideration to your ship's Caribbean itinerary when you are choosing your cruise. The length of the cruise will determine the variety and number of ports you visit, but so will the type of itinerary and the point of departure. **Round-trip** cruises start and end at the same point and usually explore ports close to one another; **one-way** cruises start at one point and end at another and range farther afield.

Almost all cruises in the Caribbean are round-trip cruises. On Caribbean itineraries you often have a choice of U.S. mainland departure points. Ships sailing out of San Juan can visit up to five ports in seven days, while cruises out of Florida can reach up to four ports in the same length of time. The Panama Canal can also be combined with a Caribbean cruise: the 50-mile (83-km) canal is a series of locks, which make up for the height difference between the Caribbean and the Pacific. Increasingly popular are partial transit cruises that enter the Panama Canal, anchor in Gatún Lake for a short time, and depart through the same set of locks.

### EASTERN CARIBBEAN ITINERARIES

Eastern Caribbean itineraries consist of two or three days at sea as well as stops at some of the Caribbean's busiest cruise ports. A typical cruise will usually take in three or four ports of call, such as St. Thomas in the U.S. Virgin Islands, San Juan, or St. Maarten/St. Martin, along with a visit to the cruise line's "private" island for beach time. Every major cruise line has at least two of those popular islands on its itineraries. Some itineraries might also include others, such as Tortola, Dominica, Barbados, St. Kitts, or Martinique.

## WESTERN CARIBBEAN ITINERARIES

Western Caribbean itineraries embarking from Galveston, Fort Lauderdale, Miami, Port Canaveral, New Orleans, or Tampa might include Belize, Cozumel, or the Costa Maya Cruise Port in Mexico, Key West, Grand Cayman, or Jamaica—all perfect for passengers who enjoy scuba diving, snorkeling, and exploring Mayan ruins. Ships often alternate itineraries in the Western Caribbean with itineraries in the Eastern Caribbean on a weekly basis, offering the ability to schedule a 14-night back-to-back cruise without repeating ports.

## SOUTHERN CARIBBEAN ITINERARIES

Southern Caribbean cruises tend to be longer in duration, with more distant ports of call. They often originate in a port that is not on the U.S. mainland. Embarking in San Juan, for example, allows you to reach the lower Caribbean on a seven-day cruise with as many as four or five ports of call. Southern Caribbean itineraries might leave Puerto Rico for the Virgin Islands, Guadeloupe, Grenada, Curaçao, Barbados, Antigua, St. Lucia, Martinique, or Aruba. Smaller ships leave from embarkation ports as far south as Bridgetown, Barbados, and cruise through the Grenadines. Every major cruise line offers some Southern Caribbean itineraries, but these cruises aren't as popular as Western and Eastern Caribbean cruises.

## OTHER ITINERARIES

In recent years shorter itineraries have grown in appeal to time-crunched and budget-constrained travelers. If you are planning your first cruise in the tropics, a short sailing to the Bahamas allows you to test your appetite for cruising before you take a chance on a longer and more expensive cruise. Embarking at Fort Lauderdale, Miami, Jacksonville, or Port Canaveral, you will cruise for three to five days, taking in at least one port of call (usually Nassau or Freeport in the Bahamas) and possibly a visit to a "private" island or Key West. Four- and five-night cruises may also include a day at sea. Cruises also depart from ports farther north on the East Coast; you might depart from Charleston, Baltimore, or New York City and cruise to Bermuda or the Bahamas.

## WHEN TO GO

Average year-round temperatures throughout the Caribbean are 78°F–85°F, with a low of 65°F and a high of 95°F; downtown shopping areas always seem to be unbearably hot. Low season runs from approximately mid-September through mid-April. Many travelers, especially families with school-age children, make reservations months in advance for the most expensive and most crowded summer months and holiday periods; however, with the many new cruise ships that have entered the market, you can often book fairly close to your departure date and still find room, although you may not get exactly the kind of cabin you would prefer. A summer cruise offers certain advantages: temperatures are virtually the same as in winter (cooler on average than in parts of the U.S. mainland), island flora is at its most dramatic, the water is smoother and clearer, and although there is always a breeze, winds are rarely strong enough to rock a ship. Some Caribbean tourist facilities close down in summer, however, and many ships move to Europe, Alaska, or the northeastern United States.

Hurricane season runs a full six months of the year—from June 1 through November 30. Although cruise ships stay well out of the way of these storms, hurricanes and tropical storms—their less-powerful relatives—can affect the weather throughout the Caribbean for days, and damage to ports can force last-minute itinerary changes.

## CRUISE COSTS

The average daily price for Caribbean itineraries varies dramatically depending on several circumstances. The cost of a cruise on a luxury line such as Silversea or Seabourn may be three to four times the cost of a cruise on a mainstream line such as Carnival or even premium lines like Princess. *When* you sail will also affect your costs: published brochure rates are usually highest during the peak summer season and holidays. When snow blankets the ground and temperatures are in single digits, a Caribbean cruise can be a welcome respite and less expensive than land resorts, which often command top dollar in winter months.

Solo travelers should be aware that single cabins have virtually disappeared from cruise ships, with the exception of Norwegian Cruise Line's newest ships *Norwegian Epic, Breakaway,* and *Getaway* and a few single cabins on Royal Caribbean and Holland America Line ships. Taking a double cabin can cost twice the advertised per-person rates (which are based on double occupancy). Some cruise lines will find same-sex roommates for singles; each then pays the per-person, double-occupancy rate.

### TIPS

One of the most delicate—yet frequently debated—topics of conversation among cruise passengers involves the matter of tipping. Whom do you tip? How much? What's "customary" and "recommended"? Should parents tip the full amount for children, or is just half adequate? Why do you have to tip at all?

When transfers to and from your ship are a part of your air-and-sea program, gratuities are generally included for luggage handling. In that case, do not worry about the interim tipping. However, if you take a taxi to the pier and hand over your bags to a stevedore, be sure to tip him. Treat him with respect and pass along at least $5.

During your cruise, room-service waiters generally receive a cash tip of $1 to $3 per delivery. A 15% to 18% gratuity will automatically be added to each bar bill during the cruise. If you use salon and spa services, a similar percentage might be added to the bills there as well. If you dine in a specialty restaurant, you may be asked to provide a one-time gratuity for the service staff.

Nowadays, tips for cruise staff generally add up to about $12 to $22 per person per day, depending on the category of your accommodations. You tip the same amount for each person who shares the cabin, including children, unless otherwise indicated. Most cruise lines now either automatically add gratuities to passengers' onboard charge accounts or offer the option.

CLOSE UP

## Recommended Gratuities by Cruise Line

Each cruise line has a different tipping policy. Some allow you to add tips to your shipboard account, and others expect you to dole out the dollars in cash on the last night of the cruise. Here are the suggested tipping amounts for each line covered in this book. Gratuity recommendations are often higher if you're staying in a suite with extra services, such as a butler.

Azamara Club Cruises: No tipping expected

Carnival Cruise Lines: $12.95–$13.95 per person per day

Celebrity Cruises: $13.50–$17 per person per day

Costa Cruises: $12 per person per day

Crystal Cruises: No tipping expected

Cunard Line: $11.50–$13.50 per person per day

Disney Cruise Line: $12 per person per day

Holland America Line: $12.50–$13.50 per person per day

MSC Cruises: $12 per person per day

Norwegian Cruise Line: $13.50–$15.50 per person per day

Oceania Cruises: $16–$23 per person per day

Ponant: No tipping expected

Princess Cruises: $12.95–$13.95 per person per day

Regent Seven Seas Cruises: No tipping expected

Royal Caribbean International: $13.50–$16.50 per person per day

Seabourn Cruise Line: No tipping expected

Seadream Yacht Club: No tipping expected

Silversea Cruises: No tipping expected

Star Clippers: $8 per person per day

Viking Ocean Cruises: $15 per person per day

Windstar Cruises: $12 per person per day

### EXTRAS

Cruise fares typically include accommodations, onboard meals and snacks, and most onboard activities. Not normally included are airfare, shore excursions, tips, soft drinks, alcoholic drinks, or spa treatments. Some lines now add a room service fee; for instance Norwegian Cruise Line charges $7.95 for all room service, with the exception of suites, and Royal Caribbean adds a $3.95 fee for late-night orders. Port fees, fuel surcharges, and sales taxes are generally added to your fare at booking.

### CABINS

In years gone by, cabins were almost an afterthought. The general attitude of both passengers and the cruise lines used to be that a cabin is a cabin and is used only for changing clothes and sleeping. That's why the cabins on most older cruise ships are skimpy in size and short on amenities.

Most cabin layouts on a ship are identical or nearly so. But cabins with a commanding view fetch higher fares. But you should know that they are also more susceptible to side-to-side movement; in rough seas you could find yourself tossed right out of bed. On lower decks, you'll pay less and find more stability, particularly in the middle of the ship, but even upper-level cabins in the middle of the ship are more steady.

Some forward cabins have a tendency to be oddly shaped, as they follow the contour of the bow. They are also likely to be noisy; when the ship's anchor drops, you won't need a wake-up call. In rough seas you can feel the ship's pitch (its upward and downward motion) more in the front. Should you go for the stern location instead? You're more likely to hear engine and machinery noise there, but you may also feel the pitch and possibly some vibration. However, many passengers feel the view of the ship's wake (the ripples it leaves behind as its massive engines move it forward) is worth any noise or vibration they might encounter there.

Above all, don't be confused by all the categories listed in cruise-line brochures—the categories more accurately reflect price levels based on location than any physical differences in the cabins themselves. Shipboard accommodations fall into four basic configurations: inside cabins, outside cabins, balcony cabins, and suites.

### INSIDE CABINS

An inside cabin has no window or porthole. These are always the least expensive cabins and are ideal for passengers who would rather spend their vacation funds on excursions or other incidentals than on upgraded accommodations. Inside cabins are generally just as spacious as the lowest category of outside cabins, and decor and amenities are similar. Parents sometimes book an inside cabin for their older children and teens, while their own cabin is an outside across the hall with a window or balcony.

### OUTSIDE CABINS

A standard outside cabin has either a picture window or porthole. To give the illusion of more space, these cabins might also rely on the generous use of mirrors for an even airier feeling. Two twin beds can be joined together to create one large bed. Going one step further, standard and larger outside staterooms on modern ships are often outfitted with a small sofa or loveseat with a cocktail table or small side table. Some larger cabins may have a combination bathtub–shower instead of just a shower.

### BALCONY CABINS

A balcony—or veranda—cabin is an outside cabin with floor-to-ceiling glass doors that open onto a private deck. Although the cabin may have large expanses of glass, the balcony is sometimes cut out of the cabin's square footage (depending on the ship). Balconies are usually furnished with two chairs and a table for lounging and casual dining outdoors. However, you should be aware that balconies are not always completely private; sometimes your balcony is visible from balconies next door and also from balconies above. The furnishings and amenities of balcony cabins are otherwise much like those in standard outside cabins.

### SUITES

Suites are the most lavish accommodations afloat, and although suites are always larger than regular cabins, they do not always have separate rooms for sleeping. Suites almost always have amenities that standard cabins do not have. Depending on the cruise line, you may find a small refrigerator or minibar stocked with complimentary soft drinks, bottled water, and the alcoholic beverages of your choice. Top suites on some ships include complimentary laundry service and complex entertainment centers with large flat-screen TVs, DVD players, and CD stereo systems. An added bonus to the suite life is the extra level of services many ships offer. Little extras might include afternoon tea and evening canapés delivered to you and served by a white-gloved butler.

Although minisuites on most contemporary ships have separate sitting areas with a sofa, chair, and cocktail table, don't let the marketing skill of the cruise lines fool you: so-called minisuites are usually little more than slightly larger versions of standard balcony cabins and seldom include the extra services and elaborate amenities you can get in regular suites. They're still generally a good value for the price if space matters.

### ACCESSIBILITY ISSUES

All major cruise lines offer a limited number of staterooms designed to be wheelchair- and scooter-accessible. Booking a newer vessel will generally assure more choices. On newer ships, public rooms are generally more accessible, and more facilities have been planned with wheelchair users in mind. Auxiliary aids, such as flashers for the hearing impaired and buzzers for visually impaired passengers, as well as lifts for swimming pools and hot tubs, are sometimes available. However, more than the usual amount of preplanning is necessary for smooth sailing if you have special needs.

For example, when a ship is unable to dock—as is the case in Grand Cayman—passengers are taken ashore on tenders that are sometimes problematic even for the able-bodied to negotiate. Some people with limited mobility may find it difficult to embark or disembark the ship when docked because of the steep angle of the gangways during high or low tide at certain times of day. In some situations, crew members may offer assistance that involves carrying guests, but if the sea is choppy when tendering is a necessity, that might not be an option.

Passengers who require continuous oxygen or have service animals will have further hurdles to overcome. You can bring both aboard a cruise ship, but you should be prepared to present up-to-date records for your service animal if they are requested.

## BOOKING YOUR CRUISE

As a rule, the majority of cruisers plan their trips nine to twelve months ahead of time. It follows, then, that a longer booking window should give you the pick of sailing dates, ships, itineraries, cabins, and flights to the port city. If you're looking for a standard itinerary and aren't choosy about the vessel or dates, you could wait for a last-minute discount, but they are rare and more difficult to find than in the past.

If particular shore excursions are important to you, consider booking them when you book your cruise to avoid disappointment later.

### USING A TRAVEL AGENT

Whether it is your first or 50th sailing, your best friend in booking a cruise is a knowledgeable travel agent. The last thing you want when considering a costly cruise vacation is an agent who has never been on a cruise, calls a cruise ship "the boat," or—worse still—quotes brochure rates. The most important steps in cruise-travel planning are research, research, and more research; your partner in this process is an experienced travel agent. Booking a cruise is a complex process, and it's seldom wise to try to go it alone, particularly the first time. But how do you find a cruise travel agent you can trust?

The most experienced and reliable agent will be certified as an Accredited Cruise Counselor (ACC), Master Cruise Counselor (MCC), or Elite Cruise Counselor (ECC) by the Cruise Lines International Association (CLIA). These agents have completed demanding training programs, including touring or sailing on a specific number of ships. Your agent should also belong to a professional trade organization. In North America, membership in the American Society of Travel Agents (ASTA) indicates that an agency has pledged to follow the code of ethics set forth by the world's largest association for travel professionals. In the best of all worlds, your travel agent is affiliated with both ASTA and CLIA.

Contrary to what conventional wisdom might suggest, cutting out the travel agent and booking directly with a cruise line won't necessarily get you the lowest price. According to Cruise Lines International Association (CLIA), seven out of ten, or 70%, of all cruise bookings are still handled through travel agents. In fact, cruise-line reservation systems simply are not capable of dealing with tens of thousands of direct calls from potential passengers. Without an agent working on your behalf, you're on your own. Do not rely solely on Internet message boards for authoritative responses to your questions—that is a service more accurately provided by your travel agent.

**Travel Agent Professional Organization American Society of Travel Agents** *(ASTA).* ☎ *703/739-2782, 800/965-2782 (24-hr hotline)* ⊕ *www.travelsense.org.*

**Cruise Line Organizations Cruise Lines International Association** *(CLIA).* ☎ *202/759-9370* ⊕ *www.cruising.org.*

## BOOKING YOUR CRUISE ONLINE

In addition to local travel agencies, there are many hardworking, dedicated travel professionals working for websites. Both big-name travel sellers and mom-and-pop agencies compete for the attention of cyber-savvy clients; and it never hurts to compare prices from a variety of these sources. Some cruise lines even allow you to book directly with them through their websites or toll-free reservation call centers.

As a rule, Web-based and toll-free brokers will do a decent job for you. They often offer discounted fares, though not always the lowest, so it pays to check around. If you know precisely what you want and how much you should pay to get a real bargain—and you don't mind dealing with an anonymous voice on the phone—make your reservations when the price is right. Just don't expect the personal service you get from an agent you know. Also, be prepared to spend a lot of time and effort on the phone if something goes wrong.

# DECIPHER YOUR DECK PLAN

## LIDO DECK

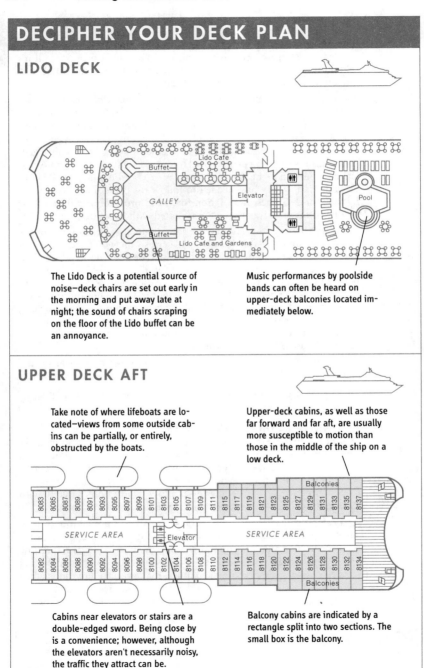

The Lido Deck is a potential source of noise—deck chairs are set out early in the morning and put away late at night; the sound of chairs scraping on the floor of the Lido buffet can be an annoyance.

Music performances by poolside bands can often be heard on upper-deck balconies located immediately below.

## UPPER DECK AFT

Take note of where lifeboats are located—views from some outside cabins can be partially, or entirely, obstructed by the boats.

Upper-deck cabins, as well as those far forward and far aft, are usually more susceptible to motion than those in the middle of the ship on a low deck.

Cabins near elevators or stairs are a double-edged sword. Being close by is a convenience; however, although the elevators aren't necessarily noisy, the traffic they attract can be.

Balcony cabins are indicated by a rectangle split into two sections. The small box is the balcony.

1

## MAIN PUBLIC DECK

Cabins immediately below restaurants and dining rooms can be noisy. Late sleepers might be bothered by early breakfast noise, early sleepers by late diners.

Theaters and dining rooms are often located on middle or lower decks.

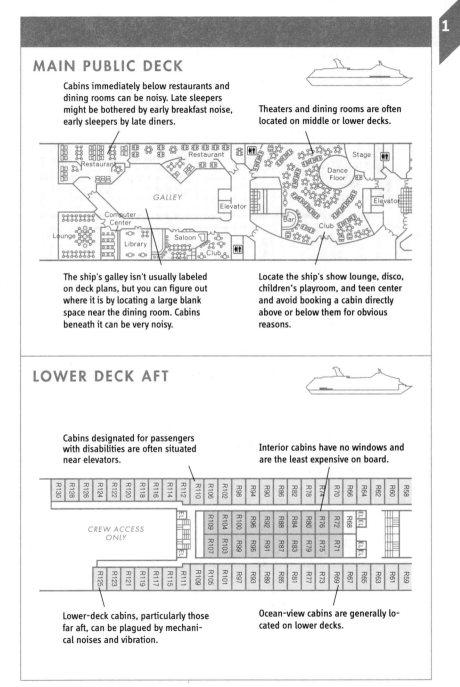

The ship's galley isn't usually labeled on deck plans, but you can figure out where it is by locating a large blank space near the dining room. Cabins beneath it can be very noisy.

Locate the ship's show lounge, disco, children's playroom, and teen center and avoid booking a cabin directly above or below them for obvious reasons.

## LOWER DECK AFT

Cabins designated for passengers with disabilities are often situated near elevators.

Interior cabins have no windows and are the least expensive on board.

Lower-deck cabins, particularly those far aft, can be plagued by mechanical noises and vibration.

Ocean-view cabins are generally located on lower decks.

CLOSE UP

## Before You Book

If you've decided to use a travel agent, ask yourself these 10 simple questions, and you'll be better prepared to help the agent do his or her job.

1. Who will be going on the cruise?

2. What can you afford to spend for the entire trip?

3. Where would you like to go?

4. How much vacation time do you have?

5. When can you get away?

6. What are your interests?

7. Do you prefer a casual or structured vacation?

8. What kind of accommodations do you want?

9. What are your dining preferences?

10. How will you get to the embarkation port?

## BEFORE YOU GO

To expedite your pre-boarding paperwork, some most cruise lines have convenient forms on their websites. As long as you have your reservation number, you can provide the required immigration information (usually your citizenship information and passport number), reserve shore excursions, and even indicate any special requests from the comfort of your home. A few less-wired cruise lines still mail pre-boarding paperwork to you or your travel agent for completion after you make your final payment, and they request that you return the forms by mail or fax. No matter how you submit them, be sure to make hard copies of any forms you fill out and bring them with you to the pier to smooth the embarkation process.

### DOCUMENTS

It is every passenger's responsibility to have proper identification. If you arrive at the embarkation port without it, you may not be allowed to board, and the line will issue no fare refund. Most travel agents know the requirements and can guide you to the proper agency to obtain what you need if you don't have it.

Everyone must have proof of citizenship and identity to travel abroad. Effective June 1, 2009, travelers were required to present a passport or other approved document denoting citizenship and identity for all land and sea travel into the United States. Like most rules, there is a confusing exception—U.S. citizens traveling within the Caribbean on closed-loop cruises (cruises that begin and end in the same port) are still permitted to depart from or enter the United States with proof of identity, which includes a government-issued photo ID, such as a driver's license, along with proof of citizenship, such as a certified birth certificate with seal issued by the state where you were born. However, you may still be required to present a passport when you dock at a foreign port, depending on the islands or countries that your cruise ship is visiting. And if your cruise begins in one U.S. port and ends in a different port, you will be required to have a passport. Check with your cruise line to ensure you have the appropriate documents for the stops you'll be making on your cruise.

Even for cruises that begin and end in the same port, cruise lines strongly recommend that all passengers travel with a valid passport, and some may very well require them. Having a valid passport will also enable you to fly from the United States to meet your ship at the first port should you miss the scheduled embarkation, as well as allow you to leave the ship without significant delays and complications before the cruise ends if you must fly back to the United States due to an emergency.

Children under the age of 18, when they are not traveling with both parents, almost always require a letter of permission from the absent parent(s). Airlines, cruise lines, and immigration agents can deny minor children initial boarding or entry to foreign countries without proper proof of identification and citizenship and a notarized permission letter from absent or noncustodial parents. Your travel agent or cruise line can help with the wording of such a letter.

## WHAT TO PACK

An absolute essential for women is a shawl or light sweater. Aggressive air-conditioning can make public rooms uncomfortable, particularly if you are sunburned from a day at the beach.

Put things you can't do without—such as prescription medication, spare eyeglasses, toiletries, a swimsuit, and change of clothes for the first day—in your carry-on. Most cruise ships provide soap, shampoo, and conditioner, so you probably won't need those.

And plan carefully. In fact, we'd strongly advise you to make a list so you don't forget anything.

## WHAT TO WEAR

In terms of your wardrobe, cruise wear falls into three categories: casual, informal, and formal. Cruise documents should include information indicating how many evenings fall into each category. You will know when to wear what by reading your ship's daily newsletter—each evening's dress code will be prominently announced.

For the day, you'll need casual wear. You'll typically need swimwear, a cover-up, and sandals for pool and beach. Time spent ashore touring and shopping calls for shorts topped with T-shirts or polo shirts and comfy walking shoes. Conservative is a rule to live by in the Caribbean (most Caribbean islands are very socially conservative), and mix-and-match will save room in your suitcase. Forget denim, which is too hot, and concentrate on lighter fabrics that will breathe in the Caribbean heat. Although jeans are allowed in the dining rooms of most mainstream ships, at night casual generally means khaki-type slacks and nice polo or sport shirts for men. Ladies' outfits are sundresses, skirts and tops, or pants outfits. By sticking to two or three complementary colors and a few accessories, you can mix up tops and bottoms for a different look every night.

Informal dress—sometimes called "resort" or "smart" casual—is a little trickier. It applies only to evening wear, and can mean different things depending on the cruise line. Informal for women is a dressier dress or pants outfit; for men it almost always includes a sport coat and sometimes a tie. Check your documents carefully.

Formal night means dressing up, but these days even that is a relative notion and found primarily on high-end ships. You will see women in everything from simple cocktail dresses to glittering formal gowns. A tuxedo or dark suit is required for gentlemen. For children, Sunday best is entirely appropriate.

### INSURANCE

It's a good idea to purchase travel insurance, which covers a variety of possible hazards and mishaps, when you book a cruise. Any policy should insure you for travel and luggage delays. A travel policy will ensure that you can get to the next port of call should you miss your ship, or replace delayed necessities secure in the knowledge that you will be reimbursed for those unexpected expenditures. Save your receipts for all out-of-pocket expenses to file your claim, and be sure to get an incident report from the airline at fault.

Insurance should also cover you for unexpected injuries and illnesses. The medical insurance program you depend on at home might not extend coverage beyond the borders of the United States. Medicare assuredly will not cover you if you are hurt or sick while abroad. It is worth noting that all ships of foreign registry are considered to be "outside the United States" by Medicare.

Nearly all cruise lines offer their own line of insurance. Compare the coverage and rates to determine which is best for you. Keep in mind that insurance purchased from an independent carrier is more likely to include coverage if the cruise line goes out of business before or during your cruise. Although it is a rare and unlikely occurrence, you do want to be insured in the event that it happens.

**U.S. Travel Insurers Allianz Travel Insurance.** ☎ *866/884–3556* ⊕ *www. allianztravelinsurance.com.* **CSA Travel Protection.** ☎ *877/243–4135* ⊕ *www. csatravelprotection.com.* **HTH Worldwide.** ☎ *610/254–8700, 888/243–2358* ⊕ *www.hthworldwide.com.* **Travelex Insurance.** ☎ *800/228–9792* ⊕ *www. travelexinsurance.com.* **Travel Guard International.** ☎ *715/345–0505, 800/826–4919* ⊕ *www.travelguard.com.* **Travel Insured International.** ☎ *800/243–3174* ⊕ *www.travelinsured.com.*

## ARRIVING AND EMBARKING

Most cruise-ship passengers fly to the port of embarkation. If you book your cruise far enough in advance, you'll be given the opportunity to purchase an air-and-sea package, which may—or may not—save you money on your flight. You might get a lower fare by booking your air independently or get considerably more convenient flight times, so it's a good idea to check for the best fare and most convenient flights available. Independent air arrangements might save you enough to cover the cost of a hotel room in your embarkation port so you can arrive early.

It's not a bad idea to arrive a day early to overcome any jet lag and avoid the possibility of delayed flights.

## GETTING TO THE PORT

If you buy an air-and-sea package from your cruise line, a uniformed cruise-line agent will meet you at baggage claim to smooth your way from airport to pier. You will need to claim your own bags and give them to the transfer driver so they can be loaded onto the bus. On arrival at the pier, luggage is automatically transferred to the ship for delivery to your cabin. The cruise-line ground transfer system can also be available to independent fliers. However, be sure to ask your travel agent how much it costs; you may find that a taxi or shuttle service is less expensive and more convenient.

In addition to the busiest embarkation ports such as Miami, Fort Lauderdale, and New York City, cruises now leave from less-familiar port cities all around the East and Gulf coasts. Galveston, Texas, and Port Canaveral, Florida, have become major home ports in recent years and are considered now to be among the nation's top 10 cruise ports. Many people prefer to drive to these ports if they are close enough to home. Secure parking is always available, either within the port itself or nearby.

## BOARDING

Procedures vary somewhat once you are greeted by staff members lined up just inside the ship's hull; however, you'll have to produce your boarding card for the security officer. At some point—either at the check-in desk or when boarding the ship for the first time—you will be photographed for security purposes; your image will display when your boarding card is "swiped" into a computer as you leave and reboard the ship in ports of call. Depending on the cruise line, you will be directed to your cabin, or a steward will relieve you of your carry-on luggage and accompany you. Stewards on high-end cruise lines not only show you the way, but hand you a glass of champagne as a welcome-aboard gesture. However, if you board early, don't be surprised if you are told cabins are not "ready" for occupancy—passageways to accommodations may even be roped off. In that case you can explore the ship, have lunch, or simply relax until an announcement is made that you can go to your cabin.

## ON BOARD

Check out your cabin to make sure that everything is in order. Try the plumbing and set the thermostat to the temperature you prefer. Your cabin may feel warm while docked but will cool off when the ship is underway. You should find a copy of the ship's daily schedule in the cabin. Take a few moments to look it over—you will want to know what time the lifeboat (or muster) drill takes place (a placard on the back of your cabin door will indicate directions to your emergency station), as well as meal hours and the schedule for various activities and entertainment.

# Fodor's Cruise Preparation Time Line

**4 TO 6 MONTHS BEFORE SAILING**
■ Check with your travel agent or the State Department for the identification required for your cruise.

■ Gather the necessary identification you need. If you need to replace a lost birth certificate, apply for a new passport, or renew one that's about to expire, start the paperwork now. Doing it at the last minute is stressful and often costly.

**60 TO 75 DAYS BEFORE SAILING**
■ Make the final payment on your cruise fare. Though the dates vary, your travel agent should remind you when the payment date draws near. Failure to submit the balance on time can result in the cancellation of your reservation.

■ Make a packing list for each person you'll be packing for.

■ Begin your wardrobe planning now. Try things on to make sure they fit and are in good repair (it's amazing how stains can magically appear months after something has been dry cleaned). Set things aside.

■ If you need to shop, get started so you have time to find just the right thing (and perhaps to return or exchange just the right thing). You may also need to allow time for alterations.

■ Make kennel reservations for your pets. (If you're traveling during a holiday period, you may need to do this even earlier.)

■ Arrange for a house sitter.

If you're cruising, but your kids are staying home:

■ Make child care arrangements.

■ Go over children's schedules to make sure they'll have everything they need while you're gone (gift for a birthday party, supplies for a school project, permission slip for a field trip).

■ If you have small children, you may want to put together a small bag of treats for them to open while you're gone—make a video of yourself reading a favorite bedtime story or singing a lullaby (as long as it's you, it will sound fantastic to them).

**30 DAYS BEFORE SAILING**
■ If you purchased an air-and-sea package, call your travel agent for the details of your airline schedule. Request seat assignments.

■ If your children are sailing with you, check their wardrobes now (do it too early and the really little kids may actually grow out of garments).

■ Make appointments for any personal services you wish to have before your cruise (for example, a haircut or manicure).

■ Get out your luggage and check the locks and zippers. Check for anything that might have spilled inside on a previous trip.

■ If you need new luggage or want an extra piece to bring home souvenirs, purchase it now.

**2 TO 4 WEEKS BEFORE SAILING**
■ Receive your cruise documents through the travel agent or print them from the cruise line's website.

■ Examine the documents for accuracy (correct cabin number, sailing date, and dining arrangements); make sure names are spelled correctly. If there's something you do not understand, ask now.

■ Read all the literature in your document package for suggestions specific to your cruise. Most cruise lines include helpful information.

■ Pay any routine bills that may be due while you're gone.

■ Go over your personalized packing list again. Finish shopping.

**1 WEEK BEFORE SAILING**
- Finalize your packing list and continue organizing everything in one area.
- Buy film or digital media and check the batteries in your camera.
- Refill prescription medications with an adequate supply.
- Make two photocopies of your passport or ID or credit cards. Leave one copy with a friend and carry the other copy separately from the originals.
- Get cash and/or traveler's checks at the bank. If you use traveler's checks, keep a separate record of the serial numbers. Get a supply of one-dollar bills for tipping baggage handlers (at the airport, hotel, pier, etc.).
- You may also want to put valuables and jewelry that you won't be taking with you in the safety deposit box while you're at the bank.
- Arrange to have your mail held at the post office or ask a neighbor to pick it up.
- Stop newspaper delivery or ask a neighbor to bring it in for you.
- Arrange for lawn and houseplant care or snow removal during your absence (if necessary).
- Leave your itinerary, the ship's telephone number (plus the name of your ship and your stateroom number), and a house key with a relative or friend.
- If traveling with young children, purchase small games or toys to keep them occupied while en route to your embarkation port.

**3 DAYS BEFORE SAILING**
- Confirm your airline flights; departure times are sometimes subject to change.
- Put a card with your name, address, telephone number, and itinerary inside each suitcase.

- Fill out the luggage tags that came with your document packet, and follow the instructions regarding when and how to attach them.
- Complete any other paperwork that the cruise line included with your documents (foreign customs and immigration forms, onboard charge application, etc.). Do not wait until you're standing in the pier check-in line to fill them in!
- Do last-minute laundry and tidy up the house.
- Pull out the luggage and begin packing.

**THE DAY BEFORE SAILING**
- Take pets to the kennel.
- Water houseplants and lawn (if necessary).
- Dispose of any perishable food in the refrigerator.
- Mail any last-minute bills.
- Set timers for indoor lights.
- Reorganize your wallet. Remove anything you will not need (local affinity cards, department store or gas credit cards, etc.), and put them in an envelope.
- Finish packing and lock your suitcases.

**DEPARTURE DAY**
- Adjust the thermostat and double-check the door locks.
- Turn off the water if there's danger of frozen pipes while you're away.
- Arrange to be at the airport a minimum of two hours before your departure time (follow the airline's instructions).
- Have photo ID and/or your passport ready for airport check-in.
- Slip your car keys, parking claim checks, and airline tickets into your carry-on luggage. Never pack these items in checked luggage.

Bon voyage gifts sent by your friends or travel agent will be delivered sometime during the afternoon. Be patient if you are expecting deliveries, particularly on megaships. Cabin stewards participate in the ship's turnaround and are extremely busy, although yours will no doubt introduce himself at the first available opportunity. It will also be a while before your checked luggage arrives, so your initial order of business is usually the buffet, if you haven't already had lunch. Bring along the daily schedule to check over while you eat.

While making your way to the Lido buffet, no doubt you'll notice bar waiters offering trays of colorful bon voyage drinks, often in souvenir glasses that you can keep. Beware—they are not complimentary! If you choose one, you will be asked to sign for it. Like the boarding photos, you are under no obligation to purchase.

Do your plans for the cruise include booking shore excursions and indulging in spa treatments? The most popular tours sometimes sell out, and spas can be busy during sea days, so your next stops should be the Shore Excursion Desk to book tours and the spa to make appointments if you didn't already book your spa visits and excursions in advance.

Dining room seating arrangements are another matter for consideration. If you aren't happy with your assigned dinner seating, speak to the maître d'. The daily schedule will indicate where and when to meet with him. If you plan to dine in the ship's specialty restaurant, make those reservations as soon as possible to avoid disappointment.

## PAYING FOR THINGS ON BOARD

Because cashless society prevails on cruise ships, during check-in an imprint is made of your credit card, or you must make a cash deposit for use against your onboard charges. Most onboard expenditures are charged to your shipboard account (via a swipe of your key card) with your signature as verification, with the exception of some casino gaming.

You'll get an itemized bill listing your purchases at the end of the voyage, and any discrepancies can be discussed at the purser's desk. To save time, check the balance of your shipboard account before the last day by requesting an interim printout of your bill from the purser to ensure accuracy. On some ships you can even access your account on your stateroom television.

## DINING

All food, all the time? Not quite, but it is possible to literally eat away the day and most of the night on a cruise. A popular cruise directors' joke is, "You came on as passengers, and you will be leaving as cargo." Although it is meant in fun, it does contain a ring of truth. Food—tasty and plentiful—is available 24 hours a day on most cruise ships, and the dining experience at sea has reached almost mythic proportions. Perhaps it has something to do with legendary midnight buffets and the absence of menu prices, or maybe it's the vast selection and availability.

## ONBOARD EXTRAS

| | |
|---|---|
| As you budget for your trip, keep these likely additional costs in mind. | Laundry: $2–$11 per piece (where self-launder facilities are unavailable) |
| Cocktails: $8–$12 | Spa treatments: $145–$265 |
| Wine by the glass: $8–$11 | Salon services: $30–$149 |
| Beer: $5–$6 | Casino gambling: 1¢ to $10 for slot machines; $5 and up for table games |
| Bottled water: $2.50–$4 | |
| Soft drinks: $2–$2.50 | Bingo: $5–$15 per card for multiple games in each session |
| Specialty ice cream and coffee: $4–$6 | |

### RESTAURANTS

Every ship has at least one main restaurant and a Lido, or casual, buffet alternative. Increasingly important are specialty restaurants. Meals in the primary and buffet restaurants are included in the cruise fare, as are most orders from round-the-clock room service, midday tea and snacks, and late-night buffets. Most mainstream cruise lines levy a surcharge for dining in alternative restaurants that may also include a gratuity, although there generally is no additional charge on luxury cruise lines.

You may also find a pizzeria or a specialty coffee bar on your ship—increasingly popular favorites cropping up on ships old and new. Although pizza is usually complimentary (though on some ships it is not when delivered by room service), expect an additional charge for specialty coffees at the coffee bar and, quite likely, in the dining room as well. You will also likely be charged for sodas and drinks other than iced tea, regular coffee, tap water, and fruit juice during meals.

There is often a direct relationship between the cost of a cruise and the quality of its cuisine. The food is sophisticated on some (mostly expensive) lines, among them Regent Seven Seas and Silversea. In the more moderate price range, Celebrity Cruises has always been known for its fine cuisine, and Oceania Cruises scores high marks as well. The trend toward featuring specialty dishes and even entire menus designed by acclaimed chefs has spread throughout the cruise industry; however, on most mainstream cruise lines the food is of the quality that you would find in any good hotel banquet—perfectly acceptable but certainly not great.

### SPECIALTY RESTAURANTS

A growing trend in shipboard dining is the emergence of sophisticated specialty restaurants that require reservations and frequently charge a fee. From as little as $29 per person for a complete steak dinner to $200 per person for an elaborate gourmet meal including fine wines paired with each course, specialty restaurants offer a refined dining option that cannot be duplicated in your ship's main restaurants. If you anticipate dining in your ship's intimate specialty restaurant, make reservations as soon as possible to avoid disappointment.

## Drinking and Gambling Ages

Many underage passengers have learned to their chagrin that the rules that apply on land are also adhered to at sea. On most mainstream cruise ships you must be 21 to imbibe alcoholic beverages. There are exceptions—for instance, on cruises departing from countries where the legal drinking age is typically lower than 21. On some cruise lines, a parent who is sailing with his or her son(s) and/or daughter(s) who is between the ages of 18 and 20 may sign a waiver allowing the 18- to 20-year-old to consume alcoholic beverages, generally limited to beer and wine. However, by and large, if you haven't achieved the magic age of 21, your shipboard charge card will be coded as booze-free, and bartenders won't risk their jobs to sell you alcohol.

Gambling is a bit looser, and 18-year-olds can try their luck on cruise lines such as Carnival, Celebrity, Holland America, Norwegian, Royal Caribbean, and Silversea; most other cruise lines adhere to the age-21 minimum.

### SPECIAL DIETS
Cruise lines make every possible attempt to ensure dining satisfaction. If you have special dietary considerations—such as low-salt, kosher, or food allergies—be sure to indicate them well ahead of time and check to be certain your needs are known by your waiter once on board. In addition to the usual menu items, so-called spa, low-calorie, low-carbohydrate, or low-fat selections, as well as children's menus, are usually available. Requests for dishes not featured on the menu can often be granted if you ask in advance.

### ALCOHOL
On all but the most upscale lines, you pay for alcohol aboard the ship, including wine with dinner. Wine typically costs about what you would expect to pay at a nice lounge or restaurant in a resort or in a major city. Wine by the bottle is a more economical choice at dinner than ordering it by the glass. Any wine you don't finish will be kept for you and served the next night. Gifts of wine or champagne ordered from the cruise line (either by you, a friend, or your travel agent) can be taken to the dining room. Wine from any other source will incur a corkage fee of approximately $10 to $25 per bottle. Some (though not all) lines will allow you to carry wine aboard when you embark for the first time; almost no line allows you to carry other alcohol on board.

### ENTERTAINMENT
Real treats are the folkloric shows or other entertainment arranged to take place while cruise ships are in port. Local performers come aboard, usually shortly before the ship sails, to present traditional songs and dances. It's an excellent way to get a glimpse of their performing arts.

Some ships also have a movie theater or offer in-cabin movies, or you may be able to rent or borrow movies to watch on your in-cabin DVD player, if you have one. The latest twist in video programming can be found on many cruise ships—huge outdoor LED screens where movies, music video concerts, news channels, and even the ship's activities are broadcast for passengers lounging poolside.

Enrichment programs have also become a popular pastime at sea. It may come as a surprise that port lecturers on many large contemporary cruise ships offer more information on shore tours and shopping than insight into the ports of call. If more cerebral presentations are important to you, consider a cruise on a line that features stimulating enrichment programs and seminars at sea. Speakers can include destination-oriented historians, popular authors, business leaders, radio or television personalities, and even movie stars.

### LOUNGES AND NIGHTCLUBS

You'll often find live entertainment in the ship lounges after dinner (and even sometimes before dinner). If you want to unleash your inner American Idol, look for karaoke. Singing along in a lively piano bar is another shipboard favorite for would-be crooners.

Other lounges might feature easy-listening or jazz performances or live music for pre- and postdinner social dancing. Later in the evening, lounges pick up the pace with music from the 1950s and '60s; clubs aimed at a younger crowd usually have more contemporary dance music during the late-night hours.

### CASINOS

On most ships, lavish casinos pulsate with activity. On ships that feature them, the rationale for locating casinos where most passengers must pass either through or alongside them is obvious—the unspoken allure of winning. In addition to slot machines in a variety of denominations, cruise-ship casinos usually have table games. Casino hours vary based on the itinerary or location of the ship; most are required to close while in port, whereas others may be able to offer 24-hour slot machines and simply close table games. Every casino has a cashier, and you may be able to charge a cash advance to your onboard account, for a fee.

### SPORTS AND FITNESS

Onboard sports facilities might include a court for basketball, volleyball, tennis—or all three—a jogging track, or even a ropes course high above the ship's top deck. Some ships are even offering innovative and unexpected features, such as rock-climbing walls, bungee trampolines, and surfing pools on some Royal Caribbean ships. For the less adventurous, there's always table tennis and shuffleboard.

Naturally, you will find at least one swimming pool, and possibly several. Cruise-ship pools are generally on the small side—more appropriate for cooling off than doing laps—and the majority contain filtered salt water. But some are elaborate affairs, with waterslides and interactive water play areas for family fun. Princess Grand–class ships have challenging, freshwater "swim against the current" pools for swimming enthusiasts who want to get their low-impact exercise while on board.

Shipboard fitness centers have become ever more elaborate, offering state-of-the-art exercise machines, treadmills, and stair steppers, not to mention weights and weight machines. As a bonus, many fitness centers with floor-to-ceiling windows have the world's most inspiring

## Will I Get Seasick?

Many first-time passengers are anxious about whether they'll be stricken by seasickness, but there is no way to tell until you actually sail. Modern vessels are equipped with stabilizers that eliminate much of the motion responsible for seasickness. On an Alaska cruise you will spend most of your time in calm, sheltered waters, so unless your cruise includes time out in the open sea (say, between San Francisco and Vancouver), you may not even feel the ship's movement—particularly if your ship is a megaliner. You may feel slightly more movement on a small ship, but not by much, as these ships ply remote bays and coves that are even more sheltered than those traveled by regular cruise ships.

If you have a history of seasickness, don't book an inside cabin. For the terminally seasick, it will begin to resemble a movable coffin in short order. If you do become seasick, you can use common drugs such as Dramamine and Bonine. Some people find anti-seasickness wristbands helpful; these apply gentle pressure to the wrist in lieu of drugs. Worn behind the ear, the Transderm Scop patch dispenses a continuous metered dose of medication, which is absorbed into the skin and enters the bloodstream. Apply the patch four hours before sailing and it will continue to be effective for three days.

sea views. Most ships offer complimentary fitness classes, but you might also find classes in Pilates, spinning, or yoga (usually for a fee). Personal trainers are usually on board to get you off on the right foot, also for a fee.

### SPAS

With all the usual pampering and service in luxurious surroundings, simply being on a cruise can be a stress-reducing experience. Add to that the menu of spa and salon services at your fingertips and you have a recipe for total sensory pleasure. Spas have also become among the most popular of shipboard areas. While high-end Canyon Ranch has made inroads with the cruise industry by opening spas on an increasing number of ships, Steiner Leisure is still the largest spa and salon operator at sea (the company also operates the Mandara and the Greenhouse spa brands), with facilities on more than 100 cruise ships worldwide.

In addition to facials, manicures, pedicures, massages, and sensual body treatments, other hallmarks of Steiner Leisure are salon services and products for hair and skin. Founded in 1901 by Henry Steiner of London, a single salon prospered when Steiner's son joined the business in 1926 and was granted a Royal Warrant as hairdresser to Her Majesty Queen Mary in 1937. In 1956 Steiner won its first cruise-ship contract to operate the salon on board the ships of the Cunard Line. By the mid-1990s Steiner Leisure began taking an active role in creating shipboard spas offering a wide variety of wellness therapies and beauty programs for both women and men.

## Safety at Sea

**1**

Safety begins with you, the passenger. Once settled into your cabin, locate your life vests if they are stored there, and review the posted emergency instructions. Make sure the vests are in good condition, and learn how to secure them properly. Make certain the ship's purser knows if you have a physical infirmity that may hamper a speedy exit from your cabin, so that in an emergency he or she can quickly dispatch a crew member to assist you. If you're traveling with children, be sure that child-size life jackets are placed in your cabin.

Before your ship leaves the embarkation port, you'll be required to attend a mandatory lifeboat drill. Do so and listen carefully. If you're unsure about how to use your vest, now is the time to ask. Some cruise lines no longer require you to bring your vest to the muster drill and instead store them near the muster station, but crew members are more than willing to assist if you have questions. Only in the most extreme circumstances will you need to abandon ship—but it has happened. The time you spend learning the procedure may serve you well in a mishap.

In actuality, the greatest danger facing cruise-ship passengers is fire. All cruise lines must meet international standards for fire safety, which require sprinkler systems, smoke detectors, and other safety features. Fires on cruise ships are not common, but they do happen, and these rules have made ships much safer. You can do your part by *not* using an iron in your cabin and taking care to properly extinguish smoking materials. Never throw a lighted cigarette overboard—it could be blown back into an opening in the ship and start a fire.

### OTHER SHIPBOARD SERVICES
### COMMUNICATIONS

Just because you are out to sea does not mean you have to be out of touch. However, ship-to-shore telephone calls can cost $2 to $15 a minute, so it makes more economic sense to use email to remain in contact with your home or office. Most ships have basic computer systems, and some newer vessels offer more high-tech connectivity—even in-cabin hookups or wireless connections for either your own laptop computer or tablet. Expect to pay an activation fee and subsequent charges in the 75¢- to $1-per-minute range for the use of these Internet services. Ships usually offer some kind of package so that you get a reduced per-minute price if you pay a fee up front.

The ability to use your own mobile phone for calls from the high seas is an alternative that is gaining in popularity. It's usually cheaper than using a cabin phone if your ship offers the service; however, it can still cost $2.50 to $5 a minute. A rather ingenious concept, the ship acts as a cell "tower" in international waters—you use your own cell phone and your own number when roaming at sea, and you can even send and receive text messages and email with some smartphones (albeit with a surcharge in addition to any roaming fees). Before leaving home, ask your cell-phone service provider to activate international roaming on your account. When in port, depending on the type of cell phone

## Crime on Ships

Crime aboard cruise ships has occasionally become headline news, thanks in large part to a few well-publicized cases. Most people never have any type of problem, but you should exercise the same precautions aboard a ship that you would at home. Keep your valuables out of sight—on big ships virtually every cabin has a small safe. Don't carry too much cash ashore, use your credit card whenever possible, and keep your money in a secure place, such as a front pocket that's harder to pick. Single women traveling with friends should stick together, especially when returning to their cabins late at night. When assaults occur, it often comes to light that excessive drinking of alcohol is a factor. Be careful about whom you befriend, as you would anywhere, whether it's a fellow passenger or a member of the crew. Don't be paranoid, but do be prudent.

Your cruise is a wonderful opportunity to leave everyday responsibilities behind, but don't neglect to pack your common sense. After a few drinks it might seem like a good idea to sit on a railing or lean over the rail to get a better view of the ship's wake. Passengers have been known to fall. "Man overboard" is more likely to be the result of carelessness than criminal intent.

you own and the agreements your mobile service-provider has established, you may be able to connect to local networks ashore. Most GSM phones are also usable in Mexico and on Caribbean islands. Rates for using the maritime service, as well as any roaming charges, are established by your mobile service carrier and are worth checking into before your trip. To avoid excessive charges, it's a good idea to turn off your phone's data roaming option while at sea.

### LAUNDRY AND DRY CLEANING

Most cruise ships offer valet laundry and pressing (and some also offer dry cleaning) service. Expenses can add up fast, especially for laundry, since charges are per item and the rates are similar to those charged in hotels, unless your ship offers a fixed-price laundry deal (all you can stuff into a bag they provide for a single fee). If doing laundry is important to you and you do not want to send it out to be done, some cruise ships have a self-service laundry room (which usually features an iron and ironing board in addition to washers and dryers). If you book one of the top-dollar suites, laundry service may be included for no additional cost. Upscale ships such as those in the Regent Seven Seas Cruises and Silversea Cruises fleets have complimentary self-service launderettes. On other cruise lines, such as Disney Cruise Line, Princess Cruises, Oceania Cruises, Carnival Cruise Lines, and some Holland America Line ships, you can do your own laundry for about $4 or less per load. None of the vessels in the Norwegian, Royal Caribbean, or Celebrity Cruises fleets has self-service laundry facilities.

# DISEMBARKATION

All cruises come to an end eventually, and the disembarkation process actually begins the day before you arrive at your ship's final port. During that day your cabin steward delivers special luggage tags to your stateroom, along with customs forms and instructions on some itineraries.

The night before you disembark, you'll need to set aside clothing to wear the next morning when you leave the ship. Many people dress in whatever casual outfits they wear for the final dinner on board, or change into travel clothes after dinner. Also, do not forget to put your passport or other proof of citizenship, airline tickets, and medications in your hand luggage. The luggage tags go onto your larger bags, which are placed outside your stateroom door for pickup during the hours indicated. Your cruise line may offer self-assist debarkation, and in that case, you do not have to put your luggage outside your stateroom the night before departure and may leave the ship early if you can take all your luggage with you.

A statement itemizing your onboard charges is delivered before you arise on disembarkation morning. Plan to get up early enough to check it over for accuracy, finish packing your personal belongings, and vacate your stateroom by the appointed hour. Any discrepancies in your onboard account should be taken care of before leaving the ship, usually at the reception desk. Breakfast is served in the main restaurant as well as the buffet on the last morning, but room service usually isn't available. Disembarkation procedures vary by cruise line, but you'll probably have to wait in a lounge or on deck for your tag color or number to be called.

Then you take a taxi, bus, or other transportation to your postcruise hotel or to the airport for your flight home. If you are flying out the day your cruise ends, leave plenty of time to go through the usual check-in, passport control/immigration, and security procedures at the airport.

## CUSTOMS AND DUTIES
### U.S. CUSTOMS

Each individual or family must fill out a customs declaration form, which will be provided before your ship docks. Be sure to keep receipts for all purchases made outside the United States; you may also be asked to show officials the receipts along with what you've bought. After showing your passport to United States immigration officials upon debarkation, you must collect your luggage from the dock.

ALLOWANCES You're always allowed to bring goods of a certain value back home without having to pay any duty or import tax. There's also a limit on the amount of tobacco and liquor you can bring back duty-free, and some countries have separate limits for perfumes; for exact figures, check with your customs department. The values of so-called duty-free goods are included in these amounts. When you shop abroad—and in the Caribbean, this means all islands except for Puerto Rico, which is considered a part of the United States for customs purposes. If the total value of your goods is more than the duty-free limit, then you'll have to pay a tax (most often a flat percentage) on the value of everything beyond that limit.

Individuals entering the United States from the Caribbean are allowed to bring in $800 worth of duty-free goods for personal use ($1,600 from the U.S. Virgin Islands), including 1 liter of alcohol (2 liters if one was produced in the Caribbean, and 5 liters from the USVI), one carton of cigarettes (or five if four were purchased in the U.S. Virgin Islands), and 100 non-Cuban cigars. Antiques and original artwork are also duty-free.

# 2

# CRUISE LINES AND CRUISE SHIPS

By Linda
Coffman

More ships sail in the Caribbean than in any other region of the world, offering passengers a wide range of choices, from mainstream to luxury, from large megaliners to small yachtlike vessels. The size of the ship will in part dictate where it can go and how passengers will enjoy their vacation. So just as with other popular cruise destinations, picking the right cruise ship is the most important decision you will make in choosing your cruise, particularly if you stick with a large ship.

Make no mistake about it: cruise ships have distinct personalities. Norwegian's lack of formality and range of dining choices and entertainment makes these ships the favorites of some and the bane of others. Even ships belonging to the same class and nearly indistinguishable from one another have certain traits that make them stand out.

That is why the most important choice you'll make when booking a cruise is the combined selection of cruise line and cruise ship. Cruise lines set the tone for their fleets, but since the cruise industry is relatively fluid, some new features introduced on one ship may not be found on all the ships owned by the same cruise line. For instance, you'll find ice-skating rinks only on the biggest Royal Caribbean ships. However, most cruise lines attempt to standardize the overall experience throughout their fleets (for example, you'll find a rock-climbing wall on *every* Royal Caribbean ship).

## ABOUT THE CRUISE LINES

Just as cruise ships differ by size and style, so do the cruise lines themselves, and finding a cruise line that matches your personality is as important as finding the right ship. Some cruise lines cater to families, others to couples, active singles, and even food and wine aficionados. Selecting the right one can mean the difference between struggling with unmet expectations and enjoying the vacation of a lifetime. Although some of the differences are subtle, most of today's cruise lines still fall into three basic categories: Mainstream, Premium, and Luxury.

### MAINSTREAM LINES

Mainstream cruise lines usually have a little something for everyone: Ships tend to be the big, bigger, and biggest at sea, carrying the highest number of passengers per available space. Cabins can be basic or fancy since most mainstream lines also offer more upscale accommodations categories, including suites. Some mainstream lines still offer traditional dining, with two assigned seatings in the main restaurant for dinner. But following the popular trend, all mainstream cruise lines have introduced variations of open seating dining and alternative restaurant options that allow passengers to dine when and with whom they please, though almost all alternative restaurants carry an extra charge.

## PREMIUM LINES

Premium lines usually offer a more subdued atmosphere and refined style: Ships tend to be newer midsize to large vessels that carry fewer passengers than mainstream ships and have a more spacious feel. Staterooms still range from more basic to more upscale, but even the basic accommodations tend to have more style and space. Cuisine on these ships tends to be a bit better, and most of these ships have à la carte options for more upscale dining for an extra charge, often higher than those on mainstream lines. There are still extra charges on the ship.

## LUXURY LINES

The air on these deluxe vessels is as rarefied as the champagne and caviar: Ships range from megayachts for only a hundred or so privileged guests to midsize vessels, which are considered large for this category. Space is so abundant that you might wonder where the other passengers are hiding. Spacious staterooms are frequently all suites; at the least, they are the equivalent to higher-grade accommodations on mainstream and premium ships. Open seating is the norm, and guests dine where and with whom they please during dinner hours. There are relatively few extra charges on these ships, except for premium wines by the bottle, spa services, and excursions, but some lines even include excursions and airfare in their prices.

## SMALL-SHIP LINES

A casual, relaxed atmosphere in intimate spaces prevails on these yacht-like vessels for fewer than a hundred passengers. Emphasis is placed on unique and flexible itineraries to off-the-beaten-path destinations with exploration leaders guiding the way to insightful encounters ashore. Accommodations are proportionately small, but basic amenities are provided. Meals often feature fresh local ingredients and are served in open seating, buffet, or family style. The dress code is always comfortable casual, and evenings on board may include a lecture, but socializing with other passengers is the most common activity. Exercise equipment is usually found on board, but kayaking and nature hikes are offered for a more adventurous workout.

## ABOUT THE SHIPS
### LARGE CRUISE SHIPS

Large cruise lines account for the majority of passengers sailing to the Caribbean. These typically have large cruise ships in their fleets with plentiful deck space and, often, a promenade deck that allows you to stroll around the ship's perimeter. In the newest vessels, traditional meets trendy with resort-style innovations; however, they still feature cruise-ship classics such as afternoon tea, and most offer complimentary room service. The smallest cruise ships in the major cruise lines' fleets carry as few as 300 passengers or less, whereas the biggest can accommodate between 1,500 and 5,000 passengers—enough people to outnumber the residents of many Caribbean islands. Large ships are a good choice if you're looking for nonstop activity and lots of options; they're especially appealing for groups and families with older kids. If you prefer a gentler pace and a chance to get to know your shipmates, try a smaller ship.

### SMALL SHIPS

Compact expedition-type vessels bring you right up to the shoreline to enter hidden coves where big ships don't fit. These cruises focus on destinations, and you'll call into smaller ports, as well as some of the better-known towns. Enrichment talks—conducted by experts in the region's natural history and local cultures—are the norm. Cabins on expedition ships can be tiny, sometimes with no phone or TV, and bathrooms are often no bigger than cubbyholes. The dining room and lounge are usually the only public areas on these vessels; however, some are luxurious with cushy cabins, comfy lounges and libraries, and hot tubs. You won't find much nightlife aboard, but what you trade space and onboard diversions for is a unique and unforgettable glimpse of the Caribbean.

Many small ships are based in Barbados or St. Marteen/St. Martin and sail the Southern Caribbean, including the Windward Islands and the Grenadines.

Small-ship cruising can be pricey, but there are few onboard charges, and, given the size of ship and style of cruise, fewer opportunities to spend money on board.

## AZAMARA CLUB CRUISES

"You'll love where we take you" is the slogan for this premium cruise line launched by parent company Royal Caribbean in 2007. The line comprises two ships, both built for now-defunct Renaissance Cruises and refitted for the deluxe-cruise crowd. Designed for exotic, destination-driven itineraries, Azamara offers a more intimate onboard experience, while allowing access to the more unusual ports of call experienced travelers want to visit. Since its launch, a number of amenities have been added to passengers' fares, with no charge for bottled water, specialty coffees and teas; shuttle bus service to/from port communities (where available); featured wines served at lunches and dinners from interesting small wineries; and complimentary self-service laundry.

Enrichment programs, from culinary demonstrations to seminars by guest speakers and experts on a wide variety of topics, are some of the best on offer. The ships are designated resort casual, so there is no necessity to weigh down your luggage with formal attire—even though your butler is on hand to unpack for you if you have booked a suite. Evening entertainment leans toward sophisticated cabaret and jazz. Azamara ships are some of the most smoke-free at sea. Only a single small section in a forward area of the pool deck is designated for smokers. No other areas on the ships allow smoking, including cabins and balconies.

**Tipping:** Housekeeping and dining gratuities are included in the fare. A standard 18% gratuity is added to beverage charges and for spa services.

**CHOOSE IF**

Your taste leans toward luxury, but your budget doesn't.

You prefer leisurely open seating dining in casual attire to the stiffness of assigned tablemates and waiters.

The manner in which you "get there" is as important to you as your destination.

**DON'T CHOOSE IF**

You want glitzy, high-energy evening entertainment.

You require the services of a butler; only suites have them.

You insist on smoking whenever and wherever you want to.

**Contacts** ☎ *877/999–9553* ⊕ *www.azamaraclubcruises.com*

## CARNIVAL CRUISE LINES

The world's largest cruise line originated the Fun Ship concept in 1972 with the relaunch of an aging ocean liner that got stuck on a sandbar during its maiden voyage. Sporting red, white, and blue flared funnels, which are easily recognized from afar, new ships are continuously added to the fleet and rarely deviate from a successful pattern. Decor tends to be over the top, though an ongoing renovation plan is toning down the glitz; each ship features numerous public rooms, bars and lounges, and huge casinos, spas, and lavish entertainment in massive show lounges.

Cabins are spacious and comfortable, often larger than on other ships in this price category, and feature the Carnival Comfort Bed sleep system consisting of plush mattresses, luxury duvets, high-quality linens, and cushy pillows. Ship decor on many ships is undergoing a softening and modernizing while new features including a new pub, rum- and tequila-based pool bars, a Guy Fieri hamburger restaurant, and comedy club have been added to most ships.

Carnival ships have both flexible dining options and casual alternative restaurants, and the quality of the food is good for a mainstream cruise line.

**Tipping:** A gratuity of $12.95 per passenger per day is automatically added to passenger accounts for standard accommodations and $13.95 for suites, and gratuities are distributed to stewards and waitstaff. Passengers may adjust the amount based on the level of service experienced and tipping is not required of children under the age of two. All beverage tabs at bars get an automatic 15% addition.

**CHOOSE IF**

You want an action-packed casino with a choice of table games and rows upon rows of clanging slot machines.

You don't mind standing in line—these are big ships with a lot of passengers, and lines are not uncommon.

You don't mind hearing announcements over the public-address system reminding you of what's next on the schedule.

### DON'T CHOOSE IF

You want an intimate, sedate atmosphere. Carnival's ships are big and bold.

You want elaborate accommodations. Carnival suites are spacious but not as feature-filled as the term "suite" may suggest.

You're turned off by men in tank tops. Casual on these ships means casual indeed.

**Contacts** ☎ *305/599–2600 or 800/227–6482* ⊕ *www.carnival.com*

## CELEBRITY CRUISES

Founded in 1989, Celebrity has gained a reputation for fine food and professional service. The cruise line has built premium, sophisticated ships and developed signature amenities, including a specialty coffee shop, martini bar, large standard staterooms with generous storage, spas, and butler service for passengers booking the top suites. Concierge-class makes certain premium ocean-view and balcony staterooms almost the equivalent of suites in terms of amenities and service.

Entertainment choices range from Broadway-style productions, captivating lounge shows, and lively discos to Monte Carlo–style casinos and specialty lounges. Multimillion-dollar art collections grace the entire fleet, which merged with Royal Caribbean International in 1997.

In early 2007 Celebrity announced plans to advance its already distinguished fleet-wide culinary program to the next level. Each ship in the fleet has highly experienced teams headed by executive chefs and food and beverage managers, who have developed their skills in some of the world's finest restaurants and hotels. An expanded cocktail program was introduced in 2013. Alternative restaurants offer fine dining, but most have an average $40 per-person supplement, much higher than on most other cruise lines.

**Tipping:** Gratuities are automatically added daily to onboard accounts in the following amounts (which may be adjusted at your discretion): $13.50 per person per day for passengers in stateroom categories; $14 per person per day for Concierge-class and Aqua-class staterooms; and $17 per person per day for suites. An automatic gratuity of 18% is added to all beverage tabs, minibar purchases, and salon and spa services.

### CHOOSE IF

You want an upscale atmosphere at a relatively reasonable fare.

You don't mind paying extra for exceptional specialty dining experiences.

You want to dine amid elegant surroundings in some of the best restaurants at sea.

### DON'T CHOOSE IF

You need to be reminded of when activities are scheduled. Announcements are kept to a minimum.

You look forward to boisterous pool games and wacky contests. These cruises are fairly quiet and sophisticated.

You think funky avant-garde art is weird. Abstract modernism abounds in the art collections.

**Contacts** ☎ *800/647–2251* ⊕ *www.celebritycruises.com*

# COSTA CRUISES

The Genoa-based Costa Crociere, parent company of Costa Cruises, had been in the shipping business for more than 100 years and in the passenger business for almost 50 years when Carnival Corporation gained sole ownership of the line in 2000, but the ships retain their original flavor. Costa's Italian-inspired vessels bring the Mediterranean vitality of La Dolce Vita to far-flung regions of the Caribbean. The ships are a combination of classic and modern design. A new vessel-building program has brought Costa ships into the 21st century with innovative, large-ship designs that reflect their Italian heritage and style without overlooking the amenities expected by modern cruisers.

Festive shipboard activities may include games of boccie and a wacky toga party, yet there is also a nod to the traditional cruise-ship entertainment expected by North Americans. Supercharged social staffs work overtime to get everyone in the mood and encourage everyone to be a part of the action.

Dining features regional Italian cuisines, a variety of pastas, chicken, beef, and seafood dishes, as well as authentic pizza. Costa dining is notable for its delicious, properly prepared pasta courses. Alternative dining is by reservation only in the upscale supper clubs, which serve choice steaks and seafood from a Tuscan steak-house menu as well as traditional Italian specialties.

**Tipping:** Gratuities are added to onboard accounts in the following amounts: $12 per adult per day; 50% of that amount for children between the ages of 4 and 14; and no charge for children under the age of 4. A 15% gratuity is automatically added to all beverage tabs.

### CHOOSE IF

You're a satisfied Carnival past passenger and want a similar experience with an Italian flavor.

You want pizza hot out of the oven whenever you get a craving for it.

You're a joiner: there are many opportunities to be in the center of the action.

### DON'T CHOOSE IF

You find announcements in a variety of languages annoying.

You want an authentic Italian cruise. The crew has grown more international than Italian as the line has expanded.

You prefer sedate splendor in a formal atmosphere; many of the ships are almost Fellini-esque in style.

**Contacts** ☎ *954/266–5600 or 800/462–6782* ⊕ *www.costacruises.com*

## CRYSTAL CRUISES

Crystal's midsize ships stand out for their modern design, amenities, and spaciousness. Built to deliver the first-rate service and amenities expected from a luxury line, including complimentary wines and premium spirits throughout the ships and open bar service in all lounges, these vessels nevertheless carry upward of 900 passengers—and have many big-ship facilities. Beginning with ship designs based on the principles of feng shui, no detail is too small to overlook to provide passengers with the best imaginable experience.

Crystal ships have long set standards for pampering—one reason these vessels often spend several days at sea rather than in port. To the typical litany of cruise-ship diversions, Crystal adds enrichment opportunities that include destination-oriented lectures and talks by scholars, political figures, and diplomats; hands-on classes in music and art; and deluxe theme cruises that emphasize such topics as food and wine or the fine arts. In 2012, Crystal became one of the last of the luxury lines to go all-inclusive.

The food is a good enough reason to book a Crystal cruise. Dining in the main restaurants is an event starring Continental-inspired cuisine served by European-trained waiters. Casual poolside dining from the grills is offered on some evenings in a relaxed, no-reservations-required option. Where service and the dishes really shine are in the specialty restaurants; each ship has Asian-inspired and Italian specialty restaurants, which are in high demand.

**Tipping:** Housekeeping and dining gratuities are included in the fare. An 18% gratuity is suggested for spa and beauty treatments and is automatically added to the bill.

### CHOOSE IF

You crave peace and quiet. Announcements are kept to a bare minimum, and the ambience is sedate.

You prefer to plan ahead. You can make spa, restaurant, shore excursion, and class reservations when you book your cruise.

You love sushi and other Asian delights—Crystal ships serve some of the best at sea.

### DON'T CHOOSE IF

You don't want to follow the dress code. Everyone does, and you'll stand out—and not in a good way—if you rebel.

You want an inside stateroom. There are none.

You want a less-structured cruise. Even with open seating dining, Crystal is a bit more regimented than other luxury lines.

**Contacts** ☎ *310/785–9300 or 888/799–4625* ⊕ *www.crystalcruises.com*

## CUNARD LINE

One of the world's most distinguished names in ocean travel since 1840, Cunard Line has a history of deluxe transatlantic crossings and worldwide cruising that is legendary for comfortable accommodations, excellent cuisine, and personal service. Though the line is now owned by Carnival Corporation, its high-end ships retain a distinctly British sensibility. Cunard offers a short season of Caribbean cruises, which are highly prized by fans of the line.

Entertainment includes nightly production shows or cabaret-style performances and even plays. An authentic pub adds to the British ambience, while a wide variety of musical styles can be found for dancing and listening in other bars and lounges. Cunard's fine enrichment programs are presented by expert guest lecturers. You can preplan your activities prior to departure by consulting the syllabus of courses available online at Cunard Line's website.

In the tradition of multiclass ocean liners, dining-room assignments are made according to the accommodation category booked, so you get the luxury you pay for. Passengers in Junior Suites are assigned to single-seating Princess Grill, while the posh Queen's Grill serves passengers booked in the most lavish suites. Some balcony accommodations receive single-seating Britannia Club dining assignments; all other passengers dine in one of two seatings in the dramatic Britannia Restaurant.

**Tipping:** Suggested gratuities of $13.50 per person per day (for Grill Restaurant accommodations) or $11.50 per person per day (all other accommodations) are automatically charged to shipboard accounts. A 15% gratuity is added to bar tabs. Direct gratuities for special service are allowed.

### CHOOSE IF

You want to boast that you have sailed on one of the world's largest ocean liners.

You enjoy a brisk walk. *Queen Mary 2* is massive, and you'll find yourself walking a great deal.

A posh English pub is your idea of the perfect place to hang out.

### DON'T CHOOSE IF

You prefer informality. Cunard ships are traditional formal liners.

You want real luxury with no add-on costs.

Your sense of direction is really bad. Nearly everyone gets lost on board *QM2* at least once.

**Contacts** ☎ *661/753–1000 or 800/728–6273* ⊕ *www.cunard.com*

## DISNEY CRUISE LINE

Disney Cruise Line launched its ships in 1998 and 1999, and expanded the fleet with a third ship in 2011; a fourth entered service in 2012. Dozens of the best ship designers, industry veterans, and Disney creative minds planned intensely for multiple years to produce these vessels, which make a positive impression on adults and children alike. Exteriors are reminiscent of the great ocean liners of the early 20th century, resplendent with two funnels and black hulls, but interiors are technologically up-to-the-minute and full of novel developments in dining, cabin, and entertainment facilities. Accommodations are especially family-friendly, and most have a split-bathroom configuration with a sink and bathtub in one section and a sink and toilet in the other.

Entertainment leans heavily on popular Disney themes and characters. Parents are actively involved in the audience with their children at shows, movies, "live" character meetings, deck parties, and dancing in the family nightclub. Teens have a supervised, no-adults-allowed club space. For adults, there are no-kids-allowed bars and lounges with live music, dancing, theme parties, and late-night comedy as well as daytime wine-tasting sessions, game shows, culinary-arts and home-entertaining demonstrations, and behind-the-scenes lectures.

Don't expect top chefs and gourmet food; the fare is all-American for the most part. In a novel twist on dining, passengers "rotate" between theme dining rooms, accompanied each night by their waitstaff. Palo, the adults-only Italian restaurant on each ship, requires reservations and has a cover charge. Similarly, adults on *Disney Dream* and *Disney Fantasy* can opt for specialty dining in Remy, Disney's first-ever premier dining restaurant serving French-inspired cuisine. Unlike on many cruise lines, fountain drinks at beverage stations and in dining rooms are complimentary.

**Tipping:** Suggested gratuity amounts are calculated on a per-person per-cruise rather than per-night basis and can be added to onboard accounts or offered in cash on the last night of the cruise. Guidelines include gratuities for your dining-room server, assistant server, head server, and stateroom host/hostess on the basis of $12 per night in the following amounts: $36 for three-night cruises, $48 for four-night cruises, and $84 for seven-night cruises. Tips for room-service delivery and the dining manager are at the passenger's discretion. An automatic 15% gratuity is added to all bar tabs and 18% is added for spa services.

### CHOOSE IF

You want to cruise with the entire family—Mom, Dad, the kids, and grandparents.

You enjoy having kids around. (There are adults-only areas to retreat to when the fun wears off.)

Your family enjoys Disney's theme parks and can't get enough wholesome entertainment.

### DON'T CHOOSE IF

You want to spend a lot of quality time bonding with your kids. Your kids may not want to leave the fun activities.

You want to dine in peace and quiet. The dining rooms and buffet can be boisterous.

You want to gamble. There are no casinos, so you'll have to settle for bingo.

**Contacts** ☎ *407/566–3500 or 888/325–2500* ⊕ *www.disneycruise.com*

# HOLLAND AMERICA LINE

Founded in 1873, Holland America Line (HAL) is one of the oldest names in cruising. Its cruises are classic, conservative affairs renowned for their grace and gentility. As its ships attract a more youthful clientele, Holland America has taken steps to shed its "old folks" image and now offers stops at a private island in the Bahamas, trendier cuisine, a culinary arts center, and an expanded children's program. Still, these are not party cruises, and Holland America has managed to preserve the refined and relaxing qualities that have always been its hallmark, even on sailings that cater more to younger passengers and families.

Luxury bedding, magnifying makeup mirrors, robes, fresh-fruit baskets, flat-screen TVs, and DVD players are found in all cabins. In addition, suites have duvets, fully stocked minibars, personalized stationery, and access to the exclusive Neptune Lounge. Explorations Café, powered by the *New York Times,* combines a coffee bar, computer center with Wi-Fi, and cozy library–reading room complete with tabletop versions of the *Times* crossword puzzles.

Food quality is generally good. In the reservations-required Pinnacle Grill ($29 dinner; $10 lunch), fresh seafood and premium cuts of beef are used to prepare creative specialty dishes. Canaletto Restaurant serves Italian favorites for dinner with a $10 cover charge. On Signature-class and Pinnacle-class ships, Tamarind offers Pan-Asian fare by reservation; there is a charge for dinner ($15), but lunch is complimentary. Pinnacle-class ships add Sel de Mer, an à la carte seafood brasserie. Delicious onboard traditions are afternoon tea, a Dutch Chocolate Extravaganza, and Holland America Line's signature bread pudding.

**Tipping:** Gratuities of $12.50 per passenger per day, or $13.50 per passenger per day for suite passengers, are automatically added to shipboard accounts, and distributed to stewards and waitstaff. Passengers may adjust the amount based on the level of service experienced. Room-service tips are usually given in cash (it's at the passenger's discretion here). Gratuities for spa and salon services can be added to the bill or offered in cash. An automatic 15% gratuity is added to bar-service tabs.

### CHOOSE IF

You crave relaxation. Grab a padded steamer chair on the teak promenade deck and watch the sea pass by.

You like to go to the movies, especially when the popcorn is free.

You want to smoke on your balcony. Holland America is the only major cruise line that allows it.

### DON'T CHOOSE IF

You want to party hard. Most of the action on these ships ends relatively early.

Dressing for dinner isn't your thing. Passengers tend to ramp up the dress code most evenings.

You want to avoid kids. Areas designed exclusively for children and teens are hot features on all ships, and more families are sailing together.

**Contacts** ☎ *206/281–3535 or 800/577–1728* ⊕ *www.hollandamerica.com*

## MSC CRUISES

With several seasons of Caribbean sailing behind them—and having redeployed one of its newest and largest ships for the Caribbean season—MSC Cruises has outgrown its newcomer status. More widely known as one of the world's largest cargo shipping companies, parent company Mediterranean Shipping Company has operated cruises with an eclectic fleet since the late 1980s, but expanded its cruising reach by introducing graceful, modern ships in the Caribbean.

While sailing Caribbean itineraries, MSC Cruises adopts activities that appeal to American passengers without abandoning those preferred by Europeans—prepare for announcements in several languages. In addition to trivia games, bingo, and cooking demonstrations, a popular option is an Italian language class. Nightly shows accentuate MSC Cruises' Mediterranean heritage—there might be an opera presentation in the main showroom and live music in the smaller lounges.

The dinner menu on MSC ships is Italian-centered. Menus list Mediterranean regional specialties and classic favorites prepared from scratch. In a nod to American tastes, chicken, sirloin steak, grilled salmon, and Caesar salad are always available in addition to the regular dinner menu. A daily highlight is the bread and pasta, freshly made on board, and Neapolitan-style pizza that is the best at sea.

**Tipping:** Gratuities are automatically charged to onboard accounts in the amount of $12 per person per day for adults (18 and over), and $6 for children (age 3 to 18). There is no gratuity charge for children age 3 and under. A 15% service charge is added to all bar purchases and spa services.

### CHOOSE IF

You appreciate authentic Italian cooking. This is the real thing, not an Olive Garden clone.

You want your ship to look like a ship. MSC's vessels are very nautical in appearance.

You want the Continental flair of a premium cruise at a fair price.

### DON'T CHOOSE IF

Announcements in more than one language get on your nerves.

You aren't able to accept things that are not always done the American way.

You prefer myriad dining choices and casual attire. MSC cruises have assigned seating and observe a dress code.

**Contacts** ☎ *800/666–9333* ⊕ *www.msccruisesusa.com*

## NORWEGIAN CRUISE LINE

Norwegian Cruise Line (NCL) was established in 1966, when one of Norway's oldest and most respected shipping companies, Oslo-based Klosters Rederi A/S, acquired the Sunward and repositioned the ship from Europe to the then-obscure Port of Miami. With the formation of a company called Norwegian Caribbean Lines, the cruise industry as we know it today was born. NCL launched an entirely new concept with its regularly scheduled cruises to the Caribbean on a single-class ship. No longer simply a means of transportation, the ship became a destination unto itself, offering guests an affordable alternative to land-based resorts.

Always a cruise-industry innovator, Norwegian Cruise Line's Freestyle cruising introduced a wider variety of dining options in a casual, free-flowing atmosphere. Noted for top-quality, high-energy entertainment and emphasis on fitness facilities and programs, NCL combines action, activities, and a resort-casual atmosphere.

Main dining rooms serve what is traditionally deemed Continental fare, although in terms of quality it's about what you would expect at a really good hotel banquet. Where NCL stands above the ordinary is in their specialty restaurants, especially the French–Mediterranean Le Bistro (on all ships), the Pan-Asian restaurants, and steak houses (on the newer ships). In addition, you may find an Italian trattoria. Most, but not all, specialty restaurants carry a cover charge and require reservations. An enhanced room service menu incurs a convenience charge of up to $7.95.

**Tipping:** A fixed service charge of $13.50 per person per day for passengers three years of age and older is added to shipboard accounts for staterooms and minisuites; for suites and The Haven, the service charge is $15.50. An automatic 18% gratuity is added to bar tabs and for spa services. Staff members may also accept cash gratuities. Passengers in suites who have access to concierge and butler services are asked to offer a cash gratuity at their own discretion.

### CHOOSE IF
Doing your own thing is your idea of a real vacation. You could remove your watch and just go with the flow.

You want to leave your formal dress-up wardrobe at home.

You're competitive. There's always a pickup game in progress on the sports courts.

### DON'T CHOOSE IF
You don't like to pay extra for food on a ship. All the best specialty restaurants have extra charges.

You don't want to stand in line. There are lines for nearly everything.

You don't want to hear announcements. They're frequent on these ships—and loud.

**Contacts** ☎ *305/436–4000 or 800/327–7030* ⊕ *www.ncl.com*

## OCEANIA CRUISES

This distinctive cruise line, founded by cruise-industry veterans with the know-how to satisfy inquisitive passengers with interesting ports of call and upscale touches for fares much lower than you would expect, is owned by Prestige Cruise Holdings. Oceania uses midsize "R-class" ships from the long-defunct Renaissance Cruises fleet, and launched a new ship class in 2011. Varied, destination-rich itineraries are an important characteristic of Oceania Cruises, and most Caribbean sailings are in the 10- to 12-night range. Before arrival in ports of call, lectures are presented on the historical background, culture, and traditions of the islands.

Intimate and cozy public spaces reflect the importance of socializing on Oceania ships. Evening entertainment leans toward light cabaret, solo artists, music for dancing, and conversation with fellow passengers; however, you'll find lively karaoke sessions as well. On sea days jazz or easy-listening melodies are played poolside.

Master chef Jacques Pépin designed the menus for Oceania, and the results are sure to please the most discriminating palate. Oceania simply serves some of the best food at sea, particularly impressive for a cruise line that charges far less than luxury rates. The main open seating restaurant offers trendy French-Continental cuisine with an always-on-the-menu steak, seafood, or poultry choice and vegetarian option. Intimate specialty restaurants require reservations, but there is no additional charge. Unlimited soft drinks, bottled water, specialty coffees and teas, and juices are complimentary.

**Tipping:** Gratuities of $16 per person per day are added to shipboard accounts for distribution to stewards and waitstaff; an additional $7 per person per day is added for occupants of suites with butler service. Passengers may adjust the amount based on the level of service experienced. An automatic 18% gratuity is added to all bar tabs for bartenders and drink servers and to all bills for salon and spa services.

**CHOOSE IF**
Socializing plays a more important role in your lifestyle than boogying the night away.

You love to read. These ships have extensive libraries that are ideal for curling up with a good book.

You have a bad back. You're sure to love the Tranquility Beds.

**DON'T CHOOSE IF**
You like the action in a huge casino. Oceania casinos are small, and seats at a poker table can be difficult to get.

You want to bring your children. Most passengers book with Oceania anticipating a kid-free atmosphere.

Glitzy production shows are your thing. Oceania's showrooms are decidedly low-key.

**Contacts** ☎ *305/514–2300 or 800/531–5658* ⊕ *www.oceaniacruises.com*

# PONANT

Ponant operates five designer ships for all-season premium yet unpretentious yacht cruising in places inaccessible to larger cruise ships. With distinctively French flair, the cruise company strikes an appealing balance between destination choice and price point on luxuriously refurbished modern sailing vessels that feature French gastronomy, elegant styling, and unique voyages with all-inclusive packages. Travel is privileged yet unpretentious aboard a small majestic three-masted sailing yacht or larger megayacht.

For experienced cruisers or newcomers, the fantasy of having one's own private yacht to sail the seven seas comes closer to reality with exotic itineraries on upscale, uncrowded ships operated by Compagnie du Ponant, which was begun in 1988 by CMA CGM, the world's third-largest container shipping company. In 2008, Compagnie du Ponant made international headlines when its smallest sailing yacht was hijacked by Somali pirates off the coast of the Seychelles in the Indian Ocean. That incident had a positive ending, and the company has since offered solid years of safe, luxury maritime travel and good reviews from discerning passengers, most of whom are European, American, and Australian globe-trotters. Expectations for substantial entertainment, perfect service, and regal accommodations should be kept realistic since these ships are limited in size. Nevertheless, Compagnie du Ponant's ambitious agenda is to provide impeccable, five-star cruising to its affluent clientele. The ships offer fine dining, outstanding attention to interior design, expedition-style cruising on eco-friendly, state-of-the-art vessels, and a sophisticated feel reminiscent of a hip boutique hotel; and these expectations are more than met for offbeat journeys draped in contemporary prestige.

Gastronomy is taken pretty seriously on Compagnie du Ponant ships. Fresh ingredients and skilled preparation by resident French chefs and bakers keep culinary standards at an outstanding level for grilled and roasted meat, fish, vegetarian meals, and desserts. Although oenophiles may be disappointed with the free table wine served for lunch and dinner, premium bottles can be ordered for a supplementary cost.

**Tipping:** All gratuities are included for restaurant, hotel, and ship staffs as well as local guides and drivers.

### CHOOSE IF

You've always dreamt of sailing on your own private yacht.

Destinations in remote ports of call and inaccessible landscapes are a priority.

You appreciate open-air cruising (large sundecks, terraces, sea-level platforms, and cabins with private balconies) and discreet elegance.

### DON'T CHOOSE IF

You seek a no-frills holiday with loud parties and prefer sandwiches for dinner.

You like to dress up in ostentatious glitz and glamorous evening wear.

Luxury travel with refined French elegance, sophistication, and language just isn't your cup of tea.

**Contacts** ☎ *888/400–1082 in U.S. and Canada or 033/488–66–64–00 in France* ⊕ *www.ponant.com*

## PRINCESS CRUISES

Rising from modest beginnings in 1965, when it began offering cruises to Mexico with a single ship, Princess has become one of the world's best-known cruise lines. Catapulted to stardom in 1977, when its flagship became the setting for *The Love Boat* television series, Princess introduced millions of viewers to the still-new concept of a seagoing vacation. Although the line does have some medium-size vessels, Princess more often follows the "bigger is better" trend. Its fleet sails to more destinations each year than any other major line.

All Princess ships feature the line's innovative Personal Choice Cruising program that gives passengers choice and flexibility in customizing their cruise experience—multiple dining locations, flexible entertainment, and affordable private balconies are all highlights. Enrichment programs feature guest lecturers and opportunities to learn new skills or crafts, but you'll still find staples such as bingo and art auctions.

Menus are varied and extensive, and the results are good to excellent. Alternative restaurants with cover charges are a staple throughout the fleet, but vary by ship class. Lido buffets on all ships are almost always open, and a pizzeria and grill offer casual daytime snack choices.

**Tipping:** Princess suggests tipping $13.95 per person per day for passengers in suites and minisuites and $12.95 per person per day for all other passengers (including children). Gratuities are automatically added to onboard accounts; 15% is added to bar bills and for spa and salon services.

### CHOOSE IF

You're a traveler with a disability. Princess ships are some of the most accessible at sea.

You like to gamble but hate a smoke-filled casino. Princess casinos are well-ventilated and spacious.

You want a balcony. Princess ships feature them in abundance at affordable rates.

### DON'T CHOOSE IF

You have a poor sense of direction. Most ships are very large.

You think Princess is still as depicted in *The Love Boat*. That was just a TV show, and it was more than three decades ago.

You're too impatient to stand in line or wait. Debarkation from the large ships can be lengthy.

**Contacts** ☎ *661/753–0000 or 800/774–6237* ⊕ *www.princess.com*

## REGENT SEVEN SEAS CRUISES

Regent Seven Seas Cruises sails an elegant fleet of vessels that offer a nearly all-inclusive cruise experience (including shore excursions) in sumptuous, contemporary surroundings. The line's spacious ocean-view staterooms have the industry's highest percentage of private balconies, and almost all drinks (except some premium brands) are now included.

Subtle improvements throughout the fleet have resulted in features such as computer service with Wi-Fi capability for your own laptop and cell phone access. New luxury bedding, Regent-branded bath amenities, flat-screen TVs, DVD players, and new clocks (a real rarity on cruise ships) have been added to all cabins. Top suites also feature iPods and Bose speakers. The ships offer exquisite service, generous staterooms with abundant amenities, a variety of dining options, and superior enrichment programs. Cruises are destination-focused, and most sailings host guest lecturers—historians, anthropologists, naturalists, and diplomats.

Menus may appear to include the usual cruise-ship staples, but the results are some of the most outstanding meals at sea. Specialty dining varies within the fleet; when available, the sophisticated Signatures features the cuisine of Le Cordon Bleu of Paris; Prime 7 offers menus that rival the finest shoreside steak and seafood restaurants. In addition, Mediterranean-inspired bistro dinners are served in the daytime casual Lido buffet restaurants. Wines chosen to complement dinner menus are freely poured each evening.

**Tipping:** Gratuities are included in the fare, and none are expected. To show their appreciation, passengers may elect to make a contribution to a crew welfare fund that benefits the ship's staff.

### CHOOSE IF

You want to learn the secrets of cooking like a Cordon Bleu chef (for a charge, of course).

You don't want the hassle of signing bar tabs or extra expense of shore excursions.

A really high-end spa experience is on your agenda.

### DON'T CHOOSE IF

Connecting cabins are a must. Very few are available, and only the priciest cabins connect.

You can't imagine a cruise without the hoopla of games in the pool; these ships are much more discreet.

You don't want to dress up for dinner. Most passengers still dress more formally than on other lines.

**Contacts** ☎ *877/505–5370* ⊕ *www.rssc.com*

## ROYAL CARIBBEAN INTERNATIONAL

Big, bigger, biggest! More than a decade ago, Royal Caribbean launched the first of the modern mega-cruise ships for passengers who enjoy traditional cruising with a touch of daring and whimsy tossed in. These large-to-giant vessels are indoor–outdoor wonders, with every conceivable activity in a resortlike atmosphere, including atrium lobbies, shopping arcades, large spas, expansive sundecks, and rock-climbing walls. Several ships have such elaborate facilities as 18-hole miniature-golf courses and ice-skating rinks. Oasis-class ships, RCI's largest ships, even have surf parks and a zip-line at sea. Plush new bedding has been installed fleet-wide.

The centerpiece of Royal Caribbean mega-ships is the multideck atrium, a hallmark that has been duplicated by many other cruise lines. The brilliance of this design is that all the major public rooms radiate from this central point, so you can learn your way around these huge ships within minutes of boarding. Ships in the Vision class are especially bright and airy, with sea views almost anywhere you happen to be. The main problem with RCI's otherwise well-conceived vessels is that there are often too many people on board, making embarkation, tendering, and disembarkation exasperating. However, Royal Caribbean is still one of the best-run and most popular cruise lines.

Royal Caribbean has made great strides in its food offerings. Although Royal Caribbean doesn't place emphasis on celebrity chefs, the line has introduced a more intimate dinner experience in the form of Italian-specialty restaurants and steak houses on most ships and has been adding more specialty dining choices fleet-wide. The Oasis-class ships feature two-dozen dining spots, ranging from a seafood café (Oasis of the Seas) or Mexican cantina (Allure of the Seas).

**Tipping:** Tips that are not prepaid when the cruise is booked are automatically added to shipboard accounts in the amount of $13.50 per person, per day ($16.50 for suites), to be shared by dining and housekeeping staff. An 18% gratuity is automatically added to all bar tabs and spa and salon services.

### CHOOSE IF

You want to see the sea from atop a rock wall—it's one of the few activities on these ships that's free.

You're active and adventurous. Even if your traveling companion isn't, there's an energetic staff on board to cheer you on.

You want your space. There's plenty of room to roam; quiet nooks and crannies are there if you look.

### DON'T CHOOSE IF

Patience is not one of your virtues. Lines are not uncommon.

You want to do your own laundry. There are no self-service facilities on any Royal Caribbean ships.

You don't want to hear announcements. There are a lot on Royal Caribbean ships.

**Contacts** ☎ *305/539–6000 or 800/5327–6700* ⊕ *www.royalcaribbean.com*

## SEABOURN CRUISE LINE

Ultraluxury pioneer Seabourn was founded on the principle that dedication to personal service in elegant surroundings would appeal to sophisticated, independent-minded passengers whose lifestyles demand the best. Its original trio of nearly identical, all-suites ships were sold to Windstar Cruises in 2013 and three larger vessels were launched in 2009, 2010, and 2011; another entered the fleet in late 2016. The "yachts" remain favorites with people who can take care of themselves but would rather do so aboard a luxury ship. Dining and evening socializing are generally more stimulating to Seabourn passengers than splashy song-and-dance reviews; however, proportionately scaled production and cabaret shows are presented in the main showroom and smaller lounge. The library stocks not only books but also movies. Daily trivia contests are taken seriously, and the competition can be fierce.

You can expect complimentary wines and spirits, elegant amenities, and even the pleasure of mini-massages while lounging poolside. Guest appearances by luminaries in the arts and world affairs highlight the enrichment program. Wine tasting, trivia contests, and other quiet pursuits might be scheduled, but most passengers prefer to simply do what pleases them.

Exceptional cuisine is prepared to order and served in open seating dining rooms. Creative menu offerings include foie gras, quail, and fresh seafood. Wines are chosen to complement each day's lunch and dinner menus, and caviar is always available. Evening dining alternatives include Restaurant 2 or The Grill, depending on ship, which serve dinner nightly; and a second—even more laid-back—choice, the Patio on each ship serves sizzling steaks and seafood some nights on deck. Themed dining in the Colonnade, the casual daytime buffet restaurant, is available nightly. All require reservations but do not charge extra.

**Tipping:** Tipping is neither required nor expected.

**CHOOSE IF**

You consider fine dining the highlight of your vacation.

You own your own tuxedo. These ships are dressy, and many men wear them on formal evenings.

You feel it's annoying to sign drink tabs; everything is included on these ships.

**DON'T CHOOSE IF**

Dressing down is on your agenda.

You absolutely must have a spacious private balcony. They are limited in number and book fast.

You need to be stimulated by constant activity.

**Contacts** ☎ *800/929–9391* ⊕ *www.seabourn.com*

## SEADREAM YACHT CLUB

Launched in 1984 as Sea Goddess mega-yachts, these boutique ships have changed hands through the years, becoming SeaDream Yacht Club in 2002. Passengers enjoy an unstructured holiday at sea doing whatever pleases them, giving the diminutive vessels the feel of true private yachts with a select guest list. Other than a pianist in the tiny piano bar, a small casino, and movies in the main lounge, there is no roster of activities. The rocking late-night place to be is the Top of the Yacht Bar, where passengers gather to share the day's experiences and kick their shoes off to dance on the teak deck. The captain hosts welcome-aboard and farewell cocktail receptions in the Main Salon each week. Otherwise, you are on your own to do as you please. A well-stocked library has books and movies for those who prefer quiet pursuits in the privacy of their staterooms.

Ports of call almost seem an intrusion on socializing amid the chic surroundings, although a picnic on a secluded beach adds the element of a private island paradise to each Caribbean cruise. While the ambience is sophisticated, all cruises are "yacht" casual, and you can leave your formal clothing at home. You can also leave your charge card in your pocket, as all beverages, including select wines and spirits, are complimentary.

Every meal is prepared to order using the freshest seafood and prime cuts of beef. Menus include vegetarian alternatives and Asian wellness cuisine for the health-conscious. Cheeses, petits fours, and chocolate truffles are offered with after-dinner coffee, and desserts are to die for. Wines are chosen to complement each luncheon and dinner menu.

**Tipping:** Tipping is neither required nor expected.

### CHOOSE IF
You enjoy dining as an event, as courses are presented with a flourish, and wine flows freely.

You don't like to hear the word *no*.

You have good sea legs. In rough seas, the SeaDream yachts tend to bob up and down.

### DON'T CHOOSE IF
You like to dress up. Although you could wear a sport coat to dinner, no one ever wears a tie on these ships.

You must have a balcony. There are none on any of Seadream's yacht-like vessels.

You need structured activities. You'll have to plan your own.

**Contacts** ☎ *305/631–6100 or 800/707–4911* ⊕ *www.seadream.com*

# SILVERSEA CRUISES

Intimate ships, paired with exclusive amenities and unparalleled hospitality, are the hallmarks of Silversea luxury cruises. Personalization is a Silversea maxim. Ships offer more activities than other comparably sized luxury vessels, with guest lecturers on nearly every cruise. A multi-tiered show lounge is the setting for classical concerts, big-screen movies, and folkloric entertainers from ashore. All accommodations are spacious outside suites—most with private verandas. Silversea ships have large swimming pools in expansive Lidos. Silversea's third generation of ships introduced even more luxurious features when the 36,000-ton *Silver Spirit* launched late in 2009.

Although these ships schedule more activities than other comparably sized luxury vessels, you can either take part or opt instead for a good book and any number of quiet spots to read or snooze in the shade. Silversea is so all-inclusive that you'll find your room key/charge card is seldom used for anything but opening your suite door.

Dishes from the galleys of Silversea's master chefs are complemented by those of La Collection du Monde, created by Silversea's culinary partner, Relais & Châteaux. Perhaps more compelling is the line's flair for originality. Nightly alternative-theme dinners in La Terrazza (by day, the buffet restaurant) feature regional specialties from the Mediterranean; an intimate dining experience aboard each vessel is Le Champagne—the Wine Restaurant, which is the only Relais & Châteaux restaurant at sea.

**Tipping:** Tipping is neither required nor expected.

### CHOOSE IF

Your taste leans toward learning and exploration.

You enjoy socializing as well as the option of live entertainment, just not too much of it.

You like to plan ahead. You can reserve shore tours, salon services, and spa treatments online.

### DON'T CHOOSE IF

You want to dress informally at all times on your cruise. Passengers on these cruises tend to dress up.

You need highly structured activities and have to be reminded of them.

You prefer the glitter and stimulation of Las Vegas to the understated glamour of Monte Carlo.

**Contacts** ☎ *954/522–2299 or 877/276–6816* ⊕ *www.silversea.com*

## STAR CLIPPERS

In 1991 Star Clippers presented a new tall-ship alternative to sophisticated travelers looking for adventure at sea, but not on board a conventional cruise ship. Star Clippers vessels are the world's largest barkentine and full-rigged sailing ships—four- and five-masted sailing beauties filled with high-tech equipment as well as amenities more often found on private yachts. The ships rely on sail power while at sea unless conditions require the assistance of the engines. Minimum heeling, usually less than 6%, is achieved through judicious control of the sails.

Star Clippers are not cruise ships in the ordinary sense, with strict agendas and pages of activities. You can lounge on deck and simply soak in the nautical ambience or learn about navigational techniques from the captain. Cabins, which are very compact, do include such amenities as hair dryers, TVs, and telephones. Star Clippers ships also have swimming pools. Other features fall somewhere between those of a true sailing yacht and the high-tech Windstar ships. The differences are more than just in the level of luxury—Star Clippers are true sailing vessels. Prices, however, are a bit more affordable and often less than you would pay on a high-end cruise ship. Onboard accounts are charged in euros, even in the Caribbean.

Not noted for gourmet fare, the international cuisine is what you would expect from a trendy shoreside bistro. Fresh fruits and fish are among the best choices from Star Clippers' galleys. In a nod to American tastes, dinner menus include an alternative steak selection. Lunch buffets are quite a spread of seafood, salads, and grilled items.

**Tipping:** Gratuities are not included in the cruise fare and are extended at the sole discretion of passengers. The recommended amount is $8 per person per day. Tips are pooled and shared; individual tipping is discouraged. You can either put cash in the tip envelope provided, and drop it at the Purser's Office, or charge gratuities to your shipboard account. An automatic 15% gratuity is added to each passenger's bar bill.

**CHOOSE IF**
You wouldn't consider a vacation on a traditional cruise ship but are a sailing enthusiast.

You love water sports, particularly snorkeling and scuba diving.

You want to anchor in secluded coves and visit islands that are off the beaten path.

**DON'T CHOOSE IF**
You have a preexisting or potentially serious medical condition. There's no physician on board.

You must have a private balcony—there are a few, but only in top accommodation categories.

You can't live without room service. Only *Royal Clipper* has it, and only in a few high-end suites.

**Contacts** ☎ *305/442–0550 or 800/276–442–0551* ⊕ *www.starclippers.com*

# VIKING OCEAN CRUISES

More widely known for their river cruises in Europe and Asia, Viking debuted Viking Ocean Cruises with their first ship in 2015. Focused on destination-centric cruising with onboard enrichment offerings, the line includes one complimentary shore experience in each port of call.

The 928-passenger, all-veranda ships have a Nordic-inspired spa, gym and yoga area, and two pools—including an infinity pool at the back of the ship and a main pool with retractable dome. Onboard amenities include a piano bar, show lounge, cinema, well-stocked library, and boutiques. Internet with Wi-Fi and laundry service are complimentary, as are all soft drinks, specialty coffees and teas, and round-the-clock room service. Wraparound promenade decks are ideal for walking or jogging.

Each ship has a variety of restaurants offering menu choices from regional specialties to heart-healthy options and American classics, as well as more alfresco dining than any other ship at sea. The Restaurant offers a daily-changing menu that highlights fresh local ingredients. The Chef's Table features a curated tasting menu with wine pairings, and the Italian Grill selections include Tuscan favorites. Each meal is accompanied by complimentary tea or coffee, and lunch and dinner service includes complimentary soft drinks, house wine, and beer. There is no reservation fee for any restaurant.

**Tipping:** Tipping is expected but considered voluntary, with suggested amounts of $15 per person, per day for onboard service; $2 per person for local city guides; and $1 per person for coach drivers. A 15% gratuity is added to bar checks, but no tips are automatically added to spa services.

**CHOOSE IF**

You prefer a nearly all-inclusive cruise at a reasonable price.

The destinations are more important to you than how you get there.

You are a satisfied Viking River Cruises passenger; Viking has brought the best features of its river cruises to sea.

**DON'T CHOOSE IF**

You must gamble because there are no casinos on these ships.

You have younger children; the minimum age for passengers is 16.

You're a fitness buff with a yen for expansive ocean views while you work out; the gyms are nicely equipped, but compact.

**Contacts** ☎ 866/984–5464 ⊕ www.vikingcruises.com

## WINDSTAR CRUISES

The original Windstar vessels are modern, masted sailing yachts, pioneers in the upscale sailing niche. Although the sails add speed, Windstar ships seldom depend on wind alone to sail. However, if you are fortunate and conditions are perfect, the total silence of pure sailing is a thrill. Although the ships' designs may be reminiscent of sailing vessels of yore, the amenities and shipboard service are among the best at sea. In something of a sea change, the line purchased Seabourn Cruises' trio of small vessels in 2013. After extensive renovations, the yacht trio completed their entry into the Windstar fleet in 2015.

In keeping with the line's exacting standards, all ocean-view staterooms and suites provide the comforts of home with sitting area, luxury linens and mattresses, DVD/CD player, Apple iPod nano with Bose Sound-Dock speakers, Wi-Fi, safe, minibar/refrigerator, international direct-dial phones, L'Occitane bath toiletries, hair dryer, plenty of closet space, and plush robes and slippers. An array of international newspapers, books, and games can be found in the library, and a wide selection of DVD titles and CDs is available for complimentary use. Life on board is unabashedly sybaritic, attracting a sophisticated, relatively young crowd who are happy to sacrifice bingo and pool games for the attractions of remote islands and water sports; even motorized water sports are included, and passengers pay extra only for scuba diving. Unfortunately, only basic non-alcoholic beverages, including specialty coffees and teas, are included in the fare.

Windstar menus offer dishes with tropical accents, using fresh local ingredients whenever possible. A mid-cruise deck barbecue featuring grilled seafood and other favorites is offered on all cruises.

**Tipping:** A service charge of $12 per person per day is automatically added to shipboard accounts. An automatic 15% gratuity is added to all bar tabs.

**CHOOSE IF**

You want a high-end experience yet prefer to dress casually every night of your vacation.

You love water sports, particularly scuba diving, kayaking, and windsurfing.

You're a romantic: tables for two are plentiful in the dining rooms.

**DON'T CHOOSE IF**

You must have a spacious private balcony. There are none.

You're bored unless surrounded by constant stimulation. Activities are purposely low-key.

You have mobility concerns. The sailing ships are simply not very good for passengers in wheelchairs.

**Contacts** ☎ *206/281–3535 or 800/258–7245* ⊕ *www.windstarcruises.com*

# PORTS OF
# EMBARKATION

Miami is the world's cruise capital, and more cruise ships are based here year-round than anywhere else. Caribbean cruises depart for their itineraries from several ports on either of Florida's coasts, as well as from cities on the Gulf Coast and East Coast of the United States.

Generally, if your cruise is on an Eastern Caribbean itinerary, you'll likely depart from Miami, Fort Lauderdale, Jacksonville, or Port Canaveral; short three- and four-day cruises to the Bahamas also depart from these ports. Most cruises on Western Caribbean itineraries depart from Tampa, New Orleans, Houston, or Galveston, though some depart from Miami as well. Cruises from farther up the East Coast of the United States, including such ports as Baltimore, Maryland; Charleston, South Carolina; and even New York City, usually go to the Bahamas or sometimes Key West and often include a private-island stop or a stop elsewhere in Florida. Cruises to the Southern Caribbean might depart from Miami if they are 10 days or longer, but more likely they will depart from San Juan, Puerto Rico, or some other port deeper in the Caribbean, often Barbados.

Regardless of which port you depart from, air connections may prevent you from leaving home on the morning of your cruise or going home the day you return to port. Or you may wish to arrive early simply to give yourself a bit more peace of mind, or you may just want to spend more time in one of these interesting port cities. Many people choose to depart from New Orleans or Galveston just to have an excuse to spend a couple of days in the city before or after their cruise.

## PORT ESSENTIALS

### CAR RENTALS
**Major Agencies Alamo.** ☎ *877/222–9075* ⊕ *www.alamo.com.* **Avis.**
☎ *800/331–1212* ⊕ *www.avis.com.* **Budget.** ☎ *800/527–0700* ⊕ *www.budget.*
*com.* **Hertz.** ☎ *800/654–3131* ⊕ *www.hertz.com.* **National Car Rental.**
☎ *877/222–9058* ⊕ *www.nationalcar.com.*

### SURCHARGES
To avoid a hefty refueling fee, fill the tank just before you turn in the car, but be aware that gas stations near rental outlets and airports may charge more than those farther away. This is a particular problem in Orlando, but it can be true in other Florida cities. If you plan to do a lot of driving (and if you can get a good price), it can sometimes be a better deal to buy a full tank of gas when you rent so you can return the car with an empty tank. However, it's never a good deal to pay the huge surcharge for not returning a tank full, unless you simply have no other choice. Other surcharges may apply if you are under 25 or over 75; if you want to add an additional driver to the contract; or if you want to drive over state borders or out of a specific radius from

## Security

All cruise lines have instituted stricter security procedures in recent years; however, you may not even be aware of all the changes.

Some of the changes will be more obvious to you. For example, only visitors who have been authorized well in advance are allowed onboard. Proper identification (a government-issued photo ID) is required in all instances to board the ship, whether you are a visitor or passenger. Ship security personnel are stationed at all points of entry to the ship. All hand-carried items are searched by hand in every port (this applies to both crew and passengers).

Some of the changes are more behind the scenes. All luggage is scanned, whether you carry it aboard with you or not, and all packages and provisions brought onboard are scanned.

In addition, every ship has added professionally trained security officers and taken many other measures to ensure the safety of all passengers. Many cruise-line security personnel are former navy or marine officers with extensive maritime experience. Some cruise lines recruit shipboard security personnel from the ranks of former British Gurkha regiments. From Nepal, the Gurkhas are renowned as soldiers of the highest caliber.

**3**

your point of rental. You'll also pay extra for child seats, which are compulsory for children under 5, and for a GPS navigation system or electronic toll pass. You can sometimes avoid the charge for insurance if you have your own, either from your own policy or from a credit card; but know what you are covered for, and read the fine print before making this decision.

### HOTELS

Whether you are driving or flying into your port of embarkation, it is often more convenient to arrive the day before or to stay for a day after your cruise. For this reason we offer lodging suggestions near each port of embarkation.

### RESTAURANTS

For each port of embarkation, we offer some restaurant suggestions that are convenient to the cruise port and the other hotels we recommend. Unless otherwise noted, the restaurants we recommend accept major credit cards and are open for both lunch and dinner.

### HOTEL AND RESTAURANT PRICES

Restaurant prices are based on the median main course price at dinner, excluding gratuity. Hotel prices are for two people in a standard double room in high season, excluding any taxes, service charges, and resort fees.

# BALTIMORE, MARYLAND

By Laura Rodini

Baltimore's charm lies in its neighborhoods. Although stellar downtown attractions such as the National Aquarium and Camden Yards draw torrents of tourists each year, much of the city's character can be found outside the Inner Harbor. Scores of Baltimore's trademark narrow redbrick row houses with white marble steps line the city's east and west sides. Some neighborhood streets are still made of cobblestone, and grand churches and museums and towering, glassy high-rises fill out the growing skyline. Now the city's blue-collar past mixes with present urban-professional revitalization. Industrial waterfront properties are giving way to high-end condos, and corner bars formerly dominated by National Bohemian beer—once made in the city—are adding microbrews to their beverage lists. And with more and more retail stores replacing old, run-down buildings and parking lots, Baltimore is one of the nation's up-and-coming cities.

## BEST BETS

- **Camden Yards.** Tour the stadium or, better yet, see an Orioles game if the team is playing while you're in town.

- **Fort McHenry.** This historic fort is where Francis Scott Key saw the Stars and Stripes flying during the War of 1812 and where he was inspired to write our National Anthem.

- **The National Aquarium.** This excellent museum is a great destination for all.

## ESSENTIALS

### HOURS

During the summer tourist season, most of Baltimore's stores and attractions usually open around 9 am and close around 9 pm.

### VISITOR INFORMATION

**Contacts Baltimore Visitor Center.** ⊠ 401 Light St., Inner Harbor ☎ 877/225–8466 ⊕ baltimore.org.

## THE CRUISE PORT

Well marked and easily accessible by major highways, the South Locust Point Cruise Terminal is about a mile from center city. Several cruise lines offer seasonal cruises from the port; Grandeur of the Seas is based here year-round. Ships dock near the main cruise building, which itself is little more than a hub for arrivals and departures. There are few facilities for passengers in the immediate port area, which is out of walking distance to Baltimore's attractions.

### AIRPORT

**Contacts Baltimore–Washington International Thurgood Marshall Airport** (BWI). ⊠ 10 miles south of Baltimore, off Rte. 295/Baltimore–Washington Pkwy., Hanover ☎ 410/859–7111 for information and paging ⊕ www.bwiairport.com.

## Baltimore Inner Harbor

**KEY**

❶ Exploring Sights

① Hotels & Restaurants

🛈 Tourist Information

### AIRPORT TRANSFERS

During cruise season, taxis are the best transportation to the downtown area. They cost about $5 one-way and frequent the port. Taxis to Baltimore–Washington International Airport charge a flat rate of $35. Rental cars are generally not necessary; if you fly into Baltimore, you can see the majority of Baltimore by taxi. Guided tours of the city range from $20 to $60.

**Contacts Airport Taxis.** ☎ 410/859–1100 ⊕ www.bwiairporttaxi.com. **Arrow Cab.** ☎ 443/575–4111. **BWI Airport rail station.** ☎ 410/672–6167 ⊕ www.bwiairport.com. **BWI SuperShuttle.** ✉ BWI Airport, Hanover ☎ 800/258–3826 ⊕ www.supershuttle.com. **Carey Limousines.** ☎ 800/336–4646, ⊕ www.carey.com. **Maryland Area Rail Commuter** (MARC). ☎ 800/325–7245, 410/539–5000 ⊕ mta.maryland.gov/marc-train. **Penn Station.** ✉ 1500 N. Charles St., Mount Vernon ☎ 800/523–8720. **Private Car/RMA Worldwide Chauffeured Transportation.** ☎ 410/519–0000, 800/878–7743 ⊕ www.rmalimo.com.

### PARKING

There's a secure parking lot next to the cruise terminal, where parking costs $15 per day. Drop off your luggage before parking.

**Contacts Baltimore Cruise Port Parking.** ⊕ www.cruise.maryland.gov/content/parking-rates.

## EXPLORING

**B&O Railroad Museum.** The famous Baltimore & Ohio Railroad was founded on the site that now houses this museum, which contains more than 120 full-size locomotives and a great collection of railroad memorabilia, from dining-car china and artwork to lanterns and signals. The 1884 roundhouse (240 feet in diameter and 120 feet high) contains exhibits and historic objects. It adjoins one of the nation's first railroad stations. Train rides are available Wednesday through Sunday (weekends only in January). TraxSide Snax serves food and drinks. ⊠ *901 W. Pratt St., West Baltimore* ☎ *410/752–2490* ⊕ *www.borail.org* ▣ *$18; $10 for train rides.*

**Fodor'sChoice**
★

**Fort McHenry.** This star-shaped brick fort is forever associated with Francis Scott Key and "The Star-Spangled Banner," which Key penned while watching the British bombardment of Baltimore during the War of 1812. Through the next day and night, as the battle raged, Key strained to be sure, through the smoke and haze, that the flag still flew above Fort McHenry—indicating that Baltimore's defenders held firm. "By the dawn's early light" of September 14, 1814, he saw the 30- by 42-foot "Star-Spangled Banner" still aloft and was inspired to pen the words to a poem (set to the tune of an old English drinking song). A visit to the fort includes a 15-minute history film, guided tour, and frequent living-history displays on summer weekends. To see how the formidable fortifications might have appeared to the bombarding British, catch a water taxi from the Inner Harbor to the fort instead of driving. ⊠ *E. Fort Ave., Locust Point* ✣ *From Light St., take Key Hwy. for 1½ miles and follow signs* ☎ *410/962–4290* ⊕ *www.nps.gov/fomc* ▣ *$10.*

**FAMILY**
**Fodor'sChoice**
★

**Maryland Science Center.** Originally known as the Maryland Academy of Sciences, this 200-year-old scientific institution is one of the oldest in the United States. Now housed in a contemporary building, the three floors of exhibits on the Chesapeake Bay, Earth science, physics, the body, dinosaurs, and outer space are an invitation to engage, experiment, and explore. The center has a planetarium, a simulated archaeological dinosaur dig, an IMAX movie theater with a screen five stories high, and a playroom especially designed for young children. ⊠ *601 Light St., Inner Harbor* ☎ *410/685–5225* ⊕ *www.mdsci.org* ▣ *$24.95.*

**Fodor'sChoice**
★

**National Aquarium in Baltimore.** The most-visited attraction in Maryland has nearly 20,000 fish, sharks, dolphins, and amphibians dwelling in 2 million gallons of water. The Blacktip Reef exhibit mimics a coral reef in the Indo-Pacific waters, featuring pufferfish, stingrays and more unusual creatures, such as the tasseled wobbegong, a carpet shark. In the Living Seashore exhibit, visitors can touch live stingrays. The aquarium also features reptiles, birds, plants, and mammals in its rain-forest environment, inside a glass pyramid 64 feet high. Atlantic bottlenose dolphins are part of several entertaining presentations that highlight their agility and intelligence. The aquarium's famed shark tank and Atlantic coral reef exhibits are spectacular. Arrive early to ensure admission, which is by timed intervals; by noon, the wait is often two to three hours, especially on weekends and holidays. ⊠ *Pier 3, Inner Harbor* ☎ *410/576–3800* ⊕ *www.aqua.org* ▣ *$39.95.*

FAMILY

Fodor's Choice

★

**Oriole Park at Camden Yards.** Home of the Baltimore Orioles, Camden Yards and the nearby area bustle on game days. Since it opened in 1992, this nostalgically designed baseball stadium has inspired other cities to emulate its neotraditional architecture and amenities. The Eutaw Street promenade, between the warehouse and the field, has a view of the stadium; look for the brass baseballs embedded in the sidewalk that mark where home runs have cleared the fence, or visit the Orioles Hall of Fame display and the monuments to retired Orioles. Daily 90-minute tours take you to nearly every section of the ballpark, from the massive, JumboTron scoreboard to the dugout to the state-of-the-art beer-delivery system. ⊠ *333 W. Camden St., Downtown* ☎ *410/685–9800 general information, 410/547–6234 tour times, 888/848–2473 tickets to Orioles home games* ⊕ *www. theorioles.com* ⊠ *Eutaw St. promenade free; tour $9.*

FAMILY

Fodor's Choice

★

**Port Discovery Children's Museum.** At this interactive museum, adults are encouraged to play every bit as much as children. A favorite attraction is the three-story KidWorks, a futuristic jungle gym on which the adventurous can climb, crawl, slide, and swing their way through stairs, slides, ropes, zip lines, and tunnels, and even across a narrow footbridge. Learn about the Earth's atmosphere as you splash around in Wonders of Water (rain slickers and shoes are provided). Cook food in Tiny's Diner, an interactive restaurant. A soccer field becomes a stage for dance-offs and virtual races. In Miss Perception's Mystery House, you can help solve a mystery surrounding the disappearance of the Baffled family by sifting through clues that appeal to your senses. Changing exhibits allow for even more play. ⊠ *35 Market Pl., Inner Harbor* ☎ *410/727–8120* ⊕ *www.portdiscovery.com* ⊠ *$14.95.*

## SHOPPING

Baltimore isn't the biggest shopping town, but it does have some malls and good stores here and there. Hampden (the "p" is silent), a neighborhood west of Johns Hopkins University, has funky shops selling everything from housewares to housedresses along its main drag, 36th Street (better known as "The Avenue"). Upscale boutiques and jewelry stores are located in the fashionable Harbor East district. Some interesting shops can be found along Charles Street in Mount Vernon and along Thames Street in Fells Point. Federal Hill has a few fun shops, particularly for furnishings and vintage items.

**Harborplace and the Gallery.** At the Inner Harbor, the Pratt Street and Light Street pavilions of Harborplace and the Gallery contain almost 200 specialty shops that sell everything from business attire to children's toys. The Gallery has Forever 21, Urban Outfitters, and the Gap, among others. ⊠ *201 E. Pratt St., Baltimore* ☎ *410/332–4191* ⊕ *www. harborplace.com.*

## NIGHTLIFE

Fells Point, just east of the Inner Harbor; Federal Hill, due south; and Canton, due east, have hosts of bars, restaurants, and clubs that draw a rowdy, largely collegiate crowd. If you're seeking quieter surroundings, head for the upscale comforts of downtown or Mount Vernon clubs and watering holes.

### BARS AND LOUNGES

**The Brewer's Art.** Housed in a turn-of-the-century brownstone that belonged to an investment banker, the Brewer's Art has a well deserved reputation for great beer. At any given time the on-site brew house produces a half-dozen Belgian-style beers. A fine such example is their Resurrection, an abbey brown ale. Upstairs is an elegant bar and lounge with ornate woodwork, marble pillars, and chandeliers, plus a dining room with terrific food; downstairs, the dimly lit subterranean bar makes a great spot for sharing secrets. ⊠ *1106 N. Charles St., Mount Vernon* ☎ *410/547–6925* ⊕ *www.thebrewersart.com.*

**Club Charles.** With its stylized art deco surroundings, the funky Club Charles is a favorite hangout for an artsy crowd, moviegoers coming from the Charles Theater across the street, and, reputation has it, John Waters. Above the bar is a large mural of the zodiac, painted in 1941, which was reclaimed from a theater in New York. For a bar, the food is surprisingly good. ⊠ *1724 N. Charles St., Station North Arts District* ☎ *410/727–8815* ⊕ *www.clubcharles.us/.*

**Grand Central.** This gay hot spot just might have the best dance floor in Baltimore. It features a fog machine, intelligent lighting, and video screens that can help you get your groove on. Strategically located bars make it easy to secure refreshment. For more relaxed entertainment, the upstairs loft has couches and pool tables. Or, you can view Charles Street's twinkling lights from the second-floor outdoor deck. ⊠ *1003 N. Charles St., Mount Vernon* ☎ *410/752–7133* ⊕ *www.grandcentral-club.com.*

**Max's Taphouse.** The enormous bar at Max's Taphouse is heaven for beer lovers—it boasts an artillery range of taps, with more than 140 draft brews and about 1,200 more in bottles. Think of it as an educational experience, as you'll want to sample a frosty pint you've never heard of before. Max's is located in the center of Fells Point, where tourists mix with locals, who often stop in to catch an Orioles or Ravens game. A tasty menu of bar favorites, such as tater tots served in a bowl with pulled pork, cheese, and sour cream, adds depth to the experience. ⊠ *737 S. Broadway, Fells Point* ☎ *410/675–6297* ⊕ *www.maxs.com.*

**Of Love and Regret.** Once a boarding house for the brewmasters of National Bohemian Brewery, which was located across the street, this is Stillwater Artisanal Ales' tasting room and restaurant. The award-winning craft brews are a far cry from Natty Boh's rather industrial taste. "Gypsy Brewer" Brian Strumke travels the world for inspiration, and the restaurant's seasonally aware menu (try the Bavarian hot pretzels with cheese) reflects his latest interests. The decor is unpretentious, from the hand-built draft tower with custom, plain taps, to the poured concrete floor and tables sourced from a 120-year-old barn. ⊠ *1028 S. Conkling St., Baltimore* ☏ *410/327-0760* ⊕ *www.ofloveandregret.com.*

**The Owl Bar.** Not much has changed since this bar opened in 1910 as an authentic speakeasy. The signature owl statues flanking the bar served a useful purpose: during Prohibition, owner Colonel Consolvo kept barrels of whiskey in the basement, so if you saw the owls' eyes blinking, you knew it was safe to order a beverage. A thoughtful cocktail list includes an Owl Bar Manhattan and a Belvedere martini. Belgian and German beers are served on tap as well as a Heavy Seas Owl Bar lager. The vibe is casual, but the atmosphere, with stately Germanic influences like leaded glass windows, iron chandeliers, and herringbone brickwork, harken to days of finer quality craftsmanship. The kitchen serves comfort foods like crab cakes, pizza, burgers, and salads. It's in the former Belvedere Hotel. ⊠ *1 E. Chase St., Baltimore* ☏ *410/347-0888* ⊕ *www.theowlbar.com.*

**13th Floor.** At the top of The Belvedere, the 13th Floor offers a great view, a long martini list, and live jazz. For a while it had been trapped in the disco era, but recent renovations have restored the space to Gatsby-esque glory, with exposed wrought-iron beams, stained glass windows, and sexy decor. ⊠ *1 E. Chase St., Mount Vernon* ☏ *410/347-0880* ⊕ *www.13floorbelvedere.com.*

## WHERE TO EAT

Baltimore loves crabs. Soft- or hardshell crabs, crab cakes, crab dip— the city's passion for clawed crustaceans seems to have no end. Flag down a Baltimore native and ask them where the best crab joint is, and you'll get a list of options. In addition to crabs and seafood, Baltimore's restaurant landscape also includes Italian, Afghan, Greek, American, Korean, Spanish, and other cuisines. The city's dining choices may not compare with those of New York, or even Washington, but it does have some real standouts. Note that places generally stop serving by 10 pm.

$   ✕ **Amicci's.** At this self-proclaimed "very casual eatery," you don't have
ITALIAN   to spend a fortune to get a satisfying taste of Little Italy. Blue jean–clad diners and walls hung with movie posters make for a fun atmosphere. Service is friendly and usually speedy, and the food comes in large portions. Try the chicken Lorenzo: breaded chicken breast covered in a marsala wine sauce, red peppers, prosciutto, and provolone. ⑤ *Average main: $18* ⊠ *231 S. High St., Little Italy* ☏ *410/528-1096* ⊕ *www. amiccis.com.*

$   ✕ **Attman's.** Open since 1915, this authentic New York–style deli near
DELI   the Jewish Museum is the only vestige of Baltimore's "Corned Beef Row" operating in its original location. Don't be put off by the long lines—they move fairly quickly, and the outstanding corned beef sandwiches are worth the wait, as are the pastrami, homemade chopped liver, and other oversized creations. Attman's closes at 6:30 pm on Monday through Saturday and 5 pm on Sunday. ⑤ *Average main: $9* ⊠ *1019 E. Lombard St., Historic Jonestown* ☏ *410/563-2666* ⊕ *www. attmansdeli.com.*

**$$**  ✕ **Bo Brooks.** Picking steamed crabs on Bo Brooks's waterfront deck as
SEAFOOD  sailboats and tugs ply the harbor is a quintessential Baltimore pleasure.
Spend a muggy summer day cracking into warm, spicy crabs and enjoy a
refreshing pitcher of beer while a cool breeze blows in from the harbor.
Brooks serves its famous crustaceans year-round, along with a menu
of Chesapeake seafood classics. Locals know to stick to the Maryland
crab soup, crab dip, jumbo lump crab cakes, and fried oysters. ⑤ *Aver-
age main: $18* ✉ *2780 Boston St., Canton* ☎ *410/558–0202* ⊕ *www.
bobrooks.com.*

**$$**  ✕ **Rusty Scupper.** A tourist favorite, the Rusty Scupper undoubtedly has
SEAFOOD  the best view along the waterfront; sunset here is magical, with the sun
sinking slowly into the harbor as lights twinkle on the city's skyscrapers.
The interior is decorated with light wood and windows from floor to
ceiling; the house specialty is seafood, particularly the jumbo lump crab
cake, but the menu also includes an Angus beef burger, grilled rockfish,
and filet mignon. Reservations are essential on Friday and Saturday and
for the popular Sunday Jazz brunch. ⑤ *Average main: $29* ✉ *402 Key
Hwy., Inner Harbor* ☎ *410/727–3678.*

## WHERE TO STAY

When booking a hotel or bed-and-breakfast in Baltimore, focus on the
Inner Harbor, where you're likely to spend a good deal of time. The
downside to staying in hotels near downtown is the noise level, which
can rise early in the morning and stay up late into the night—especially
if there's a baseball or football game. For quieter options, head to neighborhoods like Fells Point and Canton.

*For expanded reviews, facilities, and current deals, visit Fodors.com.*

**$$**  🏨 **Hilton Baltimore.** The towering Hilton has an unparalleled view of
HOTEL  Camden Yards and a skywalk that connects to the city's convention cen-
ter. **Pros:** connected to the convention center; excellent ballpark views.
**Cons:** rooms are considerably smaller than those at similarly priced
hotels in town; it's a chain hotel, albeit a nice one. ⑤ *Rooms from: $189*
✉ *401 W. Pratt St., Inner Harbor* ☎ *443/573–8700* ⊕ *www.hilton.com*
⤳ *757 rooms* 🍽 *No meals.*

**$$$**  🏨 **Hotel Monaco Baltimore.** This 202-room boutique hotel is in the his-
HOTEL  toric headquarters of the B&O Railroad—just 2½ blocks from the
FAMILY  Inner Harbor and within easy walking distance of First Mariner Arena,
Fodor'sChoice  Everyman Theatre, and Oriole Park at Camden Yards. **Pros:** a posh
★  downtown hotel at family-friendly prices. **Cons:** the reception area is
on the building's second floor. ⑤ *Rooms from: $259* ✉ *2 N. Charles St.,
Downtown* ☎ *410/692–6170* ⊕ *www.monaco-baltimore.com* ⤳ *202
rooms* 🍽 *Some meals.*

**$$$**  🏨 **Marriott Baltimore Waterfront.** The city's tallest hotel and one of a hand-
HOTEL  ful directly on the Inner Harbor, this upscale 31-story Marriott has a
neoclassical interior that uses multihue marbles, rich jewel-tone walls,
and photographs of Baltimore architectural landmarks. **Pros:** nice ame-
nities; great location and view. **Cons:** pricey compared to nearby hotels.
⑤ *Rooms from: $394* ✉ *700 Aliceanna St., Harbor East* ☎ *410/385–
3000* ⊕ *www.marriott.com* ⤳ *751 rooms* 🍽 *No meals.*

**$$$** ⚏ **Renaissance Baltimore Harborplace Hotel.** The most conveniently located
HOTEL    of the Inner Harbor hotels—across the street from the shopping pavil-
ions—the Renaissance Harborplace meets the needs of tourists, busi-
ness travelers, and conventioneers. **Pros:** snappy service. **Cons:** big and
impersonal. ⑤ *Rooms from: $224* ✉ *202 E. Pratt St., Inner Harbor*
☎ *410/547–1200, 800/468–3571* ⊕ *www.marriott.com* ⥱ *562 rooms,*
*60 suites* ⦿ *No meals.*

# CHARLESTON, SOUTH CAROLINA                                  **3**

By Eileen
Robinson
Smith

Charleston looks like a movie set,
an 18th-century etching brought to
life. The spires and steeples of more
than 180 churches punctuate her
low skyline, and tourists ride in
horse-drawn carriages that pass
grandiose, centuries-old mansions
and gardens brimming with heir-
loom plants. Preserved through the
poverty following the Civil War and
natural disasters like fires, earth-
quakes, and hurricanes, much of
Charleston's earliest public and pri-
vate architecture still stands. And
thanks to a rigorous preservation
movement and strict Board of
Architectural Review, the city's new
structures blend with the old ones.
If you're boarding your cruise ship
here, it's worth coming a few days
early to explore the historic down-
town and to eat in one of the many

### BEST BETS

■ **Viewing Art.** The city is home
to some 120 galleries, exhibiting
art from Charleston, the South,
and around the world. The Gibbes
Museum of Art and a half-dozen
other museums add to the
cultural mix.

■ **The Battery.** The views from
the point—both natural and
man-made—are the loveliest in
the city. Look west to see the
harbor; to the east you'll find
elegant Charleston mansions.

■ **Historic Homes.** Charleston's
preserved, centuries-old, stately
homes, including the Nathaniel
Russell House, are highlights.

superb restaurants. In late spring, plan in advance for the Spoleto U.S.A.
Festival. For more than 30 memorable years, arts patrons have gathered
to enjoy the international dance, opera, theater, and other performances
at venues citywide. Piccolo Spoleto showcases local and regional con-
certs, dance, theater, and comedy improvs.

### ESSENTIALS
#### HOURS
Most shops are open from 9 or 10 am to at least 6 pm, but some are
open later. A new city ordinance requires bars to close by 2 am.

#### VISITOR INFORMATION
**Contacts Charleston Visitor Center.** ✉ *375 Meeting St., Market* ☎ *843/853–*
*8000, 800/868–8118* ⊕ *www.explorecharleston.com.*

### THE CRUISE PORT
Cruise ships sailing from Charleston depart from the Union Pier Termi-
nal, which is in Charleston's historic district. If you are driving, how-
ever, and need to leave your car for the duration of your cruise, take
the East Bay Street exit off the new, majestic Ravenel Bridge on I–17

and follow the "Cruise Ship" signs. On ship embarkation days police officers will direct you to the ship terminal from the intersection of East Bay and Chapel streets. Cruise parking is located adjacent to Union Pier.

Contacts **Port of Charleston.** ⊠ *Union Pier, 280 Concord St., Market* ☎ *843/958–8298 for cruise information* ⊕ *www.port-of-charleston.com.*

### AIRPORT

Contacts **Charleston International Airport.** ⊠ *5500 International Blvd., North Charleston* ☎ *843/797–7000* ⊕ *www.chs-airport.com.*

### AIRPORT TRANSFERS

Several cab companies service the airport; expect to pay between $25 and $35 for a trip downtown. Airport Ground Transportation arranges shuttles, which cost $12 to $15 per person to the downtown area, double for a return trip to the airport. CARTA's bus No. 11, a public bus, now goes to the airport for a mere $3; it leaves downtown from the Meeting/Mary St. parking garage every 50 minutes, from 10 am until 10:30 pm, and makes a continuous loop around the airport.

Contacts **Charleston Black Cab Company.** ☎ *843/216–2627* ⊕ *charlestonblackcabcompany.com.* **Charleston Downtown Limo.** ☎ *843/723–1111, 843/973–0990* ⊕ *charlestondowntownlimo.com.* **Charleston International Airport Ground Transportation.** ⊠ *5500 International Blvd., North Charleston* ☎ *843/767–7026* ⊕ *www.chs-airport.com.*

### PARKING

Parking costs $17 per day ($119 per week) for regular vehicles, $40 per day ($280 per week) for RVs or other vehicles more than 20 feet long. A free shuttle bus takes you to the cruise-passenger terminal. Be sure to drop your large luggage off at Union Pier before you park your car; only carry-on size luggage is allowed on the shuttle bus, so if you have any bags larger than 22 inches by 14 inches, they will have to be checked before you park. Also, you'll need your cruise tickets to board the shuttle bus.

## EXPLORING

The heart of the city is on a peninsula, sometimes just called "downtown" by the nearly 60,000 residents who populate the area. Walking Charleston's peninsula is the best way to get to know the city. The main downtown historic district is roughly bounded by Lockwood Boulevard to the west, Calhoun Street to the north, the Cooper River to the east, and the Battery to the south. Nearly 2,000 historic homes and buildings occupy this fairly compact area divided into South of Broad (Street) and North of Broad. King Street, the main shopping street in town, cuts through Broad Street, and the most trafficked tourist area ends a few blocks south of the Crosstown, where U.S. 17 cuts across Upper King. If you don't wish to walk, there are bikes, pedicabs, and trolleys. Street parking is irksome, as meter readers are among the city's most efficient public servants. Parking garages, both privately and publicly owned, charge around $1.50 an hour.

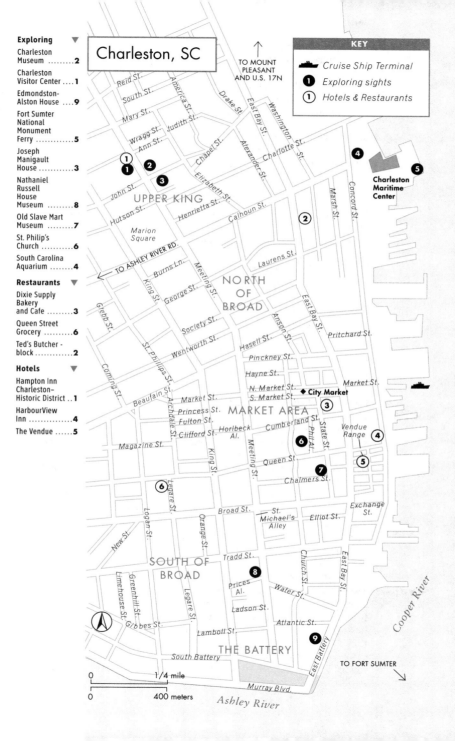

# Charleston, SC

TO MOUNT PLEASANT AND U.S. 17N

**KEY**

🚢 Cruise Ship Terminal

❶ Exploring sights

① Hotels & Restaurants

Charleston Maritime Center

UPPER KING

Marion Square

NORTH OF BROAD

TO ASHLEY RIVER RD.

MARKET AREA

◆ City Market

Vendue Range

SOUTH OF BROAD

THE BATTERY

Cooper River

Ashley River

Murray Blvd.

TO FORT SUMTER

0 __ 1/4 mile

0 __ 400 meters

**Streets:** Reid St., South St., Mary St., America St., Drake St., East Bay St., Washington St., Wragg St., Judith St., Ann St., Chapel St., Alexander St., Charlotte St., John St., Elizabeth St., Hutson St., Henrietta St., Calhoun St., Marsh St., Concord St., Laurens St., Burns Ln., Meeting St., King St., George St., Anson St., Pritchard St., Grebb St., Society St., Wentworth St., Hasell St., Pinckney St., St. Phillips St., Hayne St., Market St., Coming St., Beaufain St., Archdale St., N. Market St., S. Market St., Princess St., Fulton St., Cumberland St., State St., Phil Al., Clifford St., Horlbeck Al., Magazine St., Queen St., Chalmers St., Legare St., Broad St., St. Michael's Alley, Elliot St., Exchange St., Logan St., Orange St., New St., Tradd St., Prices Al., Water St., Limehouse St., Greenhill St., Ladson St., Atlantic St., Gibbes St., Lamboll St., Church St., East Battery, South Battery

FAMILY **Charleston Museum.** Although housed in a modern-day brick complex, this institution was founded in 1773 and is the country's oldest museum. To the delight of fans of *Antiques Roadshow,* the collection is especially strong in South Carolina decorative arts, from silver to snuffboxes. There's also a large gallery devoted to natural history (don't miss the giant polar bear). Children love the permanent Civil War exhibition and the interactive "Kidstory" area, where they can try on reproduction clothing in a miniature historic house. The Historic Textiles Gallery features rotating displays that showcase everything from uniforms and flags to couture gowns to antique quilts and needlework. Combination tickets that include the Joseph Manigault House and the Heyward-Washington House are a bargain at $28 ⊠ *360 Meeting St., Upper King* ☎ *843/722–2996* ⊕ *www.charlestonmuseum.org* ⊠ *$12, $18 ticket includes Joseph Manigault House or Heyward-Washington House; $28 for all 3 sites.*

**Charleston Visitor Center.** A 20-minute film called *Forever Charleston* makes a fine introduction to the city. ■ **TIP➡ The first 30 minutes are free at the center's parking lot, making it a real bargain.** ⊠ *375 Meeting St., Upper King* ☎ *800/774–0006* ⊕ *www.explorecharleston.com* ⊠ *Free.*

**Edmondston-Alston House.** In 1825, Charles Edmondston built this house in the Federal style on Charleston's High Battery. About 13 years later, second owner Charles Alston began transforming it into the Greek Revival structure seen today. Tours of the home—furnished with family antiques, portraits, silver, and fine china—are informative. ⊠ *21 E. Battery, South of Broad* ☎ *843/722–7171* ⊕ *www.edmondstonalston. com* ⊠ *$12.*

FAMILY **Fort Sumter National Monument.** Set on a man-made island in Charleston's
Fodor'sChoice harbor, this is the hallowed spot where the Civil War began. On April
★ 12, 1861, the first shot of the war was fired at the fort from Fort Johnson across the way. After a 34-hour battle, Union forces surrendered and Confederate troops occupied Fort Sumter, which became a symbol of Southern resistance. The Confederacy managed to hold it, despite almost continual bombardment from August 1863 to February of 1865. When it was finally evacuated, the fort was a heap of rubble. Today, the National Park Service oversees it, and rangers give interpretive talks.

To reach the fort, take a private boat or one of the ferries that depart from downtown's Fort Sumter Visitor Education Center and from Patriots Point in Mount Pleasant. There are six trips daily between mid-March and mid-August, fewer the rest of the year. ☎ *843/883–3123* ⊕ *www.nps.gov/fosu* ⊠ *Fort free; ferry $19.50.*

Fodor'sChoice **Joseph Manigault House.** An extraordinary example of Federal architec-
★ ture, this 1803 residence was designed by Gabriel Manigault for his brother, Joseph. The National Historic Landmark reflects the urban lifestyle of a well-to-do rice-planting family and the African Americans they enslaved. Engaging guided tours reveal a stunning spiral staircase; rooms that have been preserved in period style; and American, English, and French furniture from the early 19th century. Outside, stroll through the artfully maintained period garden with a classical

Gate Temple and interpretive signs that note where historic buildings once stood. ✉ *350 Meeting St., Upper King* ☎ *843/723–2926, 843/724–8481* ⊕ *www.historiccharleston.org* ✉ *$12; $18 for combination ticket including Aiken-Rhett House.*

**Fodor's**Choice
★
**Nathaniel Russell House Museum.** One of the nation's finest examples of Federal-style architecture, the Nathaniel Russell House was built in 1808 and is restored to a 19th-century aesthetic. Its grand beauty is proof of the immense wealth Russell accumulated as one of the city's leading merchants. In addition to the famous "free-flying" staircase that spirals up three stories with no visible support, the ornate interior is distinguished by Charleston-made furniture as well as paintings and works on paper by well-known American and European artists, including Henry Benbridge, Samuel F. B. Morse, and George Romney. The extensive formal garden is worth a leisurely stroll. ✉ *51 Meeting St., South of Broad* ☎ *843/724–8481* ⊕ *www.historiccharleston.org* ✉ *$12; $18 with admission to Aiken-Rhett House Museum.*

**Fodor's**Choice
★
**Old Slave Mart Museum.** This is thought to be the state's only existing building that was used for slave auctioning, a practice that ended here in 1863. It was once part of a complex called Ryan's Mart, which also contained a slave jail, kitchen, and morgue. It is now a museum that shares the history of Charleston's role in the slave trade, an unpleasant story but one that is vital to understand. Charleston was a commercial center for the South's plantation economy, and slaves were the primary source of labor both within the city and on the surrounding plantations. Galleries are outfitted with interactive exhibits, including push buttons that allow you to hear voices relating stories from the age of slavery. The museum sits on one of the few remaining cobblestone streets in town. ✉ *6 Chalmers St., Market* ☎ *843/958–6467* ⊕ *www.charleston-sc.gov* ✉ *$7.*

**Fodor's**Choice
★
**St. Philip's Church.** Founded around 1680, St. Philip's didn't move to its current site until the 1720s, becoming one of the three churches that gave Church Street its name. The first building in this location (where George Washington worshipped in 1791) burned down in 1835 and was replaced with the Corinthian-style structure seen today. A shell that exploded in the churchyard while services were being held one Sunday during the Civil War didn't deter the minister from finishing his sermon (the congregation gathered elsewhere for the remainder of the war). Amble through the churchyards, where notable South Carolinians such as John C. Calhoun are buried. If you want to tour the church, call ahead, as open hours depend upon volunteer availability. ✉ *142 Church St., Market* ☎ *843/722–7734* ⊕ *www.stphilipschurchsc.org.*

FAMILY
**Fodor's**Choice
★
**South Carolina Aquarium.** Get up-close-and-personal with more than 7,000 creatures at this waterfront attraction, where exhibits invite you to journey through distinctive habitats. Step into the Mountain Forest and find water splashing over a rocky gorge as river otters play. Enter the open-air Saltmarsh Aviary to feed stingrays and view herons, diamondback terrapins, and puffer fish. And gaze in awe at the two-story, 385,000-gallon Great Ocean Tank, home to sharks, jellyfish, and a loggerhead sea turtle. Kids love the Touch Tank and the 4-D Theater

that shows films with special effects such as wind gusts and splashes of water. Tours of the Sea Turtle Hospital are well worth the extra $10. ✉ *100 Aquarium Wharf, Upper King* ☎ *800/722–6455, 843/577–3474* ⊕ *www.scaquarium.org* ⌨ *$24.95; $29.95 with 4-D film.*

## SHOPPING

**City Market.** A cluster of shops and restaurants surrounds the old City Market. Sweetgrass basket weavers work here and you can buy their wares, although these crafts have become expensive. There are T-shirts shops as well as upscale clothing boutiques. In the covered market, vendors have stalls selling everything from jewelry to dresses and purses. You can peruse the middle section of the market in air-conditioned comfort. ✉ *E. Bay and Market Sts., Market* ⊕ *www.thecharlestoncitymarket.com.*

> ### CHARLESTON CRUISE PACKAGES
>
> For a listing of all hotel package discounts you can book along with your cruise, not to mention discounted tours (including the popular plantation tours), attractions, and shopping and dining coupons, visit www.charlestoncruisepackages.com

**Fodor's Choice** ★ **King Street.** The city's main shopping strip, King Street is divided into informal districts: Lower King (from Broad Street to Market Street) is the Antiques District, lined with high-end dealers; Middle King (from Market Street to Calhoun Street) is the Fashion District, a mix of national chains like Banana Republic and Pottery Barn and locally owned boutiques; and Upper King (from Calhoun Street to Spring Street) has been dubbed the Design District, an up-and-coming area becoming known for its furniture and interior-design stores. Check out Second Sundays on King, when the street closes to cars from Calhoun Street to Queen Street. Make sure to visit the farmers' market in Marion Square throughout the spring and summer months. ✉ *Charleston.*

## NIGHTLIFE

**Fodor's Choice** ★ **Charleston Grill.** The elegant Charleston Grill hosts live jazz seven nights a week, drawing from the city's most renowned musicians. Performers range from the internationally acclaimed Brazilian guitarist Duda Lucena to the Bob Williams Duo, a father and son who play classical guitar and violin. The place draws an urbane thirtysomething crowd. Down the hall, the neighboring Thoroughbred Club offers nightly live music and an impressive selection of bourbons. ✉ *Charleston Place Hotel, 224 King St., Market* ☎ *843/577–4522* ⊕ *www.charlestongrill.com.*

## WHERE TO EAT

$    ✕ **Dixie Supply Bakery and Cafe.** It might be buttressed by a Lil' Cricket
SOUTHERN    convenience store, but don't be fooled by the size of Dixie Supply Bakery and Cafe. It belongs to an old Charlestonian family (and by old, we mean they arrived here in 1698 or so) that seeks to honor its roots through food. It's here you'll find Lowcountry and Southern classics:

shrimp and creamy stone-ground grits, fried chicken, and a mighty fine tomato pie. Daily blue-plate specials abound, including fried green tomatoes, shrimp from nearby Wadmalaw Island, summer-squash-and-ricotta ravioli, and a steady assortment of locally plucked vegetables. If you only want a bite, the biscuits are worth grabbing to go. $ Average main: $7 ⊠ 62 State St., Market ☎ 843/722–5650 ⊕ www.dixie cafecharleston.com ⊘ No dinner.

$   ✕ **Queen Street Grocery.** For crepes and cold-pressed coffee, most folks
AMERICAN   turn to a venerable Charleston institution: Queen Street Grocery. Built in 1922, the corner building has served many purposes throughout the years: butcher shop, candy shop, and late-night convenience store. The restaurant's owners call to mind the place's roots as a neighborhood grocery store by sourcing much of the produce and other goods from local growers. Don't pass up the sweet and savory crepes, named for the islands surrounding Charleston. The place still operates as a charming bodega, perfect for picking up a bottle of wine on the way to a picnic in White Point Gardens. $ Average main: $9 ⊠ 133 Queen St., Market ☎ 843/723–4121 ⊕ www.queenstreetgrocerycafe.com.

$   ✕ **Ted's Butcherblock.** Land at Ted's on a lucky evening and you'll likely
AMERICAN   be conferred a memorable greeting: the scent of smoked meat drifting from a grill perched near the entrance. Happy day, indeed. Ted's operates as a one-stop butcher shop, supplying beef, game, seafood, and homemade sausages to complement its selection of artisanal cheeses, wine, and other specialty foods. The shop also maintains a first-rate deli counter, drawing praise from *Bon Appetit*, etc. Among the favored offerings: the house-roasted Wagyu beef panini and the ever-changing bacon-of-the-month BLT. On Friday nights there are wine tastings and a bargain prix-fixe dinner. $ Average main: $8 ⊠ 334 E. Bay St., Market ☎ 843/577–0094 ⊕ www.tedsbutcherblock.com.

## WHERE TO STAY

$$   ⚏ **Hampton Inn Charleston–Historic District.** Hardwood floors, a central
HOTEL   fireplace, and leather furnishings in the lobby of what was once an 1800s warehouse help elevate this chain hotel a bit above the rest. **Pros:** hot breakfast; located near numerous restaurant and nightlife options. **Cons:** a long walk to the Market area; rooms are smallish; no views. $ Rooms from: $199 ⊠ 345 Meeting St., Upper King ☎ 843/723–4000, 800/426–7866 ⊕ www.hamptoninn.com ⤳ 170 rooms ⎮⊙⎮ Breakfast.

$$$$   ⚏ **HarbourView Inn.** This is the only hotel facing Charleston Harbor,
HOTEL   and if you ask for a room with a view or even a private balcony, you can gaze out onto the kid-friendly fountain at the center of Waterfront Park. **Pros:** continental breakfast can be delivered to your room or the rooftop; location is tops; service is notable. **Cons:** rooms are off long, modern halls, giving the place more of a chain hotel feel. $ Rooms from: $279 ⊠ 2 Vendue Range, Market ☎ 843/853–8439 ⊕ www. harbourviewcharleston.com ⤳ 52 rooms ⎮⊙⎮ Breakfast.

$$$$   ⚏ **The Vendue.** A $4.8 million renovation transformed the Vendue into
B&B/INN   an art-filled space that feels as much like a contemporary art museum
**Fodor's** Choice   as it does a boutique hotel. **Pros:** free bike rentals; soundproofing masks
★   street noise; great restaurant and coffee shop. **Cons:** no complimentary

breakfast; some halls and spaces are small as in centuries past. $ *Rooms from: $275* ⊠ *19 Vendue Range, Market* ☎ *843/577–7970, 800/845–7900* ⊕ *www.thevendue.com* ↝ *84 rooms* ⦿ *No meals.*

# FORT LAUDERDALE, FLORIDA

By Paul Rubio

Collegians of the 1960s returning to Fort Lauderdale would be hard-pressed to recognize the onetime "Sun and Suds Spring Break Capital of the Universe." Today the beach is home to upscale shops, restaurants, and luxury resorts, while downtown has exploded with new office and luxury residential developments. The entertainment and shopping areas—Las Olas Boulevard, Riverfront, and Himmarshee Village—are thriving. And Port Everglades is giving Miami a run for its money in passenger cruising, with a dozen cruise-ship terminals, including the world's largest, hosting 34 cruise ships with some 3,000 departures annually. A captivating shoreline with wide ribbons of sand for beachcombing and sunbathing makes Fort Lauderdale and Broward County a major draw for visitors, and often tempts cruise-ship passengers to spend an extra day or two in the sun. Fort Lauderdale's 2-mile (3-km) stretch of unobstructed beachfront has been further enhanced with a sparkling promenade designed more for the pleasure of pedestrians than vehicles.

## BEST BETS

■ **The Beach.** With more than 20 miles of ocean shoreline, the scene at Greater Fort Lauderdale's best beaches, especially between Bahia Mar and Sunrise Boulevard, is not to be missed.

■ **The Everglades.** Take in the wild reaches in or near the Everglades with an airboat ride. Mosquitoes are friendly, so arm yourself accordingly.

■ **Las Olas Boulevard and the Riverwalk.** This is a great place to stroll before and after performances, dinner, libations, and other entertainment.

## ESSENTIALS

### HOURS

Many museums close on Monday.

### BOAT TOURS

A water taxi provides service along the intracoastal waterway in Fort Lauderdale between the 17th Street Causeway and Oakland Park Boulevard, and west into downtown along New River and south to Hollywood, daily from 9 am until 11 pm. A day-pass costs $26.

**Contacts Water Taxi.** ☎ *954/467–6677* ⊕ *www.watertaxi.com.*

### VISITOR INFORMATION

**Contacts Greater Fort Lauderdale Convention and Visitors Bureau.** ⊠ *101 N.E. 3rd Ave., #100, Fort Lauderdale* ☎ *954/765–4466* ⊕ *www.sunny.org.*

### THE CRUISE PORT

Port Everglades, Fort Lauderdale's cruise port (nowhere near the Everglades, but happily near the beach and less than 2 miles [3 km] from the airport), is among the world's largest, busiest ports. It's also the straightest, deepest port in the southeastern United States, meaning you'll be out to sea in no time flat once your ship sets sail. In 2009 Cruise Terminal 18 was tripled in size to accommodate Royal Caribbean's Oasis-class ships, the 5,400-passenger Oasis of the Seas and sister Allure of the Seas, both of which relocated to Port Canaveral in 2016. This made room for the latest incarnation of the world's largest cruise ship, *Harmony of the Seas,* which debuted in November 2016. The terminal's mega-size (240,000 square feet) accommodates both arriving and departing passengers and their luggage, simultaneously going through processing procedures. The port is south of downtown Fort Lauderdale, spread out over a huge area extending into Dania Beach, Hollywood, and a patch of unincorporated Broward County. A few words of caution: Schedule plenty of time to navigate the short distance from the airport, your hotel, or wherever else you might be staying, especially if you like to be among the first to embark for your sailing. Increased security (sometimes you'll be asked for a driver's license and/ or other identification, and on occasion for boarding documentation upon entering the port, other times not) combined with increased traffic, larger parking facilities, construction projects, roadway improvements, and other obstacles mean the old days of popping over to Port Everglades and running up a gangplank in the blink of an eye are history.

If you are driving, there are three entrances to the port. One is from 17th Street, west of the 17th Street Causeway Bridge, turning south at the traffic light onto Eisenhower Boulevard. Or to get to the main entrance, take either State Road 84, running east–west, to the intersection of Federal Highway and cross into the port. Or take I–595 east straight into the Port (I–595 becomes Eller Drive once inside the Port). I–595 runs east–west with connections to the Fort Lauderdale–Hollywood International Airport, U.S. 1 (Federal Highway), I–95, State Road 7 (U.S. 441), Florida's Turnpike, Sawgrass Expressway, and I–75.

**Contacts** **Port Everglades.** ✉ *1850 Eller Dr., Fort Lauderdale* ☎ *954/523–3404* ⊕ *www.porteverglades.net/cruising/.*

### AIRPORT
**Contacts** **Fort Lauderdale–Hollywood International Airport** (*FLL*). ☎ *866/435–9355* ⊕ *www.broward.org/airport.*

### AIRPORT TRANSFERS
Fort Lauderdale–Hollywood International Airport is 4 miles (6 km) south of downtown and 2 miles (3 km [about 5 to 10 minutes]) from the docks. If you haven't arranged an airport transfer with your cruise line, you can take an Uber or old-fashioned taxi to the cruise-ship terminals. The ride in a metered taxi costs about $17, depending on your departure terminal. Taxi fares for up to five passengers, regulated by the county, are $2.50 for the first 1/6 mile and 40¢ for each additional 1/6 mile, 40¢ per minute for waiting time, plus a $3 surcharge for cabs departing from the airport. Yellow Cab has a major presence, and Go Airport Shuttle provides limousine or shared-ride service to and from Port Everglades to all parts of Broward County; fares to most Fort Lauderdale beach hotels are in the $25 to $30 range.

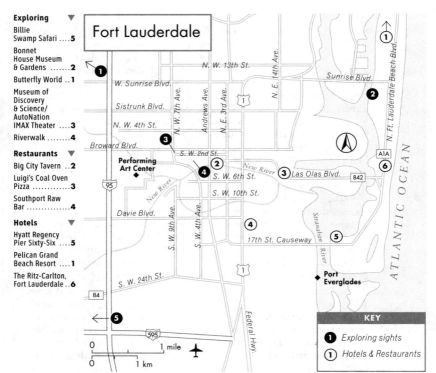

**Fort Lauderdale**

**Contacts Go Airport Shuttle.** ☎ 954/561–8888, 800/244–8252 ⊕ go-airport-shuttle.com. **Fort Lauderdale Shuttle.** ☎ 954/525–7796, 866/ 386–7433 ⊕ fortlau-derdaleshuttle.com. **Yellow Cab.** ☎ 954/777–7777 ⊕ www.yellowcabbroward.com.

**PARKING**

Two covered parking facilities close to the terminals are Northport (2,500 spaces) and Midport (2,000 spaces). Use the Northport garage if your cruise leaves from Terminal 1 or2; use Midport if your cruise leaves from Terminal 19, 21, 22/24, 25, 26, 27, or 29. The Midport Surface Lot at Terminal 18 has its own 600 spaces and the Northport Surface Lot has 172 spaces for passengers leaving from Terminal 4. The cost is $15 per day for either garage or surface lot ($19 for oversize vehicles up to 20 feet); you pay by cash or credit card when you leave. To save a few bucks on your parking tab, two separate companies, Park 'N Fly ($12 per day) and Park 'N Go ($12 per day) provide remote parking just outside Port Everglades, at the exit off I–595, with shuttles to all cruise terminals. Book ahead online for even deeper discounts.

**Contacts Park 'N Fly.** ⊠ 2200 N.E. 7th Ave., Dania Beach ✛ At Port Everglades exit off I–595 ☎ 954/779–1776 ⊕ www.pnf.com. **Park 'N Go.** ⊠ 1101 Eller Dr., Fort Lauderdale ✛ At Port Everglades exit off I–595 ☎ 954/760–4525, 888/764–7275 ⊕ www.bookparkngo.com.

# EXPLORING

Like its southeast Florida neighbors, Fort Lauderdale has been busily revitalizing for several years. In a state where gaudy tourist zones often stand aloof from workaday downtowns, Fort Lauderdale is unusual in that the city exhibits consistency at both ends of the 2-mile (3-km) Las Olas corridor. The sparkling look results from efforts to thoroughly improve both beachfront and downtown. Matching the downtown's innovative arts district, cafés, and boutiques is an equally inventive beach area with its own share of cafés and shops facing an undeveloped shoreline.

FAMILY **Billie Swamp Safari.** At the Billie Swamp Safari, experience life in the Everglades firsthand albeit in a somewhat touristy setting. Daily tours of wildlife-filled wetlands and hammocks yield sightings of deer, water buffalo, raccoons, wild hogs, hawks, eagles, and alligators. Animal and reptile shows entertain audiences. Sixty-minute ecotours are conducted aboard motorized swamp buggies, and 20-minute airboat rides are available, too. The on-site Swamp Water Café serves gator nuggets, frogs' legs, catfish, and Indian fry bread with honey. ⊠ *Big Cypress Seminole Indian Reservation, 30000 Gator Tail Trail, Clewiston* ☎ *863/983–6101, 800/949–6101* ⊕ *www.billieswamp.com* ⊠ *Swamp Safari Day Package (ecotour, shows, exhibits, and airboat ride) $50.*

Fodor'sChoice **Bonnet House Museum & Gardens.** A 35-acre oasis in the heart of the beach
★ area, this subtropical estate on the National Register of Historic Places stands as a tribute to the history of Old South Florida. This charming home, built in the 1920s, was the winter residence of the late Frederic and Evelyn Bartlett, artists whose personal touches and small surprises are evident throughout. If you're interested in architecture, artwork, or the natural environment, this place is worth a visit. After admiring the fabulous gardens, be on the lookout for playful monkeys swinging from trees. Interesting factoid: The Bonnet House was the final stop in the 2005 season of CBS's *hit television show The Amazing Race.* ⊠ *900 N. Birch Rd., Beachfront* ☎ *954/563–5393* ⊕ *www.bonnethouse.org* ⊠ *$20 for house tours, $10 for gardens only.*

FAMILY **Butterfly World.** As many as 80 butterfly species from South and Central
Fodor'sChoice America, the Philippines, Malaysia, Taiwan, and other Asian nations
★ are typically found within the serene 3-acre site inside Tradewinds Park in the northwest reaches of Broward County. A screened aviary called North American Butterflies is reserved for native species. The Tropical Rain Forest Aviary is a 30-foot-high construction, with observation decks, waterfalls, ponds, and tunnels filled with thousands of colorful butterflies. There are lots of birds, too; and kids love going in the lorikeet aviary, where the colorful birds land on every limb! ⊠ *Tradewinds Park, 3600 W. Sample Rd., Coconut Creek* ☎ *954/977–4400* ⊕ *www. butterflyworld.com* ⊠ *$26.95.*

FAMILY **Museum of Discovery & Science/AutoNation IMAX Theater.** With more
Fodor'sChoice than 200 interactive exhibits, the aim here is to entertain children—
★ *and* adults—with the wonders of science and the wonders of Florida. Exhibits include the Ecodiscovery Center with an Everglades Airboat Adventure ride, resident otters, and an interactive Florida storm center.

Florida Ecoscapes has a living coral reef, plus sharks, rays, and eels. Runways to Rockets offers stimulating trips to Mars and the moon while nine different cockpit simulators let you try out your pilot skills. The AutoNation IMAX theater, part of the complex, was renovated in 2014 and shows mainstream and educational films, some in 3-D. ⊠ *401 S. W. 2nd St., Downtown* ☎ *954/467–6637 museum, 954/463–4629 IMAX, 954/713–0930 sea turtle walks* ⊕ *www.mods. org* ⊠ *Museum $14, $19 with 1 IMAX educational screening.*

> ### SHIP NAMES
>
> Even as far back as ancient times, mariners have traditionally referred to their ships as "she." To a seaman, a ship is as beautiful and comforting as his mother or sweetheart. You could say a good ship holds a special place in his heart.

**Riverwalk.** Some lovely views prevail on this paved promenade on the New River's north bank. On the first Sunday of every month a free jazz festival attracts visitors; other days, you may be sharing the Riverwalk with Fort Lauderdale's prevalent homeless population. From west to east, the Riverwalk begins at the residential New River Sound, passes through the Arts and Science District, then the historic center of Fort Lauderdale, and wraps around the New River until it meets with Las Olas Boulevard's shopping district. ⊠ *Fort Lauderdale* ⊕ *www. goriverwalk.com.*

## BEACHES

Fort Lauderdale's beachfront offers the best of all possible worlds, with easy access not only to a wide band of beige sand but also to restaurants and shops. There are more than 20 miles of sparkling beaches, but the most popular stretch is 2 miles (3 km) south of Sunrise Boulevard along Route A1A. Here you'll have clear views, typically across rows of colorful beach umbrellas, of the sea, and of ships passing into and out of nearby Port Everglades. If you're on the beach, gaze back on an exceptionally graceful promenade.

Pedestrians rank above vehicles in Fort Lauderdale. Broad walkways line both sides of the beach road, and traffic has been trimmed to two gently curving northbound lanes, where in-line skaters skim past slow-moving cars. On the beach side, a low masonry wall doubles as an extended bench, separating sand from the promenade. At night the wall is accented with ribbons of fiber-optic color. The most crowded portion of beach is between Las Olas and Sunrise boulevards. Tackier aspects of this onetime strip—famous for the springtime madness spawned by the film *Where the Boys Are*—are now but a fading memory, with the possible exception of the icon Elbo Room, an ever-popular bar at the corner of Las Olas and A1A.

North of the redesigned beachfront are another 2 miles (3 km) of open and natural coastal landscape. Much of the way parallels the Hugh Taylor Birch State Recreation Area, preserving a patch of primeval Florida.

## SHOPPING

**Galleria Fort Lauderdale.** Fort Lauderdale's most upscale mall is just west of the Intracoastal Waterway. The split-level emporium entices with Neiman Marcus, Dillard's, Macy's, an Apple Store, plus 100 specialty shops for anything from cookware to exquisite jewelry. Chow down at Capital Grille, Truluck's, P.F. Chang's, or Seasons 52. The mall itself is open Monday through Saturday 10–9, Sunday noon–6. The stand-alone restaurants and bars are open later. ✉ *2414 E. Sunrise Blvd., Intracoastal and Inland* ☎ *954/564–1036* ⊕ *www.galleriamall-fl.com.*

Fodor's Choice
★ **Las Olas Boulevard.** Las Olas Boulevard is the heart and soul of Fort Lauderdale. Not only are 50 of the city's best boutiques, 30 top restaurants, and a dozen art galleries found along this beautifully landscaped street, but Las Olas links Fort Lauderdale's growing downtown with its superlative beaches. Though you'll find a Cheesecake Factory on the boulevard, the thoroughfare tends to shun chains and welcomes one-of-a-kind clothing boutiques, chocolatiers, and ethnic eateries. Window shopping allowed. ✉ *E. Las Olas Blvd., Downtown* ⊕ *www. lasolasboulevard.com.*

## NIGHTLIFE

Fodor's Choice
★ **Seminole Hard Rock Casino.** The glitzy, Vegas-style Seminole Hard Rock Casino is the superlative gaming and entertainment complex in Florida. Though located in a somewhat downtrodden area of inland Hollywood, once inside the Hard Rock enclave, you'll be mesmerized by the excitement radiating from the 145,000-square-foot casino, the 5,500-seat arena (Hard Rock Live), a dozen restaurants, and near dozen bars and nightclubs. The casino has blackjack, baccarat, three-card poker, more than 2,500 gaming machines, and just under 100 tables. It's open 24/7 and is connected to a hotel tower and entertainment complex, including great nightlife options such as an Improv Comedy Club, the multilevel Passion nightclub, Piano Hollywood, and Bongo's Cuban Cafe. While weekends are guaranteed party-hard mayhem, not all clubs are open on weekdays so check Hard Rock's detailed, user-friendly website for schedules. ■ **TIP→ The Seminole Hard Rock is not to be confused with its neighbor, the smoky and seedy Seminole Casino of Hollywood.** ✉ *1 Seminole Way, Hollywood* ☎ *866/502–7529* ⊕ *www.seminole hardrockhollywood.com.*

**Stache, 1920's Drinking Den.** Inspired by the Roaring Twenties, this speakeasy-style drinking den and nightclub infuses party-hard downtown Fort Lauderdale with some class and pizzazz. Expect awesome craft cocktails, inclusive of bespoke ice cubes, especially for old-school drinks like Manhattans and Side Cars. Late night on Friday and Saturday anticipate great house music and a fun, easy-on-the-eyes, young sophisticated crowd. ✉ *109 S.W. 2nd Ave., Downtown* ☎ *954/449–1044* ⊕ *www.stacheftl.com.*

**Tarpon Bend.** This casual two-story restaurant transforms into a jovial resto-bar in the early evening, ideal for enjoying a few beers, mojitos, and some great bar food. It's consistently busy, day, night, and late night with young professionals, couples, and large groups of friends. It's one place that has survived all the ups and downs of downtown Fort Lauderdale. ⊠ *200 S. W. 2nd St., Downtown* ☎ *954/523–3233* ⊕ *www. tarponbend.com.*

## WHERE TO EAT

**$$$**
MODERN
AMERICAN
FAMILY

✕ **Big City Tavern.** A Las Olas landmark, Big City Tavern is a consistent spot for good food, good spirits, and good times. The diverse menu commingles Asian entrées like shrimp pad Thai, Italian options like homemade four-cheese ravioli, and American dishes like the grilled chicken Cobb salad. Don't forget to ask about the crispy flatbread of the day, and make sure to save room for the homemade desserts. The J.G.'s Salted Caramel Ice Cream with caramel corn, the caramelized banana sundae in a mason jar, and the warm chocolate stout brownie are all heaven on Earth. ■TIP→ **Big City is open late into the night for drinks, desserts, and even offers a special late-night menu.** Ⓢ *Average main: $25* ⊠ *609 E. Las Olas Blvd., Downtown* ☎ *954/727–0307* ⊕ *www. bigcitylasolas.com.*

**$**
PIZZA
FAMILY
**Fodor's**Choice
★

✕ **Luigi's Coal Oven Pizza.** Hands down the best little pizza joint in South Florida, Luigi's Coal Oven Pizza wows with every dish on the one-page menu, including of course the full gamut of pizzas served up by Italian native Chef Luigi DiMeo, but also phenomenal salads with homemade dressings, classics like eggplant parmigiana, and oven-baked, daily fish specials. There's no substitutions or toppings allowed on the best seller—the Margherita Napoletana—a testament to the quality and flavors of the crust, cheese, and sauce of Luigi's century-old Napoli recipe. The petite eatery only has about a dozen tables, contributing to a cozy and familial vibe. Ⓢ *Average main: $15* ⊠ *1415 E. Las Olas Blvd., Downtown* ☎ *954/522–9888* ⊕ *www.luigiscoalovenpizza.com.*

**$$**
SEAFOOD

✕ **Southport Raw Bar.** You can't go wrong at this unpretentious spot where the motto, on bumper stickers for miles around, proclaims, "Eat fish, live longer, eat oysters, love longer, eat clams, last longer." Raw or steamed clams, raw oysters, and peel-and-eat shrimp are market priced. Sides range from Bimini bread to key lime pie, with conch fritters, beer-battered onion rings, and corn on the cob in between. Order wine by the bottle or glass, and beer by the pitcher, bottle, or can. Avoid the dimly lit restaurant proper, and eat outside overlooking the Intracoastal. Ⓢ *Average main: $19* ⊠ *1536 Cordova Rd., Intracoastal and Inland* ☎ *954/525–2526* ⊕ *www.southportrawbar.com.*

## WHERE TO STAY

Fort Lauderdale has a growing and varied roster of lodging options, from beachfront luxury suites to intimate B&Bs to chain hotels along the Intracoastal Waterway. If you want to be on the beach, be sure to mention this when booking your room, since many hotels advertise "waterfront" accommodations that are actually on inland waterways, not the beach.

**$$**
RESORT

⊡ **Hyatt Regency Pier Sixty-Six.** Don't let the 1970s exterior of the iconic 17-story tower fool you; this lovely 22-acre resort teems with contemporary interior-design sophistication and remains one of Florida's few hotels where a rental car isn't necessary. **Pros:** great views; plenty of activities; free shuttle to beach; easy water taxi access. **Cons:** tower rooms are far less stylish than Lanai rooms; totally retro rotating rooftop is used exclusively for private events. $ *Rooms from: $229* ✉ *2301 S.E. 17th St. Causeway, Intracoastal and Inland* ☎ *954/525–6666* ⊕ *www.pier66.hyatt.com* ⇲ *384 rooms* ⦶ *No meals.*

**$$$**
**RESORT**
**FAMILY**

**Pelican Grand Beach Resort.** Smack on Fort Lauderdale beach, this yellow spired, Key West–style, Noble House property fuses a heritage of Old Florida seaside charm with understated luxury; there are renovated rooms upstairs, an amazing beachfront, an old-fashioned emporium, and Fort Lauderdale's only lazy river. **Pros:** free popcorn in the Postcard Lounge; directly on the beach; Ocean 2000 restaurant. **Cons:** high tide can swallow most of beach area; small fitness center. $ *Rooms from: $381* ✉ *2000 N. Atlantic Blvd., Beachfront* ☎ *954/568–9431, 800/525–6232* ⊕ *www.pelicanbeach.com* ⇲ *156 rooms* ⦶ *No meals.*

**$$$$**
**HOTEL**
**Fodor'sChoice**
★

**The Ritz-Carlton, Fort Lauderdale.** Twenty-four dramatically tiered, glass-walled stories rise from the sea, forming a sumptuous Ritz-Carlton hotel with guest rooms that reinvent a golden era of luxury travel, a lavish tropical sundeck and infinity-edge pool peering over the ocean, and a Club Lounge that spans an entire floor. **Pros:** prime beach location; modern seaside elegance deviates dramatically from traditional Ritz-Carlton decor; views from Club Lounge. **Cons:** no complimentary Wi-Fi; expensive valet parking. $ *Rooms from: $649* ✉ *1 N. Fort Lauderdale Beach Blvd., Beachfront* ☎ *954/465–2300* ⊕ *www.ritzcarlton. com/FortLauderdale* ⇲ *138 rooms, 54 suites* ⦶ *No meals.*

# GALVESTON, TEXAS

By Robin
Sussman

A thin strip of an island in the Gulf of Mexico, Galveston is big sister Houston's beach playground—a year-round coastal destination just 50 miles away. Many of the first public buildings in Texas, including a post office, bank, and hotel, were built here, but most were destroyed in the Great Storm of 1900. Those that endured have been well preserved, and the Victorian character of the Historic Downtown Strand shopping district and the neighborhood surrounding Broadway is still evident. On the Galveston Bay side of the island (northeast), quaint shops and cafés in old buildings are near the Seaport Museum, harbor-front eateries, and the cruise-ship terminal. On the Gulf of Mexico side (southwest), resorts and restaurants line coastal Seawall Boulevard. The 17-foot-high seawall abuts a long ribbon of sand and provides a place for rollerblading, bicycling, and going on the occasional surrey ride. The city was badly damaged from flooding during Hurricane Ike in 2008, but businesses are now up and running, with few remnants of the storm.

Galveston is a port of embarkation for cruises on Western Caribbean itineraries. It's an especially popular port of embarkation for people living in the southeastern states who don't wish to fly to their cruise. Carnival and Royal Caribbean have ships based in Galveston, offering four-, five-, six-, and seven-day cruises along the Mexican coast and to Jamaica, Grand Cayman, Belize, Bahamas, Key West, and Honduras, plus a 14-night cruise to the Azores and Spain.

## ESSENTIALS
### HOURS
Shops in the historic district are usually open until at least 6 or 7. During peak season some stay open later. This is also the city's nightlife district, and is hopping until late.

### VISITOR INFORMATION
Contacts **Strand Visitors Center.** ⊠ *2215 Strand* ⊕ *www.galveston.com.*

### THE CRUISE PORT
The relatively sheltered waters of Galveston Bay are home to the Texas Cruise Ship Terminal. It's only 30 minutes to open water from here. Driving south from Houston on I–45, you cross a long causeway before reaching the island. Take the first exit, Harborside Drive, left after you've crossed the causeway onto Galveston Island. Follow that for a few miles to the port. Turn left on 22nd Street (also called Kempner Street); there is a security checkpoint before you continue down a driveway. The drop-off point is set up much like an airport terminal, with pull-through lanes and curbside check-in.

Contacts **Port of Galveston.** ⊠ *Harborside Dr. and 22nd St.* ☎ *409/765–9321* ⊕ *www.portofgalveston.com.*

### AIRPORT
Contacts **George Bush Intercontinental Airport.** ⊠ *2800 North Terminal Rd., Houston* ☎ *281/230–3100* ⊕ *www.fly2houston.com.* **William P. Hobby Airport.** ⊠ *7800 Airport Blvd., Houston* ☎ *713/640–3000* ⊕ *www.fly2houston.com.*

### AIRPORT TRANSFERS
The closest airports are in Houston, 50 miles from Galveston. Houston has two major airports: Hobby Airport, 9 miles (15 km) southeast of downtown, and George Bush Intercontinental, 15 miles (24 km) northeast of the city. Traffic into Galveston can be delayed because of ongoing construction.

Unless you have arranged airport transfers through your cruise line, you'll have to make arrangements to navigate the miles between the Houston airport at which you land and the cruise-ship terminal in Galveston. Galveston Limousine Service provides scheduled transportation (return reservations required) between either airport and Galveston hotels or the cruise-ship terminal. Hobby is a shorter ride (1 hour, $45 one-way, $80 round-trip), but Intercontinental (2 hours, $55 one-way, $100 round-trip) is served by more airlines, including international carriers. Taking a taxi allows you to set your own schedule, but can cost twice as much (it's also important to note that there aren't always enough taxis to handle the demands of disembarking passengers, so you might have to wait after you leave your ship). Negotiate the price before you get in.

Contacts **Galveston Limousine Service.** ☎ *800/640–4826* ⊕ *www.galvestonlimo.com.*

---

### BEST BETS

■ **Historic Homes.** The island has some lovely historic homes to explore, particularly during early May, when the Historic Homes Tour lets you into many that aren't usually open to the public.

■ **Moody Gardens.** There are enough activities at this park to keep any kid happy.

■ **The Historic Downtown Strand District.** Galveston's historic district is a great place to stroll, shop, and eat.

**PARKING**

Parking is coordinated by the Port Authority. After you drop off your checked luggage and passengers at the terminal, you receive a color-coded parking pass from the attendant, with directions to a parking lot for your cruise departure. The lots are approximately ½ mile (1 km) from the terminal. Check-in, parking, and boarding are generally allowed four hours prior to departure. A shuttle bus (carry-on luggage only) runs back and forth between the lots and the terminal every 7 to 12 minutes on cruise arrival and departure days (be sure to drop off your luggage before you park the car). The lot is closed other days. Port Authority security checks the well-lighted, fenced-in lots every two hours; there is also a limited amount of covered parking. Parking for a five-day cruise is $50, seven-day is $70 ($80 covered). Cash, traveler's checks, and credit cards (Visa and MasterCard only) are accepted for payment.

## EXPLORING

**Historic Downtown Strand District.** This shopping area is defined by the architecture of its 19th- and early-20th-century buildings, many of which survived the storm of 1900 and are on the National Register of Historic Places. When Galveston was still a powerful port city—before the Houston Ship Channel was dug, diverting most boat traffic inland—this stretch, formerly the site of stores, offices, and warehouses, was known as the Wall Street of the South. As you stroll up the Strand, you'll pass dozens of shops and cafés. ✉ *Between Strand and Postoffice St., 25th and 19th Sts., Galveston* ⊕ *www.galveston.com.*

FAMILY **Moody Gardens.** Moody Gardens is a multifaceted entertainment and educational complex inside pastel-color glass pyramids. Attractions include the 13-story Discovery Pyramid, showcasing marine life from four oceans in tanks and touch pools; Rainforest Pyramid, a 40,000-square-foot tropical habitat for exotic flora and fauna; Discovery Pyramid, a joint venture with NASA featuring more than 40 interactive exhibits; and two theaters, one of which has a space adventure ride. Outside, Palm Beach has white-sand beach, landscaped grounds, man-made lagoons, a kid-size waterslide and games, and beach chairs. ✉ *1 Hope Blvd., Galveston* ☎ *800/582–4673* ⊕ *www.moodygardens. com* ✆ *$9.95–$23.95 per venue; $59.95 day pass; $79.95 2-day pass.*

**Moody Mansion.** Moody Mansion, the residence of generations of one of Texas's most powerful families, was completed in 1895. Tour its interiors of exotic woods and gilded trim filled with family heirlooms and personal effects. ✉ *2618 Broadway, Galveston* ☎ *409/762–7668* ⊕ *www.moodymansion.org* ✆ *$10.*

**Pier 21 Theater.** At this Harborside Drive theater, watch the Great Storm of 1900 come back to life in a multimedia presentation that includes video clips of archival drawings, still photos, and narrated accounts from survivors' diaries. Also playing is a film about the exploits of pirate Jean Lafitte, who used the island as a base. ✉ *Pier 21, Harborside Dr. and 21st St., Galveston* ☎ *409/763–8808* ⊕ *www.galvestonhistory.org* ✆ *Great Storm $6; Pirate Island $6.*

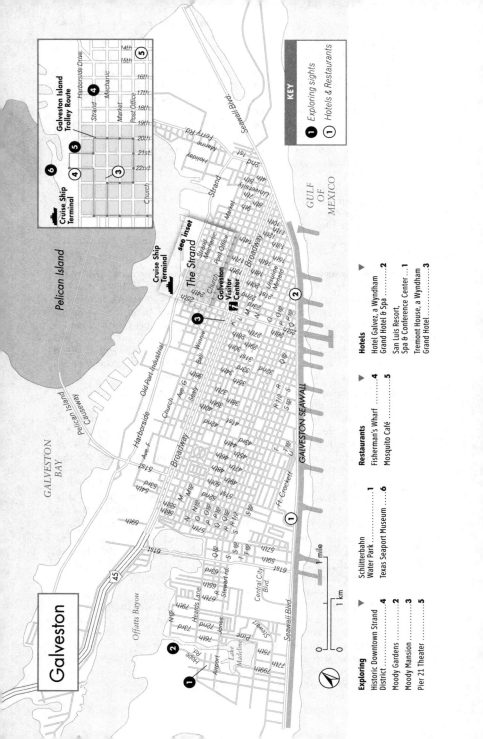

# Galveston

**Exploring** ▶

Historic Downtown Strand
District ............................ **4**
Moody Gardens .............. **2**
Moody Mansion ............. **3**
Pier 21 Theater ............. **5**
Schlitterbahn
Water Park ..................... **1**
Texas Seaport Museum ..... **6**

**Restaurants** ▶

Fisherman's Wharf ......... **4**
Mosquito Café ................ **5**

**Hotels** ▶

Hotel Galvez, a Wyndham
Grand Hotel & Spa ......... **2**
San Luis Resort,
Spa & Conference Center... **1**
Tremont House, a Wyndham
Grand Hotel .................... **3**

**KEY**

① Exploring sights

① Hotels & Restaurants

**Schlitterbahn Water Park.** The entire family will have a fun time at this water park, located on the bayside of the island. Schlitterbahn features speed slides, lazy river rides, uphill water coasters, a wave pool (with surfing), and water playgrounds for the little ones. There's even a heated indoor water park for chilly winter months. During summer, less expensive afternoon-only rates are in effect, and ticket prices drop in the off-season. Closing times vary by the season, so outside of the busiest months of June through August, verify closing times on the park's website, or call for exact hours. ⊠ *2026 Lockheed St., Galveston* ☎ *409/770–9283* ⊕ *www.schlitterbahn.com* 🖅 *$50.99.*

> **BOARDING PASSES**
>
> Modern ID cards and scanning equipment record passenger comings and goings on the majority of cruise ships these days. With a swipe through a machine (it looks much like a credit-card swipe at the supermarket), security personnel know who is on board the vessel at all times. On almost all ships passengers' pictures are recorded digitally at check-in.

**3**

**Texas Seaport Museum.** Aboard the restored 1877 tall ship *Elissa,* detailed interpretive signs provide information about the shipping trade in the 1800s, including the routes and cargoes this ship carried into Galveston. Inside the museum building is a replica of the historic wharf and a one-of-a-kind computer database containing the names of more than 133,000 immigrants who entered the United States through Galveston after 1837 ⊠ *Pier 21, Number 8, Galveston* ☎ *409/763–1877* ⊕ *www. galvestonhistory.org/Texas_Seaport_Museum.asp* 🖅 *$8.*

## BEACHES

**Galveston Island State Park.** Galveston Island State Park, on the western, unpopulated end of the island, is a 2,000-acre natural beach habitat ideal for birding, walking, and renewing your spirit. It's open daily from 8 am to 10 pm. ⊠ *14901 FM 3005, 10 miles (16 km) southwest on Seawall Blvd., Galveston* ☎ *409/737–1222* ⊕ *www.galvestonisland-statepark.org* 🖅 *$5.*

**Seawall.** The Seawall on the Gulf-side waterfront attracts runners, cyclists, and rollerbladers. Just below it is a long, free beach near many big hotels and resorts. ⊠ *Seawall Blvd., from 61st St. to 25th St., Galveston.*

**Stewart Beach Park.** Stewart Beach Park has a bathhouse, amusement park, bumper boats, miniature-golf course, and a water coaster in addition to saltwater and sand. It's open weekdays 9 to 5, weekends 8 to 6 from March through May; weekdays 8 to 6 and weekends 8 to 7 from June through September; and weekends 9 to 5 during the first two weekends of October. ⊠ *6th St. and Seawall Blvd., Galveston* ☎ *409/797–5189* 🖅 *$10–$15 per vehicle.*

## SHOPPING

**The Emporium at Eibands.** More than 50 antiques dealers are represented at The Emporium at Eibands, an upscale showroom filled with custom upholstery, bedding and draperies, antique furniture, and interesting architectural finds. ✉ *2201 Postoffice St., Galveston* ☎ *409/750–9536* ⊕ *www.galveston.com.*

**Old Strand Emporium.** Old Strand Emporium is a charming deli and grocery reminiscent of an old-fashioned ice-cream parlor and sandwich shop, with candy bins, packaged nuts, and more. ✉ *2425 Strand, Galveston* ☎ *409/515–0715.*

**Strand.** The Strand is the best place to shop in Galveston. Old storefronts are filled with gift shops, antiques stores, and one-of-a-kind boutiques. ✉ *Bounded by Strand and Postoffice Street (running east–west) and 25th and 19th streets (running north–south), Galveston* ⊕ *www. galveston.com/downtowntour/.*

## NIGHTLIFE

For a relaxing evening, choose any of the harborside restaurant–bars on piers 21 and 22 to sip a glass of wine or a frozen Hurricane as you watch the boats go by.

**The Grand 1894 Opera House.** The Grand 1894 Opera House stages musicals and hosts concerts year-round. It's worth visiting for the ornate architecture alone. Sarah Bernhardt and Anna Pavlova both performed on this storied stage. ✉ *2020 Postoffice St., Galveston* ☎ *409/765–1894, 800/821–1894* ⊕ *www.thegrand.com.*

## WHERE TO EAT

**$$$**
SEAFOOD
✕ **Fisherman's Wharf.** Even though Landry's has taken over this harborside institution, locals keep coming here for the reliably fresh seafood and reasonable prices. Dine indoors or watch the boat traffic (and waiting cruise ships) from the patio. Start with a cold combo, like boiled shrimp and grilled rare tuna. For entrées, the fried fish, shrimp, and oysters are hard to beat. ⑤ *Average main: $24* ✉ *Pier 22, 2200 Harborside Dr., Galveston* ☎ *409/765–5708* ⊕ *www.fishermanswharf galveston.com.*

**$**
AMERICAN
✕ **Mosquito Café.** This popular eatery in Galveston's historic East End serves fresh, contemporary food—including some vegetarian dishes—in a hip, high-ceilinged dining room and on an outdoor patio. Wake up to a fluffy egg frittata or a homemade scone topped with whipped cream, or try a large gourmet salad for lunch. The grilled snapper with Parmesan grits is a hit in the evening. ⑤ *Average main: $10* ✉ *628 14th St., Galveston* ☎ *409/763–1010* ⊕ *www.mosquitocafe.com* ✕ *Closed Mon. No dinner Sun.*

## WHERE TO STAY

**$$$$**  ⬚ **Hotel Galvez & Spa, a Wyndham Grand Hotel.** This renovated six-story
HOTEL  Spanish colonial hotel, built in 1911, was once called "Queen of the
Gulf." Teddy Roosevelt and Howard Hughes are just two of the many
well-known guests who have stayed here. **Pros:** directly on beach,
incredible pool area, beautiful grounds; recently renovated rooms. **Cons:**
rooms can be small (especially the bathrooms). $ *Rooms from: $269*
✉ *2024 Seawall Blvd., Galveston* ☎ *409/765–7721* ⊕ *www.wyndham.*
*com* ⇆ *231 rooms* ○| *No meals.*

**$$$$**  ⬚ **San Luis Resort, Spa & Conference Center.** A long marble staircase along-
RESORT  side a slender fountain with sculpted dolphins welcomes you to the
beachfront elegance of this resort. **Pros:** great Gulf views; nice pool area.
**Cons:** public parking (nonvalet) is not convenient. $ *Rooms from: $329*
✉ *5222 Seawall Blvd., Galveston* ☎ *409/744–1500, 800/445–0090*
⊕ *www.sanluisresort.com* ⇆ *244 rooms* ○| *No meals.*

**$$**  ⬚ **Tremont House, a Wyndham Grand Hotel.** A four-story atrium lobby,
HOTEL  with ironwork balconies and full-size palm trees, showcases an 1872
hand-carved rosewood bar in what was once a busy dry-goods ware-
house. **Pros:** beautiful, historic environment, great location; free Wi-Fi.
**Cons:** not a fun scene for young single travelers. $ *Rooms from: $139*
✉ *2300 Ship's Mechanic Row, Galveston* ☎ *409/763–0300* ⊕ *www.*
*wyndham.com* ⇆ *119 rooms* ○| *No meals.*

# JACKSONVILLE, FLORIDA

By Paul Rubio  One of Florida's oldest cities and at 758 square miles (1,926 square km)
the largest city in the continental United States in terms of land area,
Jacksonville is underrated and makes a worthwhile vacation spot for
an extra day or two before or after your cruise. It offers appealing
downtown riverside areas, handsome residential neighborhoods, the
region's only skyscrapers, a thriving arts scene, and, for football fans,
the NFL Jaguars and the NCAA Gator Bowl. Remnants of the Old
South flavor the city, especially in the Riverside/Avondale historic dis-
trict, where moss-draped oak trees frame prairie-style bungalows and
Tudor Revival mansions, and palm trees, Spanish bayonet, and azaleas
populate Jacksonville's landscape. Northeast of the city, Amelia Island
and Fernandina Beach offer some of the nicest coastline in Florida.

### ESSENTIALS

#### HOURS
Many museums close on Monday.

#### VISITOR INFORMATION
**Contacts Visit Jacksonville.** ☎ *800/733–2668* ⊕ *www.visitjacksonville.com.*

### THE CRUISE PORT
Limited in the sizes of ships it can berth, JAXPORT currently serves as
home port to the Carnival Elation, which departs weekly on four- and
five-night cruises to Key West and the Bahamas during the fall and winter
cruising seasons, with occasional weeklong sailings to Grand Turk, Half
Moon Cay, and Nassau. The facility is fairly sparse, consisting basically of
some vending machines and restrooms, but the embarkation staff receives

high marks. The terminal itself was constructed as a temporary structure, but a permanent cruise terminal has yet to be erected.

**Contacts Jacksonville Port Authority.** ✉ *9810 August Dr., Jacksonville* ☎ *904/357-3006* ⊕ *www.jaxport.com.*

### AIRPORT
JAXPORT is about 15 minutes from Jacksonville International Airport. Take I–95 South to S.R. 9-A East. Follow 9-A to Heckscher Drive (S.R. 105) west until you reach August Drive. Head south on August Drive, and follow the signs to the cruise terminal.

**Contacts Jacksonville International Airport** (*JAX*). ☎ *904/741-4902* ⊕ *www.flyjax.com.*

### AIRPORT TRANSFERS
The transfer from Jacksonville airport takes about 15 minutes and costs $30 for up to three passengers by taxi, not including tip.

**Contacts Dana's Limousine & Transportation.** ☎ *904/744-3333* ⊕ *www.danaslimo.com.*

### PARKING
There is a fenced and guarded parking lot next to the cruise terminal, within walking distance. Parking costs $15 per day for regular vehicles, $25 for RVs. You can pay in advance on the JAXPORT website, where you'll also find more parking details, or you can pay with cash or major credit card upon arrival.

---

## EXPLORING

Because Jacksonville was settled along both sides of the twisting St. Johns River, a number of attractions are on or near a riverbank. Both sides of the river, which is spanned by myriad bridges, have downtown areas and waterfront complexes of shops, restaurants, parks, and museums; some attractions can be reached by water taxi or the Skyway Express monorail system—scenic alternatives to driving back and forth across the bridges—but a car is generally necessary.

**Anheuser-Busch Jacksonville Brewery Tour.** Guided or self-guided tours give a behind-the-scenes look at how barley, malt, rice, hops, and water form the King of Beers. If you're 21 years or older, you'll receive a complimentary Budweiser at the beginning of the tour, and another beer of your choice in the Tap Room at the end of the tour. Soda or water is available for the under-21 set. Call ahead if you are interested in a guided tour. ✉ *111 Busch Dr., Jacksonville* ☎ *904/696-8373* ⊕ *www.budweisertours. com* ▣ *Free self-guided; $10 guided* ⊙ *Sept.–May closed Wed.*

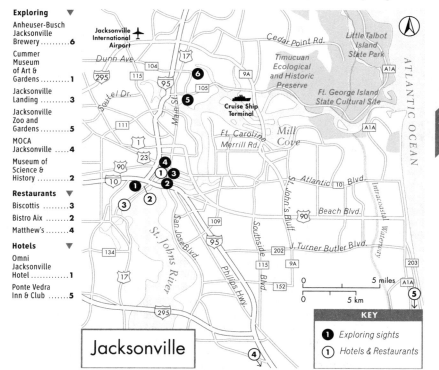

**Jacksonville**

**Cummer Museum of Art & Gardens.** The Wark Collection of early-18th-century Meissen porcelain is just one reason to visit this former estate on the St. Johns River, which includes 13 permanent galleries with more than 5,500 items spanning more than 4,000 years, and 3 acres of riverfront gardens, including a sculpture garden and outdoor plaza, that form a showcase for northeast Florida's blooming seasons and indigenous fauna. Art Connections allows kids of all ages to experience art through hands-on, interactive exhibits. The Thomas H. Jacobsen Gallery of American Art focuses on works by American artists, including Max Weber, N.C. Wyeth, and Paul Manship. Complimentary tour guide brochures at the front desk help visitors navigate the galleries, as do podcasts. ⊠ *829 Riverside Ave., Riverside* ☎ *904/356–6857* ⊕ *www. cummermuseum.org* ⌑ *$10, free Tues. 4–9.*

**Jacksonville Landing.** During the week, this riverfront market caters to locals (who sometimes arrive by boat) and tourists alike, with specialty shops, full-service restaurants—including a sushi bar, Italian bistro, Irish pub, and a steak house—and an internationally flavored food court, all of which look out over the boat traffic on the St. Johns River. Water taxis shuttle across the river between the Landing and the Southbank. The Landing hosts more than 250 weekend events each year, ranging from the good clean fun of the Lighted Boat Parade and Christmas Tree

Lighting to the just plain obnoxious Florida/Georgia game after-party, as well as live music (usually of the local cover-band variety) in the courtyard. ⊠ *2 W. Independent Dr., Downtown* ☎ *904/353–1188* ⊕ *www.jacksonvillelanding.com* ☜ *Free.*

> **BRING GEORGE**
>
> Whenever you leave for a cruise, bring a supply of one-dollar bills. They will come in handy for tipping both airport and port personnel.

FAMILY
Fodor'sChoice
★

**Jacksonville Zoo and Gardens.** The zoo offers visitors the chance to hop on a train and explore different countries through the animals that live there, from the Land of the Tiger, a 2.5-acre Asian attraction featuring Sumatran and Malayan tigers, to the Tuxedo Coast, a controlled Antarctic-like environment for a group of Magellanic penguins, and the African Plains area, which houses elephants, white rhinos, and two highly endangered leopards, in addition to other species of African birds and mammals. The Range of the Jaguar takes visitors to a 4-acre Central and South American exhibit, with exotic big cats as well as 20 other species native to the region. Among the other highlights are rare waterfowl and the African Reptile Building, which showcases some of the world's most venomous snakes. Wild Florida is a 2½-acre area with black bears, bald eagles, white-tailed deer, and other animals native to Florida, while RiverQuest reveals the ecology of the adjacent Trout River. Play Park contains a Splash Ground, forest play area, two mazes, and discovery building; Stingray Bay has a 17,000-gallon pool where visitors can pet and feed the mysterious creatures; and DinoTrek's life-size dinosaurs offer a glimpse into the past. Parking is free. ⊠ *370 Zoo Pkwy., off Heckscher Dr. E, Jacksonville* ☎ *904/757–4463* ⊕ *www.jacksonvillezoo.org* ☜ *$17.95.*

Fodor'sChoice
★

**MOCA Jacksonville.** In this loftlike, five-story, downtown building, the former headquarters of the Western Union Telegraph Company, a permanent collection of 20th-century art shares space with traveling exhibitions and a theater space. The museum, owned and managed by the University of North Florida, encompasses five galleries and ArtExplorium, a highly interactive educational exhibit for kids, as well as a funky gift shop and Nola MOCA, open for lunch on weekdays and for dinner on Thursdays. MOCA Jacksonville also hosts film series and workshops throughout the year, and packs a big art-wallop into a relatively small 14,000 square feet. A once-a-month Art Walk is free to all. ⊠ *Hemming Plaza, 333 N. Laura St., Downtown* ☎ *904/366–6911* ⊕ *www.mocajacksonville.unf.edu* ☜ *$8.*

FAMILY

**Museum of Science & History.** Known locally as MOSH, this museum is home to the Bryan-Gooding Planetarium. As a next-generation planetarium, it can project 3-D laser shows that accompany the ever-popular weekend Cosmic Concerts. For those taking in the planetarium shows, the resolution is significantly sharper than that of the biggest HDTV on the market. Whether you're a kid taking in Sesame Street's *One World, One Sky*, or an adult star-gazing in the *Skies over Jacksonville* tour of the night sky, the experience is awesome. MOSH also has a wide variety of interactive exhibits and programs that include JEA Science Theater; JEA PowerPlay: Understanding our Energy Choices; the Florida

Naturalist's Center; and the Currents of Time, where you'll navigate 12,000 years of Northeast Florida history. Nationally acclaimed traveling exhibits are featured along with signature exhibits on regional history. ⊠ *1025 Museum Circle, Jacksonville* ☏ *904/396–6674* ⊕ *www. themosh.org* ✉ *Museum $10, museum and planetarium $15, Cosmic Concerts $5; Fri. $5 all admissions.*

## SHOPPING

**San Marco Square.** More than a dozen interesting apparel, home, and jewelry stores and upscale restaurants surround the open square in 1920s Mediterranean revival–style buildings. ⊠ *San Marco and Atlantic Blvds., San Marco* ⊕ *mysanmarco.com.*

**The Shoppes of Avondale.** The highlights here include upscale clothing and accessories boutiques, art galleries, home-furnishings shops, a chocolatier, and trendy restaurants. ⊠ *St. Johns Ave., between Talbot Ave. and Dancy St., Avondale* ⊕ *www.shoppesofavondale.com.*

## WHERE TO EAT

JAXPORT's location on Jacksonville's Westside means there aren't too many nearby restaurants. But by taking a 10- to 15-minute drive south, you'll find a wealth of restaurants for all tastes and price categories.

**$$**
AMERICAN
**Fodor's**Choice
★

✕ **Biscottis.** The local artwork on the redbrick walls is a mild distraction from the jovial yuppies, soccer moms, arty types, and well-heeled professionals—all of whom are among the crowd jockeying for tables here. Elbows almost touch in the 100-seat restaurant, but no one seems to mind. The constantly changing dinner menu offers the unexpected: wild mushroom ravioli with a broth of corn, leek, and dried apricot; or curry-grilled swordfish with cucumber-fig bordelaise sauce. There are even gluten-free options. Be sure to sample from Biscottis's decadent desserts (courtesy of "b the bakery"). Brunch, a local favorite, is served until 3 on weekends. ⑤ *Average main: $21* ⊠ *3556 St. Johns Ave., Jacksonville* ☏ *904/387–2060* ⊕ *www.biscottis.net* ⚑ *Reservations not accepted.*

**$$$**
FRENCH

✕ **Bistro Aix.** Named after the French city (and pronounced simply "X"), this sophisticated bistro-bar's leather booths, 1940s brickwork, olive drapes, and intricate marbled globes, provide a perfect home for well-prepared French food. Regulars can't get enough of the creamy onion soup or escargot appetizers, prosciutto and goat cheese salad, or entrées such as oak-grilled fish Aixoise, steak frites, or mushroom and fontina wood-fired pizza. Most items (salads included) come in full or lighter-appetite portions, and you'll definitely want to save room for dessert. Aix's in-house pastry team ensures no sweet tooth leaves unsatisfied, with offerings such as profiteroles (mini cream puffs filled with vanilla ice cream and topped with chocolate and caramel sauce) and warm chocolate lava cake. Call for preferred seating. ⑤ *Average main: $28* ⊠ *1440 San Marco Blvd., San Marco* ☏ *904/398–1949* ⊕ *www.bistrox. com* ⚑ *Reservations essential.*

**$$$**  ✕ **Matthew's.** No one can accuse chef Matthew Medure of resting on his
ECLECTIC  laurels, of which there are many. Widely praised for culinary creativ-
Fodor's Choice  ity and dazzling presentation at his signature San Marco restaurant,
★  Medure's French- and Italian-inspired cuisine offers a wide range of
choices, from caviar to sweets. Highlights include a create-your-own
cheese-and-charcuterie spread "for the table"; house-made pasta with
local fish and shrimp, shiitake mushrooms, and peas; seared duck breast
with duck confit bread pudding; and espresso-smoked pork belly (an
appetizer) are among many inventive menu items. Complement your
meal with one of 450 wines (topping out at more than $1,000 per
bottle). Or if you just can't choose, the Chef's Adventure Menu gives
you a six-course tour of the menu. ⑤ *Average main: $25* ✉ *2107 Hen-
dricks Ave., San Marco* ☎ *904/396–9922* ⊕ *www.matthewsrestaurant.
com* ⊘ *Closed Sun. No lunch* ⌔ *Reservations essential.*

## WHERE TO STAY

Hotels near the cruise terminals are few and far between, so most cruis-
ers needing a room make the drive to Downtown (15 minutes) or to the
Southbank or Riverside (20 minutes).

**$**  ⌂ **Omni Jacksonville Hotel.** Jacksonville's most luxurious and glamor-
HOTEL  ous downtown hotel underwent a major update in 2015—from lobby
FAMILY  to spacious guest rooms—and offers across-the-street convenience to
the big theatrical or musical shows at the Times-Union Center. **Pros:**
award-winning on-site restaurant; downtown location; large rooms;
rooftop pool; kids' offerings. **Cons:** fee for Wi-Fi and parking; con-
gested valet area; restaurant pricey; can be chaotic when there's a show
across the street. ⑤ *Rooms from: $189* ✉ *245 Water St., Jacksonville*
☎ *904/355–6664, 800/843–6664* ⊕ *www.omnijacksonville.com* ⋰ *354
rooms, 4 two-bedroom suites* ⎰⎱ *No meals.*

**$$$**  ⌂ **Ponte Vedra Inn & Club.** Considered northeast Florida's premier resort
RESORT  for decades, this award-winning 1928 landmark continues to wow
FAMILY  guests with its stellar service and large guest rooms housed in white-
Fodor's Choice  brick, red-tile-roof buildings lining the beach. **Pros:** accommodating,
★  friendly staff; private beach; adults-only pool. **Cons:** charge for umbrellas and chaises on the beach; crowded pools at some times of year.
⑤ *Rooms from: $399* ✉ *200 Ponte Vedra Blvd., Ponte Vedra Beach*
☎ *904/285–1111, 800/234–7842* ⊕ *www.pontevedra.com* ⋰ *250
rooms, 33 suites* ⎰⎱ *No meals.*

# MIAMI, FLORIDA

By Paul Rubio  Miami is the busiest of Florida's very busy cruise ports. Because there's
so much going on in Miami these days, you'll definitely want to schedule
an extra day or two before and/or after your cruise to explore North
America's most Latin city. Downtown is a convenient place to stay if
you are meeting up with a cruise ship, but Miami Beach is still the crown
jewel of Miami. The Art Deco District in South Beach—the square-mile
section between 6th and 23rd streets—remains the heart of Miami's
vibrant nightlife and restaurant scene but Mid-Beach and Downtown

aren't too far behind. You may also want to explore beyond the beach, including the neighborhoods of Wynwood, the Design District, Little Havana, Coral Gables, and Coconut Grove.

## ESSENTIALS
### HOURS
Most of the area's attractions are open every day.

### VISITOR INFORMATION
**Contacts Greater Miami Convention & Visitors Bureau.** ✉ *701 Brickell Ave., Suite 2700, Miami* ☎ *305/539–3000, 800/933–8448 in U.S.* ⊕ *www. miamiandbeaches.com.* **Visit Miami Beach.** ✉ *Visitor Center, 1901 Convention Center Dr., Hall C, Miami Beach* ☎ *786/276–2763, 305/672–1270 Miami Beach tourist hotline* ⊕ *www.miami beachguest.com.*

---

**BEST BETS**

■ **South Beach.** A 15-minute cab from the port, South Beach is great for people-watching, an art deco tour, or a bit of sun.

■ **Bayside Marketplace.** If you want to stay close to the port, grab some outdoor drinks and eclectic eats at super-touristy Bayside Marketplace.

■ **Bill Baggs Cape Florida State Park.** Unleash your outdoor enthusiasm at Key Biscayne's Bill Baggs Cape Florida State Park.

■ **Vizcaya Museum.** One of south Florida's largest historic homes is one of the city's best museums.

---

## THE CRUISE PORT
The Port of Miami, in downtown Miami near Bayside Marketplace and the MacArthur Causeway, justifiably bills itself as the "Cruise Capital of the World." Home to 18 cruise lines (including the global headquarters for Carnival Cruise Lines, Norwegian Cruise Line, Royal Caribbean Cruises, and Oceania) and the largest year-round cruise fleet in the world, the port accommodates more than 4 million passengers a year for sailings from 3 to 14 days and sometimes longer duration. Seven air-conditioned terminals are decorated with dramatic public art installations reflecting sun-drenched waters off the Florida coastline and the Everglades ecosystems. There's duty-free shopping and limousine service. You can get taxis at all the terminals, and car-rental agencies offer shuttles to off-site lots.

If you are driving, take I–95 north or south to I–395. Follow the directional signs to the Biscayne Boulevard exit and then signs for Port Blvd and N. American Way. After passing under the tunnel, follow the directional signs to your terminal.

**Contacts PortMiami.** ✉ *1015 North American Way, Miami* ☎ *305/347–5515* ⊕ *www.miamidade.gov/portmiami.*

### AIRPORT
Subtropical, chaotic Miami International Airport (MIA), gateway to the Americas and a hub for American Airlines, is without doubt Florida's busiest airport on all counts. More than 100 international and domestic carriers are served, connecting to 150 destinations. For the travel weary, there's the rather basic but sound-proofed, 259-room Hotel MIA (smack within Concourse E). Besides "lost and found" in North Terminal D, amenities include doggie park relief areas in terminals

D, E & J, assorted ATMs including a full-service Bank of America in Terminal D, plus food and shopping opportunity galore. Data port connectors and Wi-Fi are available at assorted locations. The MIA Mover, a 1.25-mile-long people mover connects to the Miami Car Rental Center, with more than a dozen rental agencies from Hertz, Avis and leisure-leader Alamo to Dollar, Payless and Thrifty. From MIA, you also can access South Florida's Tri-Rail system connecting with Fort Lauderdale and Palm Beach airports.

> **CARRY-ON CAUTION**
>
> Airline carry-on restrictions are being updated continuously. Check with your airline before packing, and be aware that large purses will sometimes be counted as a carry-on item!

**Contacts Miami International Airport** (*MIA*). ✉ *N.E. 20th St. and LeJeune Rd., Miami* ☎ *305/876–7000* ⊕ *www.miami-airport.com.*

### AIRPORT TRANSFERS

If you have not arranged an airport transfer through your cruise line, you have a couple of options for getting to the cruise port. The first is a ride service like Uber of Lyft. Second is a taxi; fares are regulated by the county, with a flat fare of $27 from Miami International Airport (MIA). This fare is per trip, not per passenger, and includes tolls and $1 airport surcharge but not a tip. SuperShuttle vans transport passengers between MIA and local hotels, as well as the PortMiami. At MIA the vans pick up at the ground level of each concourse (look for clerks with yellow shirts, who will flag one down). SuperShuttle service from MIA is available on demand; for the return it's best to make reservations 24 hours in advance. The cost from MIA to the cruise port is $17 per person, or $65 if you want the entire van to yourselves.

**Contacts Super Shuttle.** ☎ *305/871–2000* ⊕ *www.supershuttle.com.*

### PARKING

Street-level lots are right in front of each of the cruise terminals. The port's three parking garages (each with an open-air top floor) accommodate 5,871 vehicles, with 56 spaces designated for guests with disabilities and another half-dozen or so for passengers with infants. The cost for all, payable in advance, is $20 per day ($40 for RVs, which can be parked in Lot 2, across from Terminal E) and $7 for short-term parking of less than four hours for drop-off/pick-up. You can pay with cash, credit card, or traveler's checks but not with a debit card. There is no valet parking, but a shuttle for cruise passengers (one is wheelchair-accessible) can pick you up at the parking garage/lot, take you to the appropriate terminal, and return you to your vehicle after your cruise.

## EXPLORING

In the 1950s Miami was best known for alligator wrestlers and you-pick strawberry fields or citrus groves. Well, things have changed . . . big time! Miami on the mainland is South Florida's commercial hub, while its sultry sister Miami Beach (America's Riviera) encompasses 17 islands in Biscayne Bay. Seducing winter refugees with its sunshine, beaches,

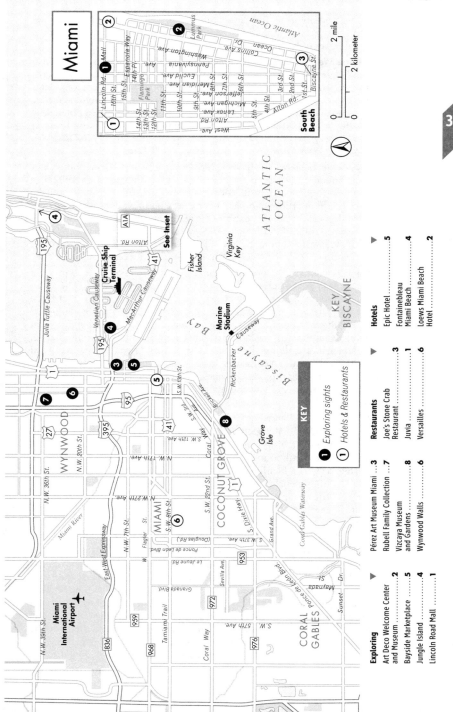

# Miami

**South Beach**

Atlantic Ocean

ATLANTIC OCEAN

KEY BISCAYNE

0 — 2 mile
0 — 2 kilometer

3

**KEY**

- 1 Exploring sights
- ① Hotels & Restaurants

## Exploring ▶

Art Deco Welcome Center
and Museum ............ 2
Bayside Marketplace ....... 5
Jungle Island ............. 4
Lincoln Road Mall ........ 1

Pérez Art Museum Miami ...3
Rubell Family Collection ...7
Vizcaya Museum
and Gardens ............. 8
Wynwood Walls .......... 6

## Restaurants ▶

Joe's Stone Crab
Restaurant ............. 3
Juvia .................. 1
Versailles .............. 6

## Hotels ▶

Epic Hotel ................ 5
Fontainebleau
Miami Beach ............. 4
Loews Miami Beach
Hotel .................. 2

palms, and nightlife, this is what most people envision when planning a trip to what they think of as Miami. If you want to do any exploring, you'll have to drive.

**Art Deco Welcome Center and Museum.** Run by the Miami Design Preservation League, the center provides information about the buildings in the district. An official Art Deco Museum opened within the center in October 2014, and a gift shop sells 1930s–50s art deco memorabilia, posters, and books on Miami's history. Several tours also start here, including a self-guided iPod audio tour and regular morning walking tours at 10:30 every day. ⊠ *1001 Ocean Dr., South Beach* ☎ *305/672–2014, 305/531–3484 for tours* ⊕ *www.mdpl.org* ⊠ *Tours $25.*

FAMILY **Bayside Marketplace.** The Bayside Marketplace, a waterfront complex of entertainment, dining, and retail stores, was en vogue circa 1992 and remains popular due to its location near PortMiami. You'll find the area awash in cruise-ship passenger chaos on most days (it's definitely *not* a draw for locals), so expect plenty of souvenir shops, a Hard Rock Cafe, and stores like Wet Seal and Sunglass Hut. Many boat tours leave from the marinas lining the festival marketplace. ⊠ *401 Biscayne Blvd., Downtown* ☎ *305/381–8972* ⊕ *www.baysidemarketplace.com.*

FAMILY **Jungle Island.** South Florida's original tourist attraction opened in 1936 and moved to its current Watson Island location in 2003. The small stretch of land between Downtown Miami and South Beach is far more than a place where cockatoos ride tricycles; this interactive zoological park is home to just about every unusual and endangered species you would want to see (if you are into seeing them in zoo-like settings that is), including a rare albino alligator, a liger (lion and tiger mix), and myriad exotic birds. With an emphasis on the experiential versus mere observation, the park offers private beaches, treetop zip lining, aquatic activities, adventure trails, and cultural activities. ⊠ *Watson Island, 1111 Parrot Jungle Trail, off MacArthur Causeway (I–395), Downtown* ☎ *305/400–7000* ⊕ *www.jungleisland.com* ⊠ *$32.95, plus $10 parking.*

FAMILY
Fodor's Choice
★
**Lincoln Road Mall.** This open-air pedestrian mall flaunts some of Miami's best people-watching. The eclectic interiors of myriad fabulous restaurants, colorful boutiques, art galleries, lounges, and cafés are often upstaged by the bustling outdoor scene. It's here among the prolific alfresco dining enclaves that you can pass the hours easily beholding the beautiful people. Indeed, outdoor restaurant and café seating take center stage along this wide pedestrian road adorned with towering date palms, linear pools, and colorful broken-tile mosaics. It's fun, lively, and friendly for people—old, young, gay, and straight—and their dogs.

Two landmarks worth checking out at the eastern end of Lincoln Road are the massive 1940s keystone building at 420 Lincoln Road, which has a 1945 Leo Birchanky mural in the lobby, and the 1921 Mission-style Miami Beach Community Church, at Drexel Avenue. The Lincoln Theatre (No. 541–545), at Pennsylvania Avenue, is a classical four-story art deco gem that now houses H &M. At Lenox Avenue, a black-and-white art deco movie house with a Mediterranean barrel-tile roof is now the Colony Theater (1040 Lincoln Road). ⊠ *Lincoln Rd., between Washington Ave. and Alton Rd., South Beach* ⊕ *www.lincolnroadmall.com.*

**Fodor'sChoice**
★
**Pérez Art Museum Miami** (*PAMM*). Opened in December 2013, the Pérez Art Museum Miami, known locally as PAMM, shines as the city's first true world-class museum. Double-story, cylindrical hanging gardens sway from high atop the museum, anchored to stylish wood trusses that help create this gotta-see-it-to-believe-it indoor/outdoor museum. Large sculptures, Asian-inspired gardens, sexy white benches, and steel frames envelop the property. Inside, the 120,000-square-foot space houses multicultural art from the 20th and 21st centuries, some of which were previously on display at the Miami Art Museum. Most of the interior space is devoted to temporary exhibitions. ■**TIP→ Admission is free every first Thursday of the month and every second Saturday of the month.** ✉ *1103 Biscayne Blvd., Downtown* ☎ *305/375–3000* ⊕ *www. pamm.org* ⊠ *$16* ⊘ *Closed Wed.*

**Fodor'sChoice**
★
**Rubell Family Collection.** Fans of edgy art will appreciate the Rubell Family Collection. Mera and Don Rubell have accumulated work by artists from the 1970s to the present, including Jeff Koons, Cindy Sherman, Damien Hirst, and Keith Haring. Admission always includes a complimentary audio tour; however, true art lovers should opt for a complimentary guided tour of the collection, offered Wednesday through Saturday at 3 pm. ✉ *95 N.W. 29th St., between N. Miami and N.W. 1st Aves., Wynwood* ☎ *305/573–6090* ⊕ *rfc.museum* ⊠ *$10.*

**Fodor'sChoice**
★
**Vizcaya Museum and Gardens.** Of the 10,000 people living in Miami between 1912 and 1916, about 1,000 of them were gainfully employed by Chicago industrialist James Deering to build this European-inspired residence. Once comprising 180 acres, this National Historic Landmark now occupies a 30-acre tract that includes a rockland hammock (native forest) and more than 10 acres of formal gardens with fountains overlooking Biscayne Bay. The house, open to the public, contains 70 rooms, 34 of which are filled with paintings, sculpture, antique furniture, and other fine and decorative arts. The collection spans 2,000 years and represents the Renaissance, baroque, rococo, and neoclassical periods. The 90-minute self-guided Discover Vizcaya Audio Tour is available in multiple languages for an additional $5. Moonlight tours, offered on evenings that are nearest the full moon, provide a magical look at the gardens; call for reservations. ✉ *3251 S. Miami Ave., Coconut Grove* ☎ *305/250–9133* ⊕ *www.vizcaya.org* ⊠ *$18* ⊘ *Closed Tues.*

**Fodor'sChoice**
★
**Wynwood Walls.** Between Northeast 25th and 26th streets on Northwest 2nd Avenue, the Wynwood Walls are a cutting-edge enclave of modern urban murals, reflecting diversity in graffiti and street art. More than 50 well-known and lesser-known artists have transformed 80,000 square feet of warehouse walls into an outdoor museum of sorts (and a photographer's dream). The popularity of the walls spawned the neighboring Wynwood Doors, an industrial space rife with metal roll-down gates also used as blank canvases. Even more recently, the Outside the Walls project is spreading the Walls love across the neighborhood, as artists are commissioned to transform Wynwood's surrounding warehouses and building spaces into singular pieces of painted art. ✉ *2520 N.W. 2nd Ave., Wynwood* ⊕ *www.thewynwoodwalls.com.*

3

## BEACHES

Fodor's Choice ★ **Bill Baggs Cape Florida State Park.** Thanks to inviting beaches, sunsets, and a tranquil lighthouse, this park at Key Biscayne's southern tip is worth the drive. In fact, the 1-mile stretch of pure beachfront has been named several times in Dr. Beach's revered America's Top 10 Beaches list. It has 18 picnic pavilions available as daily rentals, two cafés that serve light lunches that include several Cuban specialties (Lighthouse Café, overlooking the Atlantic Ocean, and the Boater's Grill, on Biscayne Bay), and plenty of space to enjoy the umbrella and chair rentals. Bill Baggs has bicycle rentals, a playground, fishing piers, and guided tours of the **Cape Florida Lighthouse,** South Florida's oldest structure. Free tours are offered at the restored cottage and lighthouse at 10 am and 1 pm Thursday to Monday. Be there a half hour beforehand. **Amenities:** food and drink; lifeguards; parking; showers; toilets. **Best for:** solitude; sunsets; walking. ⊠ *1200 S. Crandon Blvd., Key Biscayne* ☎ *305/361–5811* ⊕ *www.floridastateparks.org/park/Cape-Florida* ☷ *$8 per vehicle; $2 per pedestrian.*

Fodor's Choice ★ **South Beach.** A 10-block stretch of white sandy beach hugging the turquoise waters along Ocean Drive—from 5th to 15th streets—is one of the most popular in America, known for drawing unabashedly modelesque sunbathers and posers. With the influx of new luxe hotels and hotspots from 1st to 5th and 16th to 25th streets, the South Beach stand-and-pose scene is now bigger than ever and stretches yet another dozen plus blocks. The beaches crowd quickly on the weekends with a blend of European tourists, young hipsters, and sun-drenched locals offering Latin flavor. Separating the sand from the traffic of Ocean Drive is palm-fringed **Lummus Park,** with its volleyball nets and chickee huts (huts made of palmetto thatch over a cypress frame) for shade. The beach at **12th Street** is popular with gays, in a section often marked with rainbow flags. Locals hang out on 3rd Street beach, in an area called **SoFi** (South of Fifth) where they watch fit Brazilians play foot volley, a variation of volleyball that uses everything but the hands. Because much of South Beach leans toward skimpy sunning—women are often in G-strings and casually topless—many families prefer the tamer sections of Mid- and North Beach (save Halouver nude beach). Metered parking spots next to the ocean are a rare find. Instead, opt for a public garage a few blocks away and enjoy the people-watching as you walk to find your perfect spot on the sand. **Amenities:** food and drink; lifeguards; parking (fee); showers; toilets. **Best for:** partiers; sunrise; swimming; walking. ⊠ *Ocean Dr., from 5th to 15th Sts., then Collins Ave. to 25th St., South Beach.*

## SHOPPING

Beyond its fun-in-the-sun offerings, Miami has evolved into a world-class shopping destination. People fly to Miami from all over the world just to shop. The city teems with sophisticated malls—from multistory, indoor climate-controlled temples of consumerism to sun-kissed, open-air retail enclaves—and bustling avenues and streets, lined at once with affordable chain stores, haute couture boutiques, and one-off, "only in

Miami"–type shops. Miami's shopping centers are record breakers. Several chain stores in the massive Aventura Mall bank as the best-selling outposts in the country, while Bal Harbour Shops flaunt the most lucrative square footage of any shopping arena in the country, with its sales reaching up to $2,555 per square foot. Following the incredible success of the Bal Harbour Shops in the highest of the high-end market (Chanel, Alexander McQueen, ETRO, and Hermès), the Design District has followed suit. Beyond fabulous designer furniture showrooms, the district's tenants now include Dior Homme, Rolex, Prada and an entire LVMH (Moët Hennessy Louis Vuitton) mall.

---

| PACK IT, POST IT |
|---|
| Pack a pad of Post-It notes when you take a cruise. They come in handy when you need to leave messages for your cabin steward, family, and shipboard friends. |

**3**

## NIGHTLIFE

One of Greater Miami's most popular pursuits is barhopping. Bars range from intimate enclaves to showy see-and-be-seen lounges to loud, raucous frat parties. There's a New York–style flair to some of the newer lounges, which are increasingly catering to the Manhattan party crowd who escape to Miami and Miami Beach for long weekends. No doubt, Miami's pulse pounds with nonstop nightlife that reflects the area's potent cultural mix. On sultry, humid nights with the huge full moon rising out of the ocean and fragrant night-blooming jasmine intoxicating the senses, who can resist Cuban salsa with some disco and hip-hop thrown in for good measure? When this place throws a party, hips shake, fingers snap, bodies touch. It's no wonder many clubs are still rocking at 5 am. If you're looking for a relatively nonfrenetic evening, your best bet is one of the chic hotel bars on Collins Avenue, or a lounge in Wynwood, the Design District, or downtown.

## WHERE TO EAT

At many of the hottest spots you'll need a reservation to avoid a long wait for a table. And when you get your check, note whether a gratuity is included; most restaurants add 15%–20% (ostensibly for the convenience of—and protection from—Latin-American and European tourists who are used to this practice in their homelands and would not normally tip), but you can reduce or supplement it depending on your opinion of the service.

**$$$$**
SEAFOOD
**Fodor's** Choice
★

✕ **Joe's Stone Crab Restaurant.** In South Beach's decidedly new-money scene, the stately Joe's Stone Crab is an old-school testament to good food and good service. South Beach's most-storied restaurant started as a turn-of-the-20th-century eating house when Joseph Weiss discovered succulent stone crabs off the Florida coast. A century later, the restaurant stretches a city block and serves 2,000 dinners a day from local politicians to moneyed patriarchs. Stone crabs, served with legendary mustard sauce, crispy hash browned potatoes, and creamed spinach, remain the staple. Though stone-crab season runs from October 15 to

May 15, Joe's remains open year-round (albeit with a limited schedule) serving other phenomenal seafood dishes. Finish your meal with tart key lime pie, baked fresh daily. ■ TIP→ **Joe's famously refuses reservations, and weekend waits can be three hours long—yes, you read that correctly—so come early or order from Joe's Take Away next door.** ⑤ *Average main: $49* ⊠ *11 Washington Ave., South Beach* ☎ *305/673–0365, 305/673–4611 for takeout,* ⊕ *www.joesstonecrab.com* ❂ *No lunch Sun. and Mon. and mid-May–mid-Oct.* ⌦ *Reservations not accepted.*

**$$$$**
JAPANESE
FUSION
**Fodor's** Choice
★

✕ **Juvia.** High atop South Beach's design-driven 1111 Lincoln Road parking garage, Juvia commingles urban sophistication with South Beach seduction. Towering over the beach's art deco district, the restaurant rises as a bold amalgamation of steel, glass, hanging gardens, and purple accents—a true work of art high in the sky. Three renowned chefs unite to deliver an amazing eating experience that screams Japanese, Peruvian, and French all in the same breath, focusing largely on raw fish and seafood dishes. The see-and-be-seen crowd can't get enough; neither can we! ⑤ *Average main: $42* ⊠ *1111 Lincoln Rd., South Beach* ☎ *305/763–8272* ⊕ *www.juviamiami.com* ⌦ *Reservations essential.*

**$**
CUBAN
FAMILY
**Fodor's** Choice
★

✕ **Versailles.** *¡Bienvenido a Miami!* To the area's Cuban population, Miami without Versailles is like rice without black beans. First-timer Miami visitors looking for that "Cuban food on Calle Ocho" experience, look no further. The storied eatery, where old émigrés opine daily about all things Cuban, is a stop on every political candidate's campaign trail, and it should be a stop for you as well. Order a heaping platter of *lechon asado* (roasted pork loin), *ropa vieja* (shredded beef), or *picadillo* (spicy ground beef), all served with rice, beans, and fried plantains. It's not quite as good as true homemade Cuban food, but it's a requisite stop in Little Havana. After overeating, battle the oncoming food coma with a cup of the city's strongest *cafecito*, which comes in the tiniest of cups but packs a lot of punch. Versailles operates a bakery next door as well—take some *pastelitos* home. ⑤ *Average main: $15* ⊠ *3555 S.W. 8th St., Little Havana* ☎ *305/444–0240* ⊕ *www.versaillesrestaurant.com.*

## WHERE TO STAY

Staying in downtown Miami will put you close to the cruise terminals and show you the pulse of this growing metropolis. But for fun-in-the-sun, South Beach is still the center of the action in Miami Beach and just an Uber ride away from the port (though traffic can make this a long ride). Staying in the burgeoning Mid-Beach area, north of South Beach's Art Deco District, will put you on the beach but nominally closer to the port.

**$$$**
HOTEL

▦ **Epic Hotel.** In the heart of downtown, Kimpton's pet-friendly Epic Hotel has 411 guest rooms, each with a spacious balcony (many of them overlook Biscayne Bay) and fabulous modern amenities—Frette linens, iPod docks, spa-inspired luxury bath products—that match the modern grandeur of the trendy common areas, which include a super-sexy rooftop pool. **Pros:** sprawling rooftop pool deck; balcony in every room; complimentary wine hour, coffee, and Wi-Fi. **Cons:** some rooms have inferior views; congested valet area. $ *Rooms from: $399* ⊠ *270 Biscayne Blvd. Way, Downtown* 🕾 *305/424–5226* ⊕ *www.epichotel. com* ⟿ *411 rooms* ❙⊙❙ *No meals.*

**$$$$**
RESORT
FAMILY
**Fodor's**Choice
★

**Fontainebleau Miami Beach.** Vegas meets art deco at this colossal classic, deemed Miami's biggest hotel after its $1 billion reinvention, which spawned more than 1,500 rooms (split among 658 suites in two new all-suite towers and 846 rooms in the two original buildings), 12 renowned restaurants and lounges, LIV nightclub, several sumptuous pools with cabana islands, a state-of-the-art fitness center, and a 40,000-square-foot spa. **Pros:** excellent restaurants; historic design mixed with all-new facilities; fabulous pools. **Cons:** away from the South Beach pedestrian scene; massive size; bizarre mix of guests. $ *Rooms from: $449* ⊠ *4441 Collins Ave., Mid-Beach* 🕾 *305/535–3283, 800/548–8886* ⊕ *www. fontainebleau.com* ⟿ *846 rooms, 658 suites* ❙⊙❙ *No meals.*

**$$$$**
HOTEL
FAMILY

**Loews Miami Beach Hotel.** Loews Miami Beach, a two-tower 800-room megahotel with top-tier amenities, a massive spa, a great pool, and direct beachfront access, is a good choice for families, business-people, groups, and pet-lovers. **Pros:** excellent on-site seafood restaurant; immense spa; pets welcome. **Cons:** insanely large size; constantly crowded; pets desperate to go will need to wait several minutes to make it to the grass. $ *Rooms from: $499* ⊠ *1601 Collins Ave., South Beach* 🕾 *305/604–1601, 800/235–6397* ⊕ *www.loewshotels.com/miamibeach* ⟿ *733 rooms, 57 suites* ❙⊙❙ *No meals.*

# NEW ORLEANS, LOUISIANA

By Robin
Sussman

The spiritual and cultural heart of New Orleans is the French Quarter, where the city was settled by the French in 1718. You could easily spend several days visiting museums, shops, and eateries in this area, but you can get a small sense of the place quickly. If you have time, the rest of the city's neighborhoods, radiating out from this focal point, also make for rewarding rambling. The mansion-lined streets of the Garden District and Uptown, the aboveground cemeteries that dot the city, and the open air along Lake Pontchartrain provide a nice balance to the commercialization of the Quarter. Despite its sprawling size, New Orleans has a small-town vibe, perhaps due to locals' shared cultural habits and history.

## ESSENTIALS

### HOURS

Shops in the French Quarter tend to be open late, but stores in most of the malls close by 9. Restaurants tend to be open late as well, and many bars never close their doors.

### TOURS

Several local tour companies give two- to four-hour city tours by bus that include the French Quarter, the Garden District, uptown New Orleans, and the lakefront. Prices range from $25 to $125 per person, depending on the kind of experience. Both Gray Line and New Orleans Tours offer a longer tour that combines a two-hour city tour by bus with a two-hour steamboat ride on the Mississippi River. Gray Line and

Tours by Isabelle both offer tours of Hurricane Katrina devastation as well.

**Contacts New Orleans Tours.** ☎ 504/529–1991 ⊕ www.notours.com.

### VISITOR INFORMATION

**Contacts New Orleans Convention & Visitors Bureau.** ☎ 800/672–6124, 504/566–5011 ⊕ www.neworleanscvb.com.

### THE CRUISE PORT

The Julia Street Cruise Terminal is at the end of Julia Street on the Mississippi River; the Erato Street Terminal is just to the north. Both terminals are behind the Ernest N. Morial Convention Center. You can walk to the French Quarter from here in about 10 minutes; it's a short taxi ride to the Quarter or nearby hotels. Carnival and Norwegian base ships here year round.

If you are driving, you'll probably approach New Orleans on I–10. Take the Business 90 West/Westbank exit, locally known as Pontchartrain Expressway, and proceed to the Tchoupitoulas Street/South Peters Street exit. Continue to Convention Center Boulevard, where you will take a right turn. Continue to Henderson Street, where you will turn left, and then continue to Port of New Orleans Place. Take a left on Port of New Orleans Place to Julia Street Terminals 1 and 2, or take a right to get to the Robin Street Wharf.

**Contacts Port of New Orleans.** ⊠ Port of New Orleans Pl., at foot of Julia St., New Orleans ☎ 504/522–2551 ⊕ www.portno.com.

### AIRPORT

**Contacts Louis Armstrong New Orleans International Airport** (MSY). ☎ 504/303–7500 ⊕ www.flymsy.com.

### AIRPORT TRANSFERS

Shuttle-bus service to and from the airport and the cruise port is available through Airport Shuttle New Orleans. Buses leave regularly from the ground level near the baggage claim. Return trips to the airport need to be booked in advance. A one-way ticket is $20 per person and a round-trip ticket $38. The trip takes about 30 minutes.

A cab ride to or from the airport from uptown or downtown New Orleans costs a flat $33 for the first two passengers and $14 for each additional passenger. At the airport, pick-up is on the lower level, outside the baggage claim area. There may be an additional charge for extra baggage.

**Contacts Airport Shuttle New Orleans.** ☎ 504/522–3500, 866/596–2699 ⊕ www.airportshuttleneworleans.com.

---

**BEST BETS**

■ **Audubon Aquarium of the Americas.** Especially good for families is this fantastic aquarium on the edge of French Quarter.

■ **Eating Well.** A highlight in New Orleans is dining. If you ever wanted to splurge on a great restaurant meal, this is the place to do it. At the very least, have a beignet at Café du Mond.

■ **Bill Baggs Cape Florida State Park.** Unleash your outdoor enthusiasm at Key Biscayne's Bill Baggs Cape Florida State Park.

### PARKING

If you are spending some time in the city before or after your cruise, finding a parking space is fairly easy in most of the city, except for the French Quarter, where meter maids are plentiful and tow trucks eager. If in doubt about a space, pass it up and pay to use a parking lot. Avoid parking spaces at corners and curbs: less than 15 feet between your car and the corner will result in a ticket. Watch for temporary "No Parking" signs, which pop up along parade routes and film shoots. Long-term and overnight parking are extremely expensive at hotels and garages. Parking for the duration of your cruise is available for $16 per night and is on Erato Street; if you want, SeaCaps will take your bags directly to the ship so you just have to deal with your hand luggage. RVs can park in a lot on Poydras Street next to Terminal 2 at the Julia Street dock for $32 per night.

## EXPLORING

The French Quarter, the oldest part of the city, lives up to all you've heard: it's alive with the sights, sounds, odors, and experiences of a major entertainment hub. At some point, ignore your better judgment and take a stroll down Bourbon Street, past the bars, restaurants, music clubs, and novelty shops that have given this strip its reputation as the playground of the South. Be sure to find time to stop at Café du Monde for chicory-laced coffee and beignets. With its beautifully landscaped gardens surrounding elegant antebellum homes, the Garden District is mostly residential, but most homeowners do not mind your enjoying the sights from outside the cast-iron fences surrounding their magnificent properties.

**Garden District.** The Garden District is divided into two sections by Jackson Avenue. Upriver from Jackson is the wealthy Upper Garden District, where the homes are meticulously kept. Below Jackson, the Lower Garden District is considerably rougher. Though the homes here are often just as structurally beautiful, most of them lack the recent restorations of those of the Upper Garden District. The streets are also less well patrolled; wander cautiously. Magazine Street, lined with antiques shops and coffeehouses (ritzier along the Upper Garden District, hipper along the Lower Garden District), serves as a southern border to the Garden District; and St. Charles Avenue forms the northern border.

FAMILY
Fodor's Choice
★

**Audubon Aquarium of the Americas.** This giant aquatic showplace perched on the Mississippi riverfront has four major exhibit areas: the Amazon Rain Forest, the Mississippi River, the Gulf of Mexico, and the new Great Maya Reef gallery, all of which have fish and animals native to their respective environments. The aquarium's spectacular design allows you to feel like you're part of these watery worlds by providing close-up encounters with the inhabitants. One special treat is Parakeet Pointe, where you can spend time amidst hundreds of parakeets and feed them by hand. A gift shop and café are on the premises. Woldenberg Riverfront Park, which surrounds the aquarium, is a tranquil spot with a view of the Mississippi. You can combine tickets for the aquarium and the **Entergy IMAX Theater** ($27.50), but the best deal is the "Audubon

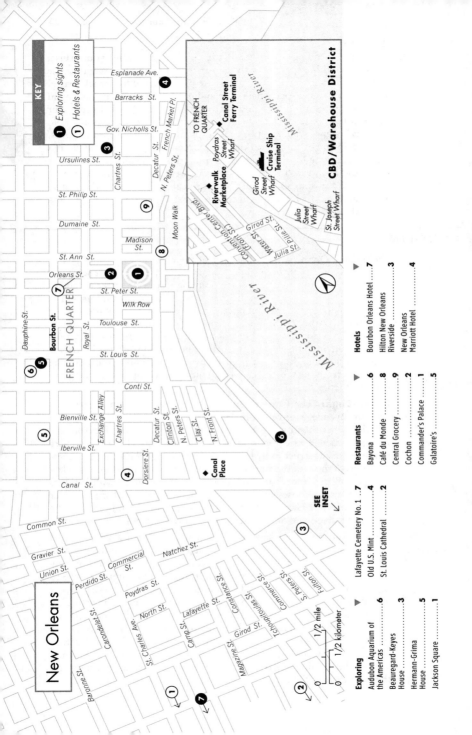

# New Orleans

## KEY

- **1** Exploring sights
- **1** Hotels & Restaurants

**FRENCH QUARTER**

**CBD/Warehouse District**

TO FRENCH QUARTER

Canal Street Ferry Terminal

Poydras Street Wharf

Cruise Ship Terminal

Girod Street Wharf

Riverwalk Marketplace

Julia Street Wharf

St. Joseph Street Wharf

Mississippi River

Canal Place

Moon Walk

Bourbon St.

SEE INSET

0    1/2 mile
0    1/2 kilometer

### Exploring

| | |
|---|---|
| Audubon Aquarium of the Americas | **6** |
| Beauregard-Keyes House | **3** |
| Hermann-Grima House | **5** |
| Jackson Square | **1** |
| Lafayette Cemetery No. 1 | **7** |
| Old U.S. Mint | **4** |
| St. Louis Cathedral | **2** |

### Restaurants ▶

| | |
|---|---|
| Bayona | **6** |
| Café du Monde | **8** |
| Central Grocery | **9** |
| Cochon | **2** |
| Commander's Palace | **1** |
| Galatoire's | **5** |

### Hotels ▶

| | |
|---|---|
| Bourbon Orleans Hotel | **7** |
| Hilton New Orleans Riverside | **3** |
| New Orleans Marriott Hotel | **4** |

Experience": aquarium, IMAX, **Audubon Insectarium**, and **Audubon Zoo** for $44.95 (tickets are good for 30 days). ⊠ *1 Canal St., French Quarter* ☎ *504/861-2537, 800/774–7394* ⊕ *www.auduboninstitute. org* ⊠ *$22.50.*

**Beauregard-Keyes House.** The Confederate general and Louisiana native P.G.T. Beauregard briefly made his home at this stately 19th-century mansion. A more long-term resident, however, was the novelist Frances Parkinson Keyes, who found the place in a sad state when she arrived in the 1940s. Keyes restored the home—today filled with period furnishings—and her studio at the back of the large courtyard remains intact, complete with family photos, original manuscripts, and her doll, fan, and teapot collections. Keyes wrote 40 novels there, all in longhand, among them local favorite *Dinner at Antoine's.* Even if you don't have time for a tour, take a peek at the beautiful walled garden through the gates at the corner of Chartres and Ursulines streets. Landscaped in the same sun pattern as Jackson Square, it blooms year-round. ⊠ *1113 Chartres St., French Quarter* ☎ *504/523–7257* ⊕ *www.bkhouse.org* ⊠ *$10.*

**Hermann-Grima House.** Noted architect William Brand built this Georgian-style house in 1831, and it's one of the largest and best-preserved examples of American architecture in the Vieux Carré. Cooking demonstrations on the open hearth of the Creole kitchen are held most Thursdays from October through May. You'll want to check out the gift shop, which has many local crafts and books. ⊠ *820 St. Louis St., French Quarter* ☎ *504/274–0746* ⊕ *www.hgghh.org* ⊠ *$12 ($15 with open-hearth cooking demo).*

FAMILY
Fodor's Choice
★

**Jackson Square.** Surrounded by historic buildings and atmospheric street life, this beautifully landscaped park is the heart of the French Quarter. **St. Louis Cathedral** sits at the top of the square, while the **Cabildo** and **Presbytère,** two Spanish colonial buildings, flank the church. The handsome brick apartments on each side of the square are the **Pontalba Buildings.** During the day, dozens of artists hang their paintings on the park fence and set up outdoor studios where they work on canvases or offer to draw portraits of passersby. Musicians, mimes, tarot-card readers, and magicians perform on the flagstone pedestrian mall, many of them day and night.

A **statue of Andrew Jackson,** victorious leader in the Battle of New Orleans in the War of 1812, commands the center of the square; the park was renamed for him in the 1850s. The words carved in the base on the cathedral side of the statue ("The Union must and shall be preserved") are a lasting reminder of the Federal troops who occupied New Orleans during the Civil War and who inscribed them. ⊠ *French Quarter* ⊕ *www.experienceneworleans.com.*

Fodor's Choice
★

**Lafayette Cemetery No. 1.** New Orleans found itself amid a large influx of Italian, German, Irish, and American immigrants from the North when this magnolia-shaded cemetery opened in 1833. Many who fought or played a role in the Civil War have plots here, indicated by plaques and headstones that detail the site of their death. Several tombs also reflect the toll taken by the yellow fever epidemic, which affected mostly children and newcomers to New Orleans; 2,000 yellow fever victims were buried here in 1852. Movies such as *Interview with the Vampire* and *Double Jeopardy* have used this walled cemetery for its eerie beauty. Save Our Cemeteries, a nonprofit, offers hour-long, volunteer-led tours daily at 10:30 am. All proceeds benefit the organization's cemetery restoration and advocacy efforts. ⊠ *1400 block of Washington Ave., Garden District* ⊕ *www.saveourcemeteries.org.*

**Old U.S. Mint.** Minting began in 1838 in this ambitious Ionic structure, a project of President Andrew Jackson's. The New Orleans mint was to provide currency for the South and the West, which it did until Louisiana seceded from the Union in 1861. Both the short-lived Republic of Louisiana and the Confederacy minted coins here. When Confederate supplies ran out, the building served as a barracks—and then a prison— for Confederate soldiers. The production of U.S. coins recommenced only in 1879; it stopped again, for good, in 1909. After years of neglect, the federal government handed the Old Mint over to Louisiana in 1966. The state now uses the building for exhibitions of the Louisiana State Museum collection, and the New Orleans Jazz National Historical Park has events here. After repairs from damage by Hurricane Katrina, the museum reopened to the public in 2007.

The first-floor exhibit recounts the history of the mint. The principal draw, however, is the second floor, dedicated to items from the **New Orleans Jazz Collection.** At the end of the exhibit, displayed in its own room like the Crown Jewels, you'll find Louis Armstrong's first cornet.

The **Louisiana Historical Center,** which holds the French and Spanish Louisiana archives, is open to researchers by appointment. At the foot of Esplanade Avenue, notice the memorial to the French rebels against early Spanish rule. The rebel leaders were executed on this spot and gave nearby Frenchmen Street its name. ⊠ *400 Esplanade Ave., French Quarter* ☎ *504/568–6993* ⊕ *louisianastatemuseum.org* ◻ *Free.*

**St. Louis Cathedral.** The oldest active Catholic cathedral in the United States, this beautiful church and basilica at the heart of the Old City is named for the 13th-century French king who led two crusades. The current building, which replaced two structures destroyed by fire, dates from 1794 (although it was remodeled and enlarged in 1851). The austere interior is brightened by murals covering the ceiling and stained-glass windows along the first floor. Pope John Paul II held a prayer service for clergy here during his New Orleans visit in 1987; to honor the occasion, the pedestrian mall in front of the cathedral was renamed Place Jean Paul Deux. Of special interest is his portrait in a Jackson Square setting, which hangs on the cathedral's inner side wall. Docents often give free tours. You can also pick up a brochure ($1) for a self-guided tour. Books about the cathedral are available in the gift shop.

■ **TIP➜ Nearly every evening in December brings a free concert at the cathedral, in addition to the free concert series throughout the year.**

The statue of the Sacred Heart of Jesus dominates St. Anthony's Garden, which extends behind the cathedral-basilica to Royal Street. The garden is also the site of a monument to 30 crewmembers of a French ship, who died in a yellow-fever epidemic in 1857. The garden has been redesigned by famed French landscape architect Louis Benech, who also redesigned the Tuileries gardens in Paris. ⊠ *615 Père Antoine Alley, French Quarter* ☎ *504/525–9585* ⊕ *www.stlouiscathedral.org* ✉ *Free* ☞ *Mass daily at 7:30 am.*

## SHOPPING

The fun of shopping in New Orleans is in the regional items available throughout the city, in the smallest shops or the biggest department stores. You can take home some of the flavor of the city: its pralines (pecan candies), seafood (packaged to go), Louisiana red beans and rice, coffee (pure or with chicory), and creole and Cajun spices (cayenne pepper, chili, and garlic). There are even packaged mixes of such local favorites as jambalaya, gumbo, beignets, and the sweet red local cocktail called the Hurricane.

> ### CALLING CARDS
>
> Print cards with your name, address, phone number, and email address to share with new friends. Stiff, business card–style paper can be purchased at nearly any office supply store, and you can make the cards on your computer at home. Having your cards handy sure beats hunting for pens and scribbling on scraps of paper to swap addresses.

Cookbooks also share the secrets of preparing distinctive New Orleans dishes. The French Quarter is well known for its fine antiques shops, located mainly on Royal and Chartres streets. The main shopping areas in the city are the French Quarter, with narrow, picturesque streets lined with specialty, gift, fashion, and antiques shops and art galleries; the Central Business District (CBD), populated mostly with jewelry, specialty, and department stores; the Warehouse District, best known for contemporary arts galleries and cultural museums; Magazine Street, home to antiques shops, art galleries, home-furnishing stores, dining venues, fashion boutiques, and specialty shops; and the Riverbend/Maple Street area, filled with clothing stores and some specialty shops.

**Jax Brewery.** A historic factory building that once produced Jax beer now holds a mall filled with local shops and a few national chain stores, like Chico's, along with a food court and balcony overlooking the Mississippi River. Shops carry souvenirs, clothing, books, artwork, and more, with an emphasis on New Orleans–themed items. The mall is open daily. On hot summer days, it's an air-conditioned refuge. ⊠ *600 Decatur St., French Quarter* ☎ *504/566–7245* ⊕ *www.jacksonbrewery.com.*

**The Shops at Canal Place.** This high-end shopping center focuses on national chains, including Saks Fifth Avenue, Michael Kors, Anthropologie, Banana Republic, Coach, J.Crew, Lululemon, and BCBG Max Azria. But the mall also includes quality local shops, such as the artists co-op RHINO ("Right Here in New Orleans"), Jean Therapy denim boutique, Wehmeier's leather goods, and Saint Germain shoes. A highlight is the Mignon Faget jewelry store, which carries the renowned local designer's full line of upscale, Louisiana-inspired creations. ⊠ *333 Canal St., Central Business District* ☎ *504/522–9200* ⊕ *www.theshopsatcanalplace.com.*

## NIGHTLIFE

No American city places such a premium on pleasure as New Orleans. From swank hotel lounges to sweaty dance clubs, refined jazz clubs and raucous Bourbon Street bars, this city is serious about frivolity. And famous for it. Partying is more than an occasional indulgence in this city—it's a lifestyle. Bars tend to open in the early afternoon and stay open into the morning hours; live music, though, follows a more restrained schedule. Some jazz spots and clubs in the French Quarter stage evening sets around 6 or 9 pm; at a few clubs, such as the Palm Court, the bands actually finish by 11 pm. But this is the exception: for the most part, gigs begin between 10 and 11 pm, and locals rarely emerge for an evening out before 10. Keep in mind that the lack of legal closing time means that shows advertised for 11 may not start until after midnight.

**Mulate's.** Across the street from the Convention Center, this large venue seats 400, and the dance floor quickly fills with couples twirling and two-stepping to authentic Cajun bands from the countryside. Regulars love to drag first-timers to the floor for impromptu lessons. The home-style Cajun cuisine is acceptable, but what matters is the nightly music. ⊠ *201 Julia St., Warehouse District* ☎ *504/522–1492* ⊕ *www.mulates.com.*

**Pat O'Brien's.** Sure, it's touristy, but there are reasons Pat O's has been a must-stop on the New Orleans drinking trail since Prohibition. Friendly staff, an easy camaraderie among patrons, and a signature drink—the pink, fruity, and extremely potent Hurricane, which comes with a souvenir glass—all make this French Quarter stalwart a pleasant afternoon diversion. There's plenty of room to spread out, from the elegant side bar and piano bar that flank the carriageway entrance to the lush (and in winter, heated) patio. Expect a line on weekend nights, and if you don't want your glass, return it for the deposit. ⊠ *718 St. Peter St., French Quarter* ☎ *504/525–4823* ⊕ *www.patobriens.com.*

FAMILY
Fodor's Choice
★
**Preservation Hall.** At this cultural landmark founded in 1961, a cadre of distinguished New Orleans musicians, most of whom were schooled by an ever-dwindling group of elder statesmen, nurture the jazz tradition that flowered in the 1920s. There is limited seating on benches—many patrons end up squatting on the floor or standing in back—and no beverages are served, although you can bring your own drink in a plastic cup. Nonetheless, legions of satisfied music lovers regard an evening at this all-ages venue as an essential New Orleans experience. Cover charge is $15 (cash only), and $20 for Friday and Saturday performances. The price can be a bit higher for special appearances. A limited number of $35 "Big Shot" tickets guarantee you a seat and let you skip the line. ⊠ *726 St. Peter St., French Quarter* ☎ *504/522–2841* ⊕ *www.preservationhall.com.*

Fodor's Choice
★
**The Spotted Cat.** Jazz, old-time, and swing bands perform nightly at this rustic club right in the thick of the Frenchmen Street action. Sets start at 4 pm on weekdays and 2 pm on weekends. Drinks cost a little more at this cash-only destination, but there's never a cover charge and the entertainment is great—from the popular bands to the cadres of young, rock-step swing dancers. ⊠ *623 Frenchmen St., Faubourg Marigny* ⊕ *www.spottedcatmusicclub.com.*

**Tipitina's.** Rub the bust of legendary New Orleans pianist Professor Longhair (or "Fess") inside this Uptown landmark named for one of the late musician's popular songs. The old concert posters on the walls read like an honor roll of musical legends, both local and national. The midsize venue boasts an eclectic and well-curated calendar, particularly during the weeks of Jazz Fest. The long-running Sunday afternoon Cajun dance party still packs the floor.

> **BRING A MUG**
>
> Take along an insulated mug with a lid that you can fill at the beverage station in the buffet area. Your drinks will stay hot or cold, and you won't have to worry about spills. Most bartenders will fill the mug with ice and water or a soft drink. With a straw, your ice will not melt instantly while you lounge at the pool.

Although the neighborhood isn't dangerous, it's far enough out of the way to require a cab trip. ✉ *501 Napoleon Ave., Uptown* ☎ *504/895–8477* ⊕ *www.tipitinas.com.*

## WHERE TO EAT

Regardless of where you decide to eat, don't miss the beignets at Café du Monde.

**$$$**
MODERN
AMERICAN
**Fodor's**Choice
★

✕ **Bayona.** "New World" is the label Louisiana native Susan Spicer applies to her cooking style, the delicious hallmarks of which include goat cheese crouton with mushrooms in madeira cream, a Bayona specialty, and Caribbean pumpkin soup with coconut. A legendary favorite at lunch is the sandwich of smoked duck, cashew peanut butter, and pepper jelly. The imaginative dishes on the constantly changing menu are served in an early-19th-century Creole cottage that glows with flower arrangements, elegant photographs, and trompe-l'oeil murals of Mediterranean landscapes. Don't skip the sweets, like the chocolate-bourbon panna cotta or roasted marshmallow ice cream bar with candied smoked pecans. ⑤ *Average main: $30* ✉ *430 Dauphine St., French Quarter* ☎ *504/525–4455* ⊕ *www.bayona.com* ☉ *Closed Sun. No lunch Mon. and Tues.*

**$**
CAFÉ
FAMILY
**Fodor's**Choice
★

✕ **Café du Monde.** No visit to New Orleans is complete without a chicory-laced café au lait paired with the addictive, sugar-dusted beignets at this venerable institution. The tables under the green-and-white-stripe awning are jammed with locals and tourists at almost every hour. If there's a wait, head around back to the takeout window, get your coffee and beignets to go, and enjoy them overlooking the river right next door or in Jackson Square. The most magical time to go is just before dawn, before the bustle begins. You can hear the birds in the crepe myrtles across the way. The metro-area satellites (there's one in the CBD at the Port of New Orleans) lack the character of the original. ⑤ *Average main: $3* ✉ *800 Decatur St., French Quarter* ☎ *504/525–4544* ⊕ *www.cafedumonde.com* ⏴ *Reservations not accepted.*

**$**
DELI
FAMILY

✕ **Central Grocery.** This old-fashioned grocery store creates authentic muffulettas, a gastronomic gift from the city's Italian immigrants. Made by filling nearly 10-inch round loaves of seeded bread with ham, salami, provolone and Emmentaler cheeses, and olive salad, the muffuletta is nearly as popular locally as the po'boy (Central Grocery also sells a vegetarian version). The sandwiches are available in wholes and halves (they're huge—unless you're starving, you'll do fine with a half). Eat at one of the counters or get your sandwich to go and dine on a bench in Jackson Square or the Moon Walk along the Mississippi riverfront. The Grocery closes at 5 pm. $ *Average main: $8* ⊠ *923 Decatur St., French Quarter* ☎ *504/523–1620* ☉ *Closed Sun. and Mon. No dinner.*

**$$**
**CAJUN**
**Fodor's Choice**
★

✕ **Cochon.** Chef-owned restaurants are common in New Orleans, but this one builds on owner Donald Link's family heritage as he, working with co-owner Stephen Stryjewski (who received a James Beard Award for his work here), prepares Cajun dishes he learned to cook at his grandfather's knee. The interior may be a bit too hip and noisy for some patrons, but the food makes up for it. The fried boudin with pickled peppers is a must—trust us on this one—then move on to turkey, black-eyed pea, and pork gumbo, and a hearty Louisiana *cochon* (pork) with turnips, cracklings, and cabbage. Despite the pork-centric reputation, all the vegetable sides, especially the smothered greens, are excellent. $ *Average main: $20* ⊠ *930 Tchoupitoulas St., Warehouse District* ☎ *504/588–2123* ⊕ *www.cochonrestaurant.com* ☉ *Closed Sun.* ⌂ *Reservations essential.*

**$$$**
**CREOLE**

✕ **Commander's Palace.** No restaurant captures New Orleans's gastronomic heritage and celebratory spirit as well as this grande dame of New Orleans fine dining. Upstairs, the Garden Room's glass walls have marvelous views of the giant oak trees on the patio below. The menu's classics include a spicy and meaty turtle soup; shrimp and tasso Henican (shrimp stuffed with ham, with pickled okra); and a wonderful pecan-crusted Gulf fish. The bread-pudding soufflé might ruin you for other bread puddings. The weekend brunch is a not-to-be-missed New Orleans tradition, complete with live jazz. The band takes requests, so come armed with tip money. Jackets are preferred at dinner; shorts and T-shirts are forbidden, and men must wear closed-toe shoes. $ *Average main: $35* ⊠ *1403 Washington Ave., Garden District* ☎ *504/899–8221* ⊕ *www.commanderspalace.com* ⌂ *Reservations essential.*

**$$$**
**CREOLE**
**Fodor's Choice**
★

✕ **Galatoire's.** With many of its recipes dating to 1905, Galatoire's epitomizes the old-style French Creole bistro. Fried oysters and bacon en brochette are worth every calorie, and the brick-red rémoulade sauce sets a high standard. Other winners include veal chops with optional béarnaise sauce, and seafood-stuffed eggplant. Downstairs in the narrow white-tablecloth dining room, lighted with gleaming brass chandeliers, is where boisterous regulars congregate, making for a lively and entertaining scene; you can only reserve a table in the renovated upstairs rooms. Friday lunch starts early and continues well into the evening. Shorts and T-shirts are never allowed; a jacket is required for dinner and all day Sunday. If the lines get too long, head to Galatoire's 33 Bar & Steak, which opened next door in 2013. It offers classic cuts and cocktails in a similarly adorned space. $ *Average main: $30* ⊠ *209 Bourbon St., French Quarter* ☎ *504/525–2021* ⊕ *www.galatoires.com* ☉ *Closed Mon.* ⌂ *Reservations essential* ⊞ *Jacket required.*

## WHERE TO STAY

You can stay in a large hotel near the cruise-ship terminal or in more intimate places in the French Quarter. Hotel rates in New Orleans tend to be on the high end, though deals abound.

**$$** ☷ **Bourbon Orleans Hotel.** This hotel's location is about as central as it
HOTEL gets, though the beautiful courtyard and pool provide welcome sanctuary from the loud, 24-hour Bourbon Street action just outside the door. **Pros:** welcome cocktail, complimentary coffee and tea in the lobby, and a free bottle of artesian water in the room; fitness center; Roux restaurant on site; live entertainment in the on-site bar. **Cons:** lobby level is often crowded; street-facing rooms can be noisy. ⑤ *Rooms from: $189 ☒717 Orleans St., French Quarter ☎504/523–2222 ⊕ www. bourbonorleans.com ↩218 rooms, 28 suites* �ⓄⅠ*No meals.*

**$$** ☷ **Hilton New Orleans Riverside.** The superb river and city views are hard
HOTEL to beat, and the guest rooms come with all the modern amenities, in
FAMILY close proximity to shops and the casino. **Pros:** well-maintained facilities; hotel runs like a well-oiled machine; great security; two heated outdoor swimming pools. **Cons:** the city's biggest hotel; typical chain service and surroundings. ⑤ *Rooms from: $199 ☒2 Poydras St., Central Business District ☎504/561–0500, 855/760–0870 ⊕ www.hiltonneworleans riverside.com ↩1622 rooms, 74 suites* ⓄⅠ*No meals.*

**$$$** ☷ **New Orleans Marriott Hotel.** This centrally located 41-story skyscraper
HOTEL boasts fabulous views of the Quarter, downtown, and the Mississippi River. **Pros:** centrally located; stunning city and river views. **Cons:** typical chain hotel; lacks charm; charge for Wi-Fi in the rooms (access is free from the lobby). ⑤ *Rooms from: $239 ☒555 Canal St., French Quarter ☎504/581–1000, 800/228–9290 ⊕ www.neworleansmarriott. com ↩1,329 rooms* ⓄⅠ*No meals.*

# NEW YORK, NEW YORK

A few cruise lines now base Caribbean-bound ships in New York City year-round; other ships do seasonal cruises to New England and Bermuda or trans-Atlantic crossings. If you're coming to the city from outside the immediate area, you can easily arrive the day before and do a bit of sightseeing and perhaps take in a Broadway show. The cruise port in Manhattan is fairly close to Times Square and Midtown hotels and theaters. But the New York City region now has three major cruise ports. You can also leave from Cape Liberty Terminal in Bayonne, New Jersey, on both Celebrity and Royal Caribbean ships. There's also a cruise terminal in Red Hook, Brooklyn, and this terminal serves Princess ships as well as Cunard's *Queen Mary 2.*

### ESSENTIALS
#### HOURS
They say that New York never sleeps, and that's particularly true around Times Square, where some stores are open until 11 pm or later even during the week. But most stores outside of the immediate Times Square area are open from 9 or 10 until 6 or 7. Many museums close on Monday.

## TOURS

You can take a hop-on hop-off bus tour of Manhattan, either uptown or downtown, but the time you waste standing still in traffic minimizes the amount you can see in a short time.

## VISITOR INFORMATION

**Contacts NYC & Company.** ⊕ *www.nycgo.com/accessibility.* **Times Square Alliance.** ✉ *Midtown West* ☎ *212/768–1560* ⊕ *www.timessquarenyc.org.*

## THE CRUISE PORT

If your cruise is leaving from "New York City" it may be leaving from any one of three cruise piers, only two of which are actually in New York City.

### BEST BETS

■ **An Art Museum.** Take your pick: the Met, MOMA, or the Frick, but museum-going is a true highlight of New York.

■ **A Broadway Show.** The theater experience in New York is arguably the best in the world.

■ **Central Park.** Even if you have time for just a stroll, come if the weather is good; it's about 30 minutes by the cruise terminal by foot.

The **Manhattan Cruise Terminal** is on the far west side of Manhattan, five very long blocks from the Times Square area, between 48th and 52nd streets; the vehicle entrance is at 55th Street. Traffic can be backed up in the area on days that cruise ships arrive and depart, so allow yourself enough time to check in and go through security. There are no nearby subway stops, though city buses do cross Midtown at 50th and 42nd streets. If you don't have too much luggage, it is usually faster and more convenient to have a taxi drop you off at the intersection of 50th Street and the West Side Highway, directly across the street from the entrance to the lower level of Pier 88 (Pier 90, also used by many ships, is next door); then you can walk right in and take the escalator or elevator up to the embarkation level.

**Cape Liberty Terminal** in Bayonne is off Route 440. From the New Jersey Turnpike, take Exit 14A, then follow the signs for 440 South, and make a left turn into the Cape Liberty Terminal area (on Port Terminal Boulevard). If you are coming from Long Island, you cross Staten Island, and after crossing the Bayonne Bridge take 440 North, making a right into the terminal area. If you are coming from Manhattan, you can also reach the terminal by public transit. Take the New Jersey Transit light-rail line from the PATH trains in Hoboken; get off at the 34th Street stop in Bayonne, and from there you can call for a taxi to the terminal (about 2 miles [3 km] away); there may be a free shuttle bus on cruise sailing dates, but confirm that with your cruise line.

The **Brooklyn Cruise Terminal** at Pier 12 in Red Hook, which opened in April 2006, is not convenient to public transportation, so you should plan to take a taxi, drive, or take the bus transfers offered by the cruise lines (the cost for this is about $45 per person from either LaGuardia or JFK). There is a secure, 500-car outdoor parking lot on-site. To reach the terminal from LaGuardia Airport, take I–278 W (the Brooklyn-Queens Expressway), Exit 26, Hamilton Avenue; the terminal entrance is actually off Browne Street. From JFK, take I–278 E (again, the Brooklyn-Queens Expressway), and then the same exit. If you arrive early, there's not much in the neighborhood, but there are a few neighborhood delis and restaurants about 15 minutes away on foot; the area is a safe place to walk around during daylight hours, though it's very industrial. Red Hook is the home of ships from the Princess and Cunard cruise lines.

**Contacts Brooklyn Cruise Terminal.** ✉ *72 Bowne St., Red Hook* ☏ *718/855–5590* ⊕ *www.nycruise.com.* **Cape Liberty Cruise Port.** ✉ *14 Port Terminal Blvd., Bayonne* ☏ *201/823–3737* ⊕ *www.cruiseliberty.com.* **Manhattan Ship Terminal.** ✉ *711 12th Ave., at W. 55th St., Midtown West* ☏ *212/641-4440* ⊕ *www.nycruise.com.*

### AIRPORT

**Contacts LaGuardia Airport** (*LGA*). ☏ *718/533–3400* ⊕ *www.laguardiaairport. com.* **JFK International Airport** (*JFK*). ☏ *718/244–4444* ⊕ *www.jfkairport. com.* **Newark Liberty International Airport** (*EWR*). ☏ *973/961–6000* ⊕ *www. newarkairport.com.*

### AIRPORT TRANSFERS

A cab to or from JFK to the New York Passenger Ship Terminal in Manhattan will cost $52 (a flat fare) plus toll and tip; expect to pay at least $35 on the meter if you are coming from LaGuardia and at least $60 or $70 (not including tolls of about $10 and the tip) from Newark in a car service (from Newark airport, it's usually more cost-effective to call for a car service to pick you up; regular taxis can be prohibitively expensive; if possible, reserve a car in advance, and call when you pick up your bags to find out where to meet it).

From Newark Airport it's approximately $30 to Cape Liberty, $90 from JFK (plus tolls and tip, so count on at least $120 and be aware that taxis are not obligated to take this route from JFK), and $90 from LaGuardia (plus tolls and tip; count on paying more than $110). Royal Caribbean offers bus service from several Mid-Atlantic and Northeast cities on sailing dates, but confirm that with the cruise line.

If your cruise is leaving from Brooklyn, the taxi fare will be much cheaper if you fly into either La Guardia (about $35) or JFK (about $45); you'll pay at least $80 for a car service from Newark Airport (not including tolls and tip, and perhaps more in a regular taxi). Cruise lines provide bus transfers from all three of the area's airports, but it may be cheaper to take a taxi if you are traveling with more than one other person. Note that all these taxi fares do not include tolls and tips. From Newark, the tolls to Brooklyn can be substantial, adding almost $20 to the fare.

**Contacts Carmel Car & Limousine Service.** ☏ *212/666–6666, 866/666–6666* ⊕ *www.carmellimo.com.* **Dial 7 Car Service.** ☏ *212/777–7777* ⊕ *www.dial7.com.* **GO Airlink NYC.** ☏ *877/599–8200, 212/812–9000* ⊕ *www.goairlinkshuttle.com.*

### PARKING

You can park at the New York Passenger Ship Terminal for a staggering $35 a day; the fee is payable in advance in cash or credit card (no Amex).

Parking at Cape Liberty Terminal in Bayonne is $19 per day, payable in cash, traveler's checks, and major credit cards.

Parking at Red Hook, Brooklyn, costs $23 for the first 24 hours and then $20 per day.

# EXPLORING

There's no way to do justice to even the most popular tourist stops in New York. Below is information about several top attractions. If you have only a day in the city, choose one or two attractions and buy a Metro card to facilitate easy transfers between the subway and bus (put on as much money as you think you'll use in a day but no less than $5.50, which is good for two rides at $2.75 each + $1 for the card, which may be shared). Times Square is approximately 20 minutes by foot from the cruise terminal; just walk straight out of the gate and east along 48th Street. There's a moving series of panels about the World Trade Center at the Ground Zero site across from the Millennium Hotel (take the 1 train to Chambers Street or the E to World Trade Center); there's another series of memorial panels underneath at the World Trade Center PATH station, which is accessible from the main, streetside memorial area.

**Fodor's Choice**
★
**American Museum of Natural History.** With 45 exhibition halls and more than 32 million artifacts and specimens, the world's largest and most important museum of natural history can easily occupy you for half a day. The dioramas might seem dated, but are fun. The dinosaur exhibits are probably the highlight. Attached to the museum is the **Rose Center for Earth and Space**, with various exhibits and housing the **Hayden Planetarium** and an **IMAX Theater**. However, the actual entry fee is a donation; you must pay something, but it can be as little as you wish. Just be aware that many of the wonderful features (not to mention special exhibits) cost extra and must be paid for in full. ✉ *Central Park W at W. 79th St., Upper West Side* ☎ *212/769–5100* ⊕ *www.amnh.org* ✎ *$22 suggested donation, includes admission to Rose Center for Earth and Space; $27 includes an IMAX or space show* Ⓜ *B, C to 81st St./ Museum of Natural History.*

**Fodor's Choice**
★
**Brooklyn Bridge.** "A drive-through cathedral" is how the journalist James Wolcott described the Brooklyn Bridge, one of New York's noblest and most recognized landmarks, perhaps rivaling Walt Whitman's comment that it was "The best, most effective medicine my soul has yet partaken." The bridge stretches over the East River, connecting Manhattan and Brooklyn. A walk across its promenade—a boardwalk elevated above the roadway, shared by pedestrians, skaters, and cyclists—takes about 40 minutes and delivers exhilarating views. If you start from Lower Manhattan, you'll end up in the heart of Brooklyn Heights (you can also take the subway to the Brooklyn side and walk back to Manhattan). It's worth noting that on evenings and weekends when the weather is nice, the narrow path gets pretty congested; it's most magical, and quietest, early in the morning. ✉ *East River Dr., Lower Manhattan* Ⓜ *4, 5, 6 to Brooklyn Bridge–City Hall; J, Z to Chambers St.; A, C to High St. (in Brooklyn).*

**FAMILY**
**Fodor's Choice**
★
**Central Park.** Without Central Park's 843 acres of meandering paths, tranquil lakes, ponds, and open meadows, New Yorkers might be a lot less sane. You can drop by the zoo (near 64th Street, on the east side) or the famous Bethesda Fountain (mid-park, at around 72nd Street), but the main draw is just to wander the lanes. Central Park has one

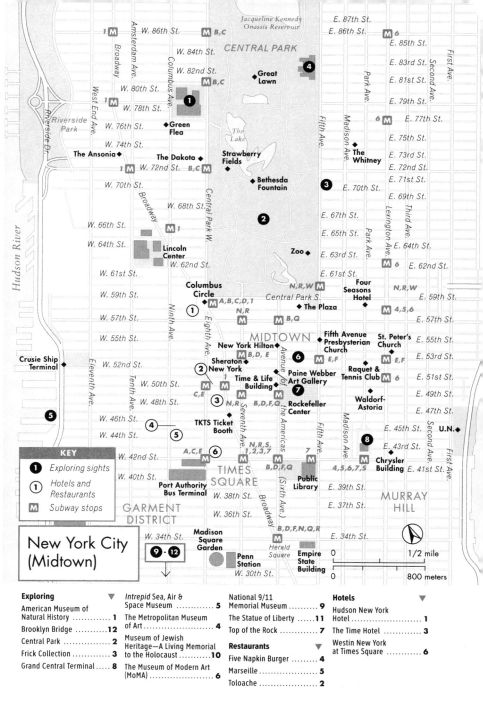

New York City (Midtown)

of the lowest crime rates in the city. Still, use common sense and stay within sight of other park visitors, and don't go into the park after dark. Directions, park maps, and events calendars can be obtained from volunteers at two 5th Avenue information booths, at East 60th Street and East 72nd Street. ⊠ *Central Park* ☎ *212/794–6564 Dairy Visitor Center, 212/360–2727 for schedule of walking tours, 646/310–6600 Central Park Conservancy* ⊕ *www.centralparknyc.org* Ⓜ *A, B, C, D, 1 to Columbus Circle; N, Q, R to 5th Ave.–59th St.*

Fodor's Choice ★
**Frick Collection.** Coke-and-steel baron Henry Clay Frick (1849–1919) amassed this superb art collection far from the soot and smoke of Pittsburgh, where he made his fortune. The mansion was designed by Thomas Hastings and built in 1913–14. It opened in 1935, but still resembles a gracious private home, albeit one with bona fide masterpieces in almost every room. This is the best small museum in town by a mile. An audio guide is included with admission. Children under 10 are not admitted, and those age 10–16 with adult only. ⊠ *1 E. 70th St., at 5th Ave., Upper East Side* ☎ *212/288–0700* ⊕ *www.frick.org* 🖼 *$20* Ⓜ *6 to 68th St.–Hunter College.*

Fodor's Choice ★
**Grand Central Terminal.** Grand Central is not only the world's largest (76 acres) and the nation's busiest (500,000 commuters and subway riders use it daily) railway station, but also one of the world's greatest public spaces ("justly famous," as critic Tony Hiss noted, "as a crossroads, a noble building . . . and an ingenious piece of engineering"). A massive four-year renovation completed in October 1998 restored the 1913 landmark to its original splendor—and then some. There's a nice audio tour for rent for $5 per adult. The Municipal Art Society (*212/935–3960 www.mas.org*) leads architectural tours of the terminal that begin here every Wednesdays from 12:30 to 2. Reservations are not required, and a $10 donation is suggested. Meet at the information booth, Main Concourse. Grand Central also has the city's largest Apple store. ⊠ *Main entrance, 42nd St. and Park Ave., Midtown East* ☎ *212/935–3960* ⊕ *www.grandcentralterminal.com* Ⓜ *4, 5, 6, 7, S to Grand Central–42nd St.*

FAMILY
**Intrepid Sea, Air & Space Museum.** Formerly the USS *Intrepid,* this 900-foot aircraft carrier is serving out its retirement as the centerpiece of Manhattan's only floating museum. An A-12 Blackbird spy plane, lunar landing modules, helicopters, seaplanes, and two dozen other aircraft are on deck. Docked alongside, and also part of the museum, are the *Growler,* a strategic-missile submarine; the *Edson,* a Vietnam-era destroyer; and several other battle-scarred naval veterans. Children can explore the ships' skinny hallways and winding staircases, as well as manipulate countless knobs, buttons, and wheels. The *Enterprise,* one of the U.S. space program's original shuttles (though this particular shuttle never flew in space) has become a big draw (and has a separate admission). This museum is within easy walking distance of the main cruise piers in Manhattan. Ticket prices are $2 cheaper if purchased online in advance, and you have the added advantage of skipping the often extensive lines. ⊠ *Pier 86, 12th Ave. at 46th St., Midtown West* ☎ *212/245–0072, 877/957–7447* ⊕ *www.intrepidmuseum.org* 🖼 *$24; $31 combo ticket with Space Shuttle* Ⓜ *A, C, E to 42nd St.–Port Authority.*

**Fodor's Choice** **The Metropolitan Museum of Art.** If Manhattan held no other museum
★ than the colossal Metropolitan Museum of Art, you could still occupy
yourself for days roaming its labyrinthine corridors. The Metropolitan Museum has more than 2 million works of art representing 5,000
years of history, so it's a good idea to plan ahead; looking at everything
here could take a week. The famous Egyptian collection (including the
Temple of Dendur) is reason enough to visit. Other don't-miss sections
include the magnificent Islamic Galleries, the collections of Impressionist
paintings, the American Wing, and the Anna Wintour Costume Center.
Admission includes same-day entry to the museum's new modern-art
outpost the Met Breuer (Madison Avenue and 75th Street), as well as
the Cloisters Museum and Gardens in northern Manhattan. ✉ *1000
5th Ave., at 82nd St., Upper East Side* ☎ *212/535–7710* ⊕ *www.met
museum.org* ✆ *$25 suggested donation; $7 for audio guide* Ⓜ *4, 5, 6
to 86th St.*

**Museum of Jewish Heritage—A Living Memorial to the Holocaust.** In a granite
hexagon rising 85 feet above Robert F. Wagner Jr. Park at the southern
end of Battery Park City, this museum pays tribute to the 6 million Jews
who perished in the Holocaust. It's one of the best such museums in
the country. The museum's east wing has a theater, memorial garden,
library, galleries, and café. A free audio guide, with narration by Meryl
Streep and Itzhak Perlman, is available at the admissions desk. ✉ *36
Battery Pl., Battery Park City, Battery Park* ☎ *646/437–4202* ⊕ *www.
mjhnyc.org* ✆ *$12 (free Wed. 4–8)* Ⓜ *4, 5 to Bowling Green; 1 to Rec-
tor St.; R to Rector St.*

**Fodor's Choice** **The Museum of Modern Art (MoMA).** The masterpieces—Monet's Water Lil-
★ ies, Picasso's Les Demoiselles d'Avignon, Van Gogh's Starry Night—are
still here, but for now the main draw at MoMA is, well, MoMA. A
"modernist dream world" is how critics have described the museum.
Unfortunately, the museum has become a victim of its own success,
which means lines are sometimes down the block. For the shortest wait,
get here before the museum opens; you can avoid some of the crowding
by entering through the 54th Street side. Be prepared for sticker shock
when you buy your ticket. Yet another expansion is underway, which
will keep construction going until 2019. ✉ *11 W. 53rd St., between
5th and 6th Aves., Midtown West* ☎ *212/708–9400* ⊕ *www.moma.org*
✆ *$25* Ⓜ *E, M to 5th Ave./53rd St.; F to 57th St.; B, D, E to 7th Ave.*

**National 9/11 Memorial Museum.** Beside the reflecting pools on the 9/11
Memorial Plaza is the glass pavilion of the Memorial Museum. The
museum descends some 70 feet down to the bedrock the Twin Towers
were built on, and displays a poignant, powerful collection of artifacts,
memorabilia, photographs, and multimedia exhibits, as well as a gallery
that takes visitors through the history of events surrounding both the
1993 and 2001 attacks. There's also a memorial wall with portraits of
those who died, pieces of the Towers' structural steel and foundations,
and remnants of the "Survivors Stairs," which allowed hundreds of people
to escape the buildings that fateful September day. Current access to the
museum is through the Memorial Plaza from the intersections of Liberty
and Greenwich Streets, Liberty and West, or West and Fulton. ✉ *180
Greenwich St., Financial District* ☎ *212/266–5211* ⊕ *www.911memorial.*

*org/museum* 🖼 *$24 (free Tues. 5–8 pm)* Ⓜ *R to Cortlandt St.; 2, 3, 4, 5, A, C, J, Z to Fulton Center; E to World Trade Center.*

**Fodor's** Choice     **The Statue of Liberty.** Though you must endure a long wait and onerous
★     security, it's worth the trouble to see one of the iconic images of New York. The narrow, double-helix stairs leading to the statue's crown closed after 9/11, but access reopened on July 4, 2009. Access to the crown is strictly limited, and tickets must be booked months in advance; otherwise, it's possible to view the museum in the pedestal, but even those tickets often sell out. Much more interesting—and well worth exploring—is the Ellis Island museum, which traces the story of immigration in New York City with moving exhibits throughout the restored processing building. Go early if you want to see everything, and allow plenty of time for security and lines. The ferry stops first at the statue and then continues to Ellis Island. ✉ *Liberty Island, Lower Manhattan* ☎ *212/363–3200, 877/523–9849 ticket reservations* ⊕ *www.liberty ellisfoundation.org* 🖼 *Free; ferry $18 round-trip (includes Ellis Island), crown tickets extra $3.*

**Fodor's** Choice     **Top of the Rock.** Rockefeller Center's multifloor observation deck, first
★     opened in 1933, and closed in the early 1980s, reopened in 2005. Though overpriced, the experience is infinitely better than that at the Empire State Building, where interminable lines spoil most of the fun. Arrive just before sunset for the best views (which include the Empire State Building). ✉ *30 Rockefeller Plaza, 50th St. entrance, between 5th and 6th Aves., Midtown West* ☎ *212/698–2000, 212/698–2000* ⊕ *www.topoftherocknyc.com* 🖼 *$32* Ⓜ *B, D, F, M to 47th–50th Sts./ Rockefeller Center; E, M to 5th Ave./53rd St.*

## SHOPPING

You can find almost any major store from virtually any designer or chain in Manhattan. High-end designers tend to be along Madison Avenue, between 55th and 86th streets. Some are along 57th Street, between Madison and 7th avenues. Fifth Avenue, starting at Saks Fifth Avenue (at 50th Street) and going up to 59th Street, is a hodgepodge of high-end stores and more accessible options, including the high-end department store Bergdorf-Goodman, at 58th Street. More interesting and individual stores can be found in SoHo (between Houston and Canal, West Broadway and Lafayette), and the East Village (between 14th Street and Houston, Broadway and Avenue A). Chinatown is chock-full of designer knockoffs, crowded streets, and dim sum palaces; though frenetic during the day, it's a fun stop. The newest group of stores in Manhattan is at the Time-Warner Center, at Columbus Circle (at 8th Avenue and 59th Street); the high-rise mall has upscale stores and some of the city's best-reviewed and most expensive new restaurants.

## BROADWAY SHOWS

Scoring tickets to Broadway shows is fairly easy except for the very top draws. For the most part, the top ticket price for Broadway musicals is now around $145; the best seats for Broadway plays can run as high as $130.

**Telecharge.** ⊠ *New York* ☎ *212/239–6200, 800/447–7400* ⊕ *www.tel-echarge.com.*

**Ticketmaster.** ⊠ *New York* ☎ *866/448–7849 for automated service, 800/745–3000* ⊕ *www.ticketmaster.com.*

**TKTS Times Square.** ⊠ *Duffy Sq., 47th St. and Broadway, Midtown West* ☎ *212/912–9770* ⊕ *www.tdf.org/tkts* Ⓜ *1, 2, 3, 7, N, Q, R, S to Times Sq.–42nd St.*

## WHERE TO EAT

The restaurants we recommend below are all in Midtown West, near Broadway theaters and hotels. Make reservations at all but the most casual places or face a numbing wait.

**$$**
BURGER
✕ **Five Napkin Burger.** This perennially packed Hell's Kitchen burger place and brasserie has been a magnet for burger lovers since day one. Bottles of Maker's Mark line the sleek, alluringly lighted bar in the back, a collection of antique butcher's scales hangs on a tile wall near the kitchen, and meat hooks dangle from the ceiling between light fixtures. Though there are many menu distractions—deep-fried pickles and warm artichoke dip, to name a few—the main attractions are the juicy burgers, like the original 10-ounce chuck with a tangle of onions, Gruyère cheese, and rosemary aioli. There's a patty option for everyone, including a ground lamb *kofta* and an onion-ring-topped ahi tuna burger. For dessert, have an überthick black-and-white malted milk shake. Ⓢ *Average main: $16* ⊠ *630 9th Ave., at 45th St., Midtown West* ☎ *212/757–2277* ⊕ *www.5napkinburger.com* Ⓜ *A, C, E to 42nd St.–Port Authority.*

**$$**
MEDITERRANEAN
✕ **Marseille.** With great food and a convenient location near several Broadway theaters, Marseille is perpetually packed. The Mediterranean creations are continually impressive, including the bouillabaisse, the signature dish of the region for which the restaurant is named—a mélange of mussels, shrimp, and whitefish in a fragrant broth, topped with a garlicky crouton and served with rouille on the side. Also worth a bite or two is the charred octopus with fennel and tomatoes. Leave room for the spongy beignets with chocolate and raspberry dipping sauces. Ⓢ *Average main: $24* ⊠ *630 9th Ave., at 44th St., Midtown West* ☎ *212/333–2323* ⊕ *www.marseillenyc.com* ⚘ *Reservations essential* Ⓜ *A, C, E to 42nd St.–Port Authority.*

**$$**
MEXICAN
✕ **Toloache.** Make a quick detour off heavily trafficked Broadway into this pleasantly bustling Mexican cantina for one of the best dining options around Times Square. The bi-level eatery has a festive, celebratory vibe, with several seating options: bar, balcony, main dining room, and ceviche bar. Foodies flock here for three types of guacamole (traditional, fruited, and spicy), a trio of well-executed ceviches, and Mexico

City–style tacos with Negra Modelo–braised brisket, and quesadillas studded with black truffle and *huitlacoche* (a corn fungus known as the "Mexican truffle"). There's an extensive tequila selection—upward of 100 brands. Adventurous palates are drawn to tacos featuring chili-studded dried grasshoppers, lobes of seared foie gras, and caramelized veal sweetbreads. There are two other locations, in Greenwich Village and on the Upper East Side. $ *Average main: $20* ⊠ *251 W. 50th St., near 8th Ave., Midtown West* ☎ *212/581–1818* ⊕ *www.toloachenyc. com* Ⓜ *1, C, E to 50th St.; N, Q, R to 49th St.*

## WHERE TO STAY

There are no real bargains in the Manhattan hotel world, and you'll find it difficult to get a decent room for under $200 during much of the year. However, occasional weekend deals can be found. All the hotels we recommend for cruise passengers are in Manhattan on the West Side, in relatively easy proximity to the Manhattan cruise ship terminal. If you are flying in the day before a cruise departing from Bayonne, you may want to stay at a Newark Airport hotel that offers free transportation to and from the airport. You can take a taxi to the Bayonne Cruise Terminal on your day of departure.

**$$** 🖼 **Hudson New York Hotel.** Budget fashionistas are drawn to this afford-
HOTEL able hotel. **Pros:** fabulous, elegant bar; gorgeous Francesco Clemente fresco in lobby; breathtaking Sky Terrace. **Cons:** staff can be condescending; tiny rooms; overpriced cocktails. $ *Rooms from: $339* ⊠ *356 W. 58th St., between 8th and 9th Aves., Midtown West* ☎ *212/554–6000* ⊕ *www.hudsonhotel.com* ⤳ *878 rooms, 67 suites* ⦿ *No meals* Ⓜ *1, A, B, C, D to 59th St.–Columbus Circle.*

**$$** 🖼 **The Time Hotel.** One of the neighborhood's first boutique hotels, this
HOTEL spot half a block from the din of Times Square is a recently refreshed and contemporary retreat. **Pros:** acclaimed and popular Serafina restaurant downstairs; surprisingly quiet for Times Square location; good turndown service. **Cons:** service is inconsistent. $ *Rooms from: $349* ⊠ *224 W. 49th St., between Broadway and 8th Ave., Midtown West* ☎ *212/246–5252, 877/846–3692* ⊕ *www.thetimeny.com* ⤳ *167 rooms, 26 suites* ⦿ *No meals* Ⓜ *1, C, E to 50th St.; N, Q, R to 49th St.*

**$** 🖼 **Westin New York at Times Square.** This giant Midtown hotel has all
HOTEL the amenities and service you expect from a reliable brand, at fairly reasonable prices. **Pros:** central for Midtown attractions; big rooms; great gym. **Cons:** congested area near Port Authority; not the best location for prime dining and nightlife. $ *Rooms from: $299* ⊠ *270 W. 43rd St., at 8th Ave., Midtown West* ☎ *212/201–2700, 866/837–4183* ⊕ *www.westinny.com* ⤳ *873 rooms* ⦿ *No meals* Ⓜ *A, C, E to 42nd St.–Port Authority.*

# NORFOLK, VIRGINIA

By Ramona Settle

Founded in 1680, Norfolk is no newcomer to the cruise business. One famous passenger, Thomas Jefferson, arrived here in November 1789 after a two-month crossing of the Atlantic. More than 200 years later, this historic seaport welcomes cruise passengers in the summer for departures to the Bahamas and Bermuda. Situated at the heart of nautical Hampton Roads, Norfolk is home to the largest naval base in the world and is also a major commercial port. Stroll through Waterside, with shops close to the water; walk to the excellent Nauticus Museum, and make sure to stop at MacArthur's burial site.

## BEST BETS

■ **Chrysler Museum of Art.** Though far from New York, Chicago, or Los Angeles, this is one of the major art museums in the United States.

■ **Nauticus.** The National Maritime Center is one of the region's most popular attractions, and especially good for families.

■ **Norfolk Naval Station.** This giant naval base, the home of the Atlantic Fleet, is an impressive site in itself.

## ESSENTIALS

### HOURS

Most stores are open weekdays from 10 to 9. Some museums close on Monday and/or Tuesday.

### VISITOR INFORMATION

**Contacts Norfolk Convention and Visitors Bureau.** ⊠ *232 E. Main St., Norfolk* ☎ *757/664–6620, 800/368–3097* ⊕ *www.visitnorfolktoday.com.*

### THE CRUISE PORT

The Half Moone Cruise and Celebration Center, as Norfolk calls its cruise terminal, is in the center of the attractive, downtown waterfront. It's within walking distance of numerous attractions and amenities. From I–264, take the City Hall exit (Exit 10). At the light, turn right on St. Paul's Boulevard, and follow the signs to the Cedar Grove parking lot.

**Contacts Half Moone Cruise and Celebration Center.** ⊠ *1 Waterside Dr., Norfolk* ⊕ *www.cruisenorfolk.org.*

### AIRPORT TRANSFERS

Norfolk International Airport (ORF) is 9 miles (15 km) and 20 minutes away from the cruise terminal. One-way, shared shuttle costs range from $7.50 to $22 per person, and a taxi costs about $18 to $25.

**Contacts Black and White Cabs.** ⊠ *6304 Sewells Point Rd., Norfolk* ☎ *757/853–0411* ⊕ *www.norfolkblackandwhitecabs.com.* **James River Transportation.** ☎ *866/823–4626* ⊕ *http://jamesrivertrans.com/.* **Yellow Cab.** ⊠ *6304 Sewells Point Rd., Norfolk* ☎ *757/727–7777* ⊕ *www.yellowcabofnorfolk.com.*

**PARKING**

Cedar Grove Parking is the designated facility for cruise passengers. The parking fee ($15 daily) is paid upon entering the lot; Visa, MasterCard, American Express, cash, and traveler's checks are accepted. Less than 1 miles (1½ km) from I-264, this lot is located on Monticello Avenue between Virginia Beach Boulevard and Princess Anne Road in Downtown Norfolk. Shuttles run regularly to the cruise terminal.

# EXPLORING

History meets high-tech in this waterfront city. From 18th-century historic homes and a major art museum to 20th-century battleships and nuclear-powered aircraft carriers, Norfolk has many interesting sites to explore, several of them free and most within walking distance of the cruise terminal.

**Chrysler Museum of Art.** By any standard, the Chrysler Museum of Art downtown qualifies as one of America's major art museums. The permanent collection includes works by Rubens, Gainsborough, Renoir, Picasso, Cézanne, Matisse, Warhol, and Pollock, a list that suggests the breadth available here. Classical and pre-Columbian civilizations are also represented. The decorative-arts collection includes exquisite English porcelain and art nouveau furnishings. The Chrysler is home to one of the most important glass collections in America, which includes glass objects from the 6th century BC to the present, with particularly strong holdings in Tiffany, French art glass, and English cameo, as well as artifacts from ancient Rome and the Near and Far East. ⊠ *One Memorial Pl., Norfolk* ☎ *757/664–6200* ⊕ *www.chrysler.org* 🎫 *Free* ☉ *Closed Mon.*

**MacArthur Memorial.** The MacArthur Memorial is the burial place of one of America's most distinguished military officers. General Douglas MacArthur (1880–1964) agreed to this navy town as the site for his monument because it was his mother's birthplace. In the rotunda of the old City Hall, converted according to MacArthur's design, is the mausoleum; 11 adjoining galleries house mementos of MacArthur's career, including his signature corncob pipe and the Japanese instruments of surrender that concluded World War II. However, this is a monument not only to General MacArthur but to all those who served in wars from the Civil to the Korean War. Its Historical Center holds 2½ million documents and more than 100,000 photographs, and assists scholars, students, and researchers from around the world. The general's staff car is on display in the gift shop, where a 24-minute biography is shown. ⊠ *Bank St. at City Hall Ave., MacArthur Sq., Norfolk* ☎ *757/441-2965* ⊕ *www.macarthurmemorial.org* 🎫 *Free (donations accepted)* ☉ *Closed Mon.*

**Moses Myers House.** The Federal redbrick Moses Myers House, built by its namesake between 1792 and 1796, is exceptional, and not just for its elegance. The furnishings, 70 precent of them original, include family portraits by Gilbert Stuart and Thomas Sully. A transplanted New Yorker as well as Norfolk's first Jewish resident, Myers made his fortune in Norfolk in shipping, then served as a diplomat and a

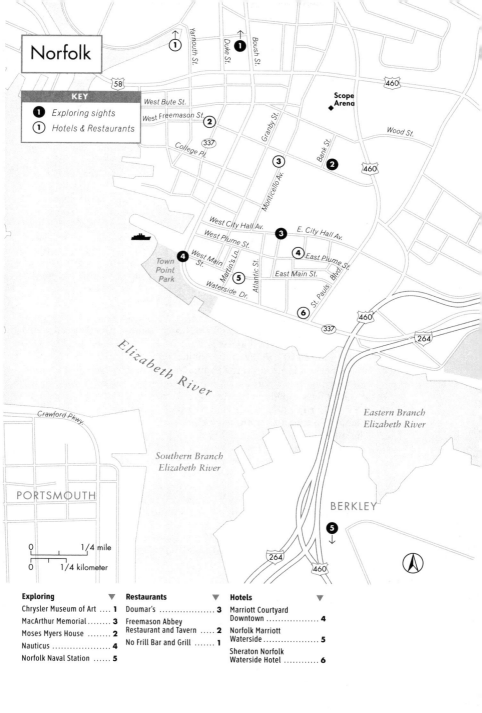

# Norfolk

**KEY**
- ❶ Exploring sights
- ①　Hotels & Restaurants

Yarmouth St.
Duke St.
Boush St.
West Bute St.
West Freemason St.
College Pl.
Granby St.
Bank St.
Wood St.
Scope Arena
Monticello Av.
West City Hall Av.
E. City Hall Av.
West Plume St.
West Main St.
Martin's Ln.
Atlantic St.
East Plume St.
St. Pauls Blvd.
East Main St.
Town Point Park
Waterside Dr.
Elizabeth River
Crawford Pkwy.
Eastern Branch Elizabeth River
Southern Branch Elizabeth River
PORTSMOUTH
BERKLEY

0　1/4 mile
0　1/4 kilometer

customhouse officer. His grandson married James Madison's grand-niece; his great-grandson served as mayor; and the family kept the house for five generations. In 2005 the home had extensive repairs to bring it back to the 19th century. Exhibits throughout the house feature letters and other artifacts from several generations of the Myers family. ☒ *323 E. Free Mason St., Norfolk* ☎ *757/333–1087* ⊕ *www.chrysler. org/about-the-museum/historic-houses/the-moses-myers-house/* ⌨ *Free* ⊘ *Closed Mon. and Tues.*

FAMILY **Nauticus.** A popular attraction on Norfolk's redeveloped downtown waterfront, Nauticus is a maritime science museum featuring hands-on exhibits, interactive theaters, and high-definition films that celebrate the local connection to the seaport. Visitors can touch a shark, learn about weather and underwater archaeology, and explore the mysteries of the Elizabeth River. A NOAA Environmental Resource Center is an invaluable stop for educational materials. Temporary exhibits in both the Changing Gallery and Forecastle Gallery keep things fresh. The Hampton Roads Naval Museum on the second floor and the battleship *Wisconsin* adjacent to the building are also popular attractions operated by the U.S. Navy, and are included in the Nauticus admission. ☒ *1 Waterside Dr., Norfolk* ☎ *757/664–1000* ⊕ *www.nauticus. org* ⌨ *$15.95* ⊘ *Closed Mon. Labor Day–Memorial Day.*

**Norfolk Naval Station.** On the northern edge of the city, the Norfolk Naval Station is an impressive sight, home to more than 100 ships of the Atlantic Fleet. The base was built on the site of the Jamestown Exposition of 1907; many of the original buildings survive and are still in use. Several large aircraft carriers, built at nearby Newport News, call Norfolk home port and can be seen from miles away, especially at the bridge-tunnel end of the base. You may see two, each with a crew of up to 6,300, beside slightly smaller amphibious carriers that discharge marines in both helicopters and amphibious assault craft. The submarine piers, floating dry docks, supply center, and air station are all worth seeing. The *Victory Rover* and *Carrie B.* provide boat tours from downtown Norfolk to the naval station; and Hampton Roads Transit operates tour trolleys most of the year, departing from the naval-base tour office. Visitor access is by tour only, and photo ID is required to enter the base (Note: you will be required to present an additional ID with a state ID from Illinois, Minnesota, Missouri, New Mexico, Washington, and American Samoa). ☒ *9079 Hampton Blvd., Norfolk* ☎ *757/444–7955* ⊕ *www.cnic.navy.mil/* ⌨ *Tour $10 (cash only; there is no ATM on premises).*

## SHOPPING

**d'Art Center.** You can meet painters, sculptors, glassworkers, jewelers, photographers, and other artists at work in their studios at the d'Art Center; the art is for sale. ☒ *Selden Arcade, 740 Duke St., Norfolk* ☎ *757/625–4211* ⊕ *www.d-artcenter.org* ⊘ *Closed Mon.*

**Ghent.** An eclectic mix of chic shops, including antiques stores, bars, and eateries, lines the streets of Ghent, a turn-of-the-20th-century neighborhood that runs from the Elizabeth River to York Street, to West Olney

Road and Llewellyn Avenue. The intersection of Colley Avenue and 21st Street is the hub. ⊠ *Norfolk.*

**Palace Shops.** In Ghent the upscale clothing and shoe boutiques at the Palace Shops are a good place to search out some finery. ⊠ *21st St. at Llewellyn Ave., Norfolk* ☎ *757/622–9999* ⊕ *www.palaceshopsghent.com.*

## WHERE TO EAT

Downtown Norfolk has many fine-dining restaurants as well as casual eateries in Waterside Festival Marketplace, where there's a versatile food court, and in the MacArthur Center Mall, including Johnny Rockets and Kincaid's—good food values for the price.

**$**
DINER
FAMILY

✕ **Doumar's.** After he introduced the world to its first ice cream cone at the 1904 World's Fair in St. Louis, Abe Doumar founded this drive-in institution in 1934. It's still operated by his family. Waitresses carry to your car the specialties of the house: barbecue, limeade, and ice cream in waffle cones made according to an original recipe. ⑤ *Average main: $3* ⊠ *20th St. at Monticello Ave., Norfolk* ☎ *757/627–4163* ⊕ *www. doumars.com* ⊗ *Closed Sun.*

**$$**
AMERICAN
**Fodor's**Choice
★

✕ **Freemason Abbey Restaurant and Tavern.** This former church near the historic business district has been drawing customers for a long time, and not without reason. It has 40-foot-high cathedral ceilings and large windows, making for an airy, and dramatic, dining experience. You can sit upstairs, in the large choir loft, or in the main part of the church downstairs. Beside the bar just inside the entrance is an informal sort of "diner" area, but with the whole menu to choose from. Regular appetizers include artichoke dip and crab stuffed mushrooms. There's a dinner special every weeknight, such as lobster, prime rib, and wild game (wild boar or alligator, for example). Vegetarian fare is also offered. ⑤ *Average main: $22* ⊠ *209 W. Freemason St., Norfolk* ☎ *757/622–3966* ⊕ *www.freemasonabbey.com.*

**$**
AMERICAN

✕ **No Frill Bar and Grill.** This expansive café is in an antique building in the heart of Ghent. Beneath a tin ceiling and exposed ductwork, a central bar is surrounded by several dining spaces with cream-and-mustard walls and wooden tables. Signature items include the ribs; the funky chicken sandwich, a grilled chicken breast with bacon, tomato, melted Swiss cheese, and Parmesan pepper dressing on rye; and the Spotswood salad of baby spinach, Granny Smith apples, and blue cheese. ⑤ *Average main: $14* ⊠ *806 Spotswood Ave., at Colley Ave., Norfolk* ☎ *757/627– 4262* ⊕ *www.nofrillgrill.com.*

## WHERE TO STAY

There are hotels within walking distance of the cruise port, or if you have a car, there are numerous chain motels on the outskirts of town where you can save a little money.

**$**
HOTEL

▣ **Marriott Courtyard Downtown.** This eight-story hotel is near everything visitors want to see and where business travelers need to be. **Pros:** convenient downtown location; walking distance to many attractions; attached shopping mall is really nice. **Cons:** parking is quite costly and shared with the mall. $ *Rooms from: $149* ⊠ *520 Plume St., Norfolk* ☎ *757/963–6000, 800/321–2211* ⊕ *www.marriott.com* ⤴ *137 rooms, 3 suites* ⁙⁙ *No meals.*

**$$** ⊞ **Norfolk Marriott Waterside.** Located in the redeveloped downtown area,
HOTEL this hotel is connected to the Waterside Festival Marketplace shopping area by a ramp, and it's close to Town Point Park, site of many festivals. **Pros:** great central location; two blocks from the Waterside Festival Marketplace. **Cons:** parking is pricey, and a walk with luggage. $ *Rooms from: $199* ⊠ *235 E. Main St., Norfolk* ☎ *757/627–4200, 800/228–9290* ⊕ *www.marriott.com* ⤴ *396 rooms, 8 suites* ⁙⁙ *No meals.*

**$$** ⊞ **Sheraton Norfolk Waterside Hotel.** Modern is the word for this hotel's
HOTEL furnishings, from the bright, spacious lobby to the ample rooms and large suites. **Pros:** the only hotel that is truly on the waterfront; nice touches such as snacks and cold water served all day; restaurant has a terrific view of Portsmouth. **Cons:** parking—for Norfolk—is pricey; overcrowded rooms may be hard to maneuver for some. $ *Rooms from: $180* ⊠ *777 Waterside Dr., Norfolk* ☎ *757/622–6664* ⊕ *www. sheratonnorfolkwaterside.com* ⤴ *426 rooms, 20 suites* ⁙⁙ *No meals.*

# PORT CANAVERAL, FLORIDA

By Paul Rubio

This once-bustling commercial fishing area is still home to a small shrimping fleet, charter boats, and party fishing boats, but its main business these days is as a cruise-ship port. Cocoa Beach itself isn't the spiffiest place around, but what is becoming quite clean and neat is the north end of the port, where the Carnival, Disney, Norweigan and Royal Caribbean cruise lines set sail, as well as Sun Cruz and Sterling casino boats. Port Canaveral is now Florida's second-busiest cruise port and home to two of the world's largest cruise ships, Royal Caribbean's *Oasis of the Seas* and sister ship, *Allure of the Seas.* Because of Port Canaveral's proximity to Orlando theme parks (about an hour away), many cruisers combine a short cruise with a stay in the area. The port is also convenient to popular Space Coast attractions such as the Kennedy Space Center and United States Astronaut Hall of Fame in Titusville.

## ESSENTIALS
### HOURS
Most of the area's attractions are open every day.

### VISITOR INFORMATION
**Contacts Space Coast Office of Tourism.** ☎ *877/572–3224, 321/433–4470* ⊕ *www.visitspacecoast.com.*

### THE CRUISE PORT
Port Canaveral sees more than 4 million passengers passing through its terminals annually, almost equal to Miami.

The port has six modern cruise terminals; a new version of Terminal 5 debuted in June 2016 after a $48 million makeover serving Carnival Cruise Lines. The port is also home to ships from Disney Cruise Line, Norweigan Cruise Lines, and Royal Caribbean International.

Other cruise lines operate seasonally. The port serves as the embarkation point for three to nine day cruises to the Bahamas, as well as Southern, Western, and Eastern Caribbean.

In Brevard County, Port Canaveral is on State Road (S.R.) 528, also known as the Beeline Expressway, which runs straight to Orlando, which has the nearest airport. To drive to Port Canaveral from there, take the north exit out of the airport, staying to the right, to S.R. 528 (Beeline Expressway) East. Take S.R. 528 directly to Port Canaveral; it's about a 45-minute drive.

| BEST BETS |
|---|
| ■ **Kennedy Space Center.** Kennedy Space Center in Titusville is the region's biggest attraction. |
| ■ **Merritt Island.** If you want to get out and commune with nature, this is the place, especially for bird-watchers. |
| ■ **Orlando Theme Parks.** With Orlando just an hour away, many cruisers combine a theme-park visit with their cruise. |

**Contacts Canaveral Port Authority.** ☎ *321/783–7831, 888/767–8226* ⊕ *www.portcanaveral.com.*

### AIRPORT TRANSFERS

If you are flying into the area, the Orlando airport is 45 minutes west from the docks. If you have not arranged airport transfers with your cruise line, you will need to make your own arrangements. Taxis are expensive, but many companies offer shared minivan and bus shuttles to Port Canaveral. They are all listed on the Canaveral Port Authority website. Some shuttles charge for the entire van, which is a good deal for groups but not for individuals or couples; some will charge a per-person rate. Expect to pay at least $38 per person round-trip, and check the Internet for coupons and special offers.

You will need to make a reservation in advance regardless of which service you use. Some cruisers who want to do some exploring before the cruise rent a car at the airport and drop it off at the port, which houses several major rental-car agencies.

**Contacts AAA Cruise Line Connection.** ☎ *407/908–5566* ⊕ *www.aasupershuttle.com.* **Busy Traveler Transport Service.** ☎ *321/453–5278, 800/496–7433* ⊕ *www.abusytraveler.com.*

### PARKING

Outdoor gated lots and a six-story parking garage are near the terminals and cost $128 per week for vehicles up to 20 feet in length and $224 per week for vehicles over 20 feet, which must be paid in advance, either in cash, traveler's checks, or by major credit card (MasterCard and Visa only).

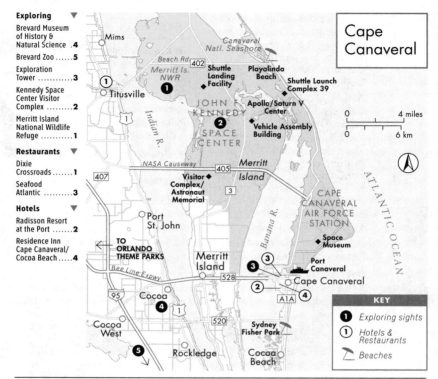

## EXPLORING

With the Kennedy Space Center just 20 minutes away, there is plenty to do in and around Cape Canaveral, though many folks opt to travel the extra hour into Orlando to visit the popular theme parks.

FAMILY **Brevard Museum of History & Natural Science.** This is the place to come to see what the lay of the local land looked like in other eras. Hands-on activities draw children, who especially migrate toward the Imagination Center, where they can act out history or reenact a space shuttle flight. Not to be missed are Ice Age era creatures such as a fully articulated mastadon, giant ground sloth, and saber-tooth cat. The Windover Archaeological Exhibit features 7,000-year-old artifacts indigenous to the region. In 1984, a shallow pond revealed the burial ground of more than 200 American Indians who lived in the area about 7,000 years ago. Preserved in the muck were bones and, to the archeologists' surprise, the brains of these ancient people. Nature lovers appreciate the museum's butterfly garden and the nature center with 22 acres of trails encompassing three distinct ecosystems—sand pine hills, lake lands, and marshlands. ⊠ *2201 Michigan Ave., Cocoa* ☎ *321/632–1830* ⊕ *www. myfloridahistory.org* 🎫 *$9* ⊘ *Closed Sun.–Tues.*

FAMILY
Fodor's Choice
★

**Brevard Zoo.** At the only Association of Zoo and Aquariums–accredited zoo built by a community, you can stroll along the shaded boardwalks and get a close-up look at rhinos, giraffes, cheetahs, alligators, crocodiles, giant anteaters, marmosets, jaguars, eagles, river otters, kangaroos, exotic birds, and kookaburras. Alligator, crocodile, and river-otter feedings are held on alternate afternoons—and no, the alligators don't dine on the otters. Stop by Paws-On, an interactive learning playground with a petting zone, wildlife detective training academy, and the Indian River Play Lagoon. Hand-feed a giraffe in Expedition Africa or a lorikeet in the Australian Free Flight Aviary; and step up to the Wetlands Outpost, an elevated pavilion that's a gateway to 22 acres of wetlands through which you can paddle kayaks and keep an eye open for the 4,000 species of wildlife that live in these waters and woods. Adventurers seeking a chimp's-eye view can zipline through the zoo on Treetop Trek. ⊠ *8225 N. Wickham Rd., Melbourne* ☎ *321/254–9453* ⊕ *www.brevardzoo.org* ⊠ *$17.95; $20.95 with train and giraffe and lorikeet food.*

FAMILY

**Exploration Tower.** The best view at Port Canaveral is no longer from the top of your cruise ship. In fact, the view from atop this towering seven-story structure, which opened in late 2013, makes the cruise ships look—well, not so massive after all. The tower, a short walk from the cruise port, is equal parts museum and scenic overlook. The seventh-floor observation deck offers impressive views of the cruise port, the Atlantic Ocean, the Banana River, and even the Vehicle Assembly Building at Kennedy Space Center. Other floors house exhibits highlighting the cultural history of the area, from space flight to surfing, bird and sea life to the rich maritime history. Kids will enjoy interactive exhibits, including a virtual ship's bridge that allows you to pilot a boat through the Canaveral Channel and into the Atlantic. A theater shows a 20-minute film dedicated to the history of Brevard County, and a small café sells refreshments and baked goods. The ground floor houses a visitor information center. ⊠ *670 Dave Nisbet Dr., Cape Canaveral* ☎ *321/394–3408* ⊕ *www.explorationtower.com* ⊠ *$6.50.*

FAMILY
Fodor's Choice
★

**Kennedy Space Center Visitor Complex.** This must-see attraction, just southeast of Titusville, is one of Central Florida's most popular sights. Located on a 140,000-acre island 45 minutes outside Orlando, Kennedy Space Center is NASA's launch headquarters. The visitor complex gives guests a unique opportunity to learn about—and experience—the past, present, and future of America's space program. Interactive programs make for the best experiences here. One such interactive program is the Heroes & Legends attraction, which opened in November 2016 and chronicles the men and women who've journeyed to space, and features the U.S. Astronaut Hall of Fame. If you want a low-key overview of the facility (and if the weather is foul) take the bus tour, included with admission. Buses depart every 15 minutes, and you can get on and off any bus whenever you like. Stops include the Launch Complex 39 Observation Gantry, which has an unparalleled view of the launchpads and Apollo/Saturn V Center, with a don't-miss presentation at the Firing Room Theatre, where the launch of America's first lunar mission, 1968's Apollo VIII, is re-created with a ground-shaking, window-rattling liftoff. The Apollo/Saturn V center also features one of three remaining Saturn V moon rockets. Astronaut Encounter Theater has two daily programs where retired NASA astronauts share their adventures in space travel and show a short film. The most moving exhibit is the Astronaut Memorial, a 70,400-pound black-granite tribute to astronauts who lost their lives in the name of space exploration.

More befitting Walt Disney World or Universal Studios (complete with the health warnings), the Shuttle Launch Experience is the center's most spectacular attraction. Designed by a team of astronauts, NASA experts, and renowned attraction engineers, the 44,000-square-foot structure uses a sophisticated motion-based platform, special-effects seats, and high-fidelity visual and audio components to simulate the sensations experienced in an actual space-shuttle launch, including MaxQ, Solid Rocker Booster separation, main engine cutoff, and External Tank separation. The journey culminates with a breathtaking view of Earth from space. The only back-to-back twin IMAX theater in the world is in the complex, too. Several add-on tours and activities are available as well if you have extra time. ⊠ *Kennedy Space Center, Rte. 405, Titusville* ☎ *877/313–2610* ⊕ *www.kennedyspacecenter.com* ⊠ *$50 (includes bus tour, IMAX movies, visitor complex shows and exhibits, and Astronaut Hall of Fame); specialty tours $21–$25; Lunch with an Astronaut $29.99.*

Fodor'sChoice  **Merritt Island National Wildlife Refuge.** Owned by the NASA, this 140,000-
★  acre refuge, which adjoins the Canaveral National Seashore, acts as a buffer around Kennedy Space Center while protecting 1,000 species of plants and 500 species of wildlife, including 15 federally considered threatened or endangered. It's an immense area dotted by brackish estuaries and marshes, coastal dunes, hardwood hammocks, and pine forests. You can borrow field guides and binoculars at the visitor center (5 miles east of U.S. 1 in Titusville on State Road 402) to track down falcons, ospreys, eagles, turkeys, doves, cuckoos, owls, and woodpeckers, as well as loggerhead turtles, alligators, wild boar and otters. A 20-minute video about refuge wildlife and accessibility—only 10,000 acres are developed—can help orient you.

You might take a self-guided driving tour along the 7-mile Black Point Wildlife Drive. On the Oak Hammock Foot Trail you can see wintering migratory waterfowl and learn about the plants of a hammock community. If you exit the north end of the refuge, look for the Manatee Observation Area just north of the Haulover Canal (maps are at the visitor center). They usually show up in spring and fall. There are also fishing camps, fishing boat ramps, and six hiking trails scattered throughout the area. If you do want to fish, a free, downloadable permit is required. Most of the refuge is closed 24 hours prior to a launch. ⊠ *Visitor Center, Rte. 402, 5 miles east of U.S. 1 across Titusville Causeway, Titusville* ☎ *321/861–0667, 321/861–0669 visitor center* ⊕ *www.fws.gov/refuge/ Merritt_Island/* ⊠ *Free; $5 per vehicle on Black Point Wildlife Dr. only.*

## ORLANDO THEME PARKS

FAMILY **SeaWorld Orlando.** In the world's largest marine adventure park, every attraction is devoted to demonstrating the ways that humans can protect the mammals, birds, fish, and reptiles that live in the ocean and its tributaries. The presentations are gentle reminders of our responsibility to safeguard the environment, and you'll find that

> **WRITE EASY**
>
> Preaddress a page of stick-on labels before you leave home; use them for postcards to the folks back home and you will not have to carry along a bulky address book.

SeaWorld's use of humor plays a major role in this education. The park is small enough that, armed with a map that lists showtimes, you can plan a chronological approach that flows easily from one attraction to the next. Near the intersection of I–4 and the Beeline Expressway; take I–4 to Exit 71 or 72 and follow signs. ✉ *7007 Sea Harbor Dr., International Drive* ☎ *888/800–5447* ⊕ *www.seaworld.com* ✉ *$99 for a 1-day ticket ($30 cheaper if bought online in advance).*

FAMILY **Universal Orlando.** The resort consists of **Universal Studios** (the original movie theme park, which includes The Wizarding World of Harry Potter–Diagon Alley), **Islands of Adventure** (the second theme park, which includes The Wizarding World of Harry Potter–Hogsmeade), and **CityWalk** (the dining-shopping-nightclub complex). Although it's bordered by residential neighborhoods and thickly trafficked International Drive, Universal Orlando is surprisingly expansive yet intimate and accessible, with two massive parking complexes, easy walks to all attractions, and a motor launch that cruises to the hotels. Universal Orlando emphasizes "two parks, two days, one great adventure," but you may find the presentation, creativity, and cutting-edge technology bring you back for more. ✉ *1000 Universal Studios Plaza, Orlando* ☎ *407/363–8000* ⊕ *www.universalorlando.com* ✉ *1-day, 1-park ticket $105.*

FAMILY **Walt Disney World.** Walt Disney World is a huge complex of theme
Fodor'sChoice parks and attractions, each of which is worth a visit. Parks include
★ the **Magic Kingdom**, a family favorite and the original here; **Epcot**, Disney's international, educational park; **Disney Hollywood Studios**, a movie-oriented theme park; and **Disney's Animal Kingdom**, which is much more than a zoo. Beyond these, there are water parks, elaborate minigolf courses, a sports center, resorts, restaurants, and nightlife. If you have only one day, you'll have to concentrate on a single park; Disney Hollywood Studios or Animal Kingdom are easiest to do in a day. Arrive early and expect to stay until park closing, which might be as early as 5 pm for Animal Kingdom or as late as 11 pm during busy seasons at the Magic Kingdom. The most direct route to the Disney Parks from Port Canaveral is S.R. 528 (the Beeline Expressway) to I–4; when you get through Orlando, follow the signs to Disney and expect traffic. ✉ *Lake Buena Vista* ☎ *407/824–4321* ⊕ *disneyworld.disney.go.com* ✉ *1-day, 1-park ticket $105 (park-hopper option extra).*

## BEACHES

**Playalinda Beach.** The southern access for the Canaveral National Seashore, remote Playalinda Beach has pristine sands and is the longest stretch of undeveloped coast on Florida's Atlantic seaboard. You can, however, see the shuttle launch pad at Cape Kennedy from the beach. Hundreds of giant sea turtles

> **EXTRA BATTERIES**
>
> Even if you don't think you'll need them, bring along extra camera batteries and change them before you think the old ones are dead.

come ashore here from May through August to lay their eggs. Fourteen parking lots anchor the beach at 1-mile intervals. From Interstate 95, take Exit 249 and head east. Bring bug repellent in case of horseflies, and note that you may see some unauthorized clothing-optional activity. **Amenities:** lifeguards (seasonal); parking (fee); toilets. **Best for:** solitude; swimming; walking. ⊠ *Rte. 402, at northern end of Beach Rd., Titusville* ☎ *321/267–1110* ⊕ *www.nps.gov/cana* ☞ *$5 per vehicle for national seashore.*

**Jetty Park.** A wonderful taste of the real Florida, this 4½-acre beach and oceanfront campground has picnic pavilions, bike paths, and a 1,200-foot-long fishing pier that doubles as a perfect vantage point from which to watch a liftoff from Cape Canaveral or to glimpse the gigantic cruise ships as they depart the port for the Bahamas. Lifeguards are on duty year-round, and all manner of equipment from beach chairs and umbrellas to boogie boards to beach wheelchairs is available for rent. A jetty constructed of giant boulders adds to the landscape, and a walkway that crosses it provides access to a less-populated stretch of beach. Real and rustic, this is Florida without the theme-park varnish. **Amenities:** food and drink; lifeguards; parking (fee); showers; toilets; water sports. **Best for:** sunrise; surfing; swimming; walking. ⊠ *400 Jetty Rd., Cape Canaveral* ☎ *321/783–7111* ⊕ *www.jettyparkbeachand campground.com* ☞ *$15 cars, $20 RVs. Cash only.*

## SHOPPING

**Cocoa Beach Surf Company.** The world's largest surf complex sits inside the Four Points by Sheraton resort, and has three floors of boards, apparel, sunglasses, and anything else a surfer, wannabe-surfer, or souvenir-seeker could need. Also on-site are a 5,600-gallon fish and shark tank and the Shark Pit Bar and Grill. You can rent surfboards, bodyboards, and wet suits, as well as umbrellas, chairs, and bikes. And staffers teach wannabes—from kids to seniors—how to surf. There are group, semi-private, and private lessons available in one-, two-, and three-hour sessions. Prices range from $40 (for a one-hour group lesson) to $120 (three-hour private). All gear is provided. ⊠ *Four Points by Sheraton, 4001 N. Atlantic Ave., Cocoa Beach* ☎ *321/799–9930* ⊕ *www.cocoabeachsurf.com.*

**Fodor's Choice** ★ **Ron Jon Surf Shop.** It's impossible to miss the flagship and original Ron Jon: it takes up nearly two blocks along Route A1A and has a giant surfboard and an art-deco facade painted orange, blue, yellow, and turquoise. What started in 1963 as a small T-shirt and bathing-suit shop has evolved into a 52,000-square-foot superstore that's open every day 'round the clock. The shop rents water-sports gear as well as chairs and umbrellas, and it sells every kind of beachwear, surf wax, plus the requisite T-shirts and flip-flops. ⊠ *4151 N. Atlantic Ave., Rte. A1A, Cocoa Beach* ☎ *321/799–8888* ⊕ *www.ronjonsurfshop.com.*

## WHERE TO EAT

The Cove at Port Canaveral has several restaurants if you are looking for a place to eat right at the port.

**$$** ✕ **Dixie Crossroads.** This sprawling restaurant is always crowded and
SEAFOOD festive, but it's not just the rustic setting that draws the throngs—it's the seafood. The specialty is rock shrimp, which are served fried, broiled, or steamed. Diners with a hearty appetite can opt for the all-you-can-eat shrimp or snow crab, or, if seafood isn't your choice, the menu offers steaks, chicken, pork and ribs. You might have to wait (up to 90 minutes) for a table, but if you don't have time to wait, you can order takeout or use the call-ahead seating option. A word to the wise: when that basket of corn fritters dusted with powdered sugar appears like magic on your table, try not to fill up on them. $ *Average main: $23* ⊠ *1475 Garden St., 2 miles east of I–95 Exit 220, Titusville* ☎ *321/268–5000* ⊕ *www.dixiecrossroads.com* ⌣ *Reservations not accepted.*

**$$** ✕ **Seafood Atlantic.** Locals think of this casual waterfront seafood mar-
SEAFOOD ket/eatery as a well-kept secret, but more and more cruise patrons are making their way here for a pre- or postcruise treat. The market is connected to the restaurant, guaranteeing not only freshness but an array of choices. You don't just order a fish sandwich or plate of steamed shrimp; you choose from at least four varieties of fish (try the Golden Tile in season) and several varieties of shrimp (the Royal Reds may be the best you've ever tasted). Seating is alfresco, with views of the Port Canaveral waterway and passing cruise ships. Best for lunch or an early dinner, the restaurant closes at 8 on Friday and Saturday, earlier other nights. $ *Average main: $19* ⊠ *520 Glen Cheek Dr., Cape Canaveral* ☎ *321/784–1963* ⊕ *www.seafoodatlantic.org* ☉ *Closed Mon. and Tues.* ⌣ *Reservations not accepted.*

## WHERE TO STAY

Many area hotels offer cruise packages that include one night's lodging, parking for the duration of your cruise, and transportation to the cruise port.

**$** ⊡ **Radisson Resort at the Port.** For cruise-ship passengers who can't wait
HOTEL to get underway, this splashy resort, done up in pink and turquoise, already feels like the Caribbean. **Pros:** cruise-ship convenience; pool area; free shuttle; free Wi-Fi. **Cons:** rooms around the pool can be noisy; loud air-conditioning in some rooms; no complimentary breakfast. $ *Rooms from: $124* ⊠ *8701 Astronaut Blvd., Cape Canaveral* ☎ *321/784–0000, 888/201–1718* ⊕ *www.radisson.com/capecanaveralfl* ⌅ *284 rooms, 72 suites* ⊚ *No meals.*

**$$** 🔲 **Residence Inn Cape Canaveral Cocoa Beach.** Billing itself as the closest
HOTEL all-suites hotel to the Kennedy Space Center, this four-story Residence
Inn, painted cheery yellow, is also convenient to other area attractions
such as Port Canaveral, the Cocoa Beach Pier, the Brevard Zoo, and
Cocoa Village, and is only an hour from the Magic Kingdom. **Pros:**
helpful staff; free breakfast buffet; free Wi-Fi; pet-friendly. **Cons:** less
than picturesque views; street noise in some rooms. ⑤ *Rooms from:
$219* ✉ *8959 Astronaut Blvd., Cape Canaveral* ☎ *321/323–1100,
800/331–3131* ⊕ *www.marriott.com* ⤵ *150 suites* ⦿ *Breakfast.*

# SAN JUAN, PUERTO RICO

By Paulina
Salach and
Julie Schwietert
Colazzo

In addition to being a major port of call, San Juan is also a common port
of embarkation for cruises on Southern Caribbean itineraries.

*For information on dining, shopping, nightlife, and sightseeing see San
Juan, Puerto Rico in Chapter 4.*

### THE CRUISE PORT

Most cruise ships dock within a couple of blocks of Old San Juan;
however, there is a second cruise pier across the bay, and if your ship
docks there you'll need to take a taxi to get anywhere on the island.
The Paseo de la Princesa, a tree-lined promenade beneath the city wall,
is a nice place for a stroll—you can admire the local crafts and stop at
the refreshment kiosks. Major sights in the Old San Juan area are mere
blocks from the piers, but be aware that the streets are narrow and
steeply inclined in places.

### AIRPORT

**Contacts Aeropuerto Internacional Luis Muñoz Marín.** ☎ *787/253–2329*
⊕ *www.aeropuertosju.com.*

### AIRPORT TRANSFERS

If you are embarking or disembarking in San Juan, the ride to or from
the Luis Muñoz Marín International Airport, east of downtown San
Juan, to the docks in Old San Juan takes about 20 minutes, depending
on traffic. The white "Taxi Turistico" cabs, marked by a logo on the
door, have a fixed rate of $19 to and from the cruise-ship piers; there
is a $1 charge for each piece of luggage. Other taxi companies charge
by the mile, which can cost a little more. Be sure the driver starts the
meter, or agree on a fare beforehand.

### VISITOR INFORMATION

**Contacts Puerto Rico Tourism Company.** ☎ *787/721–2400, 800/866–7827*
⊕ *www.seepuertorico.com.*

## WHERE TO STAY

If you are planning to spend one night in San Juan before your cruise
departs, you'll probably find it easier to stay in Old San Juan, where the
cruise-ship terminals are. But if you want to spend a few extra days in
the city, there are other possibilities near good beaches a bit farther out.
We make some nightlife suggestions in the San Juan port of call section.

$    ⬚ **The Gallery Inn.** No two rooms in this 200-year-old mansion are
B&B/INN   alike, but all have four-poster beds, handwoven tapestries, and quirky antiques in every nook and cranny. **Pros:** one-of-a-kind lodging; ocean views; wonderful classical music concerts. **Cons:** several narrow, winding staircases; an uphill walk from the rest of Old San Juan; ; sometimes raucous pet macaws and cockatoos. ⑤ *Rooms from: $160* ⊠ *204–206 Calle Norzagaray, Old San Juan* ☎ *787/722–1808* ⊕ *www.thegallery inn.com* ⇆ *20 rooms, 5 suites* ⦿ *Breakfast.*

$$    ⬚ **Hotel El Convento.** There's no longer anything austere about this
HOTEL   350-year-old former convent. **Pros:** lovely building; atmosphere to
**Fodor's**Choice   spare; plenty of nearby dining options. **Cons:** near some noisy bars;
★   small pool; small bathrooms. ⑤ *Rooms from: $285* ⊠ *100 Calle Cristo, Old San Juan* ☎ *787/723–9020* ⊕ *www.elconvento.com* ⇆ *52 rooms, 6 suites* ⦿ *No meals.*

$$    ⬚ **Sheraton Old San Juan Hotel.** Rooms facing the water at this triangular-
HOTEL   shaped hotel have spectacular views of the mammoth cruise ships that sail in and out of the nearby harbor. **Pros:** harbor views; near many dining options; good array of room types. **Cons:** chain-hotel feel to guest rooms; uphill walk to the rest of Old San Juan. ⑤ *Rooms from: $229* ⊠ *100 Calle Brumbaugh, Old San Juan* ☎ *787/289–1914* ⊕ *www. sheratonoldsanjuan.com* ⇆ *200 rooms, 40 suites* ⦿ *No meals.*

# TAMPA, FLORIDA

By Paul Rubio   It may not have the glitz of Miami or the "magic" of Orlando, but the Tampa Bay area has that elusive quality that many attribute to the "real Florida"—here you'll find some of the state's best and most unspoiled beaches and lots of history. Tampa Bay is also the state's second-largest metro area and it showcases broad cultural diversity, as well as Florida's third-busiest airport, a vibrant business community, world-class beaches, and superior hotels and resorts—many of them historic. This all adds up to an excellent place to spend a week or even a lifetime. Several ships are based here year-round and seasonally, most doing Western Caribbean itineraries.

## ESSENTIALS

### HOURS
Some museums are closed on Monday.

### VISITOR INFORMATION
**Contacts Visit Tampa Bay.** ⊠ *401 E. Jackson St., Suite 2100, Tampa* ☎ *800/448–2672, 813/223–1111* ⊕ *www.visittampabay.com.* **Ybor City Chamber Visitor Information Center.** ⊠ *1600 E. 8th Ave., Suite B104, Tampa* ☎ *813/241–8838* ⊕ *www.ybor.org.*

### THE CRUISE PORT
Tampa is the largest shipping port in the state of Florida, and it's becoming ever more important to the cruise industry, now with three passenger terminals. In Tampa's downtown area, the port is linked to nearby Ybor City and the rest of the Tampa Bay Area by the TECO streetcar line.

**Contacts Port Tampa Bay.** ⊠ *1101 Channelside Dr., Tampa* ☎ *813/905–7678, 800/741–2297* ⊕ *www.tampaport.com/cruise.*

**AIRPORT**

**Contacts Tampa International Airport.** ☎ *813/870–8700* ⊕ *www.tampaairport.com.*

**AIRPORT TRANSFERS**

SuperShuttle provides shared van service to and from the airport and the cruise terminal. Expect to pay about $13 to $14 per person.

**Contacts Blue One Transportation.** ☎ *813/282–7351* ⊕ *www.blueone transportation.com.* **SuperShuttle.** ☎ *800/258–3826* ⊕ *www.supershuttle. com.*

**PARKING**

Parking is available at the port directly across from the terminals. For Terminal 2 (Carnival Cruise Lines), parking is in a garage across the street. For Terminal 3 (Royal Caribbean and Norwegian Cruise Line), parking is also in a garage across the street. For Terminal 6 (Holland America Line), parking is outdoors in a guarded, enclosed lot. The cost is $15 a day, payable by credit card (MasterCard or Visa) or in cash in advance; valet parking is available for the same rate but with the addition of a $20 "convenience fee."

> **BEST BETS**
>
> ■ **Busch Gardens.** The area's best theme park is a good family destination.
>
> ■ **Florida Aquarium.** The aquarium is next to the cruise port, so you can just walk, making it a good option even if you have a couple of hours to kill before boarding (they'll even store your luggage if you want to visit after disembarking).
>
> ■ **The Dalí Museum.** One of the finest and most interesting museums in the United States.
>
> ■ **Ybor City.** For nightlife and restaurants, this historic district is Tampa's hot spot.

## EXPLORING

Florida's west-coast crown jewel as well as its business and commercial hub, Tampa has high-rises and heavy traffic. Amid the bustle is the region's greatest concentration of restaurants, nightlife, stores, and cultural events.

FAMILY **Adventure Island.** From spring until fall, rides named Everglides, Gulf Scream, and Key West Rapids promise heat relief at Busch Gardens' water park. Tampa's most popular "wet" park features waterslides and artificial wave pools, along with tranquil "beaches" in a 30-acre package. Try Colossal Curl, a massive thrill ride that's the tallest waterslide in the park. Another of the attraction's headliners, Riptide, challenges you to race three other riders on a sliding mat through twisting tubes and hairpin turns. Planners of this park also took the younger kids into account, with offerings such as Fabian's Funport, which has a scaled-down pool and interactive water gym. Along with a volleyball complex and a rambling river, there are cafés, snack bars, picnic and sunbathing areas, changing rooms, and private cabanas. Good discounts are sometimes offered on the park's website. ✉ *10001 N. McKinley Dr., less than 1 mile north of Busch Gardens, Central Tampa* ☎ *888/800–5447* ⊕ *www.adventureisland.com* 🎫 *$50; parking $12.*

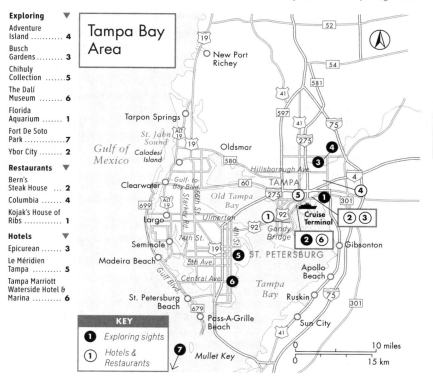

**Tampa Bay Area**

KEY

❶ Exploring sights

① Hotels & Restaurants

**FAMILY**
**Fodor's Choice**
★

**Busch Gardens.** Drawing some 4½ million visitors each year, Busch Gardens Tampa is a major theme park, with seven popular roller coasters being the biggest lure. But this is also a world-class zoo, with more than 2,000 animals, and a live entertainment venue that provides a full day (or more) of fun for the whole family. If you want to beat the crowds, start in the back of the park and work your way around clockwise. The 335-acre adventure park's habitats offer views of some of the world's most endangered and exotic animals. For the best animal sightings, go to their habitats early, when it's cooler. Catering to the shorter set, the Sesame Street Safari of Fun is a 5-acre kids' playground with Sesame-themed rides, shows, and water adventures. The Air Grover Rollercoaster takes kids (and parents) on minidives and twisty turns over the Sahara, while Rosita's Djembe Fly-Away (a swing ride) and Elmo's Safari Go-Round (carousel) get them swinging and screeching. If you're looking to cool off, your best bets are Oscar's Swamp Stomp, Zoe-Patra & the Hippos of the Nile (a flume ride), or Bert & Ernie's Water Hole—complete with bubblers, geysers, water jets, and dumping buckets. Character lunches are available (but you might want to wait until after your rides). ⊠ *10165 N. Malcolm McKinley Dr., Central Tampa* ☎ *813/987–5000, 888/800–5447* ⊕ *www.buschgardens.com* ☞ *$99; parking $15.*

**Fodor's Choice**
★

**Chihuly Collection.** In October 2016, the first permanent collection of world-renowned glass sculptor Dale Chihuly's work received a new, 10,000-square-foot home in an electrifying Albert Alfonso–designed building. Now, such impossibly vibrant, larger-than-life pieces as "Float Boat" and "Ruby Red Icicle" sit next to some of the famed sculptor's smaller and more under-the-radar works. You can tour the museum independently or with one of its volunteer docents (no added cost; tours are given hourly on the half-hour during the week). Each display is perfectly lit, which adds to the drama of Chihuly's designs. Don't miss "Mille Fiore" ("Thousand Flowers"), a spectacular, whimsical glass montage mimicking a wildflower patch, critters and all. Check out the gift shop at the end if you'd like to take some of the magic home with you. A combination ticket gets you a glimpse into Morean Arts Center's glass-blowing studio, where you can watch resident artisans create a unique glass piece before your eyes. ⊠ *720 Central Ave., Downtown* ⊕ *www.moreanartscenter.org/chihuly/* ✉ *$15.*

**Fodor's Choice**
★

**The Dalí Museum.** Inside and out, the waterfront Dalí Museum, which opened on 1/11/11 (Dali is said to have been into numerology), is almost as remarkable as the Spanish surrealist's work. The state-of-the-art building has a surreal geodesic-like glass structure called the Dalí Enigma, as well as an outdoor labyrinth and a DNA-inspired spiral staircase leading up to the collection. All this, before you've even seen the collection, which is one of the most comprehensive of its kind—courtesy of Ohio magnate A. Reynolds Morse, a friend of Dalí's.

Here, you can scope out his early impressionistic works and see how the painter evolved into the visionary he's now seen to be. The mind-expanding paintings in this downtown headliner include *Eggs on a Plate Without a Plate, The Hallucinogenic Toreador,* and more than 90 other oils. You'll also discover more than 2,000 additional works including watercolors, drawings, sculptures, photographs, and objets d'art. The museum also hosts temporary collections from the likes of Pablo Picasso and Andy Warhol. Free hour-long tours are led by well-informed docents. ⊠ *1 Dali Blvd., St. Petersburg* ☎ *727/823–3767* ⊕ *www.thedali.org* ✉ *$24.*

**FAMILY**

**Florida Aquarium.** Although eels, sharks, and stingrays are the headliners, the Florida Aquarium is much more than a giant fishbowl. This architectural landmark features an 83-foot-high, multitier, glass dome; 250,000 square feet of air-conditioned exhibit space; and more than 20,000 aquatic plants and animals representing species native to Florida and the rest of the world—from black-tip sharks to leafy sea dragons.

Floor-to-ceiling interactive displays, behind-the-scenes tours, and in-water adventures allow kids to really get hands-on—and even get their feet wet.

However, you don't have to get wet to have an interactive experience: the Ocean Commotion exhibit offers virtual dolphins and whales and multimedia displays. The Coral Reef Gallery is a 500,000-gallon tank with viewing windows, an awesome 43-foot-wide panoramic opening, and a walk-through tunnel. The Journey to Madagascar exhibit features ring-tailed lemurs, hissing cockroaches, and an Indian Ocean coral reef to showcase the nation's vast diversity of creatures and ecosystems.

If you have an extra 90 minutes, try the Wild Dolphin Adventure Cruise, which takes up to 130 passengers onto Tampa Bay in a 72-foot catamaran for an up-close look at bottlenose dolphins and other wildlife. ⊠ *701 Channelside Dr., Downtown* ☎ *813/273–4000* ⊕ *www. flaquarium.org* ⊠ *Aquarium $24.95; Aquarium/Dolphin Cruise combo $49.90; Penguins Backstage Pass combo $54.95; Behind the Scenes Combo $36.95; Stingray feeding tour combo $38.95; Dive with the Sharks $150; Swim with the Fishes $75; parking $6.*

FAMILY **Fort De Soto Park.** Spread over five small islands, 1,136-acre Fort De Soto Park lies at the mouth of Tampa Bay. It has 7 miles of waterfront (much of it beach), two fishing piers, a 4-mile hiking and skating trail, picnic-and-camping grounds, and a historic fort that kids of any age can explore. The fort for which it's named was built on the southern end of Mullet Key to protect sea lanes in the gulf during the Spanish-American War. Roam the fort or wander the beaches of any of the islands within the park. Kayaks and beach cruisers are available for rental. While most of Tampa Bay's beaches don't allow dogs, Fort De Soto has a somewhat lengthy dog beach for those who can't bear to hit the sand without their best buddy. ⊠ *3500 Pinellas Bayway St., Tierra Verde* ☎ *727/582–2267* ⊕ *www.pinellascounty.org/park/05_ft_desoto.htm* ⊠ *$5.*

**Ybor City.** Tampa's Latin quarter is one of only a few National Historic Landmark districts in Florida. Bordered by Interstate 4 to the north, 22nd Street to the east, Adamo Drive to the south, and Nebraska Avenue to the West, it has antique-brick streets and wrought-iron balconies. Cubans brought their cigar-making industry to Ybor (pronounced *ee*-bore) City in 1886, and the smell of cigars—hand-rolled by Cuban immigrants—still wafts through the heart of this east Tampa area, along with the strong aroma of roasting coffee. These days the neighborhood makes for an interesting visit as empty cigar factories and historic social clubs have been transformed into boutiques, art galleries, restaurants, and nightclubs. However, it can also be seedy and rowdy at times. ⊠ *Ybor City.*

## BEACHES

**Caladesi Island State Park.** Quiet, secluded, and still wild, this 3½-mile-long barrier island is one of the best shelling beaches on the Gulf Coast, second only to Sanibel. The park also has plenty of sights for birders—from common sandpipers to majestic blue herons to rare black skimmers—and miles of trails through scrub oaks, saw palmettos, and cacti (with tenants such as armadillos, rabbits, and raccoons). The landscape also features mangroves and dunes, and the gradual slope of the sea bottom makes this a good spot for novice swimmers and kids. You have to get to Caladesi Island by private boat (there's a 108-slip marina) or through its sister park, Honeymoon Island State Recreation Area, where you take the hourly ferry ride across to Caladesi; ferry rides cost $14 per person. You can also paddle yourself over in a kayak. **Amenities:** food and drink; showers; toilets. **Best for:** solitude; swimming.

✉ *Dunedin Causeway, Dunedin* ☎ *727/469–5918* ⊕ *floridastateparks. org/caladesiisland* 🖾 *$6 per boat; $2 per kayaker.*

FAMILY **Pass-a-Grille Beach.** At the southern tip of St. Pete Beach (past the Don
Fodor's Choice Cesar), this is the epitome of Old Florida. One of the most popular
★ beaches in the area, it skirts the west end of charming, historic Pass-a-Grille, a neighborhood that draws tourists and locals alike with its stylish yet low-key mom-and-pop motels and restaurants. There's a sunset celebration each night. On weekends, check out the Art Mart, an open-air market off the boulevard between 9th and 10th avenues that showcases the work of local artisans. **Amenities:** food and drink; parking; showers; toilets. **Best for:** sunset; windsurfing. ✉ *1000 Pass-a-Grille Way, St. Pete Beach.*

## SHOPPING

**International Plaza.** If you want to grab something at Neiman Marcus or Nordstrom, this is the place. You'll also find Gucci, Tory Burch, Burberry, Michael Kors, Louis Vuitton, and many other upscale shops. Stick around after hours, when watering holes in the mall's courtyard become a high-end club scene. ✉ *2223 N. West Shore Blvd., Airport Area* ⊕ *www.shopinternationalplaza.com.*

**Old Hyde Park Village.** It's a typical upscale shopping district in a quiet, shaded neighborhood near the water. Boutiques and upscale chains like Restoration Hardware and Anthropologie are mixed in with bistros and sidewalk cafés. ✉ *1602 W. Swann Ave., Hyde Park* ⊕ *www. hydeparkvillage.com.*

## NIGHTLIFE

Although there are plenty of boarded storefronts in Ybor City, it has the biggest concentration of nightclubs, as well as the widest variety, most of which are found along 7th Avenue. It becomes a little like Bourbon Street in New Orleans on weekend evenings.

**Gaspar's Grotto.** Spanish pirate Jose Gaspar was known for swashbuckling up and down Florida's west coast in the late 18th and early 19th century. His legend has inspired a massive, raucous street festival each winter. This Ybor City drinkery has adopted his name, and rightly so. Decked out in tons of pirate memorabilia, it's the cornerstone to any night spent barhopping on the Ybor strip. The sangria is a good choice, but the aged rums may be a better fit here. You'll also find a food menu that goes well beyond standard bar fare. ✉ *1805 E. 7th Ave., Ybor City* ☎ *813/248–5900* ⊕ *www.gasparsgrotto.com.*

**The Hub Bar.** Considered something of a dive—but a lovable one—by a loyal and young local following that ranges from esteemed jurists to nose-ring-wearing night owls. The Hub, which dates back to 1946, is known for strong drinks and a jukebox that goes well beyond the usual. ✉ *719 N. Franklin St., Downtown* ☎ *813/229–1553* ⊕ *thehub bartampa.com.*

# WHERE TO EAT

**$$$$**
STEAKHOUSE
**Fodor's**Choice
★

✕ **Bern's Steak House.** With the air of an exclusive club, this is one of—if not the—finest Florida's steak houses. Rich mahogany paneling and ornate chandeliers define the legendary circa 1956 Bern's, where the chef ages his own beef, grows much of his own produce, and roasts his own coffee. There's also a Cave Du Fromage, housing a discriminating selection of artisanal cheeses from around the world. Cuts of prime beef are sold by weight and thickness. There's a 60-ounce strip steak that's big enough to feed your pride (of lions), but for most appetites the veal loin chop or 8-ounce chateaubriand is more than enough. The wine list includes approximately 7,000 selections (with 1,000 dessert wines). After dinner, tour the kitchen and wine cellar before having dessert upstairs in a cozy booth. The dessert room is a hit. ⑤ *Average main: $36* ✉ *1208 S. Howard Ave., Hyde Park* ☎ *813/251–2421* ⊕ *www.bernssteakhouse.com* ⚓ *Reservations essential* ⛉ *Jacket and tie.*

**$$$**
SPANISH
**Fodor's**Choice
★

✕ **Columbia.** Make a date for some of the best Latin cuisine in Tampa. A fixture since 1905, this magnificent structure with an old-world air and spacious dining rooms takes up an entire city block and seems to feed the entire city—locals as well as visitors—throughout the week, but especially on weekends. The paella, bursting with seafood, chicken, and pork, is arguably the best in Florida, and the 1905 salad—with ham, olives, cheese, and garlic—is legendary. The menu has Cuban classics such as *boliche criollo* (tender eye of round stuffed with chorizo), *ropa vieja* (shredded beef with onions, peppers, and tomatoes), and *arroz con pollo* (chicken with yellow rice). Don't miss the flamenco dancing show every night but Sunday. This place is also known for its sangria. If you can, walk around the building and check out the elaborate, antique decor along every inch of the interior. ⑤ *Average main: $23* ✉ *2117 E. 7th Ave., Ybor City* ☎ *813/248–4961* ⊕ *www.columbiarestaurant.com.*

**$**
SOUTHERN

✕ **Kojak's House of Ribs.** Few barbecue joints can boast the staying power of this family-owned and -operated pit stop. Located along a shaded stretch in South Tampa, it debuted in 1978 and has since earned a following of sticky-fingered regulars who have turned it into one of the most popular barbecue stops in central Florida. It's located in a 1927 house complete with veranda, pillars supporting the overhanging roof, and brick steps. Day and night, three indoor dining rooms and an outdoor dining porch have a steady stream of hungry patrons digging into tender pork spareribs that are dry-rubbed and tanned overnight before visiting the smoker for a couple of hours. Then they're bathed in the sauce of your choice. Kojak's also has a nice selection of sandwiches, including chopped barbecue chicken and country-style sausage. ⑤ *Average main: $13* ✉ *2808 W. Gandy Blvd., South Tampa* ☎ *813/837–3774* ⊕ *kojaksbbq.net* ⊘ *Closed Mon.*

## WHERE TO STAY

If you want to be close to the cruise-ship terminal, then you'll have to stay in Tampa; but if you want to spend more time in the area and perhaps stay on the beach, St. Petersburg and the beaches are close by.

**$$**
**HOTEL**
**Fodor's Choice**
**★**

⚏ **Epicurean.** Brought to you in part by the people at Bern's Steak House (which happens to be across the street), this vibrant, cuisine-centric installment of Marriott's Autograph Collection is an absolute must for foodies, but it doesn't make nonfoodies feel left out. **Pros:** excellent service; great location; tons of amenities. **Cons:** can get pricey; exclusive vibe. ⑤ *Rooms from: $240* ⊠ *1207 S. Howard Ave., SoHo* ☎ *813/999–8700, 855/829–2536* ⊕ *epicureanhotel.com* ⤻ *137 rooms* ⏍ *No meals.*

**$$**
**HOTEL**

⚏ **Le Méridien Tampa.** A meticulous renovation transformed this historic, marble-lined former federal courthouse into Tampa's most talked-about boutique hotel. **Pros:** close to downtown attractions; fascinating for history buffs; lots of amenities. **Cons:** traffic in surrounding area can be a nightmare; all that marble makes for loud echoes in the hallways. ⑤ *Rooms from: $269* ⊠ *601 N. Florida Ave., Downtown* ☎ *813/221–9555, 877/782–0116 for reservations* ⊕ *lemeridientampa.com* ⤻ *126 rooms, 4 suites* ⏍ *No meals.*

**$**
**HOTEL**

⚏ **Tampa Marriott Waterside Hotel & Marina.** Across from the Tampa Convention Center, this downtown hotel was built for conventioneers but is also convenient to tourist spots such as the Florida Aquarium and the Ybor City and Hyde Park shopping and nightlife districts. **Pros:** great downtown location; near sights, dining, nightlife. **Cons:** gridlock during rush hour; streets tough to maneuver. ⑤ *Rooms from: $199* ⊠ *700 S. Florida Ave., Downtown* ☎ *888/268–1616 for reservations, 813/221–4900* ⊕ *www.marriott.com* ⤻ *683 rooms, 36 suites* ⏍ *No meals.*

4

# PORTS OF CALL

Nowhere in the world are conditions better suited to cruising than in the Caribbean Sea. Tiny island nations, within easy sailing distance of one another, form a chain of tropical enchantment that curves from Cuba in the north all the way down to the coast of Venezuela. There's far more to life here than sand and coconuts, however. The islands are vastly different, with a variety of cultures, topographies, and languages represented. Colonialism has left its mark, and the presence of the Spanish, French, Dutch, Danish, and British is still felt. Slavery, too, has left its cultural legacy, blending African overtones into the colonial/Indian amalgam. The one constant, however, is the weather. Despite the islands' southerly latitude, the climate is surprisingly gentle, due in large part to the cooling influence of the trade winds.

The Caribbean is made up of the Greater Antilles and the Lesser Antilles. The former consist of those islands closest to the United States: Cuba, Jamaica, Hispaniola (Haiti and the Dominican Republic), and Puerto Rico. (The Cayman Islands lie south of Cuba.) The Lesser Antilles, including the Virgin, Windward, and Leeward islands and others, are greater in number but smaller in size, and constitute the southern half of the Caribbean chain.

## GOING ASHORE

Traveling by cruise ship presents an opportunity to visit many places in a short time. The flip side is that your stay in each port of call will be brief. For this reason cruise lines offer shore excursions, which maximize passengers' time. There are a number of advantages to shore excursions arranged by your ship: in some destinations, transportation may be unreliable, and a ship-packaged tour is the best way to see distant sights. Also, you don't have to worry about missing the ship. The disadvantage of a shore excursion is the cost—you usually pay more for the convenience of having the ship do the legwork for you, but it's not always a lot more. Of course, you can always book a tour independently, hire a taxi, or use foot power to explore on your own. For each port of call included in this guide we've provided some suggestions for the best ship-sponsored excursions—in terms of both quality of experience and price—as well as some suggestions for what to do if you want to explore on your own.

## ARRIVING IN PORT

When your ship arrives in a port, it will tie up alongside a dock or anchor out in a harbor. If the ship is docked, passengers walk down the gangway to go ashore. Docking makes it easy to move between the shore and the ship.

### TENDERING

If your ship anchors in the harbor, you will have to take a small boat—called a launch or tender—to get ashore. Tendering is a nuisance, but participants in ship-sponsored shore excursions are given priority.

> ## BUYING LIQUOR AND PERFUME
>
> If you buy duty-free liquor or perfume while in a Caribbean port, don't forget that you may not bring it aboard your flight home. You will have to put it in your checked bags. Many liquor stores will pack your bottles in bubble wrap and pack them in a good cardboard box. Take advantage of this service.

**4**

Passengers wishing to disembark independently may be required to gather in a public room, get sequenced tendering passes, and wait until their numbers are called. The ride to shore may take as long as 20 minutes. If you don't like waiting, plan to go ashore an hour or so after the ship drops its anchor. On a very large ship, the wait for a tender can be quite long and frustrating.

Because tenders can be difficult to board, passengers with mobility problems may not be able to visit certain ports. The larger ships are more likely to use tenders. It is usually possible to learn before booking a cruise whether the ship will dock or anchor at its ports of call.

Before anyone is allowed to walk down the gangway or board a tender, the ship must be cleared for landing. Immigration and customs officials board the vessel to examine the ship's manifest or possibly passports and sort through red tape. It may be more than an hour before you're allowed ashore. You will be issued a boarding pass, which you'll need to get back on board.

### RETURNING TO THE SHIP

Cruise lines are strict about sailing times, which are posted at the gangway and elsewhere and announced in the daily schedule of activities. Be sure to be back on board (not on the dock waiting to get a tender back to the ship) at least an hour before the announced sailing time or you may be stranded. If you are on a shore excursion that was sold by the cruise line, however, the captain will wait for your group before casting off. That is one reason many passengers prefer ship-packaged tours.

If you're not on one of the ship's tours and the ship sails without you, immediately contact the cruise line's port representative, whose phone number is often listed on the daily schedule of activities. You may be able to hitch a ride on a pilot boat, although that is unlikely. Passengers who miss the boat must pay their own way to the next port.

## CARIBBEAN ESSENTIALS

### CURRENCY

The U.S. dollar is the official currency on Puerto Rico, the U.S. Virgin Islands, the Turks and Caicos, Bonaire, and the British Virgin Islands. On Grand Cayman you will usually have a choice of Cayman or U.S. dollars when you take money out of an ATM, and you may even be able to get change in U.S. dollars. In Cozumel, Calica, Costa Maya, and Progreso, the Mexican peso is the official currency. The euro is used in a handful of French islands (St. Barth, St. Martin, Martinique, Guadeloupe). In most Caribbean ports U.S. paper currency (not coins) is accepted readily. When you pay in dollars you'll almost always get change in local currency, so it's best to carry bills in small denominations. If you need local currency (say, for a trip to one of the French islands that uses the euro), change money at a local bank or use an ATM for the best rate. Most major credit cards are accepted all over the Caribbean, except at local market stalls and small establishments.

### KEEPING IN TOUCH

Internet cafés are now fairly common on many islands, and you'll sometimes find Internet cafés in the cruise-ship terminal itself—or perhaps in an attached or nearby shopping center. If you want to call home, most cruise-ship terminal facilities have phones that accept credit cards or local phone cards (local phone cards are almost always the cheapest option). And on most islands GSM multiband mobile phones will work, though roaming charges may be steep (some plans include Puerto Rico and the U.S. Virgin Islands in their nationwide calling regions).

### WHERE TO EAT

Cuisine on the Caribbean's islands is as varied as the islands themselves. The region's history as a colonial battleground and ethnic melting pot creates plenty of variety and adds lots of unusual tropical fruit and spices. In fact, the one quality that defines most Caribbean cooking is its spiciness, acquired from nutmeg, mace, allspice, peppers, saffron, and many other seasonings grown on the islands. Dress is generally casual, although throughout the islands beachwear is inappropriate most anywhere except on the beach. Unless otherwise noted, prices are given in U.S. dollars.

### SHORE EXCURSIONS

Typical excursions include an island or town bus tour, a visit to a beach or rum factory, a boat trip, a snorkeling or diving trip, and charter fishing. In recent years, however, shore excursions have gotten more adventurous, with mild river-rafting, parasailing, jet-skiing, hiking, and biking added to the mix. It's often easier to take a ship-arranged excursion, but it's almost never the cheapest option.

If you prefer to break away from the pack, find a knowledgeable taxi driver or tour operator—they're usually within a stone's throw of the pier—or wander around on your own. A group of four to six people will usually find this option more economical and practical than will a single person or a couple.

Renting a car is also a good option on many islands—again, the more people, the better the deal. But get a good island map before you set off, and be sure to find out how long it will take you to get around.

Conditions are ideal for water sports of all kinds—scuba diving, snorkeling, windsurfing, sailing, waterskiing, and fishing excursions abound. Your shore-excursion director can usually arrange these activities for you if the ship offers no formal excursion.

## PRIVATE ISLANDS

By Linda Coffman

When evaluating the "best" Caribbean ports of call, many repeat cruise passengers often add the cruise lines' own private islands to their lists of preferred destinations.

The cruise lines established "private" islands to provide a beach break on an island (or part of one) reserved for their exclusive use. While most passengers don't select an itinerary based solely upon calling at a private island, they usually consider them a highlight of their cruise vacation. The very least you can expect of your private island is lush foliage and a wide swath of beach surrounded by azure water. Facilities vary, but a beach barbecue, water-sports equipment rental, lounge chairs, hammocks, and restrooms are standard. Youth counselors come ashore to conduct sand-castle building competitions and lead junior pirates on swashbuckling island treasure hunts.

The use of strollers and wheelchairs equipped with all-terrain wheels may be offered on a complimentary first-come, first-served basis. However, with the exception of some participation sports on the beach, plan to pay for most water toys and activities. Costs associated with private-island fun and recreation can range from $9 for use of a snorkel vest (you may use your own snorkel equipment; however, in the event a floatation vest is required for safety, you must rent one) to $25 to $30 for rental of an entire snorkeling outfit for the day (mask, fins, snorkel vest, a mesh bag, fish identification card, and fish food). You can often take a banana-boat ride for $19 (15-minute ride), sail a small boat or catamaran for $30 to $50 (one hour), paddle a kayak for $29 to $64 (half-hour to 3½ hours), ride Jet Skis for $59 to $99 (45 minutes to one hour), parasail for a hefty $79 to $119 (10 minutes or less), or fly through the treetops on a zip line for $93. Floating mats or inner tubes are a relative bargain at $6 to $12 for all-day lounging in the water. You might also find open-air massage cabanas with pricing comparable to the spa charges onboard.

There is generally no charge for food or basic beverages such as those served onboard ship. Soft drinks and tropical cocktails can usually be charged to your shipboard account, as can paid activities like motorized water sports, stingray encounters, private cabanas, and other options that vary by cruise line. With the introduction of more resort-style amenities on private islands, there are more opportunities to spend money on things like dining in restaurants that carry a charge.

You might want to bring a small amount of cash ashore for souvenir shopping, which is almost always possible from vendors set up on or

**U.S.A.** Miami

Key West

NASSAU

T H E  B A H A M A S

HAVANA

Turks
and
Caicos
Islands

**CUBA**

Cuba

GEORGE
TOWN

Little
Cayman

Cayman
Brac

Grand
Cayman

Montego
Bay

Ocho Rios

Puerto Plata

**HAITI**

*Hispaniola*

Jamaica

KINGSTON

PORT-AU-PRINCE

G R E A T E R

*Caribbean*

Panama
Canal

Colon **PANAMA**

PANAMA CITY

Cartagena

Maracaibo

**COLOMBIA**

# Caribbean

4

ATLANTIC OCEAN

LEEWARD ISLANDS

DOMINICAN
REPUBLIC

St. John Tortola
St. Thomas    Virgin Gorda
Anguilla
St. Barthélemy
SANTO
DOMINGO    SAN JUAN
St. Maarten/
St. Martin    Saba    Barbuda
Puerto    St.    St. Eustatius
Rico    Croix    St. Kitts    Antigua
Nevis
Montserrat    Marie
Galante
Guadeloupe    WINDWARD ISLANDS

A N T I L L E S

Dominica
Martinique
FORT-DE-FRANCE
St. Lucia

Sea

St. Vincent
Bequia
The
Grenadines
Carriacou    BRIDGETOWN
Barbados

ST. GEORGE'S
WILLEMSTAD    Islas Los
Grenada
Aruba    Roques
Bonaire    Tobago
Curaçao    L E S S E R    A N T I L L E S
PORT OF SPAIN
La Guaira    Trinidad
CARACAS

VENEZUELA

0        200 miles
0        300 km

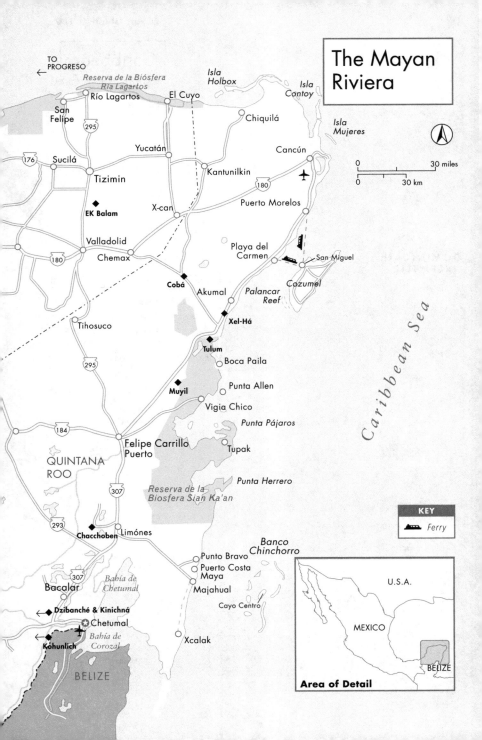

near the beach. You will also want to bring beach towels ashore and return them to the ship at the end of the day, because, as Princess Cruises reminds passengers, "Although the locals may offer to do this for you, unfortunately we seldom see the towels again!"

Even if you do nothing more than lie in a shaded hammock and sip fruity tropical concoctions, the day can be one of the most fun and relaxing of your entire cruise.

## ISLANDS BY CRUISE LINE

Carnival Cruise Lines is currently the only major cruise line without an extensive private island experience available to the entire fleet. However, select Carnival itineraries include calls at Half Moon Cay, Holland America Line's private paradise, where "Fun Ship" passengers can use all the facilities and participate in organized activities. Similarly, certain Regent Seven Seas cruises include beach days at Cayo Levantado, located off the Samaná Peninsula on the northeast coast of the Dominican Republic.

Although they do not stop at "private islands" in the strictest sense, the smaller ships of Seabourn and SeaDream offer passengers a day ashore on secluded private beaches where they can enjoy lavish barbecues and take a break from swimming and snorkeling to indulge in champagne and caviar served in the surf.

### AZAMARA CLUB CRUISES, CELEBRITY CRUISES, ROYAL CARIBBEAN

Royal Caribbean, Azamara Club Cruises, and Celebrity Cruises passengers have twice as many opportunities to visit a private island. The lines share two, and many Caribbean itineraries include one or the other.

**Coco Cay.** Coco Cay is a 140-acre island in the Berry Island chain between Nassau and Freeport. Originally known as Little Stirrup Cay, it's within view of Great Stirrup Cay (NCL's private island) and the snorkeling is just as good, especially around a sunken airplane and a replica of Blackbeard's flagship, *Queen Anne's Revenge*. In addition to activities and games ashore, Coco Cay has one of the largest Aqua Parks in the Caribbean, where children and adults alike can jump on an in-water trampoline or climb a floating sand castle before they dig into a beach barbecue or explore a nature trail. Attractions also include an inflatable 40-foot waterslide (fun for adults and kids alike) and a stingray encounter, where participants can feed and pet the gentle creatures. Rounding out the facilities are a Bahamian marketplace, several beach bars, rental cabanas, and numerous hammocks for relaxation in the sun or shade. **Activities:** scuba diving, snorkeling, jet-skiing, kayaking, parasailing, hiking, volleyball, organized games, shopping. ⊠ *Coco Cay* ⊕ *www.royalcaribbean.com.*

**Labadee.** Labadee is a 260-acre peninsula approximately 6 miles (10 km) from Cap Haitien on the secluded north coast of Haiti (the port of call is occasionally called "Hispaniola"). Passengers can step ashore on the dock, from which water taxis and five different walking paths, trails, and avenues lead to many areas throughout the peninsula, including the Labadee Town Square and Dragon's Plaza, where a welcome center and central tram station are located. In addition to swimming, water sports, an Aqua Park with floating trampolines and waterslides, and nature trails to explore, bonuses on Labadee are an authentic folkloric show presented by island performers and a market featuring work of local artists and crafters, where you might find an interesting painting or unique wood carving. Only cash is accepted, and bargaining is expected in the market. More adventurous activities include an Alpine Coaster, a thrilling roller-coaster experience, and one of the most exciting—and at 2,600 feet in length the longest—zip-line experiences in the Caribbean, which takes place 500 feet above the beaches of Labadee, where riders can reach speeds of 40 to 50 mph over the water. The use of beach chairs is complimentary; however, tipping the beach attendants for their service is always appreciated. The Barefoot Beach Club & Cabanas is reserved for top suite guests and those who rent one of the 20 cabanas, which can accommodate four to five guests. Only the nine Palm Cabanas are wheelchair-accessible, but even they have two steps to climb. **Activities:** snorkeling, jet-skiing, kayaking, parasailing, zip-lining, hiking, volleyball, organized games, shopping. ⊠ *Labadee* ⊕ *www.royalcaribbean.com.*

## COSTA CRUISES

**Catalina Island.** An unspoiled island paradise, Costa's Catalina Island is just off the coast of the Dominican Republic. Passengers can participate in Costa's "Beach Olympics," schedule a seaside massage, or just kick back on a chaise longue or a complimentary water float. Water-toy rentals, banana-boat rides, and sailing tours are available from independent concessionaires. Local vendors set up souvenir shops offering crafts and T-shirts. The ship provides the food for a lunch barbecue and tropical beverages at the beach bar. **Activities:** snorkeling, sailing, jet-skiing, waterskiing, hiking, volleyball, organized games, massages, shopping. ⊠ *Parc Nacional Isla Catalina, Isla Catalina* ⊕ *www.costacruise.com.*

## DISNEY CRUISE LINE

**Castaway Cay.** Disney's Castaway Cay has a dock, so passengers simply step ashore (rather than tendering, as is required to reach most cruise lines' private islands). Like everything associated with Disney, the line's private island is almost too good to be true. Located in the Abacos, a chain in the Bahamas, only 10% of Castaway Cay is developed, leaving plenty of unspoiled area to explore in Robinson Crusoe fashion. Trams are provided to reach separate beaches designated for children, teens, families, and adults, and areas where Disney offers age-specific activities and extensive, well-planned children's activities. Biking and hiking are so popular that two nature trails—one of them with an observation tower—are mapped out. Passengers can swim to a water platform complete with two slides or cool off in a 2,400-square-foot water-play area equipped with water jets and a splash pad. A 1,200-square-foot soft wet deck area provides freshwater fun for children with an array of pop jets, geysers, and bubblers. There is no charge for the water-play facilities. Excursions range from as passive as a glass-bottom-boat tour to the soaring excitement of parasailing. An interactive experience with stingrays is educational and safe—the gentle creatures' barbs are blunted for safety. In addition to barbecue fare served in two buffet areas with covered seating and several beverage stations, beach games, island-style music, and a shaded game pavilion, there are shops, massage cabanas by the sea, and even a post office. Popular with couples as well as families, private rental cabanas provide the luxury of a deluxe beach retreat with an option to add the personalized service of a cabana host. Teens have their own private retreat just steps from the beach. **Activities:** snorkeling, kayaking, parasailing, sailing, jet-skiing, paddleboats, water cycles, fishing, bicycles, basketball, billiards, hiking, Ping-Pong, shuffleboard, soccer, volleyball. ⊕ *disneycruise.disney.go.com.*

## HOLLAND AMERICA LINE, CARNIVAL CRUISE LINE

**Half Moon Cay.** Little San Salvador, one of the Bahamian out-islands, was renamed Half Moon Cay by Holland America Line to honor Henry Hudson's ship (depicted on the cruise line's logo) as well as to reflect the beach's crescent shape. Even after development, the island is still so unspoiled that it has been named a Wild Bird Preserve by the Bahamas National Trust. Passengers, who are welcomed ashore at a West Indies Village complete with shops and straw market, find Half Moon Cay easily accessible—all facilities are connected by hard-surfaced and packed-sand pathways and meet or exceed ADA requirements. An accessible tram also connects the welcome center with the food pavilion and bars; wheelchairs with balloon tires are available. In addition to the beach area for lazing in the sun or in the shade of a rented clamshell, the island has a post office, Bahamian-style chapel, a lagoon where you can interact with stingrays, and the Captain Morgan on the Rocks Island Bar in a "beached" pirate ship. For family fun, you'll find a beachfront water park with waterslides and fanciful sea creatures tethered to the sandy bottom of the shallow water. Massage services are available, as are fitness activities. Air-conditioned Cabanas, two-story Beach Villas with hot tubs on the second floor, and a Grand Cabana that features an eight-person hot tub and a slide from the cabana deck straight into the ocean can be rented for the day, with or without the services of your own butler. **Activities:** scuba diving, snorkeling, windsurfing, kayaking, parasailing, sailing, jet-skiing, Aqua Bikes, fishing, bicycles, basketball, hiking, horseback riding, shuffleboard, volleyball, massages, shopping. ✉ *Half Moon Cay* ⊕ *www.hollandamerica.com.*

## NORWEGIAN CRUISE LINE

**Great Stirrup Cay.** Only 120 miles east of Fort Lauderdale in the Berry Island chain of the Bahamas, much of Great Stirrup Cay looks as it did when it was acquired by Norwegian Cruise Line in 1977, with bougainvillea, sea grape, and coconut palms as abundant as the colorful tropical fish that inhabit the reef. The first uninhabited island purchased to offer cruise-ship passengers a private beach day, Great Stirrup Cay's white-sand beaches are fringed by coral and ideal for swimming and snorkeling. Permanent facilities have been added to and improved in the intervening years and a seawall was erected to reduce beach erosion and preserve the environment. A straw market, water-sports centers, bars, volleyball courts, beachside massage stations, a food pavilion, complimentary taco bar, à la carte Land Shark Bar & Grill, and a 40-feet high and 175-feet long Hippo inflatable waterslide round out the facilities. Complimentary sand wheelchairs are available on the island. For ease of access, an expansive boardwalk extends along the main beach and a paved pathway is located along the seawall. Extensive island improvements began in 2010 with the excavation of a new entrance channel for tenders and construction of tender docking facilities and a welcome pavilion that is now the site for landings. As a result, the beachfront has been expanded significantly to alleviate crowding. Private beachfront rental cabanas, two dining facilities, a kid's play area, wave runners, a floating Aqua Park with a variety of water toys, kayak tours through man-made rivers within the island, an ecocruise, and a stingray encounter experience are additional amenities. Planned for 2017 is a resort-style lagoon retreat featuring a secluded beach, luxury beach villas, and exclusive dining options. **Activities:** snorkeling, kayaking, parasailing, sailing, paddleboats, Ping-Pong, hiking, volleyball, basketball, organized games, massages, shopping. ⊠ *Great Stirrup Cay* ⊕ *www.ncl.com.*

**Harvest Caye.** Off the coast of southern Belize, Norwegian has developed the very elaborate Harvest Caye. The resort-style island stop features a pier and a large marina, which serves as a gateway for excursions to explore the mainland, including trips to Mayan ruins, river rafting, and nature tours. The heart of Harvest Caye is a 7-acre beach where 11 enclosed beach villas with concierge service, a/c, and exclusive dining and beverage services are available for rent. A resort-style pool has a swim-up bar, lounge chairs and umbrellas, and 15 cabanas for rent. A 130-foot "Flighthouse" offers a variety of aerial activities including a zip line, suspension bridges, free-fall jumps, a tandem "superman" style zip, and a fun ropes course located on a platform in the saltwater lagoon. The shopping village mixes popular name-brand retailers as well as items from local Belizean craftspeople. The island also has dining and bar options (available for an extra charge), including an indoor/outdoor Landshark Bar & Grill (an expansion of Norwegian's partnership with Jimmy Buffett's Margaritaville); street vendors, and grills at the beach and in the marina. **Activities:** kayaking, paddle boarding, and canoeing in the lagoon area, snorkeling, bird-watching, shopping.

## PRINCESS CRUISES

**Princess Cays.** Princess Cays is a 40-acre haven on the southern tip of Eleuthera Island in the Bahamas. Not quite an uninhabited island, it nevertheless offers a wide ribbon of beach, long enough for passengers to splash in the surf, relax in a hammock, or limbo to the beat of local music and never feel crowded. In a similar fashion to booking shore excursions: snorkeling equipment, sea boards, floats, kayaks, paddle wheelers, banana boat rides, aqua chairs, beach clamshells, and bungalows can be prereserved on Princess Cruises' website. All other equipment and activities must be booked onboard. Nestled in a picturesque palm grove, private bungalows with air-conditioning and ceiling fans and a deck for lounging can be rented for parties of up to six. The Sanctuary at Princess Cays, complete with bungalows for parties of four (two additional guests may be added at an additional charge), is an adults-only haven. A pirate-theme play area for children is supervised. In addition to three tropical bars and the area where a Bahamian barbecue is served, permanent facilities include small shops that sell island crafts and trinkets; but if you head around the back and through the fence, independent vendors sell similar goods for lower prices. **Activities:** snorkeling, kayaking, banana boat rides, sailing, paddleboats, Aqua Bikes, windsurfing, surf fishing, deep sea fishing, hiking, organized games, shopping. ⊠ *Princess Cays* ⊕ *www.princess.com.*

# ANTIGUA (ST. JOHN'S)

By Jordan
Simon

Some say Antigua has so many beaches that you could visit a different one every day for a year. Most have snow-white sand, and many are backed by lavish resorts that offer sailing, diving, windsurfing, and snorkeling. The largest of the British Leeward Islands, Antigua was the headquarters from which Lord Horatio Nelson (then a mere captain) made his forays against the French and pirates in the late 18th century. You may wish to explore English Harbour and its carefully restored Nelson's Dockyard, as well as tour old forts, historic churches, and tiny villages. Appealing aspects of the island's interior include a small tropical rain forest ideal for hiking and zip-lining, ancient Native American archaeological digs, and restored sugar mills. Due to time constraints, it's best to make trips this far from port with an experienced tour operator, but you can easily take a taxi to any number of fine beaches on your own and escape from the hordes descending from the ship.

**ESSENTIALS**

**CURRENCY**

Eastern Caribbean (EC) dollar. U.S. dollars are generally accepted.

**TELEPHONE**

GSM tri-band mobile phones from the United States and United Kingdom usually work on Antigua; you can also rent one from LIME (formerly Cable & Wireless) and APUA (Antigua Public Utilities Authority). Basic rental costs range between EC$25 and EC$50 per day. You can use the LIME Phone Card (available in $5, $10, and $20 denominations in most hotels and post offices) for local and long-distance calls.

**COMING ASHORE**

Though some ships dock at the deepwater harbor in downtown St. John's, most use Heritage Quay, a multimillion-dollar complex with shops, condominiums, a casino, and restaurants. Most St. John's attractions are an easy walk from Heritage Quay; the older part of the city is eight blocks away. A tourist information booth is in the main docking building.

If you intend to explore beyond St. John's, consider hiring a taxi driver–guide. Taxis meet every cruise ship. They're unmetered; fares are fixed, and drivers are required to carry a rate card. Agree on the fare before setting off (make sure you know whether the price quoted is one-way or round-trip), and plan to tip drivers 10%. Some cabbies may take you from St. John's to English Harbour and wait for a "reasonable" amount of time (about a half hour) while you look around, for about $50; you can usually arrange an island tour for around $25 per hour. Renting your own car usually isn't practical, since you must purchase a $20 temporary driving permit in addition to the car-rental fee, which is usually about $50 per day in the high season.

## EXPLORING

### ST. JOHN'S

Antigua's capital, with some 45,000 inhabitants (approximately half the island's population), lies at sea level at the inland end of a sheltered northwestern bay. Although it has seen better days, a couple of notable historic sights and some good waterfront shopping areas make it worth a visit.

At the far south end of town, where Market Street forks into Valley and All Saints roads, haggling goes on every Friday and Saturday, when locals jam the **Public Market** to buy and sell fruits, vegetables, fish, and spices. Ask before you aim a camera; your subject may expect a tip. This is old-time Caribbean shopping: a jambalaya of sights, sounds, and smells.

> **BEST BETS**
>
> ■ **Dickenson Bay Beach.** One of Antigua's best beaches.
>
> ■ **Ecotourism.** Explore the island's forested interior on foot or surrounding coves by kayak.
>
> ■ **Jolly Harbour.** A cheap day pass at the Jolly Harbour Resort is a great day at the beach.
>
> ■ **Nelson's Dockyard.** This is one of the Caribbean's best historic sights, with many stores, restaurants, and bars.
>
> ■ **St. John's.** There's excellent duty-free shopping, especially in Heritage Quay and Redcliffe Quay.

**Anglican Cathedral of St. John the Divine.** At the south gate of the Anglican Cathedral of St. John the Divine are figures of St. John the Baptist and St. John the Divine, said to have been taken from one of Napoléon's ships and brought to Antigua. The original church was built in 1681, replaced by a stone building in 1745, and destroyed by an earthquake in 1843. The present neo-baroque building dates from 1845; the parishioners had the interior completely encased in pitch pine, hoping to forestall future earthquake damage. Tombstones bear eerily eloquent testament to the colonial days. ⊠ *Between Long and Newgate Sts., St. John's* ☎ *268/461–0082.*

**Heritage Quay.** Shopaholics head directly for Heritage Quay, an ugly multimillion-dollar complex. The two-story buildings contain stores that sell duty-free goods, sportswear, down-island imports (paintings, T-shirts, straw baskets), and local crafts. There are also restaurants, a bandstand, and a casino. Cruise-ship passengers disembark here from the 500-foot-long pier. Expect heavy shilling. ⊠ *High and Thames Sts., St. John's* ⊕ *www.heritagequayantigua.com.*

**Museum of Antigua and Barbuda.** Signs at the Museum of Antigua and Barbuda say "Please touch," encouraging you to explore Antigua's past. Try your hand at the educational video games or squeeze a cassava through a *matapi* (grass sieve). Exhibits interpret the nation's history, from its geological birth to its political independence in 1981. There are fossil and coral remains from some 34 million years ago; models of a sugar plantation and a wattle-and-daub house; an Arawak canoe; and a wildly eclectic assortment of objects from cannonballs to 1920s telephone exchanges. The museum occupies the former courthouse, which dates from 1750. The superlative museum gift shop carries such unusual

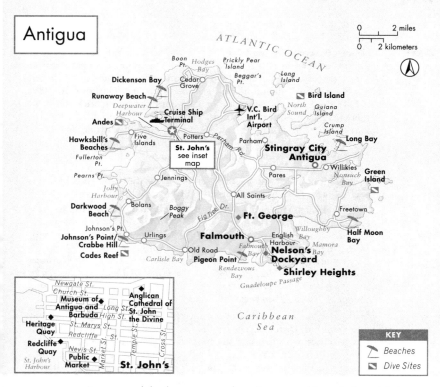

Antigua

ATLANTIC OCEAN

Boon Pt. · Hodges Bay · Prickly Pear Island · Beggar's Pt. · Long Island

Dickenson Bay · Cedar Grove
Runaway Beach · Bird Island
Deepwater Harbour · Cruise Ship Terminal · V.C. Bird Int'l. Airport · North Sound · Guiana Island
Andes
Hawksbill's Beaches · Five Islands · Potters · Parham · Crump Island · Long Bay
Fullerton Pt. · St. John's see inset map · Parham Rd. · Stingray City Antigua
Pearns Pt. · Jennings · Pares · Willikies · Green Island · Nonsuch Bay
Jolly Harbour · All Saints
Darkwood Beach · Bolans · Boggy Peak · Fig Tree Dr. · Ft. George · Freetown
Johnson's Pt. · Willoughby
Johnson's Point/ Crabbe Hill · Urlings · Falmouth · English Harbour · Mamora · Half Moon Bay
Cades Reef · Old Road · Falmouth Bay · Nelson's Bay
Carlisle Bay · Pigeon Point · Dockyard
Rendezvous Bay · Shirley Heights
Guadeloupe Passage

Caribbean Sea

0  2 miles
0  2 kilometers

**St. John's** (inset map)
Newgate St. · Church St. · Museum of Antigua and Barbuda · Long St. · High St. · Anglican Cathedral of St. John the Divine · St. Marys St. · Heritage Quay · Redcliffe St. · Redcliffe Quay · Nevis St. · Public Market · Temple St. · Market St. · Cross St. · St. John's Harbour · **St. John's**

KEY
⤢ Beaches
◥ Dive Sites

items as calabash purses, seed earrings, warri boards (warri being an African game brought to the Caribbean), and lignum vitae pipes, as well as historic maps and local books (including engrossing monographs on varied subjects by the late Desmond Nicholson, a longtime resident). ✉ *Long and Market Sts., St. John's* ☎ *268/462–1469, 268/462–4930* ⊕ *www.antiguamuseums.net* 🎟 *$3; children under 12 free.*

**Fodor's Choice** **Redcliffe Quay.** Redcliffe Quay, at the water's edge just south of Heritage
★ Quay, is the most appealing part of St. John's. Attractively restored (and superbly re-created) 19th-century buildings in a riot of cotton-candy colors house shops, restaurants, galleries, and boutiques are linked by courtyards and landscaped walkways. ✉ *Redcliffe St., St. John's* ⊕ *www.historicredcliffequay.com.*

## ELSEWHERE ON ANTIGUA

**Falmouth.** This town sits on a lovely bay backed by former sugar plantations and sugar mills. The most important historic site here is St. Paul's Church, which was rebuilt on the site of a church once used by troops during the Horatio Nelson period.

**Ft. George.** East of Liberta—one of the first settlements founded by freed slaves—on Monk's Hill, this fort was built between 1689 and 1720. Among the ruins are the sites for 32 cannons, water cisterns, the base of the old flagstaff, and some of the original buildings. ⊠ *Great Fort George Monk's Hill Trail, St. Paul.*

**Nelson's Dockyard.** Now a UNESCO World Heritage Site, Antigua's most famous attraction is the world's only Georgian-era dockyard still in use, a treasure trove for history buffs and nautical nuts alike. When the Royal Navy abandoned the station at English Harbour in 1889, it fell into a state of decay, though adventuresome yachties still lived there in near-primitive conditions. The Society of the Friends of English Harbour began restoring it in 1951; it reopened with great fanfare as Nelson's Dockyard on November 14, 1961. Within the compound are crafts shops, restaurants, and two splendidly restored 18th-century hotels. Water taxis will ferry you between points for EC$5. The Dockyard National Park also includes serene nature trails accessing beaches, rock pools, and crumbling plantation ruins and hilltop forts.

The **Dockyard Museum,** in the original Naval Officer's House, presents ship models, mock-ups of English Harbour, displays on the people who worked there and typical ships that docked, silver regatta trophies, maps, prints, antique navigational instruments, and Nelson's very own telescope and tea caddy. ⊠ *Dockyard Dr., English Harbour Town* ☎ *268/481–5027, 268/460–1379 both for Dockyard Museum, 268/481–5021 for National Parks Authority* ⊕ *www.nationalparks antigua.com* ✎ *$2 suggested donation.*

**Shirley Heights.** This bluff affords a spectacular view of English Harbour and Falmouth Harbour. The heights are named for Sir Thomas Shirley, the governor who fortified the harbor in 1781. At the top is Shirley Heights Lookout, a restaurant built into the remnants of the 18th-century fortifications. Most notable for its boisterous Sunday barbecues that continue into the night with live music and dancing, it serves dependable burgers, pumpkin soup, grilled meats, and rum punches.

Not far from Shirley Heights is the **Dows Hill Interpretation Centre,** where observation platforms provide still more sensational vistas of the English Harbour area. A multimedia sound-and-light presentation on island history and culture, spotlighting lifelike figures and colorful tableaux accompanied by running commentary and music, results in a cheery, if bland, portrait of Antiguan life from Amerindian times to the present. ⊠ *Dockyard Dr., Shirley Heights* ☎ *268/481–5045, 268/481–5021* ⊕ *www.nationalparksantigua.com* ✎ *EC$15.*

## BEACHES

**Dickenson Bay.** Along a lengthy stretch of well-kept powder-soft white sand and exceptionally calm water, you can find small and large hotels (including Siboney Beach Club, Sandals, and Rex Halcyon Cove), water sports, concessions, and beachfront restaurants (Coconut Grove and Ana's on the Beach are recommended). There's decent snorkeling at either point. **Amenities:** food and drink; water sports. **Best for:** partiers; snorkeling; swimming; walking. ⊠ *2 miles (3 km) northeast of St. John's, along main coast road.*

**Johnson's Point/Crabbe Hill.** This series of connected, deserted beaches on the southwest coast looks out toward Montserrat, Guadeloupe, and St. Kitts. Notable beach bar–restaurants include OJ's, Jacqui O's Beach-House, and Turner's. The water is generally placid, though not good for snorkeling. **Amenities:** food and drink. **Best for:** sunset; swimming; walking. ✉ *3 miles (5 km) south of Jolly Harbour complex, on main west-coast road.*

**Pigeon Point.** Near Falmouth Harbour lie two fine white-sand beaches reasonably free of seaweed and driftwood. The leeward side is calmer, the windward side is rockier, and there are sensational views and snorkeling around the point. Several restaurants and bars are nearby, though Bumpkin's (and its potent banana coladas) and the more upscale bustling Catherine's Cafe Plage satisfy most on-site needs. **Amenities:** food and drink. **Best for:** snorkeling; swimming; walking. ✉ *Off main south-coast road, southwest of Falmouth.*

## SHOPPING

Fodor'sChoice ★ **Heritage Quay,** in St. John's, has 35 shops—including many that are duty-free—that cater to the cruise-ship crowd, which docks almost at its doorstep. Outlets here include Benetton, the Body Shop, Sunglass Hut, Dolce & Gabbana, and Oshkosh B'Gosh. There are also shops along **St. John's, St. Mary's, High,** and **Long Streets.** The tangerine-and-lilac-hue four-story **Vendor's Mall** at the intersection of Redcliffe and Thames streets gathers the pushy, pesky vendors who once clogged the narrow streets. It's jammed with stalls; air-conditioned indoor shops sell some higher-price, if not higher-quality, merchandise. On the west coast the Mediterranean-style, arcaded **Jolly Harbour Marina** holds some interesting galleries and shops, as do the marinas and the main road snaking around English and Falmouth harbors.

**Redcliffe Quay,** on the waterfront at the south edge of St. John's, is by far the most appealing shopping area. Several restaurants and more than 30 boutiques, many with one-of-a-kind wares, are set around landscaped courtyards shaded by colorful trees.

## ACTIVITIES

### ADVENTURE TOURS

**Adventure Antigua.** The enthusiastic Eli Fuller, who is knowledgeable not only about the ecosystem and geography of Antigua but also about its history and politics (his grandfather was the American consul), runs Adventure Antigua. His thorough seven-hour excursion (Eli dubs it "re-creating my childhood explorations") includes stops at Guiana Island (for lunch and guided snorkeling; turtles, barracuda, and stingrays are common sightings), Pelican Island (more snorkeling), Bird Island (hiking to vantage points to admire the soaring ospreys and frigate and red-billed tropic birds), and Hell's Gate (a striking limestone rock formation where the more intrepid may hike and swim through sunken caves and tide pools painted with pink and maroon algae). The company also offers a fun "Xtreme Circumnavigation" variation on a racing boat catering to adrenaline junkies who "feel the need for speed." It also visits Stingray City and Nelson's Dockyard, and offers a more sedate Antigua Classic Yacht sail-and-snorkel experience that explains the rich West Indian history of boatbuilding. ☎ *268/727–3261, 268/726–6355* ⊕ *www.adventureantigua.com.*

FAMILY **Stingray City Antigua.** Stingray City Antigua is a carefully reproduced "natural" environment nicknamed by staffers the "retirement home," though the 30-plus stingrays, ranging from infants to seniors, are frisky. You can stroke, feed, even hold the striking gliders ("they're like puppy dogs," one guide swears), as well as snorkel in deeper, protected waters. The tour guides do a marvelous job of explaining the animals' habits, from feeding to breeding, and their predators (including man). ✉ *Seaton's Village* ☎ *268/562–7297* ⊕ *www.stingraycityantigua.com.*

## DIVING

Antigua is an unsung diving destination, with plentiful undersea sights to explore, from coral canyons to sea caves. Barbuda alone features roughly 200 wrecks on its treacherous reefs. The most accessible wreck is the 1890s bark *Andes,* not far out in Deep Bay, off Five Islands Peninsula. Among the favorite sites are **Green Island, Cades Reef,** and **Bird Island** (a national park). Memorable sightings include turtles, stingrays, and barracuda darting amid basalt walls, hulking boulders, and stray 17th-century anchors and cannon. One advantage is accessibility in many spots for shore divers and snorkelers. Double-tank dives run about $90.

**Dockyard Divers.** Owned by British ex-merchant seaman Captain A.G. "Tony" Fincham, Dockyard Divers is one of the island's most established outfits and offers diving and snorkeling trips, PADI courses, and dive packages with accommodations. They're geared to seasoned divers (two-tank dives are a quite reasonable $89), but staff work patiently with novices. Tony is a wonderful source of information on the island; ask him about the "Fincham's Follies" musical extravaganza he produces for charity. ✉ *Nelson's Dockyard, English Harbour Town* ☎ *268/460–1178* ⊕ *www.dockyard-divers.com.*

## KAYAKING

**"Paddles" Kayak Eco Adventure.** Paddles takes you on a 3½-hour tour of serene mangroves and inlets with informative narrative about the fragile ecosystem of the swamp and reefs and the rich diversity of flora and fauna. The tour ends with a hike to sunken caves and snorkeling in the North Sound Marine Park, capped by a rum punch at the fun creole-style clubhouse nestled amid botanic gardens. Experienced guides double as kayaking and snorkeling instructors, making this an excellent opportunity for novices. Conrad and Jennie's brainchild is one of Antigua's better bargains. ✉ *Seaton's Village* ☎ *268/463–1944, 268/720–4322* ⊕ *www.antiguapaddles.com.*

## ZIP-LINING

**Antigua Rainforest Canopy Tours.** Release your inner Tarzan at Antigua Rainforest Canopy Tours. You should be in fairly good condition for the ropes challenges, which require upper-body strength and stamina; there are height and weight restrictions. But anyone (vertigo or acrophobia sufferers, beware) can navigate the intentionally rickety "Indiana

Jones–inspired" suspension bridges, then fly (in secure harnesses) 200 to 300 feet above a rain forest–filled valley from one towering turpentine tree to the next on lines with names like "Screamer" and "Leap of Faith." There are 23 stations, as well as a bar–café and interpretive signage. First-timers, fear not: the "rangers" are affable, amusing, and accomplished. It's open Monday–Saturday from 8 to 6, with three scheduled tours at 9:15, 10:15, and 11:15 (other times by appointment). ⊠ *Fig Tree Dr., Wallings* ☎ *268/562–6363* ⊕ *www.antiguarainforest. com* ⧉ *From $85.*

## WHERE TO EAT

$$ ✕ **Big Banana—Pizzas in Paradise.** This tiny, often crowded spot is tucked
PIZZA into one side of a restored 18th-century rum warehouse with broad
FAMILY plank floors, wood-beam ceiling, and stone archways. Cool, Benetton-style photos of locals and musicians jamming adorn the brick walls. Big Banana serves some of the island's best pizza—try the lobster or the seafood variety—as well as fresh fruit crushes, classic pastas, wraps, burgers, and sub sandwiches bursting at the seams. There's live entertainment some nights, and a large-screen TV for sports fans. Ⓢ *Average main: $18* ⊠ *Redcliffe Quay, Redcliffe St., St. John's* ☎ *268/480–6985* ⊕ *www.bigbanana-antigua.com* ⊙ *Closed Sun.*

$$$ ✕ **Coconut Grove.** Coconut palms grow through the roof of this open-
ECLECTIC air thatched restaurant, flickering candlelight illuminates colorful local murals, waves lap the white sand, and the waitstaff provides just the right level of service. Jean-François Bellanger's dishes artfully fuse French culinary preparations with island ingredients. Top choices include pan-seared mahimahi served over cauliflower puree with fingerling potatoes and mango-pineapple chutney, and sautéed shrimp with roasted plantain and hickory bacon finished with champagne-Parmesan sauce. The signature coconut shrimp is the best lunch option. The kitchen can be uneven, the wine list is unimaginative and overpriced, and the buzzing happy-hour bar crowd lingering well into dinnertime can detract from the otherwise romantic atmosphere. Nonetheless, Coconut Grove straddles the line between casual beachfront boîte and elegant eatery with aplomb. Ⓢ *Average main: $30* ⊠ *Siboney Beach Club, Marina Bay Rd., Dickenson Bay* ☎ *268/462–1538* ⊕ *www.coconutgroveantigua. com* ⚐ *Reservations essential.*

# ARUBA (ORANJESTAD)

By Susan
Campbell

Few islands can boast the overt dedication to tourism and the quality of service that Aruba offers. The arid landscape is full of attractions to keep visitors occupied, and the island offers some of the most dazzling beaches in the Caribbean. Casinos and novelty nightclubs abound in Oranjestad, giving the capital an almost Las Vegas appeal. To keep tourists coming back year after year, the island boasts a tremendous variety of restaurants ranging from upscale French eateries to toes-in-the-sand casual dining. Aruba may not be an unexplored paradise, but hundreds of thousands of tourists make it a point to beat a path here every year. Because it's not a very large island, cruise-ship visitors can expect to see a large part of the island on their day ashore. Or they can simply see several of the beautiful beaches. Whether you're planning to be active or to simply relax, this is an ideal cruise port.

## ESSENTIALS

### CURRENCY

The Aruban florin. The florin is pegged to the U.S. dollar, and Arubans accept U.S. dollars readily. Note that the Netherlands Antilles florin used on Curaçao is not accepted on Aruba.

### TELEPHONE

You can dial international calls directly or call from the SETAR office in Oranjestad. Simply dial the seven-digit number in Aruba. AT&T customers can dial 800–8000 from special phones at the cruise dock and in the airport's arrival and departure halls. From other phones, dial 121 to contact the SETAR international operator to place a collect or calling-card call.

---

### BEST BETS

■ **Oranjestad.** Aruba's capital is pretty and easy to explore on foot, and it's impossible to get lost.

■ **Eagle Beach.** One of the most beautiful beaches in the Caribbean, with miles of white sand.

■ **Nightlife.** If your ship stays in port late, take advantage of the island's great bar scene and its many casinos.

■ **Snorkeling.** Though you can't dive here, you can snorkel to get a glimpse of what's under the sea.

■ **Windsurfing.** Constant wind allows this adrenaline sport to thrive in Aruba.

---

## COMING ASHORE

The Port of Oranjestad is a busy place and is generally full of eager tourists looking for souvenirs or a bite to eat. The Renaissance Marketplace is right on the port, as are a number of souvenir shops and some decent and inexpensive restaurants. The main shopping areas of Oranjestad are all within 10 minutes' walk of the port, but there is a free old-fashioned trolley that starts at the new cruise welcome center. It loops around the main shopping areas of Oranjestad and allows hop on/hop off.

Taxis can be flagged down on the street that runs alongside the port (look for license plates with a "TX" tag) but best to ask a doorman at resorts like the Renaissance Marina to grab you one. Rates are fixed (i.e., there are no meters; the rates are set by the government and displayed on a chart), though you and the driver should agree on the fare before your ride begins. If you want to rent a car, you can do so for a reasonable price; driving is on the right, just as in the United States; and it's pretty easy to get around, though a four-wheel-drive vehicle does help in reaching some of the more out-of-the-way places. The downtown bus terminal is within walking distance of the pier as well, and buses stop all along the most popular beaches.

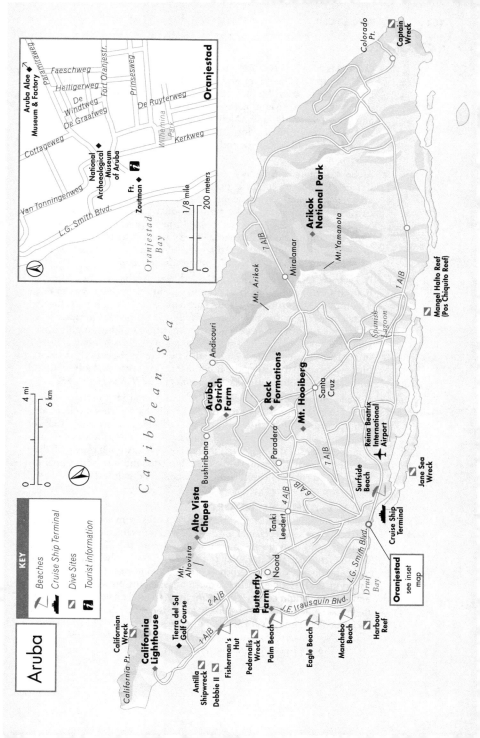

# Aruba

**KEY**
- Beaches
- Cruise Ship Terminal
- Dive Sites
- Tourist Information

0    4 mi
0    6 km

Caribbean Sea

**Oranjestad**
see inset map

Paramiraweg
Aruba Aloe
Museum & Factory
Faeschweg
Heiligweg
De Windtweg
De Graafweg
Fort Oranjestr.
Prinsesweg
Cottageweg
National Archaeological Museum of Aruba
Van Tonningenweg
De Ruyterweg
Wilhelmina Park
Kerkweg
Ft. Zoutman
L.G. Smith Blvd.
**Oranjestad**

Oranjestad Bay

0    1/8 mile
0    200 meters

Colorado Pt.
Captain Wreck

**Arikok National Park**
Mt. Yamanota
Miralamar
Mt. Arikok
7 A/B
1 A/B
Mangel Halto Reef (Pos Chiquito Reef)
Spanish Lagoon

Andicouri
**Aruba Ostrich Farm**
Bushiribana
**Rock Formations**
**Mt. Hooiberg**
Paradera
Santa Cruz
**Reina Beatrix International Airport**
7 A/B
Jane Sea Wreck

**Alto Vista Chapel**
Tanki Leendert
4 A/B
6 A/B
**Surfside Beach**
Cruise Ship Terminal

Mt. Altovista
Noord
2 A/B

**California Lighthouse**
California Pt.
Californian Wreck
Antilla Shipwreck
Debbie II
Fisherman's Hut
Pedernalis Wreck
Tierra del Sol Golf Course
1 A/B
**Butterfly Farm**
Palm Beach
J.E. Irausquin Blvd.
Eagle Beach
Manchebo Beach
Harbour Reef
Drui Bay
L.G. Smith Blvd.
**Oranjestad**
see inset map

# EXPLORING

## ORANJESTAD AND ENVIRONS

Aruba's capital is best explored by the free ecotrolley—hop on/hop off affair—and on foot. Major improvements downtown have opened up the back roads of Main Street and have created many resting spaces and pedestrian-only lanes. New small malls, restaurants, attractions, and museums can be explored there. Also worth exploring is the new linear park and boardwalk and the new outdoor art spaces along the waterfront.

**Aruba Aloe Museum & Factory.** Aruba has the ideal conditions to grow the aloe vera plant. It's an important export, and there are aloe stores all over the island. The museum and factory tour reveal the process of extracting the serum to make many products used for beauty, health, and healing; and guided or self-guided tours are available in English, Dutch, Spanish, and Papiamento. There's also a store to purchase their products on-site. Products are also available online. ⊠ *Pitastraat 115, Oranjestad* ☎ *800/952-7822* ⊕ *www.arubaaloe.com.*

**Ft. Zoutman.** One of the island's oldest edifices, Aruba's historic fort was built in 1796 and played an important role in skirmishes between British and Curaçao troops in 1803. The Willem III Tower, named for the Dutch monarch of that time, was added in 1868 to serve as a lighthouse. Over time the fort has been a government office building, a police station, and a prison; now its historical museum displays Aruban artifacts in an 18th-century house. This is also the site of the weekly Tuesday night welcome party called the Bon Bini festival, with local music, food, and dance. ⊠ *Zoutmanstraat, Oranjestad* ☎ *297/582-5199* ⊠ *$5.*

FAMILY
Fodor'sChoice
★

**National Archaeological Museum of Aruba.** Located in a multi-building complex that once housed the Ecury Family Estate, this modern, air-conditioned museum showcases the island's beginnings right back to the indigenous Arawak people, including a vast collection of farm and domestic utensils dating back hundreds of years. Among the highlights are the re-created Arawak Village, multimedia and interactive presentations, and rotating exhibits of art, history, and cultural shows. ⊠ *42 Schelpstraat, Oranjestad* ☎ *297/582-8979* ⊕ *namaruba.org* ⊠ *Free.*

## PALM BEACH AND NOORD

FAMILY
Fodor'sChoice
★

**Butterfly Farm.** Hundreds of butterflies and moths from around the world flutter about this spectacular garden. Guided tours (included in the price of admission) provide an entertaining look into the life cycle of these insects, from egg to caterpillar to chrysalis to butterfly or moth. After your initial visit, you can return as often as you like for free during your vacation. ■ TIP→ **Go early in the morning when the butterflies are most active; wear bright colors if you want them to land on you.** Early morning is also when you are most likely to see the caterpillars emerge from their cocoons and transform into butterflies or moths. ⊠ *J.E. Irausquin Blvd., Palm Beach* ✛ *Across from Divi Phoenix Aruba Beach Resort* ☎ *297/586-3656* ⊕ *www.thebutterflyfarm.com* ⊠ *$15.*

## WESTERN TIP (CALIFORNIA DUNES)

**Alto Vista Chapel.** Meaning "high view," Alto Vista was built in 1750 as the island's first Roman Catholic Church. The simple yellow and orange structure stands out in bright contrast to its stark desertlike surroundings, and its elevated location affords a wonderful panoramic view of the northwest coast. Restored in 1953, it's still in operation today with regular services and also serves as the culmination point of the annual walk of the cross at Easter. You will see small signposts guiding the faithful to the Stations of the Cross all along the winding road to its entrance. This landmark is a typical stop on most island tours. ⊠ *Alto Vista Rd., Oranjestad* ✛ *Follow the rough, winding dirt road that loops around the island's northern tip, or from the hotel strip, take Palm Beach Road through 3 intersections and watch for the asphalt road to the left just past the Alto Vista Rum Shop.*

**California Lighthouse.** Declared a national monument in 2015, the landmark lighthouse on the island's eastern tip is being restored to its original glory. It was named after a merchant ship that sunk nearby called the *Californian*, a tragedy that spawned its construction. Built in 1910, the lighthouse has been a famous Aruba attraction for decades and a typical stop on most island tours. ⊠ *Arashi, Noord.*

## SANTA CRUZ

**Mt. Hooiberg.** Named for its shape (*hooiberg* means "haystack" in Dutch), this 541-foot peak lies inland just past the airport. If you have the energy, you can climb the 562 steps to the top for an impressive view of Oranjestad (and Venezuela on clear days). ⊠ *Oranjestad.*

## ARIKOK NATIONAL PARK AND ENVIRONS

FAMILY **Arikok National Park.** There are more than 20 miles (34 km) of trails concentrated in the island's eastern interior and along its northeastern coast. Arikok Park is crowned by Aruba's second-highest mountain, the 577-foot Mt. Arikok, so you can also go climbing here.

Hiking in the park, whether alone or in a group led by guides, is generally not too strenuous. You'll need sturdy shoes to grip the granular surfaces and climb the occasionally steep terrain. You should also exercise caution with the strong sun—bring along plenty of water and wear sunscreen and a hat. At the park's main entrance, the Arikok Visitor Center houses exhibits, restrooms, and food facilities and provides maps and marked trail information, park rules, and features. Free guided mini-tours are the best way to get oriented at the park entrance. ☎ *297/585–1234* ⊕ *www.arubanationalpark.org* 🎟 *$11 per person. Children under 17 free. Yearly passes available* ⊙ *Park closes at 4 pm.*

FAMILY **Aruba Ostrich Farm.** Everything you ever wanted to know about the world's largest living birds can be found at this farm and ranch. There are emus, too! A large *palapa* (palm-thatched roof) houses a gift shop and restaurant that draws large bus tours, and tours of the farm are available every half hour. Feeding the ostriches is fun, and you can also hold an egg in your hands. ⊠ *Makividiri Rd., Paradera* ☎ *297/585–9630* ⊕ *www.arubaostrichfarm.com* 🎟 *Adults $12, children (under 12) $6.*

**Rock Formations.** The massive boulders at Ayo and Casibari are a mystery, as they don't match the island's geological makeup. You can climb to the top for fine views of the arid countryside. The main path to Casibari has steps and handrails, and you must move through tunnels and along narrow steps and ledges to reach the top. At Ayo you can find ancient pictographs in a small cave (the entrance has iron bars to protect the drawings from vandalism). At the base there is a new café/bar/restaurant open for lunch, and their dinner at night when lit up with colored lights around the rocks is surreal. Some party bus tours stop there for dinner before continuing on their barhop journey. ⚓ *Access to the rock formations at Casibari is via Tanki Hwy. 4A; you can reach Ayo via Rte. 6A. Watch carefully for the turnoff signs near the center of the island on the way to the windward side* ⊕ *www.aruba.com.*

# BEACHES

Virtually every popular Aruba beach has resorts attached, but because nearly all beaches are public, there is never a problem with access. However, lounges, showers, and shade palapas are reserved for hotel guests.

**Fodor's Choice** ★ **Eagle Beach.** Aruba's most photographed beach and the widest by far, especially in front of the Manchebo resort, Eagle Beach is not only a favorite with visitors and locals, but also of sea turtles. More sea turtles nest here than anywhere else on the island. This pristine stretch of blinding white sand and aqua surf frequently ranks among the best beaches in the world. Many of the hotels have facilities on or near the beach, and refreshments are never far away, but chairs and shade palapas are reserved for guests only. **Amenities:** food and drink; toilets. **Best for:** sunset; swimming; walking. ⊠ *J.E. Irausquin Blvd., north of Manchebo Beach.*

**Fodor's Choice** ★ **Manchebo Beach** (*Punta Brabo*). Impressively wide, the white-sand shoreline in front of the Manchebo Beach Resort is the backdrop for the numerous yoga classes now taking place under the giant palapa since the resort began offering health and wellness retreats. This sand stretch is the broadest on the island; in fact you can even get a workout just getting to the water! Waves can be rough and wild there though, so mind the current and undertow when swimming. **Amenities:** food and drink; toilets. **Best for:** bodyboarding; swimming. ⊠ *J.E. Irausquin Blvd., at Manchebo Beach Resort.*

**Fodor's Choice** ★ **Palm Beach.** This is the island's most populated and popular beach running along the high-rise resorts, and it's crammed with every kind of water sports activity and food and drink emporium imaginable. It's always crowded no matter the season, but it's a great place for people-watching, sunbathing, swimming, and partying; and there are always activities happening, such as the increasingly popular beach tennis. The water is pond calm and the sand is powder fine. **Amenities:** food and drink; shade; toilets; water sports. **Best for:** partying; people-watching; sunbathing; swimming; water sports. ⊠ *J.E. Irausquin Blvd., between Westin Aruba Resort and Marriott's Aruba Ocean Club.*

## SHOPPING

The only real duty-free shopping is in the departure area of the airport. (Passengers bound for the United States should be sure to shop before proceeding through U.S. customs in Aruba.) Downtown stores do have very low sales tax though and some excellent bargains on high-end luxury items like gold, silver, and jewelry. Major credit cards are welcome everywhere, as are U.S. dollars. Aruba's souvenir and crafts stores are full of Dutch porcelains and figurines, as befits the island's heritage. Dutch cheese is a good buy, as are hand-embroidered linens and any products made from the native aloe vera plant. Local arts and crafts run toward wood carvings and earthenware emblazoned with "Aruba: One Happy Island" and the like, but there are many shops with unique Aruban items like designer wear and artwork. Don't try to bargain unless you are at a flea market. Arubans consider it rude to haggle.

**Caya G.F. Betico Croes (Main St.).** Oranjestad's original "Main Street" (behind the Renaissance Marina Resort) had been neglected since most cruise passengers preferred to stick to the front street near the marina where the high-end shops and open-market souvenir stalls are. However, a recent massive renovation of the entire downtown region has breathed new life into the backstreets with pedestrian-only stretches, compact malls, and open resting areas. A free ecotrolley now loops all through downtown, allowing you to hop on and off to shop at all kinds of stores. Fashions, souvenirs, specialty items, sporting goods, cosmetics . . . you name it, you'll find them all on this renewed street. ⊠ *Oranjestad.*

**Fodor's**Choice ★ **Renaissance Mall.** Upscale, name-brand fashion and luxury brands of perfume, cosmetics, leather goods are what you'll find in the array of 60 stores spanning two floors in this mall located within and underneath the Renaissance Marina Resort. You'll also find specialty items like cigars and designer shoes plus high-end gold, silver, diamonds, and quality jewelry at low-duty and no-tax prices. Cafés and high-end dining, plus a casino and spa round out the offerings. Shopping until 8 pm daily. ⊠ *Renaissance Marina Resort, L.G. Smith Blvd. 82, Oranjestad* ☎ *297/582–4622* ⊕ *www.shoprenaissancearuba.com.*

FAMILY **Renaissance Marketplace.** The Renaissance Marketplace is more of a dining and gathering spot along the marina than a market. It's a lively spot with a few souvenir shops and specialty stores. There is also a modern cinema. But mostly it's full of eclectic dining emporiums and trendy cafés, and they have live music some weekends in their alfresco square. The Seaport casino is also there, and it's steps from the cruise terminal on the marina. ⊠ *L.G. Smith Blvd. 82, Oranjestad* ⊕ *www.shoprenaissancearuba.com.*

## ACTIVITIES

### BIKING

**Rancho Notorious.** One of Aruba's oldest tour operators, Rancho Notorious offers horseback riding for all levels and many different guided tours, including ATV outback adventures and mountain biking. All adventures are a great way to experience the island's rugged arid outback and scenic rocky seasides where cars cannot venture. ⊠ *Boroncana, Noord* ☏ *297/586–0508* ⊕ *www.ranchonotorious.com.*

## DIVING AND SNORKELING

With visibility of up to 90 feet, the waters around Aruba are excellent for snorkeling and diving. Advanced and novice divers alike will find plenty to occupy their time, as many of the most popular sites—including some interesting shipwrecks—are found in shallow waters ranging from 30 to 60 feet. Coral reefs covered with sensuously waving sea fans and eerie giant sponge tubes attract a colorful menagerie of sea life, including gliding manta rays, curious sea turtles, shy octopuses, and grunts, groupers, and other fish. Marine preservation is a priority on Aruba, and regulations by the Conference on International Trade in Endangered Species make it unlawful to remove coral, conch, and other marine life from the water, and the new Marine Park Foundation is ensuring the protection of the reefs. There are many snorkeling trips for all ages with large operators and DePalm Island also has excellent snorkeling.

Scuba diving operator prices vary depending on the trip. If you want to go all the way, complete open-water certification takes at least four days worth of instruction.

FAMILY **DePalm Pleasure Sail & Snorkeling.** The luxury catamaran *DePalm Plea-*
Fodor'sChoice *sure* offers three-stop snorkel trips to the island's most popular fish-filled
★ spots daily including the *Antilla* shipwreck. They also offer the option to try Snuba. Their romantic sunset sails are popular excursions. Buffet and open bar are included. Hotel pickup and drop-off are included unless they are within easy walking distance of their pier on Palm Beach. ⊠ *DePalm Pier, Palm Beach, Noord* ✛ *Between the Hilton and the Riu resorts on Palm Beach.* ☏ *297/522–4400* ⊕ *www.depalmtours.com.*

## GOLF

Fodor'sChoice **Tierra del Sol.** Stretching out to 6,811 yards, this stunning course is
★ situated on the northwest coast near the California Lighthouse and is Aruba's only 18-hole course. Designed by Robert Trent Jones Jr., Tierra del Sol combines Aruba's native beauty—cacti and rock formations, stunning views—with good greens and beautiful landscaping. Wind can also be a factor here on the rolling terrain, as are the abundant bunkers and water hazards. Greens fees include a golf cart equipped with GPS and a communications system that allows you to order drinks for your return to the clubhouse. The fully stocked golf shop is one of the Caribbean's most elegant, with an extremely attentive staff. ⊠ *Caya di Solo 10, Malmokweg* ☏ *297/586–7800* ⊕ *www.tierradelsol.com* ⅄ *18 holes, 6811 yards, par 71.*

# WHERE TO EAT

$$$ ✕ **Cuba's Cookin'.** Old Havana meets the Caribbean here with authentic
CUBAN music and food from what locals call The Big Island. The signature dish
Fodor'sChoice is the *ropa vieja,* a sautéed flank steak served with a rich sauce and it's
★ perfectly spiced and melts in your mouth. Vegetarian and gluten-free

offerings are served as well. And their boast of the best mojitos in town is a fair claim. There's hot live music every night, as well as interesting offerings like Poetry Night, when locals get up and express themselves through spoken word. The atmosphere is fun and friendly, and the location ideal for people-watching along the seaport marina. And it's the only place in town to get a famous Cuban sandwich for lunch. $ *Average main: $28* ⊠ *Renaissance Marketplace, L.G. Smith Blvd. 82, Oranjestad* ☎ *297/588–0627* ⊕ *www.cubascookin.com.*

**$$$**
CARIBBEAN

✕ **Gostoso.** Locals adore the magical mixture of Portuguese, Aruban, and international dishes on offer at this consistently excellent establishment. The decor walks a fine line between kitschy and cozy, but the atmosphere is relaxed and informal and outdoor seating is available. The *bacalhau* vinaigrette (dressed salted cod) is a delightful Portuguese appetizer and pairs nicely with most of the Aruban dishes on the menu. Meat-lovers are sure to enjoy the Venezuelan mixed grill, which includes a 14-ounce steak and chorizo accompanied by local sides like fried plantain. Service is very attentive and a table visit from the owner is par for the course. $ *Average main: $30* ⊠ *Caya Ing Roland H. Lacle 12, Oranjestad* ☎ *297/588–0053* ⊕ *www.gostosoaruba.com* ☉ *Closed Mon.* ⬧ *Reservations essential.*

# BARBADOS (BRIDGETOWN)

By Jane E. Zarem

Barbadians (Bajans) are a warm, friendly, and hospitable people, who are genuinely proud of their country and culture. Although tourism is the island's number one industry, the island has a sophisticated business community and stable government, so life here doesn't skip a beat after passengers return to the ship. Barbados is the most "British" island in the Caribbean. Afternoon tea is a ritual, and cricket is the national sport. The atmosphere, though, is hardly stuffy. This is still the Caribbean, after all. Beaches along the island's south and west coasts are picture-perfect, and all are available to cruise passengers. On the rugged east coast, the Atlantic Ocean attracts world-class surfers. The northeast is dominated by rolling hills and valleys, while the interior of the island is covered by acres of sugarcane and dotted with small villages. Historic plantations, a stalactite-studded cave, a wildlife preserve, rum distilleries, and tropical gardens are among the island's attractions. Bridgetown is the capital city, and its downtown shops and historic sites are a short walk or taxi ride from the pier.

## ESSENTIALS
### CURRENCY
The Barbados dollar (BDS$) is pegged to the U.S. dollar at the rate of BDS$1.98 to US$1. U.S. dollars (but not coins) are accepted universally across the island.

### TELEPHONE
Most U.S. cell phones will work in Barbados, though roaming charges can be expensive. Renting a cell phone or buying a local SIM card for your own unlocked phone may be a less expensive alternative if you're planning an extended stay or expect to make a lot of local calls. Top off services are available at several locations throughout the island.

## COMING ASHORE

Up to eight ships at a time can dock at Bridgetown's Deep Water Harbour, on the northwest side of Carlisle Bay near Bridgetown. The cruise-ship terminal has duty-free shops, handicraft vendors, a post office, a telephone station, a tourist information desk, and a taxi stand. To get downtown, follow the shoreline to the Careenage. It's a 15-minute walk or a $5 taxi ride.

Taxis await ships at the pier. Drivers accept U.S. dollars and appreciate a 10% tip. Taxis are unmetered and operate at an hourly rate of $35 to $40 per carload (up to three passengers). Most drivers will cheerfully narrate an island tour. You can rent a car, but rates are steep—$70 to $80 per day during the high season—and some agencies require a two-day rental. You'll also need a temporary driving permit (BDS$10). Driving is on the left, British-style.

### BEST BETS

■ **The East Coast.** The island's windward coast, with its crashing surf, is a "don't-miss" sight.

■ **Harrison's Cave.** This extensive limestone cave system is deep beneath Barbados.

■ **Mount Gay Rum Visitors Centre.** Take a tour and a tasting.

■ **Flower Gardens.** Andromeda Botanic Gardens and the Flower Forest are both scenic and fragrant.

■ **St. Nicholas Abbey.** Not an abbey at all, this is one of the oldest Jacobean-style houses in the Western Hemisphere.

## EXPLORING

### BRIDGETOWN

This bustling capital city, inscribed in 2011—along with The Garrison—onto the UNESCO World Heritage List, is a duty-free port with a compact shopping area. The principal thoroughfare is Broad Street, which leads west from National Heroes Square. A shuttle service (☎ 246/227–2200) operates between hotels and downtown during business hours.

**Nidhe Israel Synagogue.** Providing for the spiritual needs of one of the oldest Jewish congregations in the Western Hemisphere, this synagogue was formed by Jews who arrived in 1628 from Brazil and introduced sugarcane to Barbados. The adjoining cemetery has tombstones dating from the 1630s. The original house of worship, built in 1654, was destroyed in an 1831 hurricane, rebuilt in 1833, and restored in 1987 with the assistance of the Barbados National Trust. The museum, housed in a restored coral-stone building from 1750, documents the story of the Barbados Jewish community. Friday-night services are held during the winter months, but the building is open to the public year-round. Shorts are not acceptable during services but may be worn at other times. ⊠ *Synagogue La., Bridgetown* ☎ *246/436–6869* ⊕ *www. nidheisrael.com* ⌨ *Synagogue free; museum $12.50.*

## SOUTH COAST

FAMILY **Barbados Concorde Experience.** The Concorde Experience focuses on the British Airways Concorde G-BOAE (Alpha Echo, for short) that for many years flew between London and Barbados. The retired supersonic jet has made its permanent home here. Besides boarding the sleek aircraft itself, you learn about how the technology was developed and how this plane differed from other jets. It's just a two-minute walk from the terminal and a perfect place to spend about an hour if you have a long layover between flights. ⊠ *Grantley Adams International Airport, adjacent to the terminal building* ☎ *246/420–7738* ⊕ *www. barbadosconcorde.com* ✉ *$20.*

Fodor'sChoice **Sunbury Plantation House and Museum.** Lovingly rebuilt after a 1995 fire ★ destroyed everything but the thick flint-and-stone walls of this 300-year-old great house, Sunbury offers an elegant glimpse of the 18th and 19th centuries on a Barbadian sugar estate. Period furniture, old prints, and a collection of horse-drawn carriages lend an air of authenticity. A buffet luncheon ($22.50 per person, $34 on Sunday) and high tea ($14) are served daily in the Courtyard Restaurant. A five-course candlelight dinner ($100 per person, including drinks, minimum 12 people, reservations required) is served at the 200-year-old mahogany table in the dining room. ⊠ *Off Hwy. 5* ✛ *Look for the sign at Six Cross Roads Roundabout* ☎ *246/423–6270* ⊕ *www.barbadosgreathouse.com* ✉ *$7.50.*

## CENTRAL BARBADOS

Fodor'sChoice **Andromeda Botanic Gardens.** More than 600 beautiful and unusual plant ★ specimens from around the world are cultivated in 6 acres of gardens nestled among streams, ponds, and rocky outcroppings overlooking the sea above the Bathsheba coastline near Tent Bay. The gardens were created in 1954 with flowering plants collected by the late horticulturist Iris Bannochie (1914–1988). They're now administered by the Barbados National Trust. The Gallery Shop features local art, photography, and crafts. The Garden Café serves sandwiches, salads from the gardens, desserts, and drinks. ⊠ *Bathsheba* ☎ *246/433–9384* ⊕ *www.andromeda barbados.com* ✉ *$12.50.*

Fodor'sChoice **Flower Forest.** It's a treat to meander among fragrant flowering bushes, ★ canna and ginger lilies, puffball trees, and more than 100 other species of tropical flora in a cool, tranquil forest of flowers and other plants. A ½-mile (1-km) path winds through the 53.6-acre grounds, a former sugar plantation; it takes about 30 to 45 minutes to follow the path, or you can wander freely for as long as you wish. Benches throughout provide places to pause and reflect. There's also a snack bar, a gift shop, and a beautiful view of Mt. Hillaby, at 1,100 feet the island's highest point. ⊠ *Hwy. 2, Richmond* ☎ *246/433–8152* ⊕ *www.flowerforest barbados.com* ✉ *$12.50.*

FAMILY **Gun Hill Signal Station.** The 360-degree view from Gun Hill, at 700 feet, Fodor'sChoice was of strategic importance to the 18th-century British army. Using ★ lanterns and semaphore, soldiers here could communicate with their counterparts at the south coast's Garrison and the north's Grenade Hill about approaching ships, civil disorders, storms, or other emergencies.

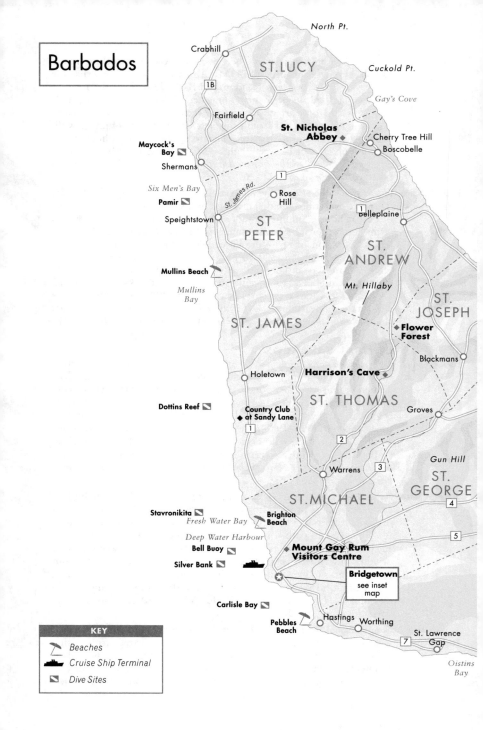

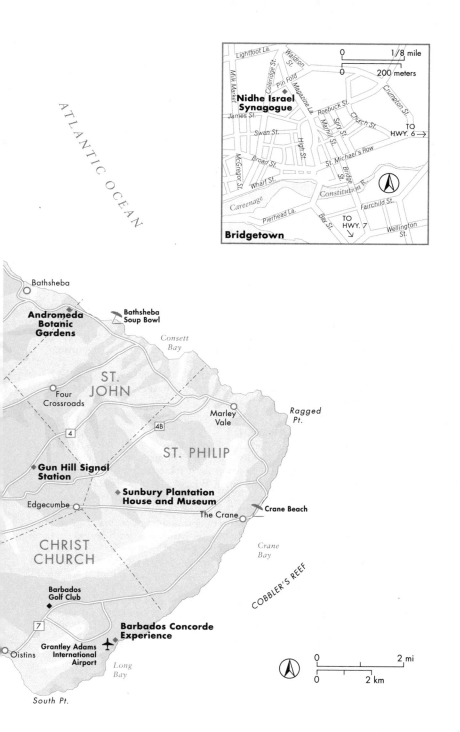

**Bridgetown**

Nidhe Israel Synagogue

Lightfoot La.
Waldron St.
Coleridge St.
Pin Fold
Magazine La.
Milk Market
James St.
Swan St.
McGregor St.
Broad St.
Wharf St.
High St.
Careenage
Pierhead La.
Roebuck St.
Church St.
Spry St.
Marhill St.
St. Michael's Row
Constitution R.
Bay St.
Bridge St.
Fairchild St.
Wellington St.
Crumpton St.

TO HWY. 6 →
TO HWY. 7 ↓

0         1/8 mile
0         200 meters

ATLANTIC OCEAN

Bathsheba

**Andromeda Botanic Gardens**

**Bathsheba Soup Bowl**

Consett Bay

ST. JOHN

Four Crossroads

Marley Vale

Ragged Pt.

4

4B

ST. PHILIP

**Gun Hill Signal Station**

**Sunbury Plantation House and Museum**

Edgecumbe

The Crane

Crane Beach

Crane Bay

CHRIST CHURCH

COBBLER'S REEF

**Barbados Golf Club**

7

**Barbados Concorde Experience**

Oistins

**Grantley Adams International Airport**

Long Bay

South Pt.

0         2 mi
0         2 km

Time moved slowly in 1868, and Captain Henry Wilkinson whiled away his off-duty hours by carving a huge lion from a single rock—on the hillside below the tower. Come for a short history lesson but mainly for the view; it's so gorgeous that military invalids were sent here to convalesce. There's a small café for refreshments. ⊠ *Fusilier Rd., Gun Hill* ☎ *246/429–1358* ⊕ *www.barbadosnationaltrust.org* ⊠ *$5.*

FAMILY

Fodor's Choice

★

**Harrison's Cave.** This limestone cavern, complete with stalactites, stalagmites, subterranean streams, and a 40-foot underground waterfall, is a rare find in the Caribbean—and one of Barbados's most popular attractions. Tours include a nine-minute video and an hour-long underground journey via electric tram. The visitor center has interactive displays, life-size models and sculptures, a souvenir shop, restaurant, and elevator access to the tram for people with disabilities. Tram tours fill up fast, so book ahead. More intrepid visitors may like the 1½-hour walking tour or 4-hour ecoadventure tour, exploring nature trails and some of the cave's natural passages. ⊠ *Hwy. 2, Welchman Hall* ☎ *246/417–3700* ⊕ *www.harrisonscave.com* ⊠ *Tram tour $30, walk-in $20, ecoadventure $101.*

**Mount Gay Rum Visitors Centre.** On this popular tour, you learn the colorful story behind the world's oldest rum, made in Barbados since 1703. Although the modern distillery is in the far north in St. Lucy Parish, tour guides here explain the rum-making process. Equipment, both historic and modern, is on display, and rows and rows of barrels are stored in this location. Tours conclude with a tasting and an opportunity to buy duty-free rum and gifts—and even have lunch or cocktails (no children on cocktail tour), depending on the time of day. ⊠ *Exmouth Gap, Brandons, Spring Garden Hwy., Bridgetown* ☎ *246/425–8757* ⊕ *www.mountgayrum.com* ⊠ *$10, $50–$62 with cocktails or lunch and transportation.*

## NORTHERN BARBADOS

Fodor's Choice

★

**St. Nicholas Abbey.** The island's oldest great house (circa 1650) was named after the original British owner's hometown, St. Nicholas Parish near Bristol, and Bath Abbey nearby. Its stone-and-wood architecture makes it one of only three original Jacobean-style houses still standing in the Western Hemisphere. It has Dutch gables, finials of coral stone, and beautiful grounds that include an "avenue" of mahogany trees, a "gully" filled with tropical trees and plantings, formal gardens, and an old sugar mill. The first floor, fully furnished with period furniture and portraits of family members, is open to the public. A fascinating home movie, shot by a previous owner's father, records Bajan life in the 1930s. Behind the great house is a rum distillery with a 19th-century steam press; cane grinding occurs Wednesdays and Thursdays, February through mid-May. Visitors can purchase artisanal plantation rum, browse the gift shop's traditional Barbadian products, and enjoy light refreshments at the Terrace Café. ⊠ *Cherry Tree Hill Rd., Moore Hill* ☎ *246/422–5357* ⊕ *www.stnicholasabbey.com* ⊠ *$20.*

# BEACHES

Geologically, Barbados is a coral-and-limestone island (not volcanic) with few rivers and, as a result, beautiful beaches, particularly along the island's southern and southeastern coastlines.

The west coast has some lovely beaches as well, but they're more susceptible to erosion after major autumn storms, if any, have taken their toll.

FAMILY **Accra Beach** (*Rockley Beach*). This popular beach, adjacent to the Accra Beach Hotel, has a broad swath of white sand with gentle surf and a lifeguard, plenty of nearby restaurants for refreshments, a playground, and beach stalls for renting chairs and equipment for snorkeling and other water sports. The Barbados Boardwalk, great for walking or running, begins here and follows the waterfront west—past private homes, restaurants, and bars—for about a mile (1.6 km) to Needham's Point. **Amenities:** food and drink; lifeguards; parking (no fee); water sports. **Best for:** snorkeling; swimming; walking. ⊠ *Hwy. 7, Rockley.*

FAMILY
Fodor's Choice
★ **Mullins Beach.** At this lovely beach just south of Speightstown, the water is safe for swimming and snorkeling. There's easy parking on the main road, and Mullins Restaurant serves snacks, meals, and drinks—and rents chairs and umbrellas. **Amenities:** food and drink; toilets. **Best for:** sunset; swimming; walking. ⊠ *Hwy. 1B, Mullins.*

FAMILY
Fodor's Choice
★ **Pebbles Beach.** On the southern side of Carlisle Bay, just south of Bridgetown, this broad half circle of white sand is one of the island's best beaches—and it can become crowded on weekends and holidays. The southern end of the beach wraps around the Hilton Barbados; the northern end is adjacent to the Radisson Aquatica Resort Barbados and a block away from Island Inn. Park at Harbour Lights or at the Boatyard Bar and Bayshore Complex, both on Bay Street, where you can also rent umbrellas and beach chairs and buy refreshments. **Amenities:** food and drink. **Best for:** snorkeling; swimming; walking. ⊠ *Off Bay St., south of Bridgetown, Garrison.*

# SHOPPING

Duty-free luxury goods—china, crystal, cameras, porcelain, leather items, electronics, jewelry, perfume, and clothing—are found at Bridgetown's Broad Street department stores and their branches, shops in the high-end Limegrove Lifestyle Centre in Holetown, the Bridgetown Cruise Terminal (for passengers only), and the departure lounge at Grantley Adams International Airport. Prices are often 30% to 40% less than full retail. To buy goods at duty-free prices, you must produce your passport, immigration form, or driver's license, along with departure information (such as flight number and date) at the time of purchase—or you can have your purchases delivered free to the airport or harbor for pickup; duty-free alcohol, tobacco products, and some electronic equipment *must* be delivered to you at the airport or harbor.

Bridgetown's **Broad Street** is the primary downtown shopping area. **DaCosta Manning Mall,** in the historic Colonnade Building on Broad Street, has more than 25 shops that sell everything from Piaget watches to postcards; across the street, **Mall 34** has 22 shops where you can buy duty-free goods, souvenirs, and snacks. At the **cruise-ship terminal** shopping arcade, passengers can buy both duty-free goods and Barbadian-made crafts at more than 30 boutiques and a dozen vendor carts and stalls. And the **airport departure lounge** is a veritable shopping mall.

**Best of Barbados.** Architect Jimmy Walker founded these shops to showcase the works of his artist wife. Products range from her framable prints, housewares, and textiles to arts and crafts in both native style and modern designs. Everything is made or designed on Barbados. Branch shops are at Chattel Village in Holetown, at Southern Palms Resort in St. Lawrence Gap, at the cruise-ship terminal, and in the airport departure lounge. ⊠ *Quayside Centre, Main Rd., Rockley* ☎ *246/622–1761* ⊕ *www.best-of-barbados.com.*

## ACTIVITIES

### FISHING

**Billfisher Deepsea Fishing.** *Billfisher III*, a 40-foot Viking Sport Fisherman, accommodates up to six passengers with three fishing chairs and five rods. Captain Winston ("The Colonel") White has been fishing these waters since 1975. His full-day charters include a full lunch; all trips include drinks and transportation to and from the boat. ⊠ *Bridge House Wharf, The Careenage, Bridgetown* ☎ *246/431–0741.*

### GOLF

**Barbados Golf Club.** The first public golf course on Barbados, an 18-hole championship course, was redesigned in 2000 by golf course architect Ron Kirby. The course has hosted numerous competitions, including the European Senior tour in 2003. Several hotels offer preferential tee-time reservations and reduced rates. Cart, trolley, club, and shoe rentals are all available. ⊠ *Hwy. 7, Durants* ☎ *246/428–8463* ⊕ *www.barbados-golfclub.com* ☎ *$105 for 18 holes; $55 for 9 holes; 3-, 5-, and 7-day passes $255, $400, $525, respectively* ⅃ *18 holes, 6805 yards, par 72.*

**Fodor's**Choice ★ **Country Club at Sandy Lane.** At this prestigious club, golfers can play the Old Nine or either of two 18-hole championship courses: the Tom Fazio–designed Country Club Course and the spectacular Green Monkey Course, which is reserved for hotel guests and club members. The layouts offer a limestone quarry setting (Green Monkey), a modern style with lakes (Country Club), and traditional small greens and narrow fairways (Old Nine). Golfers can use the driving range for free. The Country Club Restaurant and Bar, overlooking the 18th hole, is open to the public. Caddies, trolleys, clubs, and shoes are available for rent, as are GPS-equipped carts, which alert you to upcoming hazards, give tips on how to play holes, and even let you order refreshments. ⊠ *Sandy Lane, Hwy. 1, Sunset Crest* ☎ *246/444–2500* ⊕ *www.sandylane.com/ golf* ☎ *$240 for 18 holes ($200 hotel guests); $150 for 9 holes ($130 guests); 7-day pass $1,350 ($1,250 guests)* ⅃ *Green Monkey: 18 holes, 7343 yards, par 72; Country Club: 18 holes, 7060 yards, par 72; Old Nine: 9 holes, 3345 yards, par 36.*

## WHERE TO EAT

**$$**
CARIBBEAN

✕ **Shaker's.** Locals and visitors alike gather at this no-frills hangout for drinks—perhaps a Banks beer or two, a margarita, a pitcher of sangria, or whatever wets their whistle—and the delicious local food. Simple dishes like beer-battered flying fish, grilled catch of the day, barbecued chicken, grilled steak, or a solid cheeseburger deliver the goods, but the barbecued ribs are the main event. All main dishes include crisp green salad, coleslaw, and either grilled or french-fried potatoes. It's a colorful, convivial place, full of laughter and chatter—partly because the tables are so close together and partly because of the rum shop atmosphere. Arrive early or make a reservation if you want an outside table, as it fills up quickly; and be prepared to pay in cash. $ *Average main: $15* ✉ *Browne's Gap, Rockley* ☎ *246/228–8855* ⊕ *www.shakersbarbados. com* ⊟ *No credit cards* ☉ *Closed Sun. and Mon. and mid-Aug.–mid-Sept. No lunch* ⚞ *Reservations essential.*

**$$$**
CARIBBEAN
FAMILY

✕ **Waterfront Café.** This busy bistro on the walkway facing the south side of The Careenage is the perfect place to enjoy a drink, snack, or meal—and to people-watch. Locals and tourists alike gather for alfresco, all-day dining on sandwiches, salads, fish, pasta, pepper-pot stew, and tasty Bajan snacks such as buljol, fish cakes, or plantation pork (plantains stuffed with spicy minced pork). The panfried flying-fish sandwich is an especially popular lunchtime treat. Dinner is accompanied by live jazz. $ *Average main: $26* ✉ *The Careenage, Bridgetown* ☎ *246/427–0093* ⊕ *www.waterfrontcafe.com.bb* ☉ *Closed Sun. No dinner Mon.–Wed.*

# BELIZE CITY, BELIZE

By Jeffrey Van Fleet

Central America's only English-speaking nation probably has the greatest variety of flora and fauna of any country of its size in the world. Here you'll often find more iguanas or howler monkeys than humans. A few miles off the mainland is the Belize Barrier Reef, a great wall of coral stretching the entire 200-mile (333-km) length of the coast, and a sector of the Mesoamerican Barrier Reef, which stretches from Cancún to the Honduras Bay Islands. Over 200 cayes (pronounced "keys") dot the reef like punctuation marks, and three coral atolls lie farther out to sea. All are superb for diving and snorkeling. Many, like Ambergris Caye (pronounced Am-bur-griss Key) and Caye Caulker, are cheery resort islands with ample bars and restaurants, easily reachable on day trips from Belize City. The main choice you'll have to make is whether to stay in Belize City for a little stroll and shopping, and perhaps a dram at one of the Fort George hotels or restaurants, or alternatively to head out by boat, rental car, taxi, or tour on a more active adventure.

## ESSENTIALS

### CURRENCY
Since U.S. currency is universally accepted, there's no need to acquire the Belize dollar (BZ$2 to US$1).

### FLIGHTS

Especially if you are going to Ambergris Caye, you may prefer to fly, or you can water-taxi over and fly back to maximize your time. There are nearly hourly flights on two local airlines. The flight to Caulker (CUK) takes about 10 minutes and to San Pedro (SPR), on Ambergris, about 25 minutes. The cost is about BZ$190 round-trip to either island. Belize City's Municipal Airport (TZA) offers a much better selection of flights (and is much closer) than Philip S.W. Goldson International Airport (BZE) northwest of the city.

**Contacts Maya Island Air.** ☒ *Belize City Municipal Airstrip, Marine Parade Harbor Front* ☎ *223–1403 reservations* ⊕ *www.mayaislandair.com.* **Tropic Air.** ☒ *San Pedro Airstrip, San Pedro Town* ☎ *226–2626 Reservations in Belize, 800/422–3435 in U.S.* ⊕ *www.tropicair.com.*

---

**BEST BETS**

■ **Belize Zoo.** Though small, this collection of native Belize wildlife is excellent.

■ **Cave Tubing.** If you are not claustrophobic, this is an unforgettable excursion.

■ **Diving.** Belize is known as one of the world's best dive destinations. For the certified, this is a must.

■ **Snorkeling in Hol Chan.** The water is teeming with fish, and you don't need to be certified to enjoy the underwater world here.

---

### TELEPHONE

Calling locally or internationally is easy, but rates are high; around BZ$1.30 a minute for calls to the United States. To call the United States, dial 00 + 1 + the area code and number. Pay phones, which are located in the Belize Tourism Village, where you are tendered, and elsewhere downtown, accept only prepaid Belize Telemedia Limited. (BTL) phone cards are available in shops in denominations from BZ$5 to BZ$50. Your U.S.-based GSM phone will probably work on Belize's GSM 1900 system, but you will pay a high surcharge to use it abroad. Data charges can be frightfully high; look for a Wi-Fi connection or make your online time very quick. Foreign calling cards are generally blocked in Belize. Call 113 for local directory assistance, 115 for an in-country operator, and 114 for an international operator. Belize's nationwide emergency number is 911.

### VISITOR INFORMATION

**Contacts Belize Tourism Board** (BTB). ☒ *64 Regent St., Belize City* ☎ *227–2420, 800/624–0686 in U.S.* ⊕ *www.travelbelize.org.*

### COMING ASHORE

Because Belize City's harbor is shallow, passengers are tendered in. If you're going the independent route, try to get in line early for the tenders, as it sometimes takes 90 minutes or more for all the passengers to be brought ashore. ■ **TIP→ Pay attention, also, to when the last tender is scheduled back to your ship at the end of the day.** You will land at the Belize Tourism Village complex on Fort Street. It has a collection of gift shops, restaurants, and tour operators nicely situated along the harbor. Bathrooms are spick-and-span, too. Taxis, tour guides, and car-rental desks are readily available. Cabs cost BZ$7–BZ$10 for one

**Belize**

MEXICO

Buena Vista

SHIPSTERN
WILDLIFE
RESERVE

Orange
Walk

COROZAL
DISTRICT

*Bahía
de
Chetumal*
Caye

Ambergris
Caye

August Pine
Ridge

Shipyard

San Felipe

Blue Creek Village

Crooked Tree

**Crooked Tree
Wildlife
Sanctuary**

**Altun Ha**

San Pedro

**Hol Chan
Marine Reserve**

Caye Caulker

ORANGE
WALK
DISTRICT

*New River*

**Community
Baboon
Sanctuary**

Burrell
Boom

Ladyville

**Belize City**
see inset
map

Caye Chapel

**Belize
Zoo**

Burrell Boom

BELIZE
DISTRICT

Belize
City

St. George's
Caye

GUANACASTE
PARK

Hattieville

Turneffe
Islands

Spanish
Lookout

*Roaring
Creek*

Western Hwy.

*Rio Belize*

*Northern
Lagoon*

*Southern
Lagoon*

**BELMOPAN**

*Manatee
Road*

Gales
Point

**St. Herman's
Blue Hole
National Park**

*Hummingbird Hwy.*

Dangriga

0       15 miles
0       15 km

**Hummingbird
Highway**

**Museum of
Belize**

Orange St

**Swing
Bridge**

Albert

**Cathedral of
St. John
the Baptist**

**Fort George
Lighthouse
and Bliss
Memorial**

*Belize
Harbour*

**Belize City**

**House of
Culture**

person between any two points in the city, plus BZ$1 for each additional person. Taxi fares at night are slightly higher. Outside the city, and from downtown to the suburbs, you're charged by the distance you travel. Hourly rates are negotiable, but expect to pay around $30, or $150 for the day. Drivers are required to display a Taxi Federation rate card. There's no need to tip cab drivers. You can also rent a car at the Tourism Village, but rates can be high (at least $75 per day), and gas is also expensive. Green directional signs point you to nearby destinations such as the Belize Zoo. The Wet Lizard, next to the Tourism Village, also organizes tours for cruise-ship passengers.

Harvest Caye, a new $50-million port facility owned and operated by Norwegian, is being developed on Belize's southern coast near Placencia, 175 km (105 miles) south of Belize City.

## EXPLORING

Many Belize hands will tell you that the best way to see Belize City is through a rearview window. But, with an open mind to its peculiarities, and with a little caution (the city has a crime problem, but the tourist police keep a close watch on cruise-ship passengers), you may decide Belize City has a raffish, atmospheric charm rarely found in other Caribbean ports of call. The city lost out on its role as the country's capital some five decades ago, its coastal setting presenting particular vulnerability to hurricanes, but it remains the vibrant economic and cultural heart of Belize.

## BELIZE CITY

A 5- to 10-minute stroll from the colorful Belize Tourism Village brings you into the other worlds of Belize City. On the north side of Haulover Creek is the colonial-style Fort George district, where large old homes, stately but sometimes down at the heels, take the breezes off the sea and share their space with hotels and restaurants. On the south side is bustling Albert Street, the main commercial thoroughfare. But don't stroll too far since parts of Belize City are unsafe. During the daylight hours, as long as you stay within the main commercial district and the Fort George area—and ignore the street hustlers—you should have no problem.

**Fort George Lighthouse and Bliss Memorial.** Towering 15 meters (49 feet) over the entrance to Belize Harbor, the lighthouse stands guard on the tip of Fort George Point. It was designed and funded by one of the country's greatest benefactors, Baron Henry Edward Ernest Victor Bliss. The English nobleman never actually set foot on the Belizean mainland, though in his yacht he visited the waters offshore. In his will he bequeathed most of his fortune to the people of Belize, and the date of his death, March 9, is celebrated as a national holiday, now officially called National Heroes and Benefactors Day. Bliss is buried here, in a small, low mausoleum perched on the seawall, up a short run of limestone stairs. The lighthouse and mausoleum are for photo ops only—you can't enter. ⊠ *Marine Parade, near the Radisson Fort George Hotel, Fort George* ⌦ *Free.*

**House of Culture.** Formerly called Government House, the city's finest colonial structure is said to have a design inspired by the illustrious British architect Sir Christopher Wren. Built in 1814, it was once the residence of the governor-general, the British monarchy's representative in Belize. Following Hurricane Hattie in 1961, the decision was made to move the capital inland to Belmopan, and the house became a venue for social functions and a guesthouse for visiting VIPs. (Queen Elizabeth stayed here in 1985, Prince Philip in 1988.) Now it's open to the public. You can peruse its archival records, and art and artifacts from the colonial era, or mingle with the tropical birds that frequent the gardens. △ **If going here after dark, take a cab, because it's close to some of the city's most crime-ridden areas.** ⊠ *Regent St. at Southern Foreshore, opposite Cathedral of St. John the Baptist, Commercial District* ☎ *227–3050* ⊕ *www.nichbelize.org* ⌦ *BZ$10* ⊙ *Closed weekends.*

FAMILY
Fodor's Choice ★
**Museum of Belize.** This small but fascinating museum was the Belize City jail from 1857 to 1993. Permanent displays include ancient jade and other Mayan artifacts; medicinal, ink, and alcoholic-beverage bottles dating from the 1670s; Belize and British Honduran coins and colorful postage stamps; and an actual prison cell. Temporary exhibitions change periodically. ⊠ *8 Gabourel La., Belize Central Bank Compound, Fort George* ☎ *223–4524* ⊕ *www.nichbelize.org* ⌦ *BZ$10* ⊙ *Closed Sun.–Mon.*

**Cathedral of St. John the Baptist.** On Albert Street's south end is the oldest Anglican church in Central America and the only one outside England where kings were crowned. From 1815 to 1845, four kings of the Mosquito Kingdom (a British protectorate along the coast of Honduras and Nicaragua) were crowned here. The cathedral, built of brick brought here to what once was British Honduras as ballast on English ships, is thought to be the oldest surviving building in Belize from the colonial era. Its foundation stone was laid in 1812. Inside, it has whitewashed walls and mahogany pews. The roof is constructed of local sapodilla wood, with mahogany beams. Residents of the city usually refer to the cathedral as simply "St. John's." ■ TIP→ **You can combine a visit to the cathedral with a visit to the House of Culture, as they are just across the street from each other. Safe to visit during day; at night, take a taxi.** ⊠ *Albert St. at Regent St., Opposite the House of Culture, Commercial District* ☎ *227–3029* ⊠ *Free.*

**Swing Bridge.** As its name suggests, the bridge spanning Haulover Creek in the middle of Belize City actually swings. When needed to allow a boat through or by special request of visiting dignitaries, four men hand-winch the bridge a quarter-revolution so waiting boats can continue upstream (when it was the only bridge in town, this snarled traffic for blocks). The bridge, made in England, opened in 1923; it was renovated and upgraded in 1999. Outsiders' recommendations to automate the swing mechanics or—heaven forbid—rebuild the bridge entirely are always immediately rejected; no one wants to eliminate the city's most unusual landmark. Before the Swing Bridge arrived, cattle were "hauled over" the creek in a barge. The bridge appears in a scene of the 1980 movie, *The Dogs of War,* set in a fictitious African country but mostly filmed in Belize. ⊠ *Haulover Creek, where Queen and Albert sts. meet, Fort George.*

## INLAND FROM BELIZE CITY

FAMILY **Altun Ha.** A team from the Royal Ontario Museum first excavated the site in the early 1960s and found 250 structures spread over more than 1,000 square yards. At Plaza B, in the Temple of the Masonry Altars, archaeologists unearthed the grandest and most valuable piece of Mayan art ever discovered—the head of the sun god Kinich Ahau. Weighing nearly 10 pounds, it was carved from a solid block of green jade. The head is kept in a solid steel vault in the Central Bank of Belize, though it is occasionally displayed at the Museum of Belize. The jade head appears on all denominations of Belize currency. If the Masonry Altars temple looks familiar to you, it's because an illustration of the Masonry Altars structure appears on Belikin beer bottles. Because the Altun Ha site is small, it's not necessary to have a tour guide, but licensed guides may offer their services when you arrive.

Tours from Belize City, Orange Walk, and Crooked Tree also are options. Altun Ha is a regular stop on cruise ship excursions, and on days when several ships are in port in Belize City (typically midweek) Altun Ha may be crowded. Several tour operators in San Pedro and Caye Caulker also offer day trips to Altun Ha, often combined with lunch at the nearby Maruba Resort Jungle Spa. Most of these tours from the cayes are by boat, landing at Bomba Village. From here, a van makes the short ride to Altun Ha. If traveling independently or on a tour that includes it, you can stop at Maruba Resort Jungle Spa for a drink, lunch, or a spa treatment. ✉ *Rockstone Pond Rd., off Old Northern Hwy., Maskall Village* ✛ *From Belize City, take Northern Hwy. north to miles 18.9. Turn right (east) on Old Northern Hwy., which is only partly paved, and go 14 miles (23 km) to signed entrance road at Rockstone Pond Rd. to Altun Ha on left. Follow this paved road 2 miles (3 km) to visitor center.* ☎ *822–2106 NICH/Belize Institute of Archeology* ⊕ *www.nichbelize.org* ✍ *BZ$10.*

FAMILY
Fodor's Choice ★

**Belize Zoo.** Turn a sharp corner on the jungle trail, and suddenly you're face-to-face with a jaguar, the largest cat in the Western Hemisphere. The big cat growls a deep rumbling threat. You jump back, thankful that a strong but inconspicuous fence separates you and the jaguar. Plan for a visit of about two hours. Along with jaguars you'll see the country's four other wild cats: the puma, margay, ocelot, and jaguarundi. Perhaps the zoo's most famous resident is April, a Baird's tapir that is more than a quarter-century old. This relative of the horse and rhino is known to locals as the mountain cow, and is also Belize's national animal. At the zoo you'll also see jabiru storks, a harpy eagle, scarlet macaws, howler monkeys, crocodiles, and many snakes, including the fer-de-lance.

The zoo owes its existence to the dedication and drive of one gutsy woman, Sharon Matola. An American who came to Belize as part of a film crew, Matola stayed on to care for some of the semi-tame animals used in the production. She opened the zoo in 1983, and in 1991 it moved to its present location. She's also an active environmentalist. "The Zoo Lady" and her crusade against the Chalillo Dam is the subject of the 2008 book *The Last Flight of the Scarlet Macaw: One Woman's Fight To Save the World's Most Beautiful Bird* by *Outside* magazine writer Bruce Barcott. Besides touring the zoo, you can stay overnight at the Belize Zoo Jungle Lodge and hike or canoe through the 84-acre Tropical Education Center. ✉ *Mile 29, George Price Hwy., formerly Western Hwy., Belize City* ☎ *822–8000* ⊕ *www.belizezoo. org* ✍ *BZ$30 adults.*

FAMILY

**Community Baboon Sanctuary.** Spanning a 20-mile (32-km) stretch of the Belize River, the reserve was established in 1985 by a group of local farmers. The howler monkey—an agile bundle of black fur with a disturbing roar—was then zealously hunted throughout Central America and was facing extinction. Today the sanctuary is home, on some 200 private properties, to more than 2,000 black howler monkeys, as well as numerous species of birds and mammals. Thanks to ongoing conservation efforts countrywide, you can see the howler monkeys in a number of other areas, including at Lamanai in northern Belize, along the Macal, Mopan, and Belize rivers in western Belize, and near Monkey River and around Punta Gorda in southern Belize. Exploring the Community Baboon Sanctuary is easy, thanks to about 3 miles (5 km) of trails that start near a small museum and visitor center. The admission fee includes a 45-minute guided nature tour during which you definitely will see howlers. Three other themed tours—birding, canoeing, crocodiles—are priced à la carte, although the admission per couple is little more than the per-person rate. ✉ *31 miles (50 km) northwest of Belize City, Bermudian Landing* ✛ *If heading north on the Northern Highway, turn west at Mile 13.2 onto the Burrell Boom Road. Go 3 miles (5 km) and turn right just beyond the new bridge over the Belize River. Signs to Bermudian Landing mark the turn. Stay on this road approximately 12 miles (20 km) to Bermudian Landing. If going west on the Western Highway, turn north on the Burrell Boom Road at a roundabout at Mile 15½ of the Western Highway, and go 9 miles (15 km) to the new bridge over the Belize River. Just before the bridge, turn left. Signs to Bermudian Landing mark the turn. Stay on this road approximately 12 miles (20 km) to Bermudian Landing.* ☎ *245–2009* ⊕ *www.howlermonkeys.org* ✍ *BZ$14; tours from BZ$24.*

**Crooked Tree Wildlife Sanctuary.** At the end of the causeway where you pay your sanctuary admission fee, you can also arrange a guided tour of the sanctuary or rent a canoe for a do-it-yourself trip. The sanctuary, one of the country's top bird-watching spots, is managed by the Belize Audubon Society. You can also walk through the village and hike birding trails around the area. If you'd prefer to go by horseback, you pay by the hour. The visitor center has a free village and trail map. If you're staying overnight, your hotel can arrange canoe or bike rentals and set up tours and trips. Although tours can run at any time, the best time is early in the morning, when birds are most active. ✉ *Crooked Tree Village* ☎ *223–5004 Belize Audubon Society* ⊕ *www.belizeaudubon. org* ✍ *BZ$8; tours from BZ$10.*

**Hummingbird Highway.** Hands down, Hummingbird Highway is the most scenic roadway in Belize. The Hummingbird, a paved two-lane road, runs 54.5 miles (91 km) from the junction of the George Price Highway (formerly Western Highway) at Belmopan to Dangriga. Technically, only the first 32 miles (53 km) is the Hummingbird—the rest is the Stann Creek District Highway, but most people ignore that distinction. As measured from Belmopan at the junction of the Western Highway— the road has a few milepost signs running north from Dangriga, but we'll ignore them—the Hummingbird first winds through limestone hill country, passing St. Herman's Cave (Mile 12.2) and the inland Blue Hole (Mile 13.1). It then starts rising steeply, with the Maya Mountains on the west, or right side, past St. Margaret's village and Five Blue Lake (Mile 23). The views, of green mountains studded with cohune palms and tropical hardwoods, are incredible. At the Hummingbird Gap (Mile 26, elevation near 1,000 feet, with mountains nearby over 3,000 feet), you're at the crest of the highway and now begin to drop down toward the Caribbean Sea. At Middlesex village (Mile 32), technically the road becomes the Stann Creek District Highway and you're in Stann Creek District. Now you're in citrus country, with groves of grapefruit and Valencia oranges. Near Steadfast village (watch for signs around Mile 37) there's the 1,500-acre Billy Barquedier National Park, where you can hike (guide required) to waterfalls. At Mile 48.7 you pass the turn-off to the Southern Highway and at Mile 54.5 you enter Dangriga, with the sea just ahead. ■**TIP**➔ **If driving keep a watch for "sleeping policemen," speed bumps to slow down traffic near villages. Most are signed, but a few are not. Also, gas up in Belmopan, as there are no**

service stations until you approach Dangriga. ⊠ *Belmopan to Dangriga, Hummingbird Hwy., Belmopan.*

FAMILY    **St. Herman's Blue Hole National Park.** Less than a half hour south of Belmopan, the 575-acre St. Herman's Blue Hole National Park has a natural turquoise pool surrounded by mosses and lush vegetation, wonderful for a cool dip. The "inland Blue Hole" is actually part of an underground river system. On the other side of the hill is St. Herman's Cave, once inhabited by the Maya. There's a separate entrance to St. Herman's. A path leads up from the highway, but it's quite steep and difficult to climb unless the ground is dry. To explore St. Herman's cave beyond the first 300 yards or so, you must be accompanied by a guide (available at the park), and no more than five people can enter the cave at one time. With a guide, you also can explore part of another cave system here, the Crystal Cave (sometimes called the Crystalline Cave), which stretches for miles; the additional cost is BZ$20 per person for a two-hour guided tour. The main park visitor center is 12½ miles (20½ km) from Belmopan. The park is managed by the Belize Audubon Society, which administers a network of seven protected areas around the country. ⊠ *Mile 42.5, Hummingbird Hwy., Belmopan* ☎ *223–5004 Belize Audubon Society* ⊕ *www.belizeaudubon.org* ⊠ *BZ$8.*

## THE CAYES

### AMBERGRIS CAYE

Ambergris is the queen of the cayes. With a population of around 9,000, the island's only town, San Pedro, remains a small, friendly, and prosperous village. It has one of the highest literacy rates in the country and an admirable level of awareness about the fragility of the reef. The large number of substantial private houses being built on the edges of town is proof of how much tourism has enriched San Pedro. A water taxi from the Marine Terminal takes about 75 minutes and costs BZ$20 each way. You can also fly.

Fodor'sChoice    **Hol Chan Marine Reserve.** The reef's focal point for diving and snorkeling ★    near Ambergris Caye and Caye Caulker is the spectacular Hol Chan Marine Reserve (Maya for "little channel"). It's a 20-minute boat ride from San Pedro, and about 30 minutes from Caye Caulker. Hol Chan is a break in the reef about 100 feet wide and 20 to 35 feet deep, through which tremendous volumes of water pass with the tides. Shark-Ray Alley, now a part of Hol Chan, is famous as a place to swim, snorkel, and dive with sharks (nearly all are nurse sharks) and Southern sting rays.

■ TIP→ **During peak visitor periods to the cayes or when several cruise ships are docked off Belize City, snorkel tour boats can stack up at Hol Chan. Check locally to see when Hol Chan may be less busy, and consider visiting in early morning before most of the tours arrive.**

The expanded 21-square-mile (55-square-km) park has a miniature Blue Hole and a 12-foot-deep cave whose entrance often attracts the fairy basslet, an iridescent purple-and-yellow fish frequently seen here. The reserve is also home to a large moray eel population.

Varying in depth from 50 feet to 100 feet, Hol Chan's canyons lie between buttresses of coral running perpendicular to the reef, separated by white, sandy channels. You may find tunnel-like passageways from one canyon to the next. It's exciting to explore because as you come over each hill you don't know what you'll see in the "valley." Because fishing generally is off-limits here, divers and snorkelers can see abundant marine life, including spotted eagle rays and sharks. There are throngs of squirrelfish, butterfly fish, parrotfish, and queen angelfish, as well as Nassau groupers, barracuda, and large shoals of yellowtail snappers. Unfortunately, also here are lionfish, an invasive Indo-Pacific species that is eating its way—destroying small native fish—from Venezuela to the North Carolina coast. Altogether, more than 160 species of fish have been identified in the marine reserve, along with 40 species of coral, and five kinds of sponges. Hawksbill, loggerhead, and green turtles have also been found here, along with spotted and common dolphins, West Indian manatees, sting rays and several species of sharks.

⚠ **The currents through the reef can be strong here at times, so tell your guide if you're not a strong swimmer and ask for a snorkel vest or float. Also, although the nurse sharks are normally docile and very used to humans, they are wild creatures that on rare occasions have bitten snorkelers or divers who disturbed them.** ✉ *off southern tip of Ambergris Caye, Ambergris Caye* ☎ *526–2247 in San Pedro* ⊕ *www. holchanbelize.org* 🏷 *BZ$20, normally included in snorkel or dive tour charge.*

### CAYE CAULKER

On Caye Caulker, where the one village is home to around 2,000 people, brightly painted houses on stilts line the coral-sand streets. Although the island is being developed more each year, flowers still outnumber cars 10 to 1 (golf carts, bicycles, and bare feet are the preferred means of transportation). The living is easy, as you might guess from all the no shirt, no shoes, no problem signs at the bars. This is the kind of place where most of the listings in the telephone directory give addresses like "near football field." A water taxi from the Marine Terminal costs about BZ$20 each way and takes 45 minutes to an hour.

## BEACHES

Although the barrier reef limits the wave action and brings seagrass to the shore floor, the wide sandy beaches of Ambergris Caye are among the best in Belize. All beaches in Belize are public. **Mar de Tumbo,** 1½ miles (3 km) south of town near the Tropica Hotel, is the best beach on the south end of the island. **North Ambergris,** accessible by water taxi from San Pedro or by golf cart over the bridge to the north, has miles of narrow beaches and fewer people. The beach at **Ramon's Village,** across from the airstrip, is the best in the town area. The beaches on Caulker are not as good as those on Ambergris. Along the front side of the island is a narrow strip of sand, but the water is shallow and swimming conditions are poor. **The Split,** on the north end of the village (turn to your right from the main public pier), is the best place on Caye Caulker for swimming.

## SHOPPING

Belize does not have the crafts tradition of neighboring Guatemala and Mexico, and imported goods are expensive due to high duties, but hand-carved items of ziricote or other local woods make good souvenirs. Near the Swing Bridge at Market Square is the **Commercial Center**, which has some food and craft vendors on the first floor and a restaurant and shops on the second. The **Belize Tourism Village**, where the ship tenders come in, is a collection of bright and clean gift shops selling T-shirts and Belizean and Guatemalan crafts. Beside the Tourism Village is an informal **Street Vendor Market**, with funkier goods and performances by a "Brukdown" band or a group of Garifuna drummers.

**Belizean Handicraft Market Place.** Belizean Handicraft Market Place (formerly National Handicraft Center) has Belizean souvenir items, including hand-carved figurines, handmade furniture, pottery, and woven baskets. The prices are about as good as you'll find anywhere in Belize, and the sales clerks are friendly. It faces the small Memorial Park, which commemorates the Battle of St. George's Caye and is just a short stroll from the harbor front, the Belize Tourism Village, and many of the hotels in the Fort George area, including the Radisson, Chateau Caribbean, and The Great House. ⊠ 2 S. Park St., in Fort George area across from Memorial Park, Belize City ☎ 223–3627.

## ACTIVITIES

### CANOPY TOURS
You may feel a little like Tarzan as you dangle 80 feet above the jungle floor, suspended by a harness, moving from one treetop platform to another.

**Jaguar Paw Zipline.** Jaguar Paw has eight zip line platforms set 100 to 250 feet apart. At the last platform you have to rappel to the ground. There's a 240-pound weight limit. Zip line tours often are combined with cave tubing in the Caves Branch River. The cost for the zip line varies, depending on the tour and whether lunch and transportation are included. If visiting on a cruise, Chukka, the tour operator that manages Jaguar Paw, requires that you book a tour with your ship as an organized shore excursion. ⊠ Off Mile 37, George Price Hwy., Belmopan ☎ 223–4438, 877/424–8552 in U.S. ⊕ www.chukka.com ⊠ From BZ$120.

### CAVE TUBING
Very popular with cruise passengers are river-tubing trips that go through a cave, where you'll turn off your headlamp for a minute of absolute darkness, but these are not for the claustrophobic or those afraid of the dark.

**Cave-Tubing.com.** The good folks here specialize in shore excursions for cruise passengers and will plan an excursion that works with your sched-uled day in port, even when you book independently. You can choose from a basic cave-tubing outing or add a zip-line or ATV jungle tour as well. A separate zip-line tour with a visit to the ruins at Altun Ha is also available. ☎ 605–1575 ⊕ www.cave-tubing.com ⊠ From BZ$90.

### DIVING AND SNORKELING

Most companies on Ambergris Caye offer morning and afternoon single-tank dives; snorkel trips begin mid-morning or early afternoon. Dive and snorkeling trips that originate in Caye Caulker are a bit cheaper.

**Amigos del Mar.** Amigos del Mar, established in 1987, is perhaps the island's most consistently recommended dive operation. The SSI/SDI facility has a dozen dive boats and offers a range of local dives as well as trips to Turneffe Atoll and Lighthouse Reef in a fast 56-foot dive boat. You can choose from a local two-tank dive or a 12-hour trip to the Blue Hole, including the park entry fee and lunch. An open water certification course is also offered. Amigos also offers snorkel and fishing trips. Equipment rental and a 12.5% tax are extra on all tours. ⊠ *On a pier off Barrier Reef Dr., near Mayan Princess Hotel, San Pedro Town* ☎ *226–2706, 800/882–6159* ⊕ *www.amigosdivebelize. com* 💲 *From BZ$160.*

### INDEPENDENT TOURS

Several Belize City–based tour guides and operators offer custom trips for ship passengers; companies will usually meet you at the Belize Tourism Village.

**Ecological Tours & Services.** Ecological Tours specializes in shore excursions and can take you on snorkeling trips to cayes Goff, Caulker, or Ambergris. The latter includes a short flyover tour of the reef and islands. These folks also arrange a variety of cave-tubing excursions, with or without a zip-line tour. ⊠ *Belize Tourism Village, Fort St., Belize City* ☎ *625–1636* ⊕ *www.ecotoursbelize.com* 💲 *From BZ$110.*

## WHERE TO EAT

$ | ✕ **Nerie's.** Often packed with locals, Nerie's is the vox populi of dining in Belize City. The many traditional dishes on the menu include fry jacks for breakfast and cow-foot soup for lunch. Stew chicken with rice and beans and a soft drink is always an economical choice. 💲 *Average main: BZ$14* ⊠ *Queen and Daly Sts., Commercial District* ☎ *223–4028* ⊕ *www.neries.bz* ⊟ *No credit cards* ⊗ *No dinner Sun.*

CARIBBEAN

$$$ | ✕ **Riverside Tavern.** Owned and managed by the Bowen (of locally brewed Belikin-beer fame) family, Riverside Tavern is one of the city's most popular and agreeable restaurants, with dependably good food, friendly service, and safe parking. The signature hamburgers, which come in several sizes from 6 oz. to enormous, are arguably the best in Belize. The Riverside has steak and prime rib dishes, from cattle from the Bowen farm at Gallon Jug. Sit inside in air-conditioned comfort, at tables set around a huge bar, or on the outside covered patio overlooking Haulover Creek. This is one of the few restaurants in Belize with a dress code—shorts aren't allowed at night. The fenced, guarded parking lot right in front of the restaurant makes it easy and safe to park for free. 💲 *Average main: BZ$25* ⊠ *2 Mapp St., off Freetown Rd., Commercial District* ☎ *223–5640* ⊗ *Closed Sun.*

AMERICAN
Fodor'sChoice
★

# BERMUDA

By Amy
Peniston

Basking in the Atlantic, 508 miles (817 km) due east of Cape Hatteras, North Carolina, restrained and polite Bermuda is a departure from other sunny, beach-strewn isles. You won't find laid-back locals wandering around barefoot proffering piña coladas. Bermuda is somewhat formal, and despite the gorgeous weather, residents wearing stockings and heels or jackets, ties, Bermuda shorts, and knee socks are a common sight, whether on the street by day or in restaurants at night. On Bermuda's 22 square miles (57 square km) you will discover that pastel cottages, quaint shops, and manicured gardens betray a more staid, suburban way of life. A self-governing British colony since 1968, Bermuda has maintained some of its English character even as it is increasingly influenced by American culture. Most cruise ships make seven-night loops from U.S. embarkation ports, with four nights at sea and three tied up in port. Increasingly popular are round-trip itineraries originating in northeastern embarkation ports that include a single day or overnight port call in Bermuda before continuing south to the Bahamas or the Caribbean.

> **BEST BETS**
>
> ■ **Gibbs Hill Lighthouse.** Make the climb to the top, where the reward is an expansive view of the inlets and harbors.
>
> ■ **National Museum of Bermuda.** Absorb Bermuda's nautical and military history in this Royal Navy Dockyard museum.
>
> ■ **St. George's.** Attend the pierside show hosted by the town crier, where gossips and nagging wives are plunged into the water in a ducking stool.

## ESSENTIALS

### CURRENCY

The Bermuda dollar (B$) is on par with the U.S. dollar. You can use American money anywhere.

### TELEPHONE

To make a local call, simply dial the seven-digit number; Bermuda's country code is 441. International calling cards are widely available for purchase and can be used at one of Bermuda's many public telephones.

## COMING ASHORE

Three Bermuda harbors serve cruise ships: Hamilton (the capital), St. George's, and King's Wharf at the Royal Naval Dockyard.

In Hamilton, cruise ships tie up right on the city's main street, Front Street. A visitor information center is next to the ferry terminal, also on Front Street and nearby; maps and brochures are displayed in the cruise terminal itself.

St. George's accommodates a handful of smaller cruise ships every year at Penno's Wharf, located just minutes from the heart of the city. A visitor information center is at King's Square, near the Town Hall and within walking distance of the pier.

King's Wharf, in the Royal Naval Dockyard at the westernmost end of the island, is the busiest of the three cruise-ship berthing areas, and it is where the largest vessels dock. Although Dockyard appears isolated on a map, it is well connected to the rest of the island by taxi, bus, and ferry. Three visitor information centers can be found along the piers and adjacent to the ferry dock.

Taxis are the fastest and easiest way to get around the island, but they are also quite expensive. Four-seater taxis charge $7.90 for the first mile and $2.75 for each subsequent mile. A personalized taxi tour of the island costs $50 per hour for one to four people and $70 an hour for five to seven, excluding tip. If you can round up a group of people, this is often cheaper than an island tour offered by your ship. Tip drivers 15%. Rental cars are prohibited, but the island has a good bus and ferry system. You can also rent scooters, but this can be dangerous for the uninitiated and is not recommended.

## EXPLORING

### HAMILTON

Bermuda's capital since 1815, the city of Hamilton is a small, bustling harbor town. It's the economic and social center of Bermuda, with busy streets lined with shops and offices. International influences, from both business and tourism, have brought a degree of sophistication unusual in so small a city. There are several museums and galleries to explore, but the favorite pastimes are shopping in Hamilton's numerous boutiques and dining in its many upscale restaurants.

FAMILY **Bermuda Underwater Exploration Institute (BUEI).** The 40,000-square-foot Ocean Discovery Centre showcases local contributions to oceanographic research and undersea discovery. Guests can ogle the world-class shell collection amassed by resident Jack Lightbourne (three of the 1,000 species were identified by and named for Lightbourne himself); or visit a gallery honoring native-born archaeologist Teddy Tucker to see booty retrieved from Bermudian shipwrecks. The types of gizmos that made such discoveries possible are also displayed: including a replica of the bathysphere William Beebe and Otis Barton used in their record-smashing 1934 dive. A more modern "submersible," Nautilus-X2, lets wannabe explorers take a simulated seven-minute trip to the ocean floor. Pedestrians may access the facility by following the sidewalk on the waterside of Front Street. ⊠ *40 Crow La., off E. Broadway, Hamilton* ☎ *441/292–7219* ⊕ *www.buei.bm* ☎ *$15.*

**City Hall & Arts Centre.** Set back from the street, City Hall contains Hamilton's administrative offices as well as two art galleries and a performance hall. Instead of a clock, its tower is topped with a bronze wind vane—a prudent choice in a land where the weather is as important as the time. The building itself was designed in 1960 by Bermudian architect Wilfred Onions, a champion of balanced simplicity. Massive cedar doors open onto an impressive lobby notable for its beautiful chandeliers and portraits of mayors past and present. To the left is City Hall Theatre, a major venue for concerts, plays, and dance performances. To the right are the civic offices, where you can find souvenirs such as pens, T-shirts, and paperweights showing the Corporation of Hamilton's logo. A handsome cedar staircase leads upstairs to two

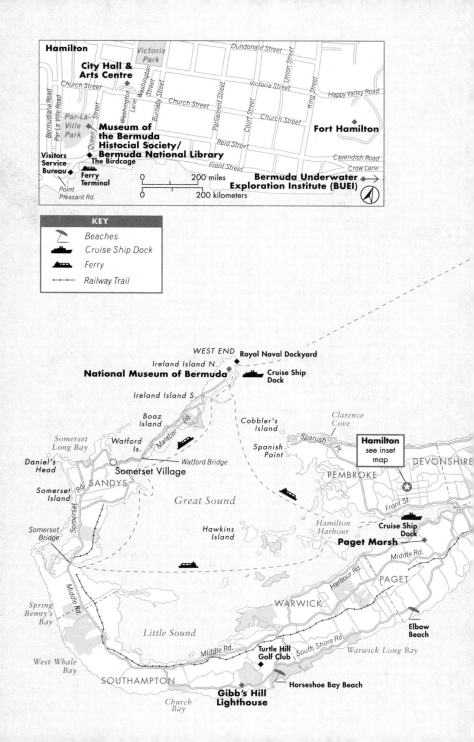

**Hamilton**

City Hall & Arts Centre

Victoria Park

Duhdonald Street

Union Street

Victoria Street

Happy Valley Road

Church Street

Bermudiana Road

Par-La-Ville Road

Washington Lane

Burnaby Street

Parliament Street

Court Street

King Street

Church Street

Church Street

Par-La-Ville Park

Queen Street

Fort Hamilton

Museum of the Bermuda Histoical Society/ Bermuda National Library

The Birdcage

Reid Street

Cavendish Road

Front Street

Crow Lane

Visitors Service Bureau

Ferry Terminal

Point Pleasant Rd.

Bermuda Underwater Exploration Institute (BUEI)

| 0 | | 200 miles |
| 0 | | 200 kilometers |

WEST END    Royal Naval Dockyard

Ireland Island N.

**National Museum of Bermuda**    Cruise Ship Dock

Ireland Island S.

Boaz Island

Cobbler's Island

Clarence Cove

Spanish Pt.

**Hamilton** see inset map

DEVONSHIRE

Watford Is.

Malabar Rd.

Spanish Point

Somerset Long Bay

Watford Bridge

PEMBROKE

Daniel's Head

Somerset Village

**Great Sound**

Hamilton Harbour

Cruise Ship Dock

Somerset Island

SANDYS

Somerset Rd.

Hawkins Island

**Paget Marsh**

Middle Rd.

Somerset Bridge

Little Sound

Harbour Rd.

PAGET

Middle Rd.

Spring Benny's Bay

WARWICK

Elbow Beach

West Whale Bay

Turtle Hill Golf Club

South Shore Rd.

Warwick Long Bay

SOUTHAMPTON

Middle Rd.

Horseshoe Bay Beach

Church Bay

**Gibb's Hill Lighthouse**

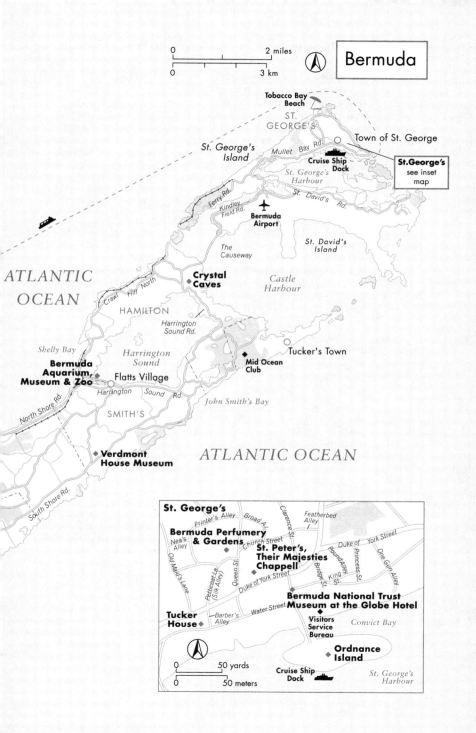

## Bermuda

0 — 2 miles
0 — 3 km

**Tobacco Bay Beach**

**ST. GEORGE'S**

St. George's Island

St. George's Harbour

*Mullet Bay Rd.*

**Cruise Ship Dock**

**Town of St. George**

**St.George's** see inset map

*Ferry Rd.*

*Kindley Field Rd.*

**Bermuda Airport**

*St. David's Rd.*

St. David's Island

**ATLANTIC OCEAN**

The Causeway

*Crawl Hill North*

**Crystal Caves**

Castle Harbour

**HAMILTON**

*Harrington Sound Rd.*

Shelly Bay

Harrington Sound

**Tucker's Town**

**Bermuda Aquarium, Museum & Zoo**

**Flatts Village**

**Mid Ocean Club**

*Harrington Sound Rd.*

*North Shore Rd.*

**SMITH'S**

*John Smith's Bay*

**Verdmont House Museum**

*South Shore Rd.*

**ATLANTIC OCEAN**

---

### St. George's

**Bermuda Perfumery & Gardens**

*Printer's Alley* — *Broad Al.*

*Clarence St.*

*Featherbed Alley*

*Nea's Alley*

*Old Maid's Lane*

*Church Street*

**St. Peter's, Their Majesties Chappell**

*Queen St.*

*Duke of York Street*

*Princess St.*

*Duke of York Street*

*One Gun Alley*

*Pound Alley*

*Bridge St.*

*King St.*

*Petticoat La. (Silk Alley)*

**Bermuda National Trust Museum at the Globe Hotel**

**Tucker House**

*Barber's Alley*

*Water Street*

**Visitors Service Bureau**

*Convict Bay*

**Ordnance Island**

0 — 50 yards
0 — 50 meters

**Cruise Ship Dock**

St. George's Harbour

upper-floor art galleries. (An elevator gets you there, too.) ✉ *17 Church St., Hamilton* ☎ *441/292–1234.*

FAMILY   **Fort Hamilton.** This imposing moat-ringed fortress has underground passageways that were cut through solid rock by Royal Engineers in the 1860s. Built to defend the West End's Royal Naval Dockyard from land attacks, it was outdated even before its completion, but remains a fine example of a polygonal Victorian fort. Even if you're not a big fan of military history, the hilltop site's stellar views and stunning gardens make the trip worthwhile. On Monday at noon, from November to March, bagpipes echo through the grounds as the kilt-clad members of the Bermuda Islands Pipe Band perform a traditional skirling ceremony. Due to one-way streets, getting to the fort by scooter can be a bit challenging. From downtown Hamilton head north on Queen Street, turn right on Church Street, then turn left to go up the hill on King Street. Make a sharp (270-degree) right turn onto Happy Valley Road and follow the signs. Pedestrians may walk along Front Street to King Street. ✉ *Happy Valley Rd., Hamilton* ☎ *441/292–1234* 🌐 *Free.*

**Museum of the Bermuda Historical Society/Bermuda National Library.** Mark Twain admired the giant rubber tree that stands on Queen Street in the front yard of this Georgian house, formerly owned by Postmaster William Bennet Perot and his family. The library was established in 1839, and its reference section has virtually every book ever written about Bermuda, as well as a microfilm collection of Bermudian newspapers dating back to 1784.

To the left of the library entrance is the Historical Society's museum. The collection is eclectic, chronicling the island's past through interesting—and in some cases downright quirky—artifacts. One display, for instance, is full of Bermudian silver dating from the 1600s; another focuses on tools and trinkets made by Boer War prisoners who were exiled here in 1901 and 1902. ✉ *13 Queen St., opposite Reid St., Hamilton* ☎ *441/299–0029 library, 441/295–2487 museum* ⊕ *www.bermuda historicalsociety.com* 🌐 *Library free; museum donations accepted* ⟲ *Tours by appointment.*

## ST. GEORGE'S

The settlement of Bermuda began in what is now the town of St. George's nearly 400 years ago, when the *Sea Venture* was shipwrecked on Bermuda's treacherous reefs on its way to the colony of Jamestown, Virginia. No trip to Bermuda is complete without a visit to this historic town and UNESCO World Heritage Site. ·

**Bermuda National Trust Museum at the Globe Hotel.** Erected as a governor's mansion around 1700, this building became a hotbed of activity during the American Civil War. From here, Confederate Major Norman Walker coordinated the surreptitious flow of guns, ammunition, and war supplies from England, through Union blockades, into American ports. It saw service as the Globe Hotel during the mid-19th century and became a National Trust property in 1951. A short video, *Bermuda, Centre of the Atlantic,* recounts the history of Bermuda, and a memorabilia-filled exhibit entitled "Rogues & Runners: Bermuda and the American Civil War" describes St. George's when it was a port for Confederate blockade runners. ⊠ *32 Duke of York St., St. George* ☎ *441/297–1423* ⊕ *www.bnt.bm* ▦ *$5; $10 combination ticket includes admission to Tucker House and Verdmont* ⊗ *Closed Fri.*

**Bermuda Perfumery & Gardens.** In 2005 this perfumery moved from Bailey's Bay in Hamilton Parish, where it had been based since 1928, to historic Stewart Hall. Although the location changed, the techniques it uses did not: the perfumery still manufactures and bottles all its island-inspired scents on-site using more than 3,000 essential oils extracted from frangipani, jasmine, oleander, and passionflower. Guides are available to explain the entire process, and there's a small museum that outlines the company's history. You can also wander around the gardens and stock up on your favorite fragrances in the showroom. ⊠ *Stewart Hall, 5 Queen St., St. George* ☎ *441/293–0627* ⊕ *www.lilibermuda. com* ▦ *Free.*

FAMILY    **Ordnance Island.** Ordnance Island, directly across from King's Square, is dominated by a splendid bronze statue of Sir George Somers, commander of the *Sea Venture*. Somers looks surprised that he made it safely to shore—and you may be surprised that he ever chose to set sail again when you spy the nearby *Deliverance*. It's a full-scale replica of one of two ships—the other was the *Patience*—built under Somers's supervision to carry survivors from the 1609 wreck onward to Jamestown. But considering her size (just 57 feet from bow to stern) *Deliverance* hardly seems seaworthy by modern standards. ⊠ *Across from King's Sq., St. George.*

Fodor's Choice ★    **St Peter's, Their Majesties Chappell.** Because parts of this whitewashed stone church date back to 1620, it holds the distinction of being the oldest continuously operating Anglican church in the Western Hemisphere. Befitting its age, St. Peter's has many treasures. The red cedar altar, carved in 1615 under the supervision of Richard Moore (a shipwright and the colony's first governor) is the oldest piece of woodwork in Bermuda. The late 18th-century bishop's throne is believed to have been salvaged from a shipwreck, and the baptismal font, brought to the island by early settlers, is an estimated 900 years old. There's also a fine collection of communion silver from the 1600s in the vestry. After viewing the interior, walk into the churchyard to see where prominent Bermudians, including Governor Sir Richard Sharples who was assassinated in 1973, are buried. A separate graveyard for slaves and free blacks (to the west of the church, behind the wall) is a poignant reminder of Bermuda's segregated past. ⊠ *33 Duke of York St., St. George* ☎ *441/297–2459* ⊕ *www.stpeters.bm* ▦ *Donations appreciated.*

**Tucker House.** Tucker House is owned and lovingly maintained as a museum by the Bermuda National Trust. It was built in the 1750s for a merchant who stored his wares in the cellar (a space that now holds an archaeological exhibit). But it's been associated with the Tucker family ever since Henry Tucker purchased it in 1775. The house is essentially a tribute to this well-connected clan whose members included a Bermudian governor, a U.S. treasurer, a Confederate navy captain, and an Episcopal bishop. Joseph Haine Rainey is thought to have operated a barber's shop in what is now the kitchen during the Civil War. As a freed slave from South Carolina, Rainey fled to Bermuda at the outbreak of the war. Afterward he returned to the United States and, in 1870, became the first black man to be elected to the House of Representatives. ⊠ *5 Water St., St. George* ☎ *441/297–0545* ⊕ *www.bnt.bm* ⊠ *$5; $10 combination ticket includes admission to National Trust Museum in Globe Hotel and Verdmont.*

## ELSEWHERE ON THE ISLAND

FAMILY
Fodor's Choice
★

**Bermuda Aquarium, Museum & Zoo** (*BAMZ*). The BAMZ, established in 1926, has always been a pleasant diversion. But following an ambitious decade-long expansion program, it rates as one of Bermuda's premier attractions. In the aquarium the big draw is the North Rock Exhibit, a 140,000-gallon tank that gives you a diver's-eye view of the area's living coral reefs and the colorful marine life it sustains. The museum section has multimedia and interactive displays focusing on native habitats and the impact humans have on them. The island-theme zoo displays more than 300 birds, reptiles, and mammals. Don't miss the "Islands of Australasia" exhibit with its lemurs, wallabies, and tree kangaroos, or "Islands of the Caribbean," a huge walk-through enclosure that gets you within arm's length of ibises and golden lion tamarins. Other popular areas include an outdoor seal pool, tidal touch tank, and cool kid-friendly Discovery Room. Take a break at Arugula, the locally sourced, farm-to-table café located on the grounds of the zoo. The food is great but it also has one of the best views. ⊠ *40 N. Shore Rd., Flatts Village, Hamilton* ☎ *441/293–2727* ⊕ *www.bamz.org* ⊠ *$10.*

FAMILY
Fodor's Choice
★

**Crystal Caves.** Bermuda's limestone caves have been attracting attention since the island was first settled. As far back as 1623, Captain John Smith (of Pocahontas fame) commented on these "vary strange, darke, and cumbersome" caverns. Nevertheless, it came as a surprise when two boys, attempting to retrieve a lost ball, discovered Crystal Cave in 1907. The hole through which the boys descended is still visible. But, thankfully, you can now view their find without having to make such a dramatic entrance. Inside, tour guides will lead you across a pontoon bridge that spans a 55-foot-deep subterranean lake. Look up to see stalactites dripping from the ceiling or down through the perfectly clear water to see stalagmites rising from the cave floor. Amateur spelunkers can also journey through geologic time at Crystal's smaller sister cave, Fantasy. After being closed to the public for decades, it reopened in 2001. Set aside 30 minutes to see one cave; 75 minutes if you plan to take in both. ⊠ *8 Crystal Caves Rd., off Wilkinson Ave., Bailey's Bay, Hamilton* ☎ *441/293–0640* ⊕ *www.caves.bm* ⊠ *One cave $22; combination ticket $30.*

FAMILY

**Gibbs Hill Lighthouse.** This cast-iron lighthouse soars above Southampton Parish. Designed in London and opened in 1846, the tower stands 117 feet high and 362 feet above the sea. The light was originally produced by a concentrated burner of four large, circular wicks. Today the beam from the 1,000-watt bulb can be seen by ships 40 miles out to sea and by planes 120 miles away at 10,000 feet. The haul up the 185 spiral stairs is an arduous one—particularly if you dislike heights or tight spaces. But en route to the top you can stop to catch your breath on eight landings, where photographs and drawings of the lighthouse help divert attention from your aching appendages. Once on the balcony, you'll be rewarded by panoramic island views. ⊠ *68 St. Anne's Rd.* ☎ *441/238–8069* ⊕ *www.bermudalighthouse.com* 🗐 *$2.50* ⊙ *Closed Feb.*

**National Museum of Bermuda.** The Maritime Museum, ensconced in Bermuda's largest fort, displays its collections in a series of old munitions warehouses that surround the parade grounds and Keep Pond. Insulated from the rest of the Dockyard by a moat and massive stone ramparts, it is entered by way of a drawbridge. At the Shifting House, right inside the entrance, you can wander through rooms filled with relics from some of the 350-odd ships wrecked on the island's reefs. Other buildings are devoted to seafaring pursuits such as whaling, shipbuilding, and yacht racing. More displays are in the 19th-century Commissioner's House, on the museum's upper grounds. Built as both home and headquarters for the Dockyard commissioner, the house later served as a barracks during World War I and was used for military intelligence during World War II. Today, after an award-winning restoration, it contains exhibits on Bermuda's social and military history. A must-see is the Hall of History, a mural of Bermuda's history covering 1,000 square feet. It took local artist Graham Foster more than 3½ years to paint. You'll also likely want to snap some photos of the sheep that graze outside the building: their job is to keep the grass well mowed. ⊠ *The Keep, Maritime La., Old Royal Naval Dockyard, Dockyard* ☎ *441/234–1418* ⊕ *www.nmb.bm* 🗐 *$15.*

**Paget Marsh.** Take a walk on the wild side at Paget Marsh: a 25-acre tract of land that's remained virtually untouched since presettlement times. Along with some of the last remaining stands of native Bermuda palmetto and cedar, this reserve—jointly owned and preserved by the Bermuda National Trust and the Bermuda Audubon Society—contains a mangrove forest and grassy savanna. These unspoiled habitats can be explored via a boardwalk that features interpretive signs describing the endemic flora and fauna. When listening to the cries of the native and migratory birds that frequent this natural wetland, you can quickly forget that bustling Hamilton is just minutes away. ⊠ *Lovers La.* ☎ *441/236–6483* ⊕ *www.bnt.bm* 🗐 *Free.*

FAMILY **Verdmont House Museum.** Even if you think you've had your fill of old houses, Verdmont deserves a look. The National Trust property, which opened as a museum in 1956, is notable for its Georgian architecture. Yet what really sets this place apart is its pristine condition. Though used as a residence until the mid-20th century, virtually no structural changes were made to Verdmont since it was erected around 1710. Former owners never even added electricity or plumbing (so the "powder room" was strictly used for powdering wigs). The house is also known for its enviable collection of antiques. Some pieces—such as the early-19th-century piano—were imported from England. However, most are 18th-century cedar, crafted by Bermudian cabinetmakers. Among the most interesting artifacts are the pint-size furnishings and period toys that fill Verdmont's upstairs nursery. A china coffee service, said to have been a gift from Napoléon to U.S. President James Madison, is also on display. The president never received it, though, since the ship bearing it across the Atlantic was seized by a privateer and brought to Bermuda. Verdmont also has its share of resident ghosts: among them, an adolescent girl who died of typhoid there in 1844. ⊠ 6 *Verdmont La., off Collector's Hill* ☎ *441/236–7369* ⊕ *www.bnt.bm* 🎫 *$5; $10 combination ticket with Bermuda National Trust Museum in Globe Hotel and Tucker House.*

## BEACHES

FAMILY **Elbow Beach.** Swimming and bodysurfing are great at this beach, which is bordered by the prime strand of sand reserved for guests of the Elbow Beach Hotel on the left, and the ultra-exclusive Coral Beach Club beach area on the right. It's a pleasant setting for a late-evening stroll, with the lights from nearby hotels dancing on the water. If you're planning a daytime visit during summer months, be sure to arrive early to claim your spot as this popular beach is often crowded. In addition to suntanners and joggers, groups of locals also gather here to play football and volleyball. Protective coral reefs make the waters some of the safest on the island, and a good choice for families. A lunch wagon sometimes sells fast food and cold drinks during the day, and Mickey's Beach Bar (part of the Elbow Beach Hotel) is open for lunch and dinner, though it may be difficult to get a table without a reservation. **Amenities:** parking (free); water sports. **Best for:** snorkeling; swimming; walking. ⊠ *Off South Rd.* Ⓜ *Bus 2 or 7 from Hamilton.*

FAMILY
**Fodor's** Choice
★

**Horseshoe Bay.** When locals say they're going to "the beach," they're generally referring to Horseshoe Bay, the island's most popular. With clear water, a 0.3-mile crescent of pink sand, a vibrant social scene, and the uncluttered backdrop of South Shore Park, Horseshoe Bay has everything you could ask of a Bermudian beach. A snack bar, changing rooms, beach-rental facilities, and lifeguards add to its appeal. The Good Friday Annual Kite Festival also takes place here. The undertow can be strong, especially on the main beach. A better place for children is **Horseshoe Baby Beach.** Before 2003's Hurricane Fabian, this beach was reached by climbing a trail over the dunes at the western end of Horseshoe Bay. Fabian's storm surge ploughed right through those dunes, creating a wide walkway for eager little beachgoers. Sheltered from the ocean by a ring of rocks, this cove is shallow and almost perfectly calm. In summer, toddlers can find lots of playmates. **Amenities:** food and drink; lifeguards; parking (free); showers; toilets. **Best for:** partiers; swimming; walking. ⊠ *Off South Shore Rd.* ☎ *441/238–2651* Ⓜ *Bus 7 from Hamilton.*

**Tobacco Bay.** The most popular beach near St. George's—about 15 minutes northwest of the town on foot—this small north-shore strand is huddled in a coral cove surrounded by rock formations. Its beach house serves burgers and salads as well as specialty cocktails. Equipment rentals including umbrellas, chairs, floaties, and snorkel sets, and ample parking are also available. It's a 10-minute hike from the bus stop in the town of St. George's, or you can flag down a taxi. In high season the beach is busy, especially midweek, when the cruise ships are docked; check their website for information on Friday night events, bonfires, and live music. **Amenities:** food and drink; parking (free); toilets; water sports. **Best for:** snorkeling; swimming. ⊠ 9 *Coot's Pond Rd., St. George* ☎ *441/297–2756 main, 441/705–7263 beach bar* ⊕ *www.tobaccobay. bm* Ⓜ *Bus 10 or 11 from Hamilton.*

## SHOPPING

**Hamilton** has the greatest concentration of shops in Bermuda, and Front Street is its pièce de résistance. Lined with small, pastel-color buildings, this most fashionable of Bermuda's streets houses sedate department stores and snazzy boutiques, with several small arcades and shopping alleys leading off it. A smart canopy shades the entrance to the 55 Front Street Group, which houses Crisson Jewelers. Modern Butterfield Place has galleries and boutiques selling, among other things, Louis Vuitton leather goods. The Emporium, a renovated building with an atrium, has a range of shops, from antiques to souvenirs.

**St. George's** Water Street, Duke of York Street, Hunters Wharf, Penno's Wharf, and Somers Wharf are the sites of numerous renovated buildings that house branches of Front Street stores, as well as artisans' studios. Historic King's Square offers little more than a couple of T-shirt and souvenir shops.

In the West End, **Somerset Village** has a few shops, but they hardly merit a special shopping trip. However, the **Clocktower Mall,** in a historic building at the Royal Naval Dockyard, has a few more shopping opportunities, including branches of Front Street shops and specialty boutiques. The Dockyard is also home to the Craft Market, the Bermuda Arts Centre, and Bermuda Clayworks.

## ACTIVITIES

### BICYCLING

The best and sometimes only way to explore Bermuda's nooks and crannies—its little hidden coves and 18th-century tribe roads—is by bicycle or motor scooter. A popular option for biking in Bermuda is the **Railway Trail,** a dedicated cycle path blissfully free of cars. Running intermittently the length of the old Bermuda Railway (old "Rattle 'n' Shake"), this trail is scenic and restricted to pedestrian and bicycle traffic. You can ask the staff at any bike-rental shop for advice on where to access the trail.

**Oleander Cycles.** This agency is known primarily for its selection of motorbikes and scooters for rent and sale. Single and double bikes are available and a $30 damage waiver is charged. Oleander Cycles' main store is in Paget, but it's Southampton location is convenient for The Reefs Resort & Club guests since it's right across the street. There are also small branches in Hamilton, near the St. George's Club, in the Royal Naval Dockyard, and down the road from Grotto Bay Beach Resort. ⊠ 6 *Valley Rd., off Middle Rd.* ☎ *441/236–5235* ⊕ *www.oleander cycles.bm.*

4

## GOLF

Golf courses make up nearly 17% of the island's 21.6 square miles. The scenery on the courses is usually spectacular, with flowering trees and shrubs decked out in multicolor blossoms against a backdrop of brilliant blue sea and sky. The layouts are remarkably challenging, thanks to capricious ocean breezes, daunting natural terrain, and the clever work of world-class golf architects.

**Mid Ocean Club.** The elite Mid Ocean Club is a 1921 Charles Blair Macdonald design revamped in 1953 by Robert Trent Jones Sr. *Golf Digest* ranks it among the top 100 courses outside the United States. The club has a genteel air, and a great sense of history. Even though it's expensive, a round of play is worthwhile, as you walk with a caddy to savor the traditional golf experience and the scenery. There are many holes near ocean cliffs, but you'll want to linger on the back tee of the last hole, where the view up the coast is spectacular. Overlooking the 18th hole and the south shore, the Mid Ocean's pink clubhouse is classically Bermudian down to the interior cedar trim. The pro shop offers a range of golfing goodies. The dining rooms are for members only, but you can have a drink in the bar. Nonmembers can play Monday, Wednesday, and Friday (except holidays). Caddies, club rentals, and shoe rentals are all available. ⊠ *1 Mid Ocean Dr., off S. Shore Rd., Tucker's Town* ☎ *441/293–1215* ⊕ *www.themidoceanclubbermuda.com* ✉ *$250 for nonmembers ($32 for cart)* ⅄. *18 holes, 6548 yards, par 71.*

**Turtle Hill Golf Club.** Spreading across the hillside below the high-rise Fairmont Southampton, this executive golf course is known for its steep terrain, giving players who opt to walk (for sunset tee times only) an excellent workout. The Ted Robinson design is a good warm-up for Bermuda's full-length courses, offering a legitimate test of wind and bunker play. The front nine has almost constant views of the ocean and is more difficult than the back nine, with tight holes calling for careful club selection. Club rentals and lessons are also available. Because the hotel and its restaurants are so close, there's no golf clubhouse per se, just a 10th-hole Golf Hut for snacks and drinks. ⊠ *Fairmont Southampton Resort, 101 South Rd.* ☎ *441/239–6952* ⊕ *www.fairmont.com/southampton-bermuda* ✉ *$89 before 3:30 pm with cart, $67 after 3:30 pm with cart or $45 walking* ⅄. *18 holes, 2684 yards, par 54.*

## SNORKELING

Snorkeling cruises are generally offered from April through September. Smaller boats, which limit capacity to 10 to 16 passengers, offer more personal attention and focus more on the beautiful snorkeling areas themselves. Guides on such tours often relate interesting historical and ecological information about the island. Some larger boats take up to 40 passengers.

**Jessie James Cruises.** Prepare for 2½-hour memorable hours with Jessie James Cruises. Depending on weather, you'll stop at two of three exciting locations: a shipwreck, a secluded island beach, and one of Bermuda's beautiful coral reefs. Snorkeling equipment, masks, and vests are provided; plus you can peer into the turquoise waters right through the glass bottom of the boat. The 31-foot *Pisces* holds up to 17 people and departs from Dockyard. ☎ *441/747–2204* ⊕ *www.jessiejames.bm* ✉ *From $65.*

## WHERE TO EAT

**$** ✗**The Docksider Pub & Restaurant.** Whether it's high noon, happy hour, or
BRITISH late Saturday night, locals love to mingle at this sprawling Front Street
sports bar. The extensive menu has all the pub fare classics—potato
skins, nachos, and local fish-and-chips. Bermudians often frequent this
restaurant to watch their favorite teams on the big screen. Go for the
English beef pie or a fish sandwich, and sip your dessert—a Dark 'n'
Stormy—out on the porch as you watch Bermuda stroll by. Food is
served until 10 pm but beware the nighttime crowd; Dockies, as it's
known locally, is generally more popular as a drinking venue and can
get quite overcrowded and loud, with live DJs common in summer
months. Stop by on weekend mornings to cure your hangover with a
hearty full English breakfast from 9 am. ⑤ *Average main: $15* ✉ *121
Front St., Hamilton* ☎ *441/296–3333* ⊕ *www.docksider.bm.*

**$$** ✗**Frog & Onion Pub.** This is a pub lover's dream, with everything on
BRITISH the menu named after old English pubs. The food is good, as are the
FAMILY ale and the atmosphere. With its vaulted limestone ceilings and thick
walls, the former Royal Naval Dockyard warehouse is a fitting place
for this nautically decorated restaurant and large arcade game room.
The selection caters to every palate and includes hearty house-made
shepherd's pie, chicken curry, and a selection of fresh local fish plates.
Fodors.com users love the bangers and mash, the fish sandwich, pan-
fried local rockfish or tuna, and the Frog & Onion burger. There's also
a gift shop where you can purchase your hot toddy mix. Call ahead to
confirm live summertime music and entertainment. ⑤ *Average main:
$25* ✉ *The Cooperage, 4 Freeport Rd., Dockyard* ☎ *441/234–2900*
⊕ *www.frogandonion.bm.*

# BONAIRE (KRALENDIJK)

By Ann L.
Phelan

Starkly beautiful Bonaire is the consummate desert island. Surrounded
by pristine waters, it is a haven for divers and snorkelers, who flock
here from around the world to take advantage of the excellent visibility,
easily accessed reefs, and bountiful marine life. Bonaire is the most
rustic of the three ABC islands, and despite its dependence on tourism
it manages to maintain its identity and simple way of life. There are
many good restaurants, most of which are within walking distance of
the port. Most of the island's 14,000-some inhabitants live in and
around Kralendijk, which must certainly qualify as one of the cutest
and most compact capitals in the Caribbean. The best shopping is to
be found along the very short stretch of road that constitutes "down-
town." Bonaire's beaches tend to be small and rocky, but there is a nice
stretch of sandy beach at Lac Bay. It is entirely possible to see almost
all of the sights and sounds of the island in one day by taking one of
the island tours on offer.

### ESSENTIALS
**CURRENCY**
U.S. dollar.

**TELEPHONE**

The country code for Bonaire is 599; 717 is the exchange for every four-digit number on the island. Phone cards from home rarely work on Bonaire. You can try AT&T by dialing 001–800/872–2881 from public phones. To call Bonaire from the United States, dial 011–599/717 plus the local four-digit number.

**COMING ASHORE**

One of the great benefits of Bonaire to cruise passengers is that the port is right in downtown Kralendijk. A four-minute walk takes you to most of the best shopping and restaurants on the island.

Bonaire lives for tourism; upon the arrival of a cruise ship, the locals are ready, and an impromptu crafts market springs up in the park across from the port entrance. Taxis wait right at the port and operate on fixed government rates. All the sights of Kralendijk are within easy walking distance, and a taxi ride to one of the larger resorts on the island will run between $10 and $17. A half-day island tour by taxi costs about $25 per hour for up to two passengers and will allow you to see most of the major sights. Fares increase by 50% between midnight and 6 am.

> **BEST BETS**
>
> ■ **Diving.** Bonaire is one of the world's top diving destinations. Shore diving is especially good.
>
> ■ **Snorkeling.** With reefs close to shore, snorkeling is good right off the beach.
>
> ■ **Flamingo spotting.** These shy, graceful birds are one of Bonaire's scenic delights.
>
> ■ **Kralendijk.** The accessible town has a nice assortment of restaurants and stores.
>
> ■ **Washington–Slagbaai National Park.** Bonaire's best land-based sight is this well-preserved national park.

## EXPLORING

Two routes, north and south from Kralendijk, the island's small capital, are possible on the 24-mile-long (39-km-long) island; either route will take from a few hours to a full day, depending on whether you stop to snorkel, swim, dive, or lounge. Those pressed for time will find that it's easy to explore the entire island in a day if stops are kept to a minimum.

**KRALENDIJK**

Bonaire's small, tidy capital city (population 3,000) is five minutes from the airport. The main drag, J.A. Abraham Boulevard, turns into **Kaya Grandi** in the center of town. Along it are most of the island's major stores, boutiques, and restaurants. Across Kaya Grandi, opposite Littman's jewelry store, is Kaya L.D. Gerharts, with several small supermarkets, a handful of snack shops, and some of the better restaurants. Walk down the narrow waterfront avenue called Kaya C.E.B. Hellmund, which leads straight to the **North and South piers.** In the center of town, the Harbourside Mall has chic boutiques. Along this route is **Ft. Oranje,** with its cannons. From December through April, cruise ships dock in the harbor once or twice a week. The diminutive ocher-and-white structure that looks like a tiny Greek temple is the produce market, where one can find plenty of fresh produce brought over from

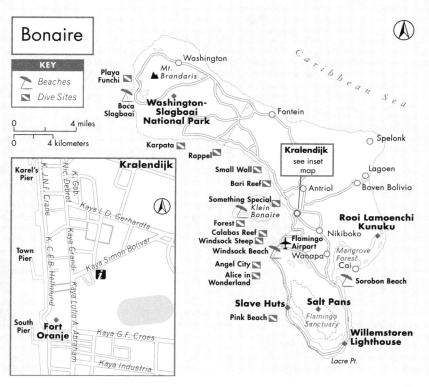

**Bonaire**

**KEY**
⛱ *Beaches*
◤ *Dive Sites*

0 ——— 4 miles
0 ——— 4 kilometers

Washington
Mt. Brandaris ▲
Playa Funchi ⛱
Boca Slagbaai ◤
**Washington-Slagbaai National Park**
Fontein
Karpata ◤
Rappel ◤
Spelonk
Lagoen
Small Wall ◤
**Kralendijk** see inset map
Antriol
Boven Bolivia
Bari Reef ◤
Something Special ◤
Klein Bonaire
**Rooi Lamoenchi Kunuku**
Forest ◤
Calabas Reef ◤
Nikiboko
Windsock Steep ◤
Windsock Beach ⛱
✈ **Flamingo Airport**
Wanapa
Mangrove Forest
Cai
Angel City ◤
Alice in Wonderland ◤
Sorobon Beach ▲
**Slave Huts** ◤
**Salt Pans** ◆
Pink Beach ⛱
*Flamingo Sanctuary*
**Willemstoren Lighthouse** ▲
Lacre Pt.

*Caribbean Sea*

**Kralendijk**

Karel's Pier
K. J.N.F. Crane
K. Gob.
K. Nic. Debrot
Kaya L.D. Gerhardts
Kaya Grandi
Kaya Lulio A. Abraham
Kaya Simon Bolivar
Town Pier
K. C. E.B. Hellmund
🛈
South Pier
**Fort Oranje**
Kaya G.F. Croes
Kaya Industria

---

Venezuela. Pick up the brochure *Walking and Shopping in Kralendijk* from the tourist office to get a map and complete list of all the monuments and sights in the town.

### SOUTH BONAIRE

The trail south from Kralendijk is chock-full of icons—both natural and man-made—that reveal part of Bonaire's history. Rent a vehicle and head out along the Southern Scenic Route. The roads wind through dramatic desert terrain, full of organ-pipe cacti and spiny-trunk mangroves—huge stumps of saltwater trees that rise from the marshes like witches. Watch for wild goats, wild donkeys, and lizards of all sizes.

FAMILY
Fodor's Choice
★

**Rooi Lamoenchi Kunuku.** Owner Ellen Herrera restored her family's homestead north of Lac Bay, in the Bonairean *kadushi* (cactus) wilderness, to educate tourists and residents about the history and tradition of authentic kunuku living and to show unspoiled terrain in two daily tours. You must make an appointment in advance and expect to spend a couple of hours. ✉ *Kaya Suiza 23* ☎ *599/717–8489* 💲 *$21.*

**Salt Pans.** Rising like mountains of snow, the salt pans are hard to miss. Harvested once a year, the "ponds" are owned by Cargill, Inc., which has reactivated the 19th-century salt industry with great success (one reason for that success is that the ocean on this part of the island is higher than the land—which makes irrigation a snap). Keep a lookout for the three 30-foot obelisks—white, blue, and red—that were used to guide the trade boats coming to pick up the salt. Look also in the distance across the pans to the abandoned solar saltworks that's now a designated flamingo sanctuary. With the naked eye you might be able to make out a pink-orange haze just on the horizon; with binoculars you will see a sea of bobbing pink bodies. The sanctuary is completely protected, and no entrance is allowed (flamingos are extremely sensitive to disturbances of any kind). ⊠ *South Bonaire.*

**Slave Huts.** The salt industry's history is revealed in Rode Pan, the site of two groups of tiny slave huts. The white huts are on the right side of the road, opposite the salt flats; the second grouping, called the red slave huts, stretches across the road toward the island's southern tip. During the 19th century, slaves worked the salt pans by day and slept in the cramped huts. Each Friday afternoon they walked many hours to Rincon to weekend with their families, returning each Sunday. The Red Slave area is a popular dive spot during low wind and calm seas. When the wind is strong and waves prevail, the local windsurf posse heads to Red Slave to catch the swell. ⊠ *South Bonaire.*

**Willemstoren Lighthouse.** Bonaire's first lighthouse was built in 1837 and is now automated (but closed to visitors). Take some time to explore the beach and notice how the waves, driven by the trade winds, play a crashing symphony against the rocks. Locals stop here to collect pieces of driftwood in spectacular shapes and to build fanciful pyramids from objects that have washed ashore. ⊠ *South Bonaire.*

## NORTH BONAIRE

The Northern Scenic Route takes you into the heart of Bonaire's natural wonders—desert gardens of towering cacti (*kadushi*, used to prepare soup, and the thornier *yatu*, used to build cactus fencing), tiny coastal coves, and plenty of fantastic panoramas. The road also weaves between eroded pink-and-black limestone walls and eerie rock formations with fanciful names such as the Devil's Mouth and Iguana Head (you'll need a vivid imagination and sharp eye to recognize them). Brazil trees growing along the route were used by Indians to make dye (pressed from a red ring in the trunk). Inscriptions still visible in several island caves were made with this dye.

A snappy excursion with the requisite photo stops will take about 2½ hours, but if you pack your swimsuit and a hefty picnic basket (forget about finding fast food), you could spend the entire day exploring this northern sector. Head out from Kralendijk on Kaya Gobernador N. Debrot until it turns into the Northern Scenic Route. Once you pass the Radio Nederland towers, you cannot turn back to Kralendijk. The narrow road becomes one-way until you get to Landhuis Karpata, and you have to follow the cross-island road to Rincon and return via the main road through the center of the island.

FAMILY

Fodor's Choice

★

**Washington–Slagbaai National Park.** Once a plantation producing divi-divi trees (the pods were used for tanning animal skins), aloe (used for medicinal lotions), charcoal, and goats, the park is now a model of conservation. It's easy to tour the 13,500-acre tropical desert terrain on the dirt roads with a jeep, but think twice about coming here if it has rained recently—the mud you may encounter will be more than inconvenient. If you're planning to hike, bring everything you may need. Goats and donkeys may dart across the road, and if you keep your eyes peeled, you may catch sight of large iguanas camouflaged in the shrubbery. Right inside the park's gate, flamingos roost on the salt pad known as **Salina Mathijs**, and exotic parakeets dot the foot of **Mt. Brandaris**, Bonaire's highest peak, at 784 feet. Some 130 species of birds fly in and out of the shrubbery in the park. Swimming, snorkeling, and scuba diving are permitted, but you're asked not to frighten the animals or remove anything from the grounds. ⌧ *Washington Slagbaai National Park* ☏ *599/717–8444* ⊕ *www.washingtonparkbonaire.org* ☒ *Free with payment of scuba diving Nature Fee ($25) or $15 with non-scuba Nature Fee ($10). Otherwise $25 for one calendar year of entry.*

**4**

## BEACHES

Although most of Bonaire's charms are underwater, there are a few beautiful beaches. Don't expect long strands of white sand, but many dive and snorkel sites have suitable entries for swimmers. Bonaire's pristine water and protected reefs offer stunning settings for sunrise or sunset viewing. Several hotels have lovely beaches that are accessible for nonguests for a nominal entrance fee. Bonaire's National Parks Foundation requires all nondivers to pay a $10 annual Nature Fee to enter the water anywhere around the island (divers pay $25). The fee can be paid at most dive shops, and the receipt will also allow access to Washington–Slagbaai National Park.

FAMILY **Klein Bonaire.** Just a water-taxi hop across from Kralendijk, this little island offers picture-perfect white-sand beaches. Klein Bonaire is one of Bonaire's most popular snorkel spots. Local boat tours frequent the island in hopes of spotting turtles. The area is protected, so absolutely no development has been allowed. Make sure to pack everything before heading to the island, including water and an umbrella to hide under because there are no refreshment stands or changing facilities, and there's almost no shade to be found. Boats leave from the Pier, across from the Rains Fishes, and the round-trip water-taxi ride costs roughly $15 per person. **Amenities:** none. **Best for:** snorkeling; solitude; swimming.

FAMILY **Sorobon Beach.** This is *the* windsurfing beach on Bonaire and one of the most beautiful beaches on the island. The sand is powdery white and the water gin-clear. It's shallow, allowing swimmers to walk up to the reef on a calm-breeze day. Here, the snorkeling is quite amazing. Keep in mind all sea life is protected, so no touching or removing shells or creatures. There are two windsurf shops on-site offering rentals and lessons. Rent a stand-up paddleboard (SUP) and cruise the shallows looking for turtles. Two on-site restaurants offer diverse menus, including tropical drinks. The public beach area near the marina has restrooms and huts for shade. **Amenities:** food and drink; parking; showers; toilets; water sports. **Best for:** snorkeling; surfing; windsurfing. ⌧ *Kaya I.R. Randolf Statuuis Van Eps, Sorobon Beach, Sorobon* ✛ *Take E.E.G. Blvd south* *from Kralendijk to Kaya I.R. Randolf Statuuis Van Eps, and then follow this route straight on to Sorobon Beach.*

**Windsock Beach.** Near the airport (just off E.E.G. Boulevard), this pretty little spot looks out toward the north side of the island and has about 200 yards of white sand along a rocky shoreline. It's a popular dive site, and swimming conditions are good. ■ **TIP→ There is often a food truck parked next door at Te Amo Beach, another great snorkeling beach.** **Amenities:** none. **Best for:** snorkeling; swimming. ⊠ *Off E.E.G. Blvd., near Flamingo Airport* ☞ *Kite City Food Truck is on-site serving delectable culinary delights.*

## SHOPPING

You can get to know all the shops in Kralendijk in an hour or so. Almost all the shops are on Kaya Grandi and adjacent streets and in tiny malls. Harbourside Mall is a pleasant, open-air mall with several fine air-conditioned shops. ■ **TIP→ Don't take home items made from tortoiseshell; they aren't allowed into the United States. Remember, too, that it's forbidden to take sea fans, coral, conch shells, and all other forms of marine life off the island.**

**JanArt Gallery.** On the main drag in town, JanArt Gallery sells unique paintings, prints, and art supplies; artist/owner Janice Huckaby has been on the island 25 years and has painted more than 1,000 original paintings of Bonaire. She also conducts art classes. ⊠ *Kaya Grandi 14, Kralendijk* ☎ *599/717–0955* ⊕ *www.janartbonaire.com.*

**Fodor'sChoice** **Littman's.** The Littmans have sold jewelry on Bonaire since 1981. Owner
★ Steven Littman handpicks many of the items available in this upscale jewelry and gift shop during his regular trips to Europe. Look for Rolex, Omega, Cartier, and Tag Heuer watches; fine gold jewelry; antique coins; nautical sculptures; resort clothing; and accessories. Typical savings are about 15% off U.S. prices. They offer watch repair and battery replacement and have another location in the Harbourside Mall. ⊠ *Kaya Grandi 33, Kralendijk* ☎ *599/717–8160* ⊕ *www.bonairelittman stores.com.*

**Richter Art Gallery.** This dedicated fine art gallery run by Linda Richter features a range of work from local artists including paintings by Linda and her late husband. In addition to paintings, the gallery also features prints and handmade jewelry. ⊠ *Kaya Statius van Eps 17, Belnem* ☎ *599/717–4112* ⊕ *www.richterart.com* ☞ *Open by appointment only.*

**Yenny's Art.** Every visitor should make a point of visiting Yenny's Art. Roam around Jenny Rijna's house, which is a replica of a traditional Bonaire town complete with her handmade life-size dolls and the skeletons of all her dead pets. Fun (and sometimes kitschy) souvenirs made out of driftwood, clay, and shells are all handmade by Jenny. ⊠ *Kaya Betico Croes 6, near post office, Kralendijk* ☎ *599/717–5004.*

# ACTIVITIES

### BICYCLING

Bonaire is generally flat, so bicycles are an easy way to get around if you are physically fit. Because of the heat, it's essential to carry water if you're planning to cycle for any distance and especially if your plans involve exploring the deserted interior. There are more than 180 miles (290 km) of unpaved routes (as well as the many paved roads) on the island.

**Tropical Travel.** This tour operator offers bikes for $11 per day or $55 per week (a $300 deposit is required). ✉ *Plaza Resort Bonaire, J.A. Abraham Blvd. 80, Kralendijk* ☎ *599/701–1232* ⊕ *www.tropicaltravel bonaire.com.*

### DIVING AND SNORKELING

Bonaire has some of the best reef diving this side of Australia's Great Barrier Reef. It takes only 5–25 minutes to reach many sites, the current is usually mild, and although some reefs have sudden, steep drops, most begin just offshore and slope gently downward at a 45-degree angle. General visibility runs 60 to 100 feet. You can see several varieties of coral: knobby-brain, giant-brain, elkhorn, staghorn, mountainous star, gorgonian, and black. You can also encounter schools of parrot fish, surgeonfish, angelfish, eel, snapper, and grouper. Shore diving is excellent just about everywhere on the leeward side. There are sites suitable for every skill level; they're clearly marked by yellow stones on the roadside.

The best snorkeling spots are on the island's leeward side, where you have shore access to the reefs, and along the west side of Klein Bonaire, where the reef is better developed. All snorkelers and swimmers must pay a $10 Nature Fee, which allows access to the waters around the island and Washington–Slagbaai National Park for one calendar year. The fee can be paid at most dive shops.

### DIVE OPERATORS

Many of the dive shops listed *below* offer PADI and NAUI certification courses and SSI, as well as underwater photography and videography courses. Some shops are also qualified to certify dive instructors. Full certification courses cost approximately $385; open-water refresher courses run about $240; a one-tank boat dive with unlimited shore diving costs about $40; a two-tank boat dive with unlimited shore diving is about $65. As for equipment, renting a mask, fin, and snorkel costs about $12 altogether; for a BC (buoyancy compensator) and regulator, expect to pay about $20.

Most dive shops on Bonaire offer a complete range of snorkel gear for rent and will provide beginner training; some dive operations also offer guided snorkeling and night snorkeling. The cost for a guided snorkel session is about $50 and includes slide presentations, transportation to the site, and a tour. Gear rental is approximately $10 per 24-hour period.

**Wannadive.** Wannadive is a casual, efficient dive company with several locations around the island, offering daily boat dives to Klein Bonaire.

They support the dive needs of beginners to professionals, from recreational to technical diving. Wannadive has an expansive rental inventory of dive and snorkel equipment and offers repair and retail at the various locations on island. ⊠ *Kaya Gobernador N. Debrot 73, Kralendijk* ☎ *599/717–8884* ⊕ *www.wannadive.com.*

## WHERE TO EAT

$ — ECLECTIC

✕ **Boudoir.** Despite the nighttime-bedroom connotation this excellent patio eatery at the Royal Palm Mall is open only for breakfast, lunch, and late-afternoon snacks. Besides having some of the best coffee on the island, Boudoir offers a range of soups, salads, sandwiches, and burgers that should please even the most discerning of diners. It's the perfect place to relax with an iced coffee and a smoked-salmon-and-capers sandwich after a day of exploring Kralendijk. ⑤ *Average main: $9* ⊠ *Royal Palm Mall, Kaya Grandi 26 F/G, Kralendijk* ☎ *599/717–4321.*

$ — CARIBBEAN FAMILY Fodor's Choice ★

✕ **Hang Out Bar.** If your vision of a Caribbean vacation includes seaside dining with balmy trade winds blowing and views of a gorgeous Caribbean bay, then Hang Out Bar is your spot. It overlooks Lac Bay, the training ground for the famous Bonaire Windsurf Team. Pros from around the globe come to train while tourists come to hone their skills and experience windsurf bliss. Hang Out Bar offers libations and tasty delights including fresh house-made smoothies and healthy and delicious salads and sandwiches, and there's always a daily special, usually fresh-caught fish. They also serve Dutch snack treats including *bitterballen* (meatballs) and *frikkendel* (hot dog). There's a lively bar scene, with a great happy hour. Free beach loungers and plenty of tables and chairs in the shade, as well as free Wi-Fi are available. Select evenings feature local and international music acts. Order a pitcher of their famous house-made sangria and you're all set. ⑤ *Average main: $10* ⊠ *Kaminda Sorobon 12, Kralendijk* ☎ *599/717–5064* ⊘ *No dinner* ⊲ *Reservations not accepted.*

# CALICA (PLAYA DEL CARMEN), MEXICO

By Jeffrey Van Fleet

Just minutes away from Calica, Playa del Carmen has become one of Mexico's fastest-growing communities, with a pace almost as hectic as Cancún's. Hotels, restaurants, and shops multiply here faster than you can say "Kukulcán." Some are branches of Cancún establishments whose owners have taken up permanent residence in Playa, while others are owned by American and European expats (predominately Italians) who came here years ago. It makes for a varied, international community. Avenida 5, the first street in town parallel to the beach, is a long pedestrian walkway with shops, cafés, and street performers; small hotels and stores stretch north from this avenue. Avenida Juárez, running east–west from the highway to the beach, is the main commercial zone for the Riviera Maya corridor. Here locals visit the food shops, pharmacies, hardware stores, and banks that line the curbs. People traveling the coast by car usually stop here to stock up on supplies—its banks, grocery stores, and gas stations are the last ones until Tulum.

## ESSENTIALS

### CURRENCY

The Mexican peso. U.S. dollars and credit cards are widely accepted in the area, from the port to Playa del Carmen, but it's best to have pesos—and small bills—when you visit ruins, where cashiers often run out of change.

### TELEPHONE

Most pay phones accept prepaid Ladatel cards, sold in 30-, 50-, or 100-peso denominations. To use the card, insert it in the pay phone's slot, dial 001 (for calls to the United States) or 01 (for calls within Mexico), followed by the area code and number. Credit is deleted from the card as you use it, and the balance is displayed on the small screen on the phone. Most tri-band mobile phones from the U.S. work in Mexico, though you must pay roaming charges.

> ### BEST BETS
>
> ■ **A Day at Xcaret.** Particularly for families, this ecological theme park is a great way to spend the day.
>
> ■ **Beaches.** The beaches in the Riviera Maya are stellar.
>
> ■ **Diving.** From Playa del Carmen it's only a short hop to some of the Yucatán's best dive sites.
>
> ■ **Shopping.** Playa del Carmen's Avenida 5 can easily keep you occupied for your day in port if you are a shopaholic.

### COMING ASHORE

The port at Calica, about 3 miles south of the town of Playa del Carmen (between Playa del Carmen and the Xcaret theme park), is small. Sometimes ships actually dock, and other times passengers are tendered to shore. There is a makeshift market at the port, where locals sell crafts. Beyond that, there is not much to do, and you'll need to head into Playa del Carmen proper to find restaurants and even tour operators. If you really want to shop, skip the vendors at the port and head to Playa del Carmen's Avenida 5, where you can easily spend an afternoon browsing shops and enjoying restaurants.

Taxis and tour buses are available at the port to take you to Playa del Carmen and other destinations, but lines often form as passengers wait for taxis, so plan accordingly if you really want to pack a lot of activity into your day. Your taxi will have you in Playa del Carmen or in Xcaret in under 10 minutes, but you'll pay a whopping $10 for the short trip.

# EXPLORING

### PLAYA DEL CARMEN

*3 miles (5 km) north of Calica*

Once upon a time, Playa del Carmen was a fishing village with a ravishing deserted beach. The villagers fished and raised coconut palms to produce copra, and the only foreigners who ventured here were beach bums and travelers catching ferries to Cozumel. That was a long time ago, however. These days the beach is far from deserted, although it is still delightful, with its alabaster-white sand and turquoise-blue waters. In fact Playa has become one of Latin America's fastest-growing

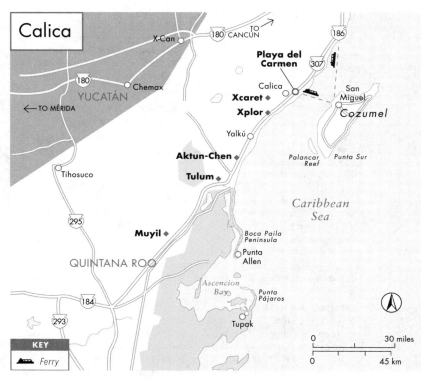

Calica

X-Can
TO CANCÚN
186
180

**Playa del Carmen**
307

Calica
San Miguel
180
Chemax

YUCATÁN
Xcaret ◆
Xplor ◆
Cozumel

← TO MÉRIDA

Yalkú

**Aktun-Chen** ◆
Palancar Reef   Punta Sur

**Tulum** ◆

Tihosuco

Caribbean Sea

295

**Muyil** ◆
Boca Paila Peninsula

QUINTANA ROO
Punta Allen

Ascension Bay
Punta Pájaros

184

293
Tupak

**KEY**
🚢 Ferry

0        30 miles
0        45 km

communities, with a population of more than 135,000 and a pace almost as hectic as Cancún's. The ferry pier, where the hourly boats arrive from and depart for Cozumel, is another busy part of town. The streets leading from the dock have shops, restaurants, cafés, a hotel, and food stands. If you take a stroll north from the pier along the beach, you'll find the serious sun worshippers. On the pier's south side is the sprawling Playacar complex. The development is a labyrinth of residences and all-inclusive resorts bordered by an 18-hole championship golf course.

## SOUTH OF CALICA

FAMILY **Aktun-Chen** (*Indiana Joes*). The name is Mayan for "the cave with cenoFodor's Choice tes inside," and these amazing underground caverns—estimated to be
★ about 5-million years old—are the area's largest. You walk through the underground passages, past stalactites and stalagmites, until you reach the cenote with its various shades of deep green. There's also an on-site canopy tour and one cenote where you can take a swim. ■TIP→ **This top family attraction isn't as crowded or touristy as Xplor, Xel-Há, and Xcaret.** ⊠ *Carretera 307, Km 107, opposite Bahia Principe resort, between Akumal and Xel-Ha, Akumal* ☎ *998/806–4962* ⊕ *www. aktun-chen.com* 🎫 *Cave tour 500 MP; cenote tour 500 MP; canopy tour 650 MP.*

**Muyil** (*Chunyaxché*). This photogenic archaeological site just 15 km (9 miles) down the 307 from Tulum, at the northern end of the Sian Ka'an biosphere reserve, is underrated. Once known as Chunyaxché, it's now called by its ancient name, Muyil (pronounced moo- *hill*). It dates from the late preclassic era, when it was connected by road to the sea and served as a port between Cobá and the Mayan centers in Belize and Guatemala. The most notable site at Muyil today is the remains of the 56-foot **Castillo**—one of the tallest on the Quintana Roo coast—at the center of a large acropolis. During excavations of the Castillo, jade figurines representing the moon and fertility goddess Ixchel were found. Recent excavations at Muyil have uncovered some smaller structures. The ruins stand near the edge of a deep-blue lagoon and are surrounded by almost impenetrable jungle—so be sure to bring insect repellent. You can drive down a dirt road on the side of the ruins to swim or fish in the lagoon. ⊠ *Carretera 307, 16 km (10 miles) south of Tulum, Sian Ka'an* ⊕ *www.inah.gob.mx* ☑ *40 MP.*

**Fodor'sChoice** **Tulum.** Tulum is one of the few Mayan cities known to have been inhab-
★ ited when the conquistadores arrived in 1518. In the 16th century it was a trade center, a safe harbor for trade goods from rival Mayan factions who considered the city neutral territory. The city reached its height when its merchants, made wealthy through trading, for the first time outranked Maya priests in authority and power. Although you can see the ruins thoroughly in two hours, you might want to allow extra time for a swim or a stroll on the beach. The largest and most-photographed structure, the Castillo (Castle), looms at the edge of a 40-foot limestone cliff just past the Temple of the Frescoes. The front wall of the Castillo has faint carvings of the Descending God and columns depicting the plumed serpent god, Kukulcán, who was introduced to the Maya by the Toltecs. A few small altars sit atop a hill at the north side of the cove, with a good view of the Castillo and the sea. ■ **TIP→ To avoid the longest lines, be sure to arrive before 11 am. Outside the entrance are dozens of vendors selling Mexican crafts, so bring some extra cash for souvenirs.** ⊠ *Carretera 307, Km 133, Tulum* ☎ *983/837–2411* ☑ *65 MP entrance; 54 MP parking; 67 MP video fee; 27 MP shuttle from parking to ruins.*

FAMILY **Xcaret.** Among the most popular attractions are the Paradise River raft tour that takes you on a winding, watery journey through the jungle; the Butterfly Pavilion, where thousands of butterflies float dreamily through a botanical garden while New Age music plays in the background; and there's an ocean-fed aquarium where you can see local sea life drifting through coral heads and sea fans. The entrance fee covers only access to the grounds and the exhibits; all other activities and equipment—from sea treks and dolphin tours to lockers and swim gear—are extra. The expensive "Plus Pass includes park entrance, lockers, snorkel equipment, food, and drinks. You can buy tickets from any travel agency or major hotel along the coast. ⊠ *Carretera 307, Km 282, Xcaret* ☎ *984/206–0038, 855/326–0682 in U.S.* ⊕ *www.xcaret. com* ☑ *Basic Pass 1780 MP; Plus Pass 2320 MP; Night Pass 1420 MP.*

FAMILY **Xplor.** Designed for thrill-seekers, this 125-acre park features underground rafting in stalactite-studded water caves and cenotes. Swim in a stalactite river, ride in an amphibious vehicle, or soar across the park on 13 of the longest zip lines in Mexico. The daytime price—valid from 9 to 5—includes all food, drink, and equipment. A separate evening admission from 5:30 to 10:30 pm includes "Xplor Fuego" activities, which includes similar things but with a nighttime theme. Mix-and-match packages can be purchased online to include both day and evening admission and/or entry to Xcaret next door. ⊠ *Carretera 307, Km 282* ☎ *984/147–6560, 888/922–7381* ⊕ *www.xplor.travel* ⊠ *Xplor: 2500 MP; Xplor Fluego: 1790 MP* ☉ *Closed Sun.*

## BEACHES

**Playa del Carmen Main Beach.** The community's most central section of beach stretches from the ferry docks up to Calle 14 at Gran Porto Real, a swath of deep white sand licked by turquoise water. The beach and water are clean, but there is some boat traffic that makes swimming less idyllic. Snorkelers aren't likely to see much here, but you can't beat the beach for convenience: countless bars and restaurants are a short walk away on Fifth Avenue, masseurs compete (discreetly) to knead out your kinks, and it's easy to find a dive shop ready to take you out to sea. The closer you get to the docks, the more people you'll find. If you're looking for seclusion, head farther north outside Playa del Carmen. **Amenities:** food and drink; water sports. **Best for:** swimming; walking. ⊠ *Between ferry docks and Calle 14, Playa del Carmen.*

## SHOPPING

Playa del Carmen's Avenida 5 between Calles 4 and 10 is the best place to shop along the coast. Boutiques sell folk art and textiles from around Mexico, and clothing stores carry lots of sarongs and beachwear made from Indonesian batiks. A shopping area called Calle Corazon, between Calles 12 and 14, has a pedestrian street, art galleries, restaurants, and boutiques.

**La Hierbabuena Artesanía.** Owner Melinda Burns offers a collection of fine Mexican clothing and crafts at La Hierbabuena Artesanía. ⊠ *Av. 5, between Calles 8 and 10, Playa del Carmen* ☎ *984/873–1741.*

## ACTIVITIES

### DIVING

**The Abyss.** PADI and SSI-affiliated, the Abyss offers introductory courses and dive trips. They also run dives in Tulum through the cenotes. ⊠ *Av. 1, between Calles 10 and 12, Playa del Carmen* ☎ *984/876–3285* ⊕ *www.abyssdivecenter.com* ⊠ *From 920 MP.*

**Tank-Ha Dive Center.** Playa's original dive outfit has PADI-certified teachers and runs diving and snorkeling excursions to the reefs and caverns. Dive packages and Cozumel trips are available, too. ⊠ *Av. 1, between Calles 20 and 22, Playa del Carmen* ☎ *984/873–0302* ⊕ *www.tankha. com* ⊠ *From 700 MP.*

## GOLF

**Grand Coral Golf Riviera Maya.** This 18-hole championship course was designed by Nick Price. Not as busy (or expensive) as neighboring courses at Mayakoba or Playacar, Grand Coral is challenging without being overly intimidating. You'll face a good amount of bunkers and water on the holes. The greens are slow, but the course is well maintained. If you can swing it, opt for the all-inclusive package that covers food and drink. Otherwise green fees cover only the cart, bottled water, and golf tees. ✉ *Grand Coral Riviera Maya, Carretera 307, Km 294, Playa del Carmen* ☎ *984/109–6025, 888/212–3209 in U.S.* ⊕ *www. grandcoralgolf.com* 🕸 *$175 for 18 holes* 🏌 *18 holes, 7043 yards, par 71.*

## WHERE TO EAT

**$$** ✕ **Babe's Noodles & Bar.** Photos and paintings of old Hollywood pin-up
**THAI** models share decor space with a large stone Buddha at this Swedish-owned Thai restaurant. It's known for fresh, interesting fare cooked to order. Try the spring rolls with peanut sauce and Korean sesame noodles, then wash it all down with a refreshing lemonade, blended with ice and mint. If you're traveling during low season, note that this restaurant usually closes from mid-September through early October. ⑤ *Average main: 175 MP* ✉ *Calle 10 between Avs. 5 and 10, Playa del Carmen* ☎ *984/879–3569* ⊕ *www.babesnoodlesandbar.com* ⊘ *Closed Mon.*

**$$** ✕ **Hot Casual Food.** This cheap streetside breakfast café with the utilitar-
**CAFÉ** ian name opens at 7 am, and it's one of the few places where you can get breakfast before early-morning sightseeing. Known for Mexican egg dishes like the chile-and-cheese omelet, which will get your day off to a spicy start, Hot also serves more pedestrian packaged muffins and pastries. Salads and sandwiches are available at lunch and dinner. Two other branches (at the Plaza Inn on Avenida 115 Norte and at the Centro Maya on the Cancún-Tulum Highway) serve the same fare and keep similar hours. ⑤ *Average main: 110 MP* ✉ *5 Av., between Calles 38 and 40, Playa del Carmen* ☎ *984/803–4268.*

# CARTAGENA, COLOMBIA

By Greg
Devilliers

Ever wondered what the "Spanish Main" refers to? This is it. Colombia's Caribbean coast invokes ghosts of conquistadors, pirates, and missionaries journeying to the New World in search of wealth, whether material or spiritual. Anchoring this shore is the magnificent colonial city of Cartagena—officially Cartagena de Indias (Cartagena of the Indies)—founded in 1533. Gold and silver passed through here en route to Spain, making the city an obvious target for pirates (including Sir Francis Drake), hence the construction of Cartagena's trademark walls and fortresses. The Ciudad Amurallada (walled city) is the near perfect historic destination—emanating history from the cobblestones, the ancient trees presiding over cool patches of respite in Plaza Bolivar, and the houses of traders, nuns, or generals that have been turned into fine boutique hotels. Cruise passengers will find that security is quite visible (without being oppressive) here in the country's top tourist destination. Take the same precautions you would visiting any city of one million people, and you should have a grand time.

## ESSENTIALS

### CURRENCY

The Colombian peso. In Colombia, peso prices are denoted with the "$" sign too. If they carry a lot of zeros, they likely are not dollar prices, but always ask.

### SAFETY

Security is tighter in Cartagena than elsewhere in Colombia, so you certainly can navigate the city on your own. (Knowing some Spanish helps.) However, beware of pickpockets in the tourist areas and avoid odd hours or being too isolated on Playa Blanca; since the completion of the bridge linking it to the mainland, muggings have become more frequent.

---

**BEST BETS**

■ **Cruise the Harbor.** A boat trip around the city's inner bay allows to you appreciate the city's formidable walls and fortresses.

■ **Islas del Rosario.** The beaches of nearby Islas del Rosario are an hour away by boat.

■ **Ride a Coche.** Take the quintessential horse-and-buggy ride through the streets.

■ **Walk Las Murallas.** Walking the city's massive stone walls is a favorite tourist pastime.

■ **Visit Palacio de la Inquisición.** Cartagena's most-visited sight is this historic—and creepy—center for the Spanish Inquisition.

---

### TELEPHONE

The Terminal de Cruceros has ample phones for your use. Local numbers in Cartagena have seven digits. For international calls, dial 009 followed by country and area codes and local number. AT&T offers roaming options in this region of Colombia for calls back to the United States; if you have a tri-band GSM phone it should work.

### COMING ASHORE

Cruise ships dock at the modern Terminal de Cruceros (cruise terminal) on Isla de Manga, an island connected by a bridge to the historic city center, about 2 miles (3 km) northwest of the docks. You'll find telephones, Internet cafés, and a duty-free shop in the terminal.

A small army of taxis waits in front of the terminal. Expect to pay 15,000 pesos for the 10-minute drive to the walled city; the same fare will get you to the nearby beaches at Bocagrande. Drivers are all too happy to take you on your own do-it-yourself guided tour. Most charge around 20,000 pesos for an hour of waiting time. Once you are in the walled city, Cartagena is so compact that walking the labyrinth of cobblestone streets is the most enjoyable way to get around, but you need to take a taxi if you visit the Cerro de la Popa.

---

## EXPLORING

Nothing says Cartagena quite like a ride in a horse-drawn carriage, or *coche,* as it is known locally. Drivers are a wealth of information about Cartagena, and many do speak English. The downside for you is that

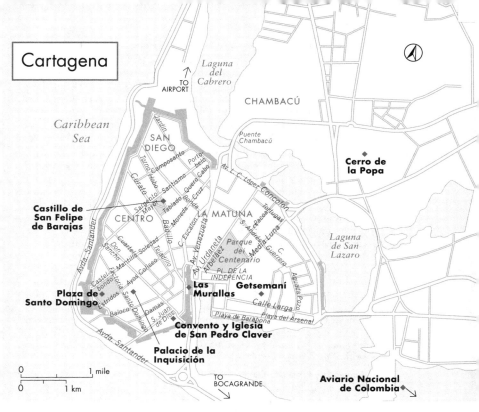

# Cartagena

Caribbean Sea

TO AIRPORT

Laguna del Cabrero

CHAMBACÚ

Puente Chambacú

Cerro de la Popa

SAN DIEGO

Jardín

Castillo de San Felipe de Barajas

CENTRO

Torno Habla
Camposanto
Portobela
Quero Cabal
Quero Cruz
Santísmo
Santa Cruz
Tablado Bonda
Moneda
Badillo
C. Escallon
Cochera
Av. L. C. López
Concolón
Tortugas
Av. Andes Pacas
C. Media Luna
S. Andrés Guerrero
C. Aguda Pozo

LA MATUNA

Parque del Centenario

PL. DE LA INDEPENCIA

Las Murallas

Getsemaní

Laguna de San Lazaro

Plaza de Santo Domingo

Estridos
Baloco Domingo
Santo Domingo
Damas
S. Juan de Dios

Calle Larga

Playa de Barahona
Playa del Arsenal

Convento y Iglesia de San Pedro Claver

Palacio de la Inquisición

0    1 mile
0    1 km

TO BOCAGRANDE

Aviario Nacional de Colombia

---

most rides begin near dusk—it's a far cooler time of the day, after all—
and your need to be back on ship may not coincide with that schedule.
Do check. You can pick up carriages at many places, including the Plaza
de los Coches, near the Puerta del Reloj in the walled city, or the Hotel
Caribe in Bocagrande. Expect to pay around $200 (in U.S. dollars) for
a two-hour tour, or around $60 for a half-hour (this kind of excursion
is best when the cost is split among a group).

FAMILY
Fodor's Choice
★

**Aviario Nacional de Colombia.** Opened early 2016, this impressive bird
sanctuary is the country's best, and in a nation famed for aviary bio-
diversity it's an opportunity not to be missed. There are three distinct
biomes—tropical jungle, coastal, and desert—as well as 21 areas to
explore that are home to 138 species of birds. ⊠ *Barú Island, Km 14.5
vía Barú, Cartagena* ✛ *Just past Barú Bridge* ☎ *5/673–4045* ⊕ *www.
aviarionacional.co* ☏ *35000 pesos.*

Fodor's Choice
★

**Castillo de San Felipe de Barajas.** What began in 1657 as a small fort
designed to protect the overland entrance to Cartagena grew over the
following century into a sprawling stone behemoth covering the entire
hill. The largest of its kind on the continent, it's a fascinating example
of asymmetrical military construction unseen in Europe. The unique
layout allowed for devastatingly efficient lines of coverage for some
63 cannons lining the walls, and the fort would never fall. Another

ingenious device was a maze of tunnels—minimally lit today to allow for spooky exploration—that connects vital points of the fort. If you don't speak Spanish, an English audio guide makes the visit infinitely richer. The fort is an easy enough walk from Getsemaní with great views of the city; the best time to go is in the afternoon. A taxi shouldn't cost more than the standard minimum 6,000 pesos, although most drivers will want to charge you 8,000. ⊠ *Av. Pedro de Heredia at Carrera 17, Cartagena* 🕾 *5/656–6803* 🖳 *25000 pesos.*

**Fodor's Choice** **Cerro de la Popa.** Make this one of your first stops on any visit to get
★ the best possible grasp of the city's geography and its role as a fortified protector of a crucial headland, as well as a more modern context for the historic center that is now surrounded by a sprawling city. Because of its strategic location, the white-walled 17th-century monastery here intermittently served as a fortress during the colonial era. It now houses a museum and a chapel dedicated to the Virgen de la Candelaria, Cartagena's patron saint, with a stunning gilded altar and religious relics up to 500 years old. Taxis charge around 10,000 pesos one way to bring you here—with the wait and return expect to pay between 40,000 and 50,000 pesos—and the sight can be included on one of Cartagena's popular *chiva* (horsedrawn carriage) tours. Under no circumstances should you walk between the city center and the hill; occasional muggings of tourists have been reported along the route. For spectacular views of Cartagena, ascend the hill around sunset. ⊠ *Barrio Pie de la Popa Cra. 29, Lomas de San Blas* ✛ *3 km (2 miles) southeast of Ciudad Amurallada* 🕾 🖳 *8000 pesos.*

**Convento y Iglesia de San Pedro Claver.** Cartagena's most impressive religious building, the church's yellow dome is an icon of the city skyline, and the carved stone facade dominates the small plaza below that is surrounded by restaurants and often filled with street vendors and musicians. Constructed at the beginning of the 17th century, the cool, peaceful interior centers around the lush green courtyard of the cloister, most of which is open to visitors, including a small museum that displays African and Haitian art and a variety of religious relics. To the right is the rather austere church, dominated by an ornate altar, which also holds the bones of San Pedro Claver, for whom the building and plaza are named. Claver was a Spanish Jesuit monk who spent 40 years in Cartagena—visitors can also enter the cell where he lived—dedicated to healing and ministering to the tens of thousands of slaves who passed through the port annually. Known as the "Slave of the Slaves," he was canonized in 1888, the first in the new world to receive this honor. There is some information in English, but we recommend hiring an English-speaking guide at the ticket office. ⊠ *Carrera 4 No. 31–00, Centro* 🕾 *5/664–4741* 🖳 *9000 pesos.*

**Fodor's Choice** **Getsemaní.** Once run-down and troubled, the Getsemaní neighborhood
★ just beyond the posher parts of the historic walled city now exudes fresh but still bohemian energy, thanks to an infusion of new restaurants and bars, as well as boutique hotels. Locals hang out and chat on the narrow streets like Callejon Angosto and gather at Plaza de la Santísima Trinidad, the heart of the neighborhood. In the plaza, look for the statue of Pedro Romero, who fought for independence from Spain. Abundant

street art along Calle de la Sierpe (and other avenues) and gritty edges keep the scene real and down to earth, at least for now. You can stroll Getsemaní day or night to check things out; weekend evenings are very lively. ✉ *Bordered by Calle del Arsenal, Av. Daniel Lemaitre, and Av. Luis Carlos López, Getsemaní.*

**Las Murallas.** Cartagena survived only because of its walls, and its *murallas* remain today the city's most distinctive feature, part of a UNESCO World Heritage Site that draws visitors to the historic and well-preserved city center full of plazas, shops, and diversions. Repeated sacking by pirates and foreign invaders convinced the Spaniards of the need to enclose the region's most important port. Construction began in 1600 and finished in 1796. The Puerta del Reloj is the principal gate to the innermost sector of the walled city. Its four-sided clock tower was a relatively late addition (1888), and has become the symbol of the city. Walking along the thick walls (you can enter at many points, and there are overpriced bars in some parts) is one of Cartagena's time-honored pastimes, especially late in the afternoon when you can watch the setting sun redden the Caribbean. ✉ *Area bounded by Bahía de las Ánimas, Laguna de San Lázaro, and Caribbean Sea, Centro.*

**Fodor's Choice**
★

**Palacio de la Inquisición.** One of Cartagena's most visited tourist sites documents the darkest period in the city's history. A baroque limestone doorway off Plaza de Bolívar marks the entrance to the 1770 Palace of the Inquisition, the headquarters of the repressive arbiters of political and spiritual orthodoxy who once exercised jurisdiction over Colombia, Ecuador, and Venezuela. Although the museum displays benign colonial and pre-Columbian artifacts and also has a brief overview of the city's history with maps and models, most people congregate on the ground floor to "Eeewww!" over the implements of torture—racks and thumbscrews, to name but two—and the displays on how to judge a witch. We recommend you hire an English-speaking guide since many displays need explanations and all signs are in Spanish. ✉ *Plaza de Bolivar, Centro* ☎ *5/664–4570* ⊕ *www.muhca.gov.co* ✉ *18000 pesos.*

**Plaza de Santo Domingo.** The eponymous church looming over the plaza is the oldest in the city and a contrast to the plaza's generally festive and bustling atmosphere. At night the area is particularly attractive as it fills up with tables from surrounding bars and restaurants. A popular, eye-catching landmark since 2000 is Colombian artist Fernando Botero's large bronze *Gertrudis*, a sculpture of a plump, naked woman. Don't pass by the Iglesia de Santo Domingo: built in 1539, the church has a simple whitewashed interior, bare limestone pillars, a raised choir, and an adjacent cloistered seminary. Local lore says the bell tower's twisted profile is the work of the Devil, who, dispirited at having failed to destroy it, threw himself into the plaza's well. For a fee you can take an audio tour. ✉ *Calle Santo Domingo and Carrera Santo Domingo, Centro.*

## BEACHES

Cartagena—although a city almost totally surrounded by water and with the Caribbean once her very walls—is quite simply not a beach destination. Time and money is much better spent here getting lost wandering cobbled streets between shady plazas and every now and then dipping into the city's ever-growing gastronomic scene. The most popular nearby beaches options have lost much of their appeal as tourism has boomed, although a great beach day can be had if you head into it with reasonable expectations.

**Bocagrande,** although a cheap taxi ride away, will disappoint most beach lovers. It offers only a strip of gray-tinged sand tucked up against a busy road lined by towering apartment buildings and hotels. Beachgoers will be constantly hassled by traders and insistent masseurs.

Though much more attractive with white sands and clear waters, the much loved **Playa Blanca** has suffered from the bridge connecting Barú Island to the mainland, seeing the beach fill up with vendors, particularly on the arrival of the tour boats from the harbor. Relaxation is often ruined by constant sales pitches for massages, beach chairs, and Jet Ski rides. Easy access has also led to an increase in petty crime, so keep an eye on your valuables at all times, and avoid being isolated or on the beach at odd hours.

The best bet to get your feet wet is a tour to the coral archipelago, **Las Islas del Rosario.** Though the coral reefs around the islands have suffered bleaching from recent high temperatures and have lost much of their previous splendor, a day out snorkeling or diving will be a pleasure for all but hardened scuba enthusiasts. Visibility is usually good, and there is still plenty of coral and sealife to be found. Daytrips to the islands can be arranged from the harbor, but the hassle and risk of scams is not worth it. Instead, you will get a much better tour—and quite possibly a better price—if you join a tour organized by your hotel.

## SHOPPING

Think "Juan Valdez" if you're looking for something to take the folks back home. Small bags of fine Colombian coffee, the country's signature souvenir, are available in most tourist-oriented shops. Colombia also means emeralds, and you'll find plenty in the jewelry shops on or near Calle Pantaleón, beside the cathedral. Don't forget the duty-free shop in the Terminal de Cruceros for those last-minute purchases.

**Las Bóvedas,** a series of arched storerooms in the Ciudad Amurallada's northern corner now houses about two-dozen shops with the best selection of local and national crafts. If you're looking for emeralds, visit the jewelry shops on or near Calle Pantaleón, beside the cathedral.

# ACTIVITIES

### DIVING

Coral reefs line the coast south of Cartagena, although warm-water currents have begun to erode them in recent years. There is still good diving to be had in the Islas del Rosario, an archipelago of 27 coral islands about 21 miles (35 km) southwest of the city.

**Fodor'sChoice**
★ **Diving Planet.** The best, friendliest, and most professional diving outfit in the city offers a good variety of dives and snorkeling expeditions. Quality gear and dive instructors make this a great choice for beginners looking to get started or experienced divers looking for the best the nearby oceans have to offer. ⊠ *Calle Estanco del aguardiente (Calle 38) #5–09, Centro* ☎ *320/230–1515* ⊕ *www.divingplanet.org.*

4

## WHERE TO EAT

**$$$**
TAPAS ✕ **Caffé Lunático.** Set on a lovely and generally calm Getsemaní street, this funky café dominated by a wall-sized graffitti mural serves the tastiest breakfast in town. Try the *arepita lunatica* for one of the best examples of the local breakfast classic. It's also an excellent choice for tapas in the evening. Ingredients are of notably good quality, and the Spanish owner/chef reliably impresses with a short menu that shows off some inventive and remarkably well-executed dishes ranging from a watermelon gazpacho with avocado and a shrimp brochette, to a corvina *tiradito* with banana and lemongrass, to a more traditional grilled octopus. All around, Lunático offers great value for the quality of the food. ⑤ *Average main: 27000 pesos* ⊠ *Calle Espiritu Santo 29–184, Getsemaní* ☎ *5/660–1735.*

**$$$**
CARIBBEAN ✕ **Cocina de Pepina.** One of the most recommended local favorites is a no-frills bastion of Cartagena cuisine built on the impressive research and

**Fodor'sChoice**
★ skill of chef and culinary historian María "Pepina" Yances. Although Doña Pepina passed away in 2014, her energy and recipe book have been carried forward by her family, and the restaurant remains a must-visit for those keen to sample local classics. The blackboard menu changes daily, although staples like the *mote de queso* (a soup of yam, coconut milk, and local cheese) and *cabeza de gato* (balls of mashed plantain and yam with a zingy tomato/onion relish) will always be on hand. Keep an eye out for the peppers stuffed with ground beef, another punchy perennial favorite. ⑤ *Average main: 35000 pesos* ⊠ *Callejon Vargas #9A–06, Getsemaní* ☎ *5/664–2944* ⊗ *Closed Sun. No dinner Mon.*

# COLÓN, PANAMA

By Jeffrey Van Fleet

When you consider the decades it took to build the canal, not to mention the lives lost and government failures and triumphs involved during its construction, it comes as no surprise that the Panama Canal is often called the Eighth Wonder of the Modern World. Best described as an aquatic bridge, the Panama Canal connects the Caribbean Sea with the Pacific Ocean by raising ships up and over Central America, through artificially created Gatún Lake, the highest point at 85 feet above sea level, and then lowering them back to sea level by using a series of locks, or water steps. A masterful engineering feat, three pairs of locks—Gatún, Pedro Miguel, and Miraflores—utilize gravity to fill and drain as ships pass through chambers 1,000 feet long by 110 feet wide that are "locked" by doors weighing 80 tons apiece, yet actually float into position. Most cruise ships pass through the canal seasonally, when repositioning from one coast to the other; however, partial transits have become an increasingly popular "destination" on regularly scheduled 10- and 11-night Caribbean itineraries. These loop cruises enter the canal from the Caribbean Sea and sail into Gatún Lake, where they remain for a few hours as passengers are tendered ashore for excursions. Ships then pass back through the locks, returning to the Caribbean and stopping at either Cristobal Pier or Colón 2000 Pier to retrieve passengers at the conclusion of their tours.

A day transiting the canal's Gatún Locks begins before dawn as your passenger ship passes through Bahía Limón and lines up with dozens of other vessels to await its turn to enter. Before your ship can proceed, two pilots and a narrator will board. The sight of a massive cruise ship being raised dozens of feet into the air by water is so mesmerizing that passengers eagerly crowd to all forward decks at the first lock. If you don't find a good viewing spot, head for the rear decks, where there is usually more room and the view is just as intriguing. If you remain aboard, as many passengers do, you'll find plenty of room up front later in the day as your ship retraces its path down to the sea. Due to the tight scheduling of the day's activities—it takes at least 90 minutes for a ship to pass through Gatún Locks—passengers who wish to go ashore early in the day are advised to sign up for one of the many available shore excursions.

### ESSENTIALS
#### CURRENCY
The U.S. dollar. Panama calls the dollar the *balboa* and designates prices with a *B/.* sign in front of the number. Panama mints its own coins, which they circulate along with U.S. coins.

#### TELEPHONE
You'll find telephones inside Colón's cruise terminal where you can purchase phone cards, a handy and inexpensive way to make calls.

### COMING ASHORE
Colón, Panama's second-largest city, has little to offer of historic interest, and is simply a jumping-off point to the rain forest and a wide variety of organized tours. Organized excursions focus on the Panama Canal or the pleasant north coast village of Portobelo, 70 km (42 miles) northeast. Infrequent cruise itineraries may include a day docked in Colón, rather than a partial canal transit. However, no matter how much time your ship spends in Colón, it is always easier (and safer) to take an organized shore excursion. ⚠ **The city itself can be quite dangerous, even during the day; under no circumstances should you wander on your own.**

Although entry time into the canal is always approximate, passenger ships have priority, and most pass through Gatún Locks early in the morning. Passengers booked on shore excursions begin the tendering process soon after the ship sets anchor, which can be as early as 8:30 am. Alternatives to excursions offered by your cruise ship are available from independent tour operators that can be arranged in advance through websites or travel agents. You will likely be informed that Panamanian regulations restrict passengers going ashore in Gatún Lake to only those who have booked the cruise line's excursions; however, anyone who has a shore-excursion reservation with a local company should be able to leave the vessel. Before making independent tour arrangements, confirm with your cruise line that you will be allowed to go ashore after presenting your private tour confirmation to the shore-excursion staff on board the ship.

> **BEST BETS**
>
> ■ **See the new Panama Canal.** The Agua Clara Visitor Center offers the best view of the new canal expansion.
>
> ■ **Kayak on Gatún Lake.** You can paddle among the many islands and mangrove forests.
>
> ■ **Panama Railway.** Take a train trip to Panama City for a quick sightseeing tour (you can come back by taxi to save some time).
>
> ■ **Portobelo.** Visit historic Panamanian forts.
>
> ■ **Rain Forest Aerial Tram.** Travel to Gamboa Rainforest Resort and see the rain forest canopy from above.

**Colón 2000.** Two blocks from the Zona Libre is the city's cruise-ship port, Colón 2000, which is basically a two-story strip mall next to the dock where ships tie up and passengers load onto buses for day trips. It has a supermarket, restaurants, and shops. A second terminal is the home port for Royal Caribbean's Enchantment of the Seas, and the Panamanian government aggressively courting other cruise companies to set up shop here, too. ⊠ *Calle El Paseo Gorgas, Colón* ☎ *447–3197.*

# EXPLORING

## COLÓN

The provincial capital of Colón, beside the canal's Atlantic entrance, has clearly seen better days, as the architecture of its older buildings attests. Its predominantly Afro-Caribbean population has long had a vibrant musical scene, and in the late 19th and early 20th centuries Colón was a relatively prosperous town. But it spent the second half of the 20th century in steady decay, and things have only gotten worse in the 21st century. ⚠ **Travelers who explore Colón on foot are simply asking to be mugged. We strongly recommend you stick with the safety of organized shore excursion here.**

**Esclusas de Gatún** (*Gatún Locks*). Twelve kilometers (7 miles) south of Colón are the Esclusas de Gatún, a triple-lock complex that's nearly a mile long and raises and lowers ships the 85 feet between sea level and Gatún Lake. There's a small visitor center with a viewing platform and information about the boats passing through is broadcast over speakers. The visitor center doesn't compare to the one at Miraflores Locks, but

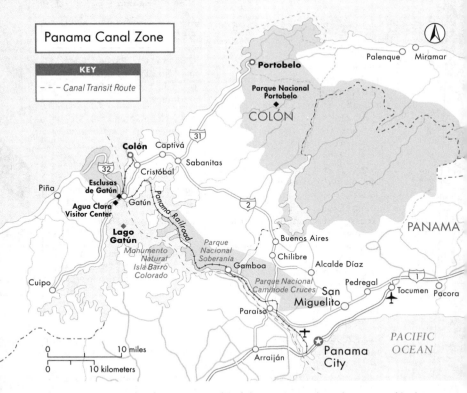

Panama Canal Zone

given the sheer magnitude of the Gatún Locks—three sets of locks, as opposed to two at Miraflores—it is an impressive sight, especially when packed with ships. You have to cross the locks on a swinging bridge to get to San Lorenzo and the Represa Gatún (Gatún Dam), which holds the water in Gatún Lake. At 2½ km (1½ miles) long, it was the largest dam in the world when it was built, a title it held for several decades. Get there by taking the first left after crossing the locks. ✉ *12 km (7 miles) south of Colón, Colón* ⊕ *visitcanaldepanama.com* ✉ *$5.*

**Agua Clara Visitor Center.** Not far from the Gatún Locks, this visitor center offers the best view of the newly completed Panama Canal expansion, which allows a new generation of larger, so-called "Post Panamax" ships to traverse the canal. A video presentation provides an introduction to the canal's history and expansion, but the open-air observation area is the most interesting part, since it offers hilltop views of the project. The facility has a playground and gift shop, as well as a pleasant, open-air restaurant operated by Panama City's El Panamá hotel, which is open daily noon–4 for lunch (call *507/215–9927* for reservations). The restaurant offers great views of Gatún Lake. ✚ *5 km (3 miles) south of Colón; turn right just before railroad tracks and make first right* ☎ *276–8325* ⊕ *www.visitcanaldepanama.com* ✉ *$5.*

## LAGO GATÚN (GATÚN LAKE)

Covering about 163 square miles, an area about the size of the island nation Barbados, Gatún Lake extends northwest from Parque Nacional Soberanía to the locks of Gatún, just south of Colón. The lake was created when the U.S. government dammed the Chagres River, between 1907 and 1910, so that boats could cross the isthmus at 85 feet above sea level. By creating the lake, the United States saved decades of digging that a sea-level canal would have required. It took several years for the rain to fill the convoluted valleys, turning hilltops into islands and killing much forest (some trunks still tower over the water nearly a century later). When it was completed, Gatún Lake was the largest man-made lake in the world. The canal route winds through its northern half, past several forest-covered islands (the largest is Barro Colorado, one of the world's first biological reserves). To the north of Barro Colorado are the Islas Brujas and Islas Tigres, which together hold a primate refuge—visitors aren't allowed. The lake itself is home to crocodiles—forego swimming here—manatees, and peacock bass, a species introduced from South America and popular with fishermen.

## PORTOBELO

Portobelo is an odd mix of colonial fortresses, clear waters, lushly forested hills, and a town of cement-block houses crowded amid the ancient walls. It holds some of Panama's most interesting colonial ruins, with rusty cannons still lying in wait for an enemy assault, and is a UNESCO World Heritage Site, together with San Lorenzo.

**Iglesia de San Felipe.** One block east of Real Aduana is the Iglesia de San Felipe, a large white church dating from 1814 that's home to the country's most venerated religious figure: the Cristo Negro (Black Christ). According to legend, that statue of a dark-skinned Jesus carrying a cross arrived in Portobelo in the 17th century on a Spanish ship bound for Cartagena, Colombia. Each time the ship tried to leave, it encountered storms and had to return to port, convincing the captain to leave the statue in Portobelo. Another legend has it that in the midst of a cholera epidemic in 1821 parishioners prayed to the Cristo Negro, and the community was spared. The statue spends most of the year to the left of the church's altar, but once a year it's paraded through town in the Festival del Cristo Negro. Each year the Cristo Negro is clothed in a new purple robe, donated by somebody who's earned the honor. Behind San Felipe are the ruins of the Iglesia de San Juan de Dios, which date from 1589. ⊠ *Calle Principal, Portobelo.*

**Parque Nacional Portobelo** (*Portobelo National Park*). Parque Nacional Portobelo is a vast marine and rain-forest reserve contiguous with Chagres National Park that protects both natural and cultural treasures. It extends from the cloud forest atop 3,212-foot Cerro Brujo down to offshore islands and coral reefs, and comprises the bay and fortresses of Portobelo.

You can't miss the remains of the three Spanish fortresses that once guarded Portobelo Bay. The first is **Fuerte Santiago de la Gloria,** with about a dozen cannons and sturdy battlements built out of blocks of coral. Portobelo's largest and most impressive fort is **Fuerte San**

**4**

Jerónimo, at the end of the bay. Surrounded by the "modern" town, it was originally built in the 1600s and rebuilt to its current state in 1758. Its large interior courtyard was once a parade ground, but it's now the venue for annual celebrations. **Fuerte San Fernando,** across the bay from Fuerte Santiago, consists of two battlements—one near the water and one on the hill above. The upper fortress affords a great view of the bay and is a good place to see birds because of the surrounding forest. Local boatmen who dock their boats next to Fuerte Santiago or Fuerte San Jerónimo can take you across the bay to explore Fuerte San Fernando for a few dollars. ✉ *Surrounding Portobelo, Portobelo* ☎ *442–8348 park office* ⊕ *www.miambiente.gob.pa* ⊠ *$5.*

**Real Aduana** (*Royal Customs House*). Near the entrance to Fuerte San Jerónimo is Real Aduana, where servants of the Spanish crown made sure that the king and queen got their cut from every ingot that rolled through town. Built in 1630, Real Aduana was damaged during pirate attacks and then destroyed by an earthquake in 1882, only to be rebuilt in 1998. It is an interesting example of colonial architecture—note the carved coral columns on the ground floor—and it houses a simple museum with some old coins, cannonballs, and displays on Panamanian folklore. ✉ *Calle de la Aduana, Portobelo* ☎ *448–2024* ⊕ *www.inac. gob.pa* ⊠ *$5.*

## SHOPPING

Both Cristobal Pier and Colón 2000 Pier have large shopping malls, where you will find Internet access, telephones, refreshments, and duty-free souvenir shops in relatively secure environments. Stores in both locations feature local crafts such as baskets, wood carvings, and toys, as well as liquor, jewelry, and the ubiquitous souvenir T-shirts. In addition to shops and cafés, Cristobal Pier features an open-air arts and craft market; Colón 2000 Pier has a well-stocked supermarket. Portobelo has a wide-ranging artisan market next to Iglesia de San Felipe.

The most unique locally made souvenirs are colorful appliquéd molas, the whimsical textile artwork created by native Kuna women, who come from the San Blas Islands; they are likely to be hand stitching new designs while they sell the ones they just completed. If you take an excursion to Portobelo, the best selection can be found in the artisan market next to Iglesia de San Felipe, where there are other locally made souvenirs that are well worth bargaining for.

## WHERE TO EAT

**$$**

SEAFOOD

✕ **Restaurante Los Cañones.** This rambling restaurant with tables among palm trees and Caribbean views is one of Panama's most attractive lunch spots. The food and service fall a little short of the setting, but not so far that you'd want to scratch it from your list. In good weather, dine at tables edging the sea surrounded by dark boulders and lush foliage. The other option is the open-air restaurant, decorated with shells, buoys, and driftwood, with a decent view of the bay and forested hills. House specialties include *pescado entero* (whole fried snapper), *langosta al ajillo* (lobster scampi), and *centolla al jengibre* (king crab in a ginger sauce). ■**TIP→ If you come here expecting to find dinner, make it an early one; the place closes at 7 pm.** ⑤*Average main: $13* ✉*2 km (1 mile) before Portobelo on left, Portobelo* ☎*448–2980* ▭*No credit cards.*

# COSTA MAYA (MAHAHUAL), MEXICO

By Jeffrey Van Fleet

Puerto Costa Maya is an anomaly. Unlike other tourist attractions in the area (the island of Cozumel being the primary Yucatán cruise port), this port of call near Mahahual has been created exclusively for cruise-ship passengers. The complex, sometimes referred to as "New Mahahual," comprises theme restaurants like Hard Rock Cafe and Señor Frog's, as well as boutique shops and chain stores such as Lapis Jewelry.

Prior to a devastating 2007 hurricane, there was no real reason to go into the small, nearby fishing village of Mahahual (pronounced *ma-ah-WAL*). Though there are still about 300 residents, post-hurricane renovations have put the village on the map; it now has its own pier as well as a smattering of hotels, restaurants, and shops. Be sure to venture beyond "New Mahahual," which lacks the charm of the nearby beachfront area. Its cement boardwalk along the beach has made Mahahual an ideal spot for a sunset stroll. The crystal-clear waters and unspoiled beaches are delightful for snorkeling, diving, and fishing.

**BEST BETS**

■ **Chacchoben.** This archaeological site is near the Belize border.

■ **Kohunlich.** This ruined city is best known for its great temples with sculpted masks.

■ **Mahahual.** This small fishing village (pronounced Ma-ha-wal) near the cruise pier has plenty of fine sand and glassy waters for a cushy afternoon in the sun.

■ **Xcalak.** This national reserve offers excellent saltwater fly-fishing and deserted beaches.

## ESSENTIALS
### CURRENCY
The Mexican peso. U.S. dollars and credit cards are widely accepted in the area.

### TELEPHONE
Most pay phones accept prepaid Ladatel cards, sold in 30-, 50-, or 100-peso denominations. To use the card, insert it in the pay phone's slot, dial 001 (for calls to the United States) or 01 (for calls within Mexico), followed by the area code and number. Credit is deleted from the card as you use it, and the balance is displayed on the small screen on the phone. Most tri-band mobile phones from the U.S. work in Mexico, though you must pay roaming charges.

### COMING ASHORE
At first glance, the port complex itself may seem to be little more than an outdoor mall. You disembark at a docking pier (which can accommodate three ships at once) and head to a 70,000-square-foot bazaar-type

compound where shops selling local crafts—jewelry, pottery, woven straw hats and bags, and embroidered dresses—are interspersed with duty-free stores and souvenir shops. There are two alfresco restaurants that serve seafood, American-friendly Mexican dishes like tacos and quesadillas, and cocktails at shaded tables. An outdoor amphitheater stages daily performances of traditional music and dance. Taxis wait at the port entrance to take you to Mahahual itself, a ride of about 5 to 10 minutes.

## EXPLORING

### MAHAHUAL

Tiny Mahahual (also spelled Majahual) has something of a split personality. With a population of only 600, it's a quiet beachfront outpost with clear, calm waters, good snorkeling and diving, and not a whole lot to do. That's just the way its Mexican and expat U.S. and Canadian residents like it. When the cruise ships are in port, however, this sleepy spot wakes up. Passengers flood its waterside palapa restaurants, beach clubs, and the boardwalk fronting the town's few blocks; it's lively but can be overwhelming.

### FURTHER AFIELD

**Chacchoben.** Excavated in 2005, Chacchoben (pronounced *cha*-cho-ben) is an ancient city that was a contemporary of Kohunlich and the most important trading partner with Guatemala north of the Bacalar Lagoon area. Several newly unearthed buildings are still in good condition. The lofty **Templo Uno**, the site's main temple, was dedicated to the Mayan sun god, Itzamná, and once held a royal tomb. (When archaeologists found it, though, it had already been looted.) Most of the site was built around AD 200, in the Petén style of the early classic period, although the city could have been inhabited as early as 200 BC. It's thought that inhabitants made their living growing cotton and extracting chewing gum and copal resin from the trees. ✉ *Felipe Carrillo Puerto* ✣ *From Carretera 307, turn right on Carretera 293 south of Cafetal, continue 9 km (5½ miles) passing Lázaro Cardenas town* ⊕ *www.inah.gob.mx* ▧ *55 MP.*

**Dzibanché-Kinichná.** The alliance between sister cities Dzibanché and Kinichná was thought to have made them the most powerful cities in southern Quintana Roo during the Mayan classic period (AD 100–1000).

At Dzibanché ("place where they write on wood," pronounced zee-ban-*che*), several carved wooden lintels have been found; the most perfectly preserved sample is in a supporting arch at the **Plaza de Xibalba**. Also at the plaza is the **Templo del Búho** (Temple of the Owl), atop which a recessed tomb was discovered—only the second of its kind in Mexico (the first was at Palenque in Chiapas). More buildings and three plazas have been restored as excavation continues. The carved stone steps at **Edificio 13** and **Edificio 2** (Buildings 13 and 2) still bear traces of stone masks. A copy of the famed lintel of **Templo IV** (Temple IV), with eight glyphs dating from AD 618, is housed in the Museo de la Cultura Maya in Chetumal. Four more tombs were discovered at **Templo I** (Temple

I). ⊠ *Carretera 186 Chetumal–Escárcega, 80 km (50 miles) west of Chetumal, Chetumal ⊹ Following Carretera 186 Chetumal–Escárcega, turn north at Km 58 and pass through town of Morocoy; continue 2 km (1 mile) farther, and turn right at sign for Dzibanché. The entrance is 7 km (4½ miles) away ☎ ⊕ www.inah.gob.mx ⊠ 55 MP.*

**Kohunlich.** Kohunlich (pronounced *ko*-hoon-lich) is renowned for the giant stucco masks on its principal pyramid, the **Edificio de los Mascarones** (Mask Building), among others. It also has one of Quintana Roo's oldest ball courts and the remains of a great drainage system at the **Plaza de las Estelas** (Plaza of the Stelae). Kohunlich was built and occupied during the classic period by various Mayan groups. This explains the eclectic architecture, which includes the Petén and Río Bec styles. Although there are 14 buildings to visit, it's thought that there are at least 500 mounds on the site waiting to be excavated. This site doesn't have a great deal of tourist traffic, so it's surrounded by thriving flora and fauna. ⊠ *Off Carretera 186, 65 km (46 miles) west of Chetumal, Chetumal ⊹ Follow Carretera 186 west of Chetumal for 65 km (40 miles); continue another 9 km (5.5 miles) south on side road to ruins ⊕ www.inah.gob.mx ⊠ 65 MP.*

**4**

# BEACHES

The cruise ships that stop here daily have made Mahahual's beach the liveliest place in town. Seaside restaurants dish out cerveza and ceviche, and several vendors offer boat tours and rental equipment like glass-bottom kayaks. The strip of beach edging the cruise complex has been outfitted with colorful lounge chairs and *hamacas* (hammocks), and may tempt you to linger and sunbathe. The main beach in the center of town has fine sand and calm waters, great for swimming and snorkeling. Some hotel owners have opened beach clubs to cater to cruise passengers looking for a day (and a drink) in the sun.

**Fodor's Choice** **Nacional Beach Club.** Many travelers stumble on this colorful beach
★ club and end up staying past sunset. For just M$170, you get a beach chair, umbrella, and access to the pool, showers, and changing facilities. Margaritas can be delivered to you beachside, or you can escape the heat by grabbing a bite in the enclosed patio. The M$40 Coronas and free Wi-Fi make this a popular spot to while away the day. There's decent snorkeling right out front, and equipment is available next door at Gypsea Divers. Even if you don't get in the water, the four shades of turquoise are breathtaking. Movies are shown under the stars on Wednesdays at 6. There are also six bungalows (from M$ 1,000) for rent if you feel like staying the night. Cash only. **Amenities:** food and drink; showers; toilets. **Best for:** partiers; snorkeling; swimming. ⊠ *Av. Mahahual, Mahahual ☎ 983/834–5719 ⊕ www.nacionalbeachclub. com ⊠ 170 MP.*

**Playa Xcalak.** This remarkably tranquil strand stretches for miles, and the isolated location means you might have it all to yourself. Much of the white sand has been eaten away by past hurricanes, narrowing the beach and making strolling a chore; however, the waters are pristine and placid. As a result, this is one of the area's best spots for swimming or kayaking. Sections of the beach connect to a network of protected mangroves frequented by manatees. Moreover, the offshore reef of nearby Banco Chinchorro is great for snorkeling, diving, and fishing. **Amenities:** food and drink. **Best for:** snorkeling; swimming. ⊠ *Xcalak.*

## SHOPPING

While most cruise passengers choose to shop in the mall at the cruise pier, in the town of Mahahual itself, vendors line the malecón (the beach walkway) and sell crafts on days when cruise ships are in town.

## ACTIVITIES

If you want to have a truly authentic Mexican experience, take advantage of the day tours offered to outlying areas. These give you a chance to see some of the really spectacular sights in this part of Mexico, many of which are rarely visited. This is one port where the shore excursion is the point, and there are no options except to purchase what your ship offers.

Among the best tours are those that let you explore the gorgeous (and usually deserted) Mayan ruin sites of Kohunlich, Dzibanché, and Chacchoben. The ancient pyramids and temples at these sites, surrounded by jungle that's protected them for centuries, are still dazzling to behold. Because the sites are some distance from the port complex—and require some road travel in one of the port's air-conditioned vans—these tours are all-day affairs. One of the most popular activities with cruise passengers is the three-hour ATV excursion along jungle roads and the Mahahual coastline. Although an adventure, the ATVs tend to be a nuisance to residents and business owners, not to mention wildlife.

## WHERE TO EAT

**$$** ╳ **Fernando's 100% Agave.** Fernando's friendly, homey restaurant—which
MEXICAN serves as a sort of ersatz visitors bureau—seems to change locations often but remains a Mahahual institution. The affordable menu features Mexican and Yucatecan specialties with a generous splash of gringo. Should you be in the market for a margarita, don't be shy; as suggested by the name, this is the place for expert guidance on all things agave. You can even buy a bottle of Fernando's homemade tequila to go. If the indoor party scene isn't lively enough for you, head to the outside tables, where cruise passengers are known to do shots. ⑤ *Average main: 190 MP* ⊠ *Plaza Martillo, between Coronado and Martillo; north of soccer field, Mahahual* ☎ *983/834-5609* ⊘ *Closed Mon.*

**$** ╳ **Cafe Karlita's.** The smell of fresh baked goods wafts onto Mahahual's
CAFÉ boardwalk from this central café. The towers of cookies, pastries, and muffins under glass domes make you forget caloric intake with the honest excuse, "I'm on vacation." For something lighter, opt for the bagel with salmon, a fruit smoothie, or organic tea. Karlita brews her own brand of coffee into cappuccinos, frappuccinos, and any other –inos you can think of. This air-conditioned pink nook has free Wi-Fi plus $1 per minute phone calls for cruise passengers wanting to call home.

If you happen to fall in love during your travels, Karlita makes wedding cakes, too. $\boxed{\$}$ *Average main: 60 MP* $\boxtimes$ *Malecón, next to Port Captain office, Mahahual* $\textcircled{\small{2}}$ *983/834–5709.*

# COZUMEL, MEXICO

By Jeffrey Van Fleet

Cozumel, with its sun-drenched ivory beaches fringed with coral reefs, fulfills the tourist's vision of a tropical Caribbean island. It's a heady mix of the natural and the commercial. Despite a miniconstruction boom in the island's sole city, San Miguel, there are still wild pockets scattered throughout the island where flora and fauna flourish. Smaller than Cancún, Cozumel surpasses its fancier neighbor in many ways. It has more history and ruins, superior diving and snorkeling, more authentic cuisine, and a greater diversity of handicrafts at better prices. The numerous coral reefs, particularly the world-renowned Palancar Reef, attract divers from around the world. On a busy cruiseship day the island can seem completely overrun, but it's still possible to get away, and some good Mayan sights are within reach on long (and expensive) shore excursions.

## BEST BETS

■ **Diving and Snorkeling.** Excellent reefs close to shore make either diving or snorkeling a must-do activity.

■ **Mayan Ruins.** Some of the most famous and dazzling ruins are reachable from Cozumel, and if you have never seen a Mayan pyramid, this is your chance.

■ **People-Watching.** You can spend hours just sitting in the main plaza (or at a sidewalk café) watching island life pass by.

## ESSENTIALS

### CURRENCY
The Mexican peso, but U.S. dollars and credit cards are widely accepted in the area.

### TELEPHONE
Most pay phones accept prepaid Ladatel cards, sold in 30-, 50-, or 100-peso denominations. To use the card, insert it in the pay phone's slot, dial 001 (for calls to the United States) or 01 (for calls within Mexico), followed by the area code and number. Credit is deleted from the card as you use it, and the balance is displayed on the small screen on the phone. Most tri-band mobile phones from the U.S. work in Mexico, though you must pay roaming charges.

### COMING ASHORE
As many as six ships call at Cozumel on a busy day, disembarking passengers at the downtown Punta Langosta pier in the center of San Miguel or docking at the two piers—referred to as the International and Puerto Maya piers—4 miles (6 km) south. (Ships will occasionally tender their passengers into the downtown pier.) From the downtown pier you can walk into town or catch the ferry to Playa del Carmen. Taxi tours are also available. A four-hour island tour (4 people maximum), including the ruins and other sights, costs about $70 to $100,

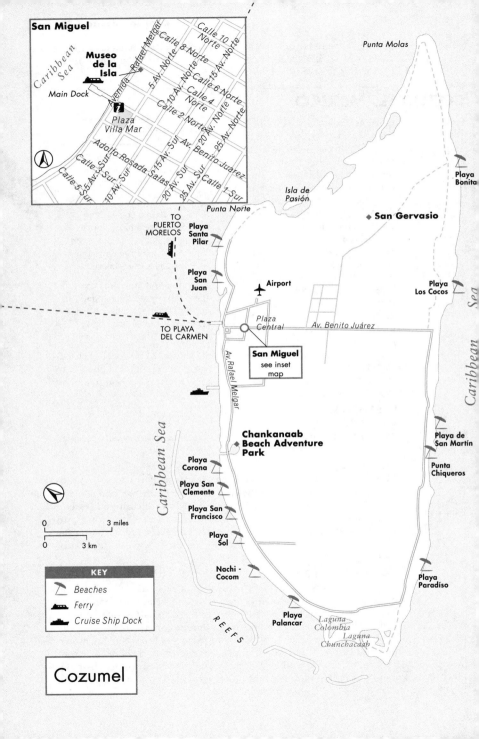

**San Miguel**

*Caribbean Sea*

**Museo de la Isla**

Main Dock

*Avenida Rafael Melgar*

Calle 10 Norte
Calle 8 Norte
Calle 6 Norte
Calle 4 Norte
Calle 2 Norte
5 Av. Norte
10 Av. Norte
15 Av. Norte
20 Av. Norte
25 Av. Norte

*Plaza Villa Mar*

Adolfo Rosada Salas
Av. Benito Juárez
Calle 1 Sur
Calle 3 Sur
Calle 5 Sur
5 Av. Sur
10 Av. Sur
15 Av. Sur
20 Av. Sur
25 Av. Sur

Punta Molas

*Isla de Pasión*

◆ **San Gervasio**

**Playa Bonita**

Punta Norte

TO PUERTO MORELOS

**Playa Santa Pilar**

**Playa San Juan**

**Playa Los Cocos**

✈ **Airport**

*Plaza Central*

TO PLAYA DEL CARMEN

**San Miguel** see inset map

*Av. Benito Juárez*

*Av. Rafael Melgar*

*Caribbean Sea*

**Chankanaab Beach Adventure Park**

**Playa de San Martín**

**Playa Corona**

**Punta Chiqueros**

**Playa San Clemente**

**Playa San Francisco**

**Playa Sol**

**Nachi-Cocom**

**Playa Paradíso**

**Playa Palancar**

*Laguna Colombia*

*Laguna Chunchacaab*

R E E F S

0      3 miles
0      3 km

**KEY**

⌒ *Beaches*
⛴ *Ferry*
🚢 *Cruise Ship Dock*

**Cozumel**

but negotiate the price before you get in the cab. The international pier is close to many beaches, but you'll need a taxi to get into town. There's rarely a wait for a taxi, but prices are high, and drivers are often aggressive, asking double or triple the reasonable fare. When in doubt, ask to see the rate card required of all taxi drivers. Expect to pay $10 for the ride into San Miguel from the pier. Tipping is not necessary.

Passenger ferries to Playa del Carmen leave Cozumel's main pier approximately every other hour from 5 am to 10 pm. They also leave Playa del Carmen's dock about every other hour on the hour, from 6 am to 11 pm (but note that service sometimes varies according to demand). The trip takes 45 minutes. Verify the times: bad weather and changing schedules can prompt cancellations.

## EXPLORING

San Miguel is not tiny, but you can easily explore the waterfront and plaza area on foot. The main attractions are the small eateries and shops that line the streets and the main square, where the locals congregate in the evening.

FAMILY **Museo de la Isla.** Filling two floors of a former hotel, Cozumel's museum has displays on natural history—the island's origins, endangered species, topography, and coral-reef ecology—as well as human history during the pre-Columbian and colonial periods. The photos of the island's transformation over the 20th and 21st centuries are especially fascinating, as is the exhibit of a typical Mayan home. Guided tours are available. ⊠ *Av. Rafael E. Melgar, between Calles 4 and 6 Norte, Cozumel* ☎ *987/872–1475* ⊕ *www.cozumelparks.com/esp/museo_isla. cfm* 🖃 *85 MP* ☉ *Closed Sun.*

FAMILY **Chankanaab Beach Adventure Park.** Chankanaab, translated as "small sea," consists of a saltwater lagoon, an archaeological park, and a botanical garden, with reproductions of a Mayan village and Olmec, Toltec, Aztec, and Mayan stone carvings scattered throughout. You can swim at the beach, plus there's plenty for snorkelers and divers to see beneath the surface—picture underwater caverns, a sunken ship, crusty old cannons and anchors, and a sculpture of la Virgen del Mar (Virgin of the Sea), all populated by parrotfish and sergeant majors galore. To preserve the ecosystem, rules forbid touching the reef or feeding the fish. You'll find dive shops, restaurants, gift shops, a snack stand, and dressing rooms with lockers and showers right on the sand. Chankanaab is also a Dolphin Discovery facility where true *Flipper* fans can swim with the much-loved marine mammals (*www.dolphindiscovery.com*). ⊠ *Carretera Sur, Km 9, Cozumel* ☎ *987/872–0093* ⊕ *www.cozumelparks. com/eng/chankanaab.cfm* 🖃 *440 MP; 295 MP, kids 3–11* ☉ *Closed Sun.*

**San Gervasio.** Rising from the jungle, these temples make up Cozumel's largest remaining Mayan and Toltec site. San Gervasio was the island's capital and ceremonial center, dedicated to the fertility goddess Ixchel. The classic- and postclassic-style buildings and temples were continuously occupied from AD 300 to 1500. Typical architectural features include limestone plazas and arches atop stepped platforms, as well as stelae and bas-reliefs. Be sure to see the temple "Las Manitas," with red hand prints all over its altar. ■TIP→ **Plaques in Mayan, Spanish, and English clearly describe each structure, but it's worth hiring a guide to fully appreciate the site.** ✉ *Benito Juarez Transversal Rd., Km 7.5, Cozumel* ✛ *From San Miguel, take cross-island road east to San Gervasio access road; turn left and follow road 7 km (4½ mile)* ☎ *987/872–0093* ⊕ *www.cozumelparks.com/eng/san_gervasio.cfm* ✈ *100 MP.*

## BEACHES

Cozumel's beaches vary from sandy treeless stretches to isolated coves to rocky shores. Most of the development is on the leeward (western) side. Beach clubs have sprung up on the southwest coast; admission, however, is usually free, as long as you buy food and drinks. Clubs offer typical tourist fare: souvenir shops, palapa restaurants, kayaks, and cold beer. A cab ride from San Miguel to most clubs costs about $15 each way. Reaching beaches on the windward (eastern) side is more difficult, but the solitude is worth it.

**Playa Palancar.** South of the resorts, down a rutted road and way off the beaten path, lies serene Playa Palancar—a long, walkable beach with hammocks hanging under coconut palms. The on-site dive shop can outfit scuba enthusiasts for trips to the famous Palancar and Columbia reefs, just offshore; boats will take snorkelers out every two hours from 9 to 5. There's also a nice open-air restaurant-bar here if you'd rather just relax. **Amenities:** food and drink; parking (free); showers; toilets; water sports. **Best for:** snorkeling; swimming; walking. ✉ *Carretera Sur, Km 19.5, Cozumel* ✈ *Free.*

**Playa San Francisco.** This busy but inviting 5-km (3-mile) expanse of sand is among the longest and finest on Cozumel. Encompassing the beaches Playa Maya and Santa Rosa, it's typically packed with cruise-ship passengers in high season. On Sunday, locals flock here to eat fresh fish. Amenities include two outdoor restaurants, a bar, dressing rooms, gift shops, beach chairs, massage treatments, and water-sports equipment rentals. **Amenities:** food and drink; parking (free); showers; toilets; water sports. **Best for:** walking; swimming. ✉ *Carretera Costera Sur, Km 14, Cozumel* ✈ *Free (136 MP minimum for food and drink).*

FAMILY **Punta Chiqueros.** Sheltered by an offshore reef, this half-moon cove is the first popular swimming area as you drive north on the coastal road. Part of a longer beach that some locals call Playa Bonita, it has fine sand, clear water, and moderate waves. At lunchtime, you can linger over fried fish at a casual eatery that's also named **Playa Bonita. Amenities:** food and drink; parking (free); toilets. **Best for:** walking; sunsets; surfing; swimming. ✉ *Carretera C–1, Km 38, Cozumel* ✈ *Free.*

## SHOPPING

Cozumel's main souvenir-shopping area is downtown along Avenida Rafael E. Melgar and on some side streets around the plaza. There are also clusters of shops at **Plaza del Sol** (east side of the main plaza) and **Vista del Mar** (✉ *Av. Rafael E. Melgar 45*). As a general rule, the newer, trendier shops line the waterfront, and the better craft shops can be found around Avenida 5a. Malls at the cruise-ship piers aim to please passengers seeking jewelry, perfume, sportswear, and low-end souvenirs at high-end prices.

Most downtown shops accept U.S. dollars; many goods are priced in dollars. To get better prices, pay with cash—some shops tack a hefty surcharge on credit-card purchases. Shops, restaurants, and streets are always crowded between 10 am and 2 pm, but get calmer in the evening. Traditionally, stores are open from 9 to 1 (except Sunday) and 5 to 9, but those nearest the pier tend to stay open all day, particularly during high season. Most shops are closed Sunday morning.

# ACTIVITIES

### DIVING AND SNORKELING

Cozumel is famous for its reefs. In addition to Chankanaab Nature Park, a great dive site is La Ceiba Reef, in the waters off La Ceiba and Sol Caribe hotels. Here lies the wreckage of a sunken airplane blown up for a Mexican disaster movie. Cozumel has plenty of dive shops to choose from.

**Blue Angel Scuba School.** The combo dive-and-snorkel excursions arranged by Blue Angel allow family members to have fun together, even if not all are scuba enthusiasts. Dedicated dive trips to local reefs and PADI courses are also offered. ✉ *Blue Angel Resort, Carretera Costera Sur, Km 2.2, Cozumel* ☎ *987/872–0819* ⊕ *www.blueangelscubaschool. com* ✉ *Snorkel trips from 660 MP; two-tank dives from 11350 MP.*

**Eagle Ray Divers.** Snorkeling trips and dive instruction are available through Eagle Ray Divers. (The three-reef snorkel trip lets nondivers explore beyond the shore.) As befits its name, the company keeps track of the eagle rays that appear off Cozumel from December to February and runs trips for advanced divers to walls where the rays congregate. Beginners can also see rays around some of the reefs. ✉ *La Caleta Marina, near Presidente InterContinental, Cozumel* ☎ *987/872–5735, 501/255–5968 in U.S.* ⊕ *www.eagleraydivers.com* ✉ *Two-tank dives from 1575 MP.*

### FISHING

You can charter high-speed fishing boats for about $420 per half-day or $600 per day (with a maximum of six people). Your hotel can help arrange daily charters—some offer special deals, with boats leaving from their own docks.

**Albatros Charters.** Half- and full-day outings that include boat and crew, tackle and bait, plus libations and lunch (quesadillas or your own fresh catch) are organized by Albatros Charters. Customized dive trips are also available. ✉ *Marina Puerto de Abrigo, Av. Rafael E. Melgar Norte, Puerto Abrigo* ☎ *987/872–7904, 888/333–4643 in U.S.* ⊕ *www. albatroscharters.com* ✉ *From 9300 MP for 6 people.*

**Tres Hermanos.** This outfit specializes in deep-sea and fly-fishing trips. It also offers scuba-diving excursions. Boats are available for group charters, allowing you to move at your own pace. ✉ *Marina Puerto de Abrigo, Av. Rafael E. Melgar Norte, Puerto Abrigo* ☎ *987/107–2030* ⊕ *www.cozumelfishing.com* ✉ *From 7875 MP for 4 people.*

## WHERE TO EAT

**$$$**   ✕**Guido's.** Chef Yvonne Villiger works wonders with fresh fish—if the
ITALIAN   wahoo with capers and black olives is on the menu, don't miss it. But
Guido's is best known for pizzas that are baked in a wood-burning oven
and served by an incredibly attentive staff. Enjoy a pitcher of delicious
sangria in the pleasant, roomy courtyard. ⑤ *Average main: 310 MP*
✉ *Av. Rafael E. Melgar 23, between Calles 6 and 8 Norte, San Miguel*
☎ *987/869–2589* ⊕ *www.guidoscozumel.com* ◷ *No lunch Sun.*

**$$$**   ✕**Pancho's Backyard.** Marimbas play beside a bubbling fountain in
MEXICAN   the charming courtyard behind one of Cozumel's best folk-art shops.
Though Pancho's is always busy, the waitstaff is patient and helpful.
Cruise-ship passengers seeking a taste of Mexico pack the place at
lunch; dinner is a bit more serene. The American-style, English menu
is geared toward tourists, but regional ingredients like smoky chipo-
tle chile make even the standard steak stand out. Other stars include
the cilantro cream soup and shrimp flambéed with tequila. ⑤ *Average
main: 218 MP* ✉ *Av. Rafael E. Melgar 27, between Calles 8 and 10
Norte, San Miguel* ☎ *987/872–2141* ⊕ *www.panchosbackyard.com*
◷ *No lunch Sun.*

# CURAÇAO (WILLEMSTAD)

By Susan
Campbell

Try to be on deck as your ship sails into Curaçao. The tiny Queen
Emma floating bridge swings aside to allow ships to pass through the
narrow channel. Pastel gingerbread buildings on shore look like doll-
houses, especially from a large cruise ship. Although the gabled roofs
and red tiles show a Dutch influence, the gleeful colors of the facades
are peculiar to Curaçao. It's said that an early governor of the island
suffered from migraines that were aggravated by the color white, so all
the houses were painted in hues from magenta to mauve. Thirty-five
miles (56 km) north of Venezuela and 42 miles (68 km) east of Aruba,
Curaçao is, at 38 miles (61 km) long and 3 to 7½ miles (5 to 12 km)
wide, the largest of the three neighboring islands. Although always
sunny, it's never stiflingly hot here because of the constant trade winds.
Water sports attract enthusiasts from all over the world, and the reef
diving is excellent.

## ESSENTIALS

### CURRENCY

Currency in Curaçao is the florin (also called the guilder) and is indicated by fl or NAf on price tags, but U.S. dollars are accepted almost
everywhere.

### TELEPHONE

To call Curaçao direct from the United States, dial 011–5999 plus
the number in Curaçao. International roaming for most GSM mobile
phones is available in Curaçao. Local companies are UTS (United Tele-
communication Services) and Digicel. You can also rent a mobile phone
or buy a prepaid SIM card for your own phone.

## COMING ASHORE

Ships dock at the terminal just beyond the Queen Emma Bridge, which leads to the floating market, cafés, and the shopping district. The walk to downtown takes less than 10 minutes. Easy-to-read maps are posted dockside and in the shopping area. The terminal has a duty-free shop, telephones, and a taxi stand.

Taxis, which meet every ship, have meters, although rates are still fixed from point to point of your journey. The government-approved rates, which do not include waiting time, can be found in a brochure called "Taxi Tariff Guide," available at the cruise-ship terminal and at the tourist board. Rates are for up to four passengers. There's a 25% sur-charge after 11 pm. It's easy to see the sights on Curaçao without going on an organized shore excursion. Downtown can be done on foot, and a taxi for up to four people will cost about $45 an hour. Taxi fares to places in and around the city range from $10 to $30. Car rentals are available but are not cheap.

### BEST BETS

■ **Diving.** After Bonaire, Curaçao has probably the best diving in the region.

■ **Punda.** Willemstad's chic and beautiful shopping area is a joy to explore on foot.

■ **Curaçao Sea Aquarium.** Explore the wonders of the ocean without getting wet.

■ **Floating Market.** This unique market is a fun destination, even though it's mostly fruits and vegetables.

■ **Kura Hulanda Museum.** This is the island's best historical museum.

# EXPLORING

## WILLEMSTAD

Dutch settlers came here in the 1630s, about the same time they sailed through the Verrazano Narrows to Manhattan, bringing with them original red-tile roofs, first used on the trade ships as ballast and later incorporated into the architecture of Willemstad. Much of the original colonial structures remain, but this historic city is constantly reinventing itself and the government monument foundation is always busy restor-ing buildings in one urban neighborhood or another. The salty air causes what is called "wall cancer," resulting in the ancient abodes continually crumbling over time. The city is cut in two by Santa Anna Bay. On one side is Punda (the point)—crammed with shops, restaurants, monu-ments, and markets and a new museum retracing its colorful history. And on the other side is Otrobanda (literally meaning the "other side"), with lots of narrow, winding streets and alleyways (called "steekjes" in Dutch), full of private homes notable for their picturesque gables and Dutch-influenced designs. In recent years the ongoing regeneration of Otrobanda has been apparent, marked by a surge in development of new hotels, restaurants, and shops; the rebirth, concentrated near the waterfront, was spearheaded by the creation of the elaborate Kura Hulanda complex. The old districts of Pietermaai and Scharloo are also

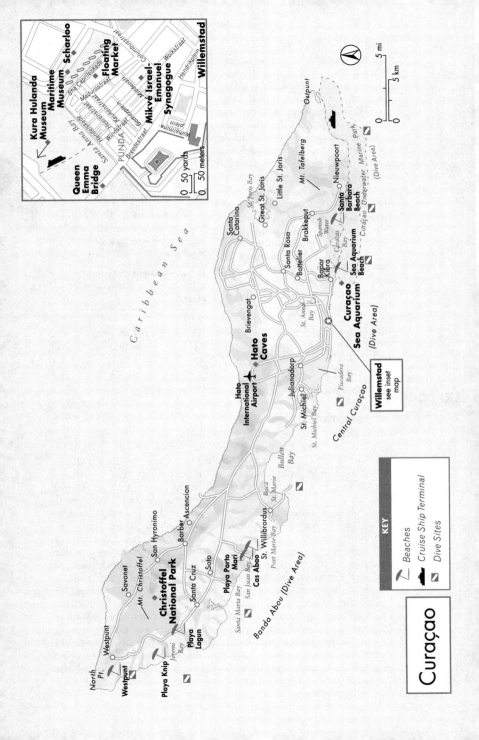

**Curaçao**

**KEY**

Beaches
Cruise Ship Terminal
Dive Sites

Willemstad
see inset
map

Central Curaçao

Curaçao Sea Aquarium
(Dive Area)

Sea Aquarium Beach
Santa Barbara Beach
Curaçao Onderwater (Underwater) Marine Park
(Dive Area)

Nieuwpoort
Ostpunt
Mt. Tafelberg
Little St. Joris
St. Joris Bay
Great St. Joris
Santa Catarina
Santa Rosa
Boca Tabla
Bapor Kibra
Caracas Bay
Spanish Water
Brakkeput
St. Anna Bay
Piscadera Bay
St. Michiel Bay
St. Michiel
Julianadorp

**Hato Caves**
Hato International Airport
Brievengat

**Christoffel National Park**
Mt. Christoffel
Savonet
San Hyronimo
Ascencion
Barber
Soto
Santa Cruz
St. Willibrordus
Cas Abao
**Playa Porto Mari**
San Juan Bay
Port Marie Bay
Santa Marta Bay
St. Marie
Boca
Bullen Bay

**Banda Abou** (Dive Area)

**Playa Lagun**
**Playa Knip**
**Westpunt**
North Pr.
Jeremi Bay

*Caribbean Sea*

5 mi
5 km

Kura Hulanda Museum
Maritime Museum
Scharloo
Floating Market
Mikvé Israel-Emanuel Synagogue
Willemstad
Queen Emma Bridge

PUNDA
Santa Anna Bay
Sha Caprileskade
Columbusstraat
Heerenstraat
Breedestraat
Madurostraat
Keukenstraat
Gomezplein
Handelskade
Wilhelmina plein
Windstraat
Walkstraat
Hendrikstraat

50 yards
50 meters

being revitalized with restored mansions and new dining, lodging, and entertainment options.

There are three ways to cross the bay: by car over the Juliana Bridge; by foot over the Queen Emma pontoon bridge (locally called "the Swinging Old Lady"); or by free ferry, which runs when the pontoon bridge is swung open for passing ships. All the major hotels outside town offer free shuttle service to town once or twice daily. Shuttles coming from the Otrobanda side leave you at Riffort. From there it's a short walk north to the foot of the pontoon bridge. Shuttles coming from the Punda side leave you near the main entrance to Ft. Amsterdam.

**Floating Market.** Curaçao is such an arid island that most of the fruit and vegetables need to be imported. The floating market consists of dozens of Venezuelan schooners laden with tropical fruits and vegetables that dock to sell their wares on the Punda side of the city. Mangoes, papayas, and exotic vegetables vie for space with freshly caught fish and herbs and spices. The buying is best at 6:30 am—too early for many people on vacation—but there's plenty of action throughout the afternoon. Vendors will stay on island for months away from their families—forming their own little community—awaiting fresh supplies each day. ⊠ *Sha Caprileskade, Punda.*

Fodor's Choice  **Kura Hulanda Museum.** Pet project of Dutch billionaire philanthropist
★  Jacob Gelt-Dekker, who brought the Otrabanda neighborhood back to life in the '90s, this fascinating anthropological museum reveals the island's diverse roots. Housed in a restored 18th-century village, the museum is built around a former mercantile square (Kura Hulanda means "Holland courtyard"), where the Dutch once housed slaves mostly before they were sold and exported. Somber exhibits of the transatlantic slave trade are tempered by sections that highlight the origins of the diaspora, including relics from West African empires, examples of pre-Columbian gold, and Antillean art. Call ahead for guided tours or rent an audio guide. ⊠ *Klipstraat 9, Otrobanda* ☎ *5999/434–7765* ⊕ *www.kurahulanda.com/en/museumx* ⊠ *$10.*

**Maritime Museum.** The museum—designed to resemble the interior of a ship—gives you a sense of Curaçao's maritime history that spans some 500 years, using model ships, historic maps, nautical charts, navigational equipment, and audiovisual displays. Topics explored in the exhibits include the development of Willemstad as a trading city, Curaçao's role as a contraband hub, the remains of *De Alphen* (a Dutch marine freighter that exploded and sank in St. Anna Bay in 1778 and was excavated in 1984), the slave trade, the development of steam navigation, and the role of the Dutch navy on the island. The museum also offers a two-hour guided tour (Wednesday and Saturday, 1 pm) on its "water bus" through Curaçao's harbor—a route familiar to traders, smugglers, and pirates. The museum is wheelchair accessible. Bar/restaurant *Sails* on-site is open for lunch. ⊠ *Van der Brandhofstraat 7, Scharloo* ☎ *5999/65–2327* ⊕ *www.curacaomaritime.com* ⊠ *Museum $6.50.*

**Mikvé Israel-Emanuel Synagogue.** The temple—the oldest in continuous use in the Western Hemisphere—is one of Curaçao's most important sights and draws thousands of visitors per year. The synagogue was dedicated in 1732 by the Jewish community, which had already grown from the original 12 families who came from Amsterdam in 1651. They were later joined by Jews from Portugal and Spain fleeing persecution from the Inquisition. White sand covers the synagogue floor for two symbolic reasons: a remembrance of the 40 years Jews spent wandering the desert, and a re-creation of the sand used by secret Jews, or *conversos,* to muffle sounds from their houses of worship during the Inquisition.

The Jewish Cultural Museum, in back of the synagogue, displays antiques and artifacts from around the world. Many of the objects are used in the synagogue, making it a "living" museum. ⊠ *Hanchi Snoa 29, Punda* 🕾 *5999/461–1067* ⊕ *www.snoa.com* ⊠ *$10; donations also accepted.*

**Fodor's Choice**
★
**Queen Emma Bridge.** Affectionately called the "Swinging Old Lady" by locals, this bridge connects the two sides of Willemstad—Punda and Otrobanda—across the Santa Anna Bay. The bridge swings open at least 30 times a day to allow passage of ships to and from the sea. The original bridge, built in 1888, was the brainchild of the American consul Leonard Burlington Smith, who made a mint off the tolls he charged for using it: 2¢ per person for those wearing shoes, free to those crossing barefoot. But though that toll distinction was meant to help the poor, the rich often saved money by crossing barefoot, and the poor would often borrow shoes to cross because they were too proud to admit they could not afford the toll! Today it's free to everyone. The bridge was dismantled and completely repaired and restored in 2005 and also restored further in 2015. ⊠ *Willemstad* ⊕ *www.curacao.com.*

**Scharloo.** The Wilhelmina Drawbridge connects Punda with the once-flourishing district of Scharloo where the early Jewish merchants built stately homes. It was a tight-knit community and the architecture along Scharlooweg (much of it from the 17th century) is magnificent. Some of the neighborhood has been restored as part of the UNESCO heritage site and the Curaçao Monuments Foundation will be restoring more old mansions in the future. This neighborhood is also home to the island's most photographed building, a light-green mansion dubbed the "Wedding Cake House" since it looks like it's been frosted with white icing. Kleine Werf—the little wharf cresting Scharloo—has now become a venue for large-scale outdoor concerts. New nightlife corners such as District 1850 are popping up there as well. ⊠ *Scharloo, Scharloo* ⊕ *www.curacao.com.*

### ELSEWHERE ON CURAÇAO

**Fodor's Choice**
★
**Christoffel National Park.** The 1,239-foot Mt. Christoffel, Curaçao's highest peak, is at the center of this 4,450-acre garden and wildlife preserve. The preserve offers guided hikes, jeep safaris, mountain biking, deer-watching (the island's elusive white-tailed deer are very shy), animal presentations, cave explorations, and special activities like full-moon nature walks. Visitors can also hike the mountain on their own. The exhilarating climb takes about two hours for a reasonably fit person. Throughout the park are eight hiking trails and a 20-mile (32-km)

network of driving trails; the old Savonet plantation house there (one of the island's first plantations) has been restored and now serves as a modern museum with exhibits retracing the region's history as far back as the original Indian inhabitants. ■TIP➜ There's a separate entrance fee to the museum but you can also get a combo-entrance pass that includes the park and museum for less. ☒ *Christoffel Park, Savonet* ☏ *5999/462–4242 for information and tour reservations* ⊕ *www.christoffelpark.org* 🗒 *$12.*

FAMILY | Fodor's Choice | ★

**Curaçao Sea Aquarium.** The Sea Aquarium is an original installation that became the island's largest marine life attraction. Though it's in the same physical location as the Dolphin Academy and Animal Encounters—all part of the Sea Aquarium Park—it operates independently. Admission allows visitors to view dolphin shows and sea lion shows, and to view marine life in the Animal Encounter lagoon from an underwater observatory. A new Sea Lion Encounter program enables visitors to get up close under the supervision of a trainer as well (additional cost). The aquarium hall has over 40 saltwater tanks full of marine life and offers visitors the opportunity to feed sharks, interact with stingrays, sea turtles, flamingos—and lots more. Extremely educational for all ages. Snack bar and souvenir shop also on-site. ☒ *Seaquarium Beach, Bapor Kibra* ☏ *5999/461–6666* ⊕ *www.curacao-sea-aquarium.com/en* 🗒 *$20 adults.*

**Hato Caves.** Stalactites and stalagmites form striking shapes in these 200,000-year-old caves. Hidden lighting adds to the dramatic effect. Indians who used the caves for shelter left petroglyphs about 1,500 years ago. More recently, slaves who escaped from nearby plantations used the caves as a hideaway. Hour-long guided tours wind down to the pools in various chambers. Keep in mind that there are 49 steps to climb up to the entrance and the occasional bat might not be to everyone's taste. A new Indian Trail walking path and cactus garden enlighten visitors about local vegetation. The space is also available for special events. Located just two minutes from Hato International Airport. ☒ *Rooseveltweg z/n, Hato* ☏ *5999/868–0379* 🗒 *$8.*

# BEACHES

FAMILY | **Cas Abao.** This white-sand gem has the brightest blue water in Curaçao, a treat for swimmers, snorkelers, and sunbathers alike. Full services include a beach bar and restaurant, lockers, changing rooms on-site, and even full massages surf-side are available. It can become crowded on weekends, especially Sunday, when local families descend in droves. You can rent beach chairs, paddle boats, and snorkeling and diving gear. The entry fee is $5–$6 per car, more on weekends, and the beach is open from 8 am to 6 pm. **Amenities:** food and drink; lifeguards; parking; showers; toilets; water sports. **Best for:** partiers; snorkeling; swimming. ☒ *West of St. Willibrordus, about 3 miles (5 km) off Weg Naar Santa Cruz* ✛ *Turn off Westpunt Hwy. at the junction onto Weg Naar Santa Cruz; follow until the turnoff for Cas Abao, and then drive along the winding country road for about 10 mins to the beach* ⊕ *www.casabaobeach.com.*

FAMILY     **Playa Knip.** Two protected coves offer crystal-clear turquoise waters. Big (Groot) Knip, also known as Playa Kenepa, is an expanse of alluring white sand, perfect for swimming and snorkeling. You can rent beach chairs and hang out under the *palapas* (thatch-roof shelters) or cool off with ice cream at the snack bar. There are restrooms here but no showers. It's particularly crowded on Sunday and school holidays. Just up the road, also in a protected cove, sister beach Little (Klein) Knip is a charmer, too, with picnic tables and palapas. There's no fee for these beaches. **Amenities:** food and drink; lifeguards; parking; toilets; water sports. **Best for:** snorkeling; sunrise; sunset; swimming. ⊠ *Just east of Westpunt, Banda Abou.*

FAMILY
Fodor'sChoice
★     **Playa PortoMari.** Set beneath an historic plantation site, you'll find calm, clear water and a long stretch of white sand and full facilities on this beach. A decent bar and restaurant, well-kept showers, changing facilities, and restrooms are all on-site; a nature trail is nearby. The double coral reef—explore one, swim past it, explore another—is a special feature that makes this spot popular with snorkelers and divers. The entrance fee is $3, children under 12 free. **Amenities:** food and drink; lifeguards; parking; showers; toilets. **Best for:** partiers; snorkeling; swimming; walking. ⊠ *Off Willibrordus Rd.* ✛ *From Willemstad, drive west on Westpunt Hwy. for 4 miles (7 km); turn left onto Willibrordus Rd. at the PortoMari billboard, and then drive 3 miles (5 km) until you see a large church; follow signs on the winding dirt road to the beach* ⊕ *www.playaportomari.com.*

## SHOPPING

From Dutch classics like embroidered linens, Delft earthenware, and cheeses to local artwork and handicrafts, shopping in Willemstad can turn up some fun finds. But don't expect major bargains on watches, jewelry, or electronics; Willemstad is not a duty-free port (the few establishments that claim to be "duty-free" are simply absorbing the cost of some or all of the tax rather than passing it on to consumers). However, if you come prepared with some comparison prices, you might still dig up some good deals. But there are new complexes out of downtown now for ultimate retail therapy—Mambo Beach Boulevard has an eclectic collection of trendy shops at the Sea Aquarium Park and the brand-new Sambil megamall is a massive multilevel shopping and entertainment complex in Veeris Commercial Park with hundreds of modern stores and trendy boutiques.

Fodor'sChoice
★     **Boolchand's.** The best-known brand for electronics in the Caribbean, Boolchand's is a legendary family-run chain, and their main store is in Punda, though they have many other outlets around Curaçao. Beyond electronics and tech, they also sell fine jewelry, Swarovski crystal, Swiss watches, cameras, and more with a good reputation for fair prices and good quality. ⊠ *Breedstraat 50, Punda* ☎ *5999/461–6233* ⊕ *www. boolchand.com/locations.*

**Cigar Emporium.** A sweet aroma permeates Cigar Emporium, where you can find the largest selection of Cuban cigars on the island, including

H. Upmann, Romeo y Julieta, and Montecristo. Visit the climate-controlled cedar cigar room. ☒ *Gomezplein 4, Punda* ☎ *5999/465–3955.*

**Fodor's**Choice ★ **Serena's Art Factory.** You might have noticed brightly painted sculptures of colorful Caribbean women with highly exaggerated physical features in many public places around the island and miniature versions of them for sale as souvenirs in many shops. These are Chichis®—creations by artist Serena Janet Israel that are unique to Curaçao. "Chi Chi" means big sister in the local lingo, and the figures are meant to exude the warmth of matronly Caribbean women. Many different local female artists have been trained by Serena to custom-paint them, but visitors are welcome to create their own for a one-of-a-kind souvenir at Serena's Art Factory near the Ostrich Farm. Group workshops and walk-in workshops for nontour visitors are available on a regular basis. A workshop is about two hours. ☒ *Jan Louis 87a* ☎ *5999/738–0648* ⊕ *www.chichi-curacao.com* ☒ *Free tour of factory.*

## ACTIVITIES

### BIKING

FAMILY **Wanna Bike Curaçao.** The island's premier biking outfit, Wanna Bike offers tours all over Curaçao with professional guides and top equipment. They are also the founders of the Mountain Bike Kids Club and organize many mountain bike clinics throughout the year. Their sister company "Wanna Go Outdoors" organizes corporate retreats and team-building events centered around biking and ecoadventures. ☒ *Jan Thiel Beach z/n, Jan Thiel, Willemstad* ☎ *5999/527–3720* ⊕ *www.wanna bike.com.*

### DIVING AND SNORKELING

The **Curaçao Underwater Marine Park** includes almost a third of the island's southern diving waters. Scuba divers and snorkelers can enjoy more than 12½ miles (20 km) of protected reefs and shores, with normal visibility from 60 to 150 feet. With water temperatures ranging from 75°F to 82°F (24°C to 28°C), wet suits are generally unnecessary. No coral collecting, spearfishing, or littering is allowed. Some of the most popular dive sites are the Mushroom Forest, the wreck of the *Superior Producer*, and the Blue Room secret cave at Westpunt. Snorkelers and divers also enjoy the little sunken tugboat at Spanish Water. Wall diving is good around the Sea Aquarium Park and they also offer open-water dives with dolphins. The north coast—where conditions are dangerously rough—is not recommended for diving.

Introductory scuba resort courses are often done in resort pools and prices vary. To become fully PADI certified, carve out at least four or five days of your holiday for instruction and practice and at least one open-water dive. Prices vary depending on operation.

**Fodor's**Choice ★ **Ocean Encounters.** This is the largest dive operator on Curaçao, and they offer a vast menu of scheduled shore and boat dives and packages as well as certified PADI instruction. They cover the island's most popular dive sites including the *Superior Producer* wreck—where barracudas hang out—an adorable little tugboat wreck, the renowned

**4**

Mushroom Forest, and much more. In July, the dive center sponsors a children's sea camp in conjunction with the Sea Aquarium, and they now run the unique Animal Encounters experience in the Sea Aquarium lagoon. They also offer Sleep & Dive packages at Lion's Dive and Sunscape Resorts. ⊠ *Sea Aquarium Park, Bapor Kibra* ☎ *5999/461–8131* ⊕ *www.oceanencounters.com.*

## WHERE TO EAT

**$$$**
ECLECTIC
**Fodor's Choice**
★

✕ **Gouverneur de Rouville Restaurant & Café.** Dine on the veranda of a restored 19th-century Dutch mansion overlooking the Santa Anna Bay and the resplendent Punda skyline. Though often busy and popular with tourists, the ambience makes it worth a visit. Intriguing soup options include Cuban banana soup and Curaçao-style fish soup. *Keshi yena* and spareribs are among the savory entrées. After dinner, you can stick around for live music at the bar, which stays open until 1 am. The restaurant is also popular for lunch and attracts crowds when cruise ships dock. Reserve ahead if you would like a balcony table. A wine tasting room is available for special events. ⑤ *Average main: $22* ⊠ *De Rouvilleweg 9, Otrobanda* ☎ *5999/462–5999* ⊕ *www.de-gouverneur.com.*

**$$**
ECLECTIC
**Fodor's Choice**
★

✕ **Primas.** In a restored plantation mansion called Landhuis Vredenberg on a lush estate, Primas is a family-run restaurant that offers authentic homemade lunch fare in a superb setting. The menu is up to the chef, but typically hearty savory meat stews, fresh fish dishes, and Curaçaon specialties like keshi yena will pop up. You can view their daily menu on their Facebook page. They're usually not open for dinner (private parties abound), but on Thursday nights Primas is one of the few places left on the island where you can sample real *rijsttafel* (rice table), an Indonesian-influenced extravaganza of dozens of small dishes served community-style. It's also worth the trip just to see the magnificent restored mansion full of exquisite antiques. Groups of 15 or more can make special dinner arrangements. ⑤ *Average main: $14* ⊠ *Bramendiweg 200, Willemstad* ☎ *5999/461–2901* ⊙ *Closed Sun. No dinner except Thurs.* ⊲ *Reservations essential.*

# DOMINICA (ROSEAU)

By Roberta
Sotonoff

In the center of the Caribbean archipelago, wedged between the two French islands of Guadeloupe to the north and Martinique to the south, Dominica is a wild place. So unyielding is the terrain that colonists surrendered efforts at colonization, but the last survivors of the Caribbean's original people, the Carib Indians, call its rugged northeast section home. Dominica—29 miles (47 km) long and 16 miles (26 km) wide—is an English-speaking island, though family and place names are a mélange of French, English, and Carib. The capital is Roseau (pronounced rose- *oh*). If you've had enough of casinos, crowds, and swim-up bars and want to take leave of everyday life—to hike, bike, trek, spot birds and butterflies in the rain forest; explore waterfalls; discover a boiling lake; kayak, dive, snorkel, or sail in marine reserves; or go out in search of the many resident whale and dolphin species—this is the place to do it.

## ESSENTIALS

### CURRENCY
The Eastern Caribbean dollar (EC$), but U.S. dollars are widely accepted.

### TELEPHONE
To call Dominica from the United States, dial the area code (767) and the local access code (44), followed by the five-digit local number. On the island, dial only the seven-digit number that follows the area code.

### COMING ASHORE
Most ships dock along Roseau's bayfront. A visitor center sits across the street from the pier in the old post office. Taxis, minibuses, and tour operators are available at the berths. Choose one that is certified and don't be afraid to ask questions. Be explicit when discussing where you want to go and how much you will pay. The drivers usually quote a fixed fare, which is regulated by the Division of Tourism and the Transportation Board, and also offer their services for tours anywhere on the island beginning at US$30 an hour for up to four people; a four- to five-hour island tour for up to four people will cost approximately US$200. You can rent a car in Roseau for about $55–$100 for a day, not including a $12 driving permit. Be aware that navigating the island is difficult, so you might opt for a guided tour.

### BEST BETS

■ **Kalinago Barana Autê.** This reserve is a great place to learn about the "fierce" Caribs.

■ **Rain-Forest Trips.** Hiking in Dominica's rain forest is the best way to experience its natural beauty.

■ **Snorkeling in Champagne.** A bubbling volcanic vent makes you feel as if you are snorkeling in champagne.

■ **Whale-Watching.** November through February offers the best whale-watching in the Caribbean.

■ **Indian River.** A rowboat ride on the river is relaxing and peaceful.

# EXPLORING

Despite the small size of this island, it can take a couple of hours to travel between the popular destinations. Many sights are isolated and difficult to find; you may be better off taking an organized excursion. If you do go it alone, drive carefully; roads can be narrow, winding, and unmarked. Plan at least eight hours to see the highlights. To fully experience the island, set aside about five days so you can enjoy the water and take some hikes.

## ROSEAU
Although it's one of the smallest capitals in the Caribbean, Roseau has the highest concentration of inhabitants of any town in the eastern Caribbean. Caribbean vernacular architecture and a bustling marketplace transport visitors back in time. Although you can walk the entire town in about an hour, you'll get a much better feel for the place on a leisurely stroll.

For some years now, the Society for Historical Architectural Preservation and Enhancement (SHAPE) has organized programs and projects

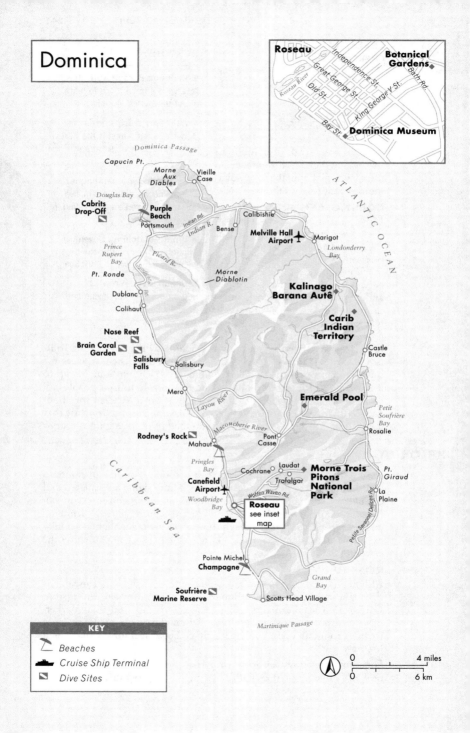

# Dominica

**Roseau**

Independence St.
Great George St.
Old St.
King George V St.
Bath Rd.
Roseau River
Bay St.

**Botanical Gardens**

**Dominica Museum**

*Dominica Passage*

Capucin Pt.

*Morne Aux Diables*

Vieille Case

Douglas Bay

**Cabrits Drop-Off**

**Purple Beach**

Portsmouth

Calibishie

Indian Rd.

Bense

Indian R.

**Melville Hall Airport**

Marigot

*Londonderry Bay*

*Prince Rupert Bay*

Picard R.

Pt. Ronde

*Morne Diablotin*

Dublanc

Sonilore Rd.

Colihaut

**Kalinago Barana Autê**

**Carib Indian Territory**

**Nose Reef**

**Brain Coral Garden**

**Salisbury Falls**

Salisbury

Castle Bruce

Mero

Layou River

**Emerald Pool**

*Petit Soufrière Bay*

Macoucherie River

Rosalie

**Rodney's Rock**

Mahaut

Pont Casse

Pringles Bay

Cochrane

Laudat

**Morne Trois Pitons National Park**

Pt. Giraud

Trafalgar

**Canefield Airport**

*Woodbridge Bay*

Wotten Waven Rd.

La Plaine

Petite Savanne/Delices Rd.

**Roseau**
see inset map

*Caribbean Sea*

Pointe Michel

**Champagne**

*Grand Bay*

**Soufrière Marine Reserve**

Scotts Head Village

*Martinique Passage*

A T L A N T I C   O C E A N

## KEY

⌇ *Beaches*

⛴ *Cruise Ship Terminal*

◣ *Dive Sites*

0 — 4 miles
0 — 6 km

to preserve the city's architectural heritage. Several interesting buildings have already been restored. **Lilac House,** on Kennedy Avenue, has three types of gingerbread fretwork, latticed veranda railings, and heavy hurricane shutters. The **J.W. Edwards Building,** at the corner of Old and King George V streets, has a stone base and a wooden second-floor gallery. The **Old Market Plaza** is the center of Roseau's historic district, which was laid out by the French on a radial plan rather than a grid, so streets such as Hanover, King George V, and Old radiate from this area. South of the marketplace is the Fort Young Hotel, built as a British fort in the 18th century; the nearby statehouse, public library, and Anglican cathedral are also worth a visit. New developments at the bayfront on Dame M.E. Charles Boulevard have brightened up the waterfront.

FAMILY **Botanical Gardens.** The 40-acre Botanical Gardens, founded in 1891 as an annex of London's Kew Gardens, is a great place to relax, stroll, or watch a cricket match. In addition to the extensive collection of tropical plants and trees, there's also a parrot aviary. At the Forestry Division office, which is also on the garden grounds, you can find numerous publications on the island's flora, fauna, and national parks. The forestry officers are particularly knowledgeable on these subjects and can also recommend good hiking guides. ⊠ *Valley Rd., Roseau* ☎ *767/266–3807, 767/266–3812* ⊕ *www.da-academy.org/dagardens.html* ✑ *Free.*

**Dominica Museum.** The old post office now houses the Dominica Museum. This labor of love by local writer and historian Dr. Lennox Honychurch contains furnishings, documents, prints, and maps that date back hundreds of years; you can also find an entire Carib hut as well as Carib canoes, baskets, and other artifacts. Normally closed on Sunday, the museum will open up when a cruise ship is in town. ⊠ *Dame M.E. Charles Blvd., opposite cruise-ship berth* ☎ *767/448–2401* ✑ *$3.*

### ELSEWHERE ON DOMINICA

FAMILY **Carib Indian Territory.** In 1903, after centuries of conflict, the Caribbean's first settlers, the Kalinago (more popularly known as the Caribs), were granted approximately 3,700 acres of land on the island's northeast coast. Here a hardened lava formation, **L'Escalier Tête Chien** (Snake's Staircase), runs down into the Atlantic. The name is derived from a snake whose head resembles that of a dog. The ocean alongside Carib Territory is particularly fierce, and the shore is full of countless coves and inlets. Approximately 3,000 natives reside here. Craftspeople have retained their knowledge of basket weaving, wood carving, and canoe building through generations. They fashion long, elegant canoes from the trunk of a single *gommier* tree. ⊕ *www.caribterritory.com.*

FAMILY **Emerald Pool.** Quite possibly the most visited nature attraction on the island, this emerald-green pool fed by a 50-foot waterfall is an easy trip to make. To reach this spot in the vast Morne Trois Pitons National Park, you follow a trail that starts at the side of the road near the reception center (it's an easy 20-minute walk). Along the way, there are lookout points with views of the windward (Atlantic) coast and the forested interior. If you don't want a crowd, check whether there are cruise ships in port before going out, as this spot is popular with cruise-ship tour groups. ⊠ *Morne Trois Pitons National Park* ✑ *US$3* *for preorganized tours; US$5 for private and stay-over visitors; US$12 weekly pass for all national parks.*

FAMILY  **Kalinago Barana Auté.** You might catch canoe builders at work at Kalinago Barana Auté, the Carib Territory's place to learn about Kalinago customs, history, and culture. A guided, 45-minute tour explores the village, stopping along the way to see some traditional dances and to learn about plants, dugout canoes, basket weaving, and cassava bread making. The path offers wonderful viewpoints of the Atlantic and a chance to glimpse Isukulati Falls. There's also a good souvenir shop. ⊠ *Crayfish River, Salibia* ☎ *767/445–7979* ⊕ *www.kalinagobaranaaute. com* ✉ *$10.*

Fodor's Choice  **Morne Trois Pitons National Park.** A UNESCO World Heritage Site, this ★  17,000-acre swath of lush, mountainous land in the south-central interior (covering 9% of Dominica) is the island's crown jewel. Named after one of the highest mountains on the island (at 4,600 feet), it contains the island's famous "boiling lake," majestic waterfalls, and cool mountain lakes. A system of trails has been developed in the park, and access to the park is possible from most points on the island, though the easiest approaches are via the small mountaintop villages of Laudat (pronounced lau- *dah*) and Cochrane.

At the base of Morne Micotrin you can find two crater lakes: the first, at 2,500 feet above sea level, is **Freshwater Lake.** According to a local legend, it's haunted by a vindictive mermaid and a monstrous serpent. Farther on is **Boeri Lake,** fringed with greenery and purple hyacinths floating on its surface.

On your way to Boiling Lake you pass through the **Valley of Desolation,** where harsh sulfuric fumes have destroyed virtually all the vegetation in what must once have been a lush forested area. At the beginning of the Valley of Desolation trail is the **TiTou Gorge,** where you can swim in the pool or relax in the hot-water springs along one side.

Also in the national park are some of the island's most spectacular waterfalls. The 45-minute hike to **Sari Sari Falls,** accessible through the east-coast village of La Plaine, can be hair-raising. But the sight of water cascading some 150 feet into a large pool is awesome. Just beyond the village of Trafalgar and up a short hill is the reception facility, where you can purchase passes to the national park and find guides to take you on a rain-forest trek to the twin **Trafalgar Falls;** the 125-foot-high waterfall is called the Father, and the wider, 95-foot-high one, the Mother. You need a guide for the arduous 75-minute hike to **Middleham Falls.** Guides for all these hikes are available at the trailheads; still, it's best to arrange a tour before setting out. ✉ *US$3 for preorganized tours; US$5 per site for private and stay-over visitors; US$12 weekly pass for all national parks*

## BEACHES

FAMILY  **Champagne.** On the west coast, just south of the village of Pointe Michel, Fodor's Choice  this stony beach is hailed as one of the best spots for swimming, diving, ★  and (especially) snorkeling. Forget the sunning, though, because the beach is strewn with rocks. Champagne gets its name from volcanic vents that constantly puff steam into the sea, which makes you feel as if you are swimming in warm champagne. A boardwalk leads to the beach from Soufrière/Scotts Head Marine Reserve. **Amenities:** none. **Best for:** snorkeling; swimming. ⊠ *Soufrière* ✛ *1 mile (1½ km) south of Pointe Michel.*

## SHOPPING

Dominicans produce distinctive handicrafts, with various communities specializing in their specific products. The crafts of the Carib Indians include traditional baskets made of dyed *larouma* reeds and water-proofed with tightly woven *balizier* leaves. These are sold in the Carib Indian Territory and Kalinago Barana Autê as well as in Roseau's shops. Vertivert straw rugs, screw-pine tableware, *fwije* (the trunk of the forest tree fern), and wood carvings are just some examples. Also notable are local herbs, spices, condiments, and herb teas. Café Dominique, the local equivalent of Jamaican Blue Mountain coffee, is an excellent buy, as are the Dominican rums Macoucherie and Soca. Proof that the old ways live on in Dominica can be found in the number of herbal rem-edies available. One stimulating memento of your visit is rum steeped with *bois bandé* (scientific name *Richeria grandis*), a tree whose bark is reputed to have aphrodisiacal properties. It's sold at shops, vendors' stalls, and supermarkets.

One of the easiest places to pick up a souvenir is the Old Market Plaza, just behind the Dominica Museum, in Roseau. Slaves were once sold here, but today handcrafted jewelry, T-shirts, spices, souvenirs, batik, and trays, plus lacquered and woven bamboo boxes are available from a group of vendors in open-air booths set up on the cobblestones. They are usually busiest when there's a cruise ship berthed across the street. On these days you can also find a vast number of vendors along the bayfront.

**Kalinago Barana Autê.** Kalinago Barana Autê sells carvings, pottery, and lovely handwoven baskets, which you can watch the women weave. ⊠ *Salybia, Carib Territory* ☎ *767/445–7979* ⊕ *www.kalinagobara-naaute.com.*

## ACTIVITIES

### ADVENTURE SPORTS

FAMILY

Fodor's Choice

★

**Wacky Rollers.** Wacky Rollers will make you feel as if you are training for the Marines as you swing on a Tarzan-style rope and grab onto a vertical rope net, rappel across zip lines, and traverse suspended log bridges, a net bridge, and four monkey bridges (rope loops). The adult course should take from 1½ to 3½ hours to conquer the 28 "games"; admission packages include transportation. There is also an abbrevi-ated kids' course (kids 10 and under). Wacky Rollers also organizes adventure tours around the island plus river-to-ocean kayaking trips and river-tubing trips. Although the office is in Roseau, the park itself is in Hillsborough Estate, 20 to 25 minutes north of Roseau. ✉ *Front St., Roseau* 📞 *767/440–4386,* ⊕ *www.wackyrollers.com* 💳 *From $75.*

## DIVING AND WHALE-WATCHING

Not only is Dominica considered one of the top 10 dive destinations in the world by *Skin Diver* and *Rodale's Scuba Diving* magazines, but it has won many other awards for its underwater sites. They are truly memorable. The west coast of the island has awesome sites, but the best are those in the southwest—within and around **Soufrière/Scotts Head Marine Reserve.** This bay is a submerged volcanic crater. The Dominica Watersports Association has worked along with the Fisheries Division for years to establish this reserve and has set stringent regulations to prevent the degradation of the ecosystem. Within ½ mile (¾ km) of the shore there are vertical drops from 800 feet to more than 1,500 feet, with visibility frequently extending to 100 feet. Shoals of boga fish, creole wrasse, and blue cromis are common, and you might even see a spotted moray eel or a honeycomb cowfish. Crinoids (rare elsewhere) are also abundant here, as are giant barrel sponges. There is a $2 fee per person to dive, snorkel, or kayak in the reserve. Other noteworthy dive sites include **Salisbury Falls, Nose Reef, Brain Coral Garden,** and—even farther north—**Cabrits Drop-Off** and **Toucari Reef.** The conditions for underwater photography, particularly macrophotography, are unparalleled. Rates start at about $55 for a single-tank dive and about $90 for a two-tank dive, or from about $75 for a resort course with one openwater dive. All scuba-diving operators also offer snorkeling. Equipment rents for $10 to $25 a day; trips with gear range from $15 to $35. A 10% tax is not included.

Dominica records the highest species counts of resident cetaceans in the southern Caribbean region, so it's not surprising that tour companies claim 90% sighting success for their excursions. Humpback whales, false killer whales, minke, and orcas are all occasionally seen, as are several species of dolphin. But the resident sperm whales (they calve in Dominica's 3,000-foot-deep waters) are truly the stars of the show. During your 3½-hour expedition, which costs about $55 plus tax, you may be asked to assist in recording sightings, data that can be shared with local and international organizations. Although there are resident whale and dolphin populations, more species can be observed from November through February. Turtle-watching trips are also popular.

**Anchorage Dive & Whale Watch Center.** The Anchorage Dive & Whale Watch Center can arrange whale-watching trips. ✉ *Anchorage Hotel, Castle Comfort* 📞 *767/448–2638, 767/440–2639* ⊕ *www.anchorage hotel.dm.*

**Dive Dominica.** Dive Dominica is a major whale-watching operator as well as a dive operator on the island. ✉ *Castle Comfort Lodge, Castle Comfort* 📞 *767/448–2188* ⊕ *www.divedominica.com.*

## HIKING

Dominica's majestic mountains, clear rivers, and lush vegetation conspire to create adventurous hiking trails. The island is crisscrossed by ancient footpaths of the Arawak and Carib Indians and of the Nègres Maroons, escaped slaves who established camps in the mountains.

Existing trails range from easygoing to arduous. To make the most of your excursion, you'll need sturdy hiking boots, insect repellent, a change of clothes (kept dry), and a guide. Hikes and tours run $25 to $80 per person, depending on destinations and duration. A poncho or light raincoat is recommended. Some of the natural attractions within the island's national parks require visitors to purchase a site pass. These are sold for varying numbers of visits. A single-entry site pass costs $5, and a week pass $12. The Discover Dominica Authority's information offices at the Bayfront (Dame Charles Boulevard) can recommend guides.

**Bertrand Jno Baptiste.** Local bird and forestry expert Bertrand Jno Baptiste leads hikes up Morne Diablotin and along the Syndicate Nature Trail; if he's not available, ask him to recommend another guide. ☎ 767/245–4768.

## WHERE TO EAT

$
ECLECTIC
FAMILY
✕ **Cocorico.** It's hard to miss this bright yellow-and-blue Parisian-style café on a prominent bayfront corner in Roseau. Breakfast crepes, croissants, baguette sandwiches, and piping-hot café au lait are available beginning at 8:30. Throughout the day you can relax indoors or out and enjoy any of the extensive menu selections with the perfect glass of wine. You can also surf the Internet on its computers. In the cellar downstairs, the Cocorico wine store has a reasonably priced selection from more than eight countries, plus a wide assortment of pâtés and cheeses, crepes, sausages, cigars, French bread, and chocolates. ⑤ *Average main: US$10 ⊠ Bay Front at Kennedy Ave., Roseau* ☎ *767/449–8686 ⊕ www. cocoricocafe.com ⊘ Closed Sun. unless a ship is in port. No dinner Mon.–Thurs. and Sun.*

$$
CARIBBEAN
✕ **Pearl's Cuisine.** Located in downtown Roseau, chef Pearl, with her robust and infectious character, prepares some of the island's best local cuisine, such as callaloo soup, fresh fish, and rabbit. Her menu changes daily, but she offers such local delicacies as souse (pickled pigs' feet), blood pudding, and rotis. When sitting down, ask for a table on the open-air gallery that overlooks Roseau. Servings are large here, but make sure you leave space for dessert. If you're on the go, enjoy a quick meal from the daily, varied menu at the back of the building on Hanover Street. You're spoiled for choice when it comes to the fresh fruit juices. ⑤ *Average main: US$12 ⊠ Sutton Place Hotel, 25 Old St., Roseau* ☎ *767/448–8707 ⊘ Closed Sun. No dinner.*

# FALMOUTH, JAMAICA

By Richard
Sitler

Falmouth, which was founded in 1769, prospered from Jamaica's status as the world's leading sugar producer. Midway between Ocho Rios and Montego Bay, and with more than 80 sugar estates nearby, the town was meticulously mapped out in the colonial tradition, with streets named after British royalty and heroes. The richness of the town's historic Georgian structures, many of which are still occupied and maintained, is reflected in its heritage. The city has long been heralded for its forward-thinking hygiene policies (the first piped water supply system in the Western Hemisphere—established here in 1799—continues to be a source of pride) and progressive politics (Falmouth was the birthplace of Jamaica's abolitionist movement in the early 19th century). The site of many slave revolts, Falmouth's residents turned scores of the town's buildings into safe houses for escaped slaves until the practice of slavery was outlawed in Jamaica in 1838.

While Falmouth is seeing a revival with the opening of a purpose-built cruise port in 2011, buildings that may seem unimpressive as they undergo restoration are still rich in history. In 1966 the Jamaican government declared Falmouth a National Monument.

---

**BEST BETS**

■ **Good Hope Plantation.** The expansive view of the plantation grounds and surrounding countryside from the front garden includes the Martha Brae River.

■ **Historic Falmouth Walking Tour.** Absorb Falmouth's Colonial-era history and discover the town's landmarks and Georgian architectural treasures.

■ **Tharp House.** Located within the Falmouth Cruise Port, the town home of sugar planter John Tharp is one of Falmouth's most historic buildings. Once a tax collector's office, it is now expected to become a maritime museum.

---

## ESSENTIALS

### CURRENCY

The Jamaican dollar, but the U.S. dollar is accepted virtually everywhere.

### TELEPHONE

Public telephones are by the bus stop at the Falmouth Cruise Terminal. Some U.S. phone companies won't permit credit-card calls to be placed from Jamaica because of problems with fraud, so collect calls are often the top option. GSM cell phones equipped with tri-band or world-roaming service will find coverage throughout the Falmouth area.

### COMING ASHORE

Cruise ships, including the world's largest, are able to dock at the Falmouth Cruise Port's two berths. A visitor information facility is in the pier area. The town is right outside the port gates, and places of interest are easily within walking distance. Currency-exchange booths are in the pier area as well as just outside the entrance gate on Seaboard Street. Further, the cruise-port area has Wi-Fi service (for a fee) for passengers with laptops. The Falmouth tourist trolley offers a half-hour tour of the town with regular departures from the Port Transportation Center. Tickets and trolley schedules are available in the trolley kiosk at the Taxi Shelter building.

For travel out of town, buses and taxis are available. Bus fare to the beach is $20 round-trip, and taxis are priced by the hour at $35 for up to four people for either a guided tour or transportation to a specific destination. Falmouth's location, about 30 minutes from Montego Bay and about an hour from Ocho Rios, makes most tours offered at those ports available from Falmouth as well. Many of the most popular and adventurous tours are operated by Chukka Caribbean and can only be

4

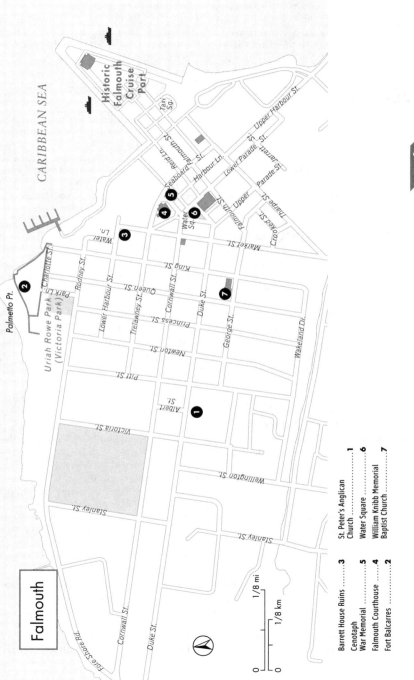

**Falmouth**

CARIBBEAN SEA

Historic Falmouth Cruise Port

Palmetto Pt.

Uriah Rowe Park (Victoria Park)

N

0    1/8 mi

0    1/8 km

Barrett House Ruins .......**3**
Cenotaph
War Memorial ........**5**
Falmouth Courthouse ......**4**
Fort Balcarres ...........**2**
St. Peter's Anglican
Church ...............**1**
Water Square ...........**6**
William Knibb Memorial
Baptist Church ........**7**

booked by cruise passengers directly with the cruise lines, as space is presold to ships for their arrival dates. Coaches for prebooked tours pick up passengers inside the Cruise Port, but authorized independent tour operators are also available there to arrange tours on the spot. Car rental isn't recommended off the main highways in Jamaica because of the narrow roads and aggressive drivers.

## EXPLORING

Falmouth's streets, which were laid out in a grid plan in the mid-1700s, are easily explored on your own. However, even with a map, finding your way around can be confusing due to a lack of street signs. If you become disoriented or require directions, look for a member of the Falmouth Tourism Courtesy Corps wearing official white shirts and hats, who are on hand to assist visitors. The one-hour trolley tour, which leaves from inside the cruise port, is an excellent way to see the historic sites and buildings and help you avoid getting lost.

Points of interest include the Falmouth Courthouse and the adjacent Cenotaph War Memorial; Water Square, where Falmouth residents got running water before New York City; Fort Balcarres, built to guard Falmouth Harbour; and Barrett House ruins, the remains of the town home of planter Edward Barrett (grandfather of Elizabeth Barrett Browning), who founded Falmouth. Also of interest is the William Knibb Baptist Church, which dates back to 1832 and was rebuilt in 1837 by Baptist missionary William Knibb, a pro-emancipation activist. St. Peter's Anglican Church is the oldest public building in Falmouth still in use.

Other sights include fine examples of Falmouth's Georgian-era architecture. These buildings are recognizable by their double-hung sash windows, keystones, columns, symmetry of facade, and full-length verandas. Constructed of a native limestone over brick, and remarkably preserved, most structures are occupied as either private residences or commercial buildings.

### NEAR FALMOUTH

Fodor's Choice ★ **Good Hope Estate.** About a 20-minute drive inland from Falmouth, this estate on more than 2,000 acres provides a sense of Jamaica's rich history as a sugar-estate island, incredible views of the Martha Brae River, and loads of fun. An adventure park offers zip-lining, river tubing, a great house tour, access to a colonial village, an aviary, swimming pool, challenge course for adults, and kids' play area with its own challenge course. Guests may get a taste of Jamaica at the Appleton Estate Jamaica Rum Tavern and Jablum Cafe or enjoy spicy goodness from the Walkerswood Jerk Hut. Adventure park passes entitle visitors to all estate activities. ⊠ *Falmouth* ☎ *876/881–6869, 876/469–3444* ⊕ *www.chukka.com* ✉ *$55.*

**Jamaica Swamp Safari Village.** With a large sign declaring that "Trespassers Will Be Eaten," this attraction on the outskirts of Falmouth will most fascinate reptile enthusiasts. The village was started as a crocodile farm in the 1970s by American Ross Kananga, who was a stunt man in the James Bond film *Live and Let Die.* Scenes from the film *Papillon,* starring Steve McQueen and Dustin Hoffman, were also shot here.

Although Ross passed away some years ago and the attraction fell into disrepair, it has recently reopened. It now houses a number of Jamaican crocodiles as well as the Jamaican yellow boa snake. There are other exotic animals from South America and colorful tropical birds in the aviary. ✉ *Foreshore Rd., Falmouth* ☎ *876/617–2798* ⊕ *www.jamaica swampsafari.com* ✄ *$38.*

## SHOPPING

Coming ashore, you will find more than four dozen shops along the cruise port's pedestrian thoroughfares housing well-known international and established Jamaican merchants. Also in the port is a covered open-air craft market, where many vendors offer their wares, including hand-carvings, and items such as T-shirts, caps, and local seasonings. In town, souvenir vendors set up on Seaboard Street near the Courthouse. Water Square is the location of the Albert George market, where artisans offer local craftwork that showcases the history and culture of the area. The upscale Shops at Rose Hall are within easy reach by taxi between Falmouth and Montego Bay.

## ACTIVITIES

Most adventure activities offered to cruise-ship passengers in Montego Bay and Ocho Rios, including water sports, trips to nearby beaches, golf, river-rafting, scuba diving, and sightseeing, are also available to cruise passengers in Falmouth. See both Montego Bay and Ocho Rios for more information. Chukka at Good Hope offers the majority of activities aimed at cruise passengers out of Good Hope Plantation.

### ADVENTURE ACTIVITIES

**Chukka at Good Hope.** This thrilling zip-line experience starts in the heart of the jungle and then flies through the rain forest and over rivers while providing spectacular mountain views. The 2½-hour tour is for ages six and older. In addition, the property offers an ATV safari, river tubing, dune buggies, and a horse-and-carriage ride. Tours of the old sugar estate, highlighting a waterwheel and trading house, are also available. ✉ *Good Hope, Falmouth* ☎ *876/619–1441 Digicel in Jamaica, 876/656–8026 Lime in Jamaica, 877/424–8552 in U.S.* ⊕ *chukka.com* ✄ *$169.*

### FISHING

**Glistening Waters Marina.** Offering deep-sea fishing and other charter trips from Glistening Waters (20 minutes east of Montego Bay), this marina also runs night tours of the lagoon, which is iridescent due to microscopic dinoflagellates that glow when they move. ✉ *North Coast Hwy., Falmouth* ☎ *876/954–3229* ⊕ *www.glisteningwaters.com.*

### GUIDED TOURS

**Falmouth Heritage Walks.** This leisurely paced walk takes you through Falmouth's commercial and residential streets while your guide shares the little-known history of the town and what made it a rich and significant port in the late 18th and early 19th centuries. Your guide will also explain how the movement to abolish slavery was essentially founded in Falmouth when you visit the former home and grave of the famous abolitionist William Knibb. The full tour takes about 2 hours 15 minutes. ⊠ *Falmouth* ☎ *876/407–2245* ⊕ *www.falmouthheritagewalks. com* ⊠ *From $25.*

**Historic Trolley Tours.** The easiest way to see the historic sites of Falmouth is on this covered trolley with a guide who offers a lively commentary about the town and its many historical buildings. The majority of these are Georgian in style and date to the 18th century. The one-hour tours leave regularly from inside the cruise port and include attractions such as Falmouth Court House, the market, Water Square, and several churches. Trams—though not motorized ones—were the mode of transport in Jamaica 300 years ago when Falmouth was in its heyday as a busy sugar port. ⊠ *Falmouth cruise port, Falmouth* ☎ *876/509–0454* ⊕ *www.falmouthtoursbytrolley.com* ⊠ *From $15.*

## WHERE TO EAT

Falmouth has a large Margaritaville restaurant and bar, which is a destination for some passengers not going on organized tours. Those planning a shopping trip to the Half Moon shopping village can eat at one of the restaurants there. Good Hope Great House also offers afternoon tea to visitors who choose to do a tour there.

$ ✕ **Club Nazz and Restaurant.** Just 100 yards west of Water Square, this
JAMAICAN restaurant is in a restored, brightly painted Georgian-style building that once served as a courthouse. Locals and visitors alike dig into Jamaican cuisine, such as curried goat, oxtail, jerk chicken or pork, and rice and peas. Shrimp and fish are done to order. For the less adventurous, there are burgers and fries. The full-service bar offers most any rum drink you can think of. Sadly, most cruise ships set sail before the nightclub scene gets underway, with performances by a cross-section of musicians. $ *Average main: $10* ⊠ *23 Market St., Falmouth* ☎ *876/615–1571* ⊟ *No credit cards.*

# FREEPORT-LUCAYA, BAHAMAS

By Jessica Robertson

Grand Bahama Island, the fourth-largest island in the Bahamas, lies 52 miles (84 km) off Palm Beach, Florida. In 1492, when Columbus first set foot in the Bahamas, Grand Bahama was already populated. Skulls found in caves attest to the existence of the peaceable Lucayans, who were constantly fleeing the more bellicose Caribs. But it was not until the 1950s, when the harvesting of Caribbean yellow pine trees (now protected by Bahamian environmental law) was the island's major industry, that American financier Wallace Groves envisioned Grand Bahama's grandiose future as a tax-free port for the shipment of goods to the United States. It was in that era that the city of Freeport and later Lucaya evolved. They are separated by a 4-mile (6-km) stretch of East Sunrise Highway, although few can tell you where one community ends and the other begins. Most of Grand Bahama's commercial activity is concentrated in Freeport, the Bahamas' second-largest city. Lucaya, with its sprawling shopping complex and water-sports reputation, stepped up to the role of island tourism capital. Resorts, beaches, a casino, and golf courses make both cities popular with visitors.

## ESSENTIALS

### CURRENCY

The Bahamian dollar (which trades one-to-one with the U.S. dollar), but the latter is universally accepted.

### TELEPHONE

Pay phones accept Bahamas Direct Prepaid cards purchased from BTC at vending machines, stores, and BTC offices. You can use these cards to call within the country or to the United States. Although most U.S. cell phones work in the Bahamas, the roaming cost can be very high, so check with your provider in advance.

## BEST BETS

■ **Diving with UNE XSO.** Simply one of the world's most respected diving facilities.

■ **The Dolphin Experience.** Choose your level of involvement.

■ **East End.** Venture beyond the city to the quiet fishing settlements east of Freeport.

■ **Lucayan National Park.** Explore caves, hike to the beach, or kayak its mangrove tidal creek.

■ **Shopping.** Duty-free shopping in the Port Lucaya Marketplace is still good; be sure to haggle if you shop at the straw markets.

## COMING ASHORE

Cruise-ship passengers arrive at Lucayan Harbour, which has a Bahamian-style look, extensive cruise-passenger terminal facilities, and an entertainment-shopping village. The harbor lies about 10 minutes west of Freeport. Taxis and limos meet all cruise ships. Two passengers are charged $20 and $27 for trips to Freeport and Lucaya, respectively. Fare to Xanadu Beach is $18; it's $33 to Taïno Beach. The price per person drops to $5–$7 per person for groups of eight or more. It's customary to tip taxi drivers 15%. Sightseeing tours range from $35 to $65 per hour depending on the area covered and the size of the vehicle needed. Grand Bahama's flat terrain and straight, well-paved roads make for good scooter riding. Rentals run $35 a day (about $15 an hour). Helmets are required and provided. Look for small rental stands in parking lots and along the road in Freeport and Lucaya and at the larger resorts. It's usually cheaper to rent a car than to hire a taxi. Automobiles, jeeps, and vans can be rented at the Grand Bahama International Airport. Some agencies provide free pickup and delivery service to the cruise-ship port and Freeport and Lucaya, but prices are still not cheap; cars begin at $65 per day.

## EXPLORING

Grand Bahama is the only planned island in the Bahamas. Its towns, villages, and sights are well laid out but far apart. Downtown Freeport and Lucaya are both best appreciated on foot. Buses and taxis can transport you the 4-mile (6-km) distance between the two. In Freeport shopping is the main attraction. Bolstered by the Our Lucaya Resort complex, Lucaya has its beautiful beach and water-sports scene, plus more shopping and a big, beautiful new casino. Outside of town, isolated fishing

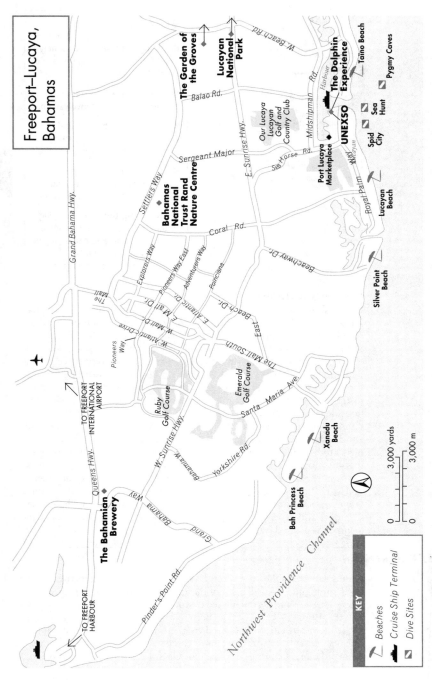

villages, beaches, natural attractions, and the once-rowdy town of West End make it worthwhile to hire a tour or rent a car. The island stretches 96 miles (154 km) from one end to the other.

## FREEPORT

**The Bahamian Brewery.** One hundred percent Bahamian owned, this 20-acre brewery opened in 2007, bringing to the Bahamian islands five new beers including Sands, High Rock Lager, Bush Crack, and Strong Back Stout. The brewery even has a signature red ale served exclusively at the Atlantis Resort on Paradise Island. The brewery does everything on-site including bottling and labeling, and offers 45-minute- to hour-long tours on weekdays that take you along each step in the brewing process. The tour ends in the tasting room where you can belly up to the bar or cocktail tables to sample each beer. Walk-ins are accepted. Beer and liquor can be purchased in the retail store; Bahamian Brewery souvenirs are available in the gift shop. ✉ *Just off Queen's Hwy., east of turn to West End, Freeport* ☎ *242/352–4070* ⊕ *www. bahamianbrewery.com* 🎟 *$8 for tours* ☾ *Closed weekends.*

**Bahamas National Trust Rand Nature Centre.** Established in 1939 on 100 acres just minutes from downtown Freeport, a half-mile of self-guided botanical trails shows off 130 types of native plants, including many plants known for their use in bush medicine. The remaining tracts of land are left natural and undisturbed to serve as wildlife habitat. The center is also one of the island's birding hot spots, where you might spy a red-tailed hawk or a Cuban emerald hummingbird. Visit Donni, the caged one-eyed Bahama parrot the center has adopted, and the two Bahamian boas, a species that inhabits most Bahamian islands, but not Grand Bahama. Guided tours are available by appointment only. The visitor center also hosts changing local art exhibits. The center survives on admissions, gift shop purchases, and donations alone, but has high hopes and plans for a future face-lift and new exhibits. ✉ *E. Settlers Way, Freeport* ☎ *242/352–5438* ⊕ *www.bnt.bs* 🎟 *$5.*

## LUCAYA

Lucaya, on Grand Bahama's southern coast and just east of Freeport, was developed as the island's resort center. These days it's booming with the megaresort complex called the Our Lucaya Resort, a fine sandy beach, championship golf courses, a casino, a first-class dive operation, and Port Lucaya's shopping and marina facilities. Most cruise ships offer excursions that include a day at Our Lucaya.

FAMILY
Fodor's Choice
★

**The Dolphin Experience.** Encounter Atlantic bottlenose dolphins in Sanctuary Bay at one of the world's first and largest dolphin facilities, about 2 miles east of Port Lucaya. A ferry takes you from Port Lucaya to the bay to observe and photograph the animals. If you don't mind getting wet, you can sit on a partially submerged dock or stand waist deep in the water and one of these friendly creatures will swim up to you. You can also engage in one of two swim-with-the-dolphins programs, but participants must be 55 inches or taller. The Dolphin Experience began in 1987, when it trained five dolphins to interact with people. Later, the animals learned to head out to sea and swim with scuba divers on the open reef. A 2½-hour dive program is available. You can buy tickets for the Dolphin Experience at UNEXSO in Port Lucaya but be sure to make reservations as early as possible. ✉ *Port Lucaya, next to Pelican Bay Hotel, Port Lucaya Marketplace* ☎ *242/373–1244, 800/992–3483* ⊕ *www.unexso.com* ✉ *Dolphin Close Encounter $85, Dolphin Swim $179, Dolphin Dive $219.*

**UNEXSO** (*Underwater Explorers Society*). This world-renowned scuba-diving facility provides rental equipment, guides, and boats. Facilities include a 17-foot-deep training pool with windows that look out on the harbor, changing rooms and showers, docks, an outdoor bar and grill, and an air-tank filling station. Daily dive excursions range from one-day discovery courses and dives, to specialty shark, dolphin, and cave diving. Both the facility and its dive masters have been featured in international and American magazines for their work with sharks and cave exploration. UNEXSO and its sister company, the Dolphin Experience, are known for their work with Atlantic bottlenose dolphins. ✉ *Port Lucaya, Lucaya* ✚ *Next to Pelican Bay Hotel* ☎ *242/373–1244, 800/992–3483* ⊕ *www.unexso.com* ☞ *One-tank reef dives $59, Discover Scuba course $129, night dives $79, dolphin dives $219, shark dives $109.*

## BEYOND FREEPORT-LUCAYA

Grand Bahama Island narrows at picturesque West End, once Grand Bahama's capital and still home to descendants of the island's first settlers. Seaside villages, with concrete-block houses painted in bright blue and pastel yellow, fill in the landscape between Freeport and West End. The East End is Grand Bahama's "back-to-nature" side. The road east from Lucaya is long, flat, and mostly straight. It cuts through a vast pine forest to reach McLean's Town, the end of the road.

**The Garden of the Groves.** This vibrant 12-acre garden and certified wildlife habitat, featuring a trademark chapel and waterfalls, is filled with native Bahamian flora, butterflies, birds, and turtles. Interpretative signage identifies plant and animal species. First opened in 1973, the park was renovated and reopened in 2008; additions include a labyrinth modeled after the one at France's Chartres Cathedral, colorful shops and galleries with local arts and crafts, a playground, and a multideck indoor and outdoor café and bar. Explore on your own or take a half hour-long guided tour at 10 am (Monday–Saturday). Enjoy the garden under twinkling lights on Friday nights only, with dinner specials and sometimes live music. ✉ *Midshipman Rd. and Magellan Dr.* ☎ *242/374–7778, 242/374–7779 Fri.-night dinner reservations* ⊕ *www.thegardenofthegroves.com* ✉ *$16.50.*

**Lucayan National Park.** In this extraordinary 40-acre land preserve, trails and elevated walkways wind through a natural forest of wild tamarind and gumbo-limbo trees, past an observation platform, over a mangrove swamp, along a postcard-worthy beach, and in and around one of the largest explored underwater cave systems in the world (more than 6 miles long). Twenty-five miles east of Lucaya, the park contains examples of the island's five ecosystems: beach, hardwood forest, mangroves, rocky coppice, and pine forest. From the designated parking lot, you can enter the caves at two access points; one is closed in June and July for bat-nursing season. Across the highway from the caves, two trails form a loop. The easier (0.2-mile) Creek Trail's boardwalk showcases impressive interpretive signage, and crosses a mangrove-clotted tidal creek to Gold Rock Beach, claimed by Grand Bahama's Ministry of Tourism to be the island's "welcome mat." This beach is a great place for a swim or picnic at low tide, but at high tide the beach all but disappears. ✉ *Grand Bahama Hwy., Freetown* ☎ *242/353–4149, 242/352–5438* ⊕ *www.bnt.bs* ✉ *$5.*

# BEACHES

Some 60 miles of magnificent, pristine stretches of sand extend between Freeport-Lucaya and the island's eastern end. Most are used only by people who live in adjacent settlements. The beaches have no public facilities, so beachgoers often headquarter at one of the local beach bars, which provide free transportation. **Lucayan Beach** is readily accessible from the town's main drag and is always lively and lovely. **Taïno Beach,** near Freeport, is fun for families, water-sports enthusiasts, and partiers. Near Freeport, **Xanadu Beach** provides a mile of white sand. **Gold Rock Beach** is about 45 minutes from the cruise port, but it's one of the most widely photographed beaches in the Bahamas; at low tide, unique sandbars and ridges form.

**4**

# SHOPPING

In the stores, shops, and boutiques on Grand Bahama you can find duty-free goods costing up to 40% less than what you might pay back home. At the numerous perfume shops fragrances are often sold at a sweet-smelling 25% below U.S. prices. Be sure to limit your haggling to the straw markets.

FAMILY **Port Lucaya Marketplace.** This quaint harbor-side shopping, dining, and entertainment village is one of the liveliest locales on the island. New owners have pumped lots of money into ongoing renovations and new shops, and restaurants continue to pop up, including a chocolate factory and a coffee shop. This marketplace already has several boutiques and restaurants in a harbor-side locale, plus an extensive straw market and 20-plus local crafts vendors. Live music and entertainment bring the center bandstand to life at night on the weekends, and additional entertainment is brought along on busy cruise ship days. ✉ *Sea Horse Rd., Lucaya* ✢ *Across from Grand Lucayan and Memories Resort* ☎ *242/373–8446* ⊕ *www.portlucaya.com.*

# ACTIVITIES

### FISHING

Private boat charters for up to four people cost $100 per person and up for a half day. Bahamian law limits the catching of game fish to six each of dolphinfish, kingfish, tuna, or wahoo per vessel.

**Reef Tours.** This family-owned company has been offering various tours on Grand Bahama since 1969. Deep-sea and bottom-reef fishing tours are three to four hours in duration. Full-day trips are also available, as are paddleboard and kayak rentals, bottom-fishing excursions, glass-bottom-boat tours, snorkeling trips, wine-and-cheese evening cruises, parasailing, and even guided tours by Segway, Harley, and 4X4. Reservations are essential. ⊠ *Port Lucaya Marketplace, Lucaya* ☎ *242/373–5880, 242/373–5891* ⊕ *www.reeftoursfreeport.com.*

### GOLF

**Reef Club Golf Course.** The Reef Course is a par-72, 6,930-yard links-style course. Designed by Robert Trent Jones Jr., it features lots of water (on 13 of the holes), wide fairways flanked by strategically placed bunkers, and a tricky dogleg left on the 18th. While it is the most expensive and nicest of the three golf courses on the island, budget constraints have left it comparable to an average municipal course in the States. Club rentals are available. ⊠ *Sea Horse Rd., Lucaya* ☎ *242/373–2002, 866/870–7148* ⊕ *www.grandlucayan.com* 💳 *$90 Dec.–Apr. and $75 May–Nov. for hotel guests; $115 Dec.–Apr. and $90 May–Nov. non-guests* ⑂ *18 holes, 6930 yards, par 72.*

**Ruby Golf Course.** This course reopened in 2008 with renovated landscaping but basically the same 18-hole, par-72 Jim Fazio design. It features a lot of sand traps and challenges on holes 7, 9, 10, and 18—especially playing from the blue tees. Hole 10 requires a tee shot onto a dogleg right fairway around a pond. This course is very tight and is more of a parkland-style course. Popular with locals, there is also a small restaurant-bar and pro shop. ⊠ *Wentworth Ave., off W. Sunrise Hwy., behind Ruby Swiss Restaurant, Freeport* ☎ *242/352–1851* 💳 *From $65 (fees are higher during the winter season)* ⑂ *18 holes, 7000 yards, par 72.*

## WHERE TO EAT

**$**
CARIBBEAN
FAMILY
**Fodor's** Choice
★

✕ **Banana Bay Restaurant.** Directly on Fortune Beach, Banana Bay is a great place for lunch or daytime cocktails, whether you sit on the restaurant's shaded deck or on a lounger in the sand. As the tide rolls out the beach grows, creating a wonderful shallow lagoon and sandbar, perfect for wading and for frolicking kids. In addition to daily fresh-fish specials, the kitchen serves up homemade warm banana bread loaves along with salads, sandwiches, wraps, and seafood appetizers like conch fritters and crab cakes. On windy days, you will have a front-row seat to kite surfers in action. A few times a week, cruise ships drop off tourists en masse, so you can expect service to get a little slow . . . which will give you more time to enjoy your piña colada. ⑤ *Average main: $12* ⊠ *Fortune Beach, Fortune Bay Dr., Lucaya* ☎ *242/373–2960* ⊗ *No dinner.*

**$$**
SUSHI
**Fodor's** Choice
★

✕ **East Sushi at Pier One.** Pier One has one of the most unique settings of any restaurant in Grand Bahama. Built on stilts above the ocean near Freeport Harbour, it offers one-of-a-kind views of magnificent sunsets, larger-than-life cruise ships departing, and sharks swimming for chum. Pier one has two levels and two menus, the best one being East's. Their menu is both creative and extensive including Japanese favorites such as miso soup, seaweed salads, tempura, and a variety of rolls—try the Bahama Mama with tempura conch, avocado, mango, and chili-lime mayo for a tropical twist. Diners can eat inside either upstairs or downstairs, but the large tables on the balcony offer the best views of the shark feedings, done every hour on the hour starting at 7 pm. For those who prefer their fish cooked or Continental fare, the other menu includes grilled fish, vegetable pasta, steaks, and chicken. ⑤ *Average main: $25* ✉ *Next to Freeport Harbour, Freeport* ☎ *242/352–6674* ⊕ *pieroneandeast.com* ۞ *No lunch Sun.*

# GRAND CAYMAN, CAYMAN ISLANDS

By Jordan Simon

The largest and most populous of the Cayman Islands, Grand Cayman is also one of the most popular cruise destinations in the Western Caribbean, largely because it doesn't suffer from the ailments afflicting many larger ports: panhandlers, hasslers, and crime. Instead, the Cayman economy is a study in stability, and the environment is healthy and prosperous. Though the island is rather featureless, Grand Cayman is a diver's paradise, with pristine waters and a colorful variety of marine life. Compared with other Caribbean ports, there are fewer things to see on land here; instead, the island's most impressive sights are underwater. Snorkeling, diving, and glass-bottom-boat and submarine rides top every ship's shore-excursion list, and can also be arranged at major aquatic shops if you don't go on a ship-sponsored excursion. Cayman is also famous for its nearly 600 offshore banks; not surprisingly, the standard of living is high, and nothing is cheap.

## ESSENTIALS

### CURRENCY

The Cayman Island dollar (CI$1 to US$1.25). The U.S. dollar is accepted everywhere, and most ATMs dispense cash in either currency.

### TELEPHONE

To dial the United States, dial 1 followed by the area code and telephone number. To place a credit-card call, dial 800/744–7777; credit-card and calling-card calls can be made from any public phone.

### COMING ASHORE

Ships anchor in George Town Harbour and tender passengers onto Harbour Drive, the center of the shopping district. If you just want to walk around town and shop or visit Seven Mile Beach, you're probably better off on your own, but the Stingray City Sandbar snorkeling trip is a highlight of many Caribbean vacations and fills up quickly on cruise-ship days, so it's often better to order that excursion from your ship, even though it will be more crowded and expensive than if you took an independent trip.

A tourist information booth is on the pier, and taxis queue for disembarking passengers. Although taxi fares may seem high, cabbies rarely try to rip off tourists. All taxis are required by law to install meters letting passengers know how much the trip costs. Taxi drivers won't usually do hourly rates for small-group tours; you must arrange a sightseeing tour with a company. Car rentals range in price from $45 to $95 per day (plus a $20 driving permit), so they are a good option if you want to do some independent exploring. You can easily see the entire island and have time to stop at a beach in a single day. ■ TIP➜ **Driving in the Cayman Islands is on the left (as in the United Kingdom), though the steering wheel may be on the left (as in the United States).**

4

## EXPLORING

### GEORGE TOWN

Begin exploring the capital by strolling along the waterfront Harbour Drive to **Elmslie Memorial United Church,** named after the first Presbyterian missionary to serve in Cayman. Its vaulted ceiling, wooden arches, and sedate nave reflect the religious nature of island residents. In front of the court building, in the center of town, names of influential Caymanians are inscribed on the **Wall of History,** which commemorates the islands' quincentennial in 2003. Across the street is the **Cayman Islands Legislative Assembly Building,** next door to the **1919 Peace Memorial Building.** In the middle of the financial district is the **General Post Office,** built in 1939. Let the kids pet the big blue iguana statues.

FAMILY
Fodor's Choice
★

**Cayman Islands National Museum.** Built in 1833, the historically significant clapboard home of the national museum has had several different incarnations over the years, serving as courthouse, jail, post office, and dance hall. It features an ongoing archaeological excavation of the Old Gaol and excellent 3-D bathymetric displays, murals, dioramas, and videos that illustrate local geology, flora and fauna, and island history. There are also temporary exhibits focusing on aspects of Caymanian culture, a local art collection, and interactive displays for kids. ⊠ *Harbour Dr., George Town* ☎ *345/949–8368* ⊕ *www.museum.ky* ☜ *$8.*

**Cayman Spirits/Seven Fathoms Rum.** Surprisingly, this growing company, established in 2008, is Cayman's first distillery. It's already garnered medals in prestigious international competitions for its artisanal small-batch rums (and is now making a splash for its smooth Gun Bay vodka as well). You can stop by for a tasting and self-guided tour (a more intensive, extensive guided tour costs $15) to learn how the rum is aged at 7 fathoms (42 feet) deep; supposedly the natural motion of the currents maximizes the rum's contact with the oak, extracting its rich flavors and enhancing complexity. Based on the results, it's not just yo-ho-hokum. ⊠ *65 Bronze Rd., George Town* ☎ *345/925–5379, 345/926–8186* ⊕ *www.caymanspirits.com, www.sevenfathomsrum. com.*

### ELSEWHERE ON THE ISLAND

FAMILY
**Camana Bay Observation Tower.** This 75-foot structure provides striking 360-degree panoramas of otherwise flat Grand Cayman, sweeping from George Town and Seven Mile Beach to the North Sound. The double-helix staircase is impressive in its own right. Running alongside the

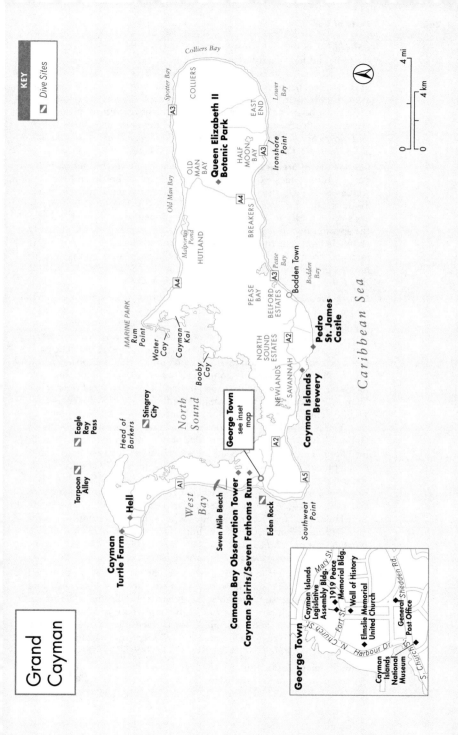

steps (an elevator is also available), a floor-to-ceiling mosaic replicates the look and feel of a dive from seabed to surface. Constructed of tiles in 114 different colors, it's one of the world's largest marine-themed mosaics. Benches and lookout points let you take in the views as you ascend. Afterward you can enjoy 500-acre Camana Bay's gardens, waterfront boardwalk, and pedestrian paths lined with shops and restaurants, or frequent live entertainment. ⊠ *Between Seven Mile Beach and North Sound, 2 miles (3 km) north of George Town, Camana Bay* ☎ *345/640–3500* ⊕ *www.camanabay.com* ⊠ *Free.*

**Cayman Islands Brewery.** In this brewery occupying the former Stingray facility, tour guides explain the iconic imagery of bottle and label as well as the nearly three-week brewing process: 7 days' fermentation, 10 days' lagering (storage), and 1 day in the bottling tank. The brewery's eco-friendly features are also championed: local farmers receive the spent grains to feed their cattle at no charge, while waste liquid is channeled into one of the Caribbean's most advanced water-treatment systems. Then enjoy your complimentary tasting knowing that you're helping the local environment and economy. ⊠ *366 Shamrock Rd., Red Bay Estate* ☎ *345/947–6699* ⊕ *caybrew.com* ⊠ *$6.*

FAMILY **Cayman Turtle Farm.** Cayman's premier attraction has been transformed into a marine theme park with souvenir shops and restaurants. Still, the turtles remain a central attraction, and you can tour ponds in the original research–breeding facility with thousands in various stages of growth, some up to 600 pounds and more than 70 years old. The park helps promote conservation, encouraging interaction and observation. The freshwater **Breaker's Lagoon**, replete with cascades plunging over moss-carpeted rocks, evokes Cayman Brac. The saltwater **Boatswain's Lagoon**, replicating all the Cayman Islands and the Trench, teems with 14,000 denizens of the deep milling about a cannily designed synthetic reef. You can snorkel here (lessons and guided tours are available). Both lagoons have underwater 4-inch-thick acrylic panels that look directly into **Predator Reef**, home to six brown sharks, four nurse sharks, and other predatory fish such as tarpons, eels, and jacks. The free-flight **Aviary**, designed by consultants from Disney's Animal Kingdom, is a riot of color and noise with feathered friends representing the entire Caribbean basin. A winding interpretive nature trail culminates in the **Blue Hole**, a collapsed cave once filled with water. Audio tours are available with different focuses, from butterflies to bush medicine. ⊠ *786 Northwest Point Rd., Box 812, West Bay* ☎ *345/949–3894* ⊕ *www. turtle.ky* ⊠ *Comprehensive, $45; Turtle Farm only, $18.*

**Hell.** The name refers to the quarter-acre of menacing shards of charred brimstone thrusting up like vengeful spirits (actually blackened and "sculpted" by acid-secreting algae and fungi over millennia). The attractions are the small post office and a gift shop where you can get cards and letters postmarked from Hell, not to mention wonderfully silly postcards titled "When Hell Freezes Over" (depicting bathing beauties on the beach). ⊠ *Hell Rd., West Bay* ☎ *345/949–3358* ⊠ *Free.*

Fodor's Choice ★ **Pedro St. James Castle.** Built in 1780, the great house is Cayman's oldest stone structure and the island's only remaining late-18th-century residence. In its capacity as courthouse and jail, it was the birthplace of Caymanian democracy, where in December 1831 the first elected parliament was organized and in 1835 the Slavery Abolition Act signed. The structure still has original or historically accurate replicas of sweeping verandas, mahogany floors, rough-hewn wide-beam ceilings, outside louvers, stone and oxblood- or mustard-color lime-wash-painted walls, brass fixtures, and Georgian furnishings. The buildings are surrounded by 8 acres of natural parks and woodlands. There's also an impressive multimedia show, on the hour, complete with smoking pots, misting rains, and two screens. ⊠ *Pedro Castle Rd., Savannah* 🕾 *345/947–3329* ⊕ *www.pedrostjames.ky* 💳 *$10.*

Fodor'sChoice   **Queen Elizabeth II Botanic Park.** This 65-acre wilderness preserve show-
★   cases a wide range of indigenous and nonindigenous tropical vegetation, approximately 2,000 species in total. Splendid sections include numerous water features and a Floral Colour Garden. A 2-acre lake and adjacent wetlands include three islets that provide a habitat and breeding ground for native birds just as showy as the floral displays. The nearly mile-long Woodland Trail encompasses every Cayman ecosystem from wetland to cactus thicket. You'll encounter birds, lizards, turtles, and agoutis, but the park's star residents are the protected endemic blue iguanas, the world's most endangered iguana, which are found only in Grand Cayman. The Trust conducts 90-minute behind-the-scenes safaris Monday–Saturday at 11 am for $30. ⊠ *367 Botanic Rd., North Side* 🕾 *345/947–9462* ⊕ *www.botanic-park.ky* 💳 *$10, children under 12 free with adult.*

## BEACHES

Fodor'sChoice   **Seven Mile Beach.** Grand Cayman's west coast is dominated by this
★   famous beach—actually a 6½-mile (10-km) expanse of powdery white sand overseeing lapis water stippled with a rainbow of parasails and kayaks. Free of litter and pesky peddlers, it's an unspoiled (though often crowded) environment. Most of the island's resorts, restaurants, and shopping centers sit along this strip. The public beach toward the north end offers chairs for rent ($10 for the day, including a beverage), a playground, water toys aplenty, beach bars, restrooms, and showers. The best snorkeling is at either end, by the Marriott and Treasure Island or off Cemetery Beach, to the north. **Amenities:** food and drink; showers; toilets; water sports. **Best for:** partiers; snorkeling. ⊠ *West Bay Rd., Seven Mile Beach.*

## SHOPPING

On Grand Cayman the good news is that there's no sales tax *and* there's plenty of duty-free merchandise. Locally made items to watch for include woven mats, baskets, jewelry made of a marblelike stone called Caymanite (from the cliffs of Cayman Brac), and authentic sunken treasure, though the latter is never cheap. In addition, there are several noteworthy local artists, some of whose atelier–homes double as galleries, such as Al Ebanks, Horacio Esteban, and Luelan Bodden. Unique items include Cayman sea salt and luxury bath salts (solar harvested in an ecologically sensitive manner) and Tortuga rum and rum cakes. Seven Fathoms is the first working distillery actually in Cayman itself, its award-winning rums aged underwater (hence the name). Cigar lovers, take note: some shops carry famed Cuban brands, but you must enjoy them on the island; bringing them back to the United States is illegal.

Although you can find black-coral products in Grand Cayman, they're controversial. Most of the coral sold here comes from Belize and Honduras; Cayman Islands' marine law prohibits the removal of live coral from its own sea, so most of it has been taken illegally. Black coral grows at a very slow rate (3 inches every 10 years) and is an endangered species. Buy other products instead.

**Guy Harvey's Gallery and Shoppe.** World-renowned marine biologist, conservationist, and artist Guy Harvey showcases his aquatic-inspired, action-packed art in every conceivable medium, from tableware to sportswear (even logo soccer balls and Zippos). The soaring, two-story 4,000-square-foot space is almost more theme park than store, with monitors playing sport-fishing videos, wood floors inlaid with tile duplicating rippling water, dangling catboats "attacked" by shark models, and life-size murals honoring such classics as Hemingway's *Old Man and the Sea*. Original paintings, sculpture, and drawings are expensive, but there's something (tile art, prints, lithographs, and photos) in most price ranges. ⊠ *49 S. Church St., George Town* ☎ *345/943–4891* ⊕ *www.guyharvey.com.*

**Tortuga Rum Company.** This company bakes, then vacuum-seals more than 10,000 of its world-famous rum cakes daily, adhering to the original, "secret" century-old recipe. There are eight flavors, from banana to Blue Mountain coffee (the new taffy also comes in eight varieties). The 12-year-old rum, blended from private stock though actually distilled in Guyana, is a connoisseur's delight for after-dinner sipping. You can buy a fresh rum cake at the airport on the way home at the same prices as at the factory store. ⊠ *Industrial Park, N. Sound Rd., George Town* ☎ *345/943–7663* ⊕ *www.tortugarumcakes.com.*

## ACTIVITIES

### DIVING AND SNORKELING

One of the world's leading dive destinations, Grand Cayman's dramatic underwater topography features plunging walls, soaring skyscraper pinnacles, grottoes, arches, swim-throughs adorned with vibrant sponges, coral-encrusted caverns, and canyons patrolled by Lilliputian grunts to gargantuan groupers, hammerheads to hawksbill turtles.

Pristine clear water, breathtaking coral formations, and plentiful marine life mark the **North Wall**—a world-renowned dive area along the North Side of Grand Cayman. **Trinity Caves,** in West Bay, is a deep dive with numerous canyons starting at about 60 feet and sloping to the wall at 130 feet. The South Side is the deepest, its wall starting 80 feet deep before plummeting, though its shallows offer a lovely labyrinth of caverns and tunnels in such sites as Japanese Gardens. The less visited, virgin East End is less varied geographically beyond the magnificent Ironshore Caves and Babylon Hanging Gardens ("trees" of black coral plunging 100 feet) but teems with "Swiss cheese" swim-throughs and exotic life in such renowned gathering spots as the Maze.

Shore-entry snorkeling spots include **Cemetery Reef,** north of Seven Mile Beach, and the reef-protected shallows of the **north and south coasts.** Ask for directions to the shallow wreck of the *Cali* in the George Town harbor area; there are several places to enter the water, including a ladder at Rackam's Pub. Among the wreckage you'll find the winch and lots of friendly fish.

**Stingray Sandbar** is one of the best snorkeling spots in the Caribbean and is always filled with boats on cruise ship days.

Fodor'sChoice **DiveTech.** With comfortable boats and quick access to West Bay, ★ DiveTech offers shore diving at its northwest-coast location, providing loads of interesting creatures, a mini-wall, and the North Wall. Technical training (a specialty of owner Nancy Easterbrook) is unparalleled, and the company offers good, personable service as well as the latest gadgetry such as underwater DPV scooters and rebreathing equipment. They even mix their own gases. Options include extended cross-training Ranger packages, Dive and Art workshop weeks, photography-video seminars with Courtney Platt, deep diving, less disruptive free diving, search and recovery, stingray interaction, reef awareness, and underwater naturalist. Snorkel and diving programs are available for children eight and up, SASY (supplied-air snorkeling, with the unit on a personal flotation device) for five and up. Multiday discounts are a bonus. ✉ *Lighthouse Point, near Boatswain's Beach, 571 Northwest Point Rd., West Bay* ☎ *345/949–1700* ⊕ *www.divetech.com.*

FAMILY **Red Sail Sports.** Daily trips leave from most major hotels, and dives are often run as guided tours, good for beginners. If you're experienced and your air lasts long, ask the captain if you must come up with the group (when the first person runs low on air). Kids' options, ages 5 to 15, include SASY and Bubblemakers. The company also operates Stingray City tours, dinner and sunset sails, and water sports from Wave Runners to windsurfing. ☎ *345/949–8745, 345/623–5965, 877/506–6368* ⊕ *www.redsailcayman.com.*

## FISHING

If you enjoy action fishing, Cayman waters have plenty to offer. Experienced, knowledgeable local captains charter boats with top-of-the-line equipment, bait, ice, and often lunch included in the price (usually $700 to $950 per half day, $1,200 to $1,600 for a full day). Options include deep-sea, reef, bone, tarpon, light-tackle, and fly-fishing. June and July are good all-around months for blue marlin, yellow- and blackfin tuna, dolphinfish, and bonefish. Bonefish have a second season in the winter months, along with wahoo and skipjack tuna.

**R&M Fly Shop and Charters.** Captain Ronald Ebanks is arguably the island's most knowledgeable fly-fishing guide, with more than 10 years' experience in Cayman and Scotland. He also runs light-tackle trips on a 24-foot Robalo. Everyone from beginners—even children—to experienced casters enjoy and learn, whether wading or poling from a 17-foot Stratos Flats boat. Free transfers are included. Captain Ronald even ties his own flies (he'll show you how). ☎ *345/947–3146, 345/946–0214* ⊕ *www.flyfishgrandcayman.com.*

### HIKING

**Mastic Trail.** This significant trail, used in the 1800s as the only direct path to the North Side, is a rugged 2-mile (3-km) slash through 776 dense acres of woodlands, black mangrove swamps, savanna, agricultural remnants, and ancient rock formations. It embraces more than 700 species, including Cayman's largest remaining contiguous ancient forest (one of the heavily deforested Caribbean's last examples). A comfortable walk depends on weather—winter is better because it's drier, though flowering plants such as the banana orchid blaze in summer. Call the National Trust to determine suitability and to book a guide ($30); tours run daily 9 to 5 by appointment and Thursdays and Fridays at 9 (sometimes earlier in summer). Or walk on the wild side with a $5 guidebook covering the ecosystems, endemic wildlife, seasonal changes, poisonous plants, and folkloric uses of flora. The trip takes about three hours. ✉ *Frank Sound Rd., entrance by fire station at botanic park, Breakers, East End* ☎ *345/749–1121, 345/749–1124 for guide reservations* ⊕ *www.nationaltrust.org.ky.*

## WHERE TO EAT

**$$** ✗ **Cimboco.** This animated space celebrates all things fun and Caribbean with walls saturated in orange, lemon, and lavender; cobalt glass fixtures; and flames dancing up the exhibition kitchen's huge wood-burning oven. The *Cimboco* was the first motorized sailing ship built in Cayman (in 1927) and for 20 years the lifeline to the outside world; National Archive photographs and old newspapers invest the space with still more character. Everything from breads (superlative bruschetta and jalapeño corn bread) to ice creams is made from scratch. Artisanal pizzas come topped with balsamic-roasted eggplant, pesto, and feta or with jerk chicken with Bermuda onions. Signature items include banana-leaf-roasted snapper and fire-roasted bacon-wrapped shrimp. Amazingly good desserts include a sinfully rich brownie. The popular breakfast and brunch are equally creative. $ *Average main: $19* ✉ *Marquee Plaza, West Bay Rd. at Harquail Bypass, Seven Mile Beach* ☎ *345/947–2782* ⊕ *www.cimboco.com.*

ECLECTIC

**$** ✗ **MacDonald's.** One of the locals' favorite burger joints—not a fast-food outlet—MacDonald's does a brisk lunch business in stick-to-your ribs basics like rotisserie chicken and fish escoveitch. Yellows and pinks predominate, with appetizing posters of food and a large cartoon chicken mounted on the wall; but decor is an afterthought to the politicos, housewives in curlers, and cops flirting shyly with the waitresses. $ *Average main: $11* ✉ *99 Shedden Rd., George Town* ☎ *345/949–4640* ⚠ *Reservations not accepted.*

CARIBBEAN

# GRAND TURK, TURKS & CAICOS ISLANDS

By Laura
Adzich-Brander

Just 7 miles (11 km) long and a little over 1 mile (1½ km) wide, Grand Turk, the political capital of the Turks and Caicos Islands, has been a longtime favorite destination for divers eager to explore the 7,000-foot coral-encrusted wall that drops down within yards of the shoreline. This tiny, quiet island is home to white-sand beaches, the National Museum, and a small population of wild horses and donkeys, which leisurely meander past the white-walled courtyards, pretty churches, and bougainvillea-covered colonial inns on their daily commute into town. The main settlement on the island is tranquil Cockburn Town, and that's where most of the small hotels, not to mention Pillory Beach, can be found. Although it has the second-largest number of inhabitants of all the Turks and Caicos Island, Grand Turk's permanent population has still not reached 4,000.

## ESSENTIALS

### CURRENCY

The official currency on the islands is the U.S. dollar.

### TELEPHONE

To make local calls, dial the seven-digit number. To make calls from the Turks and Caicos, dial 0, then 1, the area code, and the number. All telephone service is provided by LIME (formerly Cable & Wireless), and your U.S. cell phone may work on Grand Turk, but you will pay international roaming charges. Calling cards are available, or you can make a call using AT&T's USADirect by dialing 800/872–2881 to charge the call to your credit card or an AT&T prepaid calling card.

### COMING ASHORE

Cruise ships dock at the southern end of Grand Turk, just south of the airport. The $40-million cruise center is about 3 miles (5 km) from tranquil Cockburn Town, Pillory Beach, and the Ridge, and far from most of the western shore dive sites. The center has many facilities: duty free shopping, a free-form swimming pool, car-rental booths, tour operators, and even a dock from which many sea-bound excursions depart. The beautiful Governor's Beach is adjacent to the cruise-ship complex but others are right in and around Cockburn Town, as well as along the island's north shore.

If you want to visit Cockburn Town, it's reachable by taxi. Taxi rates are per person and by zone; you'll find a rate card outside the cruise terminal. You can rent a car to explore the island independently or join an organized tour by bus, scooter, or ATV.

**Grand Turk Cruise Terminal.** Head to the website for cruise schedules, a list of the shops at the terminal, and options for excursions and transportation. ✉ *South Base, on the south tip of the island, just south of the former US Airforce Base, Grand Turk Cruise Terminal* ☎ *649/946–1040* ⊕ *www.grandturkcc.com* ☉ *Closed when ships are not in port.*

**Island Auto Rentals.** Island Auto offers car, SUV, and golf cart rentals with friendly and convenient service. They also will deliver your vehicle to your hotel, and they have a convenient airport drop-off. ✉ *Grand Turk*

*Cruise Port, Grand Turk Cruise Terminal* ☎ *649/232–0933, 649/231–4214, 649/946–2042.*

## EXPLORING

Pristine beaches with vistas of turquoise waters, small local settlements, historic ruins, and native flora and fauna are among the sights on Grand Turk. Fewer than 4,000 people live on this 7½-square-mile (19-square-km) island, and it's easy to find your way around, as there aren't many roads.

### COCKBURN TOWN

The buildings in the country's capital and seat of government reflect a 19th-century Bermudian style. Narrow streets are lined with low stone walls and old street lamps. The once-vital *salinas* (natural salt pans, where the sea leaves a film of salt) have been restored, and covered benches along the sluice ways offer shady spots for observing the many wading birds, including flamingos, that frequent the shallows. Be sure to pick up a copy of the TCI Tourist Board's *Heritage Walk* guide to discover Grand Turk's rich architecture.

| BEST BETS |
|---|
| ■ **Beaches.** The sand is powdery soft, the water azure blue. |
| ■ **Diving.** If you're certified, there are several world-class dive sites within easy reach. |
| ■ **Gibb's Cay.** To swim with stingrays, take a ship-sponsored trip here; the bonus is its excellent beach. |
| ■ **Front Street.** Colorful Front Street will give you the feeling you've stepped back in time. |
| ■ **Turks and Caicos National Museum.** Small but definitely worthy. |

**Her Majesty's Prison.** This prison was built out of stone in the 1830s to incarcerate men and women who had committed mostly petty crimes. As time passed, the prison expanded, housing even modern-day drug runners until it closed in the 1990s. Through a self-guided tour, you will see the cells, solitary-confinement area, and exercise yard. The prison is open only when there is a cruise ship at the port. It is worth the stop. ✉ *Pond St., Cockburn Town* ⊕ *visittci.com* ✉ *$7.*

FAMILY
Fodor's Choice
★

**Turks and Caicos National Museum.** In one of the island's oldest stone buildings, the National Museum houses several interactive exhibits, as well as a super little gift shop with books and local handicrafts. The complete collection of preserved artifacts raised from the noteworthy Molasses Reef Wreck is here. Dating back to the early 1500s, it is the earliest European shipwreck yet excavated in the New World. Other exhibits focus on the region's natural history and environment. This is the perfect spot to start your walking tour of the historical waterfront. ✉ *Guinep House, Front St., Cockburn Town* ☎ *649/946–2160, 505/216–1795* ⊕ *www.tcmuseum.org* ✉ *$7 general admission, $5 for cruise passengers and hotel guests, children free.*

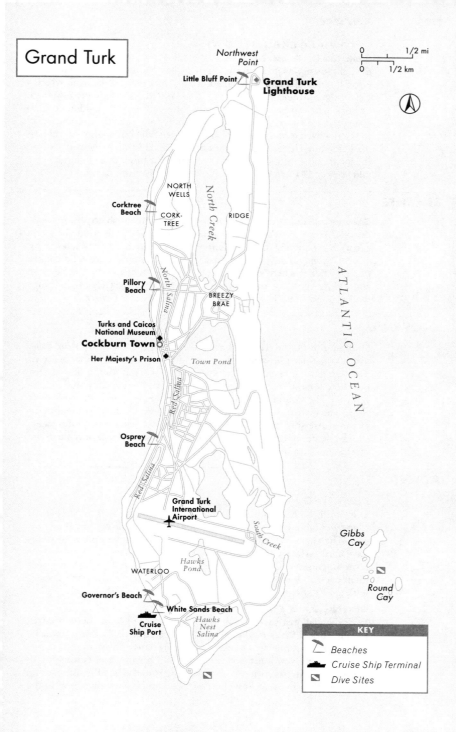

# Grand Turk

*Northwest Point*

**Little Bluff Point** **Grand Turk Lighthouse**

0        1/2 mi
0        1/2 km

NORTH WELLS

*North Creek*

**Corktree Beach**      CORK-TREE      RIDGE

*North Salina*

**Pillory Beach**

BREEZY BRAE

**Turks and Caicos National Museum**
**Cockburn Town**
**Her Majesty's Prison**          *Town Pond*

*Red Salina*

**Osprey Beach**

*Red Salina*

**Grand Turk International Airport**

*South Creek*

*Gibbs Cay*

*Hawks Pond*

WATERLOO

**Governor's Beach**

**White Sands Beach**

**Cruise Ship Port**

*Hawks Nest Salina*

*Round Cay*

ATLANTIC OCEAN

| KEY | |
|---|---|
| ⌐ | *Beaches* |
| ⛴ | *Cruise Ship Terminal* |
| ◩ | *Dive Sites* |

### BEYOND COCKBURN TOWN

**Grand Turk Lighthouse.** More than 150 years ago, the main structure of the lighthouse was prefabricated in the United Kingdom and then transported to the island; once erected, it helped prevent ships from wrecking on the northern reefs for more than 100 years, originally designed to burn whale oil as its light source. You can use this landmark as a starting point for a breezy cliff-top walk by following the donkey trails to the deserted eastern beach. Unfortunately, the cruise-ship world has made its mark here, and zip lines block the panoramic view and spoil the location's solitude. If you are stretched for time, you might want to take a pass. ⊠ *Lighthouse Rd., North Ridge* ⊕ *visittci.com.*

## BEACHES

**Governor's Beach.** Directly in front of the official British governor's residence, known as Waterloo, is a long stretch of beach framed by tall casuarina trees that provide plenty of natural shade. The beach can be a bit crowded on days when cruise ships are in port. There are a couple of picnic tables where you can enjoy a picnic lunch, and there is a decent snorkeling spot just offshore. **Amenities:** none. **Best for:** swimming; walking. ⊹ *20- to 30-min walk north of the Cruise Center.*

## SHOPPING

Shopping in Grand Turk is hard to come by—choices are slim. Let's just say that no true shopaholic would want to come here for vacation. You can get the usual T-shirts and dive trinkets at all the dive shops, but there are only a few options for more interesting shopping opportunities: The Grand Turk Inn's boutique, the National Museum's gift shop, The Gallery-Grand Turk. However, there is a duty-free mall right at the cruise-ship center, where you'll find the usual array of upscale shops, including Ron Jon's Surf Shop, the largest Margaritaville in the world, and Piranha Joe's.

## ACTIVITIES

### BICYCLING

Out of all the islands in Turks and Caicos, Grand Turk is the perfect island for biking: it's small enough that it is possible to tour it all that way. The island's mostly flat terrain isn't very taxing, and most roads have hard surfaces. Take water with you: there are few places to stop for refreshments. Most hotels have bicycles available, but you can also rent them for $20 a day from Grand Turk Diving across from the Osprey with a $200 deposit.

### DIVING AND SNORKELING

With the wall just yards off shore, diving doesn't get any better than in Grand Turk. Divers may explore undersea cathedrals, coral gardens, and countless tunnels, or watch an octopus dance down a sandy slope. But take note: you must present your valid certification before you're allowed to dive. As its name suggests, the **Black Forest** offers staggering black-coral formations as well as the occasional black-tip shark. In the

**Library** you can study fish galore, including large numbers of yellowtail snapper. The Columbus Passage separates South Caicos from Grand Turk, each side of the 22-mile-wide (35-km-wide) channel dropping 7,000 feet. From January through March, humpback whales migrate through en route to their winter breeding grounds. **Gibb's Cay**, a small cay a couple of miles off Grand Turk, is where you can swim with stingrays, making for a great excursion.

**Blue Water Divers.** In operation on Grand Turk since 1983, Blue Water Divers is the only PADI Green Star Award recipient-star dive center on the island, priding themselves on their personalized service and small group diving. The owner, Mitch, may not go diving very often anymore, but he may put some of your underwater experiences to music in the evenings when he plays at the Osprey Beach Hotel or Salt Raker Inn! In addition, Blue Water Divers offers Gibbs Cay snorkel and Salt Cay trips. ⊠ *Osprey Beach Hotel, The Atrium, 1 Duke St., Cockburn Town* ☎ *649/946–2432* ⊕ *www.grandturkscuba.com.*

**Oasis Divers.** Oasis Divers provides excellent personalized service, with full gear handling and dive site briefing included. They also supply nitrox for those who are specifically trained. In addition, Oasis Divers offers a variety of other tours, including their land-based one on Segways, as well as whale-watching when the animals migrate past. ⊠ *Duke St., Cockburn Town* ☎ *649/946–1128 direct dial, 800/892–3995 toll-free* ⊕ *www.oasisdivers.com.*

## WHERE TO EAT

$$ ✕ **Coral Cafe.** The Coral Cafe is a wonderful little gem hidden away
CAFÉ in the annex of the Osprey Beach Hotel. An amazing array of coffees
**Fodor's** Choice are served up by a barista along with freshly baked bread, scones, or
★ a delicious croissant; there's even a gluten-free option. There are great breakfasts, including fresh bagels with lox and cream cheese. For lunch, you'll find wraps, salads, and sandwiches. The staff is warm and welcoming. ⑤ *Average main: $12* ⊠ *Corner of Duke St. and Roberts Alley, Cockburn Town* ☎ *649/245–0648* ⊘ *No dinner* ⊟ *No credit cards.*

$$ ✕ **Sand Bar.** Run by two Canadian sisters, this popular beachside bar
ECLECTIC is very good value and the perfect spot to enjoy island time. No shoes or shirt required. The menu includes fresh-caught fish, lobster, and conch, as well as typical North American fare—burgers, quesadillas, and chicken and ribs—served island-style with peas and rice. The covered wooden deck juts out over the beach offering shade during the day; it's also a great place to enjoy a casual dinner while watching the sun set. The atmosphere is relaxed and the service friendly, and locals often meet here to socialize. If you're just over for a day, be sure to get there before 2:30, as they stop service for a couple of hours midday to gear up for the evening crowd. If you're staying the night, drop by for some late-evening conversation. ⑤ *Average main: $14* ⊠ *Duke St., Cockburn Town* ☎ *649/243–2666* ⊘ *Closed Sat.*

# GRENADA (ST. GEORGE'S)

By Jane E.
Zarem

Nutmeg, cinnamon, cloves, cocoa . . . those heady aromas fill the air in Grenada (pronounced gruh-nay-da). Only 21 miles (33½ km) long and 12 miles (19½ km) wide, the Isle of Spice is a tropical gem of lush rain forests, white-sand beaches, secluded coves, exotic flowers, and enough locally grown spices to fill anyone's kitchen cabinet. St. George's is one of the most picturesque capital cities in the Caribbean; St. George's Harbour is one of the most picturesque harbors; and Grenada's Grand Anse Beach is one of the region's finest beaches. The island has friendly, hospitable people and enough good shopping, restaurants, historic sites, and natural wonders to make it a popular port of call. About one-third of Grenada's visitors arrive by cruise ship, and that number continues to grow each year.

## ESSENTIALS

### CURRENCY
Eastern Caribbean (E.C.) dollar, but U.S. dollars are generally accepted.

### TELEPHONE
The area code is 473. Prepaid phone cards, which can be used for local or international calls from special card phones located throughout the Caribbean, are sold in denominations of EC$20 ($7.50), EC$30 ($12), EC$50 ($20), and EC$75 ($28) at shops, attractions, transportation centers, and other convenient outlets. For international calls using a major credit card, dial 111; to place a collect call or use a calling card, dial 800/225–5872 from any telephone. Most cell phones will work in Grenada, but international roaming charges can be high.

### COMING ASHORE
The Cruise Ship Terminal, located on the north side of St. George's, accommodates two large ships; up to four can anchor in the outer harbor. The terminal—which opens directly into the Esplanade Mall and the minibus terminus and is a block from Market Square—offers a full range of passenger facilities. You can easily tour the capital on foot, but be prepared to negotiate steep hills. If you don't want to walk up and down through town, you can find a taxi ($3 or $4 each way) or a water taxi ($4 each way) right at the terminal to take you around to the Carenage. To explore areas beyond St. George's, hiring a taxi or arranging a guided tour is more sensible than renting a car. Taxis are plentiful, and fixed rates to popular island destinations are posted at the terminal's welcome center.

A taxi ride from the terminal to Grand Anse Beach will cost $20, but water taxis are a less expensive and more picturesque way to get there; the one-way fare is about $8 per person, depending on the number of passengers. Minibuses are the least expensive way to travel between St. George's and Grand Anse; pay EC$1.50 (55¢) and hold on to your hat. They're crowded with local people getting from here to there and often make quick stops and take turns at quite a clip. Still, it's an inexpensive, fun, and safe way to travel around the island. If you want to rent a car and explore on your own, be prepared to pay $12 for a temporary driving permit (arranged by the car-rental agency) and about $75 to $85 for a day's car rental.

## EXPLORING

### ST. GEORGE'S

Grenada's capital is a bustling West Indian city, much of which remains unchanged from colonial days. Narrow streets lined with shops wind up, down, and across steep hills. Brick warehouses cling to the waterfront, and pastel-painted homes disappear into steep green hills.

Horseshoe-shape **St. George's Harbour,** a submerged volcanic crater, is arguably the prettiest harbor in the Caribbean. Schooners, ferries, and tour boats tie up along the seawall or at the small dinghy dock. **The Carenage** (pronounced car-a- *nahzh*), which surrounds the harbor, is the capital's center. Warehouses, shops, and restaurants line the waterfront. The *Christ of the Deep* statue sits on the pedestrian

> **BEST BETS**
>
> ■ **The Beach.** Grand Anse Beach is one of the Caribbean's most beautiful.
>
> ■ **Diving and Snorkeling.** Explore dozens of fish-filled sites off Grenada's southwest coast.
>
> ■ **Market Square.** Market Square is a bustling produce and spice market.
>
> ■ **Nutmeg.** Don't miss a visit to a nutmeg cooperative (and get a pocketful to take home).
>
> ■ **Waterfalls.** Concord Falls, just south of Gouyave, and Annandale Falls are among the island's most spectacular.

plaza at the center of the Carenage; it was presented to Grenada by Costa Cruise Line in remembrance of its ship, *Bianca C,* that burned and sank in the harbor in 1961. *Bianca C* is now a popular dive site.

An engineering feat for its time, the 340-foot-long **Sendall Tunnel** was built in 1895 and named for Walter Sendall, an early governor. The narrow tunnel, used by both pedestrians and vehicles, separates the harbor side of St. George's from the Esplanade on the bay side of town, where you will find the markets (produce, meat, and fish), the Cruise Ship Terminal, the Esplanade Mall, and the public bus station.

**Ft. Frederick.** Overlooking the city of St. George's and the picturesque harbor, historic Ft. Frederick provides a panoramic view of about one-fourth of Grenada. The French began construction of the fort; the British completed it in 1791. Fort Frederick was the headquarters of the People's Revolutionary Government before and during the 1983 coup. Today, it's simply a peaceful spot with a bird's-eye view of much of Grenada. ⊠ *Richmond Hill.*

FAMILY
Fodor's Choice
★

**Ft. George.** Ft. George is perched high on the hill at the entrance to St. George's Harbour. Grenada's oldest fort was built by the French in 1705 to protect the harbor, yet no shots were ever fired here until October 1983, when Prime Minister Maurice Bishop and several of his followers were assassinated in the courtyard. The fort now houses police headquarters but is open to the public daily. The 360-degree view of

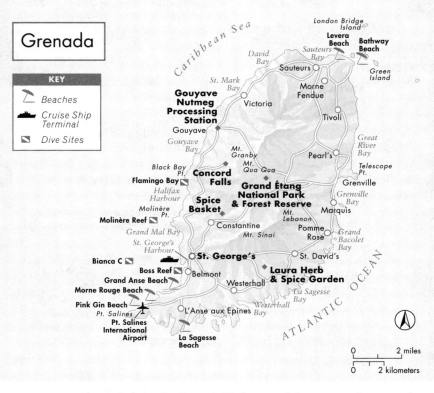

## Grenada

**KEY**

⊿ Beaches

⛴ Cruise Ship Terminal

◥ Dive Sites

Caribbean Sea

London Bridge Island
Levera Beach
Bathway Beach
David Bay
Sauteurs Bay
Green Island
Sauteurs
St. Mark Bay
Morne Fendue
Victoria
Tivoli
**Gouyave Nutmeg Processing Station**
Gouyave
Gouyave Bay
Mt. Granby
Mt. Qua Qua
Pearl's
Great River Bay
Telescope Pt.
Black Bay Pt.
Flamingo Bay
**Concord Falls**
**Grand Étang National Park & Forest Reserve**
Grenville
Halifax Harbour
**Spice Basket**
Molinère Pt.
Mt. Lebanon
Grenville Bay
Molinère Reef
Constantine
Mt. Sinai
Marquis
Grand Mal Bay
Pomme Rose
Grand Bacolet Bay
St. George's Harbour
Bianca C
**St. George's**
St. David's
Boss Reef
Belmont
**Laura Herb & Spice Garden**
Grand Anse Beach
Westerhall
Morne Rouge Beach
Ta Sagesse Bay
Pink Gin Beach
Westerhall Bay
Pt. Salines
L'Anse aux Epines
Pt. Salines International Airport
La Sagesse Beach

ATLANTIC OCEAN

0          2 miles
0          2 kilometers

the capital city, St. George's Harbour, and the open sea is spectacular. ⊠ *Church St., St. George's* 🎟 *$2.*

FAMILY **Grenada National Museum.** A block from the Carenage, the Grenada National Museum is built on the foundation of a French army barracks and prison that was originally built in 1704. The small museum has exhibitions of news items, photos, and proclamations relating to the 1983 intervention, along with fragments of Amerindian pottery, the childhood bathtub of Empress Joséphine (who was born on Martinique), and other memorabilia. ⊠ *Young and Monckton Sts., St. George's* 🕿 *473/440–3725* ⊕ *www.grenadamuseum.gd* 🎟 *$2.50.*

FAMILY **Market Square.** Definitely plan to visit St. George's Market Square, a
Fodor's Choice block from the Cruise Ship Terminal and Esplanade Mall in downtown
★ St. George's. This is the place to buy fresh spices, bottled sauces, and handcrafted gifts and souvenirs to take home. In addition to local spices and heaps of fresh produce, vendors sell baskets, brooms, clothing, knickknacks, coconut water, and more. The market is open every weekday morning but really comes alive on Saturday from 8 to noon. Market Square is also where parades begin and political rallies take place. ⊠ *Granby St., St. George's.*

## ELSEWHERE ON GRENADA

Fodor's Choice
★

**Concord Falls.** About 8 miles (13 km) north of St. George's, a turnoff from the West Coast Road leads to Concord Falls—actually three separate waterfalls. The first is at the end of the road; when the currents aren't too strong, you can take a dip under the 35-foot cascade. Reaching the two other waterfalls requires a hike into the forest reserve. The hike to the second falls (Au Coin) takes about 30 minutes. The third and most spectacular waterfall (Fontainbleu) thunders 65 feet over huge boulders and creates a small pool. It's smart to hire a guide for that trek, which can take an hour or more. The path is clear, but slippery boulders toward the end can be treacherous without assistance. ⊠ *Concord Valley, off West Coast Rd., Gouyave* ☎ *473/440–2279* ⊠ *Changing room $2.*

FAMILY
Fodor's Choice
★

**Gouyave Nutmeg Processing Station.** Touring the nutmeg-processing co-op, right in the center of the west-coast fishing village of Gouyave (pronounced *gwahv*), is a fragrant, fascinating way to spend a half hour. You can learn all about nutmeg and its uses, see the nutmegs laid out in bins, and watch the workers sort them by hand and pack them into burlap bags for shipping worldwide. The three-story plant turned out 3 million pounds of Grenada's most famous export each year before Hurricane Ivan's devastating effect on the crop in 2004, when most of the nutmeg trees were destroyed. Production has finally returned to pre-Hurricane Ivan levels. ⊠ *Central Depradine St., Gouyave* ☎ *473/444–8337* ⊕ *www.grenadanutmeg.com* ⊠ *$1.*

FAMILY
Fodor's Choice
★

**Grand Étang National Park & Forest Reserve.** A rain forest and wildlife sanctuary deep in the mountainous interior of Grenada, Grand Étang has miles of hiking trails for all levels of ability. There are also lookouts to observe the lush flora and many species of birds and other fauna (including the Mona monkey) and a number of streams for fishing. **Grand Étang Lake** is a 36-acre expanse of cobalt-blue water—1,740 feet above sea level—that fills the crater of an extinct volcano. Although legend has it that the lake is bottomless, maximum soundings have been recorded at just 18 feet. The informative **Grand Étang Forest Center** has displays on the local wildlife and vegetation. A forest ranger is on hand to answer questions; a small snack bar and souvenir stands are nearby. ⊠ *Main interior road, between Grenville and St. George's* ☎ *473/440–6160* ⊠ *$2.*

FAMILY
**Laura Herb & Spice Garden.** The 6½ acres of gardens here are part of an old plantation at Laura, near the village of Perdmontemps in St. David Parish and about 6 miles (10 km) east of Grand Anse. On the 20-minute tour, you will learn all about spices and herbs grown in Grenada—including cocoa, clove, nutmeg, pimiento, cinnamon, turmeric, and tonka beans (sometimes used in vanilla substitutes)—and how they're used for flavoring and for medicinal purposes. ⊠ *Laura Rd., Perdmontemps* ☎ *473/443–2604* ⊠ *$2.*

FAMILY
**Spice Basket.** Half of the small but fascinating museum at this cultural center and performance venue covers Grenada's heritage—its Amerindian beginnings, its geology (including samples of sand from all the different hues represented on local beaches), local birds and animals,

early tools and implements, sugar and slavery, and the 1979–1983 Grenada Revolution. The other half of the museum is dedicated to cricket, making it "the world's first and only display offering an insight into Caribbean social history through cricket." The memorabilia, some dating to the 1800s, includes uniforms, bats, equipment, and more. It's all very fascinating and definitely worth a visit. A gift shop features locally made items. Spice Basket is in the countryside, not far from Annandale Falls. ⊠ *Beaulieu* ☎ *473/437–9000, 473/232–9000* ⊕ *www.spicebasket grenada.com* ✉ *$10.*

## BEACHES

**Bathway Beach.** This broad strip of white sand on the northeastern tip of Grenada is part of Levera National Park. A natural coral reef protects swimmers and snorkelers from the rough Atlantic surf; swimming beyond the reef is dangerous. A magnet for local folks on national holidays, the beach is almost deserted at other times. Changing rooms are located at the park headquarters. A vendor or two sometimes sets up shop near the beach, but you're smart to bring your own refreshments. **Amenities:** parking (no fee); toilets. **Best for:** snorkeling; solitude; swimming; walking. ⊠ *Levera National Park, Levera.*

FAMILY  **Grand Anse Beach.** Grenada's loveliest and most popular beach is Grand
Fodor'sChoice  Anse: a gleaming 2-mile (3-km) semicircle of white sand, lapped by
★  gentle surf and punctuated by sea grape trees and coconut palms that provide shady escapes from the sun. Several resorts face the beach and have dive shops where you can arrange trips and rent snorkeling equipment. A water-taxi dock is at the midpoint of the beach, along with the Grand Anse Craft & Spice Market, where vendors also rent beach chairs and umbrellas. Restrooms and changing facilities are available at Camerhogne Park, which is the public entrance and parking lot. **Amenities:** food and drink; parking (no fee); toilets; water sports. **Best for:** sunset; swimming; walking. ⊠ *3 miles (5 km) south of St. George's, Grand Anse.*

## SHOPPING

Grenada is truly a nation of entrepreneurs, from retail businesses and processing operations, both with employees, to vendors (about one-third of the population) who personally sell their handicrafts in the markets. Note that bargaining isn't customary either in shops or markets.

Stores in Grenada are generally open weekdays from 8 to 4 or 4:30 and Saturday from 8 to 1; some close from noon to 1 during the week. Most are closed Sunday, although tourist shops usually open if a cruise ship is in port, and some mall stores, particularly supermarkets, are open for longer hours on weekends.

Some unique, locally made goods to look for in gift shops and supermarkets are locally made chocolate bars, nutmeg jam and syrup, spice-scented soaps and body oils, and (no kidding) Nut-Med Pain-Relieving Spray. Grenada's best souvenirs or gifts for friends back home, though, are spice baskets in a variety of shapes and sizes that are filled with cinnamon, nutmeg, mace, bay leaves, cloves, turmeric, and ginger. You can buy them for as little as $5 to $10 in practically every shop, at the open-air produce market at **Market Square** in St. George's, at vendor stalls along the Esplanade near the port, and at the Vendor's Craft & Spice Market on Grand Anse Beach. Vendors also sell handmade fabric dolls, coral jewelry, seashells, spice necklaces, and hats and baskets handwoven from green palm fronds.

Here's some local terminology you should know. If someone asks if you'd like a "sweetie," you're being offered a candy. When you buy spices, you may be offered "saffron" and "vanilla." The "saffron" is really turmeric, a ground yellow root, rather than the (much more expensive) fragile pistils of crocus flowers; the "vanilla" is extracted from locally grown tonka beans rather than from actual (also much more expensive) vanilla beans. No one is trying to pull the wool over your eyes; these are common local terms. That said, the U.S. Food and Drug Administration warns that "vanilla" extracts made from tonka beans can have toxic effects and may pose a significant health risk for individuals taking certain medications.

## ACTIVITIES

### DIVING AND SNORKELING

You can see hundreds of varieties of fish and some 40 species of coral at more than a dozen sites off Grenada's southwestern coast—only 15 to 20 minutes away by boat—and another couple of dozen sites around Carriacou's reefs and neighboring islets. Depths vary from 20 to 120 feet, and visibility varies from 30 to 100 feet.

For a spectacular dive, visit the ruins of *Bianca C,* a 600-foot cruise ship that caught fire in 1961, sank to 100 feet, and is now a coral-encrusted habitat for giant turtles, spotted eagle rays, barracuda, and jacks. **Boss Reef** extends 5 miles (8 km) from St. George's Harbour to Point Salines, with a depth ranging from 20 to 90 feet. **Flamingo Bay** has a wall that drops to 90 feet. It teems with fish, sponges, sea horses, sea fans, and coral. **Molinère Reef** slopes from about 20 feet below the surface to a wall that drops to 65 feet. Molinère is also the location of the **Underwater Sculpture Park,** a rather odd artificial reef consisting of more than 55 life-size figures that were sculpted by artist and scuba instructor Jason Taylor and placed on the sea bottom. An underwater bench gives divers a good view of the art gallery. Its most recent addition is a replica of *Christ of the Deep,* the statue that's on the promenade along the Carenage in St. George's. Molinère is a good dive for beginners; advanced divers can continue farther out to view the wreck of the *Buccaneer,* a 42-foot sloop.

**Aquanauts Grenada.** Every morning Aquanauts Grenada heads out on two-tank dive trips, each accommodating no more than eight divers, to both the Caribbean and Atlantic sides of Grenada. Also available: guided snorkel trips; beach snorkeling; and special activities, courses, and equipment for children. ✉ *True Blue Bay Resort, True Blue* ☎ *473/444–1126, 850/303–0330 in U.S.* ⊕ *www.aquanautsgrenada.com.*

**EcoDive.** This full-service PADI dive shop offers two trips daily for both drift and wreck dives, as well as weekly trips to dive Isle de Rhonde and a full range of diving courses. EcoDive employs two full-time marine biologists who run Grenada's marine-conservation and education center and conduct coral-reef monitoring and restoration efforts. ⊠ *Coyaba Beach Resort, Grand Anse Beach, Grand Anse* ☎ *473/444–7777* ⊕ *www.ecodiveandtrek.com.*

### FISHING

Deep-sea fishing around Grenada is excellent. The list of likely catches includes marlin, sailfish, yellowfin tuna, and dorado (also known as mahimahi or dolphin). You can arrange sport fishing trips that accommodate up to six people starting at $500 for a half day and $750 for a full day.

**True Blue Sportfishing.** British-born Captain Gary Clifford, who has been fishing since the age of six, has run True Blue Sportfishing since 1998. He offers big-game charters for up to six passengers on the 31-foot *Yes Aye.* The boat has an enclosed cabin, a fighting chair, and professional tackle. Refreshments and transportation to the marina are included. ⊠ *Port Louis Marina, Kirani James Blvd., St. George's* ☎ *473/407–4688* ⊕ *www.yesaye.com.*

## WHERE TO EAT

**$$**
CAFÉ
FAMILY
✕ **La Boulangerie.** This combination French bakery and Italian pizzeria, convenient to the hotels at Grand Anse, is perfect for an inexpensive breakfast or light meal—to eat in, take out, or have delivered. You'll find freshly baked croissants and Danish pastry, focaccia and baguette sandwiches, homemade pizza and pasta, fresh-squeezed juice or house wine, coffee and espresso, and homemade gelato. Ⓢ *Average main: $15* ⊠ *Le Marquis Complex, Across from Spiceland Mall, Grand Anse* ☎ *473/444–1131.*

**$$**
CARIBBEAN
FAMILY
✕ **The Nutmeg Bar & Restaurant.** West Indian specialties, fresh seafood, hamburgers, and a waterfront view make the Nutmeg a favorite with locals and visitors alike. It's upstairs along the Carenage, with large, open windows from which you can view the harbor activity and catch a cool breeze as you eat. Try the callaloo soup, curried lambi, fresh seafood, or a steak—or just stop by for a roti and a cold beer or rum punch, with grated nutmeg on top, of course. Ⓢ *Average main: $18* ⊠ *The Carenage, St. George's* ☎ *473/440–3654.*

# GUADELOUPE (POINTE-À-PITRE)

By Eileen Robinson Smith

On a map, Guadeloupe looks like a giant butterfly resting on the sea between Antigua and Dominica. Its two wings—Basse-Terre and Grande-Terre—are the two largest islands in the 659-square-mile (1,054-square-km) Guadeloupe archipelago. The Rivière Salée, a 4-mile (6-km) channel between the Caribbean and the Atlantic, forms the "spine" of the butterfly. A drawbridge near, the main city, connects the two islands. Gorgeous scenery awaits, as Guadeloupe is one of the most physically attractive islands in the Caribbean. If you're seeking a resort atmosphere, casinos, and nearly white sandy beaches, your target is Grande-Terre. On the other hand, Basse-Terre's Parc National de la Guadeloupe, laced with trails and washed by waterfalls and rivers, is a 74,100-acre haven for hikers, nature lovers, and anyone brave enough to peer into the steaming crater of an active volcano. The tropical beauty suggests the mythical Garden of Eden.

## ESSENTIALS

### CURRENCY

The euro. You must exchange currency at a *bureau de change,* but ATMs are your best bet if you need euros.

### TELEPHONE

To make on-island calls, dial 0590 (0690 if it is a cellular phone) and then the six-digit phone number. To call Guadeloupe from the United States, dial 00–590–590, then the local number. For cell phone numbers, dial 00–590–690, then the local number. If you're on one of the other islands in the French West Indies, dial 0590 and then the local number.

## COMING ASHORE

Ships now dock at a cruise terminal in downtown Pointe-à-Pitre, at Pier 5/6. It houses an Internet café, a duty-free shop, and the colorful Karuland Village, where cruisers can browse and buy spices, pareus, and souvenirs or just sit and listen to the local music while having coconut ice cream. It's about a five-minute walk from the shopping district. Passengers are greeted by local musicians and hostesses, usually dressed in the traditional madras costumes—and often dispensing samplings of local rum and creole specialties. These multilingual staffers operate the information booth and can pair you up with an English-speaking taxi driver for a customized island tour. To get to the main tourist office, walk along the quay to the Place de la Victoire; it is a large white Victorian building with wraparound veranda. However, at this writing, its major renovation has not been completed and it is not staffed.

Taxis are metered and expensive; during rush hour, they can be *very* expensive. Renting a car is a good way to see Guadeloupe, but it, too, is expensive and best booked in advance. Be aware that traffic around Pointe-à-Pitre can be horrible during rush hour, so allow plenty of time to drop off your rental car and get back to the ship. There are many rental agencies at the airport, but it will be at least a €30 taxi ride from the city.

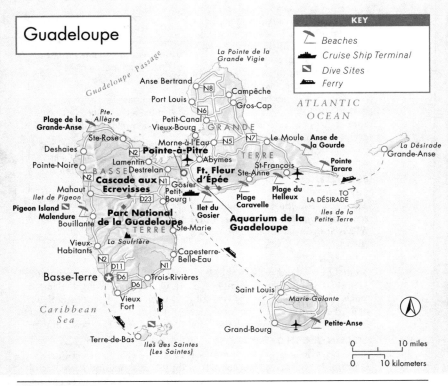

# Guadeloupe

**KEY**

↗ Beaches
🚢 Cruise Ship Terminal
◣ Dive Sites
⛴ Ferry

*La Pointe de la Grande Vigie*

*Guadeloupe Passage*

Anse Bertrand
N8
Campêche
Port Louis
Gros-Cap
N6

*ATLANTIC OCEAN*

Pte. Allègre
Petit-Canal
Vieux-Bourg
G R A N D E
**Plage de la Grande-Anse**
Ste-Rose
Morne-à-l'Eau N5 N7 Le Moule
Anse de la Gourde
*La Désirade* Grande-Anse
Deshaies
N2 **Pointe-à-Pitre**
T E R R E
Pointe-Noire
Lamentin
Abymes
St-François
**Pointe Tarare**
B A S S E Destrelan
**Ft. Fleur d'Épée** Ste-Anne
Mahaut N2 N1
**Cascade aux Ecrevisses** Gosier
Plage du Helleux LA DÉSIRADE
Ilet de Pigeon
Petit- Bourg
Plage Caravelle
TO LA DÉSIRADE
**Pigeon Island** ◣
Malendure
D23
Ilet du Gosier
Iles de la Petite Terre
Bouillante **Parc National de la Guadeloupe**
Ste-Marie
**Aquarium de la Guadeloupe**
T E R R E
Vieux-Habitants
*La Soufrière* ▲
**Basse-Terre** ⚓
Capesterre-Belle-Eau
N2 D11 N1
D6 D6 Trois-Rivières

*Caribbean Sea*

Vieux Fort
Saint Louis
*Marie-Galante*

**Petite-Anse**

Grand-Bourg

Terre-de-Bas
*Iles des Saintes (Les Saintes)*

0    10 miles
0    10 kilometers

## EXPLORING

### POINTE-À-PITRE

Although not the capital, this is the island's largest city, a commercial and industrial hub in the southwest of Grande-Terre. The Isles of Guadeloupe have 450,000 inhabitants, most of whom live in the cities. Pointe-à-Pitre is bustling, noisy, and hot—a place of honking horns and traffic jams and cars on sidewalks for want of a parking place. By day its pulse is fast, but at night, when its streets are almost deserted, you may not want to be there.

The heart of the old city is Place de la Victoire; surrounded by wooden buildings with balconies and shutters (including the tourism office) and by sidewalk cafés, it was named in honor of Victor Hugues's 1794 victory over the British. During the French Revolution Hugues ordered the guillotine set up here so that the public could witness the bloody end of 300 recalcitrant royalists, mainly the prosperous plantation owners.

Even more colorful is the bustling marketplace, between rues St-John Perse, Frébault, Schoelcher, and Peynier. It's a cacophonous place, where shoppers bargain for spices, herbs (and herbal remedies), and a bright assortment of papayas, breadfruits, christophenes, and tomatoes.

**Cathédrale de St-Pierre et St-Paul.** If you like churches, then make a pilgrimage to the imposing Cathédrale de St-Pierre et St-Paul, built in 1807. Although it has been battered by hurricanes over the years, it has fine stained-glass windows and creole-style balconies. ⊠ *Rue Alexandre Isaac at rue de l'Eglise.*

**Musée Schoelcher.** Established in a Colonial-style building, Musée Schoelcher celebrates Victor Schoelcher, an abolitionist from Alsace who fought against slavery in the French West Indies in the 19th century. The first museum in Guadeloupe, it was inaugurated in 1887, following a substantial donation in 1883 by "himself." New are 17 ethnographic objects that are part of a collection assembled by the abolitionist during his travels in the Caribbean, Egypt, and Africa, between 1830 and 1847. Presently, the museum contains many of his personal effects, and exhibits trace his life and work. ⊠ *24 rue Peynier, Pointe-à-Pitre* ☎ *0590/82–08–04* ☜ *€2.*

**Musée St-John Perse.** Those with a strong interest in French literature and culture (not your average sightseer) will want to see the Musée St-John Perse, which is dedicated to the poet Alexis Léger, Guadeloupe's most famous son. Better known as Saint-John Perse, he was the winner of the Nobel Prize for literature in 1960. Some of his finest poems are inspired by the history and landscape—particularly the sea—of his beloved Guadeloupe. This literary museum, in a restored colonial house, contains a collection of his poetry and some of his personal belongings. Before you go, look for his birthplace at 54 rue Achille René-Boisneuf. ⊠ *9 rue Nozières, Pointe-à-Pitre* ☎ *0590/90–01–92,* ☜ *€2.50.*

### ELSEWHERE ON GRANDE-TERRE

FAMILY **Aquarium de la Guadeloupe.** Unique in the Antilles, this aquarium in the marina near Pointe-à-Pitre is a good place to spend an hour. Its motto is "Visit the sea." The well-planned facility has an assortment of tropical fish, crabs, lobsters, moray eels, coffer fish, and some live coral. It's also a turtle rescue center, and the shark tank is spectacular. A restaurant serves kid-friendly fare, snacks, salads, pastas, etc. A small shop stocks marine toys and souvenirs. The aquarium also offers twice-daily half-day ecotours via small boats that travel through the mangroves, reefs, and a lagoon, with a biologist guide and a diving instructor on board. Snorkeling gear is included, and kids are more than welcome. ⊠ *Pl. Créole, off Rte. N4, Le Gosier* ☎ *0590/90–92–38, 0690/90–92–38, 0690/57–60–69 Seatours* ⊕ *www.aquariumdelaguadeloupe.com* ☜ *€11.50; ecotour €59.*

**Cascade aux Ecrevisses.** Within the Parc National de la Guadeloupe, Crayfish Falls is one of the island's loveliest (and most popular) spots. There's a marked trail (walk carefully—the rocks can be slippery) leading to this splendid waterfall, which dashes down into the Corossol River—a good place for a dip. Come early, though; otherwise you definitely won't have it to yourself. ⊠ *St-Claude* ⊕ *www.guadeloupe-parcnational.com.*

**Ft. Fleur d'Épée.** The main attraction in Bas-du-Fort is this fortress, built between 1759 and 1763. It hunkers down on a hillside behind a deep moat. The fort was the scene of hard-fought battles between the French and the English in 1794. You can explore its well-preserved dungeons and battlements and take in a sweeping view of Iles des Saintes and Marie-Galante. The free guided tour here explores the fort's history and architecture and helps explain the living conditions of the soldiers who lived here. Included on the tour is an exploration of its underground galleries, now decorated with graffiti. If a bilingual person is on duty, she will explain it all in English. Call ahead, and make certain of that day's hours. Registered as a historic monument since 1979, the fort also provides superb views for walkers. ⊠ *Bas du Fort* ☎ *0590/90–94–61* 🖾 *Free.*

**Parc National de la Guadeloupe.** This 74,100-acre park has been recognized by UNESCO as a Biosphere Reserve. Before going, pick up a *Guide to the National Park* from the tourist office; it rates the hiking trails according to difficulty, and most are quite difficult indeed. Most mountain trails are in the southern half. The park is bisected by the route de la Traversée, a 16-mile (26-km) paved road lined with masses of tree ferns, shrubs, flowers, tall trees, and green plantains. It's the ideal point of entry. Wear rubber-sole shoes and take along a swimsuit, a sweater, water, and perhaps food for a picnic. Try to get an early start to stay ahead of the hordes of cruise-ship passengers making a day of it. Check on the weather; if Basse-Terre has had a lot of rain, give it up. In the past, after intense rainfall, rock slides have closed the road for months. ⊠ *Habitation Beausoleil-Montéran, BP-93, St-Claude* ☎ *0590/80–86–00* ⊕ *www.guadeloupe-parcnational.com* 🖾 *Free.*

# BEACHES

**Plage Caravelle.** Just southwest of Ste-Anne is one of Grande-Terre's longest and prettiest stretches of sand, the occasional dilapidated shack notwithstanding. Protected by reefs, it's also a fine snorkeling spot. Club Med occupies one end of this beach, and nonguests can enjoy its beach and water sports, as well as lunch and drinks, by buying a day pass. You can also have lunch on the terrace of La Toubana Hotel & Spa, then descend the stairs to the beach or enjoy lunch at its beach restaurant, wildly popular on Sunday. **Amenities:** food and drink; parking (no fee); toilets; water sports. **Best for:** partiers; snorkeling; sunset; swimming; walking; windsurfing. ⊠ *Rte. N4, southwest of Ste-Anne, Ste-Anne.*

**Plage de la Grande-Anse.** One of Guadeloupe's widest beaches has soft beige sand sheltered by palms. To the west it's a round verdant mountain. It has a large parking area and some food stands, but no other facilities. The beach can be overrun on Sundays, not to mention littered, due to the food carts. Right after the parking lot, you can see signage for the creole restaurant Le Karacoli; if you have lunch there (it's not cheap), you can *sieste* on the chaise longues. At the far end of the beach, which is more virgin territory, is Tainos Cottages, which has a restaurant. **Amenities:** food and drink; parking (no fee). **Best for:** partiers; solitude; swimming; walking. ⊠ *Rte. N6, north of Deshaies, Deshaies.*

**Plage de Malendure.** Across from Pigeon Island and the Jacques Cousteau Underwater Park, this long, gray, volcanic beach on the Caribbean's calm waters has restrooms, a few beach shacks offering cold drinks and snacks, and a huge parking lot. There might be some litter, but the beach is cleaned regularly. Don't come here for solitude, as the beach is a launch point for many dive boats. The snorkeling's good. Le Rocher de Malendure, a fine seafood restaurant, is perched on a cliff over the bay. Food carts work the parking lot. **Amenities:** food and drink; parking (no fee); toilets. **Best for:** partiers; snorkeling; swimming. ⊠ *Rte. N6, Bouillante.*

## SHOPPING

The island has a lot of desirable French products, from designer fashions for women and men and sensual lingerie to French china and liqueurs. As for local handicrafts, you can find attractive wood carvings, madras table linens, island dolls dressed in madras, woven straw baskets and hats, and *salakos*—fishermen's hats made of split bamboo, some covered in madras—which make great wall decorations. Of course, the favorite Guadeloupean souvenir is rum. Look for *rhum vieux*, the top of the line. Be aware that the only liquor bottles allowed on planes have to be bought in the duty-free shops at the airport. Usually the shops have to deliver purchases to the aircraft. For foodies, the market ladies sell aromatic fresh spices, crisscrossed with cinnamon sticks, in little baskets lined with madras.

### AREAS AND MALLS

Bas-du-Fort's two shopping areas are the Cora Shopping Center and the marina, where there are 20 or so shops and some restaurants, many right on the water. This marina has an active social scene.

Bustling Point-à-Pitre has obtained the prestigious French label of *Ville d'Art et d'Histoire* (town of art and history). You can browse in the street stalls around the harbor quay and at the two markets (the best is the Marché de Frébault). The town's main shopping streets with lots of French merchandise, from pâté to sexy lingerie, are rue Schoelcher, rue de Nozières, and the busy rue Frébault. At the St-John Perse Cruise Terminal, there's an attractive mall with about two dozen shops.

In St-François there are more than a dozen shops surrounding the marina, some selling French lingerie, swimsuits, and fashions. The supermarket has particularly good prices on French wines and cheeses, and if you pick up a fresh baguette, you'll have a picnic. (Then you can go get lost at a secluded beach.) Don't forget some island chocolates or individual fruit and custard tarts.

## ACTIVITIES

### DIVING

The main diving area at the **Cousteau Underwater Park,** just off Basse-Terre near Pigeon Island, offers routine dives to 60 feet. The numerous glass-bottom boats and other craft make the site feel like a marine parking lot; however, the underwater sights are spectacular. Guides and instructors are certified under the French CMAS (some also have PADI, but none have NAUI). Most operators offer two-hour dives three times per day for about €50 to €55 per dive; three-dive packages are €120 to €145. Hotels and dive operators usually rent snorkeling gear.

FAMILY **Les Heures Saines.** Les Heures Saines is the premier operator for dives in the Cousteau Underwater Park. Trips to Les Saintes offer one or two dives for average and advanced divers, with plenty of time for lunch and sightseeing. Wreck, night, and nitrox diving are also available. Despite this operator's popularity, it has kept its prices moderate, with many packages available. The instructors, young and fun types from the Metropole, many of them English speakers, are excellent with children. The company also offers winter whale- and dolphin-watching trips with marine biologists as guides aboard a 60-foot catamaran. Inquire also about going canyoning and/or hiking with Les Heures Saines. ✉ *Le Rocher de Malendure, Plage de Malendure, Bouillante* ☎ *0590/98–86–63* ⊕ *www.heures-saines.gp* 🖥 *From €55.*

### HIKING

Fodor's Choice  With hundreds of trails and countless rivers and waterfalls, the **Parc**
★ **National de la Guadeloupe** on Basse-Terre is the main draw for hikers. Some of the trails should be attempted only with an experienced guide. All tend to be muddy, so wear a good pair of boots. Know that even the young and fit can find these outings arduous; the unfit may find them painful. Start off slowly, with a shorter hike, and then go for the gusto. All water sports—even canoeing and kayaking—are forbidden in the center of the park. Scientists are studying the impact of these activities on the park's ecosystem.

**Vert Intense.** Vert Intense organizes hikes in the national park and to the volcano. You move from steaming hot springs to an icy waterfall in the same hike. Guides are patient and safety-conscious, and can bring you to heights that you never thought you could reach, including the top of Le Soufrière. The volcano hike, the cheapest excursion, must be booked four days in advance. When you are under the fumaroles you can smell the sulfur (like rotten eggs) and you and your clothes will smell like sulfur until you take a shower. A mixed-adventure package spanning three days costs considerably more. The two-day bivouac and other adventures can be extreme, so before you decide to play Indiana Jones, know what is expected. The French-speaking guides, who also know some English and Spanish, can take you to other tropical forests and rivers for canyoning (climbing and scrambling on outcrops, usually along and above the water). If you are just one or two people, the company can team you up with a group. Vert Intense now has a guesthouse, les Bananes Vertes (The Green Bananas), where you can combine a stay with trekking and other activities. ✉ *Rte. de la Soufrière, St-Claude* ☎ *0590/99–34–73, 0690/55–40–47* ⊕ *www.vert-intense.com* 🖥 *From €30.*

## WHERE TO EAT

$$ ✕ **Caraïbes Café.** This sidewalk café straight out of Paris is an "in"
CAFÉ  place for lunch and also a spot for a quick breakfast, a fresh juice cocktail—try *corossel* (a tropical fruit) and mango juices, a cappuccino, *un coupe* (a sundae), or a pastis while you people-watch and listen to

French crooners. The *formule* (fixed-price menu) is always the best deal. Service is fast and friendly and may even be in English. $ *Average main: €15* ✉ *Pl. de la Victoire, Pointe-à-Pitre* ☎ *0590/82–92–23* ☉ *Closed Sun. No dinner.*

**$$$**
ECLECTIC
✕ **Café Wango.** At this alfresco hot spot, Asian wok dishes, sushi, skewers, fish carpaccios, and tartares dominate the menu, and there are no fewer than nine better-than-average salads. There are also pricey pastas and daily specials like a classic sirloin in a Roquefort-poivre sauce, but the attractive prix-fixe menus are the best choices. Kids are crazy for the ice cream and beg parents for *un coupe*. So many flavors, so little time. Facing the marina's boat slips, the modern furnishings are charcoal gray and burnt orange juxtaposed with flamingo pink walls and napkins. The seats are often filled with a fun, discerning crowd of mainly French expats; parked nearby there may be a couple of Harleys, flying tiny American flags. $ *Average main: €21* ✉ *St-François Marina, Marines 1, St-François* ☎ *0590/83–50–41* ⊕ *www.cafewango. com* ☉ *Closed June 17–July 6.*

# KEY WEST, FLORIDA

By Paul Rubio
Along with the rest of Florida, Key West—the southernmost city in the continental United States—became part of American territory in 1821. In the late 19th century it was Florida's wealthiest city per capita. The locals made their fortunes from "wrecking"—rescuing people and salvaging cargo from ships that foundered on nearby reefs. Cigar making, fishing, shrimping, and sponge gathering also became important industries. Locally dubbed the "Conch Republic," Key West today makes for a unique port of call. A genuinely American town, it nevertheless exudes the relaxed atmosphere and pace of a typical Caribbean island. Major attractions include the home of the Conch Republic's most famous residents, Ernest Hemingway and Harry Truman; the imposing Key West Museum of Art and History (situated within a former U.S. Customs House) and site of the military inquest of the USS *Maine*; and the island's renowned sunset celebrations.

## ESSENTIALS
### CURRENCY
The U.S. dollar.

### TELEPHONE
You'll be able to find plenty of public phones around Mallory Square. They're also along the major tourist thoroughfares.

### COMING ASHORE
Cruise ships dock at three different locations in Key West. Mallory Square and Pier B are within walking distance of Duval and Whitehead streets, the two main tourist thoroughfares. Passengers on ships that dock at Outer Mole Pier (aka Navy Mole) are shuttled via Conch Train or Old Town Trolley to Mallory Square. Because Key West is so easily explored on foot, there's rarely a need to hire a taxi. If you plan to venture beyond the main tourist district, a fun way to get around is by bicycle or scooter (bike rentals begin at about $12 per day). Key West

is a cycling town. In fact, there are so many bikes around that cyclists must watch out for one another as much as for cars. You can get tourist information from the Greater Key West Chamber of Commerce, which is located one block off Duval Street, at 510 Greene Street, in the old "city hall."

The Conch Tour Train can be boarded at Mallory Square or Flagler Station every half-hour; it costs $30.45 per adult for the 90-minute tour. The Old Town Trolley operates trolley-style buses starting from Mallory Square every 30 minutes for the same price, and these smaller trolleys go places the train won't fit. The Old Town Trolley also has pick up and drop off locations at numerous points around the island.

> ### BEST BETS
>
> ■ **Boat Cruise.** Being out on the water is what Key West is all about.
>
> ■ **Conch Train.** Hop aboard for a narrated tour of the town's tawdry past and rare architectural treasures.
>
> ■ **Hemingway.** Visit Ernest Hemingway's historic home for a literary treat.
>
> ■ **Duval Crawl.** Shop, eat, drink, repeat.
>
> ■ **Sunset in Mallory Square.** The nightly street party is the quintessential Key West experience.

## EXPLORING

**Audubon House and Tropical Gardens.** If you've ever seen an engraving by ornithologist John James Audubon, you'll understand why his name is synonymous with birds. See his works in this three-story house, which was built in the 1840s for Captain John Geiger and filled with period furniture. It now commemorates Audubon's 1832 stop in Key West while he was traveling through Florida to study birds. After an introduction by a docent, you can do a self-guided tour of the house and gardens. An art gallery sells lithographs of the artist's famed portraits. ⌂ *205 Whitehead St., Key West* ☎ *305/294–2116, 877/294–2470* ⊕ *www. audubonhouse.com* ✉ *$12.*

**Fodor's Choice**
★ **Custom House.** When Key West was designated a U.S. port of entry in the early 1820s, a customhouse was established. Salvaged cargoes from ships wrecked on the reefs were brought here, setting the stage for Key West to become—for a time—the richest city in Florida. The imposing redbrick-and-terra-cotta Richardsonian Romanesque–style building reopened as a museum and art gallery in 1999. Smaller galleries have long-term and changing exhibits about the history of Key West, including a Hemingway room and a permanent Henry Flagler exhibit that commemorates the arrival of Flagler's railroad to Key West in 1912. ⌂ *281 Front St., Key West* ☎ *305/295–6616* ⊕ *www.kwahs. com* ✉ *$10.*

**Fodor's Choice**
★ **The Ernest Hemingway Home and Museum.** Amusing anecdotes spice up the guided tours of Ernest Hemingway's home, built in 1801 by the town's most successful wrecker. While living here between 1931 and 1942, Hemingway wrote about 70% of his life's work, including classics like

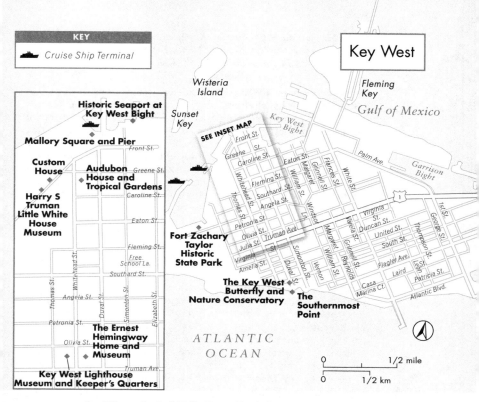

*For Whom the Bell Tolls.* Few of his belongings remain aside from some books, and there's little about his actual work, but photographs help you visualize his day-to-day life. The famous six-toed descendants of Hemingway's cats—many named for actors, artists, authors, and even a hurricane—have free rein of the property. Tours begin every 10 minutes and take 30 minutes; then you're free to explore on your own. Be sure to find out why there is a urinal in the garden! ⊠ *907 Whitehead St., Key West* ☎ *305/294–1136* ⊕ *www.hemingwayhome.com* ✉ *$13.*

**Fort Zachary Taylor Historic State Park.** Construction of the fort began in 1845 but was halted during the Civil War. Even though Florida seceded from the Union, Yankee forces used the fort as a base to block Confederate shipping. More than 1,500 Confederate vessels were detained in Key West's harbor. The fort, finally completed in 1866, was also used in the Spanish-American War. Take a 30-minute guided walking tour of the redbrick fort, a National Historic Landmark, at noon and 2, or self-tour anytime between 8 and 5. In February a celebration called Civil War Heritage Days includes costumed reenactments and demonstrations. From mid-January to mid-April the park serves as an open-air gallery for pieces created for Sculpture Key West. One of its most popular features is its man-made beach, a rest stop for migrating birds in the spring and fall; there are also picnic areas, hiking and biking trails, and a kayak launch. ☒ *Southard St., at end of street, through Truman Annex, Key West* ☏ *305/292–6713* ⊕ *www.floridastateparks.org/park/ Fort-Taylor* ☜ *$4 for single-occupant vehicles, $6 for 2–8 people in a vehicle, plus a 50¢ per person county surcharge.*

**Harry S. Truman Little White House Museum.** Renovations to this circa-1890 landmark have restored the home and gardens to the Truman era, down to the wallpaper pattern. A free photographic review of visiting dignitaries and presidents—John F. Kennedy, Jimmy Carter, and Bill Clinton are among the chief executives who passed through here—is on display in the back of the gift shop. Engaging 45-minute tours begin every 20 minutes until 4:30. They start with an excellent 10-minute video on the history of the property and Truman's visits. On the grounds of **Truman Annex**, a 103-acre former military parade grounds and barracks, the home served as a winter White House for presidents Truman, Eisenhower, and Kennedy. ■TIP➜ **The house tour does require climbing steps. Visitors can do a free self-guided botanical tour of the grounds with a brochure from the museum store.** ☒ *111 Front St., Key West* ☏ *305/294–9911* ⊕ *www.trumanlittlewhitehouse. com* ☜ *$16.13.*

**Historic Seaport at Key West Bight.** What was once a funky—in some places even seedy—part of town is now an 8½-acre historic restoration of 100 businesses, including waterfront restaurants, open-air bars, museums, clothing stores, bait shops, dive shops, docks, a marina, and watersports concessions. It's all linked by the 2-mile waterfront **Harborwalk,** which runs between Front and Grinnell streets, passing big ships, schooners, sunset cruises, fishing charters, and glass-bottom boats. ☒ *100 Grinnell St., Key West* ☏ ⊕ *www.keywestseaport.com.*

FAMILY   **The Key West Butterfly and Nature Conservatory.** This air-conditioned refuge for butterflies, birds, and the human spirit gladdens the soul with hundreds of colorful wings—more than 45 species of butterflies alone—in a lovely glass-encased bubble. Waterfalls, artistic benches, paved pathways, birds, and lush, flowering vegetation elevate this above most butterfly attractions. The gift shop and gallery are worth a visit on their own. ☒ *1316 Duval St., Key West* ☏ *305/296–2988, 800/839–4647* ⊕ *www.keywestbutterfly.com* ☜ *$12.*

**Key West Lighthouse Museum and Keeper's Quarters.** For the best view in town, climb the 88 steps to the top of this 1847 lighthouse. The 92-foot structure has a Fresnel lens, which was installed in the 1860s at a cost of $1 million. The keeper lived in the adjacent 1887 clapboard house, which now exhibits vintage photographs, ship models, nautical charts, and lighthouse artifacts from all along the Key reefs. A kids' room is stocked with books and toys. ☒ *938 Whitehead St., Key West* ☏ *305/295–6616* ⊕ *www.kwahs.com* ☜ *$10.*

**Mallory Square and Pier.** For cruise-ship passengers, this is the disembarkation point for an attack on Key West. For practically every visitor, it's the requisite venue for a nightly sunset celebration that includes street performers—human statues, sword swallowers, tightrope walkers, musicians, and more—plus craft vendors, conch fritter fryers, and other regulars who defy classification. With all the activity, don't forget to watch the main show: a dazzling tropical sunset. ⊠ *Mallory Sq., Key West.*

**The Southernmost Point.** Possibly the most photographed site in Key West (even though the actual geographic southernmost point in the continental United States lies across the bay on a naval base, where you see a satellite dish), this is a must-see. Who wouldn't want his picture taken next to the big striped buoy that marks the southernmost point in the continental United States? A plaque next to it honors Cubans who lost their lives trying to escape to America and other signs tell Key West history. ⊠ *Whitehead and South Sts., Key West.*

## BEACHES

FAMILY **Fort Zachary Taylor Beach.** The park's beach is the best and safest place to swim in Key West. There's an adjoining picnic area with barbecue grills and shade trees, a snack bar, and rental equipment, including snorkeling gear. A café serves sandwiches and other munchies. **Amenities:** food and drink; showers; toilets; water sports. **Best for:** swimming; snorkeling. ⊠ *Southard St., at end of street, through Truman Annex, Key West* ☏ *305/292–6713* ⊕ *www.floridastateparks.org/forttaylor* ➲ *$4 for 1-occupant vehicles, $6 for 2–8 people in a vehicle, plus 50¢ per person county surcharge.*

## SHOPPING

On these streets you'll find colorful local art of widely varying quality, key limes made into everything imaginable, and the raunchiest T-shirts in the civilized world. Browsing the boutiques—with frequent pub stops along the way—makes for an entertaining stroll down Duval Street. Key West is filled with art galleries, and the variety is truly amazing. Much is locally produced by the town's large artist community, but many galleries carry international artists from as close as Haiti and as far away as France. Local artists do a great job of preserving the island's architecture and spirit.

**Bahama Village.** Where to start your shopping adventure? This cluster of spruced-up shops, restaurants, and vendors is responsible for the restoration of the colorful historic district where Bahamians settled in the 19th century. The village lies roughly between Whitehead and Fort streets and Angela and Catherine streets. Hemingway frequented the bars, restaurants, and boxing rings in this part of town. ⊠ *Between Whitehead and Fort Sts. and Angela and Catherine Sts., Key West.*

## ACTIVITIES

### BOAT TOURS

**Lazy Dog.** Take a two- or four-hour guided sea kayak–snorkel tour around the mangrove islands just east of Key West. Costs include transportation, bottled water, a snack, and supplies, including snorkeling gear. Paddleboard tours and PaddleYoga and PaddleFit classes are also available, as are rentals for self-touring. ✉ *5114 Overseas Hwy., Key West* ☎ *305/295–9898* ⊕ *www.lazydog.com* ✉ *From $40.*

**Dancing Dolphin Spirit Charters.** Victoria Impallomeni, a wilderness guide and environmental marine science expert, or one of her protégés, invite up to six nature lovers—especially children—aboard the *Imp II,* a 25-foot Aquasport, for four-hour and seven-hour ecotours that frequently include encounters with wild dolphins. While island-hopping, you visit underwater gardens, natural shoreline, and mangrove habitats. For the Dolphin Day for Humans tour, you'll be pulled through the water, equipped with mask and snorkel, on a specially designed "dolphin water massage board" that simulates dolphin swimming motions. Sometimes dolphins follow the boat and swim among participants. All equipment is supplied. ✉ *MM 5 OS, Murray's Marina, 5710 Overseas Hwy., Key West* ☎ *305/304–7562, 305/745–9901* ⊕ *www.captainvictoria.com* ✉ *From $500.*

## DIVING AND SNORKELLING

The Florida Keys National Marine Sanctuary extends along Key West and beyond to the Dry Tortugas. Key West National Wildlife Refuge further protects the pristine waters. Most divers don't make it this far out in the Keys, but if you're looking for a day of diving as a break from the nonstop party in Old Town, expect to pay about $65 and upward for a two-tank dive. Serious divers can book dive trips to the Dry Tortugas.

**Captain's Corner.** This PADI–certified dive shop has classes in several languages and twice-daily snorkel and dive trips to reefs and wrecks aboard the 60-foot dive boat *Sea Eagle.* Use of weights, belts, masks, and fins is included. ✉ *125 Ann St., Key West* ☎ *305/296–8865* ⊕ *www.captainscorner.com* ✉ *From $45.*

FAMILY **Snuba of Key West.** Safely dive the coral reefs without getting a scuba certification. Ride out to the reef on a catamaran, then follow your guide underwater for a one-hour tour of the coral reefs. You wear a regulator with a breathing hose that is attached to a floating air tank on the surface. No prior diving or snorkeling experience is necessary, but you must know how to swim and be at least eight years old. The price includes beverages. ✉ *Garrison Bight Marina, Palm Ave., between Eaton St. and N. Roosevelt Blvd., Key West* ☎ *305/292–4616* ⊕ *www.snubakeywest.com* ✉ *From $109.*

## FISHING

Any number of local fishing guides can take you to where the big ones are biting, either in the backcountry for snapper and snook or to the deep water for the marlins and shark that brought Hemingway here in the first place.

**Key West Bait & Tackle.** Prepare to catch a big one with the live bait, frozen bait, and fishing equipment provided here. They even offer rod and reel rentals (starting at $15 for one day, $5 each additional day). Stop by their on-site Live Bait Lounge where you can sip $3.25 ice-cold beer while telling fish tales. ✉ *241 Margaret St., Key West* ☎ *305/292–1961* ⊕ *www.keywestbaitandtackle.com.*

**Key West Pro Guides.** This outfitter offers private charters, and you can choose four-, five-, six-, or eight-hour trips. Choose from flats, backcountry, reef, offshore fishing, and even specialty trips to the Dry Tortugas. Whatever your fishing (even spearfishing) pleasure, their captains will hook you up. ✉ *G–31 Miriam St., Key West* ☎ *866/259–4205* ⊕ *www.keywestproguides.com* ☜ *From $400.*

## WHERE TO EAT

**$**

SEAFOOD

**Fodor's**Choice

★

✕ **B.O.'s Fish Wagon.** What started out as a fish house on wheels appears to have broken down on the corner of Caroline and William streets and is today the cornerstone for one of Key West's junkyard-chic dining institutions. Step up to the wood-plank counter window and order the specialty: a grouper sandwich fried or grilled and topped with key lime sauce. Other choices include fish nuts (don't be scared, they're just fried nuggets), hot dogs, cracked conch sandwich, and shrimp or soft-shell-crab sandwich. Talk sass with your host and find a picnic table or take a seat at the plank. Grab some paper towels off one of the rolls hanging around and busy yourself reading graffiti, license plates, and irreverent signs. It's a must-do Key West experience. ⑤ *Average main: $18* ✉ *801 Caroline St., Key West* ☎ *305/294–9272* ⊕ *www.bosfishwagon.com* ☱ *No credit cards.*

**$$**

CUBAN

✕ **El Meson de Pepe.** If you want to get a taste of the island's Cuban heritage, this is the place. Perfect for after watching a Mallory Square sunset, you can dine alfresco or in the dining room on refined versions of Cuban classics. Begin with a megasized mojito while you enjoy the basket of bread and savory sauces. The expansive menu offers *tostones rellenos* (green plantains with different traditional fillings), ceviche (raw fish "cooked" in lemon juice), and more. Choose from Cuban specialties such as roasted pork in a cumin mojo sauce and *ropa vieja* (shredded beef stew). At lunch, the local Cuban population and cruise-ship passengers enjoy Cuban sandwiches and smaller versions of dinner's most popular entrées. A Latin band performs outside at the bar during the sunset celebration. ⑤ *Average main: $19* ✉ *Mallory Sq., 410 Wall St., Key West* ☎ *305/295–2620* ⊕ *www.elmesondepepe.com.*

## NIGHTLIFE

Three spots stand out for first-timers among the saloons frequented by Key West denizens. All are within easy walking distance of the cruise-ship piers.

**Capt. Tony's Saloon.** When it was the original Sloppy Joe's in the mid-1930s, Hemingway was a regular. Later, a young Jimmy Buffett sang here and made this watering hole famous in his song "Last Mango in Paris." Captain Tony was even voted mayor of Key West. Yes, this place is a beloved landmark. Stop in and take a look at the "hanging tree" that grows through the roof, listen to live music seven nights a week, and play some pool. ✉ *428 Greene St., Key West* ☎ *305/294–1838* ⊕ *www.capttonyssaloon.com.*

4

**Schooner Wharf Bar.** This open-air waterfront bar and grill in the historic seaport district retains its funky Key West charm and hosts live entertainment daily. Its margaritas rank among Key West's best, as does the bar itself, voted Best Local's Bar six years in a row. For great views, head up to the second floor and be sure to order up some fresh seafood and fritters and Dark and Stormy cocktails. ✉ *202 William St., Key West* ☎ *305/292–3302* ⊕ *www.schoonerwharf.com.*

**Sloppy Joe's.** There's history and good times at the successor to a famous 1937 speakeasy named for its founder, Captain Joe Russell. Decorated with Hemingway memorabilia and marine flags, the bar is popular with travelers and is full and noisy all the time. A Sloppy Joe's T-shirt is a de rigueur Key West souvenir, and the gift shop sells them like crazy. Grab a seat (if you can) and be entertained by the bands and by the parade of people in constant motion. ✉ *201 Duval St., Key West* ☎ *305/294–5717* ⊕ *www.sloppyjoes.com.*

---

# LA ROMANA, DOMINICAN REPUBLIC

By Eileen
Robinson
Smith

The Dominican Republic is a beautiful island bathed by the Atlantic Ocean to the north and the Caribbean Sea to the south, and some of its most beautiful beaches are in the area surrounding La Romana, notably Bayahibe Bay. The famed Casa de Campo resort and Marina will be the destination for most cruise passengers who land at La Romana's International Tourist Pier. A port call here will allow you to explore the immediate region—even take a day-trip into Santo Domingo—or simply stay and enjoy some nice (but expensive) restaurants and shops. There is also a host of activities cruise passengers can take part in on organized shore excursions.

> **BEST BETS**
>
> ■ **Altos de Chavón.** You'll find shopping and dining as well as great views.
>
> ■ **Golf.** The Teeth of the Dog is one of the Caribbean's best courses despite the cost.
>
> ■ **Horseback Riding.** Casa de Campo has an excellent equestrian center.
>
> ■ **Isla Saona.** The powder-soft beach and beautiful water are excellent.
>
> ■ **Kandela.** The tropical, Las Vegas-style review is a highlight if your ship stays late in port on a night it is performed.

## ESSENTIALS

### CURRENCY

The Dominican peso, but you can almost always use U.S. dollars.

### TELEPHONE

Telephones are available at the dock, as soon as passengers disembark, and telephone cards can be purchased there as well. Tele-cards can also be bought at the supermarket at Casa de Campo Marina. To call the United States or Canada from the D.R., just punch in 1 plus the area code and number. To make calls on the island, you must tap in the area code (809), plus the seven-digit number; if you are calling a Dominican cell phone, you must first punch in 1 then 809 or 829.

**KEY**

⌐ *Beaches*
⚓ *Cruise Ship Terminal*

Las Américas Int'l Airport
San Pedro de Macorís
La Romana International Airport
Santo Domingo
Altos de Chavón
Isla Catalina
Las Minitas
Bayahibe
Higüey
Punta Cana International Airport
Punta Cana
Punta Cana
La Romana
Parque Nacional Del Este
Bahía de Yuma
Mona Passage

*Caribbean Sea*
Isla Saona

**La Romana**

0    20 miles
0    20 kilometers

**COMING ASHORE**

Ships enter the Casa de Campo International Tourist Port (Muelle Turïstico Internacional Casa de Campo). A group of folkloric dancers and local musicians, playing merengue, greets passengers as they come down the gangway. An information booth with English-speaking staffers is there to assist cruise-ship passengers; the desk is open the entire time the ship is in port.

It is a 15-minute walk into the town of La Romana, or you can jump into a waiting taxi. It's safe to stroll around town, but it's not particularly beautiful, quaint, or even historic; however, it is a real slice of Dominican life. Most people just board the complimentary shuttle and head for the Casa de Campo Marina and/or Altos de Chavón, both of which are within the Casa de Campo resort. Shuttles run all day long.

Taxis line up at the port's docks, and some, but not all, drivers speak English. Staff members from the information kiosk will help to make taxi arrangements. Most rates are fixed and spelled out on a board: $15 to Casa de Campo Marina, $20 to Altos de Chavón. You may be able to negotiate a somewhat lower rate if a group books a taxi for a tour. You can also rent a car at Casa de Campo from National Car Rental; rates are expensive, usually more than $70 a day. Driving into Santo Domingo can be a hair-raising experience, and isn't for the faint of heart, so we don't recommend it.

## EXPLORING

Fodor'sChoice **Altos de Chavón.** This replica 16th-century Mediterranean village sits on
★ a bluff overlooking the Río Chavón, on the grounds of Casa de Campo but about 3 miles (5 km) east of the main facilities. There are cobblestone streets lined with lanterns, wrought-iron balconies, wooden shutters, courtyards swathed with bougainvillea, and **Iglesia St. Stanislaus,** the romantic setting for many a Casa de Campo wedding. More than a museum piece, this village is a place where artists live, work, and play. Emilio Robba, a famous European designer, is now directing the art studios. You can visit the ateliers and see the talented artisans making pottery, tapestry, and serigraphic art. The artists sell their finished wares

at the Art Studios Boutique. The village also has an amber museum, an archaeological museum, a handful of restaurants, and a number of unique shops. Strolling musicians enliven the rustic ambience of ceramic tiles and cobblestone terrace, but there are now more bars and nightclubs geared to Casa de Campo's guests. Big names, including Elton John, perform at the amphitheater. Christmastime is sheer magic, what with the lights, music concerts, giant Christmas tree, and Santa making a cameo appearance. ⊠ *Casa de Campo, La Romana* ⊕ *www.casadecampo.com.do.*

**Isla Catalina.** This diminutive, picture- postcard Caribbean island lies off the coast of the mainland. Catalina is about a half-hour away from Bayahibe by catamaran, and most excursions offer the use of snorkeling equipment as well as a beach barbecue. ⊠ *Isla Catalina ✛ 30 minutes from Bayahibe harbor by boat.*

**Isla Saona.** Off the east coast of Hispaniola and part of Parque Nacional del Este lies this island, inhabited by sea turtles, pigeons, and other wildlife. Indigenous people once used the caves here. The beaches are beautiful, and legend has it that Columbus once stopped over. However, the island is not nearly as pristine as one might expect for a national park. Getting here, on catamarans and other excursion boats, is half the fun, but it can be a crowded scene once you arrive. Vendors are allowed to sell to visitors, and there are a number of beach shacks serving lunch and drinks. Most boats traveling here leave out of the beach at Bayahibe Village. Most tourists book through their hotel. ⚠ **Please note that there is little to no refrigeration on the island and the sun is strong, so take caution when dining.** ⊠ *20 mins from Bayahibe harbor by boat, Bayahibe.*

**Santo Domingo.** Spanish civilization in the New World began in the 12-block Zona Colonial of Santo Domingo. Strolling its narrow streets, it's easy to imagine this old city as it was when the likes of Columbus, Cortés, and Ponce de León walked the cobblestones, pirates sailed in and out, and colonists were settling themselves. Tourist brochures tout that "history comes alive here"—a surprisingly truthful statement. A fun horse-and-carriage ride throughout the Zone costs $25 for an hour. The steeds are no thoroughbreds, but they clip right along, though any commentary will be in Spanish. The drivers usually hang out in front of the Hostal Nicolas de Ovando. History buffs will want to spend a day exploring the many "firsts" of this continent, which will be included in any cruise-ship excursion. Do wear comfortable shoes.

## BEACHES

Cruise passengers can buy a day-pass to use the beach and facilities at Casa de Campo ($75 for adults, $45 for children 4–12 years); with that, you get a place in the sun at Minitas Beach, towels, nonmotorized water sports, lunch in the Beach Club, and entrance to Altos de Chavón. Otherwise, excursions (sometimes cheaper) are available to several area beaches, including trips to Isla Catalina and Isla Saona.

**Playa Bayahibe.** Playa Bayahibe, where several seafood restaurants are situated, is somewhat thin, with hard-packed taupe sand and no lounge chairs. However, as you move away from the village, a 10-minute walk along the shoreline, you'll reach the glorious, half-moon cove where you'll find the Dreams resort. Although you'll be able to get to the cove and the soft sand, bring a towel (the resort's security won't let you use the facilities). At night, when no one is on the playa and the silver moon illuminates the phosphorescence, it's the stuff that Caribbean dreams are made of. **Amenities:** food and drink; toilets. **Best for:** partiers; sunset; swimming; walking; windsurfing. ✉ *Starts in the center of town, near the Dreams resort, Bayahibe.*

## SHOPPING

**Altos de Chavón.** Altos de Chavón is a re-creation of a 16th-century Mediterranean village on the grounds of the Casa de Campo resort, where you can find a church, art galleries, boutiques, restaurants, nightspots, and souvenir shops, and a 5,000-seat amphitheater for concerts grouped around a cobbled square. At the Altos de Chavón Art Studios you can find ceramics, weaving, and screen prints made by local and resident artists. Extra special is the Jenny Polanco Project. A top Dominican fashion designer, she has made an outlet for Dominican, Haitian, and Caribbean craftsmen to sell their wares, from Carnival masks to baskets and carved plates. Tienda Batey sells fine linens handcrafted by women from the sugar plantation *bateys* (poor villages). ✉ *Casa de Campo, La Romana.*

**Casa de Campo Marina.** Casa de Campo's top-ranked marina is home to shops and international boutiques, galleries, and jewelers scattered amid restaurants, banks, and other services. The chic shopping scene includes Luxury Shops Carmen Sol and Kiwi St. Tropez for French bathing suits. Polanco-Leon with Dominican designer Jenny Polanco's has resort wear, purses, and jewelry as well as Bibi Leon's tropical-themed home accessories. There's also a marvelous Italian antiques shop, Nuovo Rinascimento, and Club Del Cigarro (Fumo). The *supermercado* Nacional has not only groceries but sundries, postcards, and snacks. ✉ *Casa de Campo Marina, Calle Barlovento, La Romana* ⊕ *www.marinacasa decampo.com.do.*

## ACTIVITIES

Most activities available at Casa de Campo are open to cruise-ship passengers. You'll need to make reservations on the ship, particularly for golf.

### FISHING

**Casa de Campo Marina.** Casa de Campo Marina is the best charter option in the La Romana area. Yachts (22- to 60-footers) are available for deep-sea fishing charters for half or full days. Prices go from $824 for a half day on *Scorpio* to $3,555 for a full day on *Gabriella*. They can come equipped with rods, bait, dinghies, drinks, and experienced guides. Going out for the big billfish that swim the depths of the Caribbean is a major adrenaline rush. The marina hosts the annual Casa de Campo International Blue Marlin Classic Tournament in late March, which is celebrated with a round of parties. ✉ *Casa de Campo, Calle Barlovento 3, La Romana* ☎ *809/523–3333, 809/523–3333* ⊕ *www. marinacasadecampo.com.do* ✉ *Charters from $824.*

## GOLF

**Fodor's Choice**
★

**Casa de Campo Resort.** The Resort is considered by most to be the premier multiple golf resort in the Caribbean. The famed 18-hole Teeth of the Dog course at Casa de Campo, with seven holes on the sea, is usually ranked as the number-one course in the Caribbean and is among the top courses in the world. Pete Dye regards Teeth of the Dog as one of his best designs and has long enjoyed living at Casa part-time. The Teeth of the Dog requires a caddy for each round (for an additional fee). Pete Dye has designed this and two other globally acclaimed courses here. Dye Fore, now with a total of 27 holes, is close to Altos de Chavón, hugging a cliff that features commanding vistas of the sea, a river, Dominican mountains, and the marina. The Links is a gamey 18-hole inland course. Resort guests must reserve tee times for all courses at least one day in advance; nonguests should make reservations earlier. ⊠ *Casa de Campo, La Romana* ☎ *809/523–3333 resort, 809/523–8115 golf director* ⊕ *www.casadecampo.com.do* ⊠ *Teeth of the Dog: $320 per round per golfer for nonhotel guests, $250 per round per player for guests; Dye Fore: $250 for nonguests, $225 for guests; The Links: $150 for nonguests, $135 for guests ⅃. Teeth of the Dog: 18 holes, 6989 yards, par 72; Dye Fore: 18 holes, 7740 yards, par 72; The Links: 18 holes, 6664 yards, par 71.*

## HORSEBACK RIDING

**Equestrian Center at Casa de Campo.** The 250-acre Equestrian Center at Casa de Campo has something for both Western and English riders—a dude ranch, a rodeo arena (where Casa's trademark "Donkey Polo" is played), three polo fields, guided trail rides, riding, jumping, and polo lessons. There are early-morning and sunset trail rides, too. Unlimited horseback riding is included in some Casa de Campo packages. Trail rides are offered through the property's private cattle ranch, through a herd of water buffalo and passing by lakes populated with ducks and the on-site horse-breeding operation. ⊠ *Casa de Campo, La Romana* ☎ *809/523–3333* ⊕ *www.casadecampo.com.do* ⊠ *From $57.*

# WHERE TO EAT

**$$$**
ECLECTIC

**✕ Peperoni.** Although the name may sound as Italian as *amore*, this restaurant's menu is more eclectic than Italian. It has a classy, contemporary, white-dominated decor in a dreamy, marina setting. Strolling musicians perpetuate the mood, the moored yachts provide people-watching. Astounding appetizers are found under the Asian section, like the sweet plantain roll or the Peperoni roll. Pasta dishes and risottos with rock shrimp or porcini taste authentic, and the more inventive items such as house-made pear-and-goat-cheese ravioli with pine nuts are delectable. *Pulpo* (octopus) with fava beans stewed in limoncello vinaigrette is highly recommended. You can also opt for stylishly simple charcoal-grilled steaks (sauce or no), burgers, gourmet wood-oven pizzas, sandwiches, or even sushi and sashimi. Desserts are worthy here. There have been some complaints that food quality is not what it once was. ⑤ *Average main: $21* ⊠ *Casa de Campo, Plaza Portafino 16, Casa de Campo Marina, La Romana* ☎ *809/523–2227, 809/523–3333.*

# MARTINIQUE (FORT-DE-FRANCE)

By Eileen Robinson Smith

The largest of the Windward Islands, Martinique is 4,261 miles (6,817 km) from Paris, but its spirit and language are decidedly French, despite more than a soupçon of West Indian spice. Tangible, edible evidence of the fact is the island's cuisine, a superb blend of French and Creole. Martinique is lushly landscaped with tropical flowers. Trees bend under the weight of fruits such as mangoes, papayas, lemons, limes, and bright-red West Indian cherries. Acres of banana plantations, pineapple fields, and waving sugarcane stretch to the horizon. The towering mountains and verdant rain forest in the north lure hikers, while underwater sights and sunken treasures attract snorkelers and scuba divers. Martinique is also wonderful if your idea of exercise is turning over every 10 minutes to get an even tan and your taste in adventure runs to duty-free shopping. A popular excursion goes to St-Pierre, which was buried by ash when Mount Pelée erupted in 1902.

> **BEST BETS**
>
> ■ **Beaches.** If you want to relax or party, one of the most beautiful beaches is Les Salines.
>
> ■ **French food and music.** A *paradis* for Francophiles.
>
> ■ **La Route des Rhums.** Visit several distilleries and become a rum connoisseur. (Visit *www.martinique.org* for a good map.)
>
> ■ **Shopping.** Browse Fort-de-France's many upscale boutiques and department stores for French wares.
>
> ■ **St-Pierre.** Wander the narrow, winding streets of this hill town.

## ESSENTIALS

### CURRENCY

The euro. Change currency at a bureau de change, but you'll get the best rate from any ATM.

### TELEPHONE

Public phones use a télécarte, which you can buy at post offices, café-tabacs, hotels, and bureaux de change. To call the United States from Martinique, dial 00+1, the area code, and the local seven-digit number. To call locally, you now have to dial 0596 before the six-digit number. You can get the AT&T or MCI operators from blue, special-service phones at the cruise ports and in town.

### COMING ASHORE

Most cruise ships call either at Tourelles (in the old port, about 1½ miles [2 km] from Fort-de-France) or at Pointe Simon, right in downtown Fort-de-France. (It is rare to have a ship anchor in the Baie des Flamands and tender passengers ashore.) Tourist information offices are at each cruise terminal. Uniformed dispatchers assist passengers in finding English-speaking taxi drivers. Passengers who do not wish to walk 20 minutes into Fort-de-France from Tourelles can take a taxi (set rate of €8 for up to four passengers in a van, or €2 for each additional passenger). Expect to pay about €50 per hour for touring; in larger vans the price is usually €10 per person per hour. Independent cruisers can explore the capital and the nearby open-air market on their own.

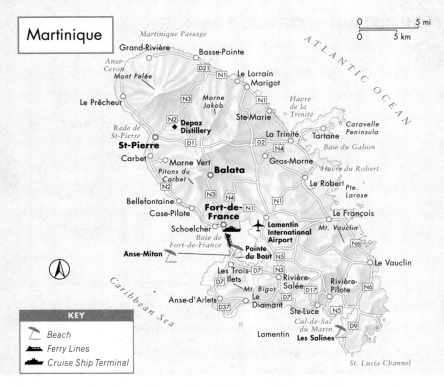

# Martinique

*Martinique Passage*

Grand-Rivière

Basse-Pointe

*Anse-Ceron*

Mont Pelée

Le Lorrain

Marigot

Le Prêcheur

N3

*Morne Jakob*

N1

*Havre de la Trinité*

Ste-Marie

Caravelle Peninsula

N2

**Depaz Distillery**

*Rade de St-Pierre*

**St-Pierre**

D1

La Trinité

Tartane

*Baie du Galion*

Carbet

Morne Vert

**Balata**

Gros-Morne

*Havre du Robert*

*Pitons du Carbet*

N2

Le Robert

Pte. Larose

Bellefontaine

N3

N4

N1

Case-Pilote

**Fort-de-France**

N1

Le François

Schoelcher

*Baie de Fort-de-France*

**Lamentin International Airport**

*Mt. Vauclin*

N6

**Anse-Mitan**

**Pointe du Bout**

N5

Le Vauclin

*Caribbean Sea*

Les Trois-Ilets

N5

D7

Rivière-Salée

D17

Rivière-Pilote

N6

*Mt. Bigot*

Anse-d'Arlets

D37

Le Diamant

D7

Ste-Luce

N5

*Cul-de-Sac du Marin*

Lamentin

**Les Salines**

D9

*St. Lucia Channel*

**ATLANTIC OCEAN**

0   5 mi

0   5 km

### KEY

⌐ Beach
Ferry Lines
Cruise Ship Terminal

Beaming and knowledgeable hostesses in creole dress greet cruise passengers. Civilian auxiliary police (in blue-and-orange uniforms) supplement the regular police.

Know that traffic in Fort-de-France can be nightmarish. If you want to go to the beach, a much cheaper option is to take a ferry from Fort-de-France. *Vedettes* (ferries) operate daily between the waterfront pier next to the public land-transport terminal and the marina in Pointe du Bout, Anse-Mitan, and Anse-à-l'Ane. Any of the three trips takes about 15 minutes, and the ferries operate about every 30 minutes on weekdays. Renting a car in Fort-de-France is possible, but the heavy traffic can be forbidding. Rates are about €80 per day (high season) for a car with manual transmission; automatics are substantially more expensive and seldom available without reservations.

## EXPLORING

If you want to see the lush island interior and St-Pierre on your own, take the N3, which snakes through dense rain forests, north through the mountains to Le Morne Rouge, then take the coastal N2 back to Fort-de-France via St-Pierre. You can do the 40-mile (64-km) round-trip in half a day, but your best option is to hire an English-speaking driver.

## FORT-DE-FRANCE

With its historic fort and superb location beneath the towering Pitons du Carbet on the Baie des Flamands, Martinique's capital—home to about one-quarter of the island's 400,000 inhabitants—should be a grand place. It hasn't been for decades but it's now coming up fast. An ambitious redevelopment project, still under way, hopes to make it one of the most attractive cities in the Caribbean. The most pleasant districts, such as Didier, Bellevue, and Schoelcher, are on the hillside, reachable only by car or taxi; there are some good shops with Parisian wares and lively street markets. Near the harbor is a marketplace where local crafts and souvenirs are sold. The urban beach between the waterfront and the fort, La Française, has been cleaned up; white sand was brought in, and many cruise-ship passengers frequent it. The new Stewards Urbaine, easily recognized by their red caps and uniforms, are able to answer most visitor questions and give directions.

**Fort St. Louis.** Fort Saint Louis (Lou-ee), an imposing stone fortress that has guarded the island's principal port city for some 375 years, offers panoramic views of the surrounding seaside urban landscape. Guided tours are available, but visitors must first check in at the Fort-de-France Office de Tourisme information kiosk 1, at the northwest corner of La Savane—at the intersection of rue de la Liberté and boulevard Alfassa. ✉ *Bd. Chevalier, Sainte-Marthe, Fort-de-France* ☎ *0596/75–41–44* ⊕ *www.tourismefdf.com* 🎫 *€8* ⊗ *Fort closed for tours Sun. and Mon.*

**La Savane.** The heart of Fort-de-France, La Savane is a 12½-acre park filled with trees, fountains, and benches. A massive revitalization made it the focal point of the city again, with entertainment, shopping, and a pedestrian mall. Attractive wooden stands have been constructed along the edge of the park that house a tourism information office, public restrooms, arts-and-crafts vendors, a crepe stand, an ice-cream stand, and numerous other eateries. Although homeless people frequent the park, they generally do not bother anyone.

Diagonally across from La Savane, you can catch the ferries for the 20-minute run across the bay to Pointe du Bout and the beaches at Anse-Mitan and Anse-à-l'Ane. It's relatively cheap as well as stress-free—much safer, more pleasant, and faster than by car. ✉ *Fort-de-France.*

**Musée d'Histoire et d'Ethnographie.** This museum is best undertaken at the beginning of your vacation, so you can better understand the history, background, and people of the island. Housed in an elaborate, former military residence (circa 1888) with balconies and fretwork, the museum displays some of the garish gold jewelry that prostitutes wore after emancipation as well as the sorts of rooms that a proper, middle-class Martinican would have lived in. Oil paintings, engravings, and old historical documents also help sketch out the island's culture. ✉ *10 bd. Général de Gaulle, Fort-de-France* ☎ *0596/72–81–87* 🎫 *€4.*

**Rue Victor Schoelcher.** Stores sell Paris fashions and French perfume, china, crystal, and liqueurs, as well as local handicrafts along this street running through the center of the capital's primary shopping district, a six-block area bounded by rue de la République, rue de la Liberté, rue Victor Severe, and rue Victor Hugo. ✉ *Fort-de-France.*

**St-Louis Cathedral.** This Romanesque cathedral with lovely stained-glass windows was built in 1878, the sixth church on this site (the others were destroyed by fires, hurricanes, and earthquakes). Classified as a historical monument, it has a marble altar, an impressive organ, and carved wooden pulpits. ☒ *Rue Victor Schoelcher, Schoelcher* ☎ *0596/60–59–00.*

## ELSEWHERE ON MARTINIQUE

### BALATA

This quiet little town has two sights worth visiting. Built in 1923 to commemorate those Martinicans who fought and died in World War I, **Balata Church** is an exact replica of Paris's Sacré-Coeur Basilica. The gardens, **Jardin de Balata,** are lovely.

**Jardin de Balata** (*Balata Gardens*). The Jardin de Balata has thousands of varieties of tropical flowers and plants; its owner is a dedicated horticulturist. There are shaded benches from which to take in the mountain views and a plantation-style house furnished with period furniture. An aerial path gives visitors an astounding, bird's-eye view of the gardens and surrounding hills, from wooden walkways suspended 50 feet in the air. There is no restaurant, though beverages are for sale. This worthy site shows why Martinique is called the Island of Flowers. It's 15 minutes from Fort-de-France, in the direction of St-Pierre. You can order anthuriums and other tropical flowers to be delivered to the airport from the mesmerizing flower boutique here. ■ TIP➔ **The gardens close at 6, but the ticket office will not admit anyone after 4:30. Children get a discount.** ☒ *Km. 10, rte. de Balata, Balata* ☎ *0596/64–48–73* ⊕ *www. jardindebalata.fr* ☒ *€12.80.*

### ST-PIERRE

The rise and fall of St-Pierre is one of the most remarkable stories in the Caribbean and one of its worst disasters. Martinique's modern history began here in 1635. By the turn of the 20th century St-Pierre was a flourishing city of 30,000, known as the Paris of the West Indies. As many as 30 ships at a time stood at anchor. By 1902 it was the most modern town in the Caribbean, with electricity, phones, and a tram. On May 8, 1902, two thunderous explosions rent the air. As the nearby volcano erupted, Mont Pelée split in half, belching forth a cloud of burning ash, poisonous gas, and lava that raced down the mountain at 250 mph. At 3,600°F, it instantly vaporized everything in its path; 30,000 people were killed in two minutes.

The **Cyparis Express,** a small tourist train, will take you around to the main sights with running narrative (in French) for an hour Monday through Saturday, starting at 11 am, with reservations (☎ *0596/55–50– 92, 0696/81–88–70*) for €12.

An Office du Tourisme is on the *moderne* seafront promenade. Stroll the main streets and check the blackboards at the sidewalk cafés before deciding where to lunch. At night some places have live music. Like stage sets for a dramatic opera, there are the ruins of the island's first church (built in 1640), the imposing theater, and the toppled statues. This city, situated on its naturally beautiful harbor and with its narrow, winding streets, has the feel of a European seaside hill town. With every footstep, you touch a page of history. Although many of the historic buildings need work, stark modernism has not invaded this burg.

**Fodor's**Choice ★
**Depaz Distillery.** An excursion to Depaz Distillery is one of the best things to do on the island. Established in 1651, it sits at the foot of the volcano. After a devastating eruption in 1902, the fields of blue cane were replanted, and in time, the rum-making began all over again. A self-guided tour includes the workers' gingerbread cottages. The tasting room sells its rums, including golden and aged rum, and liqueurs made from orange, ginger, and basil, among other flavors, that can enhance your cooking. Unfortunately, the plantation's great house, or château, is still closed to the public. Allow time and make a reservation for Depaz's restaurant, **Le Moulin a Canne** (0596/69–80–44). Open only for lunch—even on Sunday when the distillery is closed, it has the views, the service, and flavorful creole specialties as well as some French classics on the menu, plus—you guessed it—Depaz rum to wash it down. It's "on the house." ■ TIP→ **Shutters are drawn at the tasting room and the staff leaves at exactly 5 pm (or 4 on Saturday), so plan to be there at least an hour before.** ⊠ *Mont Pelée Plantation, St-Pierre* ☎ *0596/78–13–14* ⊕ *www.depazrhum.com* ✉ *Distillery free.*

FAMILY
**Musée Vulcanologique Frank Perret.** For those interested in Mont Pelée's eruption of 1902, the Musée Vulcanologique Frank Perret is a must. It was established in 1933 by Frank Perret, a noted American volcanologist. Small but fascinating and insightful, the museum houses photographs of the old town before and after the eruption, documents, and a number of relics—some gruesome—excavated from the ashy ruins, including molten glass, melted iron, the church bell, and contorted clocks stopped at 8 am. The 30-minute film is a good way to begin. An English-speaking guide is often available and may tell you that the next lava flow is expected within 50 years. (No wonder the price of real estate in St. Pierre is among the lowest on the island.) The museum requires a renovation, and some signage has become difficult to read. ⊠ *Rue Victor Hugo (D10) at rue du Theatre, St-Pierre* ☎ *0596/78–15–16* ✉ *€5.*

**Le Centre de Découverte des Sciences de la Terre.** If you want to know more about volcanoes, earthquakes, and hurricanes, check out Le Centre de Découverte des Sciences de la Terre. Housed in a sleek building that looks like a dramatic white box, this earth-science museum has high-tech exhibits and interesting films. Watch the documentary on the volcanoes in the Antilles, highlighting the eruption of the nearby Mont Pelée. Le Centre has fascinating summer programs on Wednesday on dance, food, and ecotourism. ■ TIP→ **The Depaz Distillery is nearby, and it's easy to visit both on the same day.** ⊠ *Habitation Perinelle, Quartier la Galere, St-Pierre* ☎ *0596/52–82–42* ⊕ *cdst.e-monsite.com* ✉ *€5.*

## BEACHES

**Anse-Mitan.** There are often yachts moored offshore in these calm waters. This long stretch of beach can be particularly fun on Sunday. Small, family-owned seaside restaurants are half-hidden among palm trees and are footsteps from the lapping waves. Nearly all offer grilled lobster and some form of music on weekends, perhaps a zouk band. Inexpensive waterfront hotels line the clean, golden beach, which has excellent snorkeling just offshore. Chaise longues are available for rent from hotels, and there are also usually vendors on weekends. The abandoned public housing visible from the beach has finally been razed. When you get to Pointe du Bout, take a left at the yellow office of Budget Rent-A-Car, then the next left up a hill, and park near the little white church. **Amenities:** food and drink. **Best for:** partiers; snorkeling; swimming; walking. ⊠ *Pointe du Bout, Les Trois-Îlets.*

FAMILY **Les Salines.** A short drive south of Ste-Anne brings you to a mile-long (1½-km-long) cove lined with soft white sand and coconut palms. The beach is awash with families and children during holidays and on weekends, but quiet during the week. The far end—away from the makeshift souvenir shops—is most appealing. The calm waters are safe for swimming, even for the kids. You can snorkel, but it's not that memorable. Food vendors roam the sand, and there are also pizza stands and simple seafood restaurants. From Le Marin, take the coastal road toward Ste-Anne. You will see signs for Les Salines. If you see the sign for Pointe du Marin, you have gone too far. **Amenities:** food and drink; parking; showers; toilets. **Best for:** partiers; swimming; walking. ⊠ *Ste-Anne.*

FAMILY **Pointe du Bout.** The beaches here are small, man-made, and lined with resorts. Each little strip is associated with its resident hotel, and security guards and closed gates make access difficult. However, if you take a left across from the main pedestrian entrance to the marina—after the taxi stand—then go left again, you will reach the beach for Hotel Bakoua, which has especially nice facilities and several options for lunch and drinks. If things are quiet—particularly during the week—one of the beach boys may rent you a chaise; otherwise, just plop your beach towel down, face forward, and enjoy the delightful view of the Fort-de-France skyline. The water is dead calm and quite shallow, but it eventually drops off if you swim out a bit. **Amenities:** food and drink; showers. **Best for:** snorkeling; sunset; swimming. ⊠ *Pointe du Bout, Les Trois-Îlets.*

## SHOPPING

French fragrances; designer clothes, scarves, and sunglasses; fine china and crystal; leather goods; wine (inexpensive at supermarkets); and liquor are all good buys in duty-free Fort-de-France. Purchases are further sweetened by the 20% discount on luxury items when paid for with certain credit cards. Among the items produced on the island, look for *bijoux creole* (local jewelry, such as hoop earrings and heavy bead necklaces); white, dark, and aged rum; and handcrafted straw goods, pottery, and tapestries.

The striking 215,000-square-foot Cour Perrinon Mall in Fort-de-France, bordered by rue Perrinon, houses a Carrefour supermarket, a bookstore, perfume shops, designer boutiques, a French bakery, and a café–brasserie. The area around the cathedral in Fort-de-France has a number of small shops that carry luxury goods. Of particular note are the shops on rue Victor Hugo, rue Moreau de Jones, rue Antoine

Siger, and rue Lamartine. Ongoing efforts to be more inviting to the North American market—with particular emphasis on offering English-language classes to staff—have dozens of shops participating. The **Galleries Lafayette** department store on rue Schoelcher in downtown Fort-de-France sells everything from perfume to pâté. On the outskirts of Fort-de-France, the **Centre Commercial de Cluny, Centre Commercial de Dillon, Centre Commercial de Bellevue,** and **Centre Commercial la Rond Point** are among the major shopping malls.

## ACTIVITIES

### GOLF

**Golf de l'Impératrice Josephine** (*Martinique Golf and Country Club*). Although it's named in honor of Empress Joséphine Napoléon, this Robert Trent Jones Sr. course is completely American in design, with an English-speaking pro, a pro shop, a bar, and an especially good restaurant. The best hole on the course may just be the par-five 15th. Sandwiched between two good par-3s, the 15th plays to an island fairway and then to a green situated by the shore. Try not to be mesmerized by the turquoise waters. (You can finish your visit here with foie gras torchon or a full meal at Restaurant Le Golf.) The club offers special greens fees to cruise-ship passengers. Club trolleys (called "chariots") are €6 for 18 holes, €4 for 9. There are no caddies. ⌂ *Quartier la Pagerie, Les Trois-Îlets* ☎ *0596/61–05–24* 💲 *€15 for 9 holes, €22.50 for 18; €25 for cart, 9 holes; €40 for cart, 18 holes* 🏌 *18 holes, 6640 yards, par 71.*

### HIKING

**Parc Naturel Régional de la Martinique.** Two-thirds of Martinique is designated as protected land. Trails, all 31 of them, are well marked and maintained. At the beginning of each, a notice is posted advising on the level of difficulty, the duration of a hike, and any interesting facts. The Parc Naturel Régional de la Martinique organizes inexpensive guided excursions year-round. If there have been heavy rains, though, give it up. The tangle of ferns, bamboo trees, and vines is dramatic, but during rainy season, the wet, muddy trails will temper your enthusiasm. ⌂ *9 bd. Général de Gaulle, Fort-de-France* ☎ *0596/64–45–64 communications department.*

### HORSEBACK RIDING

Horseback-riding excursions can traverse scenic beaches, palm-shaded forests, sugarcane fields, and a variety of other tropical landscapes. Trained guides often include running commentaries on the history, flora, and fauna of the island.

FAMILY **Ranch Jack.** Ranch Jack has a large stable of some 30 horses. Its trail rides (English-style) cross some beautiful country for 90 minutes to two hours; half-day excursions (inquire about transfers from nearby hotels) go through the fields and forests to the beach. Short rides ranging from an hour are also available. The company has a wonderful program to introduce kids ages three to seven to horses. Online comments reflect riders' satisfaction with the professionalism of the stable and the beautiful acreage they traverse. ⌂ *Morne habitué,*

*Les Trois-Îlets* ☎ *0596/68–37–69, 0696/92–26–58* ✎ *ranch.jack@ wanadoo.fr* ✉ *From €31.*

## WHERE TO EAT

**$$** ✕ **Le Foyaal Bar & Brasserie.** This versatile brasserie on Fort-de-France's
**BISTRO** main drag offers a large open dining space and seating on a covered terrace with a view of the sea, though traffic, noise, and dust make eating inside a safer bet. For a light lunch you could have a savory crepe and a small salad, smoked marlin, fried Camembert, or a perfect burger. If you want to go with something more substantial, and creative, there's local octopus or duck in a citrusy sauce. Some waiters speak English, and most are fun and helpful. ■ **TIP→ Foyaal serves from 7 am into the late night, 1:30 am, even on Sundays when most of the town is closed up.** Try sitting at the bar; it's fun and for a lot of French expats, this is their "Cheers." Upstairs at Le Césaire is a more refined (and expensive) dining experience. ⑤ *Average main: €20* ⊠ *Bord de Mer, 38 rue de Ernest Proges, Fort-de-France* ☎ *0596/63–00–38.*

# MONTEGO BAY, JAMAICA

By Richard Sitler

Today many explorations of MoBay are conducted from a reclining chair—frothy drink in hand—on Doctor's Cave Beach. As home of Jamaica's busiest cruise pier and the north-shore airport, Montego Bay—or Mo'Bay—is the first taste most visitors have of the island. Travelers from around the world come and go in this bustling community, which ranks as Jamaica's second-largest city. The name Montego is derived from *manteca* (lard in Spanish). The Spanish first named this Bahía de Manteca, or Lard Bay, since they once shipped hogs from this port city. Jamaican tourism began here in 1924, when the first resort opened at Doctor's Cave Beach so that health-seekers could "take the waters." If you can pull yourself away from the water's edge and brush the sand off your toes, you can find some very interesting colonial sights in the surrounding area.

### ESSENTIALS

#### CURRENCY

The Jamaican dollar, but U.S. dollars are widely accepted.

#### TELEPHONE

Public telephones (and faxes) are at the communications center at the Montego Bay Cruise Terminal. Travelers also find public phones in major Montego Bay malls, such as the City Centre Shopping Mall. Some U.S. phone companies won't permit credit-card calls to be placed from Jamaica because they've been victims of fraud, so collect calls are often the top option. GSM cell phones equipped with tri-band or worldroaming service will find coverage throughout the Montego Bay region.

#### COMING ASHORE

Ships dock at the Montego Cruise Terminal, operated by the Port Authority of Jamaica. West of Montego Bay, the cruise terminal has five berths and accommodates both cruise and cargo shipping. The terminal has shops, a communications center, a visitor information booth, and a taxi stand supervised by the Port Authority of Jamaica. The cruise port in Montego Bay is not within walking distance of the heart of town; however, there's one shopping center (the Freeport Shopping Centre) within walking distance of the docks. If you just want to visit a beach, then Doctor's Cave or the Cornwall Bathing Beach, both public beaches, are very good nearby alternatives, and they are right in town.

From the Montego Cruise Terminal both taxis and shuttle buses take passengers downtown. Taxi service is about $7 each way to downtown. Expect to pay $5 per person each way by shuttle bus to the two crafts markets, the City Centre Shopping Mall, Margaritaville, or Doctor's Cave Beach. A day pass for the shuttle bus is US$17 and allows passengers to get on and off as they wish. Jamaica is one place in the Caribbean where it's usually to your advantage to take an organized shore excursion offered by your ship unless you just want to do a bit of shopping in town. Private taxis and other transportation providers aren't particularly cheap, and a full-day tour for a small group will run $150 to $180; however, road conditions and travel time have improved significantly with the completion of the North Coast Highway.

If you take a private taxi, you should know that rates are per car, not per passenger. All licensed and properly insured taxis display red Public Passenger Vehicle (PPV) license plates. Licensed minivans also bear the red PPV plates. If you hire a taxi driver as a tour guide, be sure to agree on a price before the vehicle is put into gear. Car-rental fees in Jamaica include the cost of insurance. It is not difficult to rent a car, but driving in Jamaica is done on the left side of the road, and it can take a little getting used to.

---

## BEST BETS

■ **Doctor's Cave Beach.** This public beach club is right in the heart of Montego Bay.

■ **Dunn's River Falls.** A visit to the falls is touristy but still exhilarating.

■ **Martha Brae Rafting.** A slow rafting trip down the river is relaxing and very enjoyable.

■ **Shopping.** Mo'Bay has several good shopping centers, as well as bustling craft markets.

■ **Rose Hall.** The island's most visited great house is a peek back into the days of the plantations and its owner, the "white witch" Annie Palmer.

**4**

---

## EXPLORING

Fodor's Choice ★ **Dunn's River Falls.** A popular natural attraction that is an eye-catching sight: 600 feet of cold, clear mountain water splashing over a series of stone steps to the Caribbean Sea. The best way to enjoy the falls is to climb the slippery steps in a swimsuit (there are changing rooms at the entrance), as you take the hand of the person ahead of you. After the climb, you exit through a crowded market, another reminder that this is one of Jamaica's top tourist attractions. ■ TIP→ **Always climb with a licensed guide at Dunn's River Falls, who can be hired inside the gates, not outside (ask at the ticket window). Freelance guides might be a**

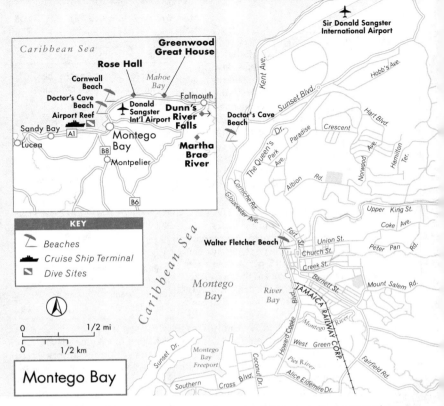

### Montego Bay

**KEY**

- ✦ Beaches
- ⛴ Cruise Ship Terminal
- ◤ Dive Sites

0 ——— 1/2 mi
0 ——— 1/2 km

little cheaper, but the experienced guides can tell you just where to plant each footstep—helping you prevent a fall. ✉ *Off Rte. A1, between St. Ann's Bay and Ocho Rios, Ocho Rios* ☎ *876/974–2857* ⊕ *www. dunnsriverfallsja.com* ✉ *$20.*

**Greenwood Great House.** Unlike Rose Hall, this historic great house has no spooky legend to titillate, but it's much better than Rose Hall at evoking life on a sugar plantation. The Barrett family, from whom the English poet Elizabeth Barrett Browning descended, once owned all the land from Rose Hall to Falmouth; on their vast holdings they built this and several other great houses. (The poet's father, Edward Moulton Barrett, "the Tyrant of Wimpole Street," was born at nearby Cinnamon Hill, later the estate of country singer Johnny Cash.) Highlights of Greenwood include oil paintings of the Barretts, china made for the family by Wedgwood, a library filled with rare books from as early as 1697, fine antique furniture, and a collection of exotic musical instruments. There's a pub on-site as well. It's 15 miles (24 km) east of Montego Bay. ✉ *435 Belgrade Ave., Montego Bay* ☎ *876/631–4701* ⊕ *www.greenwoodgreathouse.com* ✉ *$20.*

**Martha Brae River.** This gentle waterway about 25 miles (40 km) southeast of Montego Bay takes its name from an Arawak woman who killed herself because she refused to reveal the whereabouts of a local gold mine. According to legend, she agreed to take her Spanish inquisitors there and, on reaching the river, used magic to change its course, drowning herself and the greedy Spaniards with her. Her *duppy* (ghost) is said to guard the mine's entrance. Rafting on this river is a very popular activity—many operators are on hand to take you for a glide downstream. ⊠ *Trelawny.*

**Fodors** Choice
★
**Rose Hall.** In the 1700s it may well have been one of the greatest great houses in the West Indies. Today it's popular less for its architecture than for the legend surrounding its second mistress, Annie Palmer. As the story goes, she was born in 1802 in England, but when she was 10, her family moved to Haiti. Soon after, her parents died of yellow fever. Adopted by a Haitian voodoo priestess, Annie became skilled in the practice of witchcraft. She moved to Jamaica, married, and became mistress of Rose Hall, an enormous plantation spanning 6,600 acres with more than 2,000 slaves. You can take a spooky nighttime tour of the property—recommended if you're up for a scare—and then have a drink at the White Witch pub, in the great house's cellar. The house is 15 miles (24 km) east of Montego Bay. ⊠ *North Coast Hwy., St. James* ☎ *876/953–2323* ⊕ *www.rosehall.com* ✉ *$20.*

## BEACHES

FAMILY
**Doctor's Cave Bathing Club.** Located along Montego Bay's touristy Hip Strip, this famous beach first gained notoriety for waters said to have healing powers. It's a popular beach with a perpetual spring-break feel. The clubhouse has changing rooms, showers, a gift shop, and restaurant. You can rent beach chairs, pool floats, and umbrellas. Its location within the Montego Bay Marine Park—with protected coral reefs and plenty of marine life—makes it good for snorkeling and glass-bottom boat rides. Chairs, umbrellas, and pool floats are available to rent for $6 per item for the day. **Amenities:** food and drink; lifeguards; parking (fee); showers; toilets; water sports. **Best for:** partiers; snorkeling; sunset; swimming. ⊠ *Gloucester Ave., Montego Bay* ☎ *876/952–2566* ⊕ *www.doctorscavebathingclub.com* ✉ *$6.*

FAMILY
**Walter Fletcher Beach.** Although not as pretty as Doctor's Cave Beach, this strand is home to Aquasol Theme Park, which offers a large beach (with lifeguards and security personnel) and for an additional cost, glass-bottom boats, snorkeling, go-kart racing, a skating rink at night, and a bar and restaurant. Near the center of town, the beach has unusually fine swimming; the calm waters make it good for children. **Amenities:** food and drink; lifeguards; parking (no fee); showers; toilets; water sports. **Best for:** partiers; snorkeling; sunset; swimming. ⊠ *Gloucester Ave., Montego Bay* ☎ *876/979–9447* ✉ *$5.*

## SHOPPING

Jamaican artisans express themselves in silk-screening, wood carvings, resort wear, hand-loomed fabrics, and paintings. Jamaican rum makes a great gift, as do Tia Maria (the famous coffee liqueur) and Blue Mountain coffee. Wood carvings are one of the top purchases; the finest carvings are made from the Jamaican national tree, lignum vitae, or tree of life, a dense wood that talented carvers transform into dolphins, heads, or fish. Bargaining is expected with crafts vendors.

**Half Moon Shopping Village.** The bright yellow buildings at Half Moon hotel contain some of the finest and most expensive wares money can buy, as well as more affordable boutiques, a post office, bank, and restaurants. ⊠ *Half Moon, North Coast Hwy., 7 miles (11 km) east of Montego Bay, Montego Bay* ☎ *876/953–2211* ⊕ *www.halfmoon.com.*

## ACTIVITIES

### GOLF

Golfers appreciate both the beauty and the challenges offered by Jamaica's courses. Caddies are almost always mandatory throughout the island and are paid by the round, the rate varying by the course. Cart rentals are available at most courses. Some of the best courses in the country are found near MoBay.

**Half Moon Golf Course.** Swaying palms, abundant bunkering, and large greens greet you on this flat Robert Trent Jones Sr.–designed course, home of the Jamaica Open. The course was renovated in 2005 by Jones protégé Roger Rulewich to better position the hazards for today's longer hitters. The Half Moon Golf Academy offers one-day sessions, multiday retreats, and hour-long private sessions. ⊠ *Half Moon, North Coast Hwy., 7 miles (11 km) east of Montego Bay, Montego Bay* ☎ *876/953–2211* ⊕ *www.halfmoongolf.com* ⌨ *Nonguests $181 for 18 holes, $118 for 9 holes* 🏌 *18 holes, 7141 yards, par 72.*

**White Witch Golf Course.** One of the nicest courses in Montego Bay, if not Jamaica, is the White Witch course, named for Annie Palmer, the wicked 19th-century plantation mistress, whose great house looms above the course. The course was designed by Robert von Hagge and Rick Baril. Annie's Revenge is one of five tournaments hosted at the course that occupies mountainous terrain high above the sea and features bold, attractive bunkering and panoramic views. Legend has it that Annie still haunts the area, but not your golf game. Rental clubs are available for $65. Prebooking is recommended. ⊠ *Rose Hall Main Rd., Rose Hall, St. James* ☎ *876/632–7444* ⊕ *www.whitewitchgolf.com* ⌨ *$169* 🏌 *18 holes, 6758 yards, par 71.*

### RIVER RAFTING

Jamaica's many rivers mean a multitude of freshwater experiences, from mild to wild. The island's first tourist activity off the beaches was relaxing rafting trips aboard bamboo rafts poled by local boatmen, which originated on the **Rio Grande.** Jamaicans had long used rafts to transport bananas downriver. Decades ago actor and local resident Errol Flynn saw the rafts and thought they'd make a good tourist attraction. Today the slow rides are a favorite with romantic travelers and anyone looking to get off the beach for a few hours. The popularity of the Rio Grande's trips spawned similar trips down the **Martha Brae River,** about 25 miles (38 km) from Mo'Bay. Near Ocho Rios, the **Great River** has lazy river rafting as well as energetic kayaking.

**Jamaica Tours Limited.** This big tour company conducts raft trips down the Martha Brae, approximately 25 miles (38 km) east of Mo'Bay; the excursion can include lunch if requested. Price depends on number of people and pickup location. Hotel tour desks can book it. ✉ *Providence Dr., Montego Bay* ☎ *876/953–3700* ⊕ *www.jamaicatoursltd.com.*

**River Raft Ltd.** This company leads 1½-hour trips down the Martha Brae River, about 25 miles (38 km) from most Mo'Bay hotels. ☎ *876/940–7018, 876/952–0889, 876/952–0889* ⊕ *www.jamaicarafting.com* ✉ *$60.*

## WHERE TO EAT

**$$** ✗ **Biggs BBQ Restaurant & Bar.** On the Hip Strip, this authentic barbecue
BARBECUE joint, opened by a chef who got his start cooking barbecue in St. Louis, Missouri, features pulled pork, corn bread, mac-and-cheese, baked beans, and, of course, good ol' Memphis-style ribs—a taste of Americana in paradise. Diners have the option of sitting outside for amazing views of the Montego Bay coastline or inside around wooden tables draped in checkered fabric. Drinks like the must-try Bluegrass Lemonade, a heady mix of house-made lemonade and "bluebeery" vodka, are served in traditional jars, and meals are served in half-pound and one-pound portions. ⑤ *Average main: $15* ✉ *Gloucester Ave., Montego Bay* ☎ *876/952–9488* ⊕ *www.biggsbbqmobay.com.*

**$** ✗ **Scotchies.** Many call this open-air jerk eatery the best in Jamaica, but
JAMAICAN the Scotchies Too branch in Ocho Rios makes it a tough call. Both serve genuine jerk—chicken, pork, fish, sausage, and more—with fiery sauce and delectable side dishes including festival (bread similar to a hush puppy) and rice and peas. This restaurant is a favorite with Montego Bay residents and tourists; you're likely to see a slap-the-table game of dominoes. ⑤ *Average main: $10* ✉ *North Coast Hwy., across from Holiday Inn SunSpree, 10 miles (16 km) east of Montego Bay, Montego Bay* ☎ *876/794–9457.*

# NASSAU, BAHAMAS

By Jessica Robertson

Nassau, the capital of the Bahamas, has witnessed Spanish invasions and hosted pirates, who made it their headquarters for raids along the Spanish Main. The heritage of old Nassau blends the Southern charm of British loyalists from the Carolinas, the African tribal traditions of freed slaves, and a bawdy history of blockade-running during the Civil War and rum-running in the Roaring 1920s. The sheltered harbor bustles with cruise-ship hubbub, while a block away, broad, shop-lined Bay Street is alive with commercial activity. Over it all is a subtle layer of civility and sophistication, derived from three centuries of British rule. Nassau's charm, however, is often lost in its commercialism. There's excellent shopping, but if you look past the duty-free shops you'll also find sights of historical significance that are worth seeing.

## ESSENTIALS

### CURRENCY

The Bahamian dollar, which is on par with U.S. dollar, but U.S. dollars are widely accepted.

### TELEPHONE

Pay phones accept Bahamas Direct Prepaid cards purchased from BTC at vending machines, stores, and BTC offices. You can use these cards to call within the country or to the United States. Although most U.S. cell phones work in the Bahamas, the roaming coast can be very high, so check with your provider in advance.

### COMING ASHORE

Cruise ships dock at one of three piers on Prince George Wharf. Taxi drivers who meet the ships may offer you a $2 "ride into town," but the historic government buildings and duty-free shops lie just steps from the dock area. As you leave the pier, look for a tall pink tower—diagonally across from here is the tourist information office. Stop in for maps of the island and downtown Nassau. On most days you can join a one-hour walking tour ($10 per person) conducted by a well-trained guide. Tours generally start every hour on the hour from 10 am to 4 pm; confirm the day's schedule in the office. Just outside, an ATM dispenses U.S. dollars.

As you disembark from your ship, you will find a row of taxis and air-conditioned limousines. Fares are fixed by the government by zones. Unless you plan to jump all over the island, taxis are the most convenient way to get around. The fare is $9 plus $2 bridge toll between downtown Nassau and Paradise Island, $20 from Cable Beach to Paradise Island (plus $1 toll), and $18 from Cable Beach to Nassau. Fares are for two passengers; each additional passenger is $3. It's customary to tip taxi drivers 15%.

Water taxis travel between Prince George Wharf and Paradise Island during daylight hours at half-hour intervals. The one-way cost is $3 per person, and the trip takes 12 minutes.

### BEST BETS

■ **Ardastra Gardens.** Flocks of flamingos, the country's national bird, "march" in three shows daily (you can mingle with the flamboyant pink stars afterward).

■ **Atlantis.** Though very costly, the water park here is a must for families.

■ **Shopping.** To many, shopping is one of Nassau's great delights.

■ **Junkanoo Beach.** Head to this beach (aka Long Wharf Beach) and sit in the shade of a coconut palm (it's a 10-minute walk from the duty-free shops on Bay Street).

## EXPLORING

Shops angle for tourist dollars with fine imported goods at duty-free prices, yet you will find a handful of stores overflowing with authentic Bahamian crafts, foods, and other delights. Most of Nassau's historic sites are centered on downtown.

With its thoroughly revitalized downtown—the revamped British Colonial Hilton lead the way—Nassau is recapturing some of its glamour. Nevertheless, modern influence is apparent: fancy restaurants, suave

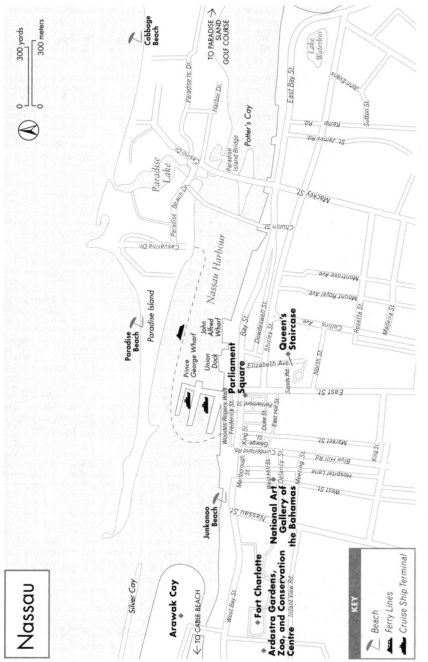

# Nassau

**KEY**

Beach
Ferry Lines
Cruise Ship Terminal

clubs, and trendy coffeehouses have popped up everywhere. This trend comes partly in response to the burgeoning upper-crust crowds that now supplement the spring-breakers and cruise passengers who have traditionally flocked to Nassau.

Today the seedy air of the town's not-so-distant past is almost unrecognizable. Petty crime is no greater than in other towns of this size, and the streets not only look cleaner but feel safer. You can still find a wild club or a rowdy bar, but you can also sip cappuccino while viewing contemporary Bahamian art or dine by candlelight beneath prints of old Nassau, serenaded by soft, island-inspired calypso music.

**Arawak Cay.** Known to Nassau residents as "The Fish Fry," Arawak Cay is one of the best places to knock back a Kalik beer, chat with locals, watch or join in a fast-paced game of dominoes, or sample traditional Bahamian fare. You can get small dishes such as conch fritters or full meals at one of the pastel-color waterside shacks. Order a fried snapper served up with a sweet homemade roll, or fresh conch salad (a spicy mixture of chopped conch—just watching the expert chopping is a show as good as any in town—mixed with diced onions, cucumbers, tomatoes, and hot peppers in a lime marinade). The two-story Twin Brothers and Goldie's Enterprises are two of the most popular places. Try their fried "cracked conch" and Goldie's famous Sky Juice (a sweet but potent gin, coconut-water, and sweet-milk concoction sprinkled with nutmeg). Local fairs and craft shows are often held in the adjacent field. ⊠ *W. Bay St. and Chippingham Rd., Nassau.*

FAMILY **Ardastra Gardens, Zoo, and Conservation Centre.** Marching flamingos? These national birds give a parading performance at Ardastra daily at 10:30, 2:15, and 4 pm. The brilliant pink birds are a delight—especially for children, who can walk among the flamingos after the show. The zoo, with more than 5 acres of tropical greenery and ponds, also has an aviary of rare tropical birds including the bright-green Bahama parrot, native Bahamian creatures such as rock iguanas and the little (and harmless) Bahamian boa constrictors, and a global collection of small animals. ⊠ *Chippingham Rd., south of W. Bay St., Nassau* ☎ *242/323–5806* ⊕ *www.ardastra.com* ☞ *$18.*

FAMILY **Fort Charlotte.** Built in 1788, this imposing fort comes complete with a waterless moat, drawbridge, ramparts, and a dungeon, where children love to see the torture device where prisoners were "stretched." Young local guides bring the fort to life. (Tips are expected.) Lord Dunmore, who built it, named the massive structure in honor of George III's wife. The fort and its surrounding 100 acres offer a wonderful view of the cricket grounds, the beach, and the ocean beyond. On Wednesday and Friday enjoy fully regaled actors reenacting life as it was in the Bahamas in the 18th and 19th centuries. An historic military parade and canon firing takes place daily at noon. ⊠ *W. Bay St. at Chippingham Rd., Nassau* ✛ *Opposite Arawak Cay* ☞ *$5* ⊘ *Closed Christmas Day.*

Fodor's Choice ★ **National Art Gallery of the Bahamas.** Opened in 2003, the museum houses the works of esteemed Bahamian artists such as Max Taylor, Amos Ferguson, Brent Malone, John Cox, and Antonius Roberts. The glorious Italianate-colonial mansion, built in 1860 and restored in the 1990s, has double-tiered verandas with elegant columns. It was the residence of Sir William Doyle, the first chief justice of the Bahamas. Don't miss the museum's gift shop, where you'll find books about the Bahamas as well as Bahamian quilts, prints, ceramics, jewelry, and crafts. ⊠ *West and W. Hill Sts., across from St. Francis Xavier Cathedral, Nassau* 🕾 *242/328–5800* ⊕ *www.nagb.org.bs* 🎟 *$10.*

**Parliament Square.** Nassau is the seat of the national government. The Bahamian Parliament comprises two houses—a 16-member Senate (Upper House) and a 38-member House of Assembly (Lower House). If the House is in session, sit in to watch lawmakers debate. Parliament Square's pink, colonnaded government buildings were constructed in the late 1700s and early 1800s by Loyalists who came to the Bahamas from North Carolina. The square is dominated by a statue of a slim young Queen Victoria that was erected on her birthday, May 24, in 1905. ⊠ *Bay St., Nassau* 🕾 *242/322–2041* 🎟 *Free.*

**Queen's Staircase.** A popular early-morning exercise regime for locals, the "66 Steps" (as Bahamians call them) are thought to have been carved out of a solid limestone cliff by slaves in the 1790s. The staircase was later named to honor Queen Victoria's reign. Pick up some souvenirs at the ad hoc straw market along the narrow road that leads to the site. ⊠ *Top of Elizabeth Ave. hill, south of Shirley St., Nassau.*

# BEACHES

New Providence is blessed with stretches of white sand studded with palm and sea grape trees. Some of the beaches are small and crescent-shape; others stretch for miles.

FAMILY

Fodor's Choice

★

**Cabbage Beach.** At this beach you'll find 3 miles of white sand lined with shady casuarina trees, sand dunes, and sun worshippers. This is the place to go to rent Jet Skis or get a bird's-eye view of Paradise Island while parasailing. Hair braiders and T-shirt vendors stroll the beach, and hotel guests crowd the areas surrounding the resorts, including Atlantis. For peace and quiet, stroll east. **Amenities:** food and drink; lifeguards; parking (fee); water sports. **Best for:** solitude; partiers; swimming; walking. ⊠ *Paradise Island.*

**Junkanoo Beach.** Right in downtown Nassau, this beach is spring-break central from late February through April. The man-made beach isn't the prettiest on the island, but it's conveniently located if you only have a few quick hours to catch a tan. Music is provided by bands, DJs, and guys with boom boxes; a growing number of bars keep the drinks flowing. **Amenities:** food and drink; parking (no fee); toilets; water sports. **Best for:** partiers; swimming. ⊠ *Immediately west of British Colonial Hilton, Nassau.*

# SHOPPING

Most of Nassau's shops are on Bay Street between Rawson Square and the British Colonial Hotel, and on the side streets leading off Bay Street. Some stores are popping up on the main shopping thoroughfare's eastern end and just west of the Cable Beach strip. Bargains abound between Bay Street and the waterfront. Upscale stores can also be found in Marina Village and the Crystal Court at Atlantis. You'll find duty-free prices—generally 25%–50% less than U.S. prices—on imported items such as crystal, linens, watches, cameras, jewelry, leather goods, and perfumes.

# ACTIVITIES

### FISHING

The waters here are generally smooth and alive with many species of game fish, which is one of the reasons why the Bahamas has more than 20 fishing tournaments open to visitors every year. A favorite spot just west of Nassau is the Tongue of the Ocean, so called because it looks like that part of the body when viewed from the air. The channel stretches for 100 miles. For boat rental, parties of two to six will pay $600 or so for a half-day, $1,600 for a full day.

**Charter Boat Association.** The Charter Boat Association has 15 boats available for fishing charters. Pickup is from Paradise Island Ferry Terminal or Nassau Harbour in front of the Straw Market. ☎ 242/393–3739.

**Chubasco Charters.** This charter company has four boats for deep-sea and light tackle sportfishing. Half- and full-day charters are available. Pickup is from Paradise Island Ferry Terminal or Nassau Harbour in front of the Straw Market. ☎ 242/324–3474 ⊕ www.chubascocharters. com.

### GOLF

**Ocean Club Golf Course.** Designed by Tom Weiskopf, the Ocean Club Golf Course is a championship course surrounded by the ocean on three sides, which means that the views are incredible, but the winds can get stiff. Call to check on current availability and up-to-date prices (those not staying at Atlantis or the One & Only Ocean Club can play at management's discretion, and at a higher rate). The course is open daily from 6 am to sunset. ⊠ One & Only Ocean Club, Paradise Island Dr., Paradise Island ☎ 242/363–6682 ⊕ oceanclub.oneandonlyresorts. com 🖾 $225–$295 for 18 holes (discounted after 1 pm); $70 club rentals ⅃. 18 holes, 6805 yards, par 72.

# WHERE TO EAT

$$ ✕ **The Green Parrot.** Two locations—Green Parrot Harbourfront and
AMERICAN Green Parrot Hurricane Hole—mean you get incomparable views of Nassau Harbour and a fresh breeze, whichever way the wind is blowing. The large burgers are a favorite at these casual, all-outdoor restaurants and bars. The menu includes burgers, wraps, quesadillas, and other simple but tasty dishes. The conch po'boy is a new favorite. The weekday happy hour from 5 to 9 and local music on Thursday, Saturday, and Sunday nights draw a lively local crowd. 🖺 Average main: $20 ⊠ E. Bay St., west of bridges to Paradise Island, Nassau ☎ 242/322–9248 ⊕ greenparrotbar.com.

**$$** ✕ **Lukka Kairi.** Lukka Kairi means "people of the Islands," and at this hot
BAHAMIAN new restaurant you can experience the food, live music, and hospital-
**Fodor's** Choice ity the Bahamian people are known for. The tapas-style menu lets you
★ sample a variety of traditional Bahamian dishes with a twist. The crispy
broccoli is a surprising favorite, and the conch fritters are among the
best around. The long bar serves up local libations until midnight—Sky
Juice with bits of toasted coconut is a must try. If you get tired of the
stunning view of Nassau Harbour, take in the larger-than-life mural
depicting the history of the Bahamas. ⑤ *Average main: $22* ⊠ *Woodes
Rodgers Walk, Nassau* ☎ *242/427–8886* ⊕ *www.lukkakairi.com.*

**$$$** ✕ **The Poop Deck.** Just east of the bridges from Paradise Island and a
BAHAMIAN quick cab ride from the center of town is this favorite local haunt
that is always busy. The conch fritters are a great start. Fish is usually
served head to tail, so if you're squeamish, ask your waiter to have the
head cut off before it comes out on your plate. If you can't decide, opt
for the Tru-tru Bahamian sampler, a delicious assortment of seafood
appetizers followed by the fried Seafood Lover's Delight or the Grilled
Fisherman's Platter. Whatever you choose, the extensive wine list will
provide the perfect accompaniment. Save room for guava duff and a
calypso coffee spiked with secret ingredients. The restaurant's popularity has resulted in a second Poop Deck on Cable Beach's west end, but,
for residents, this is still the place. ⑤ *Average main: $35* ⊠ *E. Bay St. at
Nassau Yacht Haven Marina, Nassau* ⊹ *East of bridges from Paradise
Island* ☎ *242/393–8175* ⊕ *www.thepoopdeck.com.*

# NEVIS (CHARLESTOWN)

By Jordan
Simon

In 1493, when Columbus spied a cloud-crowned volcanic isle during
his second voyage to the New World, he named it Nieves—the Spanish
word for "snows"—because it reminded him of the peaks of the Pyr-
enees. Nevis rises from the water in an almost perfect cone, the tip of
its 3,232-foot central mountain hidden by clouds. Even less developed
than sister island St. Kitts—2 miles (3 km) away at their closest point,
Nevis is known for its long beaches with white and black sand, its lush
greenery, the charming if slightly dilapidated Georgian capital of
Charlestown, mountain hikes, and its restored sugar plantations that
now house charming inns. Even on a day trip Nevis feels relaxed and
quietly upscale. You might run into celebrities at the Four Seasons or
lunching at the beach bars on Pinney's, the showcase strand. Yet Nevi-
sians (not to mention the significant expat American and British presence) never put on airs, offering warm hospitality to all visitors.

## ESSENTIALS

### CURRENCY

The Eastern Caribbean dollar (EC$), but U.S. dollars are readily
accepted.

### TELEPHONE

Phone cards, which you can buy in denominations of $5, $10, and $20,
are handy for making local phone calls, calling other islands, and access-
ing U.S. direct lines. To make a local call, dial the seven-digit number.
To call Nevis from the United States, dial the area code 869, then access

code 465, 466, 468, or 469 and the local four-digit number.

## COMING ASHORE

Cruise ships dock in Charlestown harbor; all but the smallest ships bring passengers in by tender to the central downtown ferry dock. The pier leads smack onto Main Street, with shops and restaurants steps away. Taxi drivers often greet tenders, and there's also a stand a block away. Fares are fairly expensive, but a three-hour driving tour of Nevis costs about $80 for up to four people. Several restored greathouse plantation inns are known for their lunches; your driver can provide information and arrange drop-off and pickup. Before setting off in a taxi, be sure to clarify whether the rate quoted is in EC or U.S. dollars.

If your ship docks in St. Kitts, Nevis is a 30- to 45-minute ferry ride from Basseterre. You can tour Charlestown, the capital, in a half hour or so, but you'll need three to four hours to explore the entire island. Most cruise ships arrive in port around 8 am, and the ferry schedule (figure $18 round-trip) can be irregular, so many passengers sign up for a cruise-line-run shore excursion. If you travel independently, confirm departure times with the tourist office to be sure you'll make it back to your ship on time.

## EXPLORING

### CHARLESTOWN

About 1,200 of Nevis's 10,000 inhabitants live in the capital. If you arrive by ferry, as most people do, you'll walk smack onto Main Street from the pier. It's easy to imagine how tiny Charlestown, founded in 1660, must have looked in its heyday. The weathered buildings still have fanciful galleries, elaborate gingerbread fretwork, wooden shutters, and hanging plants. The stone building with the clock tower (circa 1825, but mostly rebuilt after a devastating 1873 fire) houses the courthouse and second-floor library (a cool respite on sultry days). The little park next to the library is Memorial Square, dedicated to the fallen of World Wars I and II. Down the street from the square, archaeologists have discovered the remains of a Jewish cemetery and synagogue (Nevis reputedly had the Caribbean's second-oldest congregation), but there's little to see.

**Alexander Hamilton Birthplace.** The Alexander Hamilton Birthplace, which contains the Hamilton Museum, sits on the waterfront. This bougainvillea-draped Georgian-style house is a reconstruction of what is believed to have been the American patriot's original home, built in 1680 and likely destroyed during a mid-19th-century earthquake. Born here in 1755, Hamilton moved to St. Croix when he was about

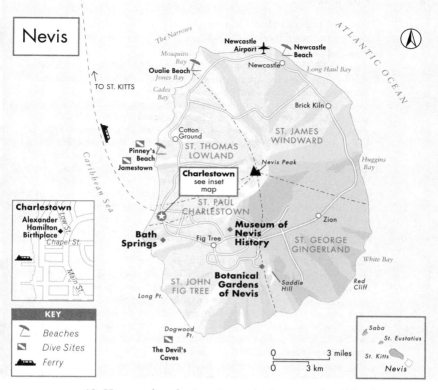

**Nevis**

THE NARROWS

Mosquito Bay

Oualie Beach
Jones Bay

↑
TO ST. KITTS

Cades Bay

Newcastle Airport ✈
Newcastle Beach
Newcastle
Long Haul Bay

ATLANTIC OCEAN

Caribbean Sea

Cotton Ground

Pinney's Beach
Jamestown

ST. THOMAS LOWLAND

Charlestown
see inset map

ST. JAMES WINDWARD

Nevis Peak

Brick Kiln ○

Huggins Bay

ST. PAUL CHARLESTOWN

Bath Springs

Fig Tree

**Museum of Nevis History**

Zion

ST. GEORGE GINGERLAND

White Bay

**Botanical Gardens of Nevis**

ST. JOHN FIG TREE

Long Pt.

Saddle Hill

Red Cliff

Dogwood Pt.

The Devil's Caves

0 ———— 3 miles
0 ———— 3 km

Saba
St. Eustatius
St. Kitts
Nevis

**Charlestown**

Alexander Hamilton Birthplace

Low St.

Chapel St.

Main St.

**KEY**

⅃ Beaches
◢ Dive Sites
🚢 Ferry

12. He moved to the American colonies to continue his education at 17; he became George Washington's Secretary of the Treasury and died in a duel with political rival Aaron Burr in 1804. The Nevis House of Assembly occupies the second floor; the museum downstairs contains Hamilton memorabilia, documents pertaining to the island's history, and displays on island geology, politics, architecture, culture, and cuisine. The gift shop is a wonderful source for historic maps, crafts, and books on Nevis. ✉ *Low St., Charlestown* ☎ *869/469–5786* ⊕ *www.nevis heritage.org, www.nevis-nhcs.org* 🎫 *$5, with admission to Museum of Nevisian History $7.*

## ELSEWHERE ON NEVIS

**Bath Springs.** The Caribbean's first hotel, the Bath Hotel, built by businessman John Huggins in 1778, was so popular in the 19th century that visitors, who included Samuel Taylor Coleridge, traveled months by ship to "take the waters" in the property's hot thermal springs. It suffered extensive hurricane and earthquake damage over the years and long languished in disrepair. Local volunteers have cleaned up the spring and built a stone pool and steps to enter the waters, though signs still caution that you bathe at your own risk, especially if you have heart problems. The development houses the Nevis Island Administration offices; there's still talk of adding massage huts, changing rooms, a restaurant, and a cultural/history center on the original hotel property. ⊠ *Charlestown* ✛ *Follow Main St. south from Charlestown.*

**Botanical Gardens of Nevis.** In addition to terraced gardens and arbors, this remarkable 7.8-acre site in the glowering shadow of Mt. Nevis has natural lagoons, streams, and waterfalls, superlative bronze mermaids, Buddhas, egrets and herons, and extravagant fountains. You can find a proper rose garden, sections devoted to orchids and bromeliads, cacti, and flowering trees and shrubs—even a bamboo garden. The entrance to the Rain Forest Conservatory—which attempts to include every conceivable Caribbean ecosystem and then some—duplicates an imposing Mayan temple. A splendid re-creation of a plantation-style great house contains the appealing Oasis in the Gardens Thai restaurant with sweeping sea views (and wonderfully inventive variations on classic cocktails utilizing local ingredients), and the upscale World Art & Antiques Gallery selling artworks, textiles, jewelry, and Indonesian teak furnishings sourced during the owners' world travels. ⊠ *Montpelier Estate* ☎ *869/469–3509* ⊕ *www.botanicalgardennevis.com* 🎟 *$13; $8 children 6–12.*

**Museum of Nevis History.** Purportedly this is the Western Hemisphere's largest collection of Lord Horatio Nelson memorabilia, including letters, documents, paintings, and even furniture from his flagship. Nelson was based in Antigua but came on military patrol to Nevis, where he met and eventually married Frances Nisbet, who lived on a 64-acre plantation here. Half the space is devoted to often-provocative displays on island life, from leading families to vernacular architecture to the adaptation of traditional African customs, from cuisine to Carnival. The shop is an excellent source for gifts, from homemade soaps to historical guides. ⊠ *Bath Rd., Charlestown* ☎ *869/469–0408* ⊕ *www.nevis-nhcs. org, www.nevisheritage.org* 🎟 *$5, with Hamilton Museum $7.*

## BEACHES

All beaches on Nevis are free to the public (the plantation inns cordon off "private" areas on Pinney's Beach for guests), but there are no changing facilities, so wear a swimsuit under your clothes.

**Oualie Beach.** South of Mosquito Bay and north of Cades and Jones Bays, this beige-sand beach lined with palms and sea grapes is where the folks at Oualie Beach Hotel can mix you a drink and fix you up with water-sports equipment. There's excellent snorkeling amid calm water and fantastic sunset views with St. Kitts silhouetted in the background. Several beach chairs and hammocks (free with lunch, $3 rental without) line the sand and the grassy "lawn" behind it. Oualie is at the island's northwest tip, approximately 3 miles (5 km) west of the airport. **Amenities:** food and drink; water sports. **Best for:** snorkeling; sunset. ⊠ *Oualie Beach.*

**Pinney's Beach.** The island's showpiece has soft golden sand on the calm Caribbean, lined with a magnificent grove of palm trees. The Four Seasons Resort is here, as are the plantation inns' beach clubs and casual beach bars such as Sunshine's, Chevy's, and the Lime (which morphs into the island's disco Friday nights). Beach chairs are gratis when you purchase a drink or lunch. Regrettably, the waters can be murky and filled with kelp if the weather has been inclement anywhere within a hundred miles, depending on the currents. **Amenities:** food and drink; water sports. **Best for:** swimming; walking. ⊠ *Pinney's Beach.*

## SHOPPING

Nevis is certainly not the place for a shopping spree, but there are some unusual and wonderful surprises, notably the island's pottery, hand-embroidered clothing, and dolls by Jeannie Rigby. Honey is another buzzing biz. Quentin Henderson, the amiable former head of the **Nevis Beekeeping Cooperative,** will even arrange trips by appointment to various hives for demonstrations of beekeeping procedures. Other than a few hotel boutiques and isolated galleries, virtually all shopping is concentrated on or just off Main Street in Charlestown. The lovely old stonework and wood floors of the waterfront Cotton Ginnery Complex make an appropriate setting for stalls of local artisans.

**CraftHouse.** This marvelous source for local specialties, from vetiver mats to leather moccasins, also has a smaller branch in the Cotton Ginnery. ⊠ *Pinney's Rd., Charlestown* ☎ *869/469–5505.*

**Nevis Handicraft Co-op Society.** This shop across from the tourist office offers works by local artisans (clothing, ceramic ware, woven goods) and locally produced honey, hot sauces, and jellies (try the guava and soursop). ⊠ *Main St., Charlestown* ☎ *869/469–1746.*

**Philatelic Bureau.** St. Kitts and Nevis are famous for their decorative, and sometimes valuable, stamps. Collectors will find real beauties here, including the butterfly, hummingbird, and marine-life series. ⊠ *Cotton Ginnery, opposite the tourist office, Charlestown* ☎ *869/469–0617.*

## ACTIVITIES

### GOLF

Fodor's Choice ★ **Four Seasons Golf Course.** The Robert Trent Jones Jr.–designed Four Seasons Golf Course is beautiful and impeccably maintained. The front 9 holes are fairly flat until hole 8, which climbs uphill after your tee shot. Most of the truly stunning views are along the back 9. The signature hole is the 15th, a 660-yard monster that encompasses a deep ravine; other holes include bridges, steep drops, rolling pitches, extremely tight and unforgiving fairways, sugar-mill ruins, and fierce doglegs. Attentive attendants canvas the course with beverage buggies, handing out chilled, peppermint-scented towels and preordered Cubanos that help test the wind. There are kids', twilight, and off-season discounts. ⊠ *Four Seasons Resort Nevis, Pinney's Beach* ☎ *869/469–1111* ⊕ *www.fourseasons.com/nevis* ⊠ *$160; rental clubs $50* ⏃ *18 holes, 6766 yards, par 72.*

### HIKING

The center of the island is Nevis Peak—also known as Mt. Nevis—which soars 3,232 feet and is flanked by Hurricane Hill on the north and Saddle Hill on the south. If you plan to scale Nevis Peak, a daylong affair, it's highly recommended that you go with a guide. Your hotel can arrange it (and a picnic lunch) for you. The 9-mile (15-km) **Upper Round Road Trail** was constructed in the late 1600s and cleared and restored by the Nevis Historical and Conservation Society. It connects the Golden Rock Plantation Inn, on the east side of the island, with Nisbet Plantation Beach Club, on the northern tip. The trail encompasses numerous vegetation zones, including pristine rain forest, and impressive plantation ruins. The original cobblestones, walls, and ruins are still evident in many places.

**Sunrise Tours.** Run by Lynell and Earla Liburd (and their son Kervin), Sunrise Tours offers a range of hiking trips, but their most popular is Devil's Copper, a rock configuration full of ghostly legends. Local people gave it its name because at one time the water was hot—a volcanic thermal stream. The area features pristine waterfalls and splendid bird-watching. They also do a Nevis village walk, a Hamilton Estate Walk, a Charlestown tour, an Amerindian walk along the wild southeast Atlantic coast, and trips to the rain forest and Nevis Peak. They love highlighting Nevisian heritage, explaining time-honored cooking techniques, the many uses of dried grasses, and medicinal plants. Hikes range from $25 to $40 per person, and you receive a certificate of achievement. ☎ *869/469–2758* ⊕ *www.nevisnaturetours.com.*

## WHERE TO EAT

**$$**
SEAFOOD
FAMILY
✗**Double Deuce.** Mark Roberts, the former chef at Montpelier, decided to chuck the "five-star lifestyle" and now co-owns this jammed, jamming bar just off Pinney's, which lures locals with fine, fairly priced fare and creative cocktails. The overgrown shack is plastered with sailing and fishing pictures, Balinese masks, fishnets, license plates, and wind chimes. Behind the cool mauve bar is a gleaming modern kitchen where Mark (and fun-loving firebrand partner Lyndeta) prepare sublime seafood he often catches himself (try the ginger garlic shrimp), as well as organic beef burgers, velvety pumpkin soup, inventive pastas, lip-smacking ribs, and some British pub standards. Stop by for free Wi-Fi and proper espresso, a game of pool, riotous karaoke on Thursdays, or Sunday bingo. ⑤ *Average main: US$18* ⊠ *Pinney's Beach* ☎ *869/469–2222* ⊕ *www.doubledeucenevis.com* ⊟ *No credit cards* ☉ *Closed Mon.* ⚁ *Reservations essential.*

**$$**
CARIBBEAN
✗**Sunshine's.** Everything about this shack overlooking (and spilling onto) the beach is larger than life, including the Rasta man Llewelyn "Sunshine" Caines himself. Flags and license plates from around the world reflect the international patrons (including an occasional movie or sports star wandering down from the Four Seasons). Picnic tables are splashed with bright sunrise-to-sunset colors; even the palm trees are painted, though "it gone upscaled," as locals say, with VIP cabanas. Fishermen cruise up with their catch—you might savor lobster rolls or snapper creole. Don't miss the lethal house specialty, Killer Bee rum punch. As Sunshine boasts, "One and you're stung, two, you're stunned, three, it's a knockout." ⑤ *Average main: US$18* ⊠ *Pinney's Beach* ☎ *869/469–5817* ⊕ *www.sunshinesnevis.com.*

# OCHO RIOS, JAMAICA

By Richard
Sitler

About 90 minutes east of Montego Bay lies Ocho Rios (often just "Ochi"), a lush destination that's favored by honeymooners for its tropical beauty. Often called the garden center of Jamaica, this community is perfumed by flowering hibiscus, bird of paradise, bougainvillea, and other tropical blooms year-round. Ocho Rios is a popular cruise port, and the destination where you'll find one of the island's most recognizable attractions: Dunn's River Falls, which invites travelers to climb in daisy-chain fashion, hand-in-hand behind a sure-footed guide. This spectacular waterfall is actually a series of falls that cascades from the mountains to the sea. That combination of hills, rivers, and sea also means many activities in the area, from seaside horseback rides to mountain biking and lazy river rafting.

> ### BEST BETS
>
> ■ **Chukka Caribbean.** Any of the great adventure tours here are sure to please.
>
> ■ **Dunn's River Falls.** A visit to the falls is touristy, but it's still exhilarating.
>
> ■ **Mystic Mountain.** Live out your *Cool Runnings* fantasies on the bobsled ride.
>
> ■ **Dolphin Cove at Treasure Reef.** Swim with a dolphin, stingray, or shark at this popular stop.
>
> ■ **Firefly.** The former home of playwright Noël Coward can be seen on a guided tour.

## ESSENTIALS

### CURRENCY

The Jamaican dollar, but the U.S. dollar is widely accepted.

### TELEPHONE

Public telephones are found at the communications center at the Ocho Rios Cruise Pier. Travelers also find public phones in major Ocho Rios malls. Some U.S. phone companies won't permit credit-card calls to be placed from Jamaica because they've been victims of fraud, so collect calls are often the top option. GSM cell phones equipped with tri-band or world-roaming service will find coverage throughout the Ocho Rios region.

### COMING ASHORE

Most cruise ships are able to dock at this port on Jamaica's North Coast, near Dunn's River Falls (a $10 taxi ride from the pier). Also less than 1 mile (2 km) from the Ocho Rios pier are Island Village (within walking distance), Taj Mahal Duty-Free Shopping Center, and the Ocean Village Shopping Center. If you're going anywhere else beyond Island Village, a taxi is recommended; expect to pay $10 for a taxi ride downtown. The pier, which includes a cruise terminal with the basic services and transportation, is also within easy walking distance of Turtle Beach.

Licensed taxis are available at the pier; expect to pay about $35 per hour for a guided taxi tour. Jamaica is one place in the Caribbean where it's usually to your advantage to take an organized shore excursion offered by your ship unless you just want to go to the beach or do

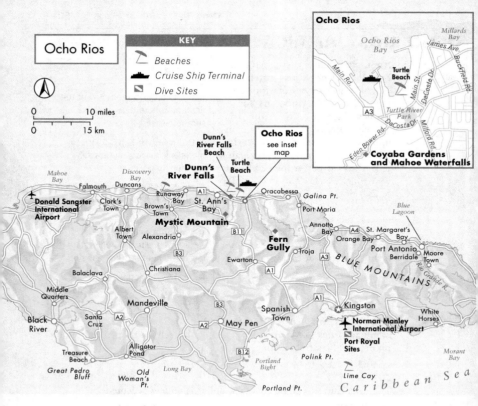

a bit of shopping in town. Car rental isn't recommended off the main highways in Jamaica because of high prices, bad roads, and aggressive drivers.

## EXPLORING

**Coyaba Gardens and Mahoe Waterfalls.** *Coyaba* is a word from the Arawaks, the original inhabitants of Jamaica, meaning paradise. Learn about Jamaican heritage and history at the museum, and then discover what makes Jamaica a natural paradise through a guided 45-minute tour through the lush 3-acre garden and also see the beautiful waterfalls and stunning views. The complex includes a crafts and gift shop and a snack bar, and Mahoe Falls is a good spot for a quiet picnic or swim. ⊠ *Shaw Park Estate, Shaw Park Ridge Rd., Ocho Rios* ☎ *876/974–6235* ⊕ *www.coyabagardens.com* ☞ *$10.*

Fodor's Choice ★ **Dunn's River Falls.** A popular natural attraction that is an eye-catching sight: 600 feet of cold, clear mountain water splashing over a series of stone steps to the Caribbean Sea. The best way to enjoy the falls is to climb the slippery steps in a swimsuit (there are changing rooms at the entrance), as you take the hand of the person ahead of you. After the climb, you exit through a crowded market, another reminder that this is one of Jamaica's top tourist attractions. ■ TIP➔ **Always climb with a** licensed guide at Dunn's River Falls, who can be hired inside the gates, not outside (ask at the ticket window). Freelance guides might be a little cheaper, but the experienced guides can tell you just where to plant each footstep—helping you prevent a fall. ⊠ *Off Rte. A1, between St. Ann's Bay and Ocho Rios, Ocho Rios* ☎ *876/974–2857* ⊕ *www. dunnsriverfallsja.com* ⊠ *$20.*

**Fern Gully.** Don't miss this natural canopy of vegetation, which sunlight barely penetrates. (Jamaica has the world's largest number of fern species—more than 570.) The winding road through the gully has been resurfaced, making for a smoother drive, and most tours of the area include a drive through this natural wonder. But to really experience it, stop and take a walk. The 3-mile (5-km) stretch of damp, fern-shaded forest includes many walking paths as well as numerous crafts vendors. ⊠ *Rte. A3, south of Ocho Rios.*

**Mystic Mountain.** This attraction covers 100 acres of mountainside rain forest near Dunn's River Falls. Visitors board the Rainforest Sky Explorer, a chairlift that soars through and over the pristine rain forest to the apex of Mystic Mountain. On top, there is a restaurant with spectacular views of Ocho Rios, arts-and-crafts shops, and the attraction's signature tours, the Rainforest Bobsled Jamaica ride and the Rainforest Zipline Canopy ride. Custom-designed bobsleds, inspired by Jamaica's Olympic bobsled team, run downhill on steel rails with speed controlled by the driver, using simple push-pull levers. Couples can run their bobsleds in tandem. The zip-line tours streak through lush rain forest under the care of an expert guide who points out items of interest. The entire facility was built using environmentally friendly techniques and materials in order to leave the native rain forest undisturbed. ⊠ *North Coast Hwy., Ocho Rios* ☎ *876/974–3990* ⊕ *www.rainforestbobsledjamaica. com* ⊠ *$47–$137.*

## BEACHES

There's a small beach right at the cruise port in Ocho Rios, with sand accessible directly from Margaritaville. Many passengers who don't want to travel are satisfed to stop here for a dip.

**Dunn's River Falls Beach.** You'll find a crowd (especially if there's a cruise ship in town) at the small beach at the foot of the falls, one of Jamaica's most-visited landmarks. Although tiny—especially considering the crowds—the beach has a great view. Look up for a spectacular vista of the cascading water, the roar from which drowns out the sea as you approach. All-day access to the beach is included in the falls' entrance fee. **Amenities:** lifeguards; parking (no fee); toilets. **Best for:** swimming. ⊠ *Rte. A1, between St. Ann's Bay and Ocho Rios, Ocho Rios* ☎ *876/974–4767* ⊕ *www.dunnsriverfallsja.com* ⊠ *$20.*

## SHOPPING

Ocho Rios has several malls that draw day-trippers from the cruise ships. The best are **Soni's Plaza** and the **Taj Mahal,** two malls on the main street with stores selling jewelry, cigars, and clothing. Another popular mall on the main street is **Ocean Village**. On the North Coast Highway slightly east of Ochos Rios are **Pineapple Place** and **Coconut Grove**.

## ACTIVITIES

### GUIDED TOURS

Half-day and full-day tours can be arranged with many taxi drivers. Be sure to agree on a price before heading out on the tour.

**Chukka Caribbean Zion Bus Tour.** A country-style bus painted in bright colors travels inland to the village of Nine Mile and the simple house where Bob Marley was born and is now buried. The five-hour tour ($104, including lunch at a jerk stand) is for those 18 and older. ⊠ *Ocho Rios* ☎ *876/619–1441 Digicel in Jamaica, 876/656–8026 Lime in Jamaica, 877/424–8552 in U.S.* ⊕ *chukka.com* ☜ *$104.*

**Jamaica Tours Limited.** This operator offers several tours with stops that include gardens and Dunn's River Falls. ☎ *876/974–6447* ⊕ *www. jamaicatoursltd.com.*

### HORSEBACK RIDING

With its combination of hills and beaches, Ocho Rios is a natural for horseback excursions. Most are guided tours taken at a slow pace and perfect for those with no previous equestrian experience. Many travelers opt to wear long pants for horseback rides, especially those away from the beach.

**Fodor's Choice** ★   **Chukka Caribbean Adventures.** The two-hour ride-and-swim tour ($159) travels along Papillion Cove (where the 1973 movie *Papillion* was filmed) as well as to locations used in *Return to Treasure Island* (1985) and *Passion and Paradise* (1988). The trail continues along the coastline to Chukka Beach and a bareback ride in the sea. Chukka has a location west of Montego Bay and handles other activities and tours, too. ⊠ *Ocho Rios* ☎ *876/619–1441 Digicel in Jamaica, 876/656–8026 Lime in Jamaica, 877/424–8552 in U.S.* ⊕ *chukka.com* ☜ *$159.*

**Hooves.** This stable offers several guided tours, including a popular 2½-hour beach ride ($95 from Boscobel, $85 from Ocho Rios, $90 from Runaway Bay—including transportation) suitable for adults and children taller than 3 feet. The trip begins with a visit to the Seville Great House estate before making its way to the beach for a ride. Hooves is home to many rescue horses that have been rehabilitated. ⊠ *Windsor Rd., St. Ann's Bay* ☎ *876/972–0905* ⊕ *www.hooves-jamaica.com.*

**Prospect Plantation.** The plantation offers horseback rides for ages eight and older, including use of helmets; reservations are required. For the adventurous, there are also guided camel rides. ⊠ *Rte. A1, about 3 miles (5 km) east of Ocho Rios* ☎ *876/974–5335* ☜ *$54.*

### RAFTING

**Chukka Caribbean Adventures.** The big activity outfitter offers the Chukka River Tubing Safari on the White River, an easy trip that doesn't require previous tubing experience. The three-hour tour lets you travel in your very own tube through gentle rapids. ⊠ *Ocho Rios* ☎ *876/619–1441 Digicel in Jamaica, 876/656–8026 Lime in Jamaica, 877/424–8552 in U.S.* ⊕ *chukka.com* ☜ *$99.*

## WHERE TO EAT

$    ✕ **Island Grill.** With 18 locations across the island, this eat-in or take-out
JAMAICAN    restaurant about a block from the main tourist area serves a Jamaican
version of fast food. Jerk chicken, rice and peas, and Jamaican stew
combo meals (called *yabbas,* an African-Jamaican term for bowl) are
all on the menu. Many meals are served with festival (fried cornbread)
and are spiced for the local palate. [$] *Average main: $4* ✉ *59 Main St.,
Ocho Rios* ☎ *876/974–3160.*

$    ✕ **Ocho Rios Jerk Centre.** This canopied, open-air eatery is a great place
JAMAICAN    for fiery jerk pork, chicken, or seafood such as fish and conch. Frosty
Red Stripe beer and cocktails such as the special Jerk Center Cooler—
a colorful mix featuring rum and vodka—are perfect complements to
the island fare. Milder barbecued meats, also sold by weight (typically,
a quarter- or half-pound makes a good serving), turn up on the daily
chalkboard menu posted on the wall. It's busy at lunch, especially when
passengers from cruise ships swamp the place. [$] *Average main: $8*
✉ *Da Costa Dr., Ocho Rios* ☎ *876/974–2549.*

# PROGRESO, MEXICO

By Jeffrey Van
Fleet

The waterfront town closest to Mérida, Progreso, is not particularly
historic. It's also not terribly picturesque; still, it provokes a certain
sentimental fondness for those who know it well. On weekdays during
most of the year the beaches are deserted, but when school is out (Easter
week, July, and August) and on summer weekends it's bustling with
families from Mérida. Progreso's charm—or lack of charm—seems to
hinge on the weather. When the sun is shining, the water looks trans-
lucent green and feels bathtub-warm, and the fine sand makes for lovely
long walks.

When the wind blows during one of Yucatán's winter *nortes,* the water
churns with whitecaps and looks gray and unappealing. Whether the
weather is good or bad, however, everyone ends up eventually at one of
the restaurants lining the main street, Calle 19. Across the street from
the oceanfront malecón, restaurants serve cold beer, seafood cocktails,
and freshly grilled fish. Most cruise passengers head immediately for
Mérida or for one of the nearby archaeological sites.

### ESSENTIALS

#### CURRENCY
The Mexican peso, but U.S. dollars are widely accepted in the area.

#### TELEPHONE
Most pay phones accept prepaid Ladatel cards, sold in 30-, 50-, or 100-
peso denominations. To use the card, insert it in the pay phone's slot,
dial 001 (for calls to the United States) or 01 (for calls within Mexico),
followed by the area code and number. Credit is deleted from the card
as you use it, and the balance is displayed on the small screen on the
phone. Most tri-band mobile phones from the U.S. work in Mexico,
though you must pay roaming charges.

## COMING ASHORE

The pier in Progreso is an astounding 5 miles long, and cruise ships dock at its end, so passengers are shuttled to the foot of the pier, where the Progreso Cruise Terminal offers visitors their first stop. The terminal houses small restaurants and shops selling locally produced crafts. These are some of the best shops in sleepy Progreso (a much wider selection is available in nearby Mérida). The beach lies just east of the pier and can easily be reached on foot. If you want to enjoy the sun and a peaceful afternoon, a drink at one of the small palapa-roof restaurants that line the beach is a good option.

### BEST BETS

■ **Chichén Itzá.** The famous Maya city is an easy day trip from Progreso and is home to the enormous and oft-photographed El Castillo pyramid.

■ **Mérida.** This delightful, though busy, town is full of life as people take to the streets for music, dance, food, and culture.

■ **Uxmal.** One of the most beautiful Mayan cities is reachable on a day trip from Progreso. If you've seen Chichén Itzá already, go here.

If you are looking to explore, there are plenty of taxis around the pier. A trip around town should not cost more than $5, but ask the taxi driver to quote you a price. If you want to see more of Progreso, a cab can also take you to the local sightseeing tour bus (which departs about every 10 minutes from the Casa de Cultura), a bright blue, open-air, double-decker bus that travels through town and costs only $2. A taxi ride from Progreso to Mérida runs about $30, and most drivers charge around $15 per hour to show you around. If you plan on renting the cab for a good part of the day, talk about the number of hours and the cost with the driver before you take off. It's difficult to rent a car, so most people just band together in a taxi.

## EXPLORING

Just south of Progreso (about 20 or 30 minutes by taxi), Mérida, the cultural and intellectual hub of the Yucatán, offers a great deal to explore. Mérida is rich in art, history, and tradition. Most streets are numbered, not named, and most run one-way. North–south streets have even numbers, which descend from west to east; east–west streets have odd numbers, which ascend from north to south. One of the best ways to see the city is to hire a calesa, a horse-drawn carriage. They congregate on the main square or at the Palacio Cantón, near the anthropology museum. Drivers charge about $25 for an hour-long circuit around downtown and up Paseo de Montejo, pointing out notable buildings and providing a little historic background along the way. An extended tour costs $35 to $50.

### MERIDA

**Casa de Montejo.** Three Franciscos de Montejo—father, son, and nephew—conquered the peninsula and founded Mérida in January of 1542, and they completed construction of this stately home on the south side of the central plaza in 1549. It's the city's oldest and finest

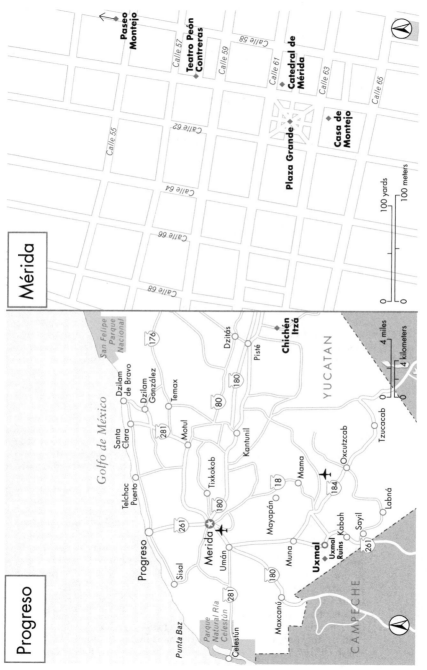

## Mérida

Paseo Montejo

Calle 57 — Teatro Peón Contreras

Calle 59

Calle 58

Calle 61

Catedral de Mérida

Calle 63

Calle 65

Calle 55

Calle 62

Plaza Grande

Casa de Montejo

Calle 64

Calle 66

Calle 68

100 yards
100 meters
0

4

## Progreso

Golfo de México

San Felipe
Parque Nacional

176

Dzilam de Bravo
Dzilam González
Temax

Dzitás
Pisté
**Chichén Itzá**

YUCATAN

281

Motul

80

180

Santa Clara

Telchac Puerto

Kantunil

Tzucacab

Tixkokob

Oxcutzcab

180

Mama

18

261

Progreso

Mayapán

184

Labná

Mérida

Muna

Kabah
Sayil

Sisal

Umán

**Uxmal**
Uxmal Ruins

261

281

180

Maxcanú

CAMPECHE

Parque Natural Ría Celestún

Punta Baz

Celestún

4 miles
4 kilometers
0

example of colonial plateresque architecture, a Spanish architectural style popular in the 16th century and typified by the kind of elaborate ornamentation you'll see here. A bas-relief on the doorway—the facade is all that remains of the original house—depicts Francisco de Montejo the younger, his wife, and daughter, as well as Spanish soldiers standing on the heads of the vanquished Maya. The building now houses a branch of the Banamex bank and the Museo del Sitio, with interesting exhibits of Meridano life in the 19th century. ⊠ *Calle 63, No. 506, Centro* ☎ *999/923–0633* ⊕ *www.casasdeculturabanamex.com* ✉ *Free* ☉ *Closed Mon.*

**Catedral de Mérida.** Begun in 1561, Mérida's archdiocesan seat is the oldest cathedral on the North American mainland (though an older one can be found in the Dominican Republic). It took several hundred Maya laborers, working with stones from the pyramids of the ravaged Mayan city, 37 years to complete it. Designed in the somber Renaissance style by an architect who had worked on the Escorial in Madrid, its facade is stark and unadorned, with gunnery slits instead of windows, and faintly Moorish spires. Inside, the black *Cristo de las Ampollas* (Christ of the Blisters) occupies a side chapel to the left of the main altar. At 23 feet tall, it's the tallest Christ figure inside a Mexican church. The statue is a replica of the original, which was destroyed during the revolution in 1910, which is also when the gold that typically decorated Mexican cathedrals was carried off. According to one of many legends, the Christ figure burned all night yet appeared the next morning unscathed—except that it was covered with the blisters for which it's named. You can hear the pipe organ play at the 11 am Sunday Mass. ⊠ *Calles 60 and 61, Centro* ☎ *999/924–7777* ⊕ *www. arquidiocesisdeyucatan.com.mx* ✉ *Free.*

**Paseo Montejo.** North of downtown, this 10-block-long street was *the* place to reside in the late 19th century, when wealthy plantation owners sought to outdo each other with the opulence of their elegant mansions. They typically opted for the decorative styles popular in New Orleans, Cuba, and Paris—imported Carrara marble, European antiques—rather than any style from Mexico. The broad boulevard, lined with tamarind and laurel trees, has lost much of its former panache; many of the mansions are now used as office buildings, while others have been or are being restored as part of a citywide, privately funded beautification program. But the street is still a lovely place to explore on foot or in a horse-drawn carriage. ⊠ *Mérida.*

**Plaza Grande.** Mérida's main square is wired as a Wi-Fi hotspot, but don't be so glued to your smartphone that you fail to take in the passing parade of activity in one of Mexico's loveliest town centers. Local people traditionally refer to it as the "Plaza Grande" or "Plaza de la Independencia"; you'll also hear it called the "Zócalo," primarily among foreigners. Whichever name you prefer, it's a good place to start a city tour, watch dance performances, listen to music, or chill in the shade of a laurel tree. Plaza Grande was laid out in 1542 on the ruins of T'hó, the Mayan city demolished to make way for Mérida; and it's still the focal point around which the most important public buildings cluster. *Confidenciales* (S-shape benches) invite intimate tête-à-têtes, and lampposts keep the park beautifully illuminated at night. ⊠ *Bordered by Calles 60, 62, 61, and 63, Centro.*

**Teatro Peón Contreras.** This 1908 Italianate theater was built along the same lines as grand turn-of-the-20th-century European theaters and opera houses. In the early 1980s, the marble staircase, dome, and frescoes were restored. Today, in addition to being a performing arts venue, the theater houses a branch of the tourist information office for the state of Yucatán. The theater's most popular attraction, however, is the café-bar spilling out into the street facing Parque de la Madre. ⊠ *Calle 60, between Calles 57 and 59, Centro* ☎ *999/924–3954* ⊕ *www.cultura yucatan.com.*

### FARTHER AFIELD

Fodor's Choice ★ **Chichén Itzá.** One of the most dramatically beautiful ancient Mayan cities, Chichén Itzá (chee- *chen* eet- *zah*) draws over one million visitors annually. Since the remains of this once-thriving kingdom were rediscovered by Europeans in the mid-1800s, many of the travelers making the pilgrimage here have been archaeologists and scholars, who study the structures and glyphs and try to piece together the mysteries surrounding them. While the artifacts here give fascinating insight into Mayan civilization, they also raise many unanswered questions.

The name of this ancient city, which means "the mouth of the well of the Itzá," is a mystery in and of itself. Although it likely refers to the valuable water sources at the site (there are several cenotes here), experts have little information about who might have actually founded the city—some structures, likely built in the 5th century, predate the arrival of the Itzá who occupied the city starting around the late 8th and early 9th centuries. Why the Itzá abandoned the city in the early 1200s is also unknown, as is its subsequent role.

Of course, most of the visitors who converge on Chichén Itzá come to marvel at its beauty. Even among laypeople, this ancient metropolis, which encompasses 6-square km (2.25-square miles), is known around the world as one of the most stunning and well-preserved Mayan sites in existence.

You've likely seen photos of the immense **El Castillo** pyramid, but they can't capture that first moment you gaze in person on the structure rising imposingly yet gracefully from the surrounding plain. El Castillo (The Castle) dominates the site both in size and in the symmetry of its perfect proportions. Open-jawed serpent statues adorn the corners of each of the pyramid's four stairways, honoring the legendary priest-king Kukulcán (also known as Quetzalcóatl), an incarnation of the feathered serpent god. More serpents appear at the top of the building as sculpted columns. At the spring and fall equinoxes, the afternoon light strikes the trapezoidal structure so that the shadow of the snake-god appears to undulate down the side of the pyramid to bless the fertile earth.

Of course, the question on everybody's lips is: "May I climb the pyramid?" The answer is a resounding "No." Disappointing though that response may be, wear and tear on the staircases and numerous injuries to visitors have necessitated an end to the climbing.

On the **Anexo del Templo de los Jaguares** (Annex to the Temple of the Jaguars), just west of El Castillo, bas-relief carvings represent more important deities. On the bottom of the columns is the rain god Tlaloc. It's no surprise that his tears represent rain—but why is the Toltec god Tlaloc honored here, instead of the Maya rain god, Chaac?

Just west of the jaguar annex, another puzzle presents itself: the auditory marvel of Chichén Itzá's main ball court. At 490 feet, this **Juego de Pelota** is the largest in Mesoamerica. Yet if you stand at one end of the playing field and whisper something to a friend at the other end, incredibly, you'll be heard. The game played on this ball court was apparently something like soccer (no hands were used), but it likely had some sort of ritualistic significance.

On the other side of El Castillo, just before a small temple dedicated to the planet Venus, a ruined *sacbé,* or raised white road, leads to the **Cenote Sagrado** (Holy Well, or Sinkhole), also probably used for ritualistic purposes.

Older Mayan structures at Chichén Itzá lie south and west of Cenote Xtaloc. Archaeologists have been restoring several buildings in this area, including the **Templo del Osario** (Ossuary Temple), which, as its name implies, concealed several tombs with skeletons and offerings. Behind the smaller **Casa Roja** (Red House) and **Casa del Venado** (House of the Deer) are the site's oldest structures, including **El Caracol** (The Snail), one of the few round buildings built by the Maya, with a spiral staircase within. Clearly built as a celestial observatory, it has eight tiny windows precisely aligned with the points of the compass rose. ⊠ *Off Carretera 180, 2 km (1½ miles) east of Pisté, Chichén-Itzá ⊕ chichenitza.inah. gob.mx ⊠ 160 MP; sound and light show 212 MP.*

Fodor's Choice
★
**Uxmal.** At 125 feet high, the **Pirámide del Adivino** is the tallest and most prominent structure at the site. Unlike most other Mayan pyramids, which are stepped and angular, this "Pyramid of the Magician" has a softer, more-refined round-corner design. The pyramid has a stairway on its western side that leads through a giant open-mouthed mask to two temples at the summit. During restoration work in 2002 the grave of a high-ranking Maya official, a ceramic mask, and a jade necklace were discovered within the pyramid. Ongoing excavations continue to reveal exciting new finds, still under study. Climbing is prohibited.

West of the pyramid lies the **Cuadrángulo de las Monjas,** often considered to be the finest part of Uxmal. It reminded the conquistadors of typical convent buildings in Old Spain (*Monjas* means nuns). You may enter the four buildings, each comprised of a series of low, gracefully repetitive chambers that look onto a central patio.

Covering 5 acres and rising over an immense acropolis, the **Palacio del Gobernador** lies at the heart of what may have been Uxmal's administrative center. It faces east while the rest of Uxmal faces west, and archaeologists suggest this allowed the structure to serve as an observatory for the planet Venus. ⚠ **In the summer months, tarantulas are a common sight on the grounds at Uxmal.** ⊠ *78 km (48 miles) south of Mérida on Carretera 261, Uxmal ⊕ www.inah.gob.mx ⊠ Site, museum, and sound-and-light show 228 MP; use of video camera 60 MP.*

# BEACHES

**Progreso Beach.** If you're looking for a pristine, Caribbean-style strand, you'd better look elsewhere. The primary draw of Progreso's main beach is its proximity to Mérida, which often leaves the sand packed with tourists and locals alike during summer weekends and holidays. Water shoes are recommended since sharp, slippery rocks lurk below the surface, making this a poor spot for diving or snorkeling. The beach is void of shade, so your best bet is to find refuge in one of the eateries lining the long malecón (boardwalk) that runs along the shore. Several restaurant owners rent beach chairs by the hour, but beware: Progreso's peddlers are relentless and leave only once they receive a small tip. Despite its drawbacks, the water here offers a refreshing escape from the bustling city. ■TIP→ **Cruise ships dock in Progreso about twice a week—to avoid the crowds, walk toward the lighthouse.** Amenities: food and drink; toilets (for restaurant patrons). **Best for:** partiers; walking. ⊠ *Av. Malecón at Calle 28, Progreso.*

# SHOPPING

In Progreso between Calle 80 and Calle 81, there is also a small downtown area that is a better place to walk than to shop. There you will find banks, supermarkets, and shops with everyday goods for locals as well as several restaurants that serve simple Mexican fare like tortas and tacos.

Mérida offers more places to shop, including colorful Mexican markets selling local goods.

**Mercado Lucas de Gálvez.** Sellers of chiles, herbs, seafood, and fruit fill this pungent and labyrinthine municipal market. In the early morning the first floor is jammed with housewives and restaurateurs shopping for the freshest fish and produce. The stairs at Calles 56 and 57 lead to the second-floor Bazar de Artesanías Municipales, where you'll find local pottery, embroidered clothes, guayabera shirts, hammocks, straw bags, sturdy leather huaraches, and piñatas in every imaginable shape and color. Note that most prices are inflated, and vendors expect you'll bargain—one way to begin is to politely request a discount. ⚠ **Be wary of pickpockets within the market.** ⊠ *Calles 56 and 67, Centro* ⊘ *Closed Sun.*

# WHERE TO EAT

$ ⤬ **Eladio's.** An outpost of lively Eladio's in Mérida, this bar and restaurant is extremely popular with cruise-ship passengers who disembark in Progreso. You can sample typical Yucatecan dishes like *longaniza asada* (baked sausage) and *pollo pibil* (citrus-pickled chicken) while seated beneath a tall palapa on the beach; as you'd expect, fresh seafood dishes are also on the menu. Tasty appetizers are free with your drinks, and there are plenty to choose from. Live music every afternoon except Tuesday adds to the party atmosphere. ⑤ *Average main: 113 MP* ⊠ *Av. Malecón s/n, at Calle 80, Centro* ☎ *969/935-5670* ⊕ *www.eladios.com.mx.*

MEXICAN

**$$**   ✕**Flamingo's.** Facing Progreso's long cement promenade, this restau-
SEAFOOD   rant is a cut above its neighbors. Service is professional and attentive;
soon after arriving, you'll get at least one free appetizer—maybe black
beans with corn tortillas or a plate of shredded shark meat stewed with
tomatoes. The creamy cilantro soup is a little too cheesy (literally, not
figuratively), but the large fish fillets are perfectly breaded and lightly
fried. A hearty breakfast kicks off each morning. There's a full bar, and
although there's no air-conditioning, large, glassless windows let in the
ocean breeze. ⑤ *Average main: 200 MP* ⊠ *Calle 19, No. 144D, at Calle
72, Progreso* ☎ *969/935–2122.*

# PUERTO LIMON, COSTA RICA

By Jeffrey Van
Fleet

Christopher Columbus became
Costa Rica's first tourist when he
landed on this stretch of coast in
1502 during his fourth and final
voyage to the New World. Expect-
ing to find vast mineral wealth, he
named the region "Costa Rica"
(rich coast). Imagine the Spaniards'
surprise eventually to find there was
none. Save for a brief skirmish
some six decades ago, the country
did prove itself rich in a long tradi-
tion of peace and democracy. No
other country in Latin America can
make that claim. Costa Rica is also
abundantly rich in natural beauty,
managing to pack beaches, volca-
noes, rain forests, and diverse animal life into an area the size of Ver-
mont and New Hampshire combined. It has successfully parlayed those
qualities into its role as one the world's great ecotourism destinations.
A day visit is short, but time enough for a quick sample.

> ### BEST BETS
>
> ■ **The Rain Forest Tram.** This
> attraction takes you up into the
> canopy of the rain forest.
>
> ■ **A Zip Line.** If you have never
> done one of these thrilling tours,
> flying from tree to tree, Costa Rica
> is the place it was invented.
>
> ■ **Tortuguero Canals.** Whether
> you go on a ship-sponsored tour
> or on your own, you see a wild
> part of Costa Rica that isn't reach-
> able by anything but boat.

### ESSENTIALS
#### CURRENCY
The colón, but U.S. dollars are widely accepted.

#### TELEPHONE
Telephone numbers have eight digits. Merely dial the number. There are
no area codes. You'll find ample phones for use in the cruise terminal.
Public phones accept locally purchased calling cards.

### COMING ASHORE
Ships dock at Limón's spacious, spiffy Terminal de Cruceros (cruise
terminal), one block south of the city's downtown. You'll find tele-
phones, Internet computers, a craft market, tourist information, and
tour operators' desks inside the terminal, as well as a small army of
manicurists who do a brisk business. Step outside and walk straight
ahead one block to reach Limón's downtown.

BARRA DEL COLORADO
NATIONAL WILDLIFE
REFUGE

Tortuguero

TORTUGUERO
NATIONAL
PARK

La Pavona

Tortuguero
Canals

Cariari

Parismina

BRAULIO
CARRILLO
NATIONAL
PARK

Santa
Clara

Guácimo

San Rafael

**Rain Forest
Adventures**

32

Costa
Flores

32

Matina

Limón
see inset
map

Sacramento

*Cordillera*

10

Stratford

♦ Zorquí

32

Bristol

Liverpool

*Isla
Uvita*

Heredia

Pacayas

*Central*

Tres Equis

**Veragua
Rainforest
Eco-Adventure**

36

**San José**

Cartago

Juan
Viñas

Turrialba

**Sloth Sanctuary
of Costa Rica**

Paraíso

Penshurt

Playa Blanca

TAPANTÍ
NATIONAL WILDLIFE
REFUGE

Cahuita

Playa
Cocles

San
Marcos

HITOY
CERERE
BIOLOGICAL
RESERVE

Bribrí

Playa Grande

Manzanillo

Santa
Maria

CA
2

**Jaguar
Rescue
Center**

Gandoca

Sixaola

Daytonia

Guabito

0 ⊢ 20 miles

0 ⊢ 20 kilometers

**Limón**

*Caribbean
Sea*

*Avenida 3*
*Avenida 2*

*Calle 4*

*Calle 2*

**Parque
Vargas**

*Caribbean
Sea*

PANAMÁ

**KEY**

⛴ *Cruise Ship Terminal*

A fleet of red taxis waits on the street in front of the terminal. Drivers are happy to help you put together a do-it-yourself tour. Most charge $100 to $150 per carload for a day of touring. There is no place to rent a car at the terminal, but you're better off leaving the driving to someone else anyway. Cruise lines offer dozens of shore excursions in Costa Rica, and if you want to go any farther afield than Limón or the coast south, we suggest you take an organized tour. The country looks disarmingly small on a map—it is—but hills give rise to mountains the farther inland you go, and road conditions range from "okay" to "abysmal." Distances are short as the toucan flies, but travel times are longer than you'd expect.

## EXPLORING

If you arrive in Limón on a cruise ship, a day in the Caribbean is yours for the taking. The Tortuguero canals, the beaches at Puerto Viejo de Talamanca, the sloth rescue center at Sloth Sanctuary of Costa Rica near Cahuita, or the Veragua Rainforest Eco-Adventure park, just a few miles away, are four popular excursions. A few hardy souls venture as far away as the Rain Forest Adventures complex north of Braulio Carrillo National Park, or even San José. (That last one makes for a *very* tiring day.) A legion of taxi drivers waits at the terminal exit if you have not arranged an organized shore excursion through your cruise company.

## LIMÓN

**Parque Vargas.** The aquamarine wooden port building faces the cruise terminal, and just to the east lies the city's palm-lined seaside park, Parque Vargas. From the promenade facing the ocean you can see the raised dead coral left stranded by the 1991 earthquake. Ten or so Hoffman's two-toed sloths live in the trees of Parque Vargas; ask a passerby to point them out, as spotting them requires a trained eye. ⊠ *Limón.*

## TORTUGUERO

The stretch of beach between the Colorado and Matina rivers was first mentioned as a nesting ground for sea turtles in a 1592 Dutch chronicle. Nearly a century earlier, Christopher Columbus compared traversing the north Caribbean coast and its swimming turtles to navigating through rocks. Because the area is so isolated—there's no road here to this day—the turtles nested undisturbed for centuries. By the mid-1900s, however, the harvesting of eggs and poaching of turtles had reached such a level that these creatures faced extinction. In 1963 an executive decree regulated the hunting of turtles and the gathering of eggs, and in 1970 the government established Tortuguero National Park; modern Tortuguero bases its economy on tourism.

In 1970 a system of canals running parallel to the shoreline was constructed to provide safer access to the region than the dangerous journey up the seacoast. You can continue up the canals, natural and man-made, that begin in Moín, near Limón, and run all the way to Tortuguero. Or you can embark at various points north of Guápiles and Siquirres, as do public transportation and most of the package tours.

### ELSEWHERE IN THE REGION

FAMILY

Fodor's Choice
★

**Jaguar Rescue Center** (*Centro de Rescate Jaguar*). Many regard a visit to the Jaguar Rescue Center as the highlight of their trip to Puerto Viejo. The name is a bit misleading. The original rescued animal here was an orphaned, injured jaguar cub that ultimately did not survive. His memory lives on in the facility's name, even if there are no other jaguars on-site. Primarily howler monkeys, sloths, and lots of snakes make up the charges of the capable staff here. The goal, of course, is to return the animals to the wild, but those that are too frail are assured a permanent home here. Your admission fee for the 90-minute tour (English or Spanish) helps fund the rescue work. ⊠ *3 km (2 miles) southeast of Puerto Viejo between Playa Cocles and Playa Chiquita, Puerto Viejo de Talamanca* ☎ *2750–0710* ⊕ *www.jaguarrescue.com* ✉ *$15.*

FAMILY

Fodor's Choice
★

**Rain Forest Adventures.** Just beyond the northeastern boundary of Braulio Carrillo National Park, about 15 km (9 miles) before the Caribbean-slope town of Guápiles, a 1,200-acre reserve houses a privately owned and operated engineering marvel: a series of gondolas strung together in a modified ski-lift pulley system. (To lessen the impact on the jungle, the support pylons were lowered into place by helicopter.) The 21 gondolas hold five people each, plus a bilingual biologist-guide equipped with a walkie-talkie to request brief stops for snapping pictures. The ride covers 2½ km (1½ miles) in 80 minutes. You can arrange a personal pickup in San José for a fee, or there are public buses (on the Guápiles line) every half hour from the Gran Terminal del Caribe in San José. Drivers know the tram as the *teleférico*. ✉ *Rain Forest Adventures, 10 km (6 miles) northeast of Braulio Carrillo National Park along Rte. 32, Braulio Carrillo National Park* ☎ *2257–5961, 866/759–8726 in North America* ⊕ *www.rainforestadventure.com* ✉ *$67; $112 includes all attractions.*

FAMILY

Fodor's Choice

★

**Sloth Sanctuary of Costa Rica.** A full-fledged nature center a few miles northwest of Cahuita is well worth a stop. Many of the sloths that live on the premises are here because of illness or injury and are not on display to the public, but Buttercup, the very first of their charges, holds court in the nature-focused gift shop. She has been joined by Leno, a Bradypus male—that's one of the two sloth species found in Costa Rica—who can be found in the aquarium. A visit is a good way to learn about these little-known animals, though numerous requests from visitors to hold or pet the sloths have to be turned down. Your admission includes a two-hour tour (no reservations are needed) and contributes to further care and research by the good-hearted folks who operate the facility. Reservations are required for a special insider's tour that takes you behind the scenes into the sloth clinic and nursery. ✉ *9 km (5 miles) northwest of Cahuita, follow signs on Río Estrella delta, Cahuita* ☎ *2750–0775* ⊕ *www.slothsanctuary.com* ✉ *$30, including 2-hr tour; Insider Tour $150.*

FAMILY

Fodor's Choice

★

**Veragua Rainforest Eco-Adventure.** Limón's hottest attraction is a 4,000-acre nature theme park, about 30 minutes west of the city. It's popular with cruise-ship passengers in port for the day and is well worth a stop if you're in the area. Veragua's great strength is its small army of enthusiastic, super-informed guides who take you through a network of nature trails and exhibits of hummingbirds, snakes, frogs, butterflies, and other insects. A gondola ride overlooks the complex and transports you through the rain-forest canopy. A branch of the Original Canopy Tour, with nine platforms rising 46 meters (150 feet) above the forest floor, is here. The zip-line tour is not included in the basic admission to the park. Packages including transportation (a minimum of two people) can be arranged to and from San José (admittedly a very long trip), to and from Puerto Viejo de Talamanca, or starting out at one and ending at the other. ✉ *Veragua de Liverpool, 15 km (9 miles) west of Limón, Limón* ☎ *2296–5056 in San José, 4000–0949* ⊕ *www.veraguarainforest.com* ✉ *Full-day tour $66; with canopy tour $99; with transportation (does not include canopy tour): from San José $149; from Puerto Viejo de Talamanca $99.*

# BEACHES

The dark-sand beaches on this sector of the coast are pleasant enough, but won't dazzle you if you've made previous stops at Caribbean islands with their white-sand strands. Nicer beaches than Limón's Playa Bonita lie farther south along the coast and can be reached by taxi or organized shore excursion. Strong undertows make for ideal surfing conditions on these shores, but risky swimming. Exercise caution.

**Playa Blanca** (*White Beach*). Costa Rica's Caribbean coast has no true white-sand beaches, but Cahuita's in-town beach is as close as it gets (*blanca* means "white" in Spanish). Right at the town entrance to the national park, you're a few steps from local eateries. The park's jungle comes right up to the beach's edge, creating one of those postcard-perfect views. The undertow can be strong here; swimmers are more likely to venture out near the center of the beach. Use caution in any case. **Amenities:** food and drink. **Best for:** sunrise; walking. ⊠ *Town center, Cahuita.*

**Playa Cocles.** The sand gets a bit lighter and the crowd slightly more upscale—it is still Puerto Viejo, though—a couple of kilometers outside of town. Fewer vendors will pester you here than in the town itself, and it'll be mostly you and other travelers. (If there's nobody around, don't linger. There's always safety in numbers.) As with all Puerto Viejo area beaches, the undertow can be strong on Cocles. Never venture out too far. **Amenities:** food and drink. **Best for:** partiers; sunrise; surfing, walking. ⊠ *2 km (1 mile) southeast of Puerto Viejo de Talamanca, Puerto Viejo de Talamanca.*

**Playa Grande.** Beyond the Atlántida Lodge, Playa Negra's black sand lightens to a dark brown. Whether this constitutes a separate beach or not is open for debate, but the lodgings out here distinguish their stretch of sand as "Playa Grande." You're much farther from town here; the beach feels even more isolated. Do be careful. As with all beaches on this coast, the undertow makes swimming risky. **Amenities:** none. **Best for:** sunrise; walking. ⊠ *Cahuita.*

# SHOPPING

The cruise-ship terminal contains an orderly maze of souvenir stands. Vendors are friendly; there's no pressure to buy. Many shops populate the restored port building across the street as well.

# ACTIVITIES

## TOURS
**Mambo Tour.** In addition to horseback riding, white-water rafting, and snorkeling or scuba diving, these folks can take you on three- to eight-hour excursions around the region, and even on an all-day trip to the Rain Forest Aerial Tram or San José. ⊠ *Terminal de Cruceros, Limón* ☏ *8997–4198* ⊕ *www.mambotour.com* 🖃 *From $30.*

# WHERE TO EAT

If you are looking for a bite to eat while off the ship, your best bet is one of the simple "sodas," small restaurants serving local food. There are several in the vicinity of the Mercado Municipal, but Limón isn't a particularly pleasant place to stroll around, so if you aren't on a more far-flung tour you may be happier returning to your ship for lunch. Most tours will include lunch.

# ROATAN, HONDURAS

By Rika Purdy  You'll swear you hear Jimmy Buffett singing as you step off the ship onto Roatán. The flavor is decidedly Margaritaville, but with all there is to do on this island off the north coast of Honduras, you'll never waste away here. Roatán is the largest and most important of the Bay Islands, though at a mere 40 miles (65 km) from tip to tip, and no more than 3 miles (5 km) at its widest; "large" is relative here. As happened elsewhere on Central America's Caribbean coast, the British got here first—the Bay Islands didn't become part of Honduras until the mid-1800s—and left an indelible imprint in the form of place names such as Coxen Hole, French Harbour, and West End, and, of course, their language, albeit a Caribbean-accented English. The eyes of underwater enthusiasts mist over at the mention of Roatán, one of the world's premier diving destinations, but plenty of topside activity will keep you busy, too.

## ESSENTIALS

### CURRENCY

The Honduran leimpira.

### TELEPHONE

All phone numbers in Honduras have eight digits. There are no area codes, so just dial the number. Public phones are hard to find, but some hotels and businesses will offer phone services to walk-up users for a small fee.

## COMING ASHORE

Roatán has two cruise terminals. Carnival and its affiliated lines own and operate an $80-million installation called Mahogany Bay, at Dixon Cove, halfway between the towns of Coxen Hole and French Harbour. The facility is designed to be entirely self-contained, with shops, restaurants, and attractions. A chairlift—$12 for a day pass—transports you to a private beach. You can partake of an entire slate of shore excursions if you wish to see more of the island, though. Other lines use the original Terminal de Cruceros (cruise terminal) in the village of Coxen Hole, the island's administrative center. You'll find telephones, Internet computers, and stands with tour information inside the terminal, as well as a flea market of crafts just outside the gate. Not to be outdone, Coxen Hole's facility is undergoing a major facelift at this writing. Periodically, schedules and weather mean cruise lines use the opposite terminal.

Taxis are readily available outside the cruise-ship docks, but be prepared to pay a premium for services there. Trips to the major tourism centers like West End and West Bay beach will cost around $20 per person, round-trip. Negotiate the price before you go, and be sure to clarify if the fare is per person and round-trip. If you would like to save money on your taxi fares, you can walk to the main highway (or into the town of Coxen Hole if you dock near there) and look for taxis marked "Colectivo." These taxis charge a flat rate of L20–L150, depending on the distance. They also pick up as many passengers as they can hold, so plan on riding with other locals or tourists. The local public-transport system consists of blue minivans that leave from Main Street in Coxen

Hole to various points on the island until 6 pm. Simply wave if you want a minivan to stop. Expect to pay L30 to French Harbour and L50 to Sandy Bay or West End.

Look for the cadre of tourist police if you need help with anything. They wear tan shirts and dark-green trousers and are evident on cruise days. You certainly can rent a car here, but the island's compact size makes it unnecessary. Taxis will happily take you anywhere; expect to pay $80 to $120 for a day's private tour, depending on how far you wish to travel.

## EXPLORING

FAMILY **Carambola Botanical Gardens.** With one of the country's most extensive orchid collections, the Carambola Botanical Gardens is home to many different varieties of tropical plants. It is also a breeding area for iguanas. There are several trails to follow, and many of the trees and plants are identified by small signs. The longest trail leads up to the top of the hill, where you find an amazing view of the West End of the island. Guides can be hired at the visitor center. ⊠ *Across from Anthony's Key Resort, Sandy Bay* ☎ *9961–3074* ⊕ *www.carambola-gardens.com* 🖼 *L220; guided tour L330.*

FAMILY **Gumbalimba Park.** This park is part nature reserve, part tourism fun. Macaws, parrots, and monkeys will land on your shoulders as iguanas scuttle around more than 200 tropical tree and plant species. Paved paths lined with boulders lead to a 91 meters (300 feet) high-hanging bridge that crosses a lagoon. The park's zip-line tour is its main attraction, with 13 lines traversing the rain-forest canopy. There is also snorkeling, SNUBA (a form of surface-supplied diving), horseback riding, kayaking, and a white sandy beach. Coxen's Cave is reminiscent of a theme park ride: recreated cave drawings line the walls; and dotting the interior are life-size pirate statues and replicas of maps, weapons, and treasure. Grab a bite at the poolside grill and take a refreshing shower in the outdoor stalls. Park admission includes the pirate cave, animal preserve, botanical gardens, and the pool. All other activities cost extra. ■ TIP→ **Avoid cruise ship days if you want to beat the crowds.** ⊠ *West Bay* ☎ *2445–1033* ⊕ *www.gumbalimbapark.com* 🖼 *From L560.*

FAMILY **Maya Key.** One of the premier day excursions—it's a great place for children—for cruisers visiting Roatán is this small, private island near Coxen Hole. The park offers a wide variety of amenities and activities, including sandy beaches, tropical gardens, a museum with cultural

---

### BEST BETS

■ **Diving and Snorkeling.** Roatán is one of the world's great diving destinations. There's snorkeling, too, most of it easily accessible from shore.

■ **Explore Garífuna Culture.** You'd never know it wandering West End, but the island has an original culture that predated the arrival of tourism, and which still dominates Roatán's eastern half.

■ **Hands-On Animal Adventures.** Macaws and monkeys scurry around you at the Gumbalimba Nature Park; dolphin encounters are available at Anthony's Key Resort.

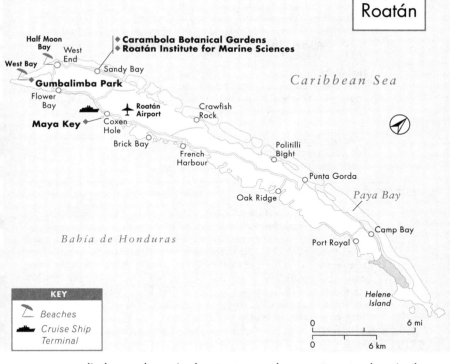

**Roatán**

Half Moon Bay
West End
West Bay
**Gumbalimba Park**
Sandy Bay
◆ **Carambola Botanical Gardens**
◆ **Roatán Institute for Marine Sciences**

*Caribbean Sea*

Flower Bay
**Maya Key**
Coxen Hole
Roatán Airport
Crawfish Rock
Brick Bay
French Harbour
Politilli Bight
Punta Gorda
Oak Ridge
*Paya Bay*
Camp Bay

*Bahía de Honduras*
Port Royal
Helene Island

KEY
⌇ Beaches
⛴ Cruise Ship Terminal

0        6 mi
0        6 km

displays, and an animal rescue center, where you can meet the animals. The 10-acre island also has spectacular snorkeling. Most cruise lines offer the island as a shore excursion, and it's the only way it can be visited; the park takes no independent bookings. It's a 3-minute water shuttle from the shuttle pier 50 yards east of the Terminal de Cruceros in Coxen Hole. ⊠ *Maya Cay, Coxen Hole* 🕾 *9995–9589* ⊕ *www.maya keyroatan.com.*

FAMILY  **Roatán Institute for Marine Sciences.** One of the attractions at Anthony's Key Resort, the Roatán Institute for Marine Sciences is an educational center that researches bottlenose dolphins and other marine animals. A dolphin show takes place every day at 4 pm. For an additional fee, you can participate in a "dolphin encounter," which allows you to interact with the dolphins while either swimming or snorkeling. There are also programs for children ages 5 to 14, including snorkeling experiences, and the "Dolphin Trainer for a Day" program. ■TIP➔ **Cruise-ship passengers must make reservations for dolphin encounters through their ship's excursion desk.** ⊠ *Anthony's Key Resort, Sandy Bay* 🕾 *9556–0212* ⊕ *www.roatanims.org* ▨ *L110.*

## BEACHES

You really can't go wrong with any of Roatán's white-sand beaches. Even those adjacent to populated areas manage to stay clean and uncluttered, thanks to efforts of residents. Water is rougher for swimming on the less-protected north side of the island.

**Half Moon Bay.** Roatán's most popular beach, Half Moon Bay is also one of its prettiest. Coconut palms and foliage come up to the crescent shoreline. The beach lies just outside the tourist-friendly West End. Crystal-clear waters offer abundant visibility for snorkeling. ⊠ *West End.*

**West Bay Beach.** Roatán is famous for the picturesque West Bay Beach. It's a de rigueur listing on every shore-excursions list. Once there, you can lounge on the beach or snorkel. ⊠ *West Bay.*

## SHOPPING

At the cruise ship dock in Coxen Hole you can find craft vendors, who set up shop outside the cruise-terminal gates; a small number of souvenir shops are scattered around the center of Coxen Hole, a short walk from the docks. Few of the souvenirs for sale here—or anywhere else on the island for that matter—were actually made in Roatán; most come from mainland Honduras. The terminal at Mahogany Bay has 22 shops as well. If you get as far as West End, there are a variety of souvenir and craft sellers in small shops lining the main sand road that runs parallel to the beach.

## ACTIVITIES

### DIVING AND SNORKELING

Most of the activity on Roatán centers on scuba diving and snorkeling, as well as the newest sensation, snuba, a cross between the two, whereby your mask is connected by a hose to an air source that remains above the water, allowing you to dive for several feet without carrying an air tank on your back. Warm water, great visibility, and thousands of colorful fish make the island a popular destination. Add to this a good chance of seeing a whale shark, and you'll realize why so many people head here each year. Dive sites cluster off the island's western and southern coasts.

One of the most popular destinations—particularly for budget travelers—is West End, offering idyllic beaches stretching as far as the eye can see. One of the loveliest spots is Half Moon Bay, a crescent of brilliant white sand. A huge number of dive shops offer incredibly low-price diving courses.

Competition among the dive shops is fierce in West End, so check out a few. West Bay has great dive sites, but few actual centers. When shopping around, ask about class size (eight is the maximum), the condition of the diving equipment, and the safety equipment on the dive boat.

FAMILY   **Native Sons.** One of the first dive shops in West End, Native Sons was started by a local diving legend, Alvin Jackson, who also helped form

Roatán Marine Park. It's now a bustling shop with beautiful dive boats, and an on-site hostel that attracts backpackers. ✉ *West End* ☎ *9670–6530* ⊕ *www.roatandivingnativesons.com.*

**Quality Time Divers.** If you want the best gear, boats, and service on the island, and you're willing to pay for it, head to Quality Time Divers. They will craft custom dive trips for you and your entire group, including dock pick-up and drop-off for those staying outside of West End. The boat captain usually fishes while heading back, and if he catches something, you'll likely be having a BBQ on the deck after you arrive back at the dock. ✉ *Behind Roatán Rentals, West End* ☎ *2445–4182* ⊕ *www.qualitytimedivers.com.*

FAMILY **Roatán Divers.** One of the most organized dive shops on the island, Roatán Divers delivers great service at affordable prices at this boutique-style shop. The owners are dive instructors themselves, and it shows in their appreciation for safety, quality, and fun. ✉ *West End* ☎ *9949–3781 from Honduras, 315/507–8656 from U.S.* ⊕ *www.roatandiver.com.*

FAMILY **West End Divers.** This shop has a youthful and fun vibe, and always seems to see the best underwater animals—check out their recent sightings board for proof. They are also the only shop in the area offering black-water dives, which are specialized late-night dives done two miles off the reef over hundreds of feet of open ocean. Cafe Escondido, located directly upstairs, is a great place to grab a quick lunch between dives. ✉ *West End* ☎ *9565–4465* ⊕ *www.westenddivers.info.*

### FISHING

FAMILY
Fodor'sChoice
★
**Wahoo Slayer Fishing Charters.** If you're more interested in catching fish than hanging out with them under water, get yourself a spot on the Wahoo Slayer. Captain Enrick Bush was raised on these waters and knows them accordingly, making sure to take you to the best places to get a good catch. Wahoo, mahimahi, and barracuda are all possibilities. Day trips to Pigeon Cay, Utila, and Cayos Cochinos are also available. ✉ *Across from Woody's Supermarket, West End* ☎ *9883–3346* ⊕ *www.wahooslayer.com* 🍴 *From L10,000.*

## WHERE TO EAT

$$
SEAFOOD
FAMILY
✕ **Bite on the Beach.** On a beautiful deck overlooking the beach, the restaurant serves up a wide selection of seafood, including conch, crab, and lobster. The menu changes often, but you'll almost always find favorites like Thai shrimp with peanut sauce and yellow coconut curry dishes. The restaurant is easily accessible by water taxi from West End, and the restaurant has Wi-Fi for guests. $ *Average main: L230* ✉ *West Bay* ☎ *9663–6317* ⊕ *www.biteonthebeach.net* ☾ *Closed Sun.*

$$
JAMAICAN
✕ **Blue Parrot Bar & Restaurant.** Once a popular beer and burger joint, the new owners now serve boldly seasoned Jamaican jerk chicken and Caribbean-inspired seafood favorites. Located next to Seadancer Condominiums, it draws a nice mix of vacationers for lunch and dinner. Tropical music plays around the clock, giving a festive atmosphere to this casual outdoor eatery. $ *Average main: L250* ✉ *Seadancer Resort, Sandy Bay* ☎ *3246–9525* ▭ *No credit cards.*

# SAMANÁ (CAYO LEVANTADO), DOMINICAN REPUBLIC

By Eileen Robinson Smith

Samaná, the name of both a peninsula in the Dominican Republic as well as the largest town on Samaná Bay, is one of the least-known regions of the country; but the international airport that opened in nearby El Catey in 2006, and the highway from Santo Domingo that has cut drive-time to two hours, are changing that perception quickly. Much development is being completed or has been completed, so a visit now will still be to a place that is not yet geared to a great deal of mainstream, mass tourism. But with the use of the port by some mega-ships, that, too, is changing rapidly. Samaná is one of the Dominican Republic's newest cruise-ship destinations, with one of the island's greatest varieties of shore excursions. You can explore caves and see an amazing waterfall. And since many humpback whales come here each year to mate and give birth, it's a top whale-watching destination from January through March. While some cruise lines still use Cayo Levantado as a private-island type of experience, for other lines it is just one of several options.

> ## BEST BETS
>
> ■ **Cayo Levantado.** This resort island puts on an excellent show for day-trippers.
>
> ■ **El Limón Waterfall.** The dazzling falls are reached by horseback.
>
> ■ **Los Haitises National Park.** The caves are filled with Taíno drawings; the mangroves are magnificent.
>
> ■ **Playa Rincón.** The perfect, quiet beach offers a river, unspoiled mountain scenery, and privacy.
>
> ■ **Whale-watching.** In season, this is the top activity in the area.

## ESSENTIALS

### CURRENCY

The Dominican peso, but you can almost always use U.S. dollars.

### TELEPHONE

Telephones are available at the dock, as soon as passengers disembark, and telephone cards can be purchased there as well. Tele-cards can also be bought at the supermarket at Casa de Campo Marina. To call the United States or Canada from the D.R., just punch in 1 plus the area code and number. To make calls on the island, you must tap in the area code (809), plus the seven-digit number; if you are calling a Dominican cell phone, you must first punch in 1 then 809 or 829.

## COMING ASHORE

Cruise ships dock at Embarcadero (name of dock) in Santa Bárbara de Samaná. Tenders will take you to one of three docks, on the Malecón, referred to as the Samaná Bay Piers. The farthest is a five-minute walk from the town center.

Renting a car, although possible, isn't a good option. Driving in the Dominican Republic can be a hectic and even harrowing experience; if you are in port one only day, don't risk it. You'll do better if you

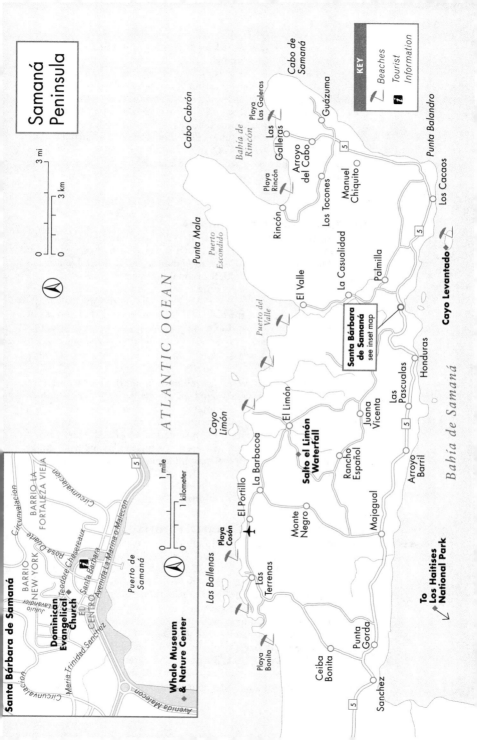

**Samaná Peninsula**

3 mi
3 km

**KEY**
Beaches
Tourist Information

ATLANTIC OCEAN

Cabo Cabrón

Punta Mala
Puerto Escondido

Bahía de Rincón

Cabo de Samaná

Playa Las Galeras

Las Galeras

Guázuma

Rincón

Playa Rincón

Arroyo del Cabo

Los Tocones

Manuel Chiquito

El Valle

Puerto del Valle

La Casualidad

Palmilla

Punta Balandro

Los Cacos

Cayo Limón

El Limón

**Salto el Limón Waterfall**

La Barbacoa

Rancho Español

Juana Vicenta

Las Pascualas

Honduras

Santa Bárbara de Samaná
see inset map

El Portillo

**Playa Cosón**

Monte Negro

Majagual

Arroyo Barril

Bahía de Samaná

**Cayo Levantado**

Las Ballenas

Las Terrenas

Punta Gorda

Ceiba Bonita

Playa Bonita

Sanchez

**To Los Haitises National Park**

**Santa Bárbara de Samaná**

Circunvalación

BARRIO LA FORTALEZA VIEJA

Julio Lavandier

Teodore Chássereaux

BARRIO NEW YORK

Rosa Duarte

Circunvalación

**Dominican Evangelical Church**

El Santa Bárbara

CENTRO

María Trinidad Sanchez

Avenida La Marina o Malecón

Puerto de Samaná

Avenida Malecón

Circunvalación

**Whale Museum & Nature Center**

1 mile
1 kilometer

combine your resources with friends from the ship and share a taxi to do some independent exploring. Negotiate prices, and settle before getting in the taxi. To give you an idea of what to expect, a minivan that can take eight people will normally charge $90 for the round-trip to Las Terrenas, including a two-hour wait while you explore or enjoy the beach. Similarly, you'll pay $80 to travel to Las Galeras round trip. Many of the drivers speak some English. Within Samaná, rickshaws are far less costly and are also fun. Called *motoconchos de carretas,* they are not unlike larger versions of the Thai tuk-tuk, but can hold up to six people. The least you will pay is RD$10. They're fine for getting around town, but don't even think about going the distance with them.

## EXPLORING

### SANTA BÁRBARA DE SAMANÁ

**Dominican Evangelical Church.** Back in 1824, a sailing vessel called the *Turtle Dove,* carrying several hundred slaves that had escaped from Philadelphia, was blown ashore in Samaná. The historic Dominican Evangelical Church is the oldest original building left in Samaná. The structure actually came across the ocean from England in 1881 in a hundred pieces and was reassembled here, serving the spiritual needs of the African-American freedmen. In 1946 a city-wide fire wiped out most of Samaná's wooden buildings and Victorian architecture; this church was miraculously saved. ⊠ *Calle Theodore Chaseurox, in front of Catholic church, 2 blocks north of the cruise ship pier, Samaná* ☎ *809/538–2579* ✑ *Donations appreciated.*

**Whale Museum & Nature Center** (*Centro de Naturaleza*). This tiny museum is dedicated to the mighty mammals of the sea. Samaná Bay is part of one of the largest marine mammal sanctuaries in the world and is a center for whale-watching during the winter migration of humpback whales. The CEBSE (Center for Conservation and Ecodevelopment of Samaná Bay and its Environment) manages this facility, which features a 40-foot female humpback skeleton. Information in English is available at the entrance. ⊠ *Av. La Marina, Tiro al Blanco, Samaná ✛ Turn left from the main section of the Malecón, en route to the hotel Bahía Príncipe Cayacoa, to find the tiny Centro de Naturaleza* ☎ *809/538–2042* ✑ *RD$100.*

### ELSEWHERE IN THE SAMANÁ PENINSULA

Fodor'sChoice ★ **Los Haitises National Park.** A highlight of any visit to the Samaná Peninsula is Los Haitises National Park (pronounced High-tee-sis), which is across Samaná Bay. The park is famous for its karst limestone formations, caves, and grottoes filled with pictographs and petroglyphs left by the indigenous Taínos. The park is accessible only by boat, and a professionally guided kayaking tour is highly recommended (a licensed guide from a tour company or the government is mandatory for any visitor). You'll paddle around dozens of dramatic rock islands and spectacular cliff faces, while beautiful coastal birds—magnificent frigate birds, brown pelicans, brown booby, egrets, and herons—swirl around overhead. A good tour will also include the caverns, where your flashlight will illuminate Taíno petroglyphs. It's a continual sensory experience, and you'll feel tiny, like a human speck surrounded by geological grandeur. DominicanShuttles (⊕ *DominicanShuttles.com*) can arrange a park tour and a stay at the adjacent, and rustic Paraiso Caño Hondo Ecolodge, which has authentic creole cuisine and multiple waterfalls. ⊠ *Samaná Bay, Samaná* 🕾 *809/472–4204* 🖘 *$4, not including mandatory use of licensed guide.*

**Salto el Limón Waterfall.** Provided that you're fit and willing to deal with a long and slippery path, an adventurous guided trip (three hours) to the spectacular Salto el Limón Waterfall is a delight. It's mostly on horseback, but includes walking down rocky, sometimes muddy trails. Horse paths are slippery, and the trek is strenuous. The well-mannered horses take you across two rivers and up mountains to El Limón, the 165-foot waterfall amid luxuriant vegetation. Some snacks and drinks are usually included, but a grilled chicken lunch is only a few more pesos. The outpost for the trek, a local guide service called Santi Rancho, is difficult to find; it's best to arrange a tour from a professional operator like **Flora Tours** (🕾 *809/240–5482* ⊕ *flora-tours.net*) in Las Terrenas. However, in times of drought, the waterfall is not as interesting. ⊠ *Santi Rancho, El Limón* 🕾 *829/923–2792 Santi Rancho.*

## BEACHES

There are no recommendable beaches in Samaná de Santa Barbara itself. You will have to travel to one of the beautiful ones elsewhere on the peninsula, another reason why the Cayo Levantado excursion is popular on most ships.

**Cayo Levantado.** There are no public beaches in Samaná town, but you can hire a boat to take you to Cayo Levantado, which has a wonderful white-sand beach on an island in Samaná Bay. Today the small island has largely been turned into a commercial enterprise to accommodate the 1,500 cruise-ship passengers who anchor here; it has dining facilities, bars, restrooms, and lounge chairs. Unfortunately, it can be extremely crowded and boisterous when there's a ship in port, so it may be best to avoid a trip to the island on those days. The beach, however, is undeniably beautiful. The island's Bahía Príncipe Cayo Levantado (*809/538–3131*), an upscale, all-inclusive resort with its own launch, sells one-day passes (adults only) for about $120. ⊠ *Samaná Bay, Samaná* 🖘 *Public beach free.*

**Fodor's** Choice
★
**Playa Cosón.** This is a long, wonderful stretch of nearly white sand and the best beach close to the town of Las Terrenas. Previously undeveloped, it's now reachable by a new highway, Carretera Cosón, and there are a number of condo developments under construction (so the current sense of solitude probably won't last). One excellent restaurant, The Beach, serves the entire 15-mile (24-km) shore, and there's the European-owned boutique hotel Casa Cosón and its restaurant and bar. If beachgoers buy lunch and/or drinks at either, then they can use the restrooms. **Amenities:** food and drink; parking; toilets. **Best for:** swimming; sunset; walking; windsurfing. ⊠ *Las Terrenas.*

4

## SHOPPING

Rum, coffee, and cigars are popular local products. You may also find good coconut handicrafts, including coconut-shell candles. Whale-oriented gift items are particularly popular. Most of the souvenir shops are on Samaná's malecón or in the market plaza; you will find more on the major downtown streets in town, all within easy walking distance of the tender piers.

## ACTIVITIES

### DIVING AND SNORKELING

In 1979 three atolls disappeared after a seaquake off Las Terrenas, providing an opportunity for truly memorable dives. Also just offshore from Las Terrenas are the Islas Las Ballenas (the Whale Islands), a cluster of four little islands with good snorkeling. A coral reef is off Playa Jackson, a beach accessible only by boat.

**Las Galeras Divers.** This is a professional, safety-conscious operation. Owner Serge is a PADI, OWSI, and nitrox instructor, and every level of PADI course is offered. Diving lessons and trips are offered in English, French, and Spanish, and diving equipment rentals are also available. Discounts are given to groups, families, and divers who want a package deal. ⊠ *Calle Principal, Las Galeras* ☎ *809/538–0220, 809/715-4111* ⊕ *www.las-galeras-divers.com* ⊠ *From $45.*

### WHALE-WATCHING

Humpback whales come to Samaná Bay to mate and give birth each year for a relatively limited period, from approximately January 15 through March 30. Samaná Bay is considered one of the top 10 destinations in the world to watch humpbacks. If you're here during the brief season, this can be the experience of a lifetime. You can listen to the male humpback's solitary courting song and witness incredible displays as the whales flip their tails and breach (humpbacks are the most active species of whales in the Atlantic).

Fodor's Choice ★ **Whale Samaná.** Owned by Kim Beddall, a Canadian who is incredibly knowledgeable about whales and Samaná in general, having lived here for decades, this operation is far and away the region's best, most professional, and environmentally sensitive. On board *Pura Mia*, a 55-foot motor vessel, a marine mammal specialist narrates and answers questions in several languages. Kim herself conducts almost all the English-speaking trips. Normal departure times are 9 for the morning trip and 1:30 for the afternoon trip; she is flexible whenever possible for cruise-ship passengers but does require advance reservations. ⊠ *Across street from town dock, beside park, Calle Sra. Morellia Kelly, Samaná* ☎ *809/538–2494* ⊕ *www.whalesamana.com* ⊠ *From $59.*

## WHERE TO EAT

$$
SEAFOOD ✕ **La Mata Rosada.** This Malecón landmark has been luring local expats and foodies since the late 1990s. Ceiling fans keep you cool as sea breezes waft in from the bay across the street. Some excellent choices

are mahimahi, shrimp, or a mix of grilled lobster and other shellfish. Go local or international, but begin with the ceviche, a specialty of this port town. ⑤ *Average main: $16* ⊠ *Av. Malecón 5B, Samaná* ☎ *809/538–2388* ⊘ *Closed June–Oct. and Wed.*

# SAN JUAN, PUERTO RICO

By Paulina Salach and Julie Schwietert Collazo

Although Puerto Rico is a commonwealth of the United States, few cities in the Caribbean are as steeped in Spanish tradition as San Juan. Within a seven-square-block area in Old San Juan are restored 16th-century buildings, museums, art galleries, bookstores, and 200-year-old houses with balustraded balconies overlooking narrow, cobblestone streets. In contrast, San Juan's sophisticated Condado and Isla Verde areas have glittering hotels, fancy boutiques, casinos, and discos. Out in the countryside is 28,000-acre El Yunque National Forest, a rain forest with more than 240 species of trees growing at least 100 feet high. You can stretch your sea legs on dramatic mountain ranges, numerous trails, in vast caves, at coffee plantations, old sugar mills, and hundreds of beaches. No wonder San Juan is one of the busiest ports of call in the Caribbean. Like any other big city, San Juan has its share of petty crime, so guard your wallet or purse, especially in crowded markets and squares.

## ESSENTIALS

### CURRENCY

The U.S. dollar.

### TELEPHONE

Calling the United States from Puerto Rico is the same as calling within the United States, and virtually all U.S. cell phone plans work here just as they do at home. You can use the long-distance telephone service office in the cruise-ship terminal, or you can use your calling card by dialing the toll-free access number of your long-distance provider from any pay phone. You'll find a phone center by the Paseo de la Princesa.

## COMING ASHORE

Most cruise ships dock within a couple of blocks of Old San Juan; however, there is a second cruise pier across the bay, and if your ship docks there you'll need to take a taxi to get anywhere on the island. The Paseo de la Princesa, a tree-lined promenade beneath the city wall, is a nice place for a stroll—you can admire the local crafts and stop at the refreshment kiosks. Major sights in the Old San Juan area are mere blocks from the piers, but be aware that the streets are narrow and steeply inclined in places.

It's particularly easy to get to Cataño and the Bacardí Rum Plant on your own; take the ferry that leaves from the cruise piers every half hour and then a taxi from the other side. Taxis, which line up to meet ships, are the best option if you want to explore beyond Old San Juan. White taxis labeled "Taxi Turístico" charge set fares of $10 to $24. Less common are metered cabs authorized by the Public Service Commission that charge an initial $1; after that, it's about 10¢ for each additional 1/13 mile. If you take a metered taxi, insist that the meter be turned on, and pay only what is shown, plus a tip of 15% to 20%. You can negotiate with taxi drivers for specific trips, and you can hire a taxi for as little as $36 per hour for sightseeing tours. If you want to see more of the island but don't want to drive, you may want to consider a shore excursion, though almost all trips can be booked more cheaply with local tour operators.

If you are embarking or disembarking in San Juan, the ride to or from the Luis Muñoz Marín International Airport, east of downtown San Juan, to the docks in Old San Juan takes about 20 minutes, depending on traffic. The white Taxi Turístico cabs, marked by a logo on the door, have a fixed rate of $19 to and from the cruise-ship piers; there is a $1 charge for each piece of luggage. Other taxi companies charge by the mile, which can cost a little more. Be sure the driver starts the meter, or agree on a fare beforehand.

> ### BEST BETS
>
> ■ **El Morro.** Explore the giant labyrinthine fort.
>
> ■ **El Yunque National Forest.** This rain forest east of San Juan is a great half-day excursion.
>
> ■ **Casa Bacardí.** Rum lovers can jump on the public ferry and then taxi over to the factory.
>
> ■ **Old San Juan.** Walk the cobblestone streets of Old San Juan.
>
> ■ **Shopping.** Within a few blocks of the port there are plenty of factory outlets and boutiques.

## EXPLORING

### OLD SAN JUAN

Old San Juan, the original city founded in 1521, contains carefully preserved examples of 16th- and 17th-century Spanish colonial architecture. More than 400 buildings have been beautifully restored. Graceful wrought-iron and wooden balconies with lush hanging plants extend over narrow streets paved with *adoquines* (blue-gray stones originally used as ballast on Spanish ships). The Old City is partially enclosed by walls that date from 1633 and once completely surrounded it. Designated a U.S. National Historic Zone in 1950, Old San Juan is chockablock with shops, open-air cafés, homes, tree-shaded squares, monuments, and people. You can get an overview on a morning's stroll, which includes some steep climbs. However, if you plan to immerse yourself in history or to shop, you'll need a couple of days.

**Alcaldía.** San Juan's city hall was built between 1602 and 1789. In 1841, extensive alterations made it resemble Madrid's city hall, with arcades, towers, balconies, and an inner courtyard. Renovations have refreshed the facade and some interior rooms, but the architecture remains true to its colonial style. Only the patios are open to public viewings. A municipal tourist information center and an art gallery with rotating exhibits are in the lobby. Call ahead to schedule a free tour. ⊠ *153 Calle San Francisco, Plaza de Armas, Old San Juan* ☎ *787/480–2910* ⊕ *www. sanjuanciudadpatria.com* ⊡ *Free.*

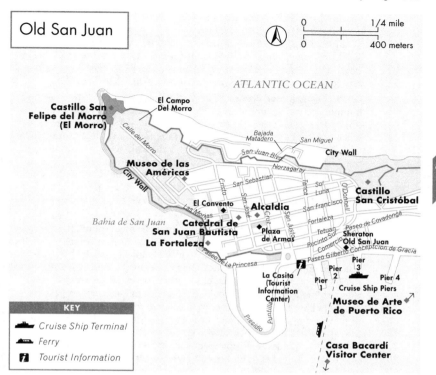

Old San Juan

0      1/4 mile

0      400 meters

ATLANTIC OCEAN

Castillo San Felipe del Morro (El Morro)

El Campo Del Morro

Calle del Morro

City Wall

Bajada Matadero

San Miguel

San Juan Blvd

Norzagaray

Museo de las Américas

San Sebastian

City Wall

Cristo

Sol

Luna

Tanca

O'Donnell

Castillo San Cristóbal

El Convento

Las Monas

Cruz

San José

San Justo

San Francisco

Alcaldía

Catedral de San Juan Bautista

La Fortaleza

Bahia de San Juan

Plaza de Armas

Fortaleza

Recinto Sur

Comercio

Tetuán

Paseo de Covadonga

Sheraton Old San Juan

Concepción de Gracia

Paseo de La Princesa

Paseo Gilberto

La Casita (Tourist Information Center)

Pier 1

Pier 2

Pier 3

Pier 4

Cruise Ship Piers

Museo de Arte de Puerto Rico

Presidio

Casa Bacardí Visitor Center

**KEY**

Cruise Ship Terminal

Ferry

Tourist Information

4

---

**FAMILY**
**Fodor's Choice**
★

**Castillo San Cristóbal.** This huge stone fortress, built between 1634 and 1790, guarded the city from land attacks from the east. The largest Spanish fortification in the New World, San Cristóbal was known in the 17th and 18th centuries as the Gibraltar of the West Indies. Five freestanding structures divided by dry moats are connected by tunnels. You're free to explore the gun turrets (with cannon in situ), officers' quarters, re-created 18th-century barracks, and gloomy passageways. Along with El Morro, San Cristóbal is a National Historic Site administered by the U.S. Park Service; it's a World Heritage Site as well. Rangers conduct tours in Spanish and English. ⌧ *Calle Norzagaray at Av. Muñoz Rivera, Old San Juan* ☎*787/729–6777* ⊕ *www.nps.gov/ saju* ⌧ *$5 includes admission to El Morro.*

**FAMILY**
**Fodor's Choice**
★

**Castillo San Felipe del Morro** (*El Morro*). At the northwestern tip of the Old City, El Morro ("the promontory") was built by the Spaniards between 1539 and 1786. Rising 140 feet above the sea, the massive six-level fortress was built to protect the port and has a commanding view of the harbor. It is a labyrinth of cannon batteries, ramps, barracks, turrets, towers, and tunnels, which you're free to wander. The cannon emplacement walls and the dank secret passageways are a wonder of engineering. A small but enlightening museum displays ancient Spanish guns and other armaments, military uniforms, and blueprints for

Spanish forts in the Americas, although Castillo San Cristóbal has more extensive and impressive exhibits. There's also a gift shop. The fort is a National Historic Site administered by the U.S. Park Service and is a World Heritage Site as well. Various tours and a video are available in English. ✉ *Calle del Morro, Old San Juan* ☎ *787/729–6960* ⊕ *www. nps.gov/saju* ☜ *$5 includes admission to Castillo San Cristóbal.*

**Catedral de San Juan Bautista.** The Catholic shrine of Puerto Rico had humble beginnings in the early 1520s as a thatch-roof, wooden structure. After a hurricane destroyed the church, it was rebuilt in 1540, when it was given a graceful circular staircase and vaulted Gothic ceilings. Most of the work on the present cathedral, however, was done in the 19th century. The remains of Ponce de León are behind a marble tomb in the wall near the transept, on the north side. The trompe l'oeil work on the inside of the dome is breathtaking. Unfortunately, many of the other frescoes suffer from water damage. ✉ *151 Calle Cristo, Old San Juan* ☎ *787/722–0861* ☜ *$1 donation suggested.*

**La Fortaleza.** Sitting atop the fortified city walls overlooking the harbor, La Fortaleza was built between 1533 and 1540 as a fortress, but it proved insufficient, mainly because it was built inside the bay. It was attacked numerous times and occupied twice, by the British in 1598 and the Dutch in 1625. When the city's other fortifications were finished, this became the governor's palace. Changes made over the past four centuries have resulted in the current eclectic yet eye-pleasing collection of marble and mahogany, medieval towers, and stained-glass galleries. Still the official residence of the island's governor, it is the Western Hemisphere's oldest executive mansion in continual use. Guided tours of the gardens and exterior are conducted several times a day in English and Spanish. Call ahead, as the schedule changes daily. Proper attire is required: no sleeveless shirts or very short shorts. Tours begin near the main gate in a yellow building called the Real Audiencia, housing the Oficina Estatal de Preservación Histórica. ✉ *Western end of Calle Fortaleza, Old San Juan* ☎ *787/721–7000* ⊕ *www.fortaleza.gobierno.pr* ☜ *Free.*

**Museo de las Américas.** On the second floor of the imposing former military barracks, Cuartel de Ballajá, this museum houses four permanent exhibits: Folk Arts, African Heritage, the Indian in America, and Conquest and Colonization. You'll also find a number of temporary exhibitions of works by regional and international artists. A wide range of handicrafts is available in the gift shop. ✉ *Calle Norzagaray and Calle del Morro, Old San Juan* ☎ *787/724–5052* ⊕ *www.museolasamericas. org* ☜ *$6.*

## ELSEWHERE IN SAN JUAN

**Casa Bacardí Visitor Center.** Exiled from Cuba, the Bacardí family built a small rum distillery here in the 1950s. Today it's the world's largest, able to produce 100,000 gallons of spirits a day and 21 million cases a year. A basic tour of the visitor center includes one free drink, or you can opt for a mixology class or rum tasting. If you don't want to drive, you can take a ferry from Pier 2 for 50¢ and then a *público* (public van service) from the ferry pier to the factory for about $3 per person.

✉ *Bay View Industrial Park, Rte. 165, Km 2.6, at Rte. 888, Cataño* ☎ *787/788–8400* ⊕ *www.visitcasabacardi.com* 🎫 *Tour $12; mixology class or rum tasting $45.*

**Fodor's Choice**  **Museo de Arte de Puerto Rico.** One of the Caribbean's biggest museums, this beautiful neoclassical building was once the San Juan Municipal Hospital. The collection of Puerto Rican art starts with the colonial era, when most art was commissioned for churches. Works by José Campeche, the island's first great painter, include his masterpiece, *Immaculate Conception,* finished in 1794. Also well represented is Francisco Oller y Cestero, who was the first to move beyond religious subjects to paint local scenes. Another room has works by artists inspired by Oller. The original building, built in the 1920s, proved too small to house the collection; a newer east wing is dominated by a five-story stained-glass window by local artist Eric Tabales. The museum also has a beautiful garden with native flora and a 400-seat theater with a remarkable hand-crocheted lace curtain. ✉ *299 Av. José de Diego, Santurce* ☎ *787/977–6277* ⊕ *www.mapr.org* 🎫 *$6; free Wed. 2–8.*

## BEACHES

The city's beaches can get crowded, especially on weekends. There's free access to all of them, but parking can be an issue in the peak sun hours—arriving early or in the late afternoon is a safer bet.

FAMILY  **Balneario de Carolina.** When people talk about a "beautiful Isla Verde beach," this is it. East of Isla Verde, this Blue Flag beach is so close to the airport that leaves rustle when planes take off. Thanks to an offshore reef, the surf is not as strong as other nearby beaches, so it's good for families. There's plenty of room to spread out underneath the palm and almond trees, and there are picnic tables and barbecue grills. Though there's a charge for parking, there's not always someone to take the money. On weekends, the beach is crowded; get here early to nab parking. **Amenities:** lifeguards; parking (fee); showers; toilets. **Best for:** swimming; walking. ✉ *Av. Los Gobernadores, Carolina* ☎ *787/791–2410* 🎫 *$3 parking.*

## SHOPPING

San Juan has the island's best range of stores (many closed on Sunday), but it isn't a free port, so you won't find bargains on electronics and perfumes. You can, however, find excellent prices on china, crystal, clothing, and jewelry. When shopping for local crafts, you'll find tacky along with treasures; in many cases you can watch the artisans at work. Popular items include *santos* (small carved figures of saints or religious scenes), hand-rolled cigars, handmade *mundillo* lace from Moca, *vejigantes* (colorful masks used during Carnival and local festivals) from Loíza and Ponce, and fancy men's shirts called guayaberas.

Old San Juan—especially Calles Fortaleza and Cristo—has T-shirt emporiums, crafts stores, bookshops, art galleries, jewelry boutiques, and even shops that specialize in made-to-order Panama hats. Calle Cristo has factory outlets, including Coach and Dooney & Bourke.

With many stores selling luxury items and designer fashions, the shopping spirit in the San Juan neighborhood of Condado is reminiscent of Miami. Avenida Ashford, the heart of San Juan's fashion district, has plenty of high-end clothing stores.

## ACTIVITIES

### GOLF

**TPC Dorado Beach.** Four 18-hole regulation courses blend Caribbean luxury and great golf at this icon with a storied tradition and were purchased by TPC in 2015. Designed by Robert Trent Jones Sr., the famous East and West courses (East was renovated by Robert Trent Jones, Jr. in 2011; West is closed for renovation) are in a secluded seaside sanctuary along 2 miles (3 km) of northeasterly shore within the former Rockefeller estate. Two Plantation Courses—the Sugarcane (more challenging) and Pineapple (easier)—complete the offerings. ⊠ *5000 Plantation Dr., Dorado* ☎ *787/262–1010* ⊕ *www.doradobeachclubs.com* 🏌 *East $282, Plantation Courses $170* 🏌 *East Course: 18 holes, 7200 yards, par 72; West Course: 18 holes, 6360 yards, par 72; Sugarcane: 18 holes, 7119 yards, par 72; Pineapple: 18 holes, 6196 yards, par 72.*

## WHERE TO EAT

**$**

**BURGER**

✕**Bistro Burger.** After exploring El Morro, head to Bistro Burger on Calle San Sebastián for what locals consider the best burgers in town. Choose from the house burgers, all named after local artists, or build your own burger with homemade ingredients. The Daphne Elvira is a great choice, made with chorizo and pork, Manchego cheese, red onion, and *acerola* (Caribbean cherry) ketchup on fresh foccacia bread. Don't leave without trying the *ropa vieja* egg rolls made with tender, stewed beef. The kitchen is open late on weekends, making Bistro Burger the perfect place to grab a bite after bar-hopping on Calle San Sebastián. ⑤ *Average main: $9* ⊠ *157 Calle San Sebastián, Old San Juan* ☎ *787/664–3626.*

**$$**

**PUERTO RICAN**

✕**La Fonda del Jibarito.** The menus are handwritten and the tables wobble, but Sanjuaneros have favored this casual, no-frills, family-run restaurant—tucked away on a quiet cobbled street—for years. The *bistec encebollado,* goat fricassee, and shredded beef stew are among the specialties on the menu of typical Puerto Rican comida criolla dishes. The tiny back porch is filled with plants, and the dining room is filled with fanciful depictions of life on the street outside. Troubadours serenade patrons, which include plenty of cruise-ship passengers when ships are in dock. ⑤ *Average main: $14* ⊠ *280 Calle Sol, Old San Juan* ☎ *787/725–8375.*

## NIGHTLIFE

Almost every ship stays in San Juan late or even overnight to give passengers an opportunity to revel in the nightlife—the most sophisticated in the Caribbean.

## BARS AND MUSIC CLUBS

**Fodor's**Choice **La Factoría.** La Factoría, the former Hijos de Borinquen, is hands-down
★ the best mixology bar in San Juan. Artisanal cocktails are crafted with
the highest-quality ingredients. Many bitters are homemade as is the
ginger beer, which is used in their popular Get Lucky Mule. Whether
its sweet, spicy, bitter, or something completely out of the box, these
drinks will blow your mind. Behind the bar, there is a secret wooden
door that leads to VINO Wine Bar, which has a great speakeasy feel.
Tasty tapas are available and can be enjoyed in the adjacent room. The
bars stays open until the sun comes, up and there is a DJ on weekends
in the back room. There's no sign on the door, so look for the terra-cotta
building on the corner of San Sebastián and San José. ⊠ *148 Calle San
Sebastián, Old San Juan* ☏ *787/594–5698.*

**The Mezzanine at St. Germain.** On top of St. Germain Bistro & Café, and
in the former headquarters of the Nationalist Party, The Mezzanine is a
contemporary take on the 1920s speakeasy. The chic space is conducive
for sipping old-fashioneds or our favorite, the Peridot, made with gin
and muddled basil and orange—very refreshing after walking the hills
of Old San Juan. Tapas are served all day. The Mezzanine also hosts one
of the best happy hours in town, Tuesday through Friday from 4 to 8.
Enjoy select tapas and cocktails for half off. You can't beat that in San
Juan! Their boozy brunch is very popular on weekends. ⊠ *156 Calle
Sol, 2nd fl., Old San Juan* ☏ *787/724–4657* ⊕ *www.themezzaninepr.
com* ⊘ *Closed Mon.*

## CASINOS

By law, all casinos must be in hotels, and most of them are in San Juan.
The government keeps a close eye on them. Dress for the larger casinos
is on the formal side, and the atmosphere is refined, particularly in the
Isla Verde resorts. Casinos set their own hours but are generally open
from noon to 4 am. In addition to slot machines, typical games include
blackjack, roulette, craps, Caribbean stud (a five-card poker game), and
*pai gow* poker (a combination of American poker and the Chinese game
pai gow). Hotels with casinos have live entertainment most weekends,
as well as restaurants and bars. The minimum age to gamble (and to
drink) is 18. Casinos set their own hours, which change seasonally,
but generally operate from noon to 4 am, although the casino in the
Conrad Condado Plaza Hotel is open 24 hours. Other hotels with
casinos include the InterContinental San Juan Resort and Casino, the
Ritz-Carlton San Juan Hotel, Spa and Casino, and the Sheraton Old
San Juan Hotel and Casino.

# SANTO DOMINGO, DOMINICAN REPUBLIC

By Eileen
Robinson
Smith

Spanish civilization in the New World began in Santo Domingo's
12-block Zona Colonial (Colonial Zone). As you stroll its narrow
streets, it's easy to imagine this old city as it was when the likes of
Columbus, Cortés, and Ponce de León walked the cobblestones, when
pirates sailed in and out of the harbor, and when colonists first started
building the New World's largest city. Tourist brochures tout that "history comes alive here"—a surprisingly truthful statement. However,

many tourists bypass the large, sprawling, and noisy city; it's their loss. The Dominican Republic's seaside capital—despite such detractions as poverty and sprawl, not to mention a population of some 2 million people—has some of the country's best hotels, restaurants, and nightlife (not to mention great casinos). Many of these are right on or near the Malecón and within the historic Zona Colonial area, which is separated from the rest of the city by Parque Independencia. If your ship calls or even embarks here, you'll be treated to a vibrant Latin cultural center unlike any other in the Caribbean.

## ESSENTIALS

### CURRENCY
The Dominican peso, but you can almost always use U.S. dollars.

### TELEPHONE
Telephones are available at the dock, as soon as passengers disembark, and telephone cards can be purchased there as well. Tele-cards can also be bought at the supermarket at Casa de Campo Marina. To call the United States or Canada from the D.R., just punch in 1 plus the area code and number. To make calls on the island, you must tap in the area code (809), plus the seven-digit number; if you are calling a Dominican cell phone, you must first punch in 1 then 809 or 829.

### COMING ASHORE
Santo Domingo has two stellar cruise-ship terminals, and has become a growing port for cruise passengers, despite the sluggish economy.

The **Don Diego Terminal** is on the Ozuma River, facing the Avenida del Puerto, and across the street are steps that lead up to the main pedestrian shopping street of the Zona Colonial, Calle El Conde. A lovely yellow-and-white building, with stained-glass windows and faux gaslights, it has a small cafeteria, and potted palms soften the cordoned-off lines where passengers wait to have their tickets checked and go through immigration. The reception area has telephones, Internet access, and a currency exchange. Just down the dock is an ATM; in front of that is a counter where you can get cold drinks and snacks.

The **Sans Souci Terminal** complex, diagonally across the Ozama River from Don Diego Terminal, on Avenida España, has been operational since 2010, but this long-term redevelopment project is still a work in progress. Its mezzanine level accommodates immigration and customs, duty-free shops, and both Internet and information centers. Like the Port of Don Diego, it has stunning lighting systems that cover the exterior and perimeter areas for greater security and visibility for visitors. When completed, the complex will have finished its marina, and have a full complement of stores, a 122-acre real-estate development, a new sports arena, and more. This major project is aimed at integrating the port area and the Zona Colonial to create an appealing destination for cruisers, yachtsmen, and high-end tourists.

### AIRPORT TRANSFERS
If you are embarking in Santo Domingo, you should fly into Las Américas International Airport (SDQ), about 15 miles (24 km) east of downtown. On arrival you will have to pay US$10 in cash for a tourist tax. Transportation into the city is usually by taxi; figure on $40

to or from hotels on the Malecón or in the Zona Colonial. You'll be greeted by a melee of hawking taxi drivers and sometimes their English-speaking solicitors (who expect to be tipped, as do the freelance porters who will undoubtedly scoop up your luggage). If you're spending a night or two in Santo Domingo before a cruise, you can arrange a driver through ⊕ *www.dominicanshuttles.com* or possibly through your hotel, so that you'll be met with someone holding a sign with your name. (It's worth the extra $10 or so to avoid the hassle.) If you're going straight to your cruise ship, do consider taking the cruise line's prearranged transfer. When you disembark from your ship, expect long lines at check-in,

and be sure to give yourself a full two hours for check-in and security. The government departure tax should be included in your airline ticket.

## EXPLORING

History buffs will want to spend a day exploring the many "firsts" of our continent. A horse-and-carriage ride throughout the Colonial Zone costs $25 an hour. The steeds are no thoroughbreds, but they clip right along, though any commentary will be in Spanish. You can also negotiate to use them as a taxi, say, down to the Malecón. The drivers hang out in front of the Hostal Nicolas de Ovando hotel.

**Alcázar de Colón.** The castle of Don Diego Colón, built in 1517, was the home to generations of the Christopher Columbus family. The Renaissance-style structure, with its balustrade and double row of arches, has strong Moorish, Gothic, and Isabelline influences. The 22 rooms are furnished in a style to which the viceroy of the island would have been accustomed—right down to the dishes and the vice regal shaving mug. The mansion's 40-inch-thick coral-limestone walls make air-conditioning impossible. Bilingual guides are on hand for tours peppered with fascinating anecdotes, like weddings once-upon-a time. Audio tours (about 25 minutes) are available in English. ⊠ *Plaza de España, off Calle Emiliano Tejera, Zona Colonial* ☎ 809/682–4750 ⊕ *www.museoalcazardecolon.com* ➲ *RD$100.*

**Basílica Catedral Menor Santa María de la Encarnación.** The coral-limestone facade of the first cathedral in the New World (Catedral Primada de América) towers over the south side of the Parque Colón. Spanish workmen began building the cathedral in 1514, but left to search for gold in Mexico. The church was finally finished in 1540. Its facade is composed of architectural elements from the late Gothic to the lavish Plateresque

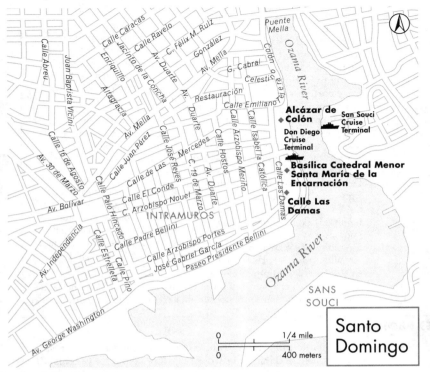

Santo Domingo

style. Inside, the high altar is made of hammered silver. A museum houses the cathedral's treasures; it's in the former jail, a yellow building just across the street. Mass times vary, so check before going there the day before. ✉ *Calle Arzobispo Meriño, Parque Colon, Zona Colonial* ☎ *809/682–3848* 🎫 *Free.*

**Calle Las Damas.** "The Ladies Street" was named after the elegant ladies of the court: in the Spanish tradition, they promenaded in the evening. Here you can see a sundial dating from 1753 and the Casa de los Jesuitas, which houses a fine research library for colonial history as well as the **Institute for Hispanic Culture**; admission is free, and it's open weekdays from 8 to 4:30. The boutique Hostal Nicolas de Ovando is on this street, across from the French Embassy. If you follow the street going toward the Malecón, you will pass a picturesque alley, fronted by a wrought-iron gate, where there are perfectly maintained colonial structures owned by the Catholic Church. ✉ *Calle las Damas, Zona Colonial.*

## BEACHES

If you are in port for just a day, you'll have a better time if you skip the beach and spend some time in the Zona Colonial and on the Malecón.

FAMILY **Playa Boca Chica.** You can walk far out into warm, calm, clear waters protected by coral reefs here. On weekends, the strip with the mid-rise resorts is busy, drawing mainly Dominican families and some Europeans. But midweek is better, when the beaches are less crowded. Sadly, on the public beach you will be pestered and hounded by a parade of roving vendors of cheap jewelry, sunglasses, hair braiders, seafood cookers, ice-cream men, and masseuses (who are usually peddling more than a simple beach massage). Young male prostitutes also roam the beach and often hook up with older European and Cuban men. The best section of the public beach is in front of Don Emilio's (the blue hotel), which has a restaurant, bar, decent bathrooms, and parking. Better, go to one of the nicer waterfront restaurants—Boca Marina Restaurant & Lounge, El Pelicano, Neptuno's Club—and skip the public beach altogether. **Amenities:** food and drink; parking; toilets. **Best for:** partiers; sunset; swimming; walking. ⊠ *Autopista Las Américas, 21 miles (34 km) east of Santo Domingo, Boca Chica.*

## SHOPPING

Exquisitely hand-wrapped cigars continue to be the hottest commodity coming out of the D.R. Only reputable cigar shops sell the real thing. Dominican rum and coffee are also good buys. Mamajuana, an herbal liqueur, is said to be the Dominican answer to Viagra. Look also for the delicate, faceless ceramic figurines that symbolize Dominican culture. Though locally crafted products are often affordable, expect to pay for designer jewelry made of amber and larimar, an indigenous semiprecious stone the color of the Caribbean. Amber, a fossilization of resin from a prehistoric pine tree, often encasing ancient animal and plant life, from leaves to spiders to tiny lizards, is mined extensively. (Beware of fakes, which are especially prevalent in street stalls.)

**Acropolis Mall,** between Avenida Winston Churchill and Calle Rafael Augusto Sanchez, has become a favorite shopping arena for the young and/or hip capitaleños. Stores like Zara and Mango (both from Spain) have today's look without breaking your budget.

One of the main shopping streets in the Zona is **Calle El Conde,** a pedestrian thoroughfare. With the advent of so many restorations, the dull and dusty stores with dated merchandise are giving way to some hip new shops. However, many of the offerings, including local designer shops, are still of a caliber and cost that the Dominicans can afford. Some of the best shops are on **Calle Duarte,** north of the Zona Colonial, between Calle Mella and Avenida de Las Américas. **El Mercado Modelo,** a covered market, borders Calle Mella in the Zona Colonial; vendors here sell a dizzying selection of Dominican crafts.

**Piantini** is a swanky residential neighborhood that has an increasing number of fashionable shops and clothing boutiques, often housed in contemporary shopping malls. Its borders run from Avenida Winston Churchill to Avenida Lope de Vega and from Calle Jose Amado Soler to Avenida 27 de Febrero.

## WHERE TO EAT

**$$$**
INTERNATIONAL

✕**Pat'e Palo European Brasserie.** Ideally located on Plaza de España across from the Alcazar de Colón, this restaurant has good claim to being the first tavern in the New World (the building itself is 500 years old) and capitalizes on its historic heritage. The alfresco dining terrace makes it perfect for watching the free cultural performances that happen across from the plaza. The innovative chef prepares a contemporary, gastro-fusion menu, offering tasting menus and cuisine-related events. Although the waiters are still dressed like pirates (with bandanas askew), the restaurant's culinary profile has only grown. The wine carte is impressive but pricey, and you can enjoy an after-dinner cigar from the humidor if you're so inclined. ⑤ *Average main: $26* ⊠ *Calle Atarazana 25, Plaza de Espana, Zona Colonial* ☎ *809/687–8089* ⊕ *www. patepalo.com.*

## WHERE TO STAY

**$**
HOTEL
**Fodor's**Choice
★

▦**Hostal Nicolas de Ovando–MGallery Collection.** This historic boutique hotel owned by the French Accor group was sculpted from the residence of the first governor of the Americas, and it just might be the best thing to happen in the Zone since Diego Columbus's palace was finished in 1517. **Pros:** lavish breakfast buffet; beautifully restored historic section; a safe haven with tight security. **Cons:** breakfast is no longer included in rates; some rooms could be larger; the restaurant is no longer the gastronomic experience it once was. ⑤ *Rooms from: $175* ⊠ *Calle Las Damas, Zona Colonial* ⊹ *Across the street from the French Embassy* ☎ *809/685–9955, 800/763–4835, 809/682–9612 direct line for reservations* ⊕ *www.mgallery.com/2975* ⇔ *97 rooms* ⦿ *No meals.*

**$**
HOTEL

▦**Renaissance Santo Domingo Jaragua Hotel & Casino.** It's remarkable what a major renovation can do to revive an iconic, albeit tired, landmark; the newly transformed Jaragua is jaw-dropping. **Pros:** security is tight and solo female travelers feel safe; large, well-appointed fitness center and spa; room service is surprisingly good. **Cons:** can be a bit noisy at times with conventions and large meetings; service in restaurants can be slow, especially with language barriers; more of a business hotel than a leisure hotel. ⑤ *Rooms from: $162* ⊠ *Av. George Washington 367, Gazcue* ☎ *809/221–2222* ⊕ *www.marriott.com* ⇔ *300 rooms* ⦿ *No meals.*

## NIGHTLIFE

Santo Domingo's nightlife is vast and ever changing. Check with the concierges and hip capitaleños. However clubs and bars must close at midnight during the week, and 2 am on Friday and Saturday nights. There are some exceptions to the latter, primarily those clubs and casinos in hotels. Sadly, the curfew has put some clubs out of business, but it has cut down on the crime and late-night noise, particularly in the Zona Colonial. Some clubs are now pushing the envelope and staying open until 3, but they do get in trouble with the authorities when caught, and you probably don't want to be there then.

# SANTO TOMÁS DE CASTILLA, GUATEMALA

By Jeffrey Van Fleet

Guatemala's short Caribbean shoreline doesn't generate the buzz of those of neighboring Belize and Mexico. The coast weighs in at a scant 74 miles (123 km), and this mostly highland country wears its indigenous culture on its sleeve and has historically looked inland rather than to the sea. You'll be drawn inland, too, with a variety of shore excursions. This is the land of the Maya, after all. But there's plenty to keep you occupied here in the lowlands. Tourist brochures tout the Caribbean coast as "The Other Guatemala." The predominantly indigenous and Spanish cultures of the highlands give way to an Afro-Caribbean tradition that listens more closely to the rhythms of far-off Jamaica rather than taking its cue from Guatemala City. Think of it as mixing a little reggae with your salsa.

> ### BEST BETS
>
> ■ **Quiriguá.** If you want to see Mayan ruins but don't want to spend an entire day on the bus, nearby Quiriguá can be impressive.
>
> ■ **Copán.** In neighboring Honduras, this Mayan site is a worthwhile day trip from Santo Tomás.
>
> ■ **Riding on the Río Dulce.** The ride on this river is one of Guatemala's most beautiful boat trips.

## ESSENTIALS

### CURRENCY

The Guatemalan quetzal; make sure you get money from the ATM in the cruise terminal in Santo Tomás de Castilla. Outside the terminal, few businesses accept U.S. dollars. Honduras's currency is the lempira for shore excursions to Copán, but U.S. dollars will suffice on an organized trip through your cruise line.

### TELEPHONE

Guatemalan phone numbers have eight digits. There are no city or area codes. Simply dial the number for any in-country call. Most towns have offices of Telgua, the national telephone company, where you can place both national and international calls. Avoid the ubiquitous public phones with signs promising "Free calls to the USA." The number back home being called gets socked with a hefty bill.

## COMING ASHORE

Cruise ships dock at the modern, spacious Terminal de Cruceros, where you'll find a bank, post office, money exchange, telephones, Internet access, a lively craft market, and an office of INGUAT, Guatemala's national tourist office. A marimba band serenades you with its clinking xylophone-like music; a Caribbean ensemble dances for you (and may even pull you in to take part).

Taxis, both vehicular and water, take you to various destinations in the area. Plan on paying $3 to Santo Tomás de Castilla proper, and $5 to Puerto Barrios. Boats transport cruise visitors to Livingston, charging about $6 for the 20-minute trip. The Amatique Bay Resort provides water taxis from port to resort of $10 per person. Vehicular taxis charge $35 per head to travel by land to the resort.

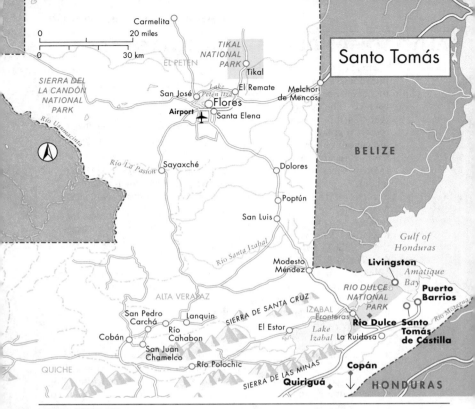

Santo Tomás

## EXPLORING

### SANTO TOMÁS DE CASTILLA

Belgian immigrants settled Santo Tomás in the 19th century, but little remains of their heritage today, save for the preponderance of French and Flemish names in the local cemetery. Most visitors move on. Santo Tomás has experienced a small renaissance as the country's most important port, receiving growing numbers of cruise and cargo ships, and serving as the headquarters of the Guatemalan navy.

### PUERTO BARRIOS

*3 miles (5 km) north of Santo Tomás de Castilla.*

Puerto Barrios maintains the atmosphere of an old banana town, humid and a tad down at the heels, perhaps longing for better days. Santo Tomás has replaced it as the country's largest port, and you'll likely zip through the Caribbean coast's biggest city on your way to somewhere else, but the cathedral and municipal market are worth a look if you find yourself here. Water taxis depart from the municipal docks for Livingston, across the bay, where you start your trip up the Río Dulce.

"Bahía de Amatique" denotes the large bay that washes the Caribbean coast of Guatemala and southern Belize just north of Puerto Barrios, but for most travelers the name is inexorably linked with the **Amatique Bay**

**Resort and Marina,** the region's only five-star hotel. The 61-room resort opens itself up for day visitors, and many cruise passengers stop by for a drink, a meal, or an entire day of swimming, watersliding, kayaking, horseback riding, or bicycling. ⊠ *6 miles (10 km) north of Santo Tomás; 14 Calle Final, Finca Pichilingo, Puerto Barrios* ☎ *7931–0000.*

## LIVINGSTON
*15 miles (25 km) by water northwest of Santo Tomás.*

Visitors compare Livingston with Puerto Barrios across the bay, and the former wins hands down, for its sultry, seductive Caribbean flavor. Wooden houses, some on stilts, congregate in this old fishing town, once an important railroad hub, but today inaccessible by land from the outside world. Livingston proudly trumpets its Garífuna heritage, a culture unique to Central America's eastern coast and descended from the intermarriage of African slaves with Caribbean indigenous people. Music and dance traditions and a Caribbean-accented English remain, even if old-timers lament the creeping outside influences, namely Spanish rap and reggae.

## RÍO DULCE
*30 miles (48 km) southwest of Santo Tomás.*

The natural crown jewel of this region is the 13,000-hectare (32,000-acre) national park that protects the river leading inland from Livingston to Lago de Izabal, Guatemala's largest lake. Pelicans, herons, egrets, and terns nest and fly along the Río Dulce, which cuts through a heavily forested limestone canyon. Excursions often approach the park by land, but we recommend making the trip upriver from Livingston to immerse yourself in the entire Indiana Jones experience. Some cruise ships offer a trip to Hacienda Tijax for the day for their activities; these trips usually include lunch.

**Castillo de San Felipe de Lara.** Once an important Mayan trade route, the Río Dulce later became the route over which the conquistadors sent the gold and silver they plundered back to Spain. All this wealth attracted Dutch and English pirates, who attacked both the ships and the warehouses on shore. Spanish colonists constructed this fortress in 1595 to guard the inland waterway from pirate incursions. A 1999 earthquake in this region destroyed the river pier and damaged portions of the fort. If you wish to visit, rather than simply see the structure from the water, you'll need to approach the park overland rather than upriver—all best accomplished on an organized shore excursion. ⊠ *Southwest of Fronteras, Río Dulce* ☎ *$3 or Q22.*

## QUIRIGUÁ
*60 miles (96 km) southwest of Puerto Barrios.*

**Quiriguá.** Quiriguá, a Mayan city that dates from the Classic period, is famous for the amazingly well-preserved stelae, or carved pillars, which are the largest yet discovered, and dwarf those of Copán, Honduras, some 50 km (30 miles) south. The stelae depict Quiriguá's ruling dynasty, especially the powerful Cauac Chan (Jade Sky), whose visage appears on nine of the structures circling the Great Plaza. Stela E, the largest of these, towers 10 meters (33 feet) high and weighs 65 tons.

4

Several monuments, covered with interesting zoomorphic figures, still stand. The most interesting of these depicts Cauac Chan's conquest of Copán and the subsequent beheading of its then-ruler, 18 Rabbit. The remains of an acropolis and other structures have been partially restored. The ruins are surrounded by a strand of rain forest—an untouched wilderness in the heart of banana country. A small museum here gives insight into Quiriguá's history. ⊠ *54 miles (90 km) southwest of Santo Tomás de Castilla, Los Amates* ⌑ *$4 or Q30.*

### COPÁN

*122 miles (203 km) southeast of Santo Tomás.*

**Copán.** Just across the border in Honduras lie the famed ruins of Copán, the center of a kingdom that rose to prominence in the Classic period (5th to 9th centuries AD).

As you stroll past towering cieba trees on your way in from the gate, you'll find the Great Plaza to your left. The ornate stelae standing around the plaza were monuments erected to glorify rulers. The most impressive—located in the middle of the plaza—depict King 18 Rabbit.

The city's most important ball court lies south of the Great Plaza. The game was more spiritual than sportslike in nature: the losers—or the winners in some cases—were killed as a sacrifice to Mayan gods.

Near the ball court lies the Hieroglyphic Stairway, containing the largest single collection of hieroglyphs in the world. The 63 steps immortalize the battles won by Copán's kings, especially those of the much revered King Smoke Jaguar.

Below the Acropolis here wind tunnels leading to some of the most fascinating discoveries at Copán. Underneath Structure 16 are the near-perfect remains of an older structure, called the Rosalila Temple, dating from AD 571. Uncovered in 1989, the Rosalila was notable in part because of the paint remains on its surface—rose and lilac—for which it was named. Another tunnel called Los Jaguares takes you past tombs, a system of aqueducts, and even an ancient bathroom.

East of the main entrance to Copán, the marvelous Museo de Escultura Maya provides a closer look at the best of Mayan artistry. ⊠ *1 km (½ mile) east of Copán Ruinas, Copán Ruinas* ☎ *2651–4018* ⌑ *Ruins $15 or L330; museum $7 or L84; tunnels $15 or L330.*

## SHOPPING

The rest of Guatemala overflows with indigenous crafts and art, but the famous market towns of the highlands are nowhere to be found in Caribbean region. Quite honestly, your best bet for shopping is the Terminal de Cruceros at Santo Tomás de Castilla, and you'll have plenty of opportunity to buy before you board your ship. What you'll find here comes from Guatemala's highlands—the coast does not have a strong artisan tradition—with a good selection of fabrics, weavings, woodwork, and basketry. Markets in Puerto Barrios and Livingston, the only real urban areas you'll encounter in this region, are more geared toward the workaday needs of residents rather than visitors.

## ACTIVITIES

### BEACHES AND WATER SPORTS

**Amatique Bay Resort & Marina.** The only real beach in the region lies within the confines of the Amatique Bay Resort & Marina, which is the only place here that has a resort atmosphere to it. Day visitors partake in swimming, waterslides, and kayaking. The resort's launch will bring you over from the cruise-ship terminal in Santo Tomás de Castilla. **Amenities:** food and drink, showers, toilets. **Best for:** walking, swimming. ⊠ *14 Calle Final, Puerto Barrios ⊹ 10 km (6 miles) north of Santo Tomás de Castilla* ☎ *7931–0000 ⊕ www.amatiquebay.net.*

### HIKING AND KAYAKING

**Hacienda Tijax.** The unusual-looking name of this eco-lodge is pronounced *tee-HAHSH*. It lies inland, near the point where the Río Dulce meets the vast Lake Izabal. The staff oversees kayaking and hiking for day visitors. ⊠ *Río Dulce ⊹ Northeast of Fronteras, near bridge that crosses over Rio Dulce* ☎ *7930–5505 ⊕ www.tijax.com.*

# ST-BARTHÉLEMY (GUSTAVIA)

By Elise Meyer

Hilly St. Barthélemy, popularly known as St. Barth (or St. Barts) is just 8 square miles (21 square km), but the island has at least 20 good beaches. What draws visitors is its sophisticated but unstudied approach to relaxation: the finest food, excellent wine, high-end shopping, and lack of large-scale commercial development. A favorite among upscale cruise-ship passengers, who also appreciate the shopping opportunities and fine dining, St. Barth isn't really equipped for megaship visits, which is why most ships calling here are from smaller premium lines. This is one place where you don't need to take the ship's shore excursions to have a good time. Just hail a cab or rent a car and go to one of the many wonderful beaches, where you will find some of the best lunchtime restaurants, or wander around Gustavia, shopping and eating. It's the best way to relax on this most relaxing of islands.

### ESSENTIALS

#### CURRENCY

The euro; however, U.S. dollars are accepted in almost all shops and in many restaurants.

#### TELEPHONE

Public telephones accept télécartes, prepaid calling cards that you can buy at the gas station next to the airport and at post offices in Lorient, St-Jean, and Gustavia. Making an international call using a télécarte is the best way to go.

### COMING ASHORE

Even medium-size ships must anchor in Gustavia Harbor and bring passengers ashore on tenders. The tiny harbor area is right in Gustavia, which is easily explored on foot. Shell Beach is accessible by a 10-minute walk, so you can take a swim during your explorations. Taxis, which meet all cruise ships, can be expensive. Technically, there's a flat rate for rides up to five minutes long. Each additional three minutes is an additional amount. In reality, however, cabbies usually name a fixed rate—and will not budge. Fares are 50% higher on Sunday and holidays. St. Barth is one port where it's really worth it to arrange a car or moped rental for a full-day exploration of the island, including the island's out-of-the-way beaches. But be aware that during high season there is often a three-day minimum, so this may not be possible except through your ship (and then you'll pay premium rates indeed). Most car-rental firms operate at the airport; however, renting on your own is usually cheaper than what you'll get if you go with one of the ship's car rentals (you may be able to find a car for $55 per day).

> **BEST BETS**
>
> ■ **Soaking up the Atmosphere.** It's the French Riviera transported to the Caribbean.
>
> ■ **Beautiful Beaches.** Pick any of the lovely, uncrowded beaches.
>
> ■ **French Food.** St. Barth has some of the best restaurants in the Caribbean.
>
> ■ **Shopping.** There is no better fashion shopping in the Caribbean, especially if you are young and slim.

## EXPLORING

With practice, negotiating St. Barth's narrow, steep roads soon becomes fun. Infrastructure upgrades and small, responsive rental cars have improved driving. Free maps are everywhere, and roads are smooth and well marked. The tourist office has annotated maps with walking tours that highlight sights of interest.

### GUSTAVIA

You can easily explore all of Gustavia during a two-hour stroll. Some shops close from noon to 3 or 4, so plan lunch accordingly, but stores stay open past 7 in the evening. Parking in Gustavia is a challenge, especially during vacation times. A good spot to park is rue de la République, alongside the catamarans, yachts, and sailboats.

FAMILY **Le Musée Territorial, Wall House.** On the far side of the harbor known as La Pointe, the charming Municipal Museum has watercolors, portraits, photographs, traditional costumes, and historic documents detailing the island's history as well as displays of the island's flowers, plants, and marine life. There are also changing contemporary art exhibitions. ⊠ *La Pointe, Gustavia* ☎ *0590/29–71–55* 🖅 *€2.*

**Le P'tit Collectionneur.** Encouraged by family and friends, André Berry opened this private museum to showcase his lifelong passion for collecting fascinating objects such as 18th-century English pipes and the first phonograph to come to the island. He will happily show you his treasures. ⊠ *La Pointe, Gustavia* 🖅 *€2.*

### COROSSOL

Traces of the island's French provincial origins are evident in this two-street fishing village with a little rocky beach.

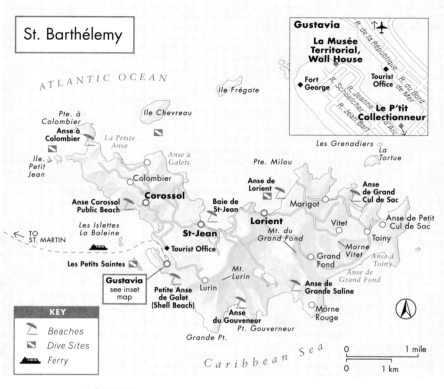

## LORIENT

Site of the first French settlement, Lorient is one of the island's two parishes; a restored church, a school, and a post office mark the spot. Note the gaily decorated graves in the cemetery.

## ST-JEAN

There is a monument at the crest of the hill that divides St-Jean from Gustavia. Called *The Arawak,* it symbolizes the soul of St. Barth. A warrior, one of the earliest inhabitants of the area, holds a lance in his right hand and stands on a rock shaped like the island; in his left hand he holds a conch shell, which sounds the cry of nature; perched beside him are a pelican (which symbolizes the air and survival by fishing) and an iguana (which represents the earth). The half-mile-long crescent of sand at St-Jean is the island's favorite beach. A popular activity is watching and photographing the hair-raising airplane landings (but it is extremely dangerous to stand at the beach end of the runway). Some of the best shopping on the island is here as are several restaurants.

## BEACHES

There is a beach in St. Barth to suit every taste. Wild surf, complete privacy in nature, a dreamy white-sand strand, and a spot at a chic beach club close to shopping and restaurants—they're all within a 20-minute drive.

There are many *anses* (coves) and nearly 20 *plages* (beaches) scattered around the island, each with a distinct personality; all are open to the public, even if they front a tony resort. Because of the number of beaches, even in high season you can find a nearly empty one, despite St. Barth's tiny size. That's not to say that all beaches are equally good or even equally suitable for swimming, but each has something to offer. Unless you are having lunch at a beachfront restaurant with lounging areas set aside for patrons, you should bring an umbrella, beach mat, and water (all of which are easily obtainable all over the island). Topless sunbathing is common, but nudism is supposedly forbidden—although both Grande Saline and Gouverneur are de facto nude beaches, albeit less than in the past. Shade is scarce.

**Anse de Grand Cul de Sac.** The shallow, reef-protected beach is nice for small children, fly-fishermen, kayakers, and windsurfers—and for the amusing pelican-like frigate birds that dive-bomb the water fishing for their lunch. There is a good dive shop. You needn't do your own fishing; you can have a wonderful lunch at one of the excellent restaurants, and use their lounge chairs for the afternoon. **Amenities:** food and drink; parking (no fee); toilets; water sports. **Best for:** swimming; walking. ⊠ *Grand Cul de Sac.*

Fodor'sChoice
★ **Anse de Grande Saline.** With its peaceful seclusion and sandy ocean bottom, this is just about everyone's favorite beach and is great for swimming, too. Without any major development, it's an ideal Caribbean strand, though there can be a bit of wind at times. In spite of the prohibition, young and old alike go nude. The beach is a 10-minute walk up a rocky dune trail, so wear sneakers or water shoes, and bring a blanket, umbrella, and beach towels. There are several good lunch restaurants near the parking area, but the beach itself is just sand, sea, and sky. The big salt ponds here are no longer in use, and the place looks a little desolate on approach, but don't despair. **Amenities:** parking (no fee). **Best for:** nudists; swimming; walking. ⊠ *Grande Saline.*

FAMILY **Baie de St-Jean.** Like a mini–Côte d'Azur—beachside bistros, terrific shopping, bungalow hotels, bronzed bodies, windsurfing, and day-trippers who tend to arrive on BIG yachts—the reef-protected strip is divided by Eden Rock promontory. Except when the hotels are filled, you can rent chaises and umbrellas at La Plage restaurant or Eden Rock, where you can lounge for hours over lunch. **Amenities:** food and drink; toilets. **Best for:** partiers; walking. ⊠ *St-Jean.*

## SHOPPING

Fodor'sChoice
★ St. Barth is a duty-free port, and its sophisticated visitors find shopping in its 200-plus boutiques a delight, especially for beachwear, accessories, jewelry, and casual wear. It's no overstatement to say that shopping for

fashionable clothing, jewels, and designer accessories is better in St. Barth than anywhere else in the Caribbean. New shops open all the time, so there's always something to discover. Some stores close from noon to 3, but they are open until 7 pm. Many are closed on Sunday. A popular afternoon pastime is strolling the two major shopping areas in Gustavia and St-Jean. While high fashion is as pricey here as everywhere, French brands sell for up to 30% less than in the U.S.

In Gustavia, boutiques pack the three major shopping streets. Quai de la République, which is right on the harbor, rivals New York's Madison Avenue or Paris's avenue Montaigne for high-end designer retail, including shops for **Louis Vuitton**, **Bulgari**, **Cartier**, **Chopard**, **Erès**, and **Hermès**. These shops often carry items that are not available in the United States. The elegant Carré d'Or plaza and the adjacent **Coeur Vendome** are great fun to explore. Shops are also clustered in **La Savane Commercial Center** (across from the airport), **La Villa Créole** (in St-Jean), and **Espace Neptune** (on the road to Lorient). It's worth working your way from one end to the other at these shopping complexes—just to see or, perhaps, be seen. Boutiques in all three areas carry the latest in French and Italian sportswear, charming children's togs, and some haute couture. Bargains may be tough to come by, but you might be able to snag that *Birkin* that has a long waiting list stateside, and in any case, you'll have a lot of fun hunting around.

For locally made art and handicrafts, the tourist office can provide information and arrange visits to studios of island artists, including Christian Bretoneiche, Robert Danet, Nathalie Daniel, Patricia Guyot, Rose Lemen, Aline de Lurin, and Marion Vinot. Gustavia, La Villa Créole, and the larger hotels have a few good gallery/craft boutiques.

## ACTIVITIES

### BOATING AND SAILING

St. Barth is a popular yachting and sailing center, thanks to its location midway between Antigua and St. Thomas.

Gustavia's harbor, 13 to 16 feet deep, has mooring and docking facilities for 40 yachts. There are also good anchorages at Public, Corossol, and Colombier. You can charter sailing and motorboats in Gustavia Harbor for as little as a half day, staffed or bareboat. Ask at the Gustavia tourist office or your hotel for a list of recommended charter companies.

**Jicky Marine Service.** This company offers private full-day outings on motorboats, Zodiacs, and 42- or 46-foot catamarans to the uninhabited Île Fourchue for swimming, snorkeling, cocktails, or lunch as well as weekly half- and full-day group cruises and twice-weekly group sunset catamaran cruises. Private fishing charters are also offered, as is private transport from St. Martin. An unskippered motorboat rental runs about €290 a day. A one-hour group Jet Ski tour of the island is also offered, as are private tours. ⊠ *26 rue Jeanne D'Arc, Gustavia* ☎ *0590/27–70–34* ⊕ *www.jickymarine.com.*

### DIVING AND SNORKELING

Several dive shops arrange scuba excursions. Depending on weather conditions, you may dive at **Pain de Sucre, Coco Island,** or toward nearby **Saba.** There's also an underwater shipwreck, plus sharks, rays, sea tortoises, coral, and the usual varieties of colorful fish. The waters on the island's leeward side are the calmest. For the uncertified, there's a shallow reef right off the beach at Anse de Cayes, which you can explore with mask and fins, and a hike down to the beach at Corossol brings you to a very popular snorkeling spot.

FAMILY **Plongée Caraïbe.** This company is recommended for its up-to-the-minute equipment, dive boat, and scuba discovery program. They offer nitrox diving and certification. It also runs two-hour group snorkeling trips on the *Blue Cat Catamaran* (€60), or you can enjoy a private charter from €490. ⊠ *Quai de la République, Gustavia* ☎ *0590/27–55–94* ⊕ *www. plongee-caraibes.com.*

## WHERE TO EAT

A service charge is always added by law, but you should leave the server 5% to 10% extra in cash. It is generally advisable to charge restaurant meals on a credit card, as the issuer will offer a better exchange rate than the restaurant.

$$ ✕ **Le Repaire.** Overlooking the harbor, this friendly classic French brasBRASSERIE serie is busy from its early-morning opening to its late-night closing.
FAMILY The flexible hours are great if you arrive on the island mid-afternoon and need a substantial snack. Grab a cappuccino, pull a captain's chair up to the street-side rail, and watch the pretty people go by. The menu ranges from cheeseburgers, served only at lunch, along with the island's best fries, to simply grilled fish and meat, pastas, risottos, mixed salads, and wonderful ice cream sundaes. ⑤ *Average main: €19* ⊠ *Rue de la République, Gustavia* ☎ *0590/27–72–48* ☉ *Closed Sun.*

$ ✕ **L'Isoletta.** This casual Roman-style pizzeria run by the popular L'Isola
PIZZA restaurant is a lively, chic lounge-style gastropub serving delicious thin-crust pizzas by the slice or the meter. There are even dessert pizzas, and excellent *tiramisu.* Lasagnas and focaccia sandwiches are also available to eat in or take out. It's open from lunch until 11 pm. ⑤ *Average main: €10* ⊠ *Rue du Roi Oscar II, Gustavia* ☎ *0590/52–02–02* ⟨ *Reservations not accepted.*

# ST. CROIX (FREDERIKSTED)

By Carol
Buchanan

St. Croix is the largest of the three U.S. Virgin Islands (USVI) that form the northern hook of the Lesser Antilles; it's 40 miles (64 km) south of its sister islands, St. Thomas and St. John. Christopher Columbus landed here in 1493, skirmishing briefly with the native Carib Indians. Since then, the USVI have played a colorful, if painful, role as pawns in the game of European colonialism. Theirs is a history of pirates and privateers, sugar plantations, slave trading, and slave revolt and liberation. Through it all, Denmark had staying power. From the 17th to the 19th century, Danes oversaw a plantation slave economy that produced molasses, rum, cotton, and tobacco. Many of the stones you tread on in the streets were once used as ballast on sailing ships, and the yellow fort of Christiansted is a reminder of the value once placed on this island treasure. Never a major cruise destination, it is still a stop for several ships each year.

### ESSENTIALS

**CURRENCY**
The U.S. dollar

**TELEPHONE**
Calling the United States from St. Croix works the same way as calling within the United States. Local calls from a public phone cost up to 35¢ for every five minutes. You can use your regular toll-free connections for long-distance services. Most U.S. cell phone plans include the Virgin Islands for no additional cost.

### COMING ASHORE

Cruise ships dock in Frederiksted, on the island's West End. You'll find an information center at the pier, and the town is easy to explore on foot. Beaches are nearby. The only difficulty is that you are far from the island's main town, Christiansted. Some cruise lines offer bus transportation there; otherwise, you are probably better off renting a car to explore the island, since both car-rental rates and gasoline prices are reasonable; just remember to drive on the left.

Taxis of all shapes and sizes are available at the cruise-ship pier and at various shopping and resort areas. Remember, too, that you can hail a taxi that's already occupied. Drivers take multiple fares and sometimes even trade passengers at midpoints. Taxis don't have meters, so you should check the list of official rates (available at the visitor centers or from drivers) and agree on a fare before you start, but there are standard rates for most trips. A taxi to Christiansted will cost about $25 for two people for transportation only; an island tour including Christiansted will cost $110 for four people.

---

> BEST BETS

■ **Buck Island.** The snorkeling trail here is fun, but go by catamaran.

■ **Christiansted.** The best shopping on the island, as well as interesting historical sights.

■ **Cruzan Rum Distillery.** This West End rum distillery gives you a tour and samples.

■ **Kayaking.** The Salt River, with few currents, is a great place to take a guided kayak trip.

■ **West End Beaches.** The island's best beaches are on the West End, and are just a short hop from the cruise pier.

---

# EXPLORING

### CHRISTIANSTED

In the 1700s and 1800s Christiansted was a trading center for sugar, rum, and molasses. Today law offices, tourist shops, and restaurants occupy many of the same buildings, which start at the harbor and go up the gently sloped hillsides. Your best bet to see the historic sights in this Danish-style town is in the morning, when it's still cool. Break for

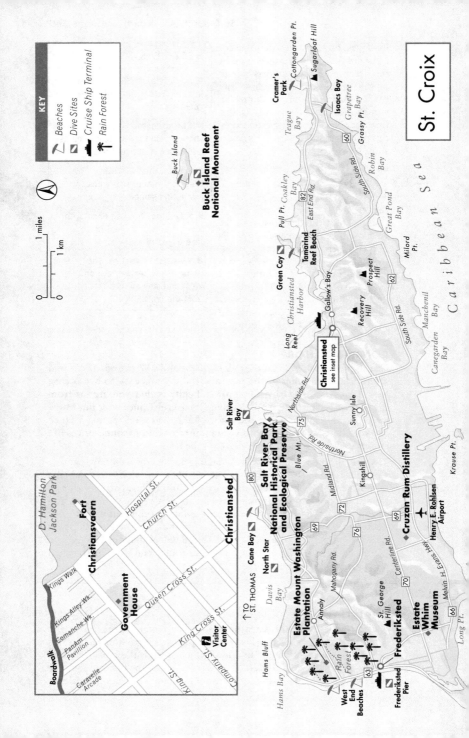

**St. Croix**

**KEY**

- Beaches
- Dive Sites
- Cruise Ship Terminal
- Rain Forest

Buck Island

**Buck Island Reef National Monument**

0    1 miles
0    1 km

Caribbean Sea

Cottongarden Pt.
Sugarloaf Hill
Cramer's Park
Isaacs Bay
Grapetree
Teague Bay
Grassy Pt. Bay
Robin Bay
60
South Side Rd.
Great Pond Bay
Milord Pt.
East End Rd.
82
Pull Pt. Coakley Bay
Tamarind Reef Beach
Green Cay
Christiansted Harbor
Long Reef
Gallow's Bay
Prospect Hill
62
Recovery Hill
Manchenil Bay
South Side Rd.
Canegarden Bay
Krause Pt.
Christiansted *see inset map*
Northside Rd.
Sunny Isle
75
Salt River Bay
**Salt River Bay National Historical Park and Ecological Preserve**
Blue Mt.
Midland Rd.
Kingshill
72
69
76
Centerline Rd.
**Cruzan Rum Distillery**
Henry E. Rohlsen Airport
70
**Estate Whim Museum**
66
Melvin H. Evans HWY
St. George Hill
**Frederiksted**
**Estate Mount Washington Plantation**
Annaly
Mahogany Rd.
Rain Forest
63
**Frederiksted Pier**
**West End Beaches**
Hams Bluff
Hams Bay
Davis Bay
**North Star**
**Cane Bay**
↑ TO ST. THOMAS
80

**Christiansted**

D. Hamilton Jackson Park
**Fort Christiansvaern**
Hospital St.
Church St.
Kings Walk
Boardwalk
Kings Alley Wk.
Comanche Wk.
Pan Am Pavillion
Caravelle Arcade
King Cross St.
King St.
Company St.
Queen Cross St.
Queen Cross St.
**Government House**
**Visitor Center**

lunch at an open-air restaurant before spending as much time as you like exploring the shopping opportunities. You can't get lost, since all streets lead back downhill to the water.

FAMILY

Fodor's Choice

★

**Fort Christiansvaern.** The large yellow fortress dominates the waterfront. Because it's so easy to spot, it makes a good place to begin a walking tour. In 1749 the Danish built the fort to protect the harbor, but the structure was repeatedly damaged by hurricane-force winds and had to be partially rebuilt in 1771. It's now a national historic site, the best preserved of the few remaining Danish-built forts in the Virgin Islands. The park's visitor center is here. Rangers are on hand to answer questions. ■TIP→ **Your paid admission also includes the Steeple Building.** ⊠ *Hospital St., Christiansted* ☎ *340/773–1460* ⊕ *www.nps.gov/chri* ⊠ *$3.*

**Government House.** One of the town's most elegant structures was built as a home for a Danish merchant in 1747. Today it houses offices. If you're here weekdays from 8 to 4:30, slip into the peaceful inner courtyard to admire the still pools and gardens. A sweeping staircase leads you to a second-story ballroom, still used for official government functions. ⊠ *King St., Christiansted* ☎ *340/773–1404.*

### EAST END

**Buck Island Reef National Monument.** Buck Island has pristine beaches that are just right for sunbathing, but there's also some shade for those who don't want to fry. The snorkeling trail set in the reef allows close-up study of coral formations and tropical fish. Overly warm seawater temperatures have led to a condition called coral bleaching that has killed some of the coral. The reefs are starting to recover, but how long it will take is anyone's guess. There's an easy hiking trail to the island's highest point, where you can be rewarded for your efforts by spectacular views of St. John. Charter-boat trips leave daily from the Christiansted waterfront or from Green Cay Marina, about 2 miles (3 km) east of Christiansted. Check with your hotel for recommendations. ⊠ *Off North Shore of St. Croix* ☎ *340/773–1460* ⊕ *www.nps.gov/buis.*

### MID ISLAND

**Cruzan Rum Distillery.** A tour of the company's factory, which was established in 1760, culminates in a tasting of its products, all sold here at good prices. It's worth a stop to look at the distillery's charming old buildings even if you're not a rum connoisseur. ⊠ *West Airport Rd., Diamond* ☎ *340/692–2280* ⊕ *www.cruzanrum.com* ⊠ *$8.*

FAMILY

Fodor's Choice

★

**Estate Whim Museum.** The restored estate, with a windmill, cook house, and other buildings, gives a sense of what life was like on St. Croix's sugar plantations in the 1800s. The oval-shape great house has high ceilings and antique furniture and utensils. Notice its fresh, airy atmosphere—the waterless stone moat around the great house was used not for defense but for gathering cooling air. If you have kids, the grounds are the perfect place for them to run around, perhaps while you browse in the museum gift shop. It's just outside of Frederiksted. ⊠ *Rte. 70, Whim* ☎ *340/772–0598* ⊕ *www.stcroixlandmarks.com* ⊠ *$10.*

4

## FREDERIKSTED AND ENVIRONS

St. Croix's second-largest town, Frederiksted, was founded in 1751. Just as Christiansted is famed for its Danish buildings, Frederiksted is known for its Victorian architecture. A stroll around its historic sights will take you no more than an hour. Allow a little more time if you want to duck into the few small shops. One long cruise-ship pier juts into the sparkling sea. It's the perfect place to start a tour of this quaint city.

**Caribbean Museum Center for the Arts.** Sitting across from the waterfront in a historic building, this small museum hosts an always-changing roster of exhibits. Many are cutting-edge multimedia efforts that you might be surprised to find in such an out-of-the way location. The openings are popular events. ⊠ *10 Strand St., Frederiksted* ☎ *340/772–2622* ⊕ *www.cmcarts.org* ⊠ *Free.*

**Estate Mount Washington Plantation.** Several years ago, while surveying the property, the owners discovered the ruins of a sugar plantation beneath the rain-forest brush. The grounds have since been cleared and opened to the public. You can take a self-guided walking tour of the mill, the rum factory, and other ruins. ⊠ *Rte. 63, Estate Mount Washington and Washington Hill.*

FAMILY **Fort Frederik.** On July 3, 1848, 8,000 slaves marched on this fort to demand their freedom. Danish governor Peter von Scholten, fearing they would burn the town to the ground, stood up in his carriage parked in front of the fort and granted their wish. The fort, completed in 1760, houses an art gallery and a number of interesting historical exhibits, including some focusing on the 1848 Emancipation and the 1917 transfer of the Virgin Islands from Denmark to the United States. It's within earshot of the Frederiksted Visitor Center. ⊠ *Waterfront, Frederiksted* ☎ *340/772–2021* ⊠ *$3.*

## NORTH SHORE

**Salt River Bay National Historical Park and Ecological Preserve.** This joint national and local park commemorates the area where Christopher Columbus's men skirmished with the Carib Indians in 1493 on his second visit to the New World. The peninsula on the bay's east side is named for the event: Cabo de las Flechas (Cape of the Arrows). Although the park is still developing, it has several sights with cultural significance. A ball court, used by the Caribs in religious ceremonies, was discovered at the spot where the taxis park. Take a short hike up the dirt road to the ruins of an old earthen fort for great views of Salt River Bay. The area also encompasses a coastal estuary with the region's largest remaining mangrove forest, a submarine canyon, and several endangered species, including the hawksbill turtle and the roseate tern. A visitor center, open in winter only, sits just uphill to the west. The water at the beach can be on the rough side, but it's a nice place for sunning. ⊠ *Rte. 75 to Rte. 80, Estate Salt River* ☎ *340/773–1460* ⊕ *www.nps.gov/sari.*

# BEACHES

**West End beaches.** There are several unnamed beaches along the coast road north of Frederiksted, but it's best if you don't stray too far from civilization. For safety's sake, most vacationers plop down their towel near one of the casual restaurants spread out along Route 63. The beach at the Rainbow Beach Club, a five-minute drive outside Frederiksted, has a bar, a casual restaurant, water sports, and volleyball. If you want to be close to the cruise-ship pier, just stroll on over to the adjacent sandy beach in front of Fort Frederik. On the way south out of Frederiksted, the stretch near Sandcastle on the Beach hotel is also lovely. **Amenities:** food and drink; water sports. **Best for:** snorkeling, swimming, walking. ⊠ *Rte. 63, north and south of Frederiksted, Frederiksted.*

# SHOPPING

Although the shopping on St. Croix isn't as varied or extensive as that on St. Thomas, the island does have several small stores with unusual merchandise. St. Croix shop hours are usually Monday through Saturday 9 to 5, but there are some shops in Christiansted open in the evening. Stores are often closed on Sunday.

The best shopping in Frederiksted is along **Strand Street** and in the side streets and alleyways that connect it with **King Street.** Most stores close on Sunday, except when a cruise ship is in port. Keep in mind that Frederiksted has a reputation for muggings, so it's best to stick to populated areas of Strand and King streets, where there are few—if any—problems.

In Christiansted the best shopping areas are the **Pan Am Pavilion** and **Caravelle Arcade,** off Strand Street, and along **King** and **Company streets.** These streets give way to arcades filled with boutiques. **Gallows Bay** has a blossoming shopping area in a quiet neighborhood.

# ACTIVITIES

## BOAT TOURS

Almost everyone takes a day trip to Buck Island aboard a charter boat. Most leave from the Christiansted waterfront or from Green Cay Marina and stop for a snorkel at the island's eastern end before dropping anchor off a gorgeous sandy beach for a swim, a hike, and lunch. Sailboats can often stop right at the beach; a larger boat might have to anchor a bit farther offshore. A full-day sail runs about $100, with lunch included on most trips. A half-day sail costs about $68.

**Big Beard's Adventure Tours.** From catamarans that depart from the Christiansted waterfront, you'll head to Buck Island for snorkeling before dropping anchor at a private beach for a barbecue lunch. ⊠ *Queen Cross St. Waterfront, Christiansted* ☎ *340/773–4482* ⊕ *www.big beards.com.*

### DIVING AND SNORKELING

**N2 the Blue.** N2 takes divers right off the beach near the Frederiksted Pier, on night dives off the Frederiksted Pier, or on boat trips to the Salt River Wall. ✉ *202 Custom House St., Frederiksted* ☎ *340/772–3483,* ⊕ *www.n2theblue.com.*

### HORSEBACK RIDING

**Paul and Jill's Equestrian Stables.** From Sprat Hall, just north of Frederiksted, co-owner Jill Hurd will take you through the rain forest, across the pastures, along the beaches, and through valleys—explaining the flora, fauna, and ruins on the way. A 1½-hour ride costs $100. ✉ *Rte. 58, Frederiksted* ☎ *340/772–2880, 340/332–0417* ⊕ *www.paulandjills. com.*

### KAYAKING

**Caribbean Adventure Tours.** These kayak tours take you on trips through Salt River Bay National Historical Park and Ecological Preserve, one of the island's most pristine areas. All tours cost $50. ✉ *Salt River Marina, Rte. 80, Estate Salt River* ☎ *340/778–1522* ⊕ *www.stcroixkayak.com.*

## WHERE TO EAT

$ | ECLECTIC
**✕ Polly's at the Pier.** With an emphasis on fresh ingredients, this very casual spot right on the waterfront serves delicious fare. The gourmet grilled-cheese sandwich comes with your choice of three cheeses as well as delicious additions like basil, fresh Bosc pears, and avocado. Salads are a specialty, and many are made with local Bibb lettuce and organic mixed greens. ⑤ *Average main: $11* ✉ *3 Strand St., Frederiksted* ☎ *340/719–9434* ☽ *No dinner.*

$$$ | ECLECTIC | FAMILY | Fodor's Choice ★
**✕ Rum Runners.** The view is as stellar as the food at this highly popular local standby. Sitting right on the Christiansted boardwalk, Rum Runners serves a little bit of everything, including a to-die-for salad of crispy romaine lettuce and tender grilled lobster drizzled with lemongrass vinaigrette. Heartier fare includes baby-back ribs cooked with the restaurant's special spice blend and Guinness stout. ⑤ *Average main: $25* ✉ *Hotel Caravelle, 44A Queen Cross St., Christiansted* ☎ *340/773–6585* ⊕ *www.rumrunnersstcroix.com.*

# ST. JOHN (CRUZ BAY)

By Lynda Lohr

St. John's heart is Virgin Islands National Park, a treasure that takes up a full two-thirds of St. John's 20 square miles (53 square km). The park helps keep the island's interior in its pristine and undisturbed state, but if you go at midday you'll probably have to share your stretch of beach with others, particularly at Trunk Bay. The island is booming, and while it can get a tad crowded at the ever-popular Trunk Bay Beach during the busy winter season, you won't find traffic jams or pollution. It's easy to escape from the fray, however: just head off on a hike. St. John doesn't have a grand major agrarian past like her sister island, St. Croix, but if you're hiking in the dry season, you can probably stumble upon the stone ruins of old plantations. The less adventuresome can visit the repaired ruins at the park's Annaberg Plantation and Caneel

Bay resort. Of the three U.S. Virgin Islands, St. John, which has 5,000 residents, has the strongest sense of community, which is primarily rooted in a desire to protect the island's natural beauty.

## ESSENTIALS

### CURRENCY
U.S. dollar.

### TELEPHONE
Both Sprint and AT&T phones work in most of St. John (take care that you're not roaming on the Tortola cell network on the island's north coast, though). It's as easy to call home from St. John as from any city in the United States. On St. John, public phones are near telephone poles midway along the Cruz Bay waterfront.

---

**BEST BETS**

■ **Hiking in the National Park.** Hiking trails that crisscross the terrain are easy enough for beginners and offer breathtaking scenery.

■ **Snorkeling Cruises.** The best snorkeling sites are reachable only by boat.

■ **Trunk Bay Beach.** St. John's national park beach is beautiful and has an underwater snorkeling trail.

---

### COMING ASHORE
Although a few smaller ships drop anchor at St. John, most people taking a cruise aboard a larger ship visit St. Thomas's sister island on a shore excursion or on an independent day trip from St. Thomas. If you prefer to not take a tour, ferries leave St. Thomas from the Charlotte Amalie waterfront and Red Hook. You'll have to take a taxi to reach the ferry dock.

If you're aboard a smaller ship that calls in St. John, your ship may simply pause outside Cruz Bay Harbor to drop you off or drop anchor if it's spending the day. You'll be tendered to shore at the main town of Cruz Bay. The shopping district starts just across the street from the tender landing. You'll find an eclectic collection of shops, cozy restaurants, and places where you can just sit and take it all in. The island has few sights to see. Your best bet is to take a tour of the Virgin Islands National Park. (If your ship doesn't offer such a tour, arrange one with one of the taxi drivers who will meet your tender.) The drive takes you past luscious beaches to a restored sugar plantation. With only a single day in port, you're better off just using the island's shared taxi vans rather than renting a car; but if you want to do some independent exploring, you can rent a car in Cruz Bay.

---

# EXPLORING

### CRUZ BAY
St. John's main town may be compact (it consists of only several blocks), but it's definitely a hub: the ferries from St. Thomas and the British Virgin Islands pull in here, and it's where you can get a taxi or rent a car to travel around the island. There are plenty of shops, a number of watering holes and restaurants, and a grassy square with benches where

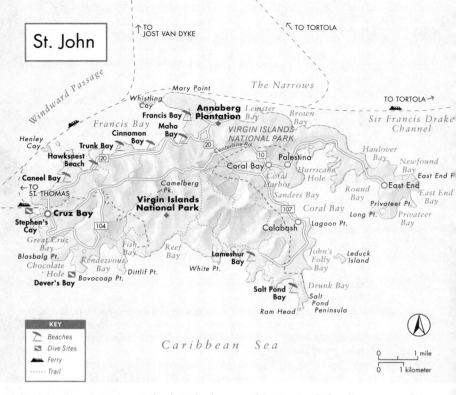

St. John

**KEY**

⚊ Beaches
⚓ Dive Sites
⛴ Ferry
····· Trail

you can sit back and take everything in. Look for the current edition of the handy, amusing "St. John Map," featuring Max the Mongoose.

**Fodor's Choice** **Virgin Islands National Park.** Virgin Islands National Park preserves the ★ island's natural environments. If you're interested in bird-watching, snorkeling, camping, history, or just strolling in beautiful environs, then Virgin Islands National Park is the place for you. At Francis Bay there's a boardwalk through the mangroves where birds may be plentiful; Salt Pond Bay offers pleasant snorkeling; Cinnamon Bay has camping facilities; and the plantation history can be explored at Annaberg Sugar Mill ruins.

There are more than 20 trails on the north and south shores, with guided hikes along the most popular routes. A full-day trip to Reef Bay is a must; it's an easy hike through lush and dry forest, past the ruins of an old plantation, and to a sugar factory adjacent to the beach. It can be a bit arduous for young kids, however. The park runs a $40 guided tour to Reef Bay that includes a safari bus ride to the trailhead and a boat ride back to the Visitors Center. The schedule changes from season to season; call for times and to make reservations, which are essential. To pick up a useful guide to St. John's hiking trails, see various large maps of the island, and find out about current Park Service programs, including guided walks and cultural demonstrations, stop by the park visitor center at the western tip of the park in Cruz Bay on North Shore Road. ⊠ *North Shore Rd., near creek, Cruz Bay* ☎ *340/776–6201* ⊕ *www.nps.gov/viis.*

## NORTH SHORE

**Fodor'sChoice** **Annaberg Plantation.** In the 18th century, sugar plantations dotted the
★ steep hills of this island. Slaves and free Danes and Dutchmen toiled to harvest the cane that was used to create sugar, molasses, and rum for export. Built in the 1780s, the partially restored plantation at Leinster Bay was once an important sugar mill. Although there are no official visiting hours, the National Park Service has regular tours, and some well-informed taxi drivers will show you around. Occasionally you may see a living-history demonstration—someone making johnnycakes or weaving baskets. For information on tours and cultural events, contact the V.I. National Park Visitors Center. ⊠ *Leinster Bay Rd., Annaberg* ☎ *340/776–6201* ⊕ *www.nps.gov/viis* ⊡ *Free.*

4

# BEACHES

**Cinnamon Bay Beach.** This long, sandy beach faces beautiful cays and abuts the national park campground. You can rent water-sports equipment here—a good thing, because there's excellent snorkeling off the point to the right; look for the big angelfish and large schools of purple triggerfish. Afternoons on Cinnamon Bay can be windy—a boon for windsurfers but an annoyance for sunbathers—so arrive early to beat the gusts. The Cinnamon Bay hiking trail begins across the road from the beach parking lot; ruins mark the trailhead. There are actually two paths here: a level nature trail (signs along it identify the flora) that loops through the woods and passes an old Danish cemetery, and a steep trail that starts where the road bends past the ruins and heads straight up to Route 10. Restrooms are on the main path from the commissary to the beach and scattered around the campground. **Amenities:** food and drink; parking; showers; toilets; water sports. **Best for:** snorkeling; swimming; walking; windsurfing. ⊠ *North Shore Rd., Rte. 20, about 4 miles (6 km) east of Cruz Bay, Cinnamon Bay* ⊕ *www.nps.gov/viis.*

**Fodor'sChoice** **Trunk Bay Beach.** St. John's most photographed beach is also the preferred
★ spot for beginning snorkelers because of its underwater trail. (Cruise-ship passengers interested in snorkeling for a day flock here, so if you're looking for seclusion, arrive early or later in the day.) Crowded or not, this stunning beach is one of the island's most beautiful. There are changing rooms with showers, bathrooms, a snack bar, picnic tables, a gift shop, phones, lockers, and snorkeling-equipment rentals. The parking lot often overflows, but you can park along the road as long as the tires are off the pavement. **Amenities:** food and drink; lifeguards; parking; toilets; water sports. **Best for:** snorkeling; swimming; windsurfing. ⊠ *North Shore Rd., Rte. 20, about 2½ miles (4 km) east of Cruz Bay, Estate Trunk Bay* ⊕ *www.nps.gov/viis* ⊡ *$5.*

## SHOPPING

Luxury goods and handicrafts can be found on St. John. Most shops carry a little of this and a bit of that, so it pays to poke around. The Cruz Bay shopping district runs from **Wharfside Village,** just around the corner from the ferry dock, to **Mongoose Junction,** an inviting shopping center on North Shore Road. (The name of this upscale shopping mall, by the way, is a holdover from a time when those furry island creatures gathered at a nearby garbage bin.) Out on Route 104, stop in at the **Marketplace** to explore its gift and crafts shops. On St. John, store hours run from 9 or 10 to 5 or 6. Wharfside Village and Mongoose Junction shops in Cruz Bay are often open into the evening.

## ACTIVITIES

### DIVING AND SNORKELING

**Cruz Bay Watersports.** Cruz Bay Watersports offers regular reef, wreck, and night dives and USVI and BVI snorkel tours. The company holds both PADI Five Star and NAUI-Dream-Resort status. There's another branch at the Westin St. John. ⊠ *Lumberyard Shopping Complex, Boulon Center Rd., Cruz Bay* ☎ *340/776–6234* ⊕ *www.cruzbaywatersports.com.*

**Low Key Watersports.** Low Key Watersports offers two-tank dives and specialty courses. It's a PADI Five Star training facility. ⊠ *1 Bay St., Cruz Bay* ☎ *340/693–8999* ⊕ *www.divelowkey.com.*

### FISHING

FAMILY **Offshore Adventures.** An excellent choice for fishing charters, Captain Rob Richards is patient with beginners—especially kids—but also enjoys going out with more experienced anglers. He runs the 40-foot center console *Mixed Bag I* and 32-foot *Mixed Bag II.* Although he's based in St. John, he will pick up parties in St. Thomas. ⊠ *Westin St. John, 3008 Chocolate Hole Rd., Estate Chocolate Hole and Great Cruz Bay* ☎ *340/513–0389* ⊕ *www.sportfishingstjohn.com.*

### HIKING

Virgin Islands National Park has more than 20 trails from which to choose. Guided trips with the park service are a popular way to explore and are highly recommended, but you can also set out on your own. To find a hike that suits your ability, stop by the park's visitor center in Cruz Bay and pick up the free trail guide; it details points of interest, trail lengths, and estimated hiking times, as well as any dangers you might encounter. Although the park staff recommends long pants to protect against thorns and insects, most people hike in shorts because it can get very hot. Wear sturdy shoes or hiking boots even if you're hiking to the beach. Don't forget to bring water and insect repellent.

## WHERE TO EAT

$$$     × **Lime Inn.** The vacationers and mainland transplants who call St. John
ECLECTIC  home like to flock to this alfresco spot for the congenial hospitality and good food, including all-you-can-eat shrimp on Wednesday night.

Fresh lobster is the specialty, and the menu also includes shrimp-and-steak dishes and rotating chicken and pasta specials. $ Average main: $30 ⊠ Lemon Tree Mall, King St., Cruz Bay ☎ 340/776–6425 ⊕ www. limeinn.com ⊙ Closed Sun.

$  ✕ **Sam and Jack's Deli.** The sandwiches are scrumptious, but this deli also dishes up wonderful to-go meals that just need heating. If the truffle–wild mushroom ravioli is on the menu, don't hesitate to order it—it's a winner. There are a few seats inside, but most folks opt to eat at the tables in front of the deli. $ Average main: $12 ⊠ Marketplace Shopping Center, Rte. 104, Cruz Bay ☎ 340/714–3354 ⊕ www.samand jacksdeli.com.

DELI
Fodor's Choice
★

# ST. KITTS (BASSETERRE)

4

By Jordan Simon

Mountainous St. Kitts, the first English settlement in the Leeward Islands, crams some stunning scenery into its 65 square miles (168 square km). Vast, brilliant green fields of sugarcane (the former cash crop, now slowly being replanted) run to the shore. The fertile, lush island has some fascinating natural and historical attractions: a rain forest replete with waterfalls, thick vines, and secret trails; a central mountain range dominated by the 3,792-foot Mt. Liamuiga, whose crater has long been dormant; and Brimstone Hill, known in the 18th century as the Gibraltar of the West Indies. St. Kitts and Nevis, along with Anguilla, achieved self-government as an associated state of Great Britain in 1967. In 1983 St. Kitts and Nevis became an independent nation. English with a strong West Indian lilt is spoken here. People are friendly but can be shy; always ask before you take photographs. Also, be sure to wear wraps or shorts over beach attire when you're in public places.

## BEST BETS

■ **Brimstone Hill Fortress.** Stop here for some of the best views on St. Kitts and historic ambience.

■ **Nevis.** A trip to Nevis is a worthwhile way to spend the day.

■ **Plantation Greathouses.** Stop for a lunch at Ottley's.

■ **Rain-forest Hikes.** Several operators on the island lead daylong hikes through the rain forest.

■ **Romney Manor.** This partially restored manor house is enhanced by the chance to shop at Caribelle Batik and watch the elaborate wax-and-dye process.

### ESSENTIALS

#### CURRENCY

Eastern Caribbean (EC) dollar, but U.S. dollars are widely accepted.

#### TELEPHONE

Phone cards, which you can buy in denominations of $5, $10, and $20, are handy for making local phone calls, calling other islands, and accessing U.S. direct lines. To make a local call, dial the seven-digit number. To call St. Kitts from the United States, dial the area code 869, then access code 465, 466, 468, or 469 and the local four-digit number.

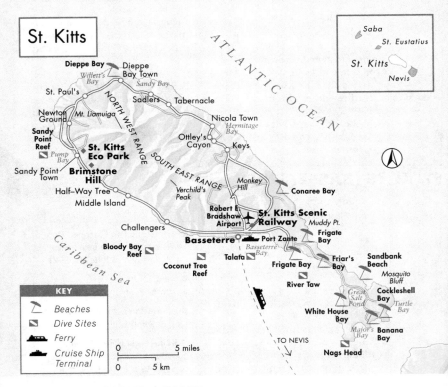

## St. Kitts

Saba
St. Eustatius
St. Kitts
Nevis

Dieppe Bay
Willett's Bay
Dieppe Bay Town
Sandy Bay
St. Paul's
Sadlers
Tabernacle
Newton Ground
Mt. Liamuiga
Nicola Town
Hermitage Bay
Sandy Point Reef
Pump Bay
St. Kitts Eco Park
Ottley's Cayon
Keys
Sandy Point Town
Brimstone Hill
Half-Way Tree
Verchild's Peak
Middle Island
Monkey Hill
Conaree Bay
Robert E. Bradshaw Airport
St. Kitts Scenic Railway
Muddy Pt.
Challengers
Basseterre
Port Zante
Frigate Bay
Bloody Bay Reef
Basseterre Bay
Talata
Coconut Tree Reef
Frigate Bay
Friar's Bay
Sandbank Beach
River Taw
Mosquito Bluff
Great Salt Pond
Cockleshell Bay
Turtle Bay
White House Bay
Major's Bay
Banana Bay
TO NEVIS
Nags Head

**NORTH WEST RANGE**
**SOUTH EAST RANGE**
ATLANTIC OCEAN
Caribbean Sea

| KEY | |
|---|---|
| ⚓ | Beaches |
| ◥ | Dive Sites |
| ⛴ | Ferry |
| 🚢 | Cruise Ship Terminal |

0        5 miles
0    5 km

## COMING ASHORE

Cruise ships calling at St. Kitts dock at Port Zante, which is a deepwater port directly in Basseterre, the capital of St. Kitts. The cruise-ship terminal is right in the downtown area, two minutes' walk from sights and shops. Taxi rates on St. Kitts are fixed, and should be posted right at the dock. If you'd like to go to Nevis, several daily ferries (30–45 minutes, $8–$10 one-way) can take you to Charlestown in Nevis; the Byzantine schedule is subject to change, so double-check times.

Taxi rates on St. Kitts are fairly expensive, and you may have to pay $32 for a ride to Brimstone Hill (for one to four passengers). A four-hour tour of St. Kitts runs about $100. It's often cheaper to arrange an island tour with one of the local companies than to hire a taxi driver to take your group around. Several restored plantation great houses are known for their lunches; your driver can provide information and arrange drop-off and pickup. Before setting off in a cab, be sure to clarify whether the rate quoted is in EC or U.S. dollars.

# EXPLORING

## BASSETERRE

On the south coast, St. Kitts's walkable capital is graced with tall palms and flagstone sidewalks; although many of the buildings appear run-down, there are interesting shops, excellent art galleries, and some beautifully maintained houses. Duty-free shops and boutiques line the streets and courtyards radiating from the octagonal **Circus,** built in the style of London's famous Piccadilly Circus.

**Independence Square.** There are lovely gardens and a fountain on the site of a former slave market at Independence Square. The square is surrounded on three sides by 18th-century Georgian buildings. ⊠ *Off Bank St., Basseterre.*

**National Museum.** In the restored former Treasury Building, the National Museum presents an eclectic collection of artifacts reflecting the history and culture of the island. ⊠ *Bay Rd., Basseterre* ☎ *869/465–5584* 💲 *$3.*

**Port Zante.** Port Zante is an ambitious, ever-growing 27-acre cruise-ship pier and marina in an area that has been reclaimed from the sea. The domed welcome center is an imposing neoclassical hodgepodge, with columns and stone arches, shops, walkways, fountains, and West Indian–style buildings housing luxury shops, galleries, restaurants, and a small casino. A second pier, 1,434 feet long, has a draft that accommodates even leviathan cruise ships. The selection of shops and restaurants (Twist serves global fusion cuisine and rocks with DJs several nights of the week) is expanding as well. ⊠ *Waterfront, behind Circus, Basseterre* ⊕ *www.portzantemarina.com.*

**St. George's Anglican Church.** This handsome stone building has a crenel-lated tower originally built by the French in 1670 that is called Nôtre-Dame. The British burned it down in 1706 and rebuilt it four years later, naming it after the patron saint of England. Since then it has suffered a fire, an earthquake, and hurricanes and was once again rebuilt in 1869. ⊠ *Cayon St., Basseterre.*

## ELSEWHERE ON ST. KITTS

**Brimstone Hill.** This 38-acre fortress, a UNESCO World Heritage Site, is part of a national park dedicated by Queen Elizabeth in 1985. After routing the French in 1690, the English erected a battery here; by 1736 the fortress held 49 guns, earning it the moniker Gibraltar of the West Indies. In 1782, 8,000 French troops laid siege to the stronghold, which was defended by 350 militia and 600 regular troops of the Royal Scots and East Yorkshires. When the English finally surrendered, they were allowed to march from the fort in full formation out of respect for their bravery (the English afforded the French the same honor when they surrendered the fort a mere year later). A hurricane severely damaged the fortress in 1834, and in 1852 it was evacuated and dismantled. The beautiful stones were carted away to build houses.

The citadel has been partially reconstructed and its guns remounted. It's a steep walk up the hill from the parking lot. A seven-minute orientation film recounts the fort's history and restoration. You can see remains of the officers' quarters, redoubts, barracks, ordnance store, and cemetery. Its museum collections were depleted by hurricanes, but some pre-Columbian artifacts, objects pertaining to the African heritage of the island's slaves (such as masks and ceremonial tools), weaponry, uniforms, photographs, and old newspapers remain. The spectacular view includes Montserrat and Nevis to the southeast; Saba and St. Eustatius to the northwest; and St. Barth and St. Maarten to the north. Nature trails snake through the tangle of surrounding hardwood forest and savanna (a fine spot to catch the green vervet monkeys—inexplicably brought by the French and now outnumbering the residents—skittering about). ⊠ *Main Rd., Brimstone Hill* ☎ *869/465–2609* ⊕ *www. brimstonehillfortress.org* ⌐ *$10.*

FAMILY   **St. Kitts Eco Park.** Created in collaboration with the Taiwanese government, St. Kitts Eco Park essentially functions as an agro-tourism demonstration farm, with soaring, light-filled glass and fiber-reinforced concrete structures that are powered by state-of-the-art solar trackers. Antique cannons and old-fashioned gas lamps lead to the handsome Victorian plantation-style visitors center, divided into Kittitian and Taiwanese sections, each selling local foodstuffs and specialty items (ceramics for St. Kitts, tea and technology for Taiwan). You can stroll through the greenhouse, viewing orchids in the working nursery, then scale the watchtower for scintillating views of the farm and the Caribbean, with Saba and Statia in the distance. Kids will love challenging the map mazes (plantings shaped like the partner nations), while parents can wander the orchards and desert garden or savor bush tea in the herb gazebo. The property provides environmental edutainment while delivering on its so-called 4G promise: greenhouse, green beauty, green energy, green landscape. ⊠ *Sir Gillies Estate, Sandy Point* ☎ *869/465–8755* ⊕ *www.ecopark.kn* ⌐ *$8.*

**St. Kitts Scenic Railway.** The old narrow-gauge train that had transported sugarcane to the central sugar factory since 1912 is all that remains of the island's once-thriving sugar industry. Two-story cars bedecked in bright Kittitian colors circle the island in just under four hours (a Rail and Sail option takes guests going or on the return via catamaran). Each passenger gets a comfortable, downstairs air-conditioned seat fronting vaulted picture windows and an upstairs open-air observation spot. The conductor's running discourse embraces not only the history of sugar cultivation but also the railway's construction, local folklore, island geography, even other agricultural mainstays from papayas to pigs. You can drink in complimentary tropical beverages (including luscious guava daiquiris) along with the sweeping rain-forest and ocean vistas, accompanied by an a cappella choir's renditions of hymns, spirituals, and predictable standards like "I've Been Workin' on the Railroad."⊠ *Needsmust Estate* ☎ *869/465–7263* ⊕ *www.stkittsscenic railway.com* ⌐ *$99.*

## BEACHES

Beaches on St. Kitts are free and open to the public (even those occupied by hotels). The best beaches, with powdery white sand, are in the Frigate Bay area or on the lower peninsula. The Atlantic waters are rougher, and many black-sand beaches northwest of Frigate Bay double as garbage dumps.

**Banana/Cockleshell Bays.** These twin connected eyebrows of glittering champagne-color sand—stretching nearly 2 miles (3 km) total at the southeastern tip of the island—feature majestic views of Nevis and are backed by lush vegetation and coconut palms. The first-rate restaurant-bar Spice Mill (next to Rasta-hue Lion Rock Beach Bar—order the knockout Lion Punch) and Reggae Beach Bar & Grill bracket either end of Cockleshell. At this writing, plans for a 125-room mixed-use Park Hyatt (with additional residential condos and villas) are back on schedule for opening by late 2016. The water is generally placid, ideal for swimming. The downside is irregular maintenance, with seaweed (particularly after rough weather) and occasional litter, especially on Banana Bay. Follow Simmonds Highway to the end and bear right, ignoring the turnoff for Turtle Beach. **Amenities:** food and drink; parking. **Best for:** partiers; snorkeling; swimming; walking. ⊠ *Banana Bay.*

**Friar's Bay.** Locals consider Friar's Bay, on the Caribbean (southern) side, the island's finest beach. It's a long, tawny scimitar where the water always seems warmer and clearer. The upscale Carambola Beach Club has co-opted roughly one third of the strand. Still, several happening bars, including Jam Rock (great grouper and jerk), ShipWreck and Sunset, serve terrific, inexpensive, local food and cheap, frosty drinks. Chair rentals cost around $3, though if you order lunch, you can negotiate a freebie. Friar's is the first major beach along Southeast Peninsula Drive (aka Simmonds Highway), approximately a mile (1½ km) southeast of Frigate Bay. **Amenities:** food and drink. **Best for:** snorkeling; swimming; walking. ⊠ *South Friar's Bay.*

**Frigate Bay.** The Caribbean side offers talcum-powder-fine beige sand framed by coconut palms and sea grapes, and the Atlantic side (a 15-minute stroll)—sometimes called North Frigate Bay—is a favorite with horseback riders. South Frigate Bay is bookended by the Timothy Beach Club's Sunset Café and the popular, pulsating Buddies Beach Hut. In between are several other lively beach spots, including Cathy's (fabulous jerk ribs), Chinchilla's, Vibes, and Mr. X Shiggidy Shack. Most charge $3 to $5 to rent a chair, though they'll often waive the fee if you ask politely and buy lunch. Locals barhop late into Friday and Saturday nights. Waters are generally calm for swimming; the rockier eastern end offers fine snorkeling. The incomparably scenic Atlantic side is—regrettably—dominated by the Marriott (plentiful dining options), attracting occasional pesky vendors. The surf is choppier and the undertow stronger here. On cruise-ship days, groups stampede both sides. **Amenities:** food and drink; water sports. **Best for:** partying; snorkeling; swimming; walking. ⊠ *Frigate Bay* ✛ *Less than 3 miles (5 km) from downtown Basseterre.*

# SHOPPING

St. Kitts has limited shopping, but several duty-free shops offer good deals on jewelry, perfume, china, and crystal. Numerous galleries sell excellent paintings and sculptures. The batik fabrics, scarves, caftans, and wall hangings of Caribelle Batik are well known. British expat Kate Spencer is an artist who has lived on the island for years, reproducing its vibrant colors on everything from silk pareus (beach wraps) and scarves to note cards. Other good island buys include crafts, jams, and herbal teas. Don't forget to pick up some CSR (Cane Spirit Rothschild), which is distilled from fresh wild sugarcane right on St. Kitts. The Brinley Gold Company has made a splash among spirits connoisseurs with its coffee, mango, coconut, lime, and vanilla rums (there is a tasting room at Port Zante).

## ACTIVITIES

### DIVING AND SNORKELING

Though unheralded as a dive destination, St. Kitts has more than a dozen excellent sites, protected by several new marine parks. The surrounding waters feature shoals, hot vents, shallows, canyons, steep walls, and caverns at depths from 40 to nearly 200 feet.

**Dive St. Kitts.** This PADI–NAUI facility offers competitive prices, computers to maximize time below, a wide range of courses from refresher to rescue, and friendly, laid-back dive masters. The Bird Rock location features superb shore diving (unlimited when you book packages): common sightings 20 to 30 feet out include octopuses, nurse sharks, manta and spotted eagle rays, sea horses, even barracudas George and Georgianna. It also offers kayak and snorkeling tours. ⊠ *2 miles (3 km) east of Basseterre, Frigate Bay* ☎ *869/465–1189, 869/465–8914* ⊕ *www. divestkitts.com.*

### GOLF

**Royal St. Kitts Golf Club.** This 18-hole links-style championship course underwent a complete redesign by Thomas McBroom to maximize Caribbean and Atlantic views and increase the challenge (there are 12 lakes and 83 bunkers). Holes 15 through 17 (the latter patterned after Pebble Beach No. 18) skirt the Atlantic in their entirety, lending new meaning to the term sand trap. The sudden gusts, wide but twisting fairways, and extremely hilly terrain demand pinpoint accuracy and finesse, yet holes such as 18 require pure power. The development includes practice bunkers, a putting green, a short-game chipping area, and the fairly high-tech Royal Golf Academy. Twilight and super-twilight discounts are offered. ⊠ *St. Kitts Marriott Resort, 858 Zenway Blvd., Frigate Bay* ☎ *869/466–2700, 866/785–4653* ⊕ *www.royalstkittsgolfclub.com* ⊠ *$150 for Marriott guests in high season, $165 for nonguests ⚐. 18 holes, 6900 yards, par 71.*

### HIKING

Trails in the central mountains vary from easy to don't-try-it-by-yourself. Monkey Hill and Verchild's Peak aren't difficult, although the Verchild's climb will take the better part of a day. Don't attempt Mt. Liamuiga without a guide. You'll start at Belmont Estate—at the west end of the island—on horseback, and then proceed on foot to the lip of the crater, at 2,600 feet. You can go down into the crater—1,000 feet deep and 1 mile (1½ km) wide, with a small freshwater lake—clinging to vines and roots and scaling rocks, even trees. Expect to get muddy.

There are several fine operators (each hotel recommends its favorite); tour rates generally range from $50 for a rain-forest walk to $95 for a volcano expedition and usually include round-trip transportation from your hotel and picnic lunch.

**Duke of Earl's Adventures.** Owner Earl "The Duke of Earl" Vanlow is as entertaining as his nickname suggests—and his prices are slightly cheaper ($50 for a rain-forest tour includes refreshments, $75 volcano expeditions add lunch; hotel pickup and drop-off is complimentary). He genuinely loves his island and conveys that enthusiasm, encouraging hikers to swing on vines or sample unusual-looking fruits during his rain-forest trip. He also conducts a thorough volcano tour to the crater's rim and a drive-through ecosafari tour ($55 with lunch). ☎ 869/465–1899, 869/663–0994.

**Greg's Safaris.** Greg Pereira of Greg's Safaris, whose family has lived on St. Kitts since the early 19th century, takes groups on half-day trips into the rain forest and on full-day hikes up the volcano and through the grounds of a private 18th-century great house. The rain-forest trips include visits to sacred Carib sites, abandoned sugar mills, and an excursion down a 100-foot coastal canyon containing a wealth of Amerindian petroglyphs. The Off the Beaten Track 4x4 Plantation Tour provides a thorough explanation of the role sugar and rum played in the Caribbean economy and colonial wars. He and his staff relate fascinating historical, folkloric, and botanical information. ☎ 869/465–4121 ⊕ www.gregsafaris.com.

### HORSEBACK RIDING

**Trinity Stables.** Guides from Trinity Stables offer beach rides ($50) and trips into the rain forest ($60), both including hotel pickup. The latter is intriguing, as guides discuss plants' medicinal properties along the way (such as sugarcane to stanch bleeding) and pick oranges right off a tree to squeeze fresh juice. The staffers are cordial but shy; this isn't a place for beginners' instruction. ✉ Palmetto Point ☎ 869/465–3226, 869/726–3098.

## WHERE TO EAT

$ ✕**El Fredo's.** This humble wood shack across from the waterfront dishes
CARIBBEAN out some of the finest local fare on St. Kitts. No surprise you'll find politicians and expats grabbing a quick lunch (it's a terrific place to eavesdrop on local gossip) alongside local workers shyly bantering with the waitresses. With just a few genre paintings for atmosphere, the decor is basic. The draw is the traditional stewed oxtail, curry goat, or swordfish creole served with heaping helpings of fungi (cornmeal), rice and peas, and dumplings. Join the locals for bounteous dishes that they swear will cure—or at least absorb—any hangover. $ *Average main: US$10* ✉ *Newtown Bay Rd. at Sanddown Rd., Basseterre* ☎ *869/764–9228* ▭ *No credit cards* ⊘ *Closed Sun. No dinner.*

$$$ ✕**Reggae Beach Bar & Grill.** Treats at this popular daytime watering
ECLECTIC hole include honey-mustard ribs, coconut shrimp, grilled lobster, decadent banana bread pudding with rum sauce, and an array of tempting tropical libations. Business cards and pennants from around the

world plaster the bar, and the open-air space is decorated with nautical accoutrements, from fishnets and turtle shells to painted wooden crustaceans. You can snorkel here, spot hawksbill turtles and the occasional monkey, visit the enormous house pig, Wilbur, laze in a palm-shaded hammock, or rent a kayak, Hobie Cat, or snorkeling gear. Beach chairs and Wi-Fi are free. Locals come Friday nights for bonfire dinners and Sunday afternoons for dancing to live bands. ⑤ *Average main: US$21* ⊠ *S.E. Peninsula Rd., Cockleshell Beach* ☏ *869/762–5050* ⊕ *www. reggaebeachbar.com* ⊘ *No dinner.*

# ST. LUCIA (CASTRIES)

By Jane E. Zarem

Magnificent St. Lucia—with its towering mountains, dense rain forest, fertile green valleys, and acres of banana plantations—lies in the middle of the Windward Islands. Nicknamed "Helen of the West Indies" because of its natural beauty, St. Lucia is distinguished from its neighbors by its unusual geological landmarks, the Pitons—the twin peaks on the southwestern coast that soar nearly ½ mile (1 km) above the ocean floor. Named a World Heritage Site by UNESCO in 2004, the Pitons are the symbol of this island. Nearby, in the former French colonial capital of Soufrière, you'll find a "drive-in" volcano, its neighboring sulfur springs that have rejuvenated bathers for nearly three centuries, and one of the most beautiful botanical gardens in the Caribbean. A century and a half of battles between the French and English resulted in St. Lucia's changing hands 14 times before 1814, when England secured possession. In 1979, the island became an independent state within the British Commonwealth of Nations. The official language is English, although most people also speak a French Creole patois.

## ESSENTIALS

### CURRENCY
Eastern Caribbean (EC) dollar, but U.S. dollars are widely accepted.

### TELEPHONE
You can make direct-dial overseas and inter-island calls from St. Lucia, and the connections are excellent. You can charge an overseas call to a major credit card with no surcharge by dialing 811. Phone cards can be purchased at many retail outlets.

### COMING ASHORE
Most cruise ships dock at the capital city of Castries, on the island's northwestern coast, at either of two docking areas: Pointe Seraphine, a port of entry and duty-free shopping complex, or Port Castries (Place Carenage), a commercial wharf across the harbor. A water taxi ($3 each way) connects the two piers. Smaller vessels occasionally call at Soufrière, on the island's southwestern coast. Ships calling at Soufrière must anchor offshore and bring passengers ashore via tender. Tourist information booths are at Pointe Seraphine, at Place Carenage, and along the waterfront on Bay Street in Soufrière. Downtown Castries is within walking distance of the pier, and the produce market and adjacent crafts and vendors' markets are the main attractions. Soufrière is a sleepy West Indian town, but it's worth a short walk around the central

square to view the French colonial architecture; many of the island's interesting natural sights are in or near Soufrière.

Taxis are available at the docks in Castries. Although they are unmetered, the standard fares are posted at the entrance to Pointe Seraphine. Taxi drivers are well informed and can give you a full tour—often an excellent one—thanks to government-sponsored training programs. From the Castries area, full-day island tours for up to four people cost $40 to $75 per person, depending on the route and whether entrance fees and lunch are included; a private sightseeing trip, including lunch, costs around $190 for two people. If you plan your own day, expect to pay the driver at least $40 per hour plus a 10% tip. Whatever your destination, negotiate the price with the driver before you depart—and be sure that you both understand whether the rate is quoted in EC or U.S. dollars.

> ### BEST BETS
>
> ■ **The Pitons.** You must see the Pitons, St. Lucia's unique twin peaks.
>
> ■ **The Rain Forest.** St. Lucia's rain forest is truly a natural wonder.
>
> ■ **Diamond Botanical Garden.** Stroll through this tropical paradise to Diamond Waterfall.
>
> ■ **Reduit Beach.** St. Lucia's broadest, most popular beach is at Rodney Bay, north of Castries.
>
> ■ **Pigeon Island National Landmark.** This national park is both a historic site and a playground.

## EXPLORING

### CASTRIES AND THE NORTH

**Castries.** The capital, a busy commercial city of about 65,000 people (one-third of the island's population), wraps around sheltered Castries Bay. Morne Fortune rises sharply to the south, creating a dramatic green backdrop. The charm of Castries lies in its liveliness rather than its architecture, since four fires between 1796 and 1948 destroyed most of the colonial buildings. Freighters (exporting bananas, coconut, cocoa, mace, nutmeg, and citrus fruits) and cruise ships come and go frequently, making Castries Harbour one of the Caribbean's busiest ports. **Pointe Seraphine** is a duty-free shopping complex on the north side of the bay, about a 20-minute walk or 2-minute cab ride from the city center; a launch ferries passengers across the harbor when cruise ships are in port. Pointe Seraphine's attractive Spanish-style architecture houses more than a dozen duty-free shops, a tourist information kiosk, and a taxi stand. **La Place Carenage,** on the south side of the harbor near the pier and markets, is another duty-free shopping complex with a dozen or more shops and a café. **Derek Walcott Square,** a green oasis bordered by Brazil, Laborie, Micoud, and Bourbon streets, honors the hometown poet who won the 1992 Nobel Prize in Literature—one of two Nobel laureates from St. Lucia. The late Sir W. Arthur Lewis won the 1979 Nobel in economics. (Interestingly, both Nobel laureates shared the same birthday, January 23!) Some of the few 19th-century buildings that survived fire, wind, and rain can be seen on Brazil Street,

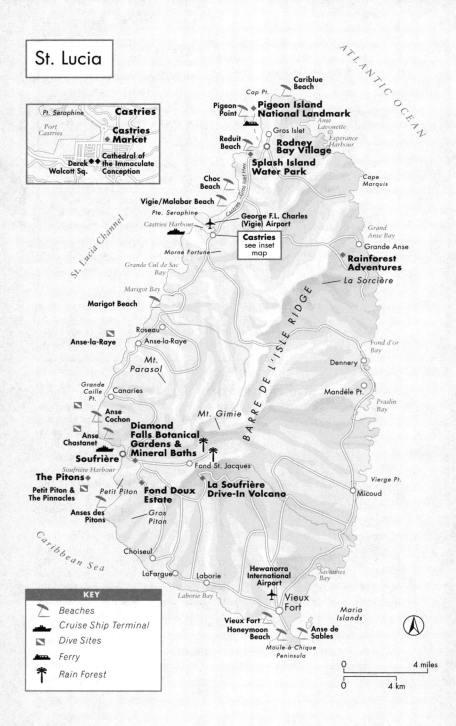

# St. Lucia

## Castries
- Pt. Seraphine
- Port Castries
- **Castries**
- **Castries Market**
- **Cathedral of the Immaculate Conception**
- Derek Walcott Sq.

ATLANTIC OCEAN

Cap Pt.

**Cariblue Beach**

**Pigeon Point**
**Pigeon Island National Landmark**

Anse Lavouette

Gros Islet

**Reduit Beach**
**Rodney Bay Village**

Esperance Harbour

**Splash Island Water Park**

Cape Marquis

**Choc Beach**

**Vigie/Malabar Beach**

Pte. Seraphine

Castries Harbour

**George F.L. Charles (Vigie) Airport**

**Castries**
see inset map

Grand Anse Bay

Grande Anse

**Rainforest Adventures**

Morne Fortune

*La Sorcière*

Grande Cul de Sac Bay

Marigot Bay

**Marigot Beach**

St. Lucia Channel

Roseau

Anse-la-Raye

**Anse-la-Raye**

Mt. Parasol

Fond d'or Bay

Dennery

BARRE DE L'ISLE RIDGE

Grande Caille Pt.

Canaries

Mandéle Pt.

Praslin Bay

Mt. Gimie

**Anse Cochon**

**Diamond Falls Botanical Gardens & Mineral Baths**

**Anse Chastanet**

**Soufrière**

Soufrière Harbour

Fond St. Jacques

**La Soufrière Drive-In Volcano**

Vierge Pt.

**The Pitons**

Micoud

**Petit Piton & The Pinnacles**

Petit Piton

**Fond Doux Estate**

**Anses des Pitons**

Gros Piton

Caribbean Sea

Choiseul

LaFargue

Laborie

**Hewanorra International Airport**

Savannes Bay

Laborie Bay

**Vieux Fort**

Maria Islands

**Vieux Fort Honeymoon Beach**

**Anse de Sables**

Moule à Chique Peninsula

## KEY
- 🏖 Beaches
- ⚓ Cruise Ship Terminal
- 🤿 Dive Sites
- ⛴ Ferry
- 🌴 Rain Forest

| 0 | | 4 miles |
|---|---|---|
| 0 | | 4 km |

the square's southern border. On the Laborie Street side, there's a huge, 400-year-old *samaan* (monkeypod) tree with leafy branches that shade a good portion of the square. Directly across Laborie Street from Derek Walcott Square is the Roman Catholic **Cathedral of the Immaculate Conception,** which was built in 1897. Though it's rather somber on the outside, colorful murals by St. Lucian artist Dunstan St. Omer decorate the interior walls. The murals were reworked prior to the visit of Pope John Paul II in 1985. The church has an active parish and is open daily for both public viewing and religious services. ⊠ *Castries.*

FAMILY
Fodor's Choice
★

**Castries Market.** Under a brilliant orange roof, this bustling market is at its liveliest on Saturday morning, when farmers bring their produce and spices to town—as they have for more than a century. (It's closed Sunday.) Next door to the produce market is the **Craft Market,** where you can buy pottery, wood carvings, handwoven straw articles, and innumerable souvenirs, trinkets, and gewgaws. At the **Vendors' Arcade,** across Peynier Street from the Craft Market, you'll find still more handicrafts and souvenirs. ⊠ *Jeremie and Peynier Sts., Castries.*

FAMILY
**Pigeon Island National Landmark.** Jutting out from the northwest coast, Pigeon Island connects to the mainland via a causeway. Tales are told of the pirate Jambe de Bois (Wooden Leg), who once hid out on this 44-acre hilltop islet—a strategic point during the French and British struggles for control of St. Lucia. Now Pigeon Island is a national park and a venue for concerts, festivals, and family gatherings. There are two small beaches with calm waters for swimming and snorkeling, a restaurant, and picnic areas. Scattered around the grounds are ruins of barracks, batteries, and garrisons that date from 18th-century French and English battles. In the Museum and Interpretative Centre, housed in the restored British officers' mess, a multimedia display explains the island's ecological and historical significance. The site is administered by the St. Lucia National Trust. ⊠ *Pigeon Island* ☎ *758/452–5005* ⊕ *www. slunatrust.org* ✉ *$7.*

FAMILY
**Rainforest Adventures.** Ever wish you could get a bird's-eye view of the rain forest? Or at least experience it without hiking up and down miles of mountain trails? Here's your chance. Depending on your athleticism and spirit of adventure, choose a two-hour aerial tram ride, a zip-line experience, or both. Either activity guarantees a magnificent view as you peacefully ride above or actively zip through the canopy of the 3,442-acre Castries Waterworks Rain Forest in Babonneau, 30 minutes east of Rodney Bay. On the tram ride, eight-passenger gondolas glide slowly among the giant trees, twisting vines, and dense thickets of vegetation accented by colorful flowers, as a tour guide explains and shares anecdotes about the various trees, plants, birds, and other wonders of nature found in the area. The zip line, on the other hand, is a thrilling experience in which you're rigged with a harness, helmet, and clamps that attach to cables strategically strung through the forest. Short trails connect 18 platforms, so riders come down to earth briefly and hike to the next station before speeding through the forest canopy to the next stop. There's even a nighttime zip-line tour. ■ TIP→ **Bring binoculars and a camera.** ⊠ *Chassin, Babonneau* ☎ *758/458–5151, 866/759–8726*

4

*in the U.S.* ⊕ *www.rainforestadventure.com* ≊ *Tram $80, zip line $80, combo $95.*

**Rodney Bay Village.** Hotels, popular restaurants, a huge mall, and the island's only casino surround a natural bay and an 80-acre man-made lagoon named for Admiral George Rodney, who sailed the British navy out of Gros Islet in 1780 to attack and ultimately destroy the French fleet. With 253 slips, Rodney Bay Marina is one of the Caribbean's premier yachting centers; each December, it's the destination of the Atlantic Rally for Cruisers, a transatlantic sailing competition for racing yachts. Yacht charters and sightseeing day trips can be arranged at the marina. Rodney Bay Village is about 15 minutes north of Castries. ⊠ *Rodney Bay.*

FAMILY
Fodor's Choice
★
**Splash Island Water Park.** The Eastern Caribbean's first open-water-sports park, installed just off Reduit Beach a dozen or so yards from the sand in front of Bay Gardens Beach Resort, thrills kids and adults alike—but mostly kids. They spend hours on the colorful, inflatable, modular features, which include a trampoline, climbing wall, monkey bars, swing, slide, hurdles, double rocker, and water volleyball net. Children must be at least six, and everyone must wear a life vest. A team of lifeguards is on duty when the park is open. ⊠ *Reduit Beach, Reduit Beach Rd., Rodney Bay* ⊹ *Facing Bay Gardens Beach Resort* ☎ *758/457–8532* ⊕ *www.stluciawaterpark.com* ≊ *$11.50 per hr; $34.50 half-day pass; $57.50 full-day pass.*

## SOUFRIÈRE AND THE WEST COAST

The oldest town in St. Lucia and the island's former colonial capital, Soufrière was founded by the French in 1746 and named for its proximity to the volcano of the same name. The wharf is the center of activity in this sleepy town (population, 9,000), particularly when a cruise ship anchors in pretty Soufrière Bay. French colonial influences are evident in the second-story verandas, gingerbread trim, and other appointments of the wooden buildings that surround the market square. The market building itself is decorated with colorful murals.

The site of much of St. Lucia's renowned natural wonders, Soufrière is the destination of most sightseeing trips. Here you can get up close to the iconic Pitons and visit St. Lucia's "drive-in" volcano, botanical gardens, working plantations, waterfalls, and countless other examples of the natural beauty for which the island is deservedly famous. Note that souvenir vendors station themselves outside some of the popular attractions in and around Soufrière, and they can be persistent. Be polite but firm if you're not interested.

Fodor's Choice
★
**Diamond Falls Botanical Gardens & Mineral Baths.** These splendid gardens are part of Soufrière Estate, a 2,000-acre land grant presented by King Louis XIV in 1713 to three Devaux brothers from Normandy in recognition of their services to France. The estate is still owned by their descendants; Joan DuBouley Devaux maintains the gardens. Bushes and shrubs bursting with brilliant flowers grow beneath towering trees and line pathways that lead to a natural gorge. Water bubbling to the surface from underground sulfur springs streams downhill in rivulets to become Diamond Waterfall, deep within the botanical gardens. Near

the falls, mineral baths are fed by the underground springs. It's claimed that the future Joséphine Bonaparte bathed here as a young girl while visiting her father's plantation nearby. In 1930 André DuBoulay had the site excavated, and two of the original stone baths were restored for his use. Outside baths were added later. For a small fee, you can slip into your swimsuit and soak for 30 minutes in one of the outside pools; a private bath costs slightly more. ⊠ *Soufrière Estate, Diamond Rd., Soufrière* ☎ *758/459–7155* ⊕ *www.diamondstlucia.com* 🖃 *$7, public bath $6, private bath $7.*

FAMILY **Fond Doux Estate.** One of the earliest French estates established by land grants (1745 and 1763), this plantation still produces cocoa, citrus, bananas, coconut, and vegetables on 135 hilly acres. The restored 1864 plantation house is still in use as well. A 30-minute walking tour begins at the cocoa fermentary, where you can see the drying process. You then follow a trail through the cultivated area, where a guide points out various fruit- or spice-bearing trees and tropical flowers. Additional trails lead to old military ruins, a religious shrine, and a vantage point for viewing the spectacular Pitons. Cool drinks and a creole buffet lunch are served at the Cocoa Pod restaurant. Souvenirs, including just-made chocolate sticks, are sold at the boutique. ⊠ *Vieux Fort Rd., Château Belair* ☎ *758/459–7545* ⊕ *www.fonddouxestate.com* 🖃 *$30, including lunch; free to resort guests.*

FAMILY **La Soufrière Drive-In Volcano.** As you approach the volcano, your nose will pick up the strong scent of sulfur from more than 20 belching pools of murky water, crusty sulfur deposits, and other multicolor minerals baking and steaming on the surface. Despite its name, you don't actually drive all the way in. Rather, you drive within a few hundred feet of the gurgling, steaming mass and then walk behind your guide—whose service is included in the admission price—around a fault in the substratum rock. It's a fascinating, educational half hour, though it can also be pretty stinky on a hot day. ⊠ *Soufrière* ☎ *758/459–7686* ⊕ *www. soufrierefoundation.org* 🖃 *$5.*

Fodor's Choice ★ **The Pitons.** Rising precipitously from the cobalt-blue Caribbean just south of Soufrière Bay, these two unusual mountains—named a UNESCO World Heritage Site in 2004—have become the iconic symbol of St. Lucia. Covered with thick tropical vegetation, the massive outcroppings were formed by a volcanic eruption 30 to 40 million years ago. They are not identical twins, since 2,619-foot Petit Piton is taller than 2,461-foot Gros Piton (Gros Piton is broader). It's possible to climb the Pitons, but it's a strenuous trek. Gros Piton is the easier climb and takes about four hours round-trip. Either climb requires permission and a guide; register at the base of Gros Piton. ⊠ *Soufrière.*

# BEACHES

FAMILY
Fodor's Choice
★
**Reduit Beach.** Many feel that Reduit (pronounced red-wee) is the island's finest beach. The long stretch of golden sand that frames Rodney Bay is within walking distance of many hotels and restaurants in Rodney Bay Village. Bay Gardens Beach Resort, Royal St. Lucia by Rex Resorts, and St. Lucian by Rex Resorts all face the beachfront; blu St. Lucia,

Harmony Suites, and Ginger Lily hotels are across the road. At the Royal's water-sports center, you can rent sports equipment and beach chairs and take windsurfing or waterskiing lessons. Kids (and adults alike) love Splash Island Water Park, an open-water inflatable playground near Bay Gardens Beach Resort with a trampoline, climbing wall, monkey bars, swing, slide, and more. **Amenities:** food and drink; toilets; water sports. **Best for:** snorkeling; sunset; swimming; walking; windsurfing. ⊠ *Rodney Bay*.

**Vigie/Malabar Beach.** This 2-mile (3-km) stretch of lovely white sand runs parallel to the George F. L. Charles Airport runway in Castries and continues on past the Rendezvous resort, where it becomes Malabar Beach. In the area opposite the airport departure lounge, a few vendors sell refreshments. **Amenities:** food and drink. **Best for:** swimming. ⊠ *Adjacent to George F.L. Charles Airport runway, Castries*.

## SHOPPING

The island's best-known products are artwork and wood carvings, straw mats, clay pottery, and clothing and household articles made from batik and silk-screened fabrics that are designed and produced in island workshops. You can also take home straw hats and baskets and locally grown cocoa, coffee, spices, sauces, and flavorings. The Castries **Craft Market** has aisles and aisles of baskets and other handmade straw work, rustic brooms made from palm fronds, wood carvings, leather work, clay pottery, and souvenirs—all at affordable prices. The **Vendors' Arcade,** across the street from the Craft Market, is a maze of stalls and booths where you can find handicrafts among the T-shirts and costume jewelry. Duty-free shopping areas are at **Pointe Seraphine,** an attractive Spanish-motif complex on Castries Harbour with a dozen shops that are open mainly when a cruise ship is in port, and **La Place Carenage,** an inviting three-story complex on the opposite side of the harbor. You can also find duty-free items at stores in **Baywalk Mall** and **J.Q.'s Rodney Bay Mall** in Rodney Bay

## ACTIVITIES

### DIVING AND SNORKELING

The coral reefs at Anse Cochon and Anse Chastanet, on the southwest coast, are popular beach-entry dive sites. In the north, Pigeon Island is the most convenient site.

**Scuba St. Lucia.** Daily beach and boat dives and resort and certification courses are available from this PADI 5-star facility located on Anse Chastanet Beach, and so is underwater photography and snorkeling equipment. Transportation from the north of the island can be arranged. ⊠ *Anse Chastanet Resort, Anse Chastanet Rd., Soufrière* ☎ *758/459–7755, 800/223–1108 in U.S.* ⊕ *www.scubastlucia.com*.

### FISHING

Sportfishing is generally done on a catch-and-release basis, but the captain may permit you to take a fish back to your hotel to be prepared for your dinner. Neither spearfishing nor collecting live fish in coastal waters is permitted. Half- and full-day deep-sea fishing excursions can be arranged at Vigie Marina. A half day of fishing on a scheduled trip runs about $85–$90 per person; a private charter costs $500–$1,200 for up to six or eight people, depending on the size of the boat and the length of time. Beginners are welcome.

**Captain Mike's.** Named for Captain Mike Hackshaw and run by his family, Bruce and Andrew, this operation has a fleet of Bertram powerboats (31 to 46 feet) that accommodate up to eight passengers for half- or full-day sportfishing charters; tackle and cold drinks are supplied. Customized sightseeing or whale/dolphin-watching trips ($50 per person) can also be arranged for four to six people. ⊠ *Vigie Marina, Vigie* ☎ *758/452–7044* ⊕ *www.captmikes.com.*

### HIKING

**St. Lucia Forestry Department.** Trails under this department's jurisdiction include the Barre de L'Isle Trail (just off the highway, halfway between Castries and Dennery), the Forestiere Trail (20 minutes east of Castries), the Des Cartiers Rain Forest Trail (west of Micoud), the Edmund Rain Forest Trail and Enbas Saut Waterfalls (east of Soufrière), the Millet Bird Sanctuary Trail (east of Marigot Bay), and the Union Nature Trail (north of Castries). Most are two-hour hikes on 2-mile (3-km) loop trails; the bird-watching tour lasts four hours. The Forestry Department provides guides ($2–$30, depending on the hike), who explain the plants and trees that you'll encounter and keep you on the right track. Seasoned hikers climb the Pitons, the two volcanic cones rising 2,461 feet and 2,619 feet from the ocean floor just south of Soufrière. Hiking is recommended only on Gros Piton, which offers a steep but safe trail to the top. The first half of the hike is moderately difficult; reaching the summit is challenging and should be attempted only by those who are physically fit. The view from the top is spectacular. Tourists are also permitted to hike Petit Piton, but the second half of the hike requires a good deal of rock climbing, and you'll need to provide your own safety equipment. Hiking either Piton requires permission and a knowledgeable guide, both arranged through the St. Lucia Forestry Department. ⊠ *Stanislaus James Bldg., Waterfront, Castries* ☎ *758/468–5648, 758/450–2231 for Piton permission* ⊕ *malff.com.*

## WHERE TO EAT

$$    ✕ **The Hummingbird.** The cheerful restaurant-bar in the Hummingbird
CARIBBEAN    Beach Resort specializes in French creole cuisine, starting with fresh seafood or chicken seasoned with local herbs and accompanied by fresh-picked vegetables from the Hummingbird's garden. Sandwiches on homemade bread and salads are also available. At lunch, sit outside by the pool for a magnificent view of the Pitons (you're welcome to take a dip). Wednesday night is Creole night, with live entertainment, dancing, and special dishes. ⑤ *Average main: US$20* ⊠ *Hummingbird Beach Resort, Anse Chastanet Rd., Soufrière* ☎ *758/459–7985* ⊕ *www. hummingbirdbeachresort.com.*

$$$$
FRENCH
**Fodor's**Choice
★
✕ **Jacques Waterfront Dining.** Chef-owner Jacky Rioux (aka Froggie Jacques) creates magical dishes in his waterfront restaurant overlooking Rodney Bay. The cooking is decidedly French, as is Rioux, but fresh produce and local spices create a memorable fusion cuisine. You might start with a bowl of Mediterranean fish soup, a grilled portobello mushroom, or tomato-and-basil tart. Main dishes include fresh-caught fish grilled with lime and olive oil, grilled rack of lamb, and breast of chicken stuffed with mushrooms and prosciutto in a Bordeaux wine reduction. The wine list is impressive. Coming by boat? You can tie up at the dinghy dock. ⑤ *Average main: US$32* ⊠ *Reduit Beach Ave., end of road, Rodney Bay* ☎ *758/458–1900* ⊕ *www.jacquesrestaurant.com* ⌫ *Reservations essential.*

# ST. MAARTEN (PHILLIPSBURG)

By Elise Meyer

St. Martin/St. Maarten: one tiny island, just 37 square miles (59 square km), with two different vibes ruled by two sovereign nations. Here French and Dutch have lived side by side for hundreds of years, and when you cross from one country to the next there are no border patrols, no customs agents. In fact, the only indication that you have crossed a border at all is a small sign and a change in road surface. It is really fun to cross from side to side experiencing all the interesting variations on tropical fun and food, especially when currently favorable exchange rates brings prices near par. St. Martin/St. Maarten epitomizes tourist islands in the sun, where services are well developed but there's still some Caribbean flavor. The Dutch side is ideal for people who like plenty to do. The French side has a more genteel ambience, and a Continental flair. The combination makes an almost ideal port. On the negative side, the island has been completely developed. It can be fun to shop, and you'll find an occasional bargain, but many goods are cheaper in the United States.

## ESSENTIALS

### CURRENCY
On the Dutch side, the NAf guilder. On the French side, the euro. However, U.S. currency is accepted almost everywhere on the island.

### TELEPHONE
Most U.S. multiband cell phones work in both St. Maarten and St. Martin, but the roaming charges will be steep. Calling from one side of the island to another is an international call. To phone from the Dutch side to the French, you first must dial 00–590–590 for local numbers, or 00–590–690 for cell phones, then the number. To call from the French side to the Dutch, dial 00–721, then the local number. To call a local number on the French side, dial 0590 plus the six-digit number. On the Dutch side, just dial the seven-digit number with no prefix.

## COMING ASHORE
Most cruise ships drop anchor off the Dutch capital of Philipsburg or dock in the marina at the southern tip of the Philipsburg harbor; a very few small or medium-size ships drop anchor in Marigot Bay and tender passengers ashore in the French capital. If your ship anchors,

tenders will ferry you to the town pier in the middle of town, where taxis await passengers. If your ship docks at the marina, downtown is a 15-minute taxi ride away. The walk is not recommended. The island is small, and most spots aren't more than a 30-minute drive from Marigot or Philipsburg.

Doing your own thing will be much less expensive here than a ship-sponsored tour, and since rental cars are cheap (starting at $35 per day for a local car rental), you can easily strike out as soon as your ship docks. This is the best thing to do if you just want to see the island and spend a little time at a beach. Compare costs of ship excursions and activities to prices offered directly by the operators on their websites to make sure you're saving the most money. Taxis are government-regulated and fairly costly, so they aren't really an option if you want to do much exploring, but if you just want to go to a beach for the day, there are taxis at the dock. Authorized taxis display stickers of the St. Maarten Taxi Association. Taxis are also available at Marigot. You may be able to negotiate a favorable deal with a taxi driver for a two- to three-hour island tour for as little as $70 for two passengers or $30 per person for more than two. Mini-buses run between major areas; destinations are posted on the front. Fare is $2 payable in cash to the driver.

---

## BEST BETS

■ **Beaches.** The island has 37 beautiful beaches, all open to the public, most with chairs to rent and beach bars and barbecues or restaurants.

■ **Butterfly Farm.** The terrarium-like Butterfly Farm is a treat for all ages.

■ **The 12-Metre Challenge.** Help sail an America's Cup yacht.

■ **Loterie Farm.** On the slopes of Pic du Paradis, an amazing eco-friendly preserve with fun activities, and great food.

■ **Shopping.** Both sides of the island are a shopper's paradise.

---

# EXPLORING

### PHILIPSBURG

The capital of Dutch St. Maarten stretches about a mile (1½ km) along an isthmus between Great Bay and the Salt Pond and has five parallel streets. Most of the village's dozens of shops and restaurants are on Front Street, narrow and cobblestone, closest to Great Bay. It's generally congested when cruise ships are in port because of its many duty-free shops and several casinos. Little lanes called *steegjes* connect Front Street with Back Street. Along the beach is a ½-mile-long (1-km-long) boardwalk with restaurants, souvenir shops, and beach concessions where you can rent chairs and umbrellas for about $15, with cold drinks included. There are many Wi-Fi hot spots.

**St. Maarten Museum.** Hosting rotating cultural exhibits addressing the history, industry, geology, and archaeology of the island, the museum contains artifacts ranging from Arawak pottery shards to objects salvaged from the wreck of the HMS *Proselyte*. An interesting exhibit about hurricanes focuses on Hurricane Luis, which devastated the

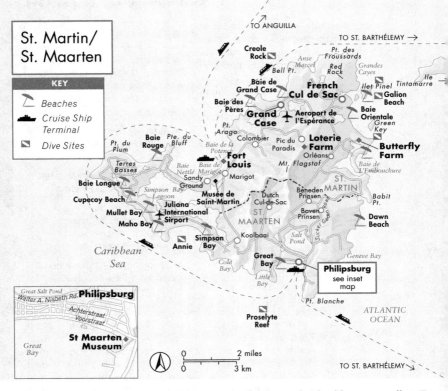

Philipsburg
see inset
map

island in 1995. There is a good reference and video library as well. ⊠ 7 *Front St., Philipsburg* ☏ *721/542–4917* ⊕ *www.museumsintmaarten. org* ⊠ *Free.*

### FRENCH CUL DE SAC

North of Orient Bay Beach, the French colonial mansion of St. Martin's mayor is nestled in the hills. Little red-roof houses look like open umbrellas tumbling down the green hillside. The area is peaceful and good for hiking. From the beach here, shuttle boats make the five-minute trip to Ilet Pinel, an uninhabited island that's fine for picnicking, snorkeling, sunning, and swimming. There are full-service beach clubs there, so just pack the sunscreen and head over.

### GRAND CASE

The Caribbean's own Restaurant Row is the heart of this French-side town, a 10-minute drive from either Orient Bay or Marigot, stretching along a narrow beach overlooking Anguilla. You'll find a first-rate restaurant for every palate, mood, and wallet. At lunchtime, or with kids, head to the casual *lolos* (open-air barbecue stands) and feet-in-the-sand beach bars. Twilight drinks and tapas are fun. At night, stroll the strip and preview the sophisticated offerings on the menus posted outside before you settle in for a long and sumptuous meal (reservations are required for some of the top restaurants). If you still have the energy, there are lounges with music (usually a DJ) that get going after 10 pm.

### ELSEWHERE IN ST. MAARTEN/ST. MARTIN

FAMILY

Fodor's Choice

★

**Butterfly Farm.** If you arrive early in the morning when the butterflies first break out of their chrysalis, you can marvel at butterflies and moths from around the world and the host plants with which each evolved. At any given time, some 40 species of butterflies—and as many as 600 individual insects—flutter inside the lush screened garden and hatch on the plants housed there. Butterfly art and knickknacks are for sale in the gift shop. In case you want to come back, your ticket, which includes a guided tour, is good for your entire stay. ⊠ *Le Galion Beach Rd., Quartier d'Orléans* ☎ *0590/87-31-21* ⊕ *www.thebutterflyfarm. com* ⊠ *$12.*

**Fort Louis.** Though not much remains of the structure itself, Fort Louis, which was completed by the French in 1789, is great fun if you want to climb the 92 steps to the top for the wonderful views of the island and neighboring Anguilla. On Wednesday and Saturday there is a market in the square at the bottom. ⊠ *Marigot.*

FAMILY

Fodor's Choice

★

**Loterie Farm.** Halfway up the road to Pic du Paradis is a peaceful 150-acre private nature preserve, opened to the public in 1999 by American expat B.J. Welch. There are trail maps, so you can hike on your own or hire a guide. Marked trails traverse native forest with tamarind, gum, mango, and mahogany trees. With luck you can see a greenback monkey. L'Eau Lounge is a lovely tropical garden with a chain of spring-fed pools and Jacuzzi area with lounge chairs, great music, roaming iguanas, and chic tented cabanas with a St. Barth–meets–Wet 'n' Wild atmosphere; groups should consider the VIP private tree house/cabanas complete with champagne and attentive service. A delicious, healthy treetop lunch or dinner can be had at **Hidden Forest Café,** and if you are brave—and over 4 feet 5 inches tall—you can try soaring over trees on one of the longest zip lines in the Western Hemisphere. There is a mild version, but people love the extreme one. "Treehab," a wild party at the end of every month, brings the island's best DJs; and the Garden Groove Party enlivens every Saturday night in June, July, and August. ⊠ *103 rte. de Pic du Paradis, Rambaud* ☎ *0590/87-86-16* ⊕ *www. loteriefarm.com* ⊠ *Hiking €5, guide €25, zip line €40–€60.*

## BEACHES

FAMILY

**Baie des Pères** *(Friar's Bay).* This quiet, somewhat rocky cove close to Marigot has beach grills and bars, with chaises and umbrellas, calm waters, and a lovely view of Anguilla. Kali's Beach Bar, open daily for lunch and (weather permitting) dinner, has a Rasta vibe and color scheme. It's the best place to be on the full moon, with music, dancing, and a huge bonfire, but you can get lunch, beach chairs, and umbrellas anytime. Friar's Bay Beach Café is a French bistro on the sand, open from breakfast to sunset. To get to the beach, take National Road 7 from Marigot, go toward Grand Case to the Morne Valois hill, and turn left on the dead-end road at the sign. **Amenities:** food and drink; toilets. **Best for:** partiers; swimming; walking. ⊠ *Anse des Pères.*

**Fodors** Choice  **Baie Orientale** (*Orient Bay*). Many consider this the island's most beauti-
★  ful beach, but its 2 miles (3 km) of champagne sand, underwater marine
reserve, variety of water sports, beach clubs, and hotels also make it one
of the most crowded. Lots of "naturists" take advantage of the clothing-
optional policy, so don't be shocked. Early-morning nude beach walking is de rigueur for the guests at Club Orient, at the southeastern end
of the beach. Plan to spend the day at one of the clubs; each bar has
different color umbrellas, and all boast terrific restaurants and lively
bars. You can have an open-air massage, try any sea toy you fancy, and
stay until dark. To get here from Marigot, take National Road 7 past
Grand Case, past the Aéroport de L'Espérance, and watch for the left
turn. **Amenities:** food and drink; parking; toilets; water sports. **Best for:**
nudists; partiers; swimming; walking; windsurfing. ⊠ *Baie Orientale.*

FAMILY  **Ilet Pinel.** A protected nature reserve, this kid-friendly island is a five-
**Fodors** Choice  minute ferry ride from French Cul de Sac ($7 per person round-trip).
★  The ferry runs every half hour from mid-morning until 4 pm. The water
is clear and shallow, and the shore is sheltered. Snorkelers can swim a
trail between both coasts of this pencil-shaped speck in the ocean. You
can rent equipment on the island or in the parking lot before you board
the ferry for about $12. Two beach clubs offer lunch: Karibuni (closed
September) has the freshest fish, great salads, tapas, and drinks—try
the frozen mojito and homemade ice cream. Yellow Beach has more of
a party vibe with cocktail tables in the water. Chairs and umbrellas can
be rented for $25 for two. **Amenities:** food and drink; parking. **Best for:**
snorkeling; swimming. ⊠ *Ilet Pinel.*

## SHOPPING

Shopaholics are drawn to the array of stores, and jewelry in particular is
big business on both sides of the island. Duty-free shops can offer substantial savings—about 15% to 30% below U.S. and Canadian prices—
on cameras, expensive jewelry, watches, liquor, cigars, and designer
clothing, but not always, so make sure you know U.S. prices to know
if you're getting a deal; and be prepared to bargain hard. Stick with
the big vendors that advertise in the tourist press, and you will be more
likely to avoid today's ubiquitous fakes and replicas. On both sides of
the island, be alert for idlers. They can snatch unwatched purses.

Prices are in dollars on the Dutch side, in euros on the French side. As
for bargains, there are more to be had on the Dutch side; prices on the
French side may be higher than those back home, and being in euros
doesn't help. Merchandise may not be from the newest collections, especially with regard to clothing; there are items available on the French
side that are not available on the Dutch side.

Philipsburg's **Front Street** has reinvented itself. Now it's mall-like, with a
redbrick walk and streets, palm trees lining the sleek boutiques, jewelry
stores, souvenir shops, outdoor restaurants, and the old reliables, such
as McDonald's and Burger King. Here and there a school or a church
appears to remind visitors there's more to the island than shopping.
On Back Street, the **Philipsburg Market Place** is a daily open-air market
where you can haggle on handicrafts, souvenirs, and beachwear. **Old**

**Street,** near the end of Front Street, has stores, boutiques, and open-air cafés offering French crepes, rich chocolates, and island mementos.

## ACTIVITIES

### DIVING AND SNORKELING

Diving in St. Maarten/St. Martin is mediocre at best, but those who want to dive will find a few positives. The water temperature here is rarely below 70°F (21°C) and visibility is often 60 to 100 feet. The island has more than 30 dive sites, from wrecks to rocky labyrinths. Right outside Philipsburg, 55 feet under the water, is the HMS *Proselyte,* once explored by Jacques Cousteau. Although it sank in 1801, the boat's cannons and coral-encrusted anchors are still visible. Off the north coast, in the protected and mostly current-free Grand Case Bay, is **Creole Rock.** The water here ranges in depth from 10 feet to 25 feet. Other sites off the north coast include **Ilet Pinel,** with its good shallow diving; **Green Key,** with its vibrant barrier reef; and **Tintamarre,** with its sheltered coves and geologic faults. On average, one-tank dives start at $58; two-tank dives are about $100. Certification courses start at about $450.

**Dive Safaris.** Certified divers who have dived within the last two years can watch professional feeders give reef sharks a little nosh in a half-hour shark-awareness dive. The company also offers a full PADI training program and can tailor dive excursions and sophisticated, sensitive instruction to any level. ⊠ *16 Airport Rd., Simpson Bay* ☎ *721/545–2401* ⊕ *www.divesafarisstmaarten.com.*

### FISHING

You can angle for yellowtail snapper, grouper, marlin, tuna, and wahoo on deep-sea excursions. Costs range from $150 per person for a half day to $250 for a full day. Prices usually include bait and tackle, instruction for novices, and refreshments. Ask about licensing and insurance.

**Lee's Deepsea Fishing.** When you return from an excursion with this outfit, Lee's Roadside Grill will cook the tuna, wahoo, or mahimahi you catch. Rates start at $800 for a half day trip for six people. ⊠ *84 Welfare Rd., Cole Bay* ☎ *721/544–4233* ⊕ *www.leesfish.com.*

**Rudy's Deep Sea Fishing.** One of the more experienced sport-angling outfits runs private charter trips. Half-day excursions for up to four people start at $575, $50 each additional for up to six. Three-quarter- and full-day trips are also available. ■ **TIP→ Check the website for great tips on fishing around St. Maarten.** ⊠ *14 Airport Rd., Simpson Bay* ☎ *721/545–2177* ⊕ *www.rudysdeepseafishing.com.*

## WHERE TO EAT

$$ ✕ **Cynthia's Talk of the Town.** Although St. Martin is known for upscale
CARIBBEAN  dining, each town has its barbecue stands, called *lolos*—even Grand
FAMILY  Case. Locals flock to the half-dozen stands in the middle of town, on the
Fodor's Choice  water side, for a fun, relatively cheap, and iconic St. Martin meal. With
★  plastic utensils and paper plates, Cynthia's couldn't be more informal. The menu includes everything from succulent grilled ribs to stewed

conch, fresh snapper, and grilled lobster at the most reasonable prices on the island. All come with several tasty sides, like plantains, curried rice, beans, and coleslaw. Don't miss the johnnycakes. The service is friendly, if a bit slow; sit back with a $1.50 beer and enjoy the experience. On weekends there is often live music. At this writing, a 1:1 euro-dollar exchange rate is offered. ■TIP→ **Come earlier in the day for fresher fare.** ⑤ *Average main: €14* ⊠ *Bd. de Grand Case, Grand Case* ☎ *0590/35–67–84* ▭ *No credit cards* ⚖ *Reservations not accepted.*

$$

ECLECTIC

FAMILY

✕**Taloula Mango's.** Ribs and burgers are the specialty at this casual beachfront restaurant, but the jerk chicken and thin-crust pizza, not to mention a few vegetarian options like tasty falafel, are not to be ignored. On weekdays lunch is accompanied by (warning: loud) live music; every Friday during happy hour a DJ spins tunes. In case you're wondering, the restaurant got its name from the owner's golden retriever. ⑤ *Average main: $17* ⊠ *Sint Rose Shopping Mall, off Front St. on boardwalk, Philipsburg* ☎ *721/542–1645* ⊕ *www.taloulamango.com.*

# ST. THOMAS (CHARLOTTE AMALIE)

By Carol
Bareuther

St. Thomas is the busiest cruise port of call in the Caribbean. Up to eight mega ships may visit in a single day. Don't expect an exotic island experience: St. Thomas is as American as any place on the mainland, complete with McDonald's and HBO. The positive side of all this development is that there are more tours here than anywhere else in the Caribbean, and every year the excursions get better. Of course, shopping is the big draw in Charlotte Amalie, but experienced travelers remember the days of "real" bargains. Today so many passengers fill the stores that it's a seller's market. On some days there are so many cruise passengers on St. Thomas that you must book a ship-sponsored shore excursion if you want to do more than just take a taxi to the beach or stroll around Charlotte Amalie.

## ESSENTIALS

### CURRENCY
U.S. dollar.

### TELEPHONE
Both GSM and Sprint phones work in St. Thomas (and the USVI are normally included in most U.S. cell phone plans). It's as easy to call home from St. Thomas and St. John as from any city in the United States. On St. Thomas, public phones are easily found, and AT&T has a telecommunications center across from the Havensight Mall.

### COMING ASHORE
Depending on how many ships are in port, cruise ships drop anchor in the harbor at Charlotte Amalie and tender passengers directly to the waterfront duty-free shops, dock at the Havensight Mall at the eastern end of the crescent bay, or dock at Crown Bay Marina a few miles west of town (Holland America almost always docks at Crown Bay).

The distance from Havensight to the duty-free shops is 1½ miles (3 km), which can be walked in less than half an hour; a taxi ride there costs

$6 per person ($5 for each additional person). Tourist information offices are at the Havensight Mall (across from Building No. 1) for docking passengers and downtown near Fort Christian (at the eastern end of the waterfront shopping area) for those coming ashore by tender. Both offices distribute free maps. From Crown Bay it's also a half-hour walk or a $5-per-person cab ride ($4 for each additional person). V.I. Taxi Association drivers offer a basic two-hour island tour for $29 per person for two or more people. You can rent a car in St. Thomas, but with all the tour options it's often easier and cheaper to take an organized excursion or just hop in a cab.

| BEST BETS |
| --- |
| ■ **Coral World Ocean Park.** This aquarium attraction is a great bet for families, and it's on one of the best snorkeling beaches. |
| ■ **Magens Bay Beach.** St. Thomas has one of the most picture-perfect beaches you'll ever see. It's great for swimming. |
| ■ **St. John.** It's easy to hop on the ferry to St. John for a day of hiking, then relax for an hour or two on the beach afterward. |
| ■ **Shopping.** Charlotte Amalie is one of the best places in the Caribbean to shop. |

## EXPLORING

### CHARLOTTE AMALIE

St. Thomas's major burg is a hilly shopping town. There are also plenty of interesting historic sights—so take the time to see at least a few.

FAMILY **Fort Christian.** St. Thomas's oldest standing structure, this remarkable building was built between 1672 and 1680 and now has U.S. National Landmark status. Over the years, it was used as a jail, governor's residence, town hall, courthouse, and church. In 2005, a multimillion-dollar renovation project started to stabilize the structure and halt centuries of deterioration. This project is still ongoing, but you can see historic features from the outside like the four renovated faces of the famous 19th-century clock tower. ⊠ *Waterfront Hwy., east of shopping district, Charlotte Amalie* 🕾 *340/774–5541* ⊕ *stthomashistoricaltrust.org.*

**Hassel Island.** East of Water Island in Charlotte Amalie harbor, Hassel Island is part of the Virgin Islands National Park. On it are the ruins of a British military garrison (built during a brief British occupation of the USVI during the 1800s) and the remains of a marine railway (where ships were hoisted into dry dock for repairs). Daily guided kayak tours to the island are available from VI Ecotours. The St. Thomas Historical Trust leads three-hour walking tours throughout the year. ⊠ *Charlotte Amalie harbor, Charlotte Amalie* 🕾 *340/776–6201 Virgin Islands National Park main office* ⊕ *www.nps.gov/viis.*

**99 Steps.** This staircase "street," built by the Danes in the 1700s, leads to the residential area above Charlotte Amalie and to Blackbeard's Castle, a U.S. national historic landmark. If you count the stairs as you go up, you'll discover, as thousands have before you, that there are more than the name implies. ⊠ *Look for steps heading north from Government Hill, Charlotte Amalie.*

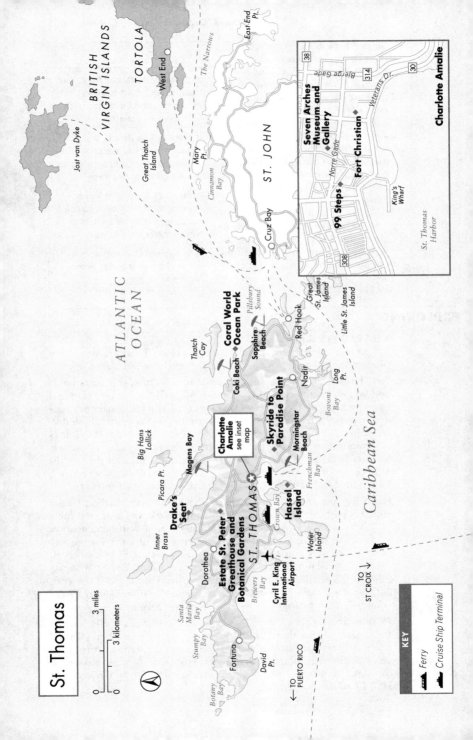

**Seven Arches Museum and Gallery.** This restored 18th-century home is a striking example of classic Danish–West Indian architecture. There seem to be arches everywhere—seven to be exact—all supporting a "welcoming arms" staircase that leads to the second floor and the flower-framed front doorway. The Danish kitchen is a highlight: it's housed in a separate building away from the main house, as were all cooking facilities in the early days (for fire prevention). Inside the house you can see mahogany furnishings and gas lamps and colorful abstract canvases painted by the museum's curator, a local artist. ⊠ *Government Hill, 3 buildings east of Government House, 18A–B Dronningens Gade, Charlotte Amalie* ☎ *340/774–9295* ⊕ *www.sevenarchesmuseum.com* ☞ *$5 donation.*

### ELSEWHERE ON ST. THOMAS

FAMILY

Fodor's Choice

★

**Coral World Ocean Park.** This interactive aquarium and water-sports center lets you experience a variety of sea life and other animals. There's a new 2-acre dolphin habitat under construction, as well as several outdoor pools where you can pet baby sharks, feed stingrays, touch starfish, and view endangered sea turtles. During the Sea Trek Helmet Dive, you walk along an underwater trail wearing a helmet that provides a continuous supply of air. You can also try "snuba," a cross between snorkeling and scuba diving. Swim with a sea lion and have a chance at playing ball or getting a big, wet, whiskered kiss. You can also buy a cup of nectar and let the cheerful lorikeets perch on your hand and drink. The park also has an offshore underwater observatory, an 80,000-gallon coral reef exhibit (one of the largest in the world), and a nature trail with native ducks and tortoises. Daily feedings take place at most exhibits. ⊠ *Coki Point north of Rte. 38, 6450 Estate Smith Bay, Frydendal* ☎ *340/775–1555* ⊕ *www.coralworldvi.com* ☞ *$19 general admission; combination tickets from $41.*

**Drake's Seat.** Sir Francis Drake was supposed to have kept watch over his fleet, looking for enemy ships from this vantage point. The panorama is especially breathtaking (and romantic) at dusk, and if you arrive late in the day, you can miss the hordes of day-trippers on taxi tours who stop here to take pictures. ⊠ *Rte. 40, located ¼ mile (½ km) west of the intersection of Rtes. 40 and 35, Mafolie.*

**Estate St. Peter Greathouse and Botanical Gardens.** This unusual spot is perched on a mountainside 1,000 feet above sea level, with views of more than 20 islands and islets. You can wander through a gallery displaying local art, sip a complimentary rum punch while looking out at the view, or follow a nature trail that leads you past nearly 70 varieties of tropical plants, including 17 varieties of orchids. ⊠ *Rte. 40, directly across from Tree Limin' Extreme Zipline, Estate St. Peter* ☎ *340/774–4999* ⊕ *www.greathousevi.com* ☞ *$8.*

FAMILY

**Skyride to Paradise Point.** Fly skyward in a seven-minute gondola ride to Paradise Point, an overlook with breathtaking views of Charlotte Amalie and the harbor. You'll find several shops, a bar, a restaurant, and a wedding gazebo. A ¼-mile (½-km) hiking trail leads to spectacular views of St. Croix. Wear sturdy shoes, as the trail is steep and rocky. You can also skip the $21 gondola ride and taxi to the top for $7 per person from the Havensight Dock. ⊠ *Rte. 30, across from Havensight Mall, Havensight* ☎ *340/774–9809* ⊕ *www.ridetheview.com* ✉ *$21.*

## BEACHES

FAMILY

Fodor'sChoice

★

**Coki Beach.** Funky beach huts selling local foods such as pâtés (fried turnovers with a spicy ground-beef filling), quaint vendor kiosks, and a brigade of hair braiders and taxi men make this beach overlooking picturesque Thatch Cay feel like a carnival. But this is the best place on the island to snorkel and scuba dive. Fish, including grunts, snappers, and wrasses, are like an effervescent cloud you can wave your hand through. **Amenities:** food and drink; lifeguards; parking; restrooms; showers; water sports. **Best for:** partiers; snorkeling. ⊠ *Rte. 388, next to Coral World Ocean Park, Estate Smith Bay.*

FAMILY

Fodor'sChoice

★

**Magens Bay.** Deeded to the island as a public park, this heart-shape stretch of white sand is considered one of the most beautiful in the world. The bottom of the bay is flat and sandy, so this is a place for sunning and swimming rather than snorkeling. On weekends and holidays the sounds of music from groups partying under the sheds fill the air. There's a bar, snack shack, and beachwear boutique; and bathhouses with restrooms, changing rooms, and saltwater showers are close by. Sunfish, kayaks, and paddleboards are the most popular rentals at the water-sports kiosk. East of the beach is Famous Delite (formerly Udder Delite), a one-room shop that serves a Virgin Islands tradition—a milk shake with a splash of Cruzan rum. (Kids can enjoy virgin versions, which have a touch of soursop, mango, or banana flavoring). If you arrive between 8 am and 5 pm, you pay an entrance fee of $4 per person, $2 per vehicle; it's free for children under 12. **Amenities:** food and drink; lifeguards; parking (fee); restrooms; showers; water sports. **Best for:** partiers; swimming; walking. ⊠ *Magens Bay, Rte. 35, at end of road on north side of island* ☎ *340/777–6300* ⊕ *www.magensbay authority.com.*

## SHOPPING

Fodor'sChoice

★

St. Thomas lives up to its billing as a duty-free shopping destination. Even if shopping isn't your idea of how to spend a vacation, you still may want to slip in on a quiet day (check the cruise-ship listings—Monday and Sunday are usually the least crowded) to browse. Among the best buys are liquor, linens, china, crystal (most stores will ship), and jewelry. The amount of jewelry available makes this one of the few items for which comparison shopping is worth the effort. Local crafts include shell jewelry, carved calabash bowls, straw brooms, woven baskets, and dolls. Spice mixes, hot sauces, and tropical jams and jellies are other native products.

On St. Thomas stores on Main Street in Charlotte Amalie are open weekdays and Saturday 9 to 5. The hours of the shops in the Havensight Mall (next to the cruise-ship dock) and the Crown Bay Commercial Center (next to the Crown Bay cruise-ship dock) are the same, though occasionally some stay open until 9 on Friday, depending on how many cruise ships are anchored nearby. You may also find some shops open on Sunday if cruise ships are in port. Hotel shops are usually open evenings as well.

There's no sales tax in the USVI, and you can take advantage of the $1,200 duty-free allowance per family member (remember to save your receipts). Although you can find the occasional salesclerk who will make a deal, bartering isn't the norm.

The prime shopping area in **Charlotte Amalie** is between Post Office and Market squares; it consists of two parallel streets that run east–west (Waterfront Highway and Main Street) and the alleyways that connect them. Particularly attractive are the historic **A.H. Riise Alley, Drake's Passage, Royal Dane Mall, Palm Passage,** and pastel-painted **International Plaza.**

**Vendors Plaza,** on the waterfront side of Emancipation Gardens in Charlotte Amalie, is a central location for vendors selling handmade earrings, necklaces, and bracelets; straw baskets and handbags; T-shirts; fabrics; African artifacts; and local fruits. Look for the many brightly colored umbrellas.

## ACTIVITIES

### DIVING AND SNORKELING

FAMILY **Coki Dive Center.** Snorkeling and dive tours in the fish-filled reefs off Coki Beach are available from this PADI Five Star outfit, as are classes, including one on underwater photography. It's run by the avid diver Peter Jackson. ⊠ *Rte. 388, at Coki Point, Frydendal* ☎ *340/775–4220* ⊕ *www.cokidive.com.*

FAMILY **Snuba of St. Thomas.** In snuba, a snorkeling and scuba-diving hybrid, a 20-foot air hose connects you to the surface. The cost is $74. Children must be eight or older to participate. ⊠ *Rte. 388, at Coki Point, Estate Smith Bay* ☎ *340/693–8063* ⊕ *www.visnuba.com.*

### FISHING

FAMILY
Fodor's Choice
★
**Double Header Sportfishing.** This company offers trips out to the North Drop on its 40-foot sportfisher and half-day reef and bay trips aboard its two speedy 35-foot center consoles. ⊠ *Sapphire Bay Marina, Rte. 38, Sapphire Bay* ☎ *340/777–7317* ⊕ *www.doubleheadersportfishing.net.*

### GOLF

Fodor's Choice
★
**Mahogany Run Golf Course.** The Mahogany Run Golf Course is the only course in St. Thomas, and it attracts golfers who are drawn by its spectacular view of the British Virgin Islands and the challenging three-hole Devil's Triangle of holes 13–15. This Tom and George Fazio–designed course is not particularly long, but in addition to the scenery, you will experience lots of natural flora and fauna. There's a fully stocked pro shop, snack bar, and open-air clubhouse. Walking is not permitted and the course enforces a dress code. It's open daily, and there are frequently informal weekend tournaments. ⊠ *Rte. 42, Lovenlund* ☎ *340/777–6006, 800/253–7103* ⊕ *www.mahoganyrungolf.com* ✉ *$165 for 18 holes; $115 for 9 holes during peak winter season* ⏆ *18 holes, 6022 yards, par 70.*

## WHERE TO EAT

**$$**      ✕**Cuzzin's Caribbean Restaurant and Bar.** In a 19th-century livery stable
CARIBBEAN on Back Street, this restaurant is hard to find but well worth it if you
want to sample bona fide Virgin Islands cuisine. For lunch, order tender
slivers of conch stewed in a rich onion-and-butter sauce, shrimp creole,
or savory stewed chicken. At dinner the island-style mutton, served in
thick gravy and seasoned with locally grown herbs, offers a tasty treat
that's deliciously different. Side dishes include peas and rice, boiled
green bananas, fried plantains, and potato stuffing. $ *Average main:
$15* ✉ *7 Wimmelskafts Gade, also called Back St., Charlotte Amalie*
☎ *340/777–4711* ⊕ *cuzzinsvi.com* ☾ *Closed Sun.*

**$$**      ✕**Gladys' Cafe.** Even if the local specialties—conch in butter sauce, jerk
CARIBBEAN pork, panfried yellowtail snapper—didn't make this a recommended
**Fodor's**Choice café, it would be worth coming for Gladys's smile. Her cozy alleyway
★      restaurant is rich in atmosphere with its mahogany bar and native stone
walls, making dining a double delight. While you're here, pick up a
$5 or $10 bottle of her special hot sauce. There are mustard-, oil and
vinegar–, and tomato-based versions; the tomato-based sauce is the hottest. $ *Average main: $14* ✉ *Waterfront, 28A Dronningens Gade, west
side of Royal Dane Mall, Charlotte Amalie* ☎ *340/774–6604* ⊕ *www.
gladyscafe.com* ☾ *No dinner* ⌁ *Only Amex credit cards accepted.*

# ST. VINCENT (KINGSTOWN)

By Jane E.
Zarem

You won't find glitzy resorts or flashy discos in St. Vincent. Rather,
you'll be fascinated by its busy capital, mountainous beauty, and fine
sailing waters. St. Vincent is the largest and northernmost island in the
Grenadines archipelago; Kingstown, the capital city of St. Vincent and
the Grenadines, is the government and business center and major port.
Except for one barren area on the island's northeast coast—remnants
of the 1979 eruption of La Soufrière, one of the last active volcanoes
in the Caribbean—the countryside is mountainous, lush, and green. St.
Vincent's topography thwarted European settlement for many years.
As colonization advanced elsewhere in the Caribbean, in fact, the island
became a refuge for Carib Indians—descendants of whom still live in
northeastern St. Vincent. After years of fighting and back-and-forth
territorial claims, British troops prevailed by overpowering the French
and banishing Carib warriors to Central America. Independent since
1979, St. Vincent and the Grenadines remains a member of the British
Commonwealth.

### ESSENTIALS

#### CURRENCY

Eastern Caribbean (EC) dollar, but U.S. dollars are widely accepted.

#### TELEPHONE

Your cell phone should operate in St. Vincent, but roaming charges can
be hefty. Pay phones are readily available and best operated with the
prepaid phone cards that are sold at many stores. Telephone services
are available at the Cruise Ship Complex in Kingstown. For an international operator, dial 115; to charge your call to a credit card, call 117.

## COMING ASHORE

The Cruise Ship Complex at Kingstown, St. Vincent's capital city, accommodates two cruise ships; additional vessels anchor offshore and transport passengers to the jetty by launch. The facility has about two dozen shops that sell duty-free items and handicrafts. There's a communications center, post office, tourist information desk, restaurant, and food court.

Buses and taxis are available at the wharf. Taxi drivers are well equipped to take you on an island tour; expect to pay $30 per hour for up to four passengers. The ferry to Bequia (one hour each way, with frequent daily service) is at the adjacent pier. Renting a car for just one day isn't advisable, since car rentals are expensive (at least $55 per day) and require a $24 temporary driving permit on top of that. It's almost always a better deal to take a tour, though you don't have to limit yourself to excursions offered by your ship.

### BEST BETS

■ **Island Tour.** Tour the greater Kingstown area, then travel up the leeward coast to Wallilabou.

■ **Falls of Baleine.** An all-day boat trip to the 60-foot falls is a beautiful way to spend a day.

■ **Ferry to Bequia.** Laid-back Bequia is one hour by ferry from St. Vincent.

■ **Hiking.** Whether you hike in the rain forest or do the more difficult climb of La Soufrière, it's worth exploring some of the island's rugged terrain.

# EXPLORING

You can explore Kingstown's shopping and business district, historic churches and cathedrals, and other points of interest in a half day, with another couple of hours spent in the Botanic Gardens. The coastal roads of St. Vincent offer spectacular panoramas and scenes of island life. The Leeward Highway follows the scenic Caribbean coastline; the Windward Highway follows the more dramatic Atlantic coast. A drive along the windward coast requires a full day. Exploring La Soufrière or the Vermont Nature Trails is also a major undertaking, requiring a very early start and a full day of strenuous hiking.

FAMILY
Fodor'sChoice
★
**Botanic Gardens.** One of the oldest botanical gardens in the Western Hemisphere is just north of downtown Kingstown—a few minutes by taxi. The garden was created in 1765 by General Robert Melville, governor of the British Caribbean islands, after Captain Bligh—of *Bounty* fame—brought the first breadfruit tree to this island for landowners to propagate. The prolific bounty of the breadfruit trees was used to feed the slaves. You can see a direct descendant of the original tree among the specimen mahogany, rubber, teak, and other tropical trees and shrubs in the 20 acres of gardens. Two dozen rare St. Vincent parrots (*Amazona guildingii*), confiscated from illegal collections, live in the small aviary. Guides explain all the medicinal and ornamental trees and shrubs; they also appreciate a tip (about $5 per person) at the end of the tour. A gift shop, open Monday through Friday, has local crafts, artwork, books,

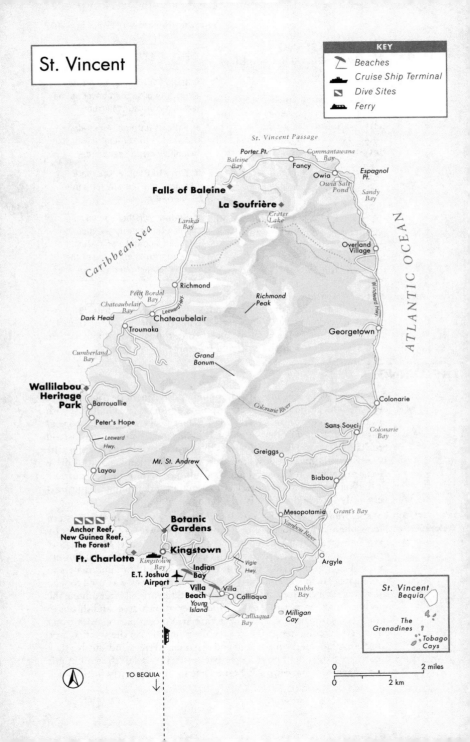

# St. Vincent

**KEY**

Beaches

Cruise Ship Terminal

Dive Sites

Ferry

*St. Vincent Passage*

Porter Pt.
*Baleine Bay*
Fancy
*Commantawana Bay*
Owia
*Espagnol Pt.*

**Falls of Baleine**
*Owia Salt Pond*
**La Soufrière**
*Sandy Bay*

*Larikai Bay*
*Crater Lake*

Overland Village

Richmond
*Richmond Peak*

*Caribbean Sea*

*Petit Bordel Bay*
*Chateaubelair Bay*
*Leeward Hwy.*
**Dark Head**
**Chateaubelair**
Troumaka

Georgetown

ATLANTIC OCEAN

*Cumberland Bay*

*Grand Bonum*

**Wallilabou Heritage Park**
Barrouallie
Peter's Hope
*Colonarie River*
Colonarie

*Leeward Hwy.*
Sans Souci
*Colonarie Bay*

Layou
*Mt. St. Andrew*
Greiggs

Biabou

Mesopotamia
*Grant's Bay*

**Botanic Gardens**
*Yambou River*

**Anchor Reef, New Guinea Reef, The Forest**
**Kingstown**
**Ft. Charlotte**
*Kingstown Bay*
**Indian Bay**
*Vigie Hwy.*
**E.T. Joshua Airport**
**Villa Beach**
Villa
Argyle
*Young Island*
Calliaqua
*Stubbs Bay*
*Calliaqua Bay*
Milligan Cay

*St. Vincent*
*Bequia*

*The Grenadines*

*Tobago Cays*

N

TO BEQUIA

0      2 miles
0      2 km

confections, and a traditional creole lunch menu. ⊠ *Off Leeward Hwy., northeast of town, Montrose* ☎ *784/453–1623* ⊡ *Free.*

**Falls of Baleine.** The falls are impossible to reach by car, so book an escorted, all-day boat trip from Villa Beach. The boat ride along the coast offers scenic island views. When you arrive, you have to wade through shallow water to get to the beach. Then local guides help you make the easy 10-minute trek to the 60-foot falls and the rock-enclosed freshwater pool that the falls create. Wear a bathing suit. ⊠ *Baleine Bay, at the northern tip of the island.*

FAMILY
Fodor's Choice
★

**Ft. Charlotte.** Started by the French in 1786 and completed by the British in 1806, the fort was ultimately named for Britain's Queen Charlotte, wife of King George III. It sits on Berkshire Hill, a dramatic promontory 2 miles (3 km) north of Kingstown and 636 feet above sea level, affording a stunning view of the capital city and the Grenadines. Interestingly, its cannons face inland, as the fear of attack—by the French and their Carib allies—from the ridges above Kingstown was far greater than any threat approaching from the sea. In any case, the fort saw no action. Nowadays, it serves as a signal station for ships; the ancient cells house historical paintings of the island by Lindsay Prescott. ⊠ *Berkshire Hill, 2 miles (3 km) north of town, Kingstown.*

**Kingstown.** The capital of St. Vincent and the Grenadines, a city of 13,500 residents, wraps around Kingstown Bay on the island's southwestern coast; a ring of green hills and ridges studded with homes forms a backdrop for the city. This is very much a working city, with a busy harbor and few concessions to tourists. Kingstown Harbour is the only deepwater port on the island.

A few gift shops can be found on and around **Bay Street,** near the harbor. Upper Bay Street, which stretches along the bayfront, bustles with daytime activity—workers going about their business and housewives doing their shopping. Many of Kingstown's downtown buildings are built of stone or brick brought to the island as ballast in the holds of 18th-century ships (and replaced with sugar and spices for the return trip to Europe). The Georgian-style stone arches and second-floor overhangs on former warehouses—which provide shelter from midday sun and the brief, cooling showers common to the tropics—have earned Kingstown the nickname "City of Arches."

**Grenadines Wharf,** at the south end of Bay Street, is busy with ships loading supplies and ferries loading people bound for the Grenadines. The **Cruise-Ship Complex,** just south of the commercial wharf, has a mall with a dozen or more shops, plus restaurants, communications facilities, and a taxi stand.

A huge selection of produce fills the **Kingstown Market,** a three-story building that takes up a whole city block on Upper Bay, Hillsboro, and Bedford streets in the center of town. It's noisy, colorful, and open Monday through Saturday—but the busiest times (and the best times to go) are Friday and Saturday mornings. In the courtyard, vendors sell local arts and crafts. On the upper floors, merchants sell clothing, household items, gifts, and other products.

**St. George's Cathedral,** on Grenville Street, is a pristine, creamy-yellow Anglican church built in 1820. The dignified Georgian architecture includes simple wooden pews, an ornate chandelier, and beautiful stained-glass windows; one was a gift from Queen Victoria, who actually commissioned it for London's St. Paul's Cathedral in honor of her first grandson. When the artist created an angel with a red robe, she was horrified by the color and sent the window abroad. The markers in the cathedral's graveyard recount the history of the island. Across the street is **St. Mary's Roman Catholic Cathedral of the Assumption,** built in stages beginning in 1823. The strangely appealing design is a blend of Moorish, Georgian, and Romanesque styles applied to black brick. Nearby, freed slaves built the **Kingstown Methodist Church** in 1841. The exterior is brick, simply decorated with quoins (solid blocks that form the corners), and the roof is held together by metal straps, bolts, and wooden pins. **Scots Kirk** was built from 1839 to 1880 by and for Scottish settlers but became a Seventh-Day Adventist church in 1952. ⊠ *Kingstown.*

**La Soufrière.** This towering volcano, which last erupted in 1979, is 4,048 feet high and so huge in area that its surrounding mountainside covers virtually the entire northern third of the island. The eastern trail to the rim of the crater, a two-hour ascent, begins at Rabacca Dry River. ⊠ *Rabacca Dry River, Rabacca.*

FAMILY **Wallilabou Heritage Park.** The Wallilabou Estate, halfway up the island's leeward coast, once produced cocoa, cotton, and arrowroot. Today, it is Wallilabou Heritage Park, a recreational site with a river and small waterfall, which creates a small pool where you can take a freshwater plunge. You can also sunbathe, swim, picnic, or buy your lunch at Wallilabou Anchorage—a favorite stop for boaters staying overnight. The *Pirates of the Caribbean* movies left their mark on Wallilabou (pronounced wally-la- *boo*), a location used for filming the opening scenes of *The Curse of the Black Pearl* in 2003. Many of the buildings and docks built as stage sets remain, giving Wallilabou Bay (a port of entry for visiting yachts) an intriguingly historic (yet ersatz) appearance. ⊠ *Wallilabou Bay.*

## BEACHES

St. Vincent's origin is volcanic, so its beaches range in color from golden-brown to black. Swimming is recommended only in the lagoons and bays along the leeward coast. By contrast, beaches on Bequia and the rest of the Grenadines have pure white sand, palm trees, and crystal-clear aquamarine water; some are even within walking distance of the jetty.

**Indian Bay Beach.** South of Kingstown and separated from Villa Beach by a rocky hill, Indian Bay has golden sand but is slightly rocky; it's very good for snorkeling. Grand View Hotel, high on a cliff overlooking Indian Bay Beach, operates a beach bar and grill. **Amenities:** food and drink. **Best for:** snorkeling; swimming. ⊠ *Villa Beach.*

**Villa Beach.** The long stretch of sand in front of the row of hotels facing the Young Island Channel (Mariners, Paradise Beach, Sunset Shores, and Beachcombers on the "mainland" and Young Island Resort across the channel) varies from 20 to 25 feet wide to practically nonexistent. The broadest, sandiest part is in front of Beachcombers Hotel, which is also the perfect spot for sunbathers to get lunch and liquid refreshments. Villa Beach is a popular beach destination for cruise-ship passengers when a ship is in port. **Amenities:** food and drink; water sports. **Best for:** swimming. ⊠ *Villa Beach*.

## SHOPPING

The 12 small blocks that hug the waterfront in **downtown Kingstown** make up St. Vincent's main shopping district. Among the shops that sell goods to fulfill household needs are a few that sell local crafts, gifts, and souvenirs. Bargaining is neither expected nor appreciated. The **cruise-ship complex,** on the waterfront in Kingstown, has a collection of a dozen or so boutiques, shops, and restaurants that cater primarily to cruise-ship passengers but welcome all shoppers. The best souvenirs of St. Vincent are intricately woven straw items, such as handbags, hats, slippers, baskets, and grass mats that range in size from place mats to room-size floor mats. If you're inclined to bring home a floor mat, they aren't heavy and roll or fold rather neatly; wrapped tightly and packed in an extra (soft-sided) suitcase or tote, it can be checked as luggage for the flight home. Local artwork and carvings are available in galleries, from street vendors, and in shops at the cruise-ship complex. Hot sauce and other condiments, often produced in St. Vincent and sold in markets and gift shops, make tasty souvenirs to bring back home.

## ACTIVITIES

### DIVING AND SNORKELING

Novices and advanced divers alike will be impressed by the marine life in the waters around St. Vincent—brilliant sponges, huge deepwater coral trees, and shallow reefs teeming with colorful fish. Many sites in the Grenadines are still virtually unexplored. It can't be emphasized enough, however, that the coral reef is extremely fragile; you must only look and never touch.

A day-trip to the pristine waters surrounding the **Tobago Cays,** in the southern Grenadines, provides a spectacular diving or snorkeling experience.

**Dive Fantasea.** Earl Halbich takes guests on dive and snorkeling trips along the St. Vincent coast and to the Tobago Cays on his custom-built 42-foot snorkel/dive boat, *Get Wet.* ⊠ *Paradise Beach Hotel, Windward Hwy., Villa Beach* ☎ *784/457–4477* ⊕ *www.fantaseatours.com.*

**Dive St. Vincent.** Two PADI-certified dive masters offer beginner and certification courses for ages eight and up, advanced water excursions along the St. Vincent coast and to the southern Grenadines for diving connoisseurs, and an introductory scuba course for novices. ⊠ *Young Island Dock, Villa Beach* ☎ *784/457–4714* ⊕ *www.divestvincent.com.*

### GUIDED TOURS

Several operators on St. Vincent offer sightseeing tours on land or by sea. You can also arrange for informal land tours through taxi drivers, who double as knowledgeable guides. Expect to pay $30 per hour for up to four people.

**Fantasea Tours.** A fleet of four powerboats—ranging from a 28-foot Bowen to a 60-foot party catamaran—are ready to take you on a cruise to Bequia and Mustique, along the St. Vincent coast, whale- or dolphin-watching, or snorkeling in the Tobago Cays and Mayreau. Alternatively Fantasea offers land tours along the windward coast to Owia Salt Pond, along the leeward coast to Dark View Falls, or hikes either along the Vermont Nature Trail or up La Soufrière volcano. ⊠ *Villa Beach* ☎ *784/457–4477* ⊕ *www.fantaseatours.com.*

**Sailor's Wilderness Tours.** Options from this company include a comfortable sightseeing drive (by day or by moonlight), mountain biking on remote trails, or a strenuous hike up La Soufrière volcano—and the tours are usually under the expert guidance of Trevor "Sailor" Bailey himself. ⊠ *Upper Middle St., Kingstown* ☎ *784/457–1712* ⊕ *www.sailors wildernesstours.com.*

**Sam's Taxi Tours.** In addition to half- and full-day tours of St. Vincent, Sam's also offers hiking tours to La Soufrière and scenic walks along the Vermont Nature Trails. Also available: a day-trip to Mustique and a tour on Bequia that includes snorkeling at Friendship Bay. ⊠ *Sion Hill, Kingstown* ☎ *784/456–4338, 703/738–6461 in U.S.* ⊕ *www.sam taxiandtours.com.*

---

## WHERE TO EAT

**$$$**
CARIBBEAN
✕ **Basil's Bar and Restaurant.** It's not just the air-conditioning that makes this restaurant cool. Basil's, at street level at the Cobblestone Inn, is owned by Basil Charles, whose Basil's Beach Bar on Mustique is a hangout for the vacationing rich and famous. This is the Kingstown power-lunch venue. Local businesspeople gather for the daily buffet (weekdays) or full menu of salads, sandwiches, barbecued chicken, or fresh seafood platters. Dinner entrées of pasta, local seafood, and chicken are served at candlelit tables. $ *Average main: $24* ⊠ *Upper Bay St., below Cobblestone Inn, Kingstown* ☎ *784/457–2713* ⊕ *www. basilsbar.com* ⊘ *Closed Sun.*

**$$**
CARIBBEAN
✕ **Cobblestone Roof-Top Bar & Restaurant.** To reach what is perhaps the most pleasant, the breeziest, and the most satisfying breakfast and lunch spot in downtown Kingstown, diners must climb the equivalent of three flights of interior stone steps within the historic Cobblestone Inn. But getting to the open-air rooftop restaurant is half the fun, as en route diners get an up-close view of a 19th-century sugar (and later arrowroot) Georgian warehouse that's now a very appealing boutique inn. A full breakfast menu is available to hotel guests and the public alike. The luncheon menu ranges from homemade soups, salads (tuna, chicken, fruit, or tossed), sandwiches, or burgers and fries to full meals of roast beef, stewed chicken, or grilled fish served with rice, plantains, macaroni pie, and fresh local vegetables. $ *Average main: $15* ⊠ *Cobblestone*

*Inn, Upper Bay St., Kingstown* ☎ *784/456–1937* ⊕ *www.thecobble-stoneinn.com* ☾ *No dinner.*

# TORTOLA (ROAD TOWN)

By Carol Bareuther

Once a sleepy backwater, Tortola is definitely busy these days, particularly when several cruise ships tie up at the Road Town dock. Passengers crowd the streets and shops, and open-air jitneys filled with cruise-ship passengers create bottlenecks on the island's byways. That said, most folks visit Tortola to relax on its deserted sands or linger over lunch at one of its many delightful restaurants. Beaches are never more than a few miles away, and the steep green hills that form Tortola's spine are fanned by gentle trade winds. The neighboring islands glimmer like emeralds in a sea of sapphire. Tortola doesn't have many historic sights, but it does have abundant natural beauty. Beware of the roads, which are extraordinarily steep and twisting, making driving demanding. The best beaches are on the north shore.

## ESSENTIALS

### CURRENCY
U.S. dollar.

### TELEPHONE
To call anywhere in the BVI once you've arrived, dial all seven digits. A local call from a pay phone costs 25¢, but such phones are sometimes on the blink. An alternative is a Caribbean phone card, available in $5, $10, and $20 denominations. They're sold at most major hotels and many stores, and can be used to call within the BVI as well as all over the Caribbean, and to access USADirect from special phone-card phones. If you're coming ashore at the cruise-ship dock, you'll find pay phones right on the dock. If a tender drops you right in Road Town at the ferry dock, phones are located in the terminal.

AT&T has service in nearby St. John, USVI, so it's possible to get service from there in some spots in Road Town and along the waterfront highway that leads to the West End. You may not have to pay international roaming charges on some U.S. cell-phone plans if you can connect with this network.

### COMING ASHORE
Large cruise ships either anchor in Road Town Harbor and bring passengers ashore by tender or tie up at Tortola Pier Park, which opened in 2016. Either way, it's a short stroll to Road Town. If your ship isn't going to Virgin Gorda, you can make the 12-mile (19-km) trip by ferry from the dock in Road Town in about 30 minutes for about $30 round-trip, but you'll still have to take a taxi to get to The Baths for swimming and snorkeling, so it's not necessarily a bad deal to go on your ship's shore excursion.

There are taxi stands at Wickham's Cay and in Road Town. Taxis are unmetered, and there are minimums for travel throughout the island, so it's usually cheaper to travel in groups. Negotiate to get the best fares, as there is no set fee schedule. If you are in the islands for just a day, it's usually more cost-effective to share a taxi with a small group than to rent a car, since you'd have to pay an agency at Wickham's Cay or in Road Town car-rental charges of at least $50 a day. You must be at least age 25 to rent a car.

## EXPLORING

### AROUND ROAD TOWN

The bustling capital of the BVI looks out over Road Harbour. It takes only an hour or so to stroll down Main Street and along the waterfront, checking out the traditional West Indian buildings painted in pastel colors and with corrugated-tin roofs, bright shutters, and delicate fretwork trim. For sightseeing brochures and the latest information on everything from taxi rates to ferry schedules, stop in at the BVI Tourist Board office. Or just choose a seat on one of the benches in Sir Olva Georges Square, on Waterfront Drive, and watch the people come and go from the ferry dock and customs office across the street.

> **BEST BETS**
>
> ■ **The** *Rhone*. For certified divers, this is one of the best wreck dives in the Caribbean.
>
> ■ **Sage Mountain**. The highest peak in the Virgin Islands has breathtaking views and is a great hiking destination.
>
> ■ **Sailing Trips**. Because of its proximity to small islets and good snorkeling sights, Tortola is the sailing capital of the Caribbean.
>
> ■ **Virgin Gorda**. Ferries link Tortola and Virgin Gorda, making a half-day trip to the Baths quite possible (just be sure to check the ferry schedules before heading out).

**Dolphin Discovery.** Get up close and personal with dolphins as they swim in a spacious seaside pen. There are three different programs. In the Royal Swim, dolphins tow participants around the pen. The less expensive Adventure and Discovery programs allow you to touch the dolphins. ⊠ *Waterfront Dr., Road Town* ⊹ *Located at Prospect Reef* ☎ *284/494–7675, 888/393–5158* ⊕ *www.dolphindiscovery.com* 🕬 *Royal Swim $149, Adventure $99, Discovery $79.*

**Fort Burt.** The most intact historic ruin on Tortola was built by the Dutch in the early 17th century to safeguard Road Harbour. It sits on a hill at the western edge of Road Town and is now the site of a small hotel and restaurant. The foundations and magazine remain, and the structure offers a commanding view of the harbor. ⊠ *Waterfront Dr., Road Town* 🕬 *Free.*

**J.R. O'Neal Botanic Gardens.** Take a walk through this 4-acre showcase of lush plant life. There are sections devoted to prickly cacti and succulents, hothouses for ferns and orchids, gardens of medicinal herbs, and plants and trees indigenous to the seashore. From the tourist office in Road Town, cross Waterfront Drive and walk one block over to Main Street and turn right. Keep walking until you see the high school. The gardens are on your left. ⊠ *Botanic Station, Road Town* ☎ *284/494–2069* ⊕ *www.bvinationalparkstrust.org* 🕬 *$3.*

**Fodor's Choice**
★    **Old Government House Museum.** The official government residence until 1997, this gracious building now displays a nice collection of artifacts

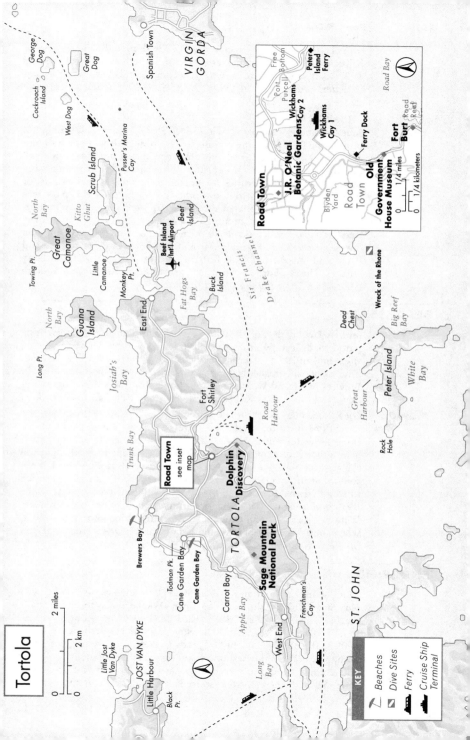

from Tortola's past. The rooms are filled with period furniture, hand-painted china, books signed by Queen Elizabeth II on her 1966 and 1977 visits, and numerous items reflecting Tortola's seafaring legacy. ⊠ *Waterfront Dr., Road Town* ☎ *284/494–4091* ⊕ *www.oghm.org* 🖅 *$5.*

### MID-ISLAND

**Sage Mountain National Park.** At 1,716 feet, Sage Mountain is the highest peak in the BVI. From the parking area, a trail leads you in a loop not only to the peak itself (and extraordinary views) but also to a small rain forest that is sometimes shrouded in mist. Most of the forest was cut down over the centuries for timber, to create pastureland, or for growing sugarcane, cotton, and other crops. In 1964 this park was established to preserve what remained. Up here you can see mahogany trees, white cedars, mountain guavas, elephant-ear vines, mamey trees, and giant bullet woods, to say nothing of such birds as mountain doves and thrushes. Take a taxi from Road Town or drive up Joe's Hill Road and make a left onto Ridge Road toward Chalwell and Doty villages. The road dead-ends at the park. ⊠ *Ridge Rd., Sage Mountain* ☎ *284/852–3650* ⊕ *www.bvinpt.org* 🖅 *$3.*

## BEACHES

**Brewers Bay Beach.** This beach is easy to find, but the steep, twisting paved roads leading down the hill to it can be a bit daunting. An old sugar mill and ruins of a rum distillery are off the beach along the road. You can actually reach the beach from either Brewers Bay Road East or Brewers Bay Road West. **Amenities:** none. **Best for:** snorkeling; swimming. ⊠ *Brewers Bay Rd. E, off Cane Garden Bay Rd., Brewers Bay.*

Fodor's Choice ★ **Cane Garden Bay Beach.** A silky stretch of sand, Cane Garden Bay has exceptionally calm, crystalline waters—except when storms at sea turn the water murky. Snorkeling is good along the edges. Casual guesthouses, restaurants, bars, and shops are steps from the beach in the growing village of the same name. The beach is a laid-back, even somewhat funky place to put down your towel. It's the closest beach to Road Town—one steep uphill and downhill drive—and one of the BVI's best-known anchorages (unfortunately, it can be very crowded). Water-sports shops rent equipment. **Amenities:** food and drink; toilets; water sports. **Best for:** snorkeling; swimming. ⊠ *Cane Garden Bay Rd., off Ridge Rd., Cane Garden Bay.*

## SHOPPING

Many shops and boutiques are clustered along and just off Road Town's **Main Street.** You can shop in Road Town's **Wickham's Cay I** adjacent to the marina. The **Crafts Alive Market** on the Road Town waterfront is a collection of colorful West Indian–style buildings with shops that carry items made in the BVI. You might find pretty baskets or interesting pottery or perhaps a bottle of home-brewed hot sauce. A growing number of art and clothing stores are opening at **Soper's Hole** in West End. Expanded shopping at the new Tortola Cruise Pier is under development.

## ACTIVITIES

### DIVING AND SNORKELING

Clear waters and numerous reefs afford some wonderful opportunities for underwater exploration. In some spots visibility reaches 100 feet, but colorful reefs teeming with fish are often just a few feet below the sea surface. The BVI's system of marine parks means the underwater life visible through your mask will stay protected.

The *Chikuzen,* sunk northwest of Brewers Bay in 1981, is a 246-foot vessel in 75 feet of water; it's home to thousands of fish, colorful corals, and big rays. In 1867 the **RMS *Rhone,*** a 310-foot royal mail steamer, split in two when it sank in a devastating hurricane. It's so well preserved that it was used as an underwater prop in the 1977 movie *The Deep.* You can see the crow's nest and bowsprit, the cargo hold in the bow, and the engine and enormous propeller shaft in the stern. Its four parts are at various depths, from 30 to 80 feet. Get yourself some snorkeling gear and hop aboard a dive boat to this wreck near Salt Island (across the channel from Road Town). Every dive outfit in the BVI runs scuba and snorkel tours to this part of the BVI National Parks Trust; if you have time for only one trip, make it this one. Rates start at around $85 for a one-tank dive and $130 for a two-tank dive.

**Blue Water Divers.** If you're chartering a sailboat, Blue Waters Divers will meet yours at Peter, Salt, Norman, or Cooper Island for a rendezvous dive. The company teaches resort, open-water, rescue, and advanced diving courses, and also makes daily dive trips. Rates include all equipment as well as instruction. Reserve two days in advance. ⊠ *Nanny Cay Marina, Nanny Cay* ☎ *284/494–2847* ⊕ *www.bluewaterdiversbvi.com.*

### FISHING

Most of the boats that take you deep-sea fishing for blue marlin, white marlin, wahoo, tuna, and dolphinfish (mahimahi) leave from nearby St. Thomas, but local anglers like to fish the shallower water for bonefish. A half day for two people runs about $480, a full day around $890. Wading trips are $345.

**Caribbean Fly Fishing.** ⊠ *Nanny Cay Marina, Nanny Cay* ☎ *284/494– 4797, 284/499–1590* ⊕ *www.caribflyfishing.com.*

### SAILING

If a day sail to some secluded anchorage is more your cup of tea, the BVI have numerous boats of various sizes and styles that leave from many points around Tortola. Prices start at around $90 per person for a full-day sail, including lunch and snorkeling equipment.

**Aristocat Charters.** This company's 48-foot catamarans, *Aristocat* and *Lionheart,* set sail daily to Jost Van Dyke, Norman Island, and other small islands. *Aristocat* sails out of Soper's Hole (Frenchman's Cay), West End, and *Lionheart* sails out of Village Cay Marina in Road Town. ☎ *284/499–1249* ⊕ *www.aristocatcharters.com.*

## WHERE TO EAT

**$$**
**ITALIAN**
**Fodor's Choice**
**★**

✕**Capriccio di Mare.** Stop by this casual, authentic Italian outdoor café for an espresso, a fresh pastry, a bowl of perfectly cooked penne, or a crispy tomato-and-mozzarella pizza. Drink specialties include a mango Bellini, an adaptation of the famous cocktail served at Harry's Bar in Venice. ⑤ *Average main: $19* ⊠ *Waterfront Dr., Road Town* ☎ *284/494–5369* ⊘ *Closed Sun.* ⚑ *Reservations not accepted.*

**$$**
**ECLECTIC**
**FAMILY**

✕**Pusser's Road Town Pub.** Almost everyone who visits Tortola stops here at least once to have a bite to eat and to sample the famous Pusser's Rum Painkiller (fruit juice and rum). The nonthreatening menu includes cheesy pizza, shepherd's pie, fish-and-chips, and hamburgers. Dine inside in air-conditioned comfort or outside on the veranda, which looks out on the harbor. ⑤ *Average main: $15* ⊠ *Waterfront Dr., Road Town* ☎ *284/494–3897* ⊕ *www.pussers.com.*

# VIRGIN GORDA (THE VALLEY)

By Carol
Bareuther

Virgin Gorda, or "Fat Virgin," received its name from Christopher Columbus. The explorer envisioned the island as a pregnant woman in a languid recline with Gorda Peak being her big belly and the boulders of the Baths her toes. Different in topography from Tortola, with its arid landscape covered with scrub brush and cactus, Virgin Gorda has a slower pace of life, too. Goats and cattle own the right-of-way, and the unpretentious friendliness of the people is winning. The top sight (and beach for that matter) is the Baths, which draws scores of cruise-ship passengers and day-trippers to its giant boulders and grottoes that form a perfect snorkeling environment. While ships used to stop only in Tortola, saving Virgin Gorda for shore excursions, smaller ships are coming increasingly to Virgin Gorda directly.

### ESSENTIALS

#### CURRENCY
U.S. dollar.

#### TELEPHONE
To call anywhere in the BVI once you've arrived, dial all seven digits. There are no longer any pay phones on Virgin Gorda. Instead, get a Caribbean phone card, available in $5, $10, and $20 denominations. They're sold at most major hotels and many stores, and can be used to call within the BVI, as well as all over the Caribbean. Your own cell phone may work in the BVI, but you'll probably pay a hefty roaming fee.

#### COMING ASHORE
Ships often dock off Spanish Town, Leverick Bay, or in North Sound and tender passengers to the ferry dock. A few taxis will be available at Leverick Bay and at Gun Creek in North Sound—you can set up an island tour for about $45 for two people—but Leverick Bay and North Sound are far away from The Baths, the island's must-see beach, so a shore excursion is often the best choice. If you are tendered to Spanish Town, then it's possible to take a shuttle taxi to The Baths for as little as $4 per person each way. If you are on Virgin Gorda for just a day,

it's usually more cost-effective to share a taxi with a small group than to rent a car, since you'd have to pay car-rental charges of at least $50 a day. You must be at least age 25 to rent a car.

## EXPLORING

One of the most efficient ways to see Virgin Gorda is by sailboat. There are few roads, and most byways don't follow the scalloped shoreline. The main route sticks resolutely to the center of the island, linking The Baths on the southern tip with Gun Creek and Leverick Bay at North Sound. The craggy coast, cut through with grottoes and fringed by palms and boulders, has a primitive beauty. If you drive, you can hit all the sights in one day. The best plan is to explore the area near your hotel (either Spanish Town or North Sound) first, then take a day to drive to the other end. Stop to climb Gorda Peak, which is in the island's center. There are few signs, so come prepared with a map.

> **BEST BETS**
>
> ■ **The Baths.** This unique beach strewn with giant boulders and grottos is a favorite snorkeling destination.
>
> ■ **Virgin Gorda Peak.** This lofty peak has excellent views and is a great hiking destination.
>
> ■ **Sailing Trips.** Like Tortola, Virgin Gorda is within easy reach of many small islets and good snorkeling sights.

FAMILY
Fodor's Choice
★

**The Baths National Park.** At Virgin Gorda's most celebrated sight, giant boulders are scattered about the beach and in the water. Some are almost as large as houses and form remarkable grottoes. Climb between these rocks to swim in the many placid pools. Early morning and late afternoon are the best times to visit if you want to avoid crowds. If it's privacy you crave, follow the shore northward to quieter bays—Spring Bay, the Crawl, Little Trunk, and Valley Trunk—or head south to Devil's Bay. ⊠ *Off Tower Rd., Spanish Town* ☎ *284/852–3650* ⊕ *www.bvinationalparkstrust.org* ⊠ *$3.*

**Copper Mine Point.** A tall stone shaft silhouetted against the sky and a small stone structure that overlooks the sea are part of what was once a copper mine, now in ruins. Established 400 years ago, it was worked first by the Spanish, then by the English, until the early 20th century. The route is not well marked, so turn inland near LSL Restaurant and look for the hard-to-see sign pointing the way. ⊠ *Copper Mine Rd., Spanish Town* ⊕ *www.bvinpt.org* ⊠ *Free.*

**Spanish Town.** Virgin Gorda's peaceful main settlement, on the island's southern wing, is so tiny that it barely qualifies as a town at all. Also known as The Valley, Spanish Town has a marina, some shops, and a couple of car-rental agencies. Just north of town is the ferry slip. At the Virgin Gorda Yacht Harbour you can stroll along the dock and do a little shopping. ⊠ *Spanish Town.*

**Virgin Gorda Peak National Park.** There are two trails at this 265-acre park, which contains the island's highest point, at 1,359 feet. Signs on North Sound Road mark both entrances. It's about a 15-minute hike from either entrance up to a small clearing, where you can climb

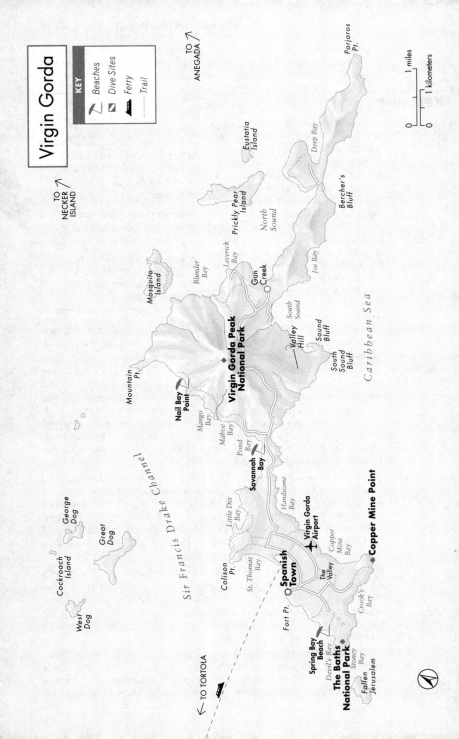

# Virgin Gorda

**KEY**

⟍ Beaches
◨ Dive Sites
⚓ Ferry
⋯⋯ Trail

TO NECKER ISLAND

TO ANEGADA

TO TORTOLA

West Dog

Cockroach Island

George Dog

Great Dog

Sir Francis Drake Channel

Mosquito Island

Blunder Bay

Leverick Bay

Prickly Pear Island

North Sound

Gun Creek

Eustatia Island

Deep Bay

Bercher's Bluff

Parjaros Pt.

Mountain Pt.

**Nail Bay Point**

Mango Bay

Mahoe Bay

Pond Bay

**Savannah Bay**

**Virgin Gorda Peak National Park**

Valley Hill

South Sound

Sound Bluff

South Sound Bluff

Caribbean Sea

Handsome Bay

Little Dix Bay

Colison Pt.

St. Thomas Bay

**Spanish Town**

Fort Pt.

The Valley

**Virgin Gorda Airport**

Copper Mine Bay

**Copper Mine Point**

Crook's Bay

**Spring Bay Beach**

Devil's Bay

**The Baths National Park**

Stoney Bay

Fallen Jerusalem

0 — 1 miles
0 — 1 kilometers

a ladder to the platform of a wooden observation tower to see a spectacular 360-degree view. ⊠ *North Sound Rd., Gorda Peak* ⊕ *www.bvinpt.org* ⌨ *Free.*

## BEACHES

**The Baths Beach.** This stunning maze of huge granite boulders extending into the sea is usually crowded midday with day-trippers. The snorkeling is good, and you're likely to see a wide variety of fish, but watch out for dinghies coming ashore from the numerous sailboats anchored offshore. Public bathrooms and a handful of bars and shops are close to the water and at the start of the path that leads to the beach. Lockers are available to keep belongings safe. **Amenities:** food and drink; parking; toilets. **Best for:** snorkeling; swimming. ⊠ *Tower Rd., about 1 mile (1½ km) west of Spanish Town ferry dock, Spanish Town* ☏ *284/852–3650* ⊕ *www.bvinpt.org* ⌨ *$3.*

**Savannah Bay Beach.** This is a wonderfully private beach close to Spanish Town. It may not always be completely deserted, but you can find a spot to yourself on this long stretch of soft, white sand. Bring your own mask, fins, and snorkel, as there are no facilities. Villas are available through rental property agencies. The view from above is a photographer's delight. **Amenities:** none. **Best for:** solitude; snorkeling; swimming. ⊠ *Off N. Sound Rd., ¾ mile (1¼ km) east of Spanish Town ferry dock, Savannah Bay* ⌨ *Free.*

**Spring Bay Beach.** This national-park beach gets much less traffic than the nearby Baths, and has the similarly large, imposing boulders that create interesting grottoes for swimming. It also has no admission fee, unlike the more popular Baths. The snorkeling is excellent, and the grounds include swings and picnic tables. Guavaberry Spring Bay Vacation has villas and cottages right near the beach. **Amenities:** none. **Best for:** snorkeling; swimming. ⊠ *Spanish Town* ☏ *284/852–3650* ⊕ *www.bvinpt.org* ⌨ *Free.*

## SHOPPING

Most boutiques are within hotel complexes or at Virgin Gorda Yacht Harbour. One of the best is at Little Dix Bay. Other properties—the Bitter End and Leverick Bay—have small but equally good boutiques.

## ACTIVITIES

### DIVING AND SNORKELING

The dive companies are all certified by PADI. Costs vary, but count on paying about $85 for a one-tank dive and $130 for a two-tank dive. All dive operators offer introductory courses as well as certification and advanced courses. There are some terrific snorkel and dive sites off Virgin Gorda, including areas around The Baths, the North Sound, and the Dogs. The Chimney at Great Dog Island has a coral archway and canyon covered with a wide variety of sponges. At Joe's Cave, an underwater cavern on West Dog Island, huge groupers, eagle rays, and other colorful fish accompany divers as they swim. At some sites you can see 100 feet down, but divers who don't want to go that deep and snorkelers will find plenty to look at just below the surface.

**Dive BVI.** In addition to day trips, Dive BVI also offers expert instruction and certification. ☒ *Virgin Gorda Yacht Harbour, Lee Rd., Spanish Town* ☎ *284/495–5513, 800/848–7078* ⊕ *www.divebvi.com.*

**Sunchaser Scuba.** Resort, advanced, and rescue courses are all available here. ☒ *Bitter End Yacht Club, North Sound* ☎ *284/495–9638, 800/932–4286* ⊕ *www.sunchaserscuba.com.*

## SAILING AND BOATING

The BVI waters are calm and terrific places to learn to sail. You can also rent sea kayaks, waterskiing equipment, dinghies, and powerboats, or take a parasailing trip.

**Double "D" Charters.** If you just want to sit back, relax, and let the captain take the helm, choose a sailing or power yacht from Double "D" Charters. Rates run from $110 for a day trip. Private full-day cruises or sails for up to eight people run from $1,100. ☒ *Virgin Gorda Yacht Harbour, Lee Rd., Spanish Town* ☎ *284/499–2479* ⊕ *www.doubledbvi.com.*

# WHERE TO EAT

**$$**
ECLECTIC
✕ **Bath and Turtle.** You can sit back and relax at this informal tavern with a friendly staff (or enjoy the outdoor Rendezvous Bar on the waterfront), although the noise from the television can sometimes be a bit much. Well-stuffed sandwiches, homemade pizzas, pasta dishes, and daily specials such as conch soup round out the casual menu. Local musicians perform many Wednesday and Sunday nights. ⑤ *Average main: $19* ☒ *Virgin Gorda Yacht Harbour, Lee Rd., Spanish Town* ☎ *284/495–5239* ⊕ *www.bathandturtle.com.*

**$$$**
ECLECTIC
FAMILY
✕ **Top of the Baths.** At the entrance to The Baths, this popular restaurant has tables on an outdoor terrace or in an open-air pavilion; all have stunning views of the Sir Francis Drake Channel. The restaurant starts serving at 8 am for breakfast; for lunch, hamburgers, coconut chicken sandwiches, and fish-and-chips are among the offerings. Sushi is served 11 am to 3 pm every day except Sunday. For dessert, the key lime pie is excellent. The Sunday barbecue, served from noon until 3 pm, is an island event. ⑤ *Average main: $23* ☒ *Spanish Town* ☎ *284/495–5497* ⊕ *www.topofthebaths.com.*

# INDEX

## PHOTO CREDITS

**Front cover:** Danny Lehman/Getty Images [Description: Cruise Ship Docked at Ocho Rios, Jamaica]. Back cover, from left to right: Sara Winter/iStockphoto; Onepony | Dreamstime.com; Wildroze/iStockphoto. Spine: Ginosphotos | Dreamstime.com **Chapter 1, Cruise Primer:** 7, Andy Newman/Carnival Cruise Lines. **Chapter 2, Cruising the Caribbean:** 33, Regent Seven Seas Cruises. **Chapter 3, Ports of Embarkation:** 57, Royal Caribbean International. **Chapter 4, Ports of Call:** 143, Celebrity Cruises.

# ABOUT OUR WRITERS

Linda Coffman is a freelance travel writer and the originator of CruiseDiva.com, her Web site, which has been dishing out cruise-travel advice and information since 2000. Before that, she was the cruise guide for About.com. Her columns and articles have appeared in *Cruise Travel, Porthole, Consumers Digest,* and other regional and national magazines; the *Chicago Sun-Times, Denver Post;* and on numerous Web sites, including those for USA Today, Fodors.com, and the Travel Channel. She's an avid cruiser, who enjoys sailing on ships of every size to any port worldwide but spends most of her time cruising the Caribbean. Linda thinks cruising is in her Norwegian blood and credits her heritage for a love of all things nautical. When not at sea, she makes her home in Augusta, Georgia, with her husband, Mel. Linda is the primary cruise correspondent for Fodor's and updated all the cruise line and cruise ship sections for this edition as well as our coverage of the cruise line private islands.

The following writers updated coverage and contributed valuable insights for the Caribbean cruise ports of call: Laura Adzich-Brander (Grand Turk), Carol M. Bareuther (St. Thomas, Tortola, Virgin Gorda), Carol Buchanan (St. Croix), Susan Campbell (Aruba, Curaçao), Greg Devilliers (Cartagena), Lynda Lohr (St. John), Elise Meyer (St. Barthélemy, St. Maarten), Amy Peniston (Bermuda), Ann L. Phelan (Bonaire), Rika Purdy (Roatan), Jessica Robertson (Freeport-Lucaya, Nassau), Laura Rodini (Baltimore), Paul Rubio (Fort Lauderdale, Key West, Miami, Jacksonville, Port Canaveral, Tampa), Paulina Salach (San Juan), Julie Schwietert Collazo (San Juan), Jordan Simon (Antigua, Grand Cayman, Nevis, St. Kitts), Richard Sitler (Falmouth, Montego Bay, Ocho Rios), Eileen Robinson Smith (Charleston, Guadeloupe, La Romana, Martinique, Samaná, Santo Domingo), Roberta Sotonoff (Dominica), Robin Sussman (Galveston, New Orleans), Jeffrey Van Fleet (Belize City, Calica, Colón, Costa Maya, Cozumel, Progreso, Puerto Limón, Santo Tomás de Castillo), Jane E. Zarem (Barbados, Grenada, St. Lucia, St. Vincent).